Master

Keys

to

Spiritual

Freedom

Master

Keys

to

Spiritual

Freedom

Kim Michaels

More to Life Publishing

Master Keys to Spiritual Freedom
by Kim Michaels.
Copyright © 2007 by Kim Michaels and
More to Life Publishing. www.morepublish.com

ISBN-10: 0-9766971-7-3
ISBN-13: 978-0-9766971-7-6

Other books by Kim Michaels:

I Love Jesus, I Hate Christianity
The Least You Should Know About Life
Master Keys to the Abundant Life
Beyond Religious Conflict
I Am a Thinking Christian
The Secret Coming of Christ
The Jesus Koans
Save Your Planet
Save Yourself!
The Inner Path of Light
The Christ Is Born in You

Table of Contents

Introduction
What this book will and will not do for you

This book is not for everyone—for the simple reason that not everyone is ready for the teachings that will be revealed in this book. This book is a gift from the spiritual teachers of humankind to those who want the full truth about the path to spiritual freedom. There are, of course, numerous religious and spiritual organizations which claim they have this truth and that it has already been defined by their doctrines. Yet it is a fact that such earthly organizations too often restrict people's spiritual freedom through a set of rigid doctrines and rituals. This book is for those who are willing to consider the cause of the readily observable phenomenon that religion often reduces people's spiritual freedom rather than giving them greater freedom. The book will expose the hidden forces that operate in the religious life of this planet, forces that often pervert the original purpose of religion. That purpose is to set human beings free to be – while still on Earth – the spiritual beings they were created to be.

When I say that not everyone is ready for this book, my statement does not in any way imply a value judgment. I am not trying to hint that those who are ready are more sophisticated or spiritual than those who are not ready. We who are the true spiritual teachers of humankind have no reason to judge and we have no human values. The simple reason is that we have risen above the condition of duality from which all judgment springs, a condition that will be clearly explained in the coming chapters. In fact, because we are above duality, we have no need to play the game of pretending that is so common among the members of religious movements. Thus, I am not trying to appeal to the pride of those who are using spirituality to satisfy their need to feel better than others.

My statement is meant to insert a dose of practical realism. I know that not everyone is ready for this book, yet I also know that everyone has the potential to become ready—if they are willing to make the necessary adjustments. Which then leads us to a discussion of what it will take for you to get the maximum benefit from this book.

The basic dilemma faced by all seekers of truth

When you look at humankind, it is obvious that many people display no interest in the spiritual side of life. Some actively deny that there is a spiritual realm beyond the material universe, while others are indifferent, focusing all of their attention on the material world and its pleasures or problems. Based on this observation, many people reason that the spiritual teachers of humankind evaluate people based on their outer interest in spirituality. Many people seem to think that God loves the most outwardly religious people – specifically the members of their religion – more than others. Such people might reason that this book is aimed at those who are openly religious or spiritual.

In reality, a spiritual teacher does not evaluate people based on outer appearances. Instead, we look beyond all such appearances and look at the inner condition of a person's total being. Our concern is not what people currently believe or don't believe with the outer mind. Our only concern is to what degree a person is willing to look beyond his or her existing beliefs and belief system. We are spiritual teachers, so our calling is to teach. And in order to teach people anything, people must be teachable. In order to be teachable, a person must be willing to look beyond his or her existing mental box. Why is this so?

One might think that all of the people who see themselves as religious or spiritual people should be open to a higher understanding of the spiritual reality, and thus they should be teachable. Unfortunately, this is not always the case. In order to be teachable, you must be open to the possibility that there is more to know about the spiritual side of life than what is defined by your current belief system, your current mental box. As can readily be observed by anyone willing to take an honest look, those who already have a spiritual or religious belief system often close their minds to any knowledge that goes beyond the mental box defined by their belief system. For example, many religious people are afraid to consider ideas that contradict or go beyond the official doctrines of their religion. They think it is dangerous to consider such ideas and that various calamities might befall them if they open their minds to anything beyond the "safe" framework of their belief system—which they consider to be the only true religion. Thus, it is an unfortunate fact that religion often closes people's minds to a higher understanding of life, making them unreachable for the true spiritual teachers who are always seeking to raise humankind to a higher understanding.

We now see the basic dilemma faced by any seeker of truth. You already have a certain knowledge about the spiritual side of life, and you have likely received that knowledge through one or more outer religions, gurus or teachings. This knowledge forms a belief system, a mental box, and it gives you a sense of security, even a sense of who you are. Yet if you have started reading this book, you must consider yourself a seeker of truth, meaning that you have questions about spiritual topics that have not been answered. You must have an inner knowing that your search for truth has not been ultimately fulfilled. You sense that there is more to know, and you are longing for a higher understanding. Thus, the central dilemma that determines whether you are teachable is a battle, a tug of war, between two forces in your own psyche:

- There is a force that seeks to make you cling to what you already know. This force has an insatiable need for security, for feeling that it is already saved, and it wants you to believe that by following an outer belief system, your salvation is guaranteed. This force is what I will call the ego, and I will describe it in greater detail later in the book. The important point at this stage is to understand that those who follow the voice of the ego will read a spiritual book primarily to get their existing beliefs confirmed. Thus, when they come across statements that contradict or go beyond their existing beliefs, they will judge the book as being false, often using one statement as justification for rejecting an entire book. Such people obviously are not teachable, and this book is not written for them.

- There is a force that is never attached to any knowledge expressed in the words and images of this world. This force always seeks to inspire you to look beyond your current mental box and increase your understanding. This force is the voice of your Higher Self, your spiritual self, and it will also be described in detail. People who listen to this voice are always seeking to expand their mental boxes, and some have even understood that the ultimate goal of spiritual growth is to escape all human boxes.

We now see that the factor that determines whether you are teachable is the balance between these two forces. To what degree do you cling to your existing beliefs and to what degree are you willing to look beyond your current mental box?

It might help you to recognize the fundamental reality that guides all human progress. What keeps people trapped in limitations and suffering is ignorance. Human society has progressed beyond the stage of the cave dwellers precisely because modern people have a greater understanding of all facets of life than people did in prehistoric times. So the key to your spiritual progress is that you must expand your understanding of the spiritual side of life—with all thy getting, get understanding (Proverbs 4:7). Yet how can you expand your understanding? Where can a higher understanding be found? Well, a higher understanding can be found *only* by looking beyond your existing beliefs, your current mental box. If the higher understanding was found inside your current mental box, you would already have that understanding and your questions would be answered. Thus, it remains a basic fact of life that only those who are willing to look beyond their mental boxes will rise to a higher level of understanding. Being teachable means being willing to look beyond your current mental box—not indiscriminately, but with discernment, as will be explained later.

Which voice will you follow?

The question of whether you are teachable can – of course – not be answered by me. It can be answered only by you. Yet let me offer you some guidance. The spiritual teachers of humankind have a saying which states, "When the student is ready, the teacher appears." The meaning is that you will not be able to find a spiritual teaching – or recognize the validity of it – until you are ready to take a step higher on the spiritual path. Being ready is truly a matter of the inner condition of your total being. However, it is quite possible – and common – that people are ready for a higher teaching at inner levels of their beings, yet their outer minds block the acceptance of the new teaching, causing them to cling to what is familiar.

For example, if you have found this book and read to this point, I can assure you that – at the higher levels of your being – you are ready for the teachings that will be given in this book. However, it is possible that a part of your outer mind, your ego, will resist your reading of this book or your acceptance of its teachings. In order to overcome this resistance, you need to become aware of the voice of the ego, which will seek to block your acceptance of ideas that can set you free from its control. The ego can be a very loud voice that seeks to play on your fear, by making you fear that certain ideas in this book are false and will take you to hell. Yet the ego can also be a very subtle and persuasive voice that seeks to make you believe you don't really have to question or expand your current mental box. It will make you think you already know all you need to know or that the teachings in this book are inferior to your existing beliefs. The message is that you can safely stay where you are comfortable, meaning where the ego has you under its control.

Take note of what I am saying here. I am in no way asking you to blindly accept the teachings I give in this book. What I am truly saying is that if you have found this book, your own higher being knows that this book can give you the keys to your spiritual freedom. Yet that freedom cannot be won by blindly believing in what is stated in this book. It can be won only by using the teachings in this book as a key to unlocking the inner understanding that you already have in your higher being. In other words, the real key to spiritual growth is to bring your outer mind into alignment with your higher being—a concept I will later explain in greater detail. For now I simply want to make you aware that I am not asking you to believe me or my statements in this book. I am asking you to carefully look beyond the outer mind and connect to your own higher being. I am asking you to neither believe the outer teachings in this book nor the outer teachings to which your ego is attached. I am asking you to go within yourself and unlock your inner ability to know what is valid, to know what will take you to a higher level of understanding.

The real key to having the maximum benefit from this book is to engage in a process of self-examination. As you read this book, examine your reactions to the statements in it. Be aware of the voice of the ego, which will always resist your growth. And be aware of the subtle, inner voice that always inspires you to look beyond your mental box and reach for the greater freedom that comes only from inner knowing. That inner knowing is not the automatic result of believing an outer teaching. However, you can use an outer teaching to stimulate the process of getting answers from within. More on this later in the book.

The outer savior versus the inner path

Let us consider how the two forces described above have been outplayed in the religious life of this planet. Many religions have followed a distinct pattern, and although I will later talk about this in
greater detail, I want to make you aware of it at this early stage. Most
religions have been started by one person who attained a direct connection to the spiritual realm. This person then became the open door
through which the spiritual teachers of humankind brought forth a
new spiritual teaching. That teaching was aimed at giving people
spiritual freedom, meaning that it was designed to help people establish their own inner connections to their higher selves and the spiritual realm. The new teaching was – in its original form – the voice
that called people to go beyond their old mental boxes and open their
minds to a higher understanding. The leader of the new religion was
meant to be an example to follow rather than an exception. He was
meant to show that all people can go within and attain a higher understanding.

Yet for practically all religions, the ego eventually took over and
turned the founder into someone who was so above and beyond other
human beings that no one can follow in his footsteps. The ego's
desire for security, its desire for a guaranteed salvation, turned the
original teaching into a rigid doctrine that presents an outer church or
an outer savior as the only road to salvation. For example, when Jesus
said, "I am the way, the truth and the life, no man cometh to the
Father but by me" (John 14:6), he did not mean that the outer religion
of Christianity is the only road to salvation. This is clearly seen by
another statement in which Jesus said that the kingdom of God is
within you (Luke 17:21). When you take these two statements
together, you see that the only road to the Father, the only road to salvation, is to become one with Christ, with the Christ consciousness
that Jesus embodied and thus exemplified for all who have eyes to
see. The true meaning is that no man comes to the Father except by
becoming one with the Christ consciousness, by letting that mind be
in you which was also in Christ Jesus (Philippians 2:5).

My point here is to show you that being saved – or whatever you
want to call the ultimate transcendence of human limitations – is not
an outer, mechanical process. It is not a matter of being a member of a
particular church, believing its doctrines and following its rituals. It is
an inner, creative process that requires you to fundamentally change

your consciousness, to be spiritually reborn, as Jesus explained (John 3:3). As true spiritual teachers, we have a desire to see you rise above the human condition, but we know this must happen within the framework of the ultimate law of this universe, namely the Law of Free Will. I cannot change your consciousness *for* you—only *you* can change your own consciousness. You must do so consciously by understanding how to rise above the duality that leads to all suffering.

The bottom line is that for a person to be teachable, he or she must realize that the only road to spiritual freedom is through a change in consciousness. And that change can be brought about only by *you*. I can give you the keys to spiritual freedom, as I will do in this book. Yet the locks are located in your mind, so you must decide to insert the keys into the locks and open the doors that lead to freedom. I cannot do this *for* you and neither can anyone else. Thus, you will not truly place yourself on the path to spiritual freedom until you accept this fact and take responsibility for changing what is – or should be – your personal domain, namely your mind. It is only when you are willing to acknowledge the need to change your state of consciousness – and accept your responsibility for doing so – that you become fully teachable. And only when you are fully teachable, will you get the full benefit from this book.

The purpose of this introduction is to tell you what this book will and will not do for you, and you now have a clearer picture. This book will give you the keys to spiritual freedom, but it will not give you spiritual freedom. You must use the keys in this book to unlock the locks in your mind that block your freedom. And this is a work that neither a book nor a spiritual teacher (whether on Earth or in the spiritual realm) can do for you. Thus, it remains an inescapable fact – a fact that the ego will deny to the end – that you are ultimately responsible for attaining spiritual freedom. No one can change your consciousness *for* you, for your consciousness is *your* responsibility.

Who am I?

Let me give you a clearer picture of who I am. If you look at history, you will see that over the centuries and millennia human beings have progressed in their understanding of themselves and the world · which they live. You will even see a progression in nature ʈ⸱ more and more complex life-forms. It should therefore bᴇ for most people to reason that planet Earth is a schoolroo.

human beings – as individuals and as a whole – can progress toward higher levels of understanding. But what is the end of this progress?

Every now and then a person appears on the world stage who seems to have progressed beyond the norm. While many people are quick to label such people as insane or elevate them to the status of an idol, this is just one more example of people's unwillingness to take responsibility for their own lives. The fact is that people such as the Buddha, Krishna or Jesus were not fundamentally different from yourself. They were merely further advanced in the learning process offered on Earth. In fact, they demonstrated the last steps toward the final graduation, steps that all human beings have the potential to take if they are willing to leave all human limitations behind.

After you pass the final exam – which I will describe in more detail later in this book – you will permanently ascend to a higher level of learning. You will take up your abode in a realm that spiritual people call heaven but which we – using the terminology of science – could also call a higher vibrational spectrum, a higher dimension, even a parallel universe. Once ascended to this realm, you have two options. You can continue to grow in God's never-ending cycles of expanded awareness. Or you can choose to remain with Earth, seeking to help those of your spiritual brothers and sisters, those who have not yet passed the final exam—even those who have been brought up to believe there is no final exam or that they cannot pass it on their own.

There are many beings in the spiritual realm who have made the decision to help people on Earth raise their level of consciousness and pass the final exam. We have been known by many names, but in this context I prefer to call us the "Ascended Host." This name indicates that we have ascended from a lower to a higher realm and thus are not fundamentally different from those who are still unascended. I am one member of the Ascended Host, and I have been known to students in both East and West as Lord Maitreya. Let it be known that the Garden of Eden was a cosmic schoolroom, a mystery school, in which I was the main teacher. I was what the Bible calls "God" but which was not God in the highest sense but a representative of God, serving as the main teacher of a specific group of lifestreams. Thus, I have an intimate understanding of what caused the Fall of Man and how you can overcome the effects of that event, an event that affects everyone embodying on Earth.

It has also been my privilege to serve as the personal teacher for the lifestream you know as Jesus. When Jesus referred to his Father, he was sometimes referring to me and sometimes to the Creator. Jesus did not come to be elevated to the idol of being the only son of God. He came to demonstrate the teacher-student relationship, so that he could take up his rightful role and become a world teacher. I will later explain how this purpose was subverted by setting Jesus up as an exception rather than as an example to follow, and I will show you how you can stop dancing around this golden calf and have no other teachers before the Living Christ (Exodus 20:3).

I hold several spiritual offices, and one of them is the office of the "Great Initiator." In earthly terms, you might think of this as the secretary of education. I serve as the overseer for how the evolutions on Earth are taught, or initiated, into the deeper mysteries of life. It is as an extension of my office that I offer this book. It has been determined by our councils that it is time to offer the evolutions on Earth the full and unmasked truth about God, religion and their relationship with God.

Why this book is different

The purpose of this book is to offer you a living truth that has never before been publicly offered on this planet. The reason is that when we give a spiritual teaching, we normally adapt it to the level of consciousness of the intended recipients. The reasoning behind this approach should be clear when you look at the religious landscape on this planet. Many people ask the fundamental questions of life, but they limit the kind of answers they are willing to receive. And in most cases people use an existing belief system – be it religious or scientific in origin – as their basis for restricting their willingness to receive living answers. Because of this human tendency, we of the Ascended Host – we who serve as the spiritual teachers for the evolutions of Earth – are practical realists. When we give a spiritual teaching, we are *not* seeking to give people the absolute and infallible truth about God. We are carefully targeting the teaching to a specific group of people, and we are seeking to give them a teaching that they can accept with their current level of consciousness but which can still take them beyond that level of consciousness.

It is always our hope that people will use any given teach· rise above their current level of consciousness—that they v·

ply their talents. When people do rise, we can then give them a more sophisticated understanding. When you look at the history of religion on this planet, you will see that so far we have been severely limited by people's willingness to look beyond their existing beliefs and their willingness to change their lives in order to receive a higher truth. Fortunately, this has begun to change, and it has been determined by our councils that planet Earth has reached a critical mass. There are now enough people in embodiment who are open to the Living Truth that we have decided to release the full truth about religion on this planet.

In all past teachings we have always left certain questions unaddressed, and this gave certain people the opportunity to hide behind surface appearances. People could study a teaching – and understand it intellectually – without actually looking in the mirror and applying it to themselves. That is why you have seen so many religious people who did not live their beliefs, who did not walk their talk. That is why there has so far been room for so much hypocrisy in religion. That is why so many religions have followed the same pattern of becoming rigid and dogmatic, offering ready-made answers while denying people the key of knowledge (Luke 11:52) that can give them living answers.

The teachings I offer you in this book will go far beyond this approach and will not leave room for anyone to hide behind intellectual interpretations. The basic dynamic of life on Earth will be exposed so that only those who are completely blind will fail to see the beam in their own eyes. Truth is a two-edged sword, and one edge is always pointing toward yourself, ready to cut through the illusions you hold about yourself and God. Only those who are willing to let go of such illusions, will find this book liberating. Those who cling to their illusions, will find that their egos will be working overtime on trying to come up with excuses for rejecting this book.

Wise are the students who monitor themselves and expose the ego that opposes their progress on the path toward full oneness with the Living Truth. Yet fear not, for I will give you the knowledge to unmask and leave behind the ego and all forces that oppose your path toward the final exam—whereby you become an initiate who understands the essential mystery of life on Earth, the mystery that has so far been unspoken. Yet in this book that mystery shall be spoken publicly for the first time, so that those who are willing can overcome that last enemy—which the Bible called death (1Corinthians 15:26) but whose true identity few have understood.

I want to make it clear that this book is given as part of a whole. The other part of the whole is the book released by Mother Mary, called *Master Keys to the Abundant Life*. These two books together form a polarity that represents the two basic forces, the Alpha and Omega, of creation. Mother Mary's book takes the Omega approach of starting with people's present level of consciousness and explaining how to systematically rise above it. This book takes the Alpha approach of giving you the big picture, the overall view. Other books will follow to complete the task and incorporate all four elements of God's Being.

This book will not in any way cater to or adapt to people's existing beliefs or belief systems. This book breaks new ground in that it is not adapted to a particular group of people with a particular belief system. It states truth in a universal way and leaves it completely up to the reader how he or she will respond to that truth. Thus, the responsibility is placed where it belongs, namely on you. Let those who are willing to go beyond their existing beliefs discover the higher truth of who they are and from whence they came.

Key 1
How to find answers to life's questions

This book is a gift to those who consider themselves seekers of truth, meaning that they have come to the conscious realization that they want real answers to the fundamental questions of life:

- Who am I, where did I come from and why am I here—meaning both in existence and here on this planet called Earth?

- What is the purpose of life in general and what is the specific purpose for my personal life?

- Who is God and what is God like?

- What is my relationship with God and how can I deepen it?

- What is the ideal role of religion in my relationship with God and why does religion so often limit rather than expand my relationship with God?

What do I mean when I talk about *real* answers? There are numerous belief systems that claim they have complete, absolute and infallible answers to the fundamental questions of life. Let it be made clear that it is *not* the purpose of this book to create another belief system to compete with the many systems that claim to have the exclusive answers to life's questions.

This book will *not* give you the answers to life's questions. It is designed to assist you in receiving these answers from the only place they *can* be received, namely a source inside yourself. That source is the Spirit of Truth (John 4:24), and the answers you get from it are living answers, the Living Truth that is beyond words.

As a true spiritual seeker, it is essential for you to recognize the limitations of words. Words are inherently ambiguous, and the same statement can trigger mutually exclusive interpretations from different people. That is why most of the people who claim to be religious are caught in the age-old game of thinking that their particular expression of "truth" is superior to others. Thus, they have abandoned the quest for the Living Truth in favor of seeking to prove the superiority of a dead truth, a truth that has been frozen in time by being clothed in words. Let it be understood, therefore, that as soon as a spiritual concept has been reduced to words, it has entered the realm of duality, and from that point it is subject to interpretation by a specific part of the human mind, namely the analytical mind that is so easily controlled by the ego.

One of the main purposes of this book is to explain – in a way never done before – how the human ego interferes with your relationship with God. This will take some time, but what you need to be aware of from the beginning is how the ego uses words to block your growth, while your Higher Self seeks to help you see beyond the words to the hidden meaning:

- The ego will seek to make you interpret any statement I make at the level of the words by taking it literally. It will seek to make you compare the statement to your existing belief system and reject anything that contradicts or goes beyond what you already believe. The ego is always seeking to put your mind in a mental box in which it feels it has you under its control. Once you are there, it seeks to prevent you from expanding the box or stepping outside the box. There are billions of people who claim to be religious but who have not realized that their egos have used their religion to build a mental prison for their minds. Thus, this book is a gift to those who have realized or are willing to realize that there is a force in their own psychology which seeks to hinder their search for the Living Truth. In order to find truth, one must transcend this force.

- Your Higher Self is seeking to help you look beyond the outer words and use them as a springboard for reaching for a direct, inner experience of the Spirit of Truth. The truth you receive from this inner source is the Living Truth that cannot be confined to words. Nevertheless, it can be experienced through your intuitive faculties, and this experience can be triggered by words. When you do experience the Living Truth, you realize that it cannot be confined to any belief system. Thus, the quest to prove the superiority of one belief system is futile. In reality, many belief systems can serve as stepping stones for the direct experience of the Living Truth. When used as such, they serve their rightful purpose, but when used as weapons to prove the ego's superiority, they form an impenetrable barrier between you and God.

This book is a gift for those who have passed one of the most important turning points on the spiritual path, namely where you realize that you want the Living Truth over anything offered on this planet, including the many dead "truths" that come from the duality consciousness of the ego. You want truth more than the comfortability and seeming security offered by the mental box of the ego or a ready-made belief system. You have realized that the outer "truth" offered by so many belief systems will never satisfy your inner longing for truth. I hope you will also realize that the reason for this is that only the Living Truth will satisfy your longing. And this truth can be known *only* through a direct, inner experience.

***

What does it take to have an experience of the Spirit of Truth? It is likely that you have already had at least glimpses of this living experience. However, most people are not quite able to have a clear experience of the Spirit of Truth, for they do – as Saint Paul expressed it – see through a glass darkly (1Corinthians 13:12). That filter – which stands between your conscious mind and the Spirit of Truth – is created by the ideas and beliefs that your ego and the world have programmed into your mind. It is therefore an eternal dilemma that in order to have a progressively clearer experience of the Spirit of Truth, you must be willing to gradually purify your mind from beliefs that spring from a lower source—and rest assured that I will expose this source and its illusions as the book progresses. One of the most important abilities on the quest for truth is the willingness to examine one's beliefs and let go of all beliefs that are found to limit one's quest for the Living Truth.

It remains the greatest limitation for humankind's spiritual teachers that so many of those who sincerely seek truth have not yet recognized the conflict in their own psyches. If you do not recognize the existence of the ego, it can so easily cause you to doubt and rationalize away the directions you get from your Higher Self or your direct experiences of the Living Truth. If you are still caught in the trap of seeking to fit every new insight into the framework of your existing beliefs – seeking to defend your world view rather than expand it –

then you will be your own worst enemy, going back and forth without ever finding satisfying answers to life's questions. The challenge for any seeker of truth is whether to cling to what is familiar and seems safe or whether to reach for an understanding that simply cannot fit within the confines of one's existing beliefs.

***

I have done everything I can to make sure this book can trigger a direct encounter with the Spirit of Truth. I can do no more, as I respect God's Law of Free Will and have no desire to make decisions for you. Yet if you make the decision to reach beyond the words in this book, seeking honestly for an encounter with the Spirit of Truth, I will work with you as will your own Higher Self. Thus, the experience you get from reading this book can become a two-way street, a figure-eight flow, between you as the student below and I as the spiritual teacher above. This student-teacher relationship is – and always has been – the very essence of how life progresses on this planet. It is the God-ordained means to raise the consciousness of those who are still in a physical body but know they are more than the body. It is a sacred relationship that has been described in many spiritual and religious traditions. And even though many orthodox religions have replaced it with an outer institution, it has always remained as an option for those who are willing to seek first the kingdom of God and then let the teacher add all other things to them as they are ready for it (Matthew 6:33). Even though orthodoxy has downplayed it, let it be known that Jesus clearly recognized his own relationship to his teacher, as he stated, "I and my father are one" (John 10:30), "I can of my own self do nothing" (John 5:30) and "My father worketh hitherto and I work" (John 5:17).

As mentioned, it is an eternal truth that when the student is ready, the teacher appears. However, this is a subtle statement with hidden meanings. The real question is what kind of teacher you are ready for at any given moment? For you will inevitably attract to you a teacher that corresponds not only to your current level of consciousness but also to your willingness to transcend that level of consciousness. If you are only ready to look for truth in a teaching expressed in words, then you will attract a teacher who thinks truth can be confined to words. Yet when you are ready to go beyond the level of words, you will attract a spiritual teacher who can take you beyond words to the Living Truth itself. I am such a teacher, and through this book I offer my guidance to anyone who is willing to self-transcend.

I have only one intention for offering you this book. That is to offer you the tools you need in order to set yourself free from your human limitations and be who you really are. Yet in order to *be* who you are, you have to *know* who you are. Thus, you must take up the ancient challenge:

Human, know thyself!

I have conquered that challenge. I know who I am and I am being who I am. Thus, I am qualified to help you discover who you are. Yet for me to help you, you must be willing to accept my offering. You must be willing to consider my teachings with an open mind and heart. You must be willing to look beyond your present beliefs and question what you have so far been unable or unwilling to question.

How strongly do you want to know who you are and how many of your current illusions are you willing to give up in order to find out who you really are? How strongly do you want to *be* who you are and how much of your current sense of limitation – your sense of what you cannot *do* and cannot *be* – are you willing to give up in order to be who you really are?

I can only offer you the tools that can set you free. I cannot force you to use them. There are numerous books that offer you knowledge, even understanding. Yet it is an eternal fact that the knowledge that can be put in a book will do nothing to change your life. As an old Indian proverb states, "The knowledge that is in the books stays in the books." Knowledge coming from an external source will not change your life. Only knowledge coming from within yourself will produce positive change. That is why I stress the importance of seeing this book as a stepping stone to a direct experience of the Spirit of Truth. Only such an experience will provide the impetus for a change in your consciousness.

To be, or not to be is still the question. By making use of this book, you will be able to answer that question. You will be able to be here below all that you are above—and MORE!

***

Most people take one of the following approaches to finding answers to life's questions:

- They think answers *don't* exist or that it is beyond the capacity of human beings to find such answers or to determine what constitutes true answers.

- They think answers *do* exist, but you cannot find them on your own, let alone from a source inside yourself. You need an external source with the proper authority to tell you what is true. And such an authority can be found only within the context of an established belief system with some superhuman authority.

 The result of either approach is that people adopt a passive approach to finding answers. They either give up trying to find answers or they confine their search to the doctrines of a particular belief system. Therefore, many people *do* ask the fundamental questions of life, but in seeking answers they impose – consciously or subconsciously – restrictions on how the answers can be given. In other words, people are only open to answers that do not go beyond or challenge their existing beliefs.

Why do people take this approach? There can be only one explanation. They are not willing to take full responsibility for their lives, their growth, even their "salvation." They are not willing to take full responsibility for finding their own answers by activating their inherent ability to get understanding. With all their getting, they are not willing to get true understanding and internalization (Proverbs 4:7). They are not willing to recognize and admit that they *do* have the ability to find answers from within themselves. They are not willing to acknowledge that they can find living answers only by looking beyond their existing belief system.

Such people are not willing to truly change themselves – to expand their beliefs, question their belief system, change their approach to life – in order to find answers. Instead, they want someone else to give them ready-made answers, answers that do not "rock their boat" and require them to change the beliefs and the approach to life that make them comfortable. Such people may claim that they want answers to life's questions, but in reality they do not want answers. They want confirmation that they can continue to live their lives as they do now. Obviously, such people are not teachable and cannot even recognize a true spiritual teacher.

***

Jesus talked about the truth that will make you free (John 8:32), and it is a basic fact that for every human limitation there is a higher understanding that will set you free from that limitation. Yet in order to claim this freedom, you must be willing to change your actions, your beliefs and your approach to life based on your new understanding. And to do that, you must be willing to let go of some aspect of your current beliefs, even your current limitations. And before you can let go of your limitations, you must overcome your fear of freedom, your fear of the unknown.

Before you can be set free from a physical prison, you must be willing to leave behind your cell. Before you can be set free from a mental prison, you must be willing to leave behind the belief system that makes you feel like you have your life under some degree of control. The problem is that many people are afraid of total spiritual freedom, and they cling to the limitations that are familiar and give them a sense of comfortability. As a result of this fear, they are reluctant to acknowledge the truth that can make them free from their current limitations. For example, it is far easier to let an external authority give you ready-made answers than to seek living answers inside yourself. It is easier to think that you can be saved by following an external authority than it is to take full responsibility for your own spiritual growth.

My point being that as long as people refuse to take full responsibility for their lives, they will resist knowing the full truth about life. They might be seeking answers, but they do not really want the truth. They want a "truth" that fits within the confines of their accepted belief system—so that they can feel comfortable in continuing their present lifestyle.

If this is your approach, then this book will do nothing but agitate you. This book will systematically challenge every aspect of your current beliefs, no matter what those beliefs might be. How can I say this? Because this book will give you an understanding of life that has never before been released on this planet and thus cannot be found – in full – within any of the existing belief systems. This book can help you only if you are willing to look beyond your current belief system and if you are willing to let a higher understanding change your approach to life. If you truly seek such fundamental changes to your life, then I welcome you to my heart. If you do not, I bid you go in peace and I do not judge or condemn you in any way. I want you to know that you are always welcome to come back to me when you decide that you are willing to accept responsibility for your own destiny. I am a cosmic teacher, and I am always willing to teach those who have made the decision that makes them teachable—the decision that they are willing to go beyond their current mental boxes.

***

Before you can find answers, you must be willing to ask questions, questions that go beyond your existing beliefs. Yet it is a fact that many spiritual and religious people are reluctant to ask such questions. Too often a religion has the effect of closing people's minds to questions that are not within the framework defined by official doctrine. People seem to believe that God has something to hide and does not want them to ask certain questions. Let it be made clear, then, that there are no stupid or forbidden questions. What is unfortunate is when people are not willing to open their minds to find living answers to the questions they ask.

It is a fact that all questions have answers. Any question you could possibly ask has an answer that will increase your understanding of the topic. However, not all questions can be answered the way they are asked. The reason is that when you ask a question, the way you formulate the question is a product of your current state of consciousness, which includes your current belief system. Most people are unaware of this fact and thus do not understand that the state of consciousness from which they ask the question often prevents them from finding a meaningful answer.

As an example, consider the age-old question, "What is the meaning of life?" In today's world many people subscribe to a scientific, materialistic belief system. This belief system states that there is nothing beyond the material world and that if a theory proposes a non-materialistic cause, the theory is unscientific. It follows that life on Earth is a product of a random process, and thus the question of the meaning of life simply cannot be answered within the context of the materialistic belief system. If everything is random, how could life possibly have any meaning?

Other people subscribe to an orthodox religion which states that everything is the product of the will of an external deity, often portrayed as an angry being in the sky. Yet if you have no freedom to choose your own path in life, how can your life have any meaning? If you are nothing more than a puppet on a string, there is no meaning to your individual existence. If you cannot choose and learn from your choices, how can you possibly grow? And without conscious growth, how can life have meaning?

In both cases, people's state of consciousness, and their belief systems, prevent them from finding a meaningful answer to the question about the meaning of life. This has caused many people to ignore the question, while others use their belief system to define an "infallible" answer or define the question as irrelevant. Yet it is a fact that human beings have been wondering about the meaning of life for a very long time. Thus, the very fact that people continue to ask this question should be an indicator that somewhere in your being is an inner knowledge that the question has an answer.

The reason you have not discovered the answer is that this answer cannot be found within the confines of your current belief system and world view. Thus, you face the simple choice that is the precursor to all human progress. Will you look beyond your existing beliefs in order to find the higher understanding that will open the door for your question to be answered, or will you cling to your present beliefs and close the door to the answer? Humankind moved beyond the stage of the cave dwellers only because some people were willing to look beyond their existing world view and consider that there could be a better way to live. Only those who are willing to do this will benefit from this book—or any other book about the deeper mysteries of life.

***

In medieval Europe your options for finding answers to life's questions were rather limited. You could either accept or reject the official Catholic doctrine, which claimed to give infallible answers to all the questions you were allowed to ask. If the doctrine could not answer a particular question, it was because you were not allowed to know. No alternative theories were available, having been suppressed by the Church, often through violent means. While this situation was simple, it obviously was not free, for how can there be freedom without choices and how can there be choice when freedom of expression – even freedom of thought – is forcefully suppressed?

In today's world your options for finding answers are infinitely more complex. Thanks to the internet, there is now so much information, so many competing and often mutually exclusive belief systems, that it is overwhelming to most people. Truly, you have greater freedom to search for answers, but unless you have a way to distinguish between true and false information, how can you exercise that freedom? Both too little information and too much information can limit your ability to find answers that help you transcend your current level of consciousness. Thus, as has always been the case, the true key to finding useful answers is the ability to discern between what is real and what is unreal. Where does this ability come from?

All religions on this planet talk about the existence of a realm beyond the material universe. Even the latest discoveries of science have opened up for the existence of such a parallel universe or dimension. Most religions state that there is one or more intelligent beings living in this higher realm. These immortal beings are not bound by the limitations that imprison people on Earth. All human beings have the potential to pass the final exam in Earth's schoolroom and ascend to the spiritual realm. When you go through this ascension process, all of the questions you have on Earth will be answered in an absolute and final way. You will acquire a new understanding of life, a broader view of life, that will make your former questions obsolete.

What does it really mean to have a question answered in a final way? As I said earlier, every question you ask is a reflection of a certain state of consciousness. In that state of consciousness, there is something you cannot see, something you do not understand—which is why you have a question about that something. Yet you only have the question because you have a limited vision of reality. Once you attain a broader vision, your question fades away and becomes irrelevant. There was a time when many people considered the question of whether the Earth was flat. Yet today people have an expanded world view, and in this larger world view the question of whether the Earth is flat has become obsolete. Take note that modern people do not simply have the answer to the question of whether the Earth is flat. They have a vastly broader understanding of life, an entirely different view of life, than people in medieval times. Thus, modern people have a higher level of consciousness, giving them a more mature approach to life—at least compared to their ancestors.

My point is that the only way to find a final answer to a question is for you to rise above the state of consciousness – the state of ignorance – that gave birth to the question. Thus, only by rising above the state of ignorance that entraps most people on Earth will you find final answers to the questions people have on Earth. Rising above your present state of consciousness is the highest possible outcome of asking questions. Thus, your questions should be seen as the stepping stones for your growth in consciousness, your spiritual progress.

**

When you go through the process of the ascension, you will find final answers to every question you ever had while on Earth. You find these answers by connecting to – and eventually becoming one with – a larger mind than the mind you are aware of right now. This larger mind, this greater state of awareness, can be called by several valid names, but I would like to call it the "Christ mind." I am aware that because Christianity has fallen into the typical pattern of becoming a rigid and exclusivist religion, many people do not see the word "Christ" as a universal term. Yet I have no intention of catering to people's biases, and thus I simply state the fact that the term "Christ" refers to a universal state of mind, a universal state of consciousness. The function of this mind – which I will later describe in more detail – is to store all knowledge that is true, real and valid in an absolute sense. The knowledge stored in the universal Christ mind is in complete harmony with the reality of God—we might say it is true in an absolute sense. In contrast, much of the knowledge found on Earth – even in the world's religions and science – is out of harmony with the reality of God—it is false or at best incomplete.

Again, I will give you more detail later, but for now let me point out that most of the religions found on this planet talk about the fact that human beings have descended or fallen into a state of consciousness in which they cannot see the truth and the reality of God. They are trapped behind a veil of ignorance, illusion or sin that prevents them from seeing the absolute reality. The absolute reality that many religions talk about (using different names) is the truth that is stored in the universal Christ mind. The image I would like to impart to you is that in a higher vibrational spectrum there is a "database" containing all of the true knowledge found in this universe. Your mind is currently separated from this fount of knowledge by a veil of illusions and ignorance. Yet this is not the way things need to remain. You do indeed have the option of connecting to the universal Christ mind, and by doing so you will gain the ability to discern whether the knowledge you find on Earth is true and valid in an absolute sense.

In reality, all of the true spiritual teachers who have been sent to Earth by the Ascended Host have had as their mission to help people connect to the source of truth. The Buddha said that people's minds are trapped behind a veil of maya, or illusions, and he described a path that leads to enlightenment—meaning that you see reality as it truly is. Jesus gave a similar concept and talked about the "key of knowledge" (Luke 11:52). He chastised the lawyers for refusing to use the key of knowledge and even trying to prevent others from using it. The lawyers were those who focused on the outer doctrines of a particular belief system and refused to reach beyond their current level of consciousness. They wanted to keep their existing world view – their graven image (Exodus 20:4) – and refused to connect to the Living Truth. They did not want to take ultimate responsibility for their own salvation and placed responsibility with the external God, the external savior. Unfortunately, many modern Christians have taken on the mindset of the lawyers. They now use Jesus' own teachings to justify staying in a state of illusion, ignoring the call to establish a connection to the universal Christ mind. This call was verbalized by Paul, but inspired by Jesus himself, in the statement, "Let this mind be in you which was also in Christ Jesus" (Philippians 2:5).

Ultimately, both the Buddha and Jesus demonstrated the final stages of the path, where you go beyond having a connection to the universal Christ mind and unite with that mind. Your mind becomes an individual identity existing within the whole of the universal mind, and only at that point have you fully risen above the consciousness that traps people on Earth. Only then will your earthly questions be fully and finally answered.

***

How can you establish a personal connection to the universal Christ mind, to the source of truth? The fact is that you have separated yourself from the universal Christ mind (through a process I will describe later), and thus you need a mediator. That mediator has two aspects, two forms. There is the external teacher, namely an ascended being or a teacher on Earth who serves as your personal guide. And there is the inner teacher, namely what I would like to call your Christ self or Higher Self. Your Christ self has become part of your own mind, or being, and it knows you in intimate detail. Thus, it is capable of guiding you in all of life's situations, and it can give you answers that are carefully adapted to your current state of consciousness.

My point is that all sincere seekers of understanding already have a personal connection to the universal Christ mind, to the source of truth. And that connection is located inside themselves, not in some outer guru, organization or doctrine. This is truly why Jesus said that the kingdom of God is within you (Luke 17:21). He meant that you already have – inside yourself – the key to God's kingdom—which is a state of consciousness. You already have the key of knowledge, namely your personal Christ self, which Jesus called the Comforter. He also said, "But the Comforter… he shall teach you all things, and bring all things to your remembrance, whatsoever I have said unto you" (John 14:26). Truly, your Christ self can teach you all things and answer all of your questions.

The fact that you are open to this book demonstrates that you already have some connection to your Christ self. You might know it as intuition, your inner guide, the still small voice, an inner sense of knowing what is right or perhaps a sense of warning that something is wrong. You simply need to increase your awareness of this connection and perhaps use suitable techniques for expanding it. Such techniques are offered in Mother Mary's book and on Jesus' website.*

***

In order to make full use of your personal connection to the universal Christ mind, you need to understand that the knowledge stored in this higher mind is not stored in the form of words, at least not the words known on Earth. On this planet people currently use words in a very

* See the website *www.askrealjesus.com*.

ambiguous and linear way. Two people can read the same statement and come away with two different, even mutually exclusive, interpretations. In fact, the conflicting interpretations of religious scriptures is one of the major sources of conflict on this planet. How sad it is when people who claim to be religious fight each other over the interpretation of an outer scripture, both sides refusing to use the key of knowledge that is the open door to an inner understanding that can resolve all conflict.

Obviously, such conflicts cannot exist in heaven, and one consequence is that your Christ self does not communicate in a linear way. Your Christ self does not communicate the same way as your intellect, nor does it follow the norms of society. Your Christ self communicates in a spherical, non-linear way that gives you the overall picture. And this often comes to you in the form of a mental image or an intuitive sensation. My point is that you cannot expect that you will always get a linear, verbal expression of truth from your Christ self, and this is especially true when it comes to the deeper questions of life. Words are simply too linear, too imprecise, to ambiguous to convey a real understanding of the deeper mysteries of life.

Obviously, the limitations of words apply to this book as well. Human beings love to elevate their chosen religious scripture to the status of an infallible or absolute truth, but the reality is that no teaching expressed in words can ever be absolute or infallible. I have no intention of claiming that this book states an absolute truth. On the contrary, let it be made clear that this book is an attempt to do the impossible, namely to explain the – nonlinear, spherical – truth about life through linear words. Thus, this book is not meant to give you everything you need in order to understand these mysteries. This book can merely serve as an outer stimulant that will help you gain insights directly from your Christ self. These insights will often come to you as non-verbal, spherical sensations that an idea in the book is true, but the insights go beyond the outer words.

Be careful not to fall into the age-old trap of thinking that the truth I describe in this book can be expressed only through the words I am using. I am deliberately giving this book in the straightforward, rational, direct and linear language that is commonly used in the modern Western world. However, the same truth can be expressed in many other ways that can be equally valid in different contexts. For example, it would be possible to express the same concepts by using

the symbolism and language of many ancient forms of poetry, such as
the Iliad, the Upanishads or other epic poems.

My point is that if you are to make full use of this book, you must
not focus too much on the outer words. You must use the key of
knowledge to reach beyond the outer words and allow your Christ
self to give you an inner, spherical image that goes beyond words.
You must watch for the inner sensation of resonance, whereby you
feel that the statements made in this book are true because they reso-
nate – at a level deeper than words – with the truth stored in the universal Christ mind, the truth found in the kingdom of God within you.

***

For the serious student of the deeper mysteries, it is absolutely essential to be aware that there are forces that seek to oppose your progress
on the path toward a higher state of consciousness. I will later
describe these forces in greater detail, and this knowledge will
remove your fear of such forces. Yet for now, you need to know that
these forces want to control you, and they can control you only
through ignorance or illusions. Thus, it is always their modus operandi to prevent you from discovering or internalizing the truth that
will set you free (John 8:32). In your present state of consciousness,
these forces have some degree of control over you. Were you to discover a higher understanding, you would rise above your present state
of consciousness, and thus you would diminish their control. Because
they do not want to lose control, these forces are always trying to prevent you from finding, accepting or internalizing a higher understanding than your current belief system. They are generally trying to make
it seem like you do not need to change your lifestyle or approach to
life but that you should continue living as you do now, knowing what
you know now.

To escape this control, it is essential to realize that when you are
presented with new information, such as this book or any other spiritual teaching that goes beyond your present belief system, there are
forces that seek to make you reject the "dangerous" information. You
have an inner teacher and an outer teacher who are seeking to help
you grow by presenting you with a higher understanding. Likewise,
you have an inner false teacher and an outer false teacher who are try-

ing to prevent you from accepting any liberating truth presented by your true teachers.

The outer false teacher is made up of the mass consciousness and certain forces that I will describe later. The inner false teacher is what is commonly called the human ego, and it is the impostor of your Christ self. The ego will always seek to make you reject information that could set you free from its control. The ego will often do this by referring to its current belief system as the unfailing standard against which all new information must be measured. The ego has an extreme need for security, and one aspect of this is that it clings to a belief system that it claims is infallible. The ego believes that by being a member of a particular religion or believing a certain outer doctrine, you will automatically be saved. Thus, when you are presented with a new spiritual idea, your ego will immediately compare it to its "infallible" belief system, using any real or perceived differences to argue – loudly and with great confidence or subtly and with great powers of persuasion – that the new idea is false or dangerous.

As a serious student, you need to learn to recognize the voice of the ego. And you need to learn to recognize the subtle, gentle voice of your Christ self that gives you the inner recognition that a teaching is true. As you read this book, you will no doubt hear both voices. Yet if you are not aware of the voice of the ego, it is all too easy for you to let this voice draw your attention away from the still, small voice within.

If you read the New Testament, you will see that Jesus often talked about those who were blind, were without understanding or did not have ears to hear. Even Jesus felt frustrated over the fact that so many people – even his disciples – did not grasp his message. The situation faced by the spiritual teachers of humankind is that human beings see everything through the filter of their ego-based belief systems. Imagine that every human being had been wearing colored contact lenses since birth, lenses that prevented them from seeing the world as it really is. We who are the spiritual teachers are constantly trying to get people to take off the contact lenses. Yet most people allow their egos to convince them that what they see through the filter is the only true vision. Thus, instead of seeking to take off the contact lenses, most people spend their lives trying to convince everyone else that their particular kind of contact lenses is the only one showing the world as it really is.

Your benefit from reading this book depends entirely on whether you listen to the voice of the ego or the voice of your Christ self. In the end, this comes down to choices that only *you* can make. As I said, I can only present you with the key of knowledge. I cannot force you to use it to unlock the door in your mind that leads you to a higher state of consciousness. Thus, once again, I place all responsibility where it belongs, namely on you. I have done my part by bringing forth this book. It is now up to you what you do with it. Will you multiply the talents I offer you or will you bury them in the ground and cover them over with your present beliefs?

Key 2
Seeing beyond the graven images of God

Does God exist? People have been pondering this question for eons. While some claim to have found proof that God exists in a particular form, others claim there is no final proof and still others claim to have proof that God does not exist. This controversy has given rise to the related question, "If God does indeed exist, why hasn't he given human beings some irrefutable proof that he exists?" This question is worth pondering before we go any further.

Let us begin by considering how God could possibly give such a proof. How could any proof be irrefutable? Or rather, how could there ever be a proof or fact that could not be doubted by the human mind? When you look at the variety of ideas and belief systems found on Earth, it is not difficult to see that for every idea or belief there is a counter-idea that seems to invalidate or at least question the original idea. Today, it seems completely obvious to most people that the Earth is round. Yet only a few centuries ago, this now accepted fact was disputed by most people.

The logical conclusion is that most human beings are in a state of consciousness that is dominated by an interplay of two opposites—truth and falsity, count and counter-point, black and white. These two opposites are – or seem to be – mutually exclusive. A statement cannot be true and false at the same time—or so it seems to the human mind. And thus, it seems that people must choose between one of the opposing viewpoints. They either accept that God exists or they accept that he does not exist, and in either case they cite evidence to "prove" their belief—evidence that can be debated and disputed endlessly without ever finding a final answer. So instead of finding the final answer to the question of God's existence, people continue to debate the evidence, and they continue to seek to convince others that their evidence constitutes a final, absolute and infallible proof.

Is there an alternative approach to the question of God's existence? Let us step back from the debate. Let us recognize that most of the people who argue for or against the existence of God do so based on a particular mental image of God or of "reality." For example,

materialists argue that there is no God because they claim to have discovered an evolutionary mechanism in nature that supposedly can
account for the appearance of today's multitude of species. Thus, if
everything could have come from a random process, there is no need
for an intelligent creator. However, this theory is based on certain
assumptions, and these assumptions are based on a particular view of
the world. One such assumption is that a highly structured and
orderly universe – and science continues to discover deeper layers of
complexity and order – could actually have arisen from a completely
random process. In other words, they say randomness can – by
chance – produce order and it can – randomly – uphold an ordered
process of evolution that – over billions of years – leads from less
complex to more complex life forms, such as human beings. Obviously, this cannot be proven in an ultimate way (if everything is random, how can an ordered process be proven?), and thus the entire
world view of materialistic science rests on an assumption.

What is an assumption? It is a mental image of reality that you
choose to create even though you have no direct experience or proof
to demonstrate that the image is correct. You assume your image is
true, and therefore, an assumption is a chosen rather than a necessary
or infallible mental image. If you have a strong desire to prove your
assumption, you might see only evidence that supports it and over-
look evidence that goes beyond it. You see what you want to see,
because you have used your assumption to form a mental image and
you are now seeking to project that image upon reality.

Most religions argue that God does exist, but in reality they are
not arguing for a universal or transcendental concept of God. They
are arguing for a specific concept or image of God, as defined by their
sacred scriptures and by their current interpretations of those scriptures, their preferred doctrines. They are arguing that *their* God exists
and that he/she/it is the only true God. For example, the mainstream
Christian churches argue that God is omnipotent and thus he could
not have created anything imperfect. Yet everyone can observe that
conditions on Earth are not perfect because they produce much suffering. So either an omnipotent God created human beings to suffer
or something must have prevented God's original intent from being
manifest on this planet. Either way, there is no absolute proof that
God is omnipotent, so this is another example of an assumption that is
chosen and not the only possible assumption.

If we are to prove the existence of God in an ultimate way, we have to go beyond theories that are based on assumptions, assumptions that can be disputed based on people's chosen view of "reality." We have to go beyond theories that are expressed in words, words that can be interpreted differently by different people. We have to find a way to prove God's existence that is beyond the human mind, the level of consciousness dominated by the two relative opposites. We have to find something that is beyond truth and error, something that cannot be influenced by the dualistic mind, the mind that sees everything in terms of opposites. To find absolute proof, we must turn to experience, but not just any experience.

***

Most people believe in the existence of atoms, and most people believe in the existence of apples. Most people have never seen an atom, so their belief in the reality of atoms does not rest on direct experience. Instead, it rests on a process that takes place entirely in the mind, a process that has led most people to accept that everything they see is made of invisible building blocks that look like miniature solar systems. Yet because most people have not seen an actual atom, their belief in atoms rests on the creation of a mental image. After they became aware of this mental image, they used the mind's reasoning faculties to accept that the image must be accurate and therefore atoms must exist. The point is that people's acceptance of the existence of atoms requires the intermediate step of a mental image.

In contrast, people's belief in the reality of apples is not based on any kind of reasoning process. People do not have to reason in order to accept the existence of apples, they simply have to draw upon experience. They have all seen an apple, felt its smooth skin, heard the sound of their fingers rubbing that skin, smelled its fragrance and experienced the taste of the sweet juice. Thus, few would seriously dispute that apples are real. The point being that although people have a mental image of apples, they do not need this image in order to accept the existence of apples. They have had a direct experience of the phenomenon they call an apple, and their acceptance is based on this experience with no intermediary in the form of a mental image.

As discussed above, people who believe in the non-existence of God have no experiential proof for this belief. It is not possible to experience that God *does not* exist—it is only possible to fail to have the experience that God *does* exist. It is not possible to experience the non-existence of something, as it is not possible to logically prove that something does not exist. You can experience an apple, but you cannot experience the non-existence of apples. You can say that at this point you have not had the experience of apples, but that does not prove you could never have this experience. Likewise, all one can say is that one has not experienced the existence of God. One can never rule out that such an experience could be attained in the future. Thus, people who believe God does not exist do so based on a mental image, a mental image that portrays a world in which God is not needed. The point being that this non-belief in God is not based on direct experience but requires the intermediary of a mental image.

Most religious people have not experienced the Presence of God. Their belief in God rests entirely on a mental image defined by a particular religion. The point being that whether people believe in God or do not believe in God, their belief is based on a mental image and not on direct experience. If people were to have a direct experience of the Presence of God, their view of God would no longer be based on belief, would no longer be based on the acceptance or non-acceptance of a mental image. Thus, the existence of God would be no more mysterious than the existence of apples.

We might say that when you *believe* in something, your belief is based on a mental image. The mental image is subject to belief or non-belief, and it can be debated endlessly by the dualistic mind without ever finding a conclusive answer. When you experience something, you go beyond the mental image to a direct perception. Yet even experience is not absolute. It is possible that your experience can be colored by your mental images, as if you are seeing the world through colored glasses. Thus, you can refine your experience, but seeking direct experience is still better than clinging to a mental image. We might say that only those who are willing to seek for a direct experience have the potential to answer the question of God's existence. A mental image can never prove or disprove anything.

Can human beings have a direct experience of the Presence of God? Many people – from every religion, even some from no religious background – have had spiritual or mystical experiences. In fact, the statement in the Old Testament that human beings were created "in the image" and "after the likeness" of God (Genesis 1:26) is an indication that human beings were designed with the capacity to have a direct experience of God's Presence. Yet this ability to experience God is not based on the physical senses, which is why most people have experienced apples but they have not experienced God. You can experience God only by going beyond the physical senses and even beyond the entire consciousness that creates mental images of reality, the consciousness that operates with relative opposites.

***

It is a fact that the physical senses cannot detect the Presence of God. While some have used this to reason that God does not exist, most people know that the physical senses are easily deceived by appearances. For example, most people have seen the optical illusion to the right.

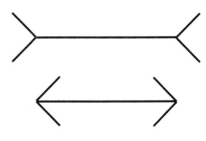

It seems to the human eye that the upper line is longer than the lower line, while in reality the two lines have the same length. Most people use this well-known example to reason that the physical senses are not reliable, but this is not entirely true. Your eyes are not telling you that one line is longer than the other. Your eyes are simply passing on an arrangement of light waves. It is your mind that transforms these light waves into a mental image. It is your mind that names parts of this image as lines, creates the concept of length and reasons that one line appears to be longer than the other. Your eyes do not operate with the concept of lines and thus have no idea that one could be longer than the other. Only your mind creates this mental image and imposes it upon the light waves detected by your eyes. The point being that it really is the mind that is unreliable and not the senses. Your senses simply do what they were designed to do, namely detect the energy waves that make up the material universe. Your senses do not make any judgments about whether there is anything beyond what they detect—only your mind can do that. What makes the mind unreliable is the tendency to impose mental images upon the impressions detected by the senses. If these mental images are out of touch with reality, the mind will base its view of reality, its world view, upon a set of illusions.

Obviously, the senses have certain limitations. For example, your eyes can only detect light waves that fall within a certain spectrum of frequencies. Science has shown that there are many light waves that vibrate at higher or lower frequencies. Yet this discovery was based on using scientific instruments to extend the range of the physical senses. Thus, people can prove the existence of something that cannot be experienced directly by the senses. Many people have seen an X-ray image and thus have a direct experiential proof that such light rays exist.

Materialistic science has greatly extended the range of the physical senses. However, because science has focused on the material world, it has not gone any further. It is possible to extend human experience beyond the physical senses and even beyond the reasoning mind, the mind that creates mental images of the world. In fact, it is possible to create a spiritual science that systematically uses the faculties that are built into the consciousness of every human being. These faculties can give people a direct experience of a level of reality that is beyond the material universe. Thus, a mystical experience is not mystical. It is a perfectly natural experience that uses a built-in ability to reach beyond the level of the physical senses, even beyond the vibrational spectrum of the material universe. When you make use of this faculty, you can have a direct experience of a level of reality beyond the material world. As the faculty is sharpened, you can even have a direct experience of the Presence, the Being, of God. At that point, the question of whether God exists has become obsolete.

If someone tells you about a fruit that grows in a far-away land, you can choose to believe or not to believe in this testimony. When you hear about the fruit and its properties, you form a mental image of it, and thus your belief or non-belief is based on this mental image. There is nothing wrong with this, as you do not have the opportunity for direct experience. The ability to form a mental image is useful in many ways. One way is that the mental image gives you an opportunity to build the desire to travel to the far country to prove or disprove the existence of the fruit. Yet the danger is that a mental image can also take away all desire to go beyond it and compare it to reality.

The true purpose of religion is to give you a mental image of God that can serve as the basis for developing a desire to have a direct experience of God's Presence. When you hold a fruit in your hand and take a bite of it, you no longer doubt its existence. Likewise, when you actually experience God as a Living Presence, your doubts will give way to the certainty that can only come from direct experience. The problem comes in when people misuse their ability to form mental images by deciding that their current image represents the truth and that it is infallible, meaning that it never needs to be proven through experience. In that case, people become the slaves of their mental images and the images prevent them from knowing reality.

The direct experience of God can only come when you are willing to reach beyond the senses and beyond the reasoning mind. You must be willing to reach beyond the mental images created by the reasoning mind, even the images expressed in the world's religions. To understand this, consider the first two of the Ten Commandments given to Moses. The first is that you shall have no other gods before the one true God (Exodus 20:3). The second is that you shall not create any graven image of that God (Exodus 20:4). The meaning is clear. If you use any words or images from this world to create a mental image of God, you will be creating a false image, and you will worship this idol instead of the true God. Thus, these two commandments were meant as guidelines for how you can attain a direct experience of God.

Why is it so important not to use words or images from this world in order to create an image of God? Because the one true God is beyond the material world. As Jesus clearly stated, God is a Spirit and you must worship him in Spirit and in truth (John 4:24). And precisely because God is beyond this world, the words or images found in this world cannot give a complete or an accurate portrayal of God. This is a concept we will explore further.

***

Imagine that you meet a person who has grown up on a remote island where there are no apple trees. Your task is to help this person know what an apple tastes like—and you can use only words to do so. If you think about this task, you will realize that the taste of an apple is a sensory experience that cannot be accurately conveyed in words. Some of the greatest poets of all time have attempted to use words to convey a direct experience, but their success has been limited. In fact, if you were to describe the taste of an apple with words, you would quickly start comparing the taste of an apple to a taste with which the person is familiar. This is what most poets have done in trying to convey experiences through words—they seek to invoke people's memory of a similar experience. They seek to find words that will trigger the memory of an actual experience and thus give people the impression that they are experiencing what the poet describes. Yet while having tasted pears and plums and cherries can give you some idea of what an apple tastes like, an apple does not taste exactly like any of these other fruits. Thus, only by actually tasting an apple will you know its taste.

The point here is that if you describe the taste of an apple by comparing it to the taste of other fruits, the person will build a mental image of what an apple might taste like. The person will then project this mental image upon the concept of an apple, and the person might eventually begin to believe that the mental image is complete and accurate. People can convince themselves that they know exactly what an apple tastes like, and thus there is no reason to taste an actual apple. People have an ability to substitute their mental images for direct experience, even to the point of preferring the image for the real experience. This is especially true when it comes to the existence of God. Most people are quite willing to create a mental image of God (or the non-existence of God) but very few are willing to put their image to the test through direct experience. Sure, many people have a mental image of God that makes them think such direct experience is impossible or reserved for the few, but they are still not willing to test the validity of this belief by asking God to prove or disprove it. And while some are willing to ask, most of them are not willing to ask with an open mind and heart—meaning that you let go of and look beyond *all* of your mental images of God in order to experience the transcendent reality of God. In other words, while some people pray for God to show himself to them, they expect him to appear in the form of their preferred mental image—their idol.

This is an essential feature of the human consciousness, the consciousness that operates with relative opposites. It is incapable of experiencing anything beyond the material world. Yet it is not incapable of creating a mental image of something beyond the material world. And because it cannot compare its mental images of God to direct experience, it becomes completely convinced that its graven image of God is correct. It therefore refuses to question its image, and this refusal to look beyond the image prevents the person from having a direct experience of anything beyond the material world. Thus, the human consciousness becomes a closed system, a spiritual catch-22, that can keep you trapped behind a veil of illusions for an indefinite period of time. People think they know all they need to know about God, and this belief prevents them from seeking a direct experience to confirm or expand their knowledge of God.

In fact, it is important to realize the reality behind the Biblical statement that God created human beings in his image and after his likeness. It is true that human beings were originally created in the likeness of God, in the sense that human beings have the capacity – the key of knowledge – to have a direct experience of God's Presence and God's Living Truth. Yet, as I mentioned earlier, most religions contain the concept that people have fallen into a different state, which truly means a lower state of consciousness. This is the consciousness in which people no longer see the one truth of God and only see the dualistic struggle between two opposing views. I will later describe this state of consciousness in greater detail, but for now let it be enough to say that the dualistic state of consciousness creates mental images and projects them upon everything. This includes God. The reality is that after human beings fell into the dualistic state of consciousness, they started creating a "god" in the image and after the likeness of their own dualistic state of mind. Thus, many of the images of God found in this world – even the images promoted by some of the major world religions – are the products of the dualistic state of mind. They are false or incomplete images that people have projected unto the concept of God, and over time large segments of humanity have accepted these images as real without ever comparing them to direct experience.

This has happened precisely because when people cannot experience a "thing" directly, they tend to create a mental image of that thing by comparing it to something they *do* experience. In other words, after people fell into the lower state of consciousness, they could only experience the material world. Thus, they started creating a mental image of God based on what they experienced in the material world. And since they experienced life as a struggle, they created the image of an angry God who is seeking to punish them for their sins by making them struggle for everything. In reality, this human struggle was not created by God and it is not God's punishment. It is an entirely self-created condition, as I will later explain in greater detail.

The essential question now becomes whether you will cling to your mental images of God or whether you are willing to let go of all such images in order to experience God's Presence? Jesus described this dilemma by saying that if you seek to save your life – meaning the mortal sense of life that is based on mental images instead of reality – you will lose your life (Matthew 16:25). Only if you are willing to let your mental images – your mortal sense of identity – die for the sake of experiencing God directly, will you have the eternal life that comes only through experiencing – eventually becoming one with – the Presence of God. We can also say that it is people's mental images of God that take away their spiritual freedom. The ultimate spiritual freedom can be attained only by going beyond all graven images of God until you experience God's Spirit directly and with no intermediary. How can you be free as long as you are separated from your source?

**

The essential point is that God is a Spirit, meaning that God is beyond the material universe. Something that is beyond this universe cannot be limited to or fit into any of the belief systems found in this world. No words or mental images can accurately describe the reality and the Presence of God. They can only give approximations that point to a deeper reality. No matter how elaborate a theory or doctrine you might create, God will always be more than your description.

The essential problem with religion on this planet is that human beings have used religion to create mental images of God, and then they have attempted to force the transcendental Spirit of God into their mental boxes. Not only is this impossible, and thus futile, but it has the inevitable effect that people force themselves into their own mental boxes. They think that unless they live their lives according to the standards defined by their mental boxes, they will go to hell or eternal damnation. They think that their entry into heaven is dependent upon them living up to certain conditions on Earth.

In reality, such people have created a set of conditions based on the dualistic state of consciousness and they have projected a mental image upon the real God. These dualistic images are either partially or completely out of touch with the transcendent reality of God, and thus the conditions people have created on Earth have little or no bearing on their getting into heaven. People might think they are righteous according to their own dualistic standard, but their self-created righteousness has no effect on their entry into the higher realms. However, by clinging to their self-created conditions, they will inevitably keep themselves trapped in their mental boxes, and this will serve to keep them away from the direct experience of the Presence of God—the direct experience that is the only entry point into the eternal life of the spiritual realm. This is precisely why Jesus said that unless your righteousness exceeds the righteousness of the scribes and Pharisees – meaning those who cling to their mental images and refuse to seek the direct experience – you cannot enter the kingdom – the consciousness – of God (Matthew 5:20). That is also why he said that you will find eternal life only by letting your mortal sense of life – meaning the sense of identity based on mental images – die (John 12:25).

My point here is that it is not in itself limiting to study a religious teaching that talks about the spiritual realm or about God. I am not trying to say that you should shy away from any spiritual teaching or any description of God. What I am saying, however, is that you must never forget that any teaching expressed in the words and images from this world can never give you a complete or infallible description of God. Therefore, you must *never* turn an outer teaching into a graven image. A graven image means a mental image that is never changing, that you see as absolute or infallible. As long as you are here on Earth, you will not be able to fathom the totality of God's Being. You can have a direct experience of God's Presence, but you cannot fathom the totality of God's Being while you are still in a physical body. Thus, you must never allow yourself to think that you have found a complete image of God. You must be willing to always look beyond any images in this world and strive for a more and more pure experience of God's Presence.

All true spiritual teachings were originally given by the Ascended Host for the purpose of helping people attain a direct experience of God's Presence. A spiritual teaching was never intended to be turned into a religious doctrine that supposedly gives the only true and infallible description of God. When you use a spiritual teaching to create a mental box around your mind, you have betrayed the purpose behind that spiritual teaching. You have created a dualistic illusion that is constantly being threatened by its dualistic opposite. And in order to uphold your illusion of infallibility, you must seek to destroy the threat. This is what has lead to all of the religious conflicts seen on this planet. And as long as you are trapped in the dualistic state of thinking – in which you believe your relationship to God can be threatened by or depends upon anything on Earth – you cannot enter the kingdom of God. As Jesus said, the kingdom of God is within you because it is a state of consciousness.

My point for starting the book with this discussion is to show you that you have a choice to make. You must choose whether you will cling to your current mental image of God or whether you will allow me to give you a higher understanding of the reality of God. If you cling to your existing image, the rest of this book will be a constant agitation to you. Only if you are willing to look beyond your current image of God is there any possibility that this book will help you attain the direct experience that will answer your questions about God. In the following chapters I will give you the unmasked truth about the nature of God, the purpose of this universe and how human beings have obscured that purpose by creating their own mental images and projecting them upon the screen of life. My explanation can set you free from all of the mental boxes – the mental prisons – created by human beings throughout the ages. Yet you will be free only if you are willing to walk through the prison door on your own. I can show you the door but I cannot – nor do I want to – force you to walk through it. Thus, I AM the open door, but you must walk through it of your own free-will choosing.

Because you were created in the image and likeness of God, it is natural for you to have a direct experience of God's Presence. In other words, *not* having this experience is unnatural, and this happens only because the experience is being blocked. What is blocking your direct experience of God's Presence? Well, it is the mental images of God that fill up your mind so there is no room for the direct experience to penetrate to your conscious awareness. Therefore, attaining spiritual freedom means doing some housecleaning so you can remove the mental images that block the direct experience of the Spirit of God. Will you allow me to help you remove your dualistic images or will you cling to the images with which you are familiar?

Key 3
Why there is no irrefutable proof that God exists

Let us return to the previous question, "If God does indeed exist, why hasn't he given human beings some irrefutable proof that he exists?" We now see that God has indeed given an irrefutable proof of his existence by giving all human beings the ability – the key of knowledge – to have a direct experience of God's Presence. Once you have such an experience, the question of whether or not God exists becomes obsolete. Yet to have such an experience, you must be willing to go beyond the state of consciousness that creates mental images, projects them upon reality and claims that the image is more real than reality itself.

We will later talk in more detail about the importance of free will, but for now let us simply conclude that God has given people the ability to prove his existence, but he has left it up to the free will of the individual whether he or she will make use of this ability. The determining factor is the individual's willingness to look beyond his or her mental images and adjust them according to a direct experience of a reality that is beyond the image. Thus, as we shall see later, God has given you the ability to find proof without violating his own Law of Free Will, which gives you the right to create your own image of reality and cling to it until the end of your time. This gives people the option to live on Earth and deny the existence of God. If God had given an irrefutable proof that he exists, people would not have had this option, and this would – as we will see – have been against the very purpose for this universe.

We have seen that God – in the ultimate sense – is a transcendent reality, meaning that no words or images from this world can accurately describe God. That is why Jesus said that those who worship God must do so in Spirit and in truth. You cannot worship a transcendent God exclusively through words, mental images or practices that are of this world.

Yet we have also seen that it is not pointless to have spiritual teachings that describe facets of God. You simply need to avoid falling into the age-old trap of thinking that a particular doctrine gives a complete or infallible description of God. No matter how extensive or detailed a spiritual teaching might be, God will always be more than what is described in the earthly teaching. This "more" can be known only through a direct experience. A spiritual teaching is *not* meant to replace the direct experience of God's Presence but to facilitate such an experience. Thus, following or studying a particular religious or spiritual teaching is only a stepping stone to a direct experience of God's Presence and a direct, personal relationship with Beings in the spiritual realm.

***

Having said that no words can fully describe the transcendental nature of God, this book will of necessity use words to give a description that can help you develop a more mature concept of God's nature. As a starting point for this discussion, let us begin by looking at the fact that most religions on Earth teach that there is at least one aspect of reality that is beyond the material universe. This realm is often called "heaven" or the spiritual realm, and in various religions it has specific names. This gives us the concept that the totality of the world you live in can be divided into layers, or levels. In fact, many religions teach that the spiritual realm is not one-dimensional or uniform. It has various levels, or layers, ranging from the lowest heaven to the highest heaven.

At this point, we need to take a step aside to clear up a misconception that has crept into several religions, namely the idea that heaven and Earth are fundamentally different or that there is an impenetrable barrier between them. To better understand the reality of the situation, it will be helpful to look at the findings of modern science. The idea that science is in opposition to religion springs from the dualistic state of consciousness, and we will later discuss why – in an enlightened society – there should be no real conflict between these two parallel – and potentially complementary – ways of describing the world.

I have stated that the human consciousness is dualistic, meaning that it thinks in terms of two relative opposites. One of the major achievements of science is that it has systematically undermined this dualistic view of the world and pointed to an underlying reality that is not defined by relative opposites. For example, scientists used to believe – partly based on sensory experience – that the world was made of two different substances, namely solid matter and fluid energy. Modern physicists have discovered that the material universe is not made from two fundamentally different substances. In reality, everything is energy. Even what your senses perceive as "solid" matter is made from energy. Energy is a form of vibration that is detected as waves. You can measure the vibrational properties of waves, such as their frequency, and the only real difference between different forms of waves is their vibration. Scientists have proven that the only difference between a material substance, such as gold, and a non-material "substance," such as thoughts, is a difference in the vibration of the energy waves.

Scientists have measured many different types of energy waves, and there is no theoretical barrier to the existence of energy waves of such high vibrations that they cannot be measured by current scientific instruments. In other words, scientists can no longer in good faith reject the existence of a realm – call it a different dimension or a parallel universe, if you like – that exists alongside the material universe and is simply made of vibrations that make it undetectable by current instruments. In fact, given that everything is energy, science cannot rule out that there could be an interchange of energy waves between such a high-vibration realm and the low-vibration realm that people call the material universe. To put the matter more directly, modern science has – at least on the theoretical level – shown that religions could be correct in talking about a heaven world beyond the material universe.

What is important about the findings of science is that they have proven that there is no fundamental difference between the spiritual realm and the material world. Everything is made from the same basic substance, namely what scientists call energy. The material world is made from energies that vibrate within a certain spectrum. The spiritual realm is made from the same basic type of energy; it simply vibrates in a higher spectrum. We can find mention of this concept in many religious scriptures. Take for example the account of creation given in Genesis. It states that in the beginning God created the heaven and the Earth (Genesis 1:1), namely two realms as part of the same creation. At first, the Earth was without form and void, obviously setting it apart from heaven, which was different from the void. Then, God created light (Genesis 1:3). Light is a substance that

God can mold into any form, and thus we might compare the Biblical concept of light to the scientific concept of energy. In reality, they are one and the same. Before God created any material form, he had to create a substance that could be molded into form, and thus light is the "building block" of the material universe.

We will later talk about this process in greater detail, but for now let it be stated that the light described in Genesis is simply light that vibrates within the vibrational spectrum of the material universe. Thus, this light can be molded into material forms, including the atoms that form the physical building blocks for all matter. Yet there is also light in the heaven world, and it is the same basic substance that simply has higher vibrational properties. Thus, it cannot be used to build material forms until it has been lowered in vibration. The process of lowering the vibration of spiritual light is, in fact, the very process that led to the creation of the material universe. As we will see later, even human beings can be part of this creation process, which is why they were created in God's image and likeness and have the potential to have dominion (Genesis 1:26) over "the Earth"—meaning the light from which all matter is made.

***

For now, let us stay with the image of a layered world. As most people learned in school, red light vibrates at a lower frequency than blue or violet light. Thus, the material universe is made from light of various frequencies. Some of this light has been lowered in vibration until your senses detect it as a "solid" substance that people call matter. Yet, as modern physics has proven, when you go into the deeper layers of matter, you reach a line where the distinction between matter particles and energy waves becomes blurred. What physicist, especially quantum physicists, have detected is the invisible line that marks the division between the highest vibrations in the material vibrational spectrum and the lowest vibrations in a higher spectrum. As you cross that line, one might say – if one uses a linear description – that you exit the material universe and enter a higher realm. In reality, the situation is not as linear, as we will discuss later.

When we realize that everything is created from the same basic substance, we see that there is no impenetrable barrier between the material world and the spiritual realm. However, we also realize that when people are trapped in a lower state of consciousness, there might seem to be such a barrier. If people identify themselves as material beings, they can perceive the world only through their physical senses, and these senses cannot detect the higher vibrations that are beyond the material realm. Thus, such people cannot have a direct experience of anything beyond the material world—not because such an experience is impossible but because these people cannot detect any vibrations beyond the range of the senses. Some of these people obviously belong to the religion called scientific materialism. Yet some of them can be seemingly religious people who believe in the existence of a heaven world. Yet they consider it impossible that "ordinary" people could have a direct experience of this world. They believe a true religion must be based on the account of heaven given by a unique person who was the only one with the ability to know God directly.

In reality, such people must inevitably violate the first two commandments, and thus they worship idols. The reason is that if people rely on a description of heaven without having any direct experience, they will inevitably base their beliefs on a mental image. This mental image can never be complete, and if they elevate it to the status of an infallible doctrine, they have created an idol. By believing that people are separated from heaven by an impenetrable barrier, they have put themselves in a closed box from which they – seemingly – cannot escape on their own.

In reality, all beings that were created in God's image and likeness have the potential to perceive vibrations that are beyond the material spectrum. We might say that all people are equipped with spiritual "senses" that can detect higher vibrations. This fact accounts for the innumerable instances of extra-sensory perception, spiritual or mystical visions, near-death experiences or paranormal experiences. Some religious people reject such experiences as do scientific materialists. Yet, as we have seen, their rejection is not based on direct evidence. It is based on the fact that their refusal to develop or use their spiritual senses has turned them into self-fulfilling prophecies. They see what they want to see, and thus the world appears to be flat—or at least one-dimensional.

The reality is that there is a spiritual world beyond the material universe, and you can have a direct experience of this world by developing your "spiritual senses." This has an important impact on the way you view religion.

***

Anyone who is a sincerely religious or spiritual person ought to be concerned by the fact that religion has caused so much conflict and bloodshed on this planet. Thus, any sincere person should be willing to consider what causes religious conflict. Unfortunately, many prefer to play the age-old game of looking at the mote in the eye of another and ignoring the beam in their own eyes (Matthew 7:5). Yet for those open to this book, it should be easy to see that the general cause of all religious conflict is what we might call extremism or fanaticism. Most people are aware of extreme examples of what religious fanaticism can lead to, such as the willingness to kill others in the name of one's idolatrous image of God. However, as we shall see later, this fanaticism is only the extreme expression of a psychological mechanism that is part of the consciousness of virtually every human being. This is a fear-based state of mind that causes the need for a sense of absolute security, which leads to the belief that your religion is the only true one, and as a member you are guaranteed to go to heaven. The main effect of this frame of mind is an unwillingness to consider that one's religious world view might be partially (or even fully) based on mental images that are out of touch with the reality of God. People in this state of mind are not willing to subject their mental images to the test of comparing them to a direct experience of God's Presence.

For those who are willing to consider that there might be more to know about God and religion, I suggest you start by considering that God's purpose for giving people religion might be entirely different from the purpose perceived by most religious people. I have already stated that all true spiritual teachings are given by the spiritual teachers of humankind, namely the Ascended Host. Our purpose for giving a spiritual teaching is *not* to give an absolute, complete and infallible description of God—for we know this is not possible. Our purpose for giving a specific teaching is to reach a specific group of people who are trapped at a particular level of consciousness. The teaching we give must meet two requirements. One is that it must be acceptable to the target audience, meaning that it is adapted to their present beliefs—even if those beliefs are based on incorrect mental images. The other is that it must contain enough new concepts and tools that people can rise above their limited state of consciousness.

My point here is that it is *never* our purpose to create an ultimate or superior religion. We have no desire to bring forth the "one true" religion on Earth. The "one true" religion is a direct experience of God's Being, and this experience is beyond any teaching expressed in words. Our purpose for giving people spiritual teachings is to help them rise above the dualistic state of consciousness that causes them to compare one religion to another and gives them the need to feel that one religion – and thus themselves as followers of that religion – is superior to others. Unfortunately, people who are too attached to their mental images find it almost impossible to understand or accept this fact. Thus, they tend to use any spiritual teaching to create a religious doctrine and organization that they elevate to the status of infallibility. I will later explain why this happens, but for now let us simply recognize that it *does* happen and that the effect is to trap people more firmly in the dualistic state of consciousness rather than raising them above that frame of mind. In other words, what was given as a tool to set people free has now been turned into a tool for imprisoning them behind even thicker mental walls.

When you begin to recognize that our purpose for giving a spiritual teaching is to set people free from a certain state of consciousness, you also see that the way a teaching is given is designed to support this goal. In other words, when we give a teaching, we do so in a way that demonstrates that a person on Earth can rise above the limited state of consciousness addressed by the teaching. As an example, consider the well-known but sometimes ignored fact that no religious scripture ever fell from the sky. Even though some people seem to think the opposite, even the Bible did not fall from the sky. It is the result of a very long process, and the different books in the Bible were brought forth through human beings who received them as a form of inspiration or inner revelation. In reality, the many people who received the books in the Bible were not fundamentally different from you. However, they were all willing to look beyond the particular state of consciousness that blinded most of the people of their time. In other words, they were simply further advanced in the learning process offered in Earth's schoolroom, the process aimed at raising people above the dualistic state of consciousness.

Even when you look at Jesus, you will see this outpictured. Jesus did not bring forth the highest possible spiritual teaching that could ever be brought forth on this planet. His teachings were carefully adapted to the consciousness of humankind – and to some degree the Jewish culture – as it was 2,000 years ago. Surely, the teachings of Jesus contained many timeless and universal elements that are applicable today. Yet it is a fact that there was a limit to what Jesus could say publicly 2,000 years ago, as clearly demonstrated by this quote, "I have yet many things to say unto you, but ye cannot bear them now" (John 16:12).

My purpose is to show you that it is pointless to be looking for the "one true religion." There will never be an absolute and infallible spiritual teaching on this planet. Thus, you face the choice of whether you will spend your life defending an outer teaching – inevitably becoming more rigid and fanatical in the process – or whether you will look beyond the outer teaching and use it as a stepping stone for having a direct experience of God's transcendent reality. This truly is the essential question that will determine whether you attain spiritual freedom or continue to be imprisoned by your mental images.

***

Let us take this discussion one step further. I have said that the true goal of your spiritual quest should be a direct experience of a higher level of reality. Yet it is essential for you to realize that even such an experience should never be considered as absolute and infallible. There are indeed several factors that can influence such an experience and the description of it.

First of all, let us return to the idea that there are several levels in the spiritual realm. Over the cause of history, many people have had direct experiences of one level of the spiritual realm. Yet only few people have had the flexibility of mind to experience several, let alone all, of the levels in the spiritual realm. Thus, it is entirely possible that two people could have different spiritual visions, yet both of the visions are valid. In fact, because each of the major world religions were aimed at people in a specific culture and state of consciousness, each of them is based on visions of a different level of the spiritual realm. Therefore, there is no real conflict between the visions of heaven from the Jewish, Buddhist, Hindu, Muslim and Christian religions.

Let us now consider that it is one thing to have a direct experience of the spiritual realm, but it is another to describe this experience to other people. When you have a spiritual experience, it is a total experience, much like standing on the shore of the ocean. You take in the ocean with all of your senses, and if you were to describe the experience in words, you would find it very difficult to convey the totality of the experience. Likewise, people who have been given spiritual experiences find it very difficult to adequately describe the experience in words. And when they do describe an experience in words, it is inevitable that their use of words is adapted to their culture. It should be obvious that Jesus used many parables adapted to an agricultural society. Had he appeared in a major city in today's world, do you think his parables would have used the exact same words and imagery?

As I said, the people who brought forth the spiritual teachings that form the basis for most major – and many minor – religions have reached a higher level of consciousness than the average person. Yet many other people have had spiritual experiences, and they did not necessarily have the same purity of mind. In fact, regardless of your purity, it is inevitable that your culture and belief system will have some influence on your spiritual visions. If you were wearing colored glasses, your eyes would pass on a colored image. Likewise, the contents of your consciousness will form a filter that will be superimposed upon your spiritual experience. Depending on how dense or pure your consciousness is, your experience might be colored to a greater or lesser degree. In other words, some people have had a vision of a level of reality beyond the material vibrational spectrum, but their vision has not been pure. Likewise, their interpretation and description of the vision can be colored by their state of consciousness.

Does it seem strange that I encourage you to have transcendental experiences and then question the validity of such experiences? In reality, I am not questioning the validity of the experience. As I said earlier, your eyes simply pass on an image of light rays. It is your mind that imposes a mental image upon what your eyes see and then attaches a certain interpretation to the image. So my point here is to show you that the very foundation for knowing a higher truth is to have a direct experience. However, until you reach the highest level of the schoolroom of Earth – until your consciousness has been completely purified – it is extremely wise to *never* see your experiences as complete or infallible. A wise student is always aware that his or her consciousness can influence the experience and the interpretation of it. The very purpose of having a spiritual experience is to contact a level of reality that is beyond the dualistic mind. Yet if you allow your dualistic mind to influence the experience, you defeat that purpose.

You need to recognize that getting to know God's true Being is a gradual process that will take time. Yet if you are willing to apply the proper approach and the proper tools, you will gradually purify your consciousness. You will gradually attain purer and purer experiences, experiences that cannot be colored by any of the mental images that human beings have created upon this planet. And as you clear your inner vision of all such dualistic images, you will eventually come to know the pure, unmasked Being and Presence of God. I can assure you that having this experience is well worth the effort you have to put forth. In fact, I can assure you that even the most elaborate graven images created by man are as nothing compared to the transcendent reality of the Living God.

Let me give you an illustration of why it is so important to avoid becoming fixated on one particular expression of spiritual truth. You have no doubt heard the ancient myth of a pot of gold at the end of the rainbow, and you know no one has ever found it. Most people would say the reason is that there is no gold, but the real reason is that there is no rainbow. A rainbow is created by sunlight being split by the prisms formed by raindrops in the air. Yet this split can be seen only from a specific angle. Thus, when you see a rainbow, that rainbow has no universal existence in that it is visible only from a certain vantage point. If you were several miles away, you might see no rainbow or you might see a rainbow, but it would be a different rainbow. Likewise, if you move closer to the rainbow, it will move in front of you and you can never catch up. A spiritual or religious teaching should be seen as a rainbow. It gives a view of God's transcendent and illusive reality, and although the view is valid, it shows the transcendent reality only from a certain viewing angle. Thus, it is possible to look at the same reality from a different angle and get a teaching that is different but still valid. So it is futile to fight over which rainbow is the best one, when the purpose of the teaching is merely to point to the transcendent reality beyond it. The real purpose of a spiritual teaching is to get you to look for the pot of gold, which is a direct, inner experience of the transcendent Spirit of God.

***

Another purpose for this discussion is to help you develop a higher approach to religion. Obviously, you were brought up in a certain culture, and you were exposed to one, perhaps several, belief systems. In fact, most people in the Western world were exposed to the schizophrenic conflict between orthodox Christianity and materialistic science, thus being forced – from a very early age – to deal with two mutually exclusive explanations of their identity and purpose for being.

As I have mentioned, most people need some sense of security, some stable platform for their journey in an insecure world. Thus, most people develop a certain belief system, and it gives them a sense of comfort and stability. The effect is that having to question your belief system can be a disturbing experience, and it can lead to the fear-based reaction that causes people to close their minds to new ideas. Obviously, those who read this book are not completely trapped in this fear-based approach to religion. Yet it is prudent to monitor your reaction to this book, so that you can avoid closing your mind to ideas that are too far beyond your existing beliefs.

In the hope of assisting you in developing an approach to religion that is not based on fear, let me offer you some thoughts. When Jesus was asked what was the most important point of the spiritual law, he said that it is to love God with all your heart, soul and mind (Matthew 22:37). As we will see later, the Living God is a God of unconditional love, and he is nothing like the mental images of an angry and judgmental being in the sky. Jesus clearly demonstrated that he loved the Living God before any graven images, and he also showed that his love for God was unconditional. When you love God unconditionally, you want to know and experience the Living God. Thus, you will not let any graven images – any conditions – stand between you and a direct experience of God's Presence.

There are many religious people who would say that they love God, but their love for God is a human form of love that is conditional. This is demonstrated by the fact that they cling to the mental image of God given by their particular religion. They cling to this image because they have come to believe that it is the only true one, and they fear that if they look at any other image, they will be condemned. In other words, their approach to God and religion is not truly based on love. It is based on a perversion of love, namely fear—which causes them to impose conditions upon their relationship with God, in essence seeking to control God. We will later explain the cause of fear, but for now let us simply consider that you can put all spiritual and religious people on a scale. On one end you have people whose approach to God and religion is based entirely on fear, and on the other end you have those whose approach is based entirely on love. The goal of all truly spiritual people should be to move toward an approach to God that is entirely based on unconditional love. As Jesus said, "Blessed are the pure in heart, for they shall see God" (Matthew 5:8).

As you read this book, monitor your reactions to the ideas I present. If you find yourself resisting an idea, consider whether your resistance springs from a fear-based reaction. Do you resist the idea because it goes too far beyond your existing beliefs and thus seems to threaten the sense of security provided by your existing belief system? Those who will get the greatest growth from reading this book will be those who are willing to recognize their fear-based reactions and then look beyond them. Consider that even though you can build a sense of security from a fear-based approach to religion, it is a false security, a house built on sand (Matthew 7:26). Jesus stated clearly that unless your righteousness exceeds the righteousness of the scribes and Pharisees, you will not enter the kingdom – the consciousness – of heaven (Matthew 5:20). The scribes and Pharisees took the fear-based approach to religion and they were sure they would go to heaven. Yet they based their sense of security on their belief in outer doctrines and a rigid adherence to the rules defined in those doctrines. Jesus said that this was not enough, and based on our previous discussion, you should be able to see the deeper meaning.

Jesus knew that the real key to entering heaven is to raise your state of consciousness beyond the dualistic state of mind that is the cause of fear. Thus, he came to show people how to attain the Christ mind that empowers you to see beyond duality. When you use the mind of Christ to purify your mind of dualistic beliefs, you will develop an approach to God that springs from unconditional love.

Thus, you can be secure in knowing that your understanding of God is based on the rock of Christ vision, rather than the shifting sands of the dualistic state of consciousness. This is true security because you now experience the perfect love that will cast out all fear (1John 4:18). If you are willing to let me lead you beyond your dualistic, graven images of God, you will surely open your mind and heart to this love.

As I said, all I can do is to offer you the love-based truth that will make you free. I cannot force you to accept my unconditional love, for unconditional love knows no force. Thus, once again, the responsibility rests on you. Will you let me show you the true Presence of the God of unconditional love or will you prefer a fear-based graven image of a conditional god?

Key 4
The purpose of this universe

Now that we have set an adequate foundation, we can go into a more direct discussion about the nature of God and the purpose for this universe. The purpose of this discussion is to expand your mental image of God so that – if you are willing – you can avoid having your mental image block a direct experience of God's Presence. In other words, it is my hope that I can expand both your understanding of God and your direct perception of God. As an ascended Being I perceive the reality of God. I can describe my perception of God's reality, but I have no desire to have you settle for my description. I want you to have a direct perception of God's reality. Yet as we have discussed, this requires you to purify your mind of fixed, or graven, images that block your perception. Thus, let us consider the differences between how you – as an unascended being on Earth – and I – as an ascended being in the spiritual realm – perceive the level of reality in which we live, move and have our being.

As I have said, the material universe is made from the same basic substance as the spiritual realm. Yet the light in the material universe has been lowered to a different vibrational spectrum. We might also say that the lower vibration makes the light less intense, and thus it is not – yet – able to fill the material universe with light. That is why the space between solar systems and galaxies appears to be empty. It appears as if there are huge areas with no light and that only certain localized areas – your sun being one example – radiate light from within themselves. We might say that there is still more darkness than light in the material universe. The effect is that you cannot see energies above a certain vibration, and thus you cannot see that physical matter is actually made from finer energies that stream into the material universe from a higher vibrational spectrum. We might say that there is an observation horizon beyond which most people cannot perceive with their current level of consciousness.

The density of matter makes it possible for people to create and maintain the illusion that there is no God or that they are separated from God by an impenetrable barrier. This sense of separation from

God inevitably leads people to see themselves as separate, independent beings. People can see themselves as being separate from other people, which gives rise to the illusion that you can harm other people, other forms of life and even the physical planet, without harming yourself. This, of course, is the essential cause of all human conflict and atrocities, for if people knew they were hurting themselves by hurting others, most of them would modify their behavior accordingly. Only a few very disturbed people would deliberately hurt themselves, but in reality, even they do not fully understand what they are doing. We might say that the purpose of life in the material realm is to overcome the limited perception of reality, so that you can experience directly that you are not a separate being but an extension of your source, of your Creator.

In contrast to the material universe, the spiritual realm is made from energy of a higher vibration, and thus a higher intensity. Even in the lowest level of the spiritual realm, there is no empty space. Everything appears filled with light, and you see yourself as moving in an ocean of light. You perceive directly that everything is made from light, meaning that it radiates light from within itself or allows light to shine through it. Thus, you perceive that you too radiate light from within yourself. If you care to look more closely, you will see that the light in your vibrational spectrum streams into your world from a higher realm. And if you follow the direction of the light, you will see that it originated as the pure light that was created by the Being who created this particular world of form. Thus, you will know that there is a God and that "without him was not anything made that was made" (John 1:3), including yourself.

Your direct perception that everything is light and that light comes from God does not take away your free will. In fact, it gives you true freedom of choice. A Being in the spiritual realm can still choose to go against the Creator's laws and creative intent. Yet it cannot do so based on ignorance, it cannot do so without knowing that by hurting others it is hurting itself. On Earth, it is harder to have a direct experience of God's existence, and thus it is more likely that beings can choose to go against what they do not understand or do not believe to be real. People can believe they can hurt others without harming themselves.

Imagine that you come to a fork in the road and you have to choose which way to go. You cannot see that one road leads to an abyss and another leads to a hospitable kingdom. No one is forcing you to take either road, but can you really make a free choice when you do not know where both roads lead? If you do not know or fully understand the consequences of your choices, can you really make a free choice? Thus, can those who violate God's laws or deny God's existence without perceiving God directly really be said to be making free choices? If you have not perceived God, or at least God's light, can you really choose freely whether you will follow or go against God's intent for creating this universe? That is why the Bible talks about a way that seems right to a human being, but the ends thereof are the ways of death (Proverbs 14:12).

***

The reality of God is not linear but because the human mind is so programmed to think in linear images, let us look at a linear representation. Let us start with your perception of the material universe. Science has already discovered that there is something beyond the material universe and that the human mind has an ability to perceive something beyond the material universe. Yet few scientists have been willing to put the two together and recognize that when people see something beyond, they are not – at least not always – hallucinating. They are seeing something that is really there. Science will one day recognize that one of the major characteristics of the mind is the ability to perceive and that the mind's perception is far more sophisticated than perception based on the physical senses. Most people have been brought up to direct the mind's perceptive ability exclusively through the physical senses. That is why they see nothing beyond the material universe—or rather, they *do* see it but their minds filter it out as unnecessary information before it reaches the conscious level. Yet the mind can be retrained to direct its perceptive abilities beyond the senses. Intuition is the first step, but others can follow. My point being that your mind has the ability to perceive all of the spiritual realms created by your Creator. You can start by perceiving the lowest spiritual realm and can gradually work your way up to perceiving the highest level of the world of form. You can even take a step beyond and experience the Creator itself.

Many people have already done this, although few have the ability to perceive details of the higher realms. Yet most people who are spiritually interested have the ability to sense that there is something beyond the material universe, and thus they know – through direct experience or inner knowing – that the spiritual world is real. Likewise, you can have a direct experience that there is a Presence, a Being, that is beyond even the highest spiritual realm. Thus, you can *know* that God exists.

Once you have the sense that something is real, you can use another of the mind's abilities to increase your understanding of that something, even though you do not perceive the details directly. This is the mind's ability to imagine, to conceptualize, that which is not perceived in detail but only as "something real." This ability is – or should be – coupled with the ability to rationalize, whereby you can extend your understanding beyond what is directly perceived. This, of course, is where spiritual teachings have a function in terms of helping you develop a more detailed understanding of the spiritual world. In other words, outer teachings can assist your growth by clarifying your direct experiences—as long as you do not use an outer teaching to block the experience.

Let me now ask you to imagine that you travel up through the various levels of the spiritual realm until you reach the highest level. This is the level described in the Bible as God saying, "I am Alpha and Omega, the beginning and the ending" (Revelation 21:6). This is the highest level of the world of form, because it is the first level of the Creator expressing itself in form. The Creator starts by expressing itself as two polarities, the Alpha and the Omega, the beginning and the ending, the expanding and the contracting forces, the out-breath and the in-breath, the Yang and the Yin. On the human level, these forces are often seen as the Father and the Mother or the masculine and feminine, although they are far beyond human sexuality.

The point is that as the first level of expression, the One Creator expresses itself as two polarities. These are not opposites, and they do not cancel out each other. They are complementary forces that supplement and enhance each other. When they meet in a balanced manifestation, they multiply each other and become more. The whole is more than the sum of its parts, and thus a new expression of life is created. This is how all the succeeding levels of the world of form are created, as we will later explore. My point here is to show that the One Creator manifests itself as two polarities, yet beyond the highest level of the world of form there is still the One Creator. In other words, there is only One God, and although "without him was not anything made that was made" the One God never ceases to be One, the indivisible whole.

Many religions on Earth talk about this One God, simply using different names and slightly different descriptions for the same reality. Yet before we can go any further, we need to address a misconception that has crept into several religions. This misunderstanding states that there is nothing beyond the One God, that this superior or ultimate God is all there is to God. This is partly due to a lack of perception and understanding of anything beyond. Yet it is also caused by the human ego's need for superiority. Many religious people have a need to feel that their religion is the only true one and is superior to any other religion. And if your religion is the only true one and is the only one worshiping the ultimate God, then it must be the best religion on Earth—or so the ego reasons. This war of religions has prevented the Ascended Host from releasing a higher understanding of God on this planet. Yet a critical mass has been reached, and we have determined to release this higher understanding for those who have eyes to see.

***

Again, reality is not linear, but I will give you a linear image. Imagine a figure-eight. It has an upper figure, a lower figure and a center—the point in the nexus. Your Creator is represented by the nexus, the meeting point between the upper and the lower figure. The lower figure is a representation of the world of form that is created by your Creator and in which you live. The upper figure is – a highly inadequate – representation of a level of God, a reality of God, that is beyond your Creator. This level of God I would like to call the Pure Being of God or the Allness of God's Presence.

What is this Allness? It is something that cannot be accurately described or represented by any of the linear words and images that the human mind can fathom. It is beyond the world of form and cannot be represented by anything in the world of form. In this world you find separate forms that are set apart from each other, and thus they are defined by their differences. These differences are also limitations that set limits for each form and set it apart from the whole. Naturally, this causes people to focus on the differences and prevents them from seeing this world as a coherent whole. They see the trees but not the forest. In the Allness, there are no separate forms, no contradictions and no limitations. Yet the human mind finds it difficult to fathom a world without separateness, and thus it might be the wiser course of action to say nothing about it. Yet you need to understand certain things in order to understand why your universe was created.

In this universe you are used to having a separate sense of existence. You clearly see yourself as an individual being who is separated from other people. You are separated from nature and the rest of the vast universe in which you live. You experience that you have a separate will, and therefore you can create – by using the mind's ability to imagine and conceptualize – the illusion that you can harm others without harming yourself. You can conceptualize that there is a God, but you tend to see yourself as separated from God. Thus, you tend to see his will as being outside of, possibly in opposition to, your own. You might conceptualize that God has laws, but you tend to see them as put upon you by an external authority and you might see them as restricting your free-

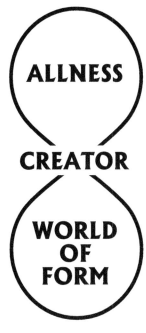

dom to do what you want as a separate being. As you walk the spiritual path, you might build a stronger connection to this external God. You may eventually build a sense of oneness with your God, as Jesus expressed when he said, "I and my Father are one" (John 10:30). Yet you still see yourself as an "I" that has become one with the "It" or the greater "I."

In the Allness, no such sense of separation is possible. There are individual Beings – I prefer to call them Presences – in the Allness. They do have a sense of individual awareness, but they also have an awareness of not only being one with the Allness, but *being* the Allness. They can focus their awareness at a particular "point" – although time and space have no meaning in the Allness – and they can focus on a particular quality of the Allness. Yet they can never lose their ability to be one with, to be everywhere in, the Allness. They can make decisions, so they have freedom of choice. But they cannot make separate decisions in the sense that they can never say that they want to do something that benefits themselves while hurting others. Nor can they seek to elevate themselves as being better or more important than other Beings. Such concepts have no meaning in the Allness. The Presences in the Allness do not have a sense of one-ness with God—they *are* God. It would be unthinkable that they would see God's laws as put upon them by an external authority. Consequently, it would be unthinkable for them to go against God's laws or the purpose of creation. They *are* that law and they define that purpose.

I realize this is difficult to fathom with the linear mind, yet the image I want to give you is that in the Allness, a separate existence simply is not possible. You may think, "Well, but I prefer to be a separate individual." And that is precisely why you – still – find yourself in this universe. Let me explain.

A Presence in the Allness can experience absolutely everything that is in the Allness—and it can experience it all at once if it so chooses. Yet in the Allness there is nothing that is separated from the Allness. Thus, a Presence in the Allness cannot experience something that is outside of or less than the Allness. Yet such a Presence also has the ability to imagine or conceptualize something that it does not experience. So, some of the Presences in the Allness imagined the concept of something that was separated from the Allness. What would it be like to experience a "world" that was separated from the Allness? Such Presences realized that it really has no meaning to talk about something being outside the Allness since the Allness is all there is, and thus it is everywhere. So they realized that any sense of being separated from the Allness could not exist as a reality, but only as a perception in the mind. Yet they still imagined that a sphere could be set aside from the Allness and that a Being could enter or be born in this sphere in order to take on the illusion of a separate existence.

In the Allness there is no sense of lack. Presences in the Allness have everything they could want, because their thoughts can instantly be manifest if they will it. From your viewpoint, on a planet characterized by lack, you might wonder why any Being in the Allness would want to experience anything less than the Allness. Yet the Presences in the Allness realized that by experiencing something different, you can more fully appreciate what you have.

The Presences in the Allness conceived of setting aside a sphere from the Allness. A Presence could then project itself into that sphere and focus itself as a separate Being. It could then create a separate world in that sphere, and this could be a valuable learning experience for this Being. Yet once you have created a sphere in which a separate existence is possible, another possibility opens up. The Being that projects itself into the sphere still has a memory of its existence in the Allness. Yet this being can now create self-conscious extensions of itself, beings that are created without any memory of the Allness, and thus – from their inception – see themselves as separate beings. Because they are created out of the consciousness of their Creator, the Creator can still experience the world through their individual minds. Thus, the Creator can experience what it is like to be a separate being.

Yet precisely because these beings are extensions of the consciousness of the Creator, they have the potential to expand their individual sense of identity until they attain a sense of oneness with their Creator. They can then have the option to take on the role of a Creator, and they can even go beyond and enter the Allness as individual Presences. Because they started out their self-awareness as separate beings, they can enter the Allness with the memory of what it is like to be separated from the Allness, giving them a special sense of appreciation for the Allness. They can then share this appreciation with the Presences that remained in the Allness, and thus everyone grows from the interplay between the Allness and that which is less than the Allness.

In short, the Presences in the Allness realized that there is value in creating a process through which a being can start out with the sense of identity as a separate and limited being who is focused on itself in a world that is separated from the Allness. This being can then gradually grow in self-awareness until it expands its sense of self to encompass the Allness. The being can then enter the Allness with the memory of what it is like to climb toward the Allness, thus having a greater sense of appreciation than a being who has never experienced anything but the Allness. This process is what I will call the Path of Oneness to signify that it takes you from a sense of separation toward a sense of oneness with the Allness, oneness with all life.

**

How was your particular universe created? A Presence in the Allness decided that it wanted to experience what it is like to be separated from the Allness and create forms that are separated from the Allness. It started by projecting a spherical boundary around itself, creating the illusion of a division within the Allness.

Within this sphere, the Presence now contracted its consciousness – in the Allness everything is consciousness – into a single point, a singularity, within the center of the sphere. This created a sphere that was not filled with the Allness, and thus it opened up the potential for creating separate forms within this sphere. Yet in the beginning there were no separate forms in the sphere, neither was there the fullness of the Allness. Thus, the sphere was void, which is a concept that you find in several religions.

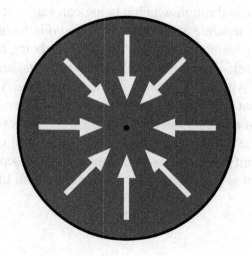

The singularity in the center of the void now became the focal point for the Being that is the Creator of your universe. You might notice that the concept of a singularity in the center of a void is similar to the theory of the Big Bang, developed by modern science. Science says that before the Big Bang, all of the matter and energy in the material universe was compressed into a singularity. From there, it expanded outward in a giant and uncontrolled explosion that gradually gave rise to an incredibly complex system of galaxies and solar systems—yet this complexity has arisen spontaneously from a random process. In reality, the picture is very different, as we will see later.

In the singularity of the Creator, there was no matter as it is known in the material universe where you live. There was only pure consciousness, pure Being. The creative process began when the Creator projected its own Being, its own consciousness, outward. This did not happen in an uncontrolled and unplanned explosion. On the contrary, the Creator first projected itself as a substance that we have earlier called Light. By the creation of this light, the Creator had formed the first polarity, namely between itself and the Light. The Creator is the active, expanding or Alpha principle, whereas the Light is the passive, contracting or Omega principle. If we follow a traditional religious imagery and call the Creator for God the Father, then the Light becomes God the Mother, or the Mother Light, the Ma-ter Light.

The Mother Light is in itself formless, but it has the potential to take on absolutely any form. The Mother Light is created out of the Creator's own consciousness and Being, so the Mother Light has consciousness. Yet it does not have consciousness as an individual being that is separated from the Creator. It has awareness as a Being that is an extension of the Creator. The consequence is that the Mother Light cannot – in and of itself – create any manifest or separate form. The Mother Light can take on form only when it is acted upon by the Creator or by self-conscious, separate beings created by the Creator. In the most general sense, we can call such a being a co-creator although – as we will discus later – there are various types of self-conscious beings in the world of form.

In the beginning, the Mother Light existed only as a concept – a state of pure consciousness – and there was not yet any manifest, or expressed, light. As the first act of manifest creation, the Creator projected itself outward in the form of the Mother Light. By using the

Mother Light, the Creator created a sphere that was set apart from the void. In the void is nothingness (as opposed to Allness), and the Creator now created a sphere in the center of the void. This sphere had a certain intensity of light, setting it apart from the nothingness of the void yet still being far away from the intensity of light found in the Allness.

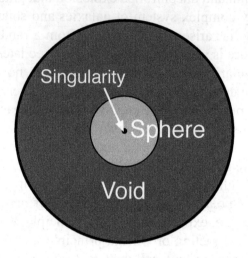

As the next act of creation, the Creator created certain structures in the first sphere. These structures were quite different from what you find in the material universe, but the main point is that they provided a platform for life, for intelligent, self-conscious beings. Thus, the Creator now projected itself into the first sphere in the form of such self-conscious beings. These beings were extensions of the Creator, individualizations created from the Creator's consciousness. Yet they were created as separate beings with a separate sense of identity. They did not have the full self-awareness of the Creator, and their self-awareness was focused upon their separate beings. They did not have an awareness of the Allness, and they were focused on the sphere in which they came into being. They did not have a direct awareness of themselves as being extensions of the Creator. However, they did have a direct connection to the Creator in the sense that the Creator served as a teacher or tutor for them.

The first self-conscious beings were sent into the new sphere with the command to "Multiply and have dominion!" They were given the gifts of individuality, self-awareness, imagination, free will and rational thinking. They were given the ability to command the Mother Light through the power of their minds, and they were given a certain amount of light that was theirs to command as a start. By using their creative faculties, they could create more structures in the sphere, thus gradually filling it to greater intensity and complexity. By multiplying their talents (Matthew 25:14), they would receive more light, which would increase their creative powers and also increase the intensity of the light in their own beings. As they used that light and projected it around themselves, they would increase the intensity of the light in their sphere, so that it was further set apart from the nothingness of the void and came closer to the Allness. In doing so, these lifestreams would grow in self-awareness.

They would first realize that their teacher was the Creator. They would then accept themselves as individualizations of God the Father, as extensions of the Creator. They would realize that they were living in the cosmic womb of God the Mother. As the Father and Mother elements came into oneness within their beings, a new self-awareness was born, and they attained a sense of oneness with their Creator without losing their individual awareness. As this oneness became complete, they could eventually make a choice to enter the Allness or they could become creators of their own worlds of form.

After the first sphere had reached a certain intensity of light, the Creator called the self-conscious beings who had mastered the lessons presented by the first sphere – let us call them masters – to participate with it in creating a second sphere. The Creator then projected the Mother Light out from the first sphere to create a second sphere that was set apart from the void. The masters of the first sphere then created certain inanimate structures in this sphere in order to provide a platform for intelligent life. After that, the masters of the first sphere created self-conscious extensions of themselves who were sent into the second sphere with the command to "Multiply and have dominion!"

You can now see the pattern. When the second sphere had reached a critical intensity of light, it too was used as the platform for creating the next sphere. This process of gradually expanding God's kingdom of light by taking in more and more of the void has gone through a number of stages. The material universe in which you live is the latest stage of this process. In other words, the universe in which you live is the newest sphere in God's creation. It is still relatively young, which is why there appears to be empty space or darkness left. So far, only relatively few beings in this world have become self-luminous and have ascended to the higher realms.

The Mother Light that makes up the material universe still vibrates at such low frequencies and has such low intensity that it is possible to create the illusion that there is nothing beyond the material universe. Yet your world is nevertheless the extension of a series of concentric, interpenetrating and coexisting spheres that started with the singularity of the Creator. Your world was created out of the same basic substance as the higher spheres, namely the Mother Light, which is made out of the Creator's consciousness. Without him was not anything made that was made.

***

Let us consider the meaning of consciousness. In the Allness, everything is made from one mind, from one consciousness. We might call it the Mind of God, but if you project human images upon the concept "God," you will not be able to fathom the consciousness that is the Allness. In the Allness everything is consciousness, meaning that everything is conscious. There are individual Presences in the Allness, and they focus on a particular quality. From your view in this universe, you might see them as the Presence of Infinite Light, the Presence of Unconditional Love, the Presence of God's Will, the Presence of Oneness etcetera. However, such individual Presences do not see themselves as separated from the Allness or from each other. They are fully aware that they are extensions of the Allness and that they are part of the same whole. Thus, they are all one in the Allness. Likewise, they do not see themselves as extensions of a remote God. They *are* God, meaning that the Pure Being of God is not *in* the Allness but *is* the Allness. In the Allness everything is God and everything is self-aware, meaning that everything is aware of itself as God.

In the created realm in which you live, the world of form, it is possible to create something that is not self-aware. As I said, everything is created out of the consciousness of the Creator, meaning that everything has a form of consciousness. That is why Jesus said that if men should refuse to defend the Christ, the stones would cry out (Luke 19:40). Everything is created from the Mother Light, so everything has – or *is* – consciousness. Yet it takes a certain complexity before a form can become the focus of self-awareness.

In the Allness, there is nothing that is not self-aware. In the world of form, it is possible to create inanimate forms and animate beings that do not have self-awareness. It is also possible to have self-aware beings who are not aware of their connection to anything beyond themselves, thus not aware that they are extensions of their Creator or aware of the Allness. This makes it possible that in the world of form you can have beings who have a limited self-awareness but have the potential to expand that self-awareness until they attain oneness with the All.

In other words, the entire purpose for this world of form is to give *you* the opportunity to experience yourself as a separate being with a narrowly focused self-awareness. When you have had enough of this experience, you can step unto a systematic path that will gradually expand your self-awareness, until you can enter the Allness with the memory of what it is like to be outside the Allness, giving you a unique appreciation for the Allness.

***

Where does the process of expanding the spheres of light end? Naturally, it ends when the entire void has been turned into a sphere of light and when every part of that sphere has reached the intensity of light that is the Allness. In other words, what used to be separate and less than the Allness has now become the Allness. Yet this will not – as some religions portray – happen automatically or through some kind of inevitable process. It will happen only as a result of the free-will choices made by the self-aware beings who inhabit God's spheres. This means that the darkness and limitations found in the world of form will not disappear completely until all self-aware beings have had their full opportunity to experience what it is like to be separate beings living in a world of – self-created – limitations.

You are an extension of your Creator, yet your Creator gave you a sense of identity as a separate being. Your Creator wants you to come home by expanding your sense of self until you attain full oneness with your Creator and with all life. Your Creator knows that coming back to Oneness is the only way for you to feel fully happy, fully whole, fully at peace. Yet your Creator wants you to do this out of a free choice that is based on love. Thus, your Creator has great – although not unlimited – patience with your choices and will allow you to experiment with limitations for a very long time if you prefer.

I know these concepts are most likely far beyond your present religious beliefs and understanding. I understand that it can take some time and contemplation to fully understand these ideas and integrate them. In the coming chapters, I will give you additional teachings to help you make full use of these concepts and relate them to your present situation on Earth. Yet for now I ask you to consider what these concepts can teach you about the meaning of life, the purpose of life. So many people have asked the questions about where they come from, where they are going and whether life truly has any meaning. I hope you can now begin to at least glimpse that these questions actually have meaningful answers.

As you begin to integrate these answers, you will find that an entirely new world, an entirely new world view, opens up to you. You are not a miserable sinner thrust into a hostile universe by some angry God. You are not all alone in a hostile environment where everyone is out to get you. You are not limited to who you are or what you experience right now.

You are an extension of your God. You are your God experiencing itself as a separate being who is on a journey from a lower level of consciousness to the highest level of consciousness that is the All-ness. Everything you have experienced here on Earth can give you a valuable perspective on your journey, on yourself and on life. Even the most unpleasant of circumstances can be turned into an opportunity to learn, an opportunity to raise your consciousness and expand your self-awareness. Thus, you have the potential to raise yourself above any circumstances you might be experiencing.

The entire purpose of life is to rise above your present sense of self and attain a greater sense of self. No matter what circumstances you have experienced or do experience, you can never lose the ability to overcome them, to rise higher. Thus, if you do not like your present circumstances, you can unlock your inner potential to overcome them. If you do not like who you are, you can expand your sense of who you are until you transcend *any* limitation in the material universe.

If this does not give you a different perspective on your current limitations, there can be only one reason. You have not yet had enough of experiencing these circumstances, and thus you have not summoned the will to leave them behind. You are miserable because you want to experience what it is like to be miserable, and you will continue to experience this "reality" until you decide that you have had enough and want to experience a different, a greater, reality. I know this can sound harsh to people who are suffering, so let us move on to consider how you can make use of your ability to transcend any limitation in the world of form.

Key 5
ɔ be MORE, or to be less—that is the real question

If you are to understand the dynamics that shape your experience in the material universe, you need to keep in mind that the entire world of form was created for a very specific purpose. That purpose was to open up for an experience of what it is like to be less than – separated from – the Allness. Yet it was never God's intention to make this experience permanent. This world was created as being less but also created to follow a path of gradually becoming more, until it again merges into the Allness from which it came and from which it was never truly set apart.

Your Creator has projected itself into the world of form as two polarities. One is the Mother Light, which obediently takes on any form projected upon it by the other polarity, namely the self-conscious beings with co-creative abilities. It is essential to understand that your Creator experiences the world of form through you. The Creator has a memory of the Allness and has a sense of oneness with the Allness that can never be lost. So when you experience limitations in the world of form, your Creator – through you – experiences what it is like to be less than and separated from the Allness. Your Creator created you partly in order to have this experience. Thus, for your Creator, any experience you have contributes to the Creator's experience of what it is like to be less than the Allness. Why is this important? Because while your Creator can have – through you – an experience of being less than the Allness, the Creator can never be lost in this experience. The Creator can experience the illusion of being separated from the Allness, but the Creator can never fully believe that this appearance of separation, the appearance of less, is real or permanent. The reason is that your Creator's sense of self-awareness did not originate inside the world of form, and thus it could never be confined to this world. Your Creator knows with an absolute knowing that it is *more* than the world of form. In contrast, you do not know what it is like to be less than the Allness, for you have not experienced the Allness. Thus, you can become lost in the world of form, thinking it is all there is and that you have no way of rising above your separate and limited sense of identity. Obviously, this is not what the Creator wants for you.

Let me illustrate this point with an analogy. Imagine yourself in a theater as one of the actors in a play. You are fully aware that you started life outside the theater. You entered the building and put on a costume. In order to give a convincing performance, you set aside your normal personality and take on the personality of the character you are playing. Yet when the performance is over, you take off the costume, revert back to your normal personality and leave the theater—returning to the "real" world or at least the world of your long-term sense of identity. Now imagine that a person has been born inside a theater and has never seen the world outside. The person has seen people entering and leaving the theater but has never really thought about what is outside. Thus, the person has come to believe that the theater is all there is to reality and that the world of the theater is real in an ultimate sense. The person might even believe that he or she has no life separate from the theater and has no identity apart from the role he or she is currently playing.

You are a self-aware being and you are an extension of your Creator. Yet you are not created simply as a puppet, as a toy, for your Creator. Your Creator has given you the gift of life, meaning that you have self-awareness, imagination and free will—you have the ability to create your own experience, even your own material circumstances, by using the Mother Light. And you have free will to design this experience according to your imagination and your own choosing. Your Creator did not originate within its own creation, and the Creator can never fall prey to the illusion that the world of form is the only reality. Yet because you *did* originate within the world of form, you can come to believe that what you have created is the ultimate reality and that you have no way to escape it. Thus, while the Creator can never become lost in its own creation, you *can*. You can believe that you really are a limited human being, living on a planet where life is suffering.

It is understandable that you might accept this illusion, and God does not blame you for identifying fully with the role you are now playing in the theater called planet Earth. Yet your Creator also knows that you have the potential to expand your sense of self-awareness beyond what you experience right now. Because you are an extension of the consciousness of the Creator, you have the potential to reach the full awareness of the Creator.

You might have heard about a holographic image. It is a type of photograph, but it is unique in that the whole image is comprised of individual parts and each part has a smaller replica of the whole. We might say that you are created as one part of the holographic image that is the Creator expressing itself as the world of form. Your individual consciousness contains within it a replica of the whole, and by magnifying your awareness of the whole, you can become one with the whole, you can become all that the whole is, you can become the All. This is the highest potential that comes with the gift of life.

Here is the essential point. You were created as a separate being, living inside the world of form. Yet it was never your Creator's intention that you should become permanently lost in the world of form, in your separate identity. Your Creator wants you to realize that the material world is just a theater in which you have taken on a particular role in a play. Your Creator never wanted you to permanently identify yourself with and as that part or think there is nothing more to life than the play. Why not? Because your Creator knows that this world is incredibly limited compared to the Allness. The Creator knows that the material universe, at its current level of development, is incredibly limited compared to the spiritual realm. You are an extension of the Creator and your Creator loves you as itself because you *are* itself. Thus, the Creator has no desire to see you permanently trapped in a limited world in which you experience life as suffering.

Remember that the Creator experiences separation through you because you are an extension of the Creator's Being. However, this works both ways, meaning that you can experience the Creator's Being while in this limited state. You can experience that you are the Creator experiencing limitations through your lower being. When you have this experience of expanded awareness, you will no longer be lost in separation and you will no longer be identified with the limitations that cause suffering. You will rise above all identification with this world, and this is called enlightenment—the state of knowing who you truly are.

You might ask why your Creator then created you as a limited being that is trapped on a planet with so much suffering. The overall answer is that your Creator did not create you with your current sense of – human – identity nor did it create the Earth with its current level of imperfection and suffering. So who created the separate being – the separate sense of identity – that you see yourself as being today? *You did!* Who created the world that you live in today? Humankind did so collectively! I will give further explanation of this fact, but I will approach it gradually.

***

Let me try to make this as clear as possible. You were created as a self-aware being with a separate sense of identity that is more or less narrowly focused on your sense of self. With your current sense of self, you probably see yourself as separate from other beings in your environment and from the Creator. This is not necessarily wrong, but since you are a spiritual person, you need to become more aware of your potential to expand your sense of self. In other words, while you were created as a separate being, you have the potential to grow beyond that. You can follow a path that expands your sense of self until you attain a sense of oneness with your source – your Creator – and with all life.

You were created as a separate being, but you were not created to *remain* a separate being. You were created to start out as a separate being and then follow a path of growing in self-awareness, until you overcome separateness and become one with the All without losing your sense of individuality. In other words, the underlying theme in the world of form is to grow from separateness to oneness. What many religious people call salvation is this exact process of growing from a separate sense of identity to an expanded sense of identity, in which you realize the oneness of all life and live accordingly. As I have said, everything is created from the Creator's consciousness, which has been temporarily projected into a limited, separate form. Yet the Creator does not want its own Being to remain trapped in such limitations forever. Thus, all that was created out of the Creator's consciousness is meant to return to the Creator. You too can return, the difference being that in this return you will not lose your identity but will magnify it until you can enter the Allness or become a creator for your own universe. Thus, the real purpose of life is to transcend your current sense of identity until you reach what we might call full God consciousness.

We might say that all separate beings were created as "self-transcending beings." As we will see later, there are various evolutions in the world of form, but they are all created to self-transcend, going from separateness to oneness.

***

Always keep in mind that the world of form is designed to be different from the Allness. Yet because it is designed by a Being *from* the Allness, there are also some similarities. One similarity is a oneness in purpose. Both worlds are set up to facilitate the growth in the self-awareness of individual beings. A self-conscious, or self-aware, being grows by expressing its creative abilities and divine individuality, and then learning from experiencing the reactions generated by its actions.

One of the main differences between the two worlds is that in the Allness individual Beings do not see themselves as separate from each other or the whole. Thus, it is inconceivable that one Being would choose to do something that would hurt another or that is aimed at making itself seem better than others. In the Allness, all Beings are not only *created* equal, they *are* equal in every way because they are all part of the same whole. Thus, a Being in the Allness could never conceive of using its will to go against the whole or the purpose of creation. It could never see its will as being in opposition to the purpose of life or the will of other beings. Such a being has self-awareness, but it is not a separate self-awareness.

In the world of form self-conscious beings start out with a self-awareness as separate beings. You are meant to grow from separateness to oneness, but you have imagination, so it is possible to envision a scale upon which one being is better or more important than others. You have free will, so it is possible to use that will to try to create the appearance that you are more important or more powerful than others. In doing so, you might seek to limit others in order to make yourself look better. You might even seek to destroy others if they oppose your attempt to control them. My point is that when your Creator created self-conscious beings with a limited self-awareness and endowed them with imagination and free will, a very specific concern was brought into being. That concern is how to balance the individual will of separate beings with the overall purpose of the world of form. How can you make it possible for beings to express their imagination and will without destroying themselves or each other in the process? When you look at the wars and atrocities that this small planet has witnessed in its relatively short existence, I am sure you can see that this is a rather important consideration. Thus, we will look at it in greater detail.

Let us begin by considering what it really means to make free choices. I have already stated that if you do not know what your options entail, you cannot make truly free choices. In the Allness, all Presences know that they are one with the Allness and thus one with each other. If one Presence was to do something that hurt another Presence, it would literally be hurting itself at the same time. A Presence in the Allness does have free will, but it would never conceive of using it to hurt or limit itself. We might say that a Presence in the Allness cannot use its free will as if it was a separate being. From your present viewpoint that might seem like a limitation, but consider that it is the inconsiderate use of free will that is the cause of all suffering on Earth. So perhaps this is not really a limitation.

Because a Presence in the Allness sees itself as one with every aspect of the Allness, it would never do something to hurt others. It knows that it is perfectly possible to raise up itself and at the same time raise up all life. And because of its sense of oneness with all life, it has no desire to raise itself compared to others. It knows that the only true way to raise itself is to raise all life. In the Allness comparisons have no meaning and neither do value judgments. Although Presences in the Allness have unrestricted free will, they would never conceive of using their will as a separate will or as something that was out of harmony with what is best for the All—meaning themselves.

In the world of form, you have beings who were created with a separate sense of identity. And because the material universe has not reached the intensity of light found in higher realms, it is possible for a being to truly believe that it is separated from other forms of life. Thus, it can fall prey to the illusion that it can hurt others without hurting itself. It might even think it can benefit from doing something that hurts others. As I have said, everything in the world of form is created out of the Mother Light, which is an expression, an extension, of the consciousness of the Creator. Thus, everything is connected at the level of the Mother Light, but this connection is hidden from the conscious awareness of those who focus their attention on separation. The more you focus on the appearance that you are a separate being, the more unable you are to see any deeper connection between yourself and the All. If you choose to harm or limit other people, you are in all reality harming yourself as well. Yet you will not be able to perceive this and you might not be able to conceptualize it either. In other words, you are not making a truly free choice when you hurt others. You are making such choices because you are trapped in an illusion, the illusion of separateness that prevents you from seeing that you are hurting yourself by hurting others.

**

My point is that the fact that you see yourself as a separate being makes it possible for you to use your will as if you really *were* a separate being. Thus, you can convince yourself that your actions do not have consequences that affect you. You can even convince yourself that your actions do not have any (negative) consequences at all. What is the deciding factor between those who are trapped inside this illusion and those who have seen beyond it? It is the level of self-centeredness. The more self-centered you become – the more attached you are to your separate sense of identity – the more blind you are to the reality that all life is one interconnected whole. Thus, you begin to believe that you have a right to do whatever you want and that you can get away with doing whatever you want. If you look at history, you will see that some of the worst human atrocities were perpetrated by the most self-centered people on the planet. One of the inescapable consequences of giving separate beings free will is that it is possible that one being can build the illusion that it is the center of the universe, that it is the only being that matters and that it has a right to do whatever it wants without considering how it affects others. A separate being might even believe that all other separate beings are here only to serve its own needs.

This leads to an interesting conclusion. If your Creator had given all self-transcending beings free will without setting up any safety mechanism to guide the use of that free will, it would have given an unfair advantage to those who had become self-centered. The more self-centered you become, the more willing you are to disregard how your actions affect others. You are willing to control others and to destroy those who will not be controlled. So the more insensitive and aggressive you become, the more willing you are to use your free will to control, harm or destroy others. If there was no mechanism to restrain the most self-centered beings, this world of form could have descended into anarchy with no hope of ever emerging from this state of chaos. I know it might seem as if the law of the jungle reigns supreme on Earth, but that is not actually the case, as we will see.

Let us remember that the purpose of this world of form is to give you the opportunity to start out with a separate sense of identity and gradually expand your sense of self until you become the Allness. Yet because you have free will, it is possible for you to go in the opposite direction. In the process of doing so, you might imprison or destroy other self-transcending beings before you finally destroy yourself. In other words, free will gives you the opportunity to create a downward spiral that traps you behind a wall of self-created illusions. This can make you blind to the consequences of your choices. Thus, once you have become blinded by self-centeredness, you can no longer choose to pull yourself out. You are now hurting yourself without fully realizing what you are doing, and thus you are not truly making free choices.

An intelligent and loving Creator obviously would not want this to happen to any of the extensions of itself. Thus, it was necessary to set up certain laws that could accompany the Law of Free Will, creating a safety net that could give separate beings all possible opportunities for *not* destroying themselves.

***

Before we move on, let us summarize what we have discussed so far. We have said that as a self-transcending being with unrestricted imagination and free will, you have the potential to follow two roads, two paths, in life. You were created to start your journey at a particular level of the world of form. Some beings were created at the highest level of the world of form, while others were created to start in the material universe, which is currently the lowest level of the world of form.

The purpose of the world of form is to give beings the opportunity to start out as separate beings in a limited world and then grow from there toward full self-awareness as being one with the All. In other words, the basic design of the universe is that you start at a certain level of the world of form and then work your way up from there. Jesus described this process in his parable about the talents, where those who multiplied their talents were rewarded by receiving greater creative powers. To him that has, more shall be given (Matthew 25:29).

If you multiply the talents you were given when you were created, God will multiply your offering and thus you will have more. In other words, if you use your imagination and free will as intended, you will place yourself on a path that leads to greater abundance and self-awareness. This is the path of becoming MORE than you are, more than you were created to be.

On the other hand, you have free will, so you have the potential to imagine that you could bury your talents in the ground and become less than you were created to be. In fact, you will become less even by not multiplying what you were given. As Jesus' parable describes, you live in a universe that is meant to expand and grow. Thus, the entire world of form is constantly becoming MORE. As an individual, you can go *with* the flow or you can go *against* the flow. Yet stillstand is not an option in the sense that if you do not go with the flow, you will fall behind. We might say that you have a right to refuse to grow, refuse to multiply your talents and become MORE, but you do not have a right to demand that the rest of the universe stops its growth in order to accommodate you.

My point here is that the alternative to the path of becoming MORE is the path of becoming less. Instead of expanding your self-awareness, you now restrict your self-awareness. Instead of becoming aware of the self as the greater Self, the All, you create a sense of self that is less than what you were originally given. You become more and more centered on that lesser self, you become more and more selfish and unable or unwilling to see beyond your short-sighted self-interest.

We can also say that the path of becoming MORE is the path of abundance. It is what Jesus called the kingdom of God or the abundant life (Luke 12:32). It is what the Buddha called the state of enlightenment and what many other religions have described as a form of paradise. In contrast, the path of becoming less will give you the opposite of abundance. You will experience all kinds of limitations, and this will cause you to feel that life is a struggle. Thus, the path of becoming less is the path of suffering. You might know that the Buddha defined the four noble truths, and the first of them is that life is suffering. Well, life is only truly suffering when you walk the path of becoming less. And as the Buddha pointed out, there is an alternative, namely to walk the path of becoming MORE – what he called the Middle Way – leading you to enlightenment, which is truly a state of realistic self-awareness as a self-transcending being.

I hope you can now see that we have reached an understanding that can dramatically change your life. Many of the world's religions have hinted at this explanation, but none have expressed it with full clarity. Yet once you understand and fully acknowledge that you must choose between two paths, you can completely change your outlook on life, religion, God and yourself. You can then quickly expand your understanding until you can make a truly free – meaning a fully informed – choice about whether you want to continue on the path of becoming less or whether you will make a decisive effort to place yourself firmly on the path of becoming MORE. If you decide to follow the path of less, you will inevitably lose your spiritual freedom, so the only way to attain true spiritual freedom is to follow the Path of MORE.

I have no intention of making the choice for you or even telling you what to choose. However, I will give you a greater understanding of the mechanisms that affect you no matter which path you take.

Key 6
Understanding the purpose of God's laws

If you take an impersonal look at the world of form, you might say that the purpose of this world is to have the light grow in intensity until it fills up the void and eventually reaches the same intensity as the Allness, thus becoming – or merging back into – the Allness. Yet this world was not created for an impersonal or mechanical purpose. It was created for a personal purpose, namely to give self-transcending beings the opportunity to start out as separate, self-centered beings and grow in self-awareness until they can enter the Allness with a memory of being less than the Allness. Thus, life is not a treadmill of creating a void, filling that void, creating a new void, filling that void and so on. Life is a creative process wherein self-conscious beings receive a unique opportunity to grow in awareness until they reach the same level of consciousness as God itself. You are, so to speak, a God in the making, which is why Jesus said, "Ye are Gods" (John 10:34).

Imagine the conditions found before anything was created in the void. Your Creator had projected itself as a singularity in the middle of a vast void in which there was absolutely nothing. Your Creator could create absolutely anything it could envision. There were no rules or limitations, for it was up to the Creator to define its own rules. This was actually a challenge for your Creator, for when you can create anything without having any prior experience or reference to guide you, you can feel a bit lonely and lost. Obviously, your Creator had the full memory of the Allness and saw itself as an extension of the Allness, so the emptiness of the void was not scary to the Creator. Yet imagine that the Creator had created a number of self-conscious beings and had sent them into the void with the command to create anything they wanted. These beings would not have had any memory of the Allness and no sense of connection to it. Neither would they have had any prior experience to guide their creative efforts. Naturally, they would have felt alone and quite possibly lost. You might have heard of people who lose their memory and how traumatic that can be. You might even have heard of torture where people are deprived of sensory experiences, thus feeling like they are alone in a world of nothingness. This can very quickly lead to a mental breakdown, even permanent insanity.

Your Creator had no desire to put its offspring through that experience, so it created a protected sphere that was set apart from the void. Within that sphere, the Creator created certain structures and set up certain creative principles – or laws – to guide the growth of that sphere. When a basis for life had been created, the Creator created self-transcending beings and gave them the command to "multiply" and "have dominion" (Genesis 1:28). Instead of throwing these beings into nothingness, the Creator gave them a foundation and told them to build upon it. They could do this by multiplying what they had been given and by learning how to use the laws defined by the Creator, thereby taking dominion over their sphere through self-mastery.

When they had mastered life in their native sphere, the self-transcending beings became masters who helped co-create the next sphere. And in doing so, they had greater creative freedom in terms of designing structures in that sphere. Thus, they had the opportunity to create anything they wanted, but they had guidelines and a basis of experience from which to create. In other words, only the Creator creates from "nothing," whereas all other beings have a foundation for their creative efforts. The Creator creates, whereas you expand your sense of self within the framework defined by the Creator. We might say that you co-create.

***

We have seen that the purpose of this world is to give self-conscious beings the opportunity to grow in self-awareness. This growth must take place gradually, or in stages. Why is this so? Because at any given time you have a sense of who you are. You might experience a situation that causes you to expand your sense of who you are, but it will take time for you to integrate that new sense of identity. That is why a child on Earth needs time to grow up and why children who are forced to "grow up" too quickly can experience severe psychological problems. If change happens too abruptly, people can lose their sense of who they are and they will find it difficult to cope with life.

My point is that sustainable growth must be balanced growth. You are, so to speak, meant to lose your separate sense of identity. Yet you are not meant to lose it all at once so that you have no identity left. You are meant to lose your separate sense of identity only as the result of a process whereby it is replaced by an expanded sense of identity. If the growth happened too quickly, you would lose your sense of stability and continuity, possibly even all sense of identity. If the growth happened too slowly, you might become so attached to a particular way of life that you would refuse to grow beyond that level of awareness. In order to achieve the best possible growth, everything in your life should be balanced. What does balance mean?

We have seen that the Creator created the void by contracting all of its consciousness and Being into a single point. This set the stage for the creation of the world of form by creating the void. Yet the actual creation began when the Creator projected part of its own consciousness outward. These are the two basic forces involved in creation, namely the contracting force and the expanding force. Imagine that the contracting force was the dominant force. In that case, nothing could be created. As soon as the Creator projected energy out into the void, the contracting force would instantly return it to the center. Now imagine that the expanding force was dominant. In that case all of God's Being would be released in one giant outburst, instantly filling the void. In either case a balanced and gradual growth would not be possible, thus leaving little opportunity for lifestreams to gradually grow in self-awareness. We can conclude that this world is not built on an all-or-nothing approach but on a careful balance between the two forces.

From a human perspective it might seem as if the expanding and the contracting forces are opposite each other. Yet true opposites cancel out each other. If opposites meet, they either destroy each other or one destroys the other and only one is left. In reality, the expanding and contracting forces are complementary, meaning that they supplement, even magnify, each other. Only when both forces are present is it possible to create a sustainable form.

The point is that the only way to create a sustainable structure – yet a structure that is growing – is to have a state of balance between the expanding and the contracting forces. They must coexist but they must be balanced so they keep each other in check without canceling out each other. And they must be balanced in such a way that they do not stop the growth that is the very purpose of the world of form. Balance is not something static. The balance of the universe is a dynamic balance, leading in a balanced way toward a higher goal. What is it that creates the balance between the two basic forces of creation?

***

Imagine that you are the Creator. You have the entire void in front of you, and you can create anything you want. The end goal is to fill up the void with light of such intensity that the void blends back into the Allness. Yet to reach that goal, you can potentially take an infinite number of different paths. There is an infinite variety of forms that you can create within the void, and many of them can lead to the end goal of filling the void. In other words, there is more than one way to design a universe.

We now realize that although the Creator is an infinite Being with unlimited power, even the Creator faces certain limitations. In the world of form, everything is characterized by having form, meaning that every form is different from other forms. A distinct form is set apart from the void and set apart from other forms. Let us use an example with which you are familiar. There is an almost infinite variety of ways in which you can design a table. Yet a table has certain basic properties that set it apart from a chair. You might create a table that is similar to a chair, and you might be able to sit on that table. Yet the concept of a table is still different from the concept of a chair. So when you are in the wood-shop, you have to decide whether you want to build a table or a chair.

My point is that once you design something in the world of form, you run into the fact that a form is distinct, meaning that it cannot be two things at the same time. The result is that even the Creator has to make certain choices. The Creator can create anything it can imagine, but it cannot create everything at once. The Creator has to decide which type of universe it wants to create, and once it has decided on a design, it has to stick with it until the end goal of filling that portion of the void is accomplished. (I am not saying your Creator is the only Creator and that your world is the only world of form. In reality there are a large number of worlds representing many different basic designs, but that is another story that goes beyond the scope of this book.)

The Creator could potentially fill the void instantly, but that would defeat the purpose of creating the void as separate from the Allness. The Creator could also create a static universe that never changed, but that would also defeat the purpose of creating a process that leads from separateness back to oneness with the Allness. So the Creator is faced with the task of creating a gradual process that leads toward an end goal. You might never have considered what it would take to design such a gradual, goal-oriented process, so I ask you to do it now.

The first thing you realize is that you need certain principles, or laws, that can guide the progress toward the goal in an orderly and balanced manner. Imagine that you have no such principles. You simply send a burst of light into the void. The light will keep expanding out into the void but no organized structures will form. Consider the theory of the Big Bang. It states that all of the matter in the universe was compressed into a singularity and then expanded outward in a giant explosion. Yet after a short time, organized structures started forming within the chaos of the initial explosion. Why did such structures begin to form and why did they take the form they did? Why didn't the energy simply continue to expand in a random explosion? There can be only one explanation, namely that there are certain laws that guide the formation of organized structures. In fact, modern science can be described as an attempt to uncover and understand the laws that guide the unfoldment of the material universe. As a side note, the existence of laws proves that the world is not the product of a random process, for how could randomness give rise to consistent laws? And how could laws arise unless there was an intelligent being who defined the laws by making choices? Thus, science truly *has* pointed to the existence of an intelligent creator.

Now imagine that you *do* create certain laws but they are not consistent. If you allow randomness or contradictions, how can you make sure your end goal will be reached? The creative process might stall before the void is filled. Or you might have an inversion that destroys organized structures and moves backward toward an empty void. Or you could go back and forth without ever reaching the end goal.

We now see that if your goal is to be fulfilled, you need certain guiding principles that can make sure your creation proceeds in an organized and balanced manner. Yet an infinite Creator could potentially design many different types of worlds that had consistent laws and thus would all lead toward filling the void. So once again, we see that in order to design the particular world in which you live, your Creator had to make certain choices. And once those choices were made, this world of form was set on a track. Only by continuing on that track will this world reach its end goal.

***

Let us now look at another level of consideration. Your Creator created this world of form for the purpose of experiencing what it is like to be a separate being that is set apart from the Allness. In order to facilitate this experience, your Creator creates a sphere that is set apart from the void, creates structures in that sphere and then projects itself into that sphere in the form of a number of self-conscious, separate beings. Yet you are not created as a mere robot or a clone of the Creator. You are given the gift of life, meaning that you have the potential to grow toward the point where your individuality becomes permanent. We might say that you are created as a temporary lifestream, but you can grow toward receiving immortality, or what Jesus called eternal life.

What will it take for you to complete that process? You will start out by following the laws defined by your Creator. As a new being you do not have the experience or level of awareness to define your own laws, so the Creator has given you a foundation for your journey. These laws are not set up to restrict your creativity or freedom. They are defined to facilitate your growth toward the ultimate goal of becoming an immortal being who is one with the Allness. So you start out by mastering the laws defined by your Creator, using them to transcend your limited sense of identity until you reach the ultimate state of self-awareness that human beings call God. When you attain this God awareness, you can then create your own void and define whatever laws you like within that sphere. Yet to reach that point, you must begin by mastering the laws defined by your Creator.

Let us look at an analogy. In some parts of the Earth, there is an abundance of natural stones that can be used for building houses. There are a large number of house designs that can be built with natural stones. Yet natural stones have certain characteristics that set rules for how you can build a stone house. Does this actually limit your creativity, or does it merely channel it in certain directions? Say you get tired of the irregularity of natural stones. You decide to build a brick house instead, and this opens up new design possibilities. Yet even bricks have certain characteristics that set rules for how you can design a brick house, and the same is true for any other building material. There are many possible building materials and by exploring all of them, you could potentially overcome virtually all restrictions on how to design a house. What cannot be done with natural stones can be done with glass and so on. Yet all of the different materials found on Earth have something in common. They all exist within a larger framework, namely the law of gravity. No matter which material you use to build a house, you must find ways to counterbalance the pull of gravity so the house does not collapse.

Yet is the law of gravity really a restriction of your creative freedom? Consider what would happen if there was no gravity. How would you build a house when all of the materials would float off into empty space? My point is that the law of gravity does not restrict your creative freedom. It actually gives you a foundation for expressing your creative freedom. Likewise, even particular building materials do not truly restrict your freedom. They simply set up rules that allow you to channel your creativity in certain directions. Each material has its characteristics, but rather than being limitations, they actually give the material its charm. A house built from natural stone has a charm that is different from a house built from logs. One is not necessarily better or more attractive than the other and both materials give you numerous opportunities for expressing your creativity.

My overall point is that it is more constructive to learn how to make use of God's laws than to resist those laws. You have been given free will, so you have the option of refusing to work within the framework of the laws chosen by your Creator. Yet in doing so, you will inevitably limit yourself because you choose the path of becoming less—the path without balance between the two basic forces. This world of form was designed according to certain principles that ensure balanced growth, and it is only by working within the framework of those laws that you will self-transcend and become MORE. You may not agree with the choices made by your Creator when it designed this world. Yet by working *with* those laws, you can attain God consciousness and you can then create your own world in which you can design the laws as you choose. However, in order to get to that point, you have to pass the exam in *this* schoolroom. In order to transcend the laws of your Creator, you have to work *with* those laws, learning how to use them to their full capacity. Doing this will give you experience and insight that will empower you to create a world that does not self-destruct.

***

We now need to realize that this world of form was not created exclusively for *your* sake. You are not the center of the universe. You are an individual being but you are not the only one. Your Creator created many self-transcending beings, and this opens up for another level of consideration, namely how to balance the individual and the whole.

You are designed to start out as a separate being and gradually expand your self-awareness until you see that you are part of a larger whole. This does not mean that you lose your individuality, it actually means that you find your true individuality as an immortal spiritual being. You go from a very narrowly focused sense of self-awareness toward an awareness of yourself as part of the timeless process of life that is God. You start out seeing yourself as a separate being and can eventually develop the sense that you are connected to a remote God. You then gradually realize that the kingdom of God is within you, meaning that you are an extension of God. Eventually, you even realize that you are one with God, meaning that your sense of self-awareness can be expanded to be everywhere in the consciousness of God. At that point, you also realize that you are one with all life, because the Creator has become the many without ceasing to be the One.

For you to go through this process of expanded self-awareness, you need to start out as a separate being. You see yourself as being apart from your Creator and apart from other separate beings. In order to grow in self-awareness, you must be given imagination and free will. This is what gives you the potential to choose between the path of becoming MORE and the path of becoming less. Yet if you do choose the path of becoming less, you will reinforce the sense that you are separate from other beings. This increases the possibility that you will begin to see yourself as being in competition with or in opposition to other lifestreams. And then you might actually start interfering with their growth by seeking to control their imagination and free will according to your self-centered desires. You might also separate yourself from the Creator's overall purpose of creation and refuse to grow in self-awareness. The point is that you need free will and imagination in order to grow in self-awareness. However, you can potentially use these abilities to contract in self-awareness, thereby going against the purpose for your own life and even seeking to prevent others from growing.

Your Creator did not create you with the casualness of someone rolling a dice. Your Creator does not want you to contract in self-awareness until you destroy yourself. So your Creator did design certain principles that would increase the likelihood that all lifestreams would – eventually – choose the path of becoming MORE over the path of becoming less. In other words, your Creator has set up certain laws to balance your individual creativity with that of other self-transcending beings and with the overall purpose of the world of form. This is not done to restrict your free will but to guide your free will so you do not destroy yourself or other beings—who are truly expressions of your own greater Self, namely the Creator.

***

There is one overall principle that guides the unfoldment of the world of form. That principle is what balances the expanding and the contracting forces. As you might remember, only when these two forces are balanced do you have a sustainable form. Thus, when your Creator defined the design of this world of form, it decided on a particular balance between the expanding and contracting forces. It is much like a composer who decides on the basic musical key of a symphony. Once decided, the entire symphony builds upon the foundation and thus there will be perfect harmony between the different parts of the composition. Even though many individual musicians play different instruments, their efforts form a harmonious whole as long as they stay true to the key defined by the composer. Likewise, there is a basic note or sound that defines the balance for this particular world. Some spiritual teachings have called it the "cosmic hum" and you can tune in to it by reciting the sound OM or AUM.

The Creator knew full well the implications of giving self-transcending beings a separate sense of identity and free will. Thus, the Creator decided that as the very first act of creation it would create a state of mind that could contain – in an unerasable form – the Creator's blueprint for the world of form. This state of consciousness records the entire purpose and intention behind the creation of the void, including the goal of filling the void and seeing separate beings grow to full God consciousness. It also records all of the choices made by the Creator regarding the basic design of the world of form. This includes all of the principles that the Creator defined as a guide for the unfoldment of this particular world.

We might say that these principles define the *only* way in which this particular design can unfold and come to full fruition. As we saw earlier, many designs were possible, but your Creator had to choose one. Thus, once the design was chosen, this particular world of form was set on a track. Only by following that track can this world fulfill its purpose. There is still room for infinite creativity within the framework defined by the basic design. Yet only by staying within that framework, will you be able to express your individual creativity in a way that is in alignment with the overall purpose and design of the world in which you live. And only then will you grow toward the fulfillment of your individual reason for being, namely to attain full God consciousness.

If you stay within the framework defined by your Creator, anything you create will have the necessary balance between the expanding and contracting forces. If you go against that framework, you will inevitably create an imbalance between the two basic forces, and thus your creation simply is not sustainable. An imbalance between the basic forces will eventually cause your creation to be blown apart in over-expansion or collapse in over-contraction. And this causes you to experience life as an ongoing process of imbalance, conflict and suffering.

If you stay within the basic framework of this world, there will be balance between your individual creativity and the whole. Your efforts will not only raise yourself but will also raise the whole, thus causing the sphere in which you live to increase in organization, complexity and intensity of light. This is what Jesus described when he said that if he was lifted up, he would draw all people unto him (John 12:32). This is the abundant life in which you constantly experience an expansion of your joy and happiness, and thus you have complete peace of mind. When you follow God's design, you are on the path of becoming MORE, whereby you also work to make your entire sphere MORE. Obviously, if you take the path of becoming less, you not

only limit yourself but also work to pull down the entire sphere in
which you live.

What do we call the universal state of consciousness that is
designed to keep the entire world of form on track toward victory? As
mentioned before, if we call the Creator God the Father, we can call
the balancing principle the Son, the only begotten son or the firstborn
son. Obviously, we find these expressions in Christianity, but unfortunately orthodox Christianity has made the error of creating a man-
made doctrine according to which Jesus was the *only* Son of God.
The reality is that the universal Christ consciousness is the only Son
of God, the only begotten of the Father. Jesus is an example of a person who has united with that universal Christ mind and has attained
individual Christhood. Through this union, Jesus deserves the title of
the Son of God, or rather the SUN of God. Yet Jesus is not the only
one who could attain this title. In fact, all human beings have that
potential, and Jesus came specifically to set forth an example of how
to become the Christ on Earth. That is why the Gospel of John contains the following words—that are often ignored or misinterpreted
by orthodox Christians, "But as many as received him, to them gave
he power to become the sons of God, even to them that believe on his
name (John 1:12).

How do you attain Christhood? By expanding your sense of self-
awareness until you see who you truly are – namely an individualization of your Creator – and thus you exclaim with Jesus, "I and my
father are one" (John 10:30). At that point, your sense of identity has
become immortalized and you have attained eternal life through oneness with your source, your Creator. You have overcome the sense of
self as a separate, mortal being and you have been reborn into a new
sense of self as an immortal being who is one with the All.

You might remember that Jesus said, "All things are delivered
unto me of my Father: and no man knoweth the Son, but the Father;
neither knoweth any man the Father, save the Son, and he to whomso-
ever the Son will reveal him" (Matthew 11:27). The true meaning is
that you can know God only through the universal Christ mind. Only
this mind knows that you are an extension of the Creator and only this
mind knows the laws defined by the Creator. Thus, it is only by
attaining the Christ consciousness that you can bring yourself into
alignment with the purpose of creation and the basic design of your
world. If you go outside the mind of Christ, you set yourself up

against the world. Your life will inevitably become a struggle because everything you do will be a fight *against* the basic forces of creation. When you return to the Christ consciousness, you enter the abundant life because everything you do will enhance both yourself and all life. You are moving *with* the basic forces of creation and thus these forces magnify everything you do instead of opposing it. More on this as we move on.

We might say that the main function of the universal Christ mind is to create and maintain oneness within the world of form. It is through the Christ mind that you can establish oneness with your Creator, with the Creator's purpose and with the Creator's laws. Once you attain some sense of oneness with your Creator, you will see that all other self-transcending beings, and indeed everything in the world of form, is created from God's Being and substance. This will open up for a sense of oneness with all life, and this is the only factor that can bring harmony and unity among individual beings. Thus, one of the main functions of the Christ mind is to help individual beings establish a sense of unity and oneness amongst themselves. This is the *only* factor that can overcome competition and conflict, so that individual beings do not work against each other but work together on raising up all life. When you have the Christ consciousness, you know that the only way to raise yourself is to raise the whole of which you are a part. Thus, individual Christ consciousness gives rise to the realization that all beings are part of the one Body of God on Earth.

***

There are a number of specific laws that guide the unfoldment of the material universe. For each sphere in the spiritual realm, there are laws that are specific to that sphere. Yet all of these laws function within the framework of one single law. That law is the Law of Love, which can also be called the Law of Oneness. In order to understand the Law of Love, we first need to take a closer look at love itself. When we talk about the Law of Love, we are talking about divine love, which is quite different from human love. Let us contrast the two:

- Human love is often focused on the individual self. Divine love is focused on everything within God's creation. We might say it is focused on the All or that it is focused on the larger Self that *is* the All.

- Human love is conditional. You set up conditions in your mind for who is worthy to receive your love. And you set up conditions which say that in certain situations it is not possible to respond with love. Divine love knows no conditions. It is given freely to all, as Jesus explained when he said that God lets the sun rise upon the evil and the good (Matthew 5:45). Likewise, divine love accepts no conditions for when it should be expressed and when it should be held back. Divine love always flows and is always in the process of becoming MORE.

- Human love is possessive. It seeks to gather to itself, and once it has taken possession of something, it wants to keep it. People with possessive love are seeking to prevent change because they are afraid of loss.

- According to human love, perfection is a static state in which nothing can change. Divine love does not seek to own any particular thing because it is one with the All—it *is* everything. It does not seek to gather to itself, it seeks to raise the All by freely giving of itself. Divine love is not seeking to *stop* growth in order to keep what it has. It is seeking to *speed up* growth in order to become more than it is right now.

- Human love seeks to *have* more. Divine love seeks to *be* MORE. Divine love knows it does not become more by taking from others but by giving of itself to others, thus raising the All.

- Human love is often aimed at raising up the individual in comparison to others, it is aimed at fulfilling self-interest. It seeks to raise the individual self rather than the larger Self. Divine love knows it is one with the larger Self. It knows that it becomes more only when the All becomes more. Thus, it is seeking the enlightened self-interest that comes from realizing you are one with the All.

- Human love is based on fear, the fear of not being good enough, the fear of loss. Human love makes you fear to give because you fear that you will lose what you have. Divine love has no element of fear in it whatsoever. It is the perfect love that casts out all fear (1John 4:12). Divine love knows it is one with the

All, and thus it could never lose by giving. When you give with unconditional love, God will multiply your gift so that you will end up having more to give.

***

Why did your Creator create this universe? Out of love, unconditional love! If you have grown up in a religious culture, you have probably been given the concept of a better world beyond the material universe. You might have seen it as a form of paradise with various positive properties. If you take these positive aspects and multiply them a billion times, you will have some idea of what the Allness is like. In other words, your Creator was completely happy and fulfilled in the Allness.

It is true that your Creator had a desire to experience being outside the Allness, but that was not a self-centered desire. The reason being that the Creator cannot experience what it is like to be outside the Allness—this can happen only when the Creator projects itself as individual, separate beings. Thus, the Creator's desire was actually focused on giving you – and many other self-transcending beings – the opportunity to grow in self-awareness until you too become one with the Allness. For this growth to happen, a Presence from the Allness must dedicate itself to setting itself apart from the Allness. It must then create a world out of its own Being, meaning that the infinite Being of the Creator is – so to speak – imprisoned in the finite world of form. The Creator even allows the extensions of itself to do whatever they want with that part of its Being over which they have power.

My point is that your Creator did make a type of sacrifice by creating you, namely by setting itself apart from the Allness and giving you power to do with its own Being as you see fit. However, the Creator does not see it as a sacrifice but as a service to life. The desire to serve life can spring from only one source, namely unconditional love. Thus, the very motivation behind the creation of the world of form is unconditional love. And this force of unconditional love is built into every aspect of this world. That is why the Law of Love is the basic law of the universe.

What exactly does the Law of Love say? It says that the very purpose of life is to grow toward the Allness, from less to MORE. If you have unconditional love, you do not want any conditions to stop this growth toward the ultimate source of fulfillment and joy. Thus, you do not want any self-transcending being to become stuck in a limited sense of self-awareness. You want all beings to be on the path of becoming MORE so they are constantly growing toward God consciousness. In other words, the Law of Love states that stillstand is not possible. You are either moving forward toward the infinite self-awareness of God or you are moving backward toward the infinitely limited self-awareness of being apart from God. You are either becoming MORE or you are becoming less, for there is nothing in between. It is much like a light switch that is either ON or OFF.

In order to better understand this, let us consider the relationship between the individual and the whole. Everything ever created by your Creator is created out of the consciousness of the Creator. Thus, it came from the same source and it is united through that common origin. Everything in the world of form makes up an interconnected whole, which is what I call the All. Everything is created for the same purpose and follows the same basic design principles. Thus, we might say that the All is a whole that is moving toward a particular goal. We can compare this to a river in which individual drops of water are moving toward the common goal of uniting with the ocean. Everything that is in harmony with the basic purpose of creation forms what I will call the "River of Life." This is a coherent whole that is moving in unison – by following the laws defined by the Creator – toward the common goal of merging with – of *becoming* – the Allness.

As an individual being, you have the option of choosing the path of becoming MORE or the path of becoming less. When you choose the Path of MORE, you join the River of Life and you are moving in harmony with everyone else who has chosen to unite with the purpose of creation. This does not mean that you lose your free will or creativity. It means that you are expressing your creativity in harmony with the purpose of creation, and thereby everything you create is multiplied. This is the abundant life where you are constantly becoming MORE and thus receiving more abundance. I can assure you that the vast majority of the self-transcending beings found in the world of form have – out of love – chosen to join this River of Life. Thus, there is a vast momentum in this movement, created by all of the individual beings who have added their creative powers to the forward movement of the All.

If you choose the path of less, you set yourself outside the River of Life. Thus, you are going against the basic purpose of creation, and you are also going against the momentum generated by those who are in the River of Life. You have free will, so you have the right to set yourself apart from the River of Life. Yet your free will does not supersede or cancel out the free will of other beings. You have a right to step outside the River of Life, but you do not have the right to demand that the river should slow down in order to wait for you. In other words, the River of Life moves on, and because all life is created from the same source and is interconnected, the forward momentum of the River of Life will pull on you to move along with it. The result is that you can remain outside the River of Life only by resisting this pull, and that is why your life becomes a constant struggle—like swimming upstream in a river. Because the River of Life is constantly moving forward, stepping outside of it does not mean that you stand still. You will be falling behind the River, and you will be falling behind the place in the river where you would have been if you had stayed on the Path of MORE.

In summary, the Law of Love states that the very purpose of life is to become MORE. You have a right to go against that purpose, but the Law of Love mandates that the rest of the world of form does not have to follow your choices. Other self-transcending beings have a right to continue on the Path of MORE and thus add to the momentum that makes it harder for you to resist the forward movement of the River of Life. As I have explained, everything is created from the same source and is interconnected. Separation is an illusion that exists only in the mind of individual beings. So when you choose this illusion, you are not separated from the River of Life in reality but only in your own mind, which is why you have to struggle to maintain the illusion. More on this later.

As a side note let me mention that following along with the River of Life does not mean that you blindly follow the crowd. The beings who are in the River of Life are all on the Path of MORE, which means that they are constantly transcending themselves and expanding their sense of identity. This is a highly creative process and it cannot be done by passively following others. Your task is to expand your unique individuality, and that cannot be done by imitating or following someone else.

***

The Law of Love has two aspects. There is an Alpha aspect that corresponds to the expanding force and an Omega aspect that corresponds to the contracting force. The Alpha aspect is the Law of MORE, the law of self-transcendence. This law states that the purpose of life is growth. You start out in a limited world with a limited sense of self-awareness. Yet it is not the purpose of life that your world or your self-awareness should remain in that limited state or descend below it. The purpose is that both your world and your self-awareness should transcend limitations until they reach the fullness of the Allness.

The Law of MORE states that you do not have a right to remain in limbo, to remain at a standstill. If you are not transcending your limitations, those limitations are becoming more defined, more restricting. Thus, if you do not expand your sense of awareness, you will inevitably contract your self-awareness until your own refusal to grow takes away your creative freedom. Your imagination and free will eventually become so narrowly focused that you no longer have the ability to create anything. You have put yourself in a box and you have continued to make the box smaller until you have no more room to move. You are boxed in by your own limited sense of self-awareness.

The Omega aspect of the Law of Love is the Law of the ONE, which states that because all life came from the same source, it is connected at the deepest level. All life is meant to move forward as one interconnected whole, namely the River of Life. You can refuse to become MORE, and in doing so you can set yourself outside the River of Life created by those who are on the Path of MORE. Yet you cannot set yourself outside the basic oneness of all life. This means that you do not have the right to demand that all other self-transcending beings slow down in order to accommodate you. Nor can you escape the fact that the oneness of all life means that everything is pulling on everything else. If you can create a downward pull that is stronger than the upward pull of those who are on the Path of MORE, you can slow down the progression of life, at least temporarily. Yet if other beings create a stronger upward pull, you cannot avoid being affected by that force. Thus, it will require more and more effort on your part to stay separated from the River of Life. You have a right to set yourself outside the Sphere of Oneness in order to experience what it is like to be separated from your source. However, you do not have the right to do this forever, for the Creator's own Being is embedded within you and the Creator does not want to be separated from itself forever.

The combined effect of the Law of MORE and the Law of the ONE is to maintain a balanced growth toward the ultimate goal of creation. The Law of MORE upholds the forward movement of life, whereas the Law of the ONE makes this movement gradual and balanced. The two laws make it easier for any being to stay balanced in the use of both the expanding or the contracting force. These laws pull you back toward the center, back toward balance, yet they do not restrict your creative freedom. They merely channel your creativity in a direction that ensures your own growth and the growth of the All.

As we have seen, free will is a foundational element in your growth toward God consciousness. The Creator has no desire to force you to do what is best for yourself. The Creator wants you to come to a point of truly understanding what is best for yourself, so that you can choose it out of love and with no sense of being forced. The Creator gives you almost unlimited freedom in terms of which path you will follow toward the point of enlightenment, where you fully realize what is best for yourself and thus choose to join the River of Life out of unconditional love.

We might express this in another way by saying that the Creator has given you the right to always do what you see as best for yourself. Yet the Creator has set up laws that pull on you to expand your sense of self. If you follow those laws, you will expand your sense of self until you see that what is best for yourself is what is best for the All— for your ultimate sense of self *is* the All.

***

You learn from your experience, so the question is what kind of experiences you personally need in order to come to the point of enlightenment. If you need the experience of using either the expanding or the contracting force in an unbalanced way, then the Law of Free Will allows this to happen. Yet the Law of Free Will also has an Alpha and an Omega aspect. The Alpha aspect is that you have a right to create for yourself any experience you want, yet because you have self-awareness you cannot escape experiencing what you create. We can call this law the Law of Cause and Effect, meaning that if you set in motion an unbalanced cause – through an unbalanced use of either creative force – you will inevitably experience an unbalanced effect in your life. The Omega aspect is that you must balance any unbalanced effect that you create so that you bring the universe back to the state of balance it was in before your unbalanced action. This is the Law of Balance, which in some religions is called the Law of Karma.

What happens if a self-transcending being uses the expanding force in an unbalanced manner? Such beings will often grow faster and accelerate beyond the level of awareness of other beings in their sphere. While such beings are often motivated by a true desire to do well, the crucial distinction is whether they eventually come to understand the Law of the ONE. If they do, they will realize that they need to start using their own attainment to help others. If they do not, they simply engage in a quest to prove themselves better than others, as if life was a cosmic competition.

In most cases, such unbalanced beings will eventually run out of steam and will come back to a level of growth that is sustainable because it is the balanced growth of the River of Life. Yet if several beings have attained a higher level of creative power and if they work together, it is possible that they can misuse the expanding force to such an extent that they break the tie to the other beings in their sphere. We earlier saw that the spheres created by the Creator are concentric, making it possible that a being can attain mastery of one sphere and then ascend to a higher sphere. Yet for this to happen, the being must be completely balanced in its use of both creative forces. In other words, only those who are balanced and contribute to the growth of the All – only those who are acting from love – can work their way up through the spheres toward God consciousness.

If beings use the expanding force with sufficient imbalance, they can come to a point where they can no longer stay in their native sphere, yet the lack of balance makes it impossible for them to ascend to the spiritual realm. They can then catapult themselves into the sphere that is being created as their own sphere ascends. They can continue to exist here until the new sphere ascends and they face the same choice again. Yet eventually they will lose their opportunity to exist as separate beings, if not sooner then when the void is finally filled with light.

What happens if a being uses the contracting force in an unbalanced way? Such a being will not accelerate its own growth beyond other beings but will seek to slow down their growth by controlling them. Such beings can also create their own world within a world, and they can continue to seek to set themselves up as the superior leaders – controlling everyone within their reach – until their sphere begins to ascend.

For both types of imbalances, there will come a point when the self-transcending beings in that sphere have created such a momentum of the River of Life that the intensity of the light in their sphere reaches a critical level. At that point, the unbalanced beings can no longer remain. Thus, they are faced with the choice that they must either step up to the path of becoming MORE or they must move to the sphere that is below them and thus still has sufficient darkness left for them to exist there. If a being decides to misuse either force after the critical light intensity is reached in its sphere, it will immediately fall from that sphere to a lower sphere.

If a group of beings misuse either force in order to set themselves apart from others, they can create a downward spiral within their sphere (providing it has sufficient darkness left). This spiral can become quite powerful and can even overpower other beings and draw them into it. Such a spiral can no longer exist in any of the spheres that make up the spiritual realm. Only in the latest sphere – your sphere – is there still enough darkness left for a downward spiral of selfishness to exist.

Such a downward spiral is what many religions call hell. It is created by beings who are using their creative abilities to make themselves more powerful compared to others instead of working to raise the All. Thus, they create a spiral in which the contracting or the expanding force becomes gradually more concentrated. This has the effect of focusing the imagination and free will around themselves and around the goals defined by the most powerful beings in the downward spiral. These goals are completely selfish, meaning that the less powerful beings in the spiral end up working for the glorification of the most powerful beings (instead of everyone working to raise the All). The effect is that many beings actually lose their free will and imagination after entering such a spiral. They are simply so overpowered by the more aggressive beings that they lose their sense of self and become like robots working for the leaders—the blind following the blind (Matthew 15:14).

We will later talk about this in more detail. For now, let it be enough to say that the downward spiral will eventually reach such intensity that even the leaders lose their free will and imagination because they are so focused on themselves that they cannot think about anything else. This causes the unbalanced force to intensify until it reaches a level where it begins to break down any organized structure. If unbalanced beings continue to misuse the contracting force, they can create such a powerful spiral that any organized structure collapses in upon itself, even destroying their own self-awareness. This has the appearance of a fiery inferno that burns up everything, and it is the reality behind the various conceptions of hell found in religions on Earth. Similarly, if unbalanced beings continue to misuse the expanding force, they can create such a powerful spiral that any organized structure is blown apart. In either case, the Mother Light is then returned to its original purity, but the self-awareness of the beings in the spiral is irretrievably lost.

***

The laws we have described so far form the framework for the overall growth of both individual beings and the spheres of God. The basic principle is relatively simple, as described in Jesus' parable about the servants who received talents from their master. As a new self-transcending being, you are given a certain amount of light energy as a gift. It is, so to speak, your investment account in the cosmic bank and you can draw on it to live and to exercise your creative powers. You start out with a sizeable amount of light in your account, and it can sustain you for a long time.

When you make choices that are self-centered, you can still use the light in your account. Yet self-centered actions will do nothing to raise the All, which means that you are not multiplying your talents, your light. If you are not multiplying what you have been given, the Law of MORE makes it impossible for you to receive more. Thus, you will end up spending what you have in the account without getting more. On the other hand, when you make choices that are not self-centered, you will use your light to raise up the All and increase the intensity of light in your sphere. You have now multiplied your talents and will be given more light from above. By being balanced, you can exercise your creativity without depleting your account. Instead, you will add to what is in the account.

The Law of MORE was described by Jesus when he said, "For whosoever hath, to him shall be given, and he shall have MORE abundance: but whosoever hath not, from him shall be taken away even that he hath" (Matthew 13:12). In other words, when you take light from your cosmic account and use it to raise the All, you multiply that light instead of burying it in the ground (of self-glorification or the fear of loss). The law will then multiply what you have given and you will have more light in your cosmic account. Obviously, this will then add to the intensity of light in your sphere, and when many beings do this, they create an upward spiral, which is what I have called the River of Life. When you are in this stream of life, you have no fear of loss, and thus you know that the more you give, the more you will receive.

As such an upward spiral continues to build, it will increase the intensity of the light in that sphere. Eventually, a critical mass is reached and the sphere now has no room for darkness. This means that there is no more room for beings who are unbalanced in their use of the basic creative forces. The sphere has now become part of the spiritual realm. If there are beings in that sphere who are not in the River of Life, they will have to descend to the next lower sphere. Such a new sphere is created when one sphere reaches the critical intensity of light.

The point is that these laws ensure the balanced progression of the world of form while giving self-transcending beings the greatest possible opportunities for exercising their free will without destroying themselves or each other. The main goal is for all beings to learn from their experience. You are not expected to be perfect from the beginning, and you are allowed to go against the laws of God. Yet when you do so, you will inevitably limit your self-awareness and turn your life into a struggle. Thus, because the Creator loves you unconditionally, the laws are set up to do everything possible to help you get back to a balanced state. The laws make sure that the more unbalanced you become, the more you have to struggle to maintain your unbalanced state. Thus, you will hopefully come to the point of tiring of the continued struggle so you start asking yourself whether there is a better way. As Jesus said to Paul, "It is hard for thee to kick against the pricks" (Acts 9:5). And when you realize that you are *creating* the pricks, you might decide that it is time to learn by going *with* the laws of God rather than going *against* them. You will then enter the Path of MORE that leads you toward enlightenment and beyond.

In summary, we might say that Plan A for this universe was that all self-transcending being should start out at a certain level and only go up from there, never falling below the level at which they came into being. In other words, suffering was not part of the Creator's original design. As we will see, not all self-conscious beings decided to go along with this vision. Thus, a Plan B was created.

Key 7
Understanding the cosmic growth process

In the preceding chapters I have given teachings that give you the big picture for the entire world of form and all beings in it. I will now focus specifically on helping you understand your situation as a human being on Earth.

Let us begin by summarizing the process of how a sphere is created. The first step is that a sphere is set apart from the void. Masters from the higher spheres create certain structures in the new sphere and, within the larger framework of the laws defined by the Creator, they define certain specific laws for the new sphere. Self-aware beings are then created to help the new sphere ascend, either by working from the spiritual realm (angels) or by helping to co-create it from within (co-creators). As the sphere reaches a critical intensity of light and organization, it "ascends" and becomes a permanent part of the spiritual realm.

When a sphere ascends, it becomes so filled with light that there is no longer room for the illusion of separateness. The beings who were sent into the sphere started out with a separate sense of identity, yet by transcending themselves they helped raise up their sphere. When a critical mass of beings reach the mastery of oneness with their source, they have brought their sphere to the point of ascension. As one sphere goes through the process of ascending, a new sphere is created by being set apart from the void. The ascending sphere is becoming so filled with light that the illusion of a separate identity cannot be maintained by the beings in that sphere. Yet in the newly created sphere, there is still such a low intensity of light that darkness or shadows can exist, and thus the illusion of a separate existence is possible. A new "generation" of beings is born and sent into the new sphere, beings who start out with a limited sense of identity and an awareness of themselves as separate beings.

I have explained that the very first sphere was created by the Creator itself. Thus, the beings who were sent into – or rather created in – that sphere were created directly by the Creator. The first sphere was designed in such a way that the structures in it were less defined, more fluid or less dense than what you see in the material world. We might say that the Ma-ter Light out of which the first sphere was created vibrated at a higher level and therefore everything in that sphere was more transparent than matter in your sphere. The consequence is that although the beings in the first sphere started out with a separate sense of self, it was far easier for them to overcome separateness than it is for the beings in the material universe. The first beings could easily see that there was something beyond their sphere, that it was created by a Being beyond themselves and that it was sustained by a constant stream of spiritual light that originated with the Creator and was stepped down to their level of vibration. They knew they were not alone and that there was something or someone beyond their own sphere. In other words, it was relatively easy for the first beings to ascend and attain the mastery of oneness with their source.

When the next sphere was created, the beings who had attained mastery in the first sphere helped create the second sphere. It was the Creator who set the second sphere apart from the void, and he also defined the laws for that sphere. Within that framework, the masters from the first sphere designed certain structures that could serve as a platform for life in the second sphere. These structures were more specific, more defined, than the structures in the first sphere. The masters from the first sphere used their own experiences to design these structures. It was part of the Creator's plan that the structures in the second sphere should be more defined, more complex, more dense, than in the first sphere. In this way the second sphere would be one step further removed from oneness, making it more challenging for the beings in the second sphere to overcome separation.

If the beings in the second sphere had been created as the beings in the first sphere, the density of the second sphere might have been difficult for them to overcome. It would have been similar to taking a group of children and asking them to run a country. Yet the beings in the second sphere were created out of the consciousness of the masters from the first sphere. Thus, these second generation beings were designed based on the experience of these masters, meaning that they had a basis for overcoming the greater separation. This equipped them to deal with the density of the second sphere, making it possible that the Creator – through the second generation beings – could experience a greater sense of separation while minimizing the risk that these beings would become lost in separation. This is somewhat similar to the school system on Earth. Students start out by learning addition and subtraction, which gives them a basis for learning multiplication. This in turn gives them a basis for learning more advanced math, eventually leading to the university level.

The plan of the Creator is that the spheres are created as a continuum from less dense to more dense, from closer to oneness to further removed from oneness, from less complex to greater complexity. The specific structures in each succeeding sphere are designed by those who attained mastery in the previous sphere, but beings in all previous spheres are involved in the design of a new sphere. This means that each new sphere becomes more sophisticated, more specific, more expressed, which necessitates that the Ma-ter Light has a lower vibration. Greater complexity means a greater variety of different forms, and only light of a denser vibration can give rise to greater differentiation. We might say that the matter that makes up the material universe is more dense than the "stuff" in the spiritual realm. Matter is so dense that you cannot see that it is made from vibrating energy, that it is made from spiritual light that has been stepped down in vibration. You cannot directly perceive – at least not with the state of consciousness that is currently considered normal on Earth – that there is something beyond the material universe.

The higher density makes it more challenging for the beings sent into the new sphere to overcome separateness and come into oneness. Yet in their striving to overcome separation, they can lean on the beings who have gone before them in higher spheres. Thus, any given being is not truly separate – no man is an island – but has access to the entire hierarchy of beings that have gone before it and out of which it is the latest expression. It is somewhat like a family tree that gives you access to the experience of all previous generations, giving you the option of learning from the mistakes of others so you do not have to reinvent the wheel or repeat the same mistakes.

**

We will later consider that people on Earth started out their journey from many different points of origin. However, what I want to do here is to give you a universal description of how beings first descended to this particular sphere and eventually came to be in embodiment on the physical Earth. By describing this process, you will also gain a greater understanding of how you can ascend from this sphere and win your immortality as a spiritual being.

As I have explained, the material universe is the most dense part of the world of form, even the most dense part ever created in the world of form. The density of physical matter makes separate forms appear fully separate, which also makes self-conscious beings appear fully separate. Thus, it is more difficult for such beings to overcome the illusion of separation and follow the Path of Oneness that leads them to a higher sense of identity that is based on oneness with all life.

When a being enters a physical body on planet Earth, it will generally forget that it had any existence prior to this particular lifetime. I earlier explained that when the Creator created the first self-aware beings, it did not want to throw them into a vacuum with no sense of identity or continuity. Thus, it was not the original plan that any being would start out its journey in this sphere by being sent directly into physical embodiment. Beings were meant to start out in a protected environment in which they were offered the guidance of spiritual teachers who had attained the greater oneness with the All. Thus, beings would enter this latest sphere through a kind of cosmic or spiritual schoolroom in which they were offered a structured program to help them anchor themselves firmly on the Path of Oneness.

Such a program has existed in all higher spheres, and it has been successful in raising new beings up to a sense of oneness with their source. As I said, all beings are created as extensions of higher beings, forming a Chain of Being that reaches back to the Creator. Thus, the key to attaining oneness with your source is to begin by attaining oneness with the beings who are right above you in the Chain of Being. Obviously, this is far easier for a new lifestream than attaining oneness with the Creator who is far above it.

Once you are in a physical body, it really does not matter so much where you came from. What is truly important is that if you are to attain immortality, you have to follow the Path of Oneness that leads you to overcome the illusion of separation. Yet most people are not born with any awareness of this path, and there is hardly any religion on Earth that teaches the path. We must therefore conclude that on the physical Earth, knowledge of the Path of Oneness has been lost. It is important for you to understand how and why this happened, so that you can overcome the effects of this loss and rediscover the true path to eternal life. We will consider this topic in the coming chapters.

***

Once you have descended into physical embodiment, you have – regardless of where your lifestream originated – taken on the role that was designed for human beings. Human beings were designed to serve as co-creators with God who could help complete the creation of the Earth by building upon the foundation set by masters in the spiritual realm. We might say that the masters created the Earth from above and human beings are meant to co-create it from within. To help you understand your role as a human being, I would like to give you a general understanding of the role of co-creators.

We can talk about two types of co-creators, namely those who have attained mastery and those who are moving toward mastery. Obviously, both types were created to be co-creators, and we might say that those who are helping to design a new sphere are master co-creators, but let us avoid confusion and call them masters. The task of these beings is to create a new sphere from above, from their own sphere, which is now part of the spiritual realm. In other words, they are not meant to descend into the new sphere and co-create it from within. Doing this is the task of the beings I will call co-creators. Although they are created out of the beings of the masters, they start out in the new sphere with a separate sense of identity. Yet they do not start out by simply being tossed into a new sphere with no guidance. On the contrary, all new co-creators start out in a spiritual school-room in which they are guided by representatives of the masters out of whose beings they were born.

As I explained earlier, the universal Christ mind is the means set up to ensure that new co-creators do not get lost in separation but find their rightful places in the process of creation. The masters who have attained oneness with the Christ mind serve as guides for new co-creators, and they represent the Christ mind to the students. They are the link through which new co-creators can overcome separation and attain their own oneness with the Christ mind, thereby attaining immortality. We now have the foundation for taking a closer look at the situation of a new co-creator.

When a co-creator first comes into existence, it has a separate sense of identity, but it has a clear inner sense that it is connected to something greater than itself. It also has a direct connection to the universal Christ mind through its teachers from a higher realm. It does not have the full Christ consciousness but it has a foundation for developing this awareness through its own efforts—by multiplying the talents it has been given. We might say that a new co-creator is given the seed of Christ consciousness, and by nourishing it, the seed will grow into the fullness of individual Christhood.

A co-creator is born into a protected environment in which it has the direct guidance of a spiritual teacher. When the Creator created the very first sphere in the void, the first co-creators had guidance directly from the Creator. Since then, the co-creators in any given sphere have had direct guidance from masters in the sphere right above their own. However, there are also teachers who descend to the level of the new co-creators, so that the students can interact directly with these teachers. The point being that a new co-creator always has a foundation upon which it can build, it has a path it can follow out of separation and into oneness.

***

Any self-aware being is created in innocence, meaning that while it has free will, it has no built-in propensity for going against the basic laws of the Creator. In other words, the common belief in some religions that human beings are created in sin or with a propensity to sin is not correct. It has some basis in truth when you look at yourself only in terms of your current sense of identity as a human being (as we will later discuss in greater detail). However, the reality is that you were born as a spiritual being, meaning you were born in innocence and without even the knowledge that you could go against the laws of the Creator.

As new co-creators grew in self-awareness by following the path they were offered, they would face certain tests, certain initiations, and one of these was the possibility of going against the laws of God. We might say that all co-creators were created in a protected environment, much like the Garden of Eden. However, rather than the static paradise that many people envision, the Garden of Eden was a school in which co-creators had the opportunity to learn how to use their creative abilities in harmony with the laws of God. The teacher in such a spiritual schoolroom was not the Creator but a master from a higher realm. The fruits in the Garden represented various initiations on the path to Christhood.

As students in a spiritual school walk the path of initiation, they become more consciously aware of their own identity and of the laws of God. They start out by following the directions giving by their spiritual teacher, and thereby they are following the laws of God through obedience. As they move toward understanding God's laws, they eventually start following the laws with full awareness of how they work and why following them is enlightened self-interest. They then follow God's laws out of love—love for God, love for all life and love for themselves as part of the All.

If a student passes all of the tests in the cosmic schoolroom, it will continue to grow in self-awareness until it attains Christ consciousness. This does not mean that it loses its free will but that it can now make truly free choices. It now has full awareness of God's law and the consequences of following it or going against it. If a student continues to stay within God's law, it will continue to experience only abundance. It will continue to raise itself up while raising up all life. Thus, it will take part in the creative process of filling its own sphere with light until it has attained full mastery of that sphere. It can then use this mastery in co-creating the next sphere and thus rise even higher in Christ consciousness. This process can continue until the being attains full God consciousness and now becomes a Creator in its own right.

One of the fruits in the Garden of Eden was the fruit of the knowledge of good and evil. This fruit represents the awareness that a student can go against the laws of God. Because a student has free will, it is inevitable that it must face the temptation to use that will to go against the laws of God. Only by facing this temptation – and overcoming it – can a student attain the Christhood that makes it one with the Creator, the Creator's purpose and with all life. Yet it is possible that a student can fail the test represented by the knowledge of good and evil and can choose either relative evil or relative good over the absolute reality of God. A student can choose to go against the laws of God and separate itself from the Creator. We will later explore what happens when a student chooses the path of becoming less.

***

Let us take a closer look at the situation of a new student. The path of an individual student can be divided into stages. At this point we will talk about three main stages, although each of them can be subdivided into several steps:

- **Pre-graduation.** The first stage is from the student's entry into the school (which for a new co-creator is its birth as an individual being) until it graduates from the spiritual schoolroom. In order to graduate, a student has to attain the enlightenment that makes it realize who it is, namely an individualization of a greater spiritual Being who ultimately – through the Chain of Being – is an individualization of the Creator. At that point the student has the option to consciously – and motivated only by love – join the River of Life. It has then attained the first level of individual Christhood, which means it has an awareness of the oneness of all life.

- **Post-graduation.** The second stage is after a student has chosen to join the River of Life. It now leaves the schoolroom and goes out to apply what it has learned by working to raise up its native sphere and all life in it. The first phase is, so to speak, the Alpha phase of reaching for oneness with its higher being, and the second phase is the Omega phase of reaching for oneness with all life.

- **Ascension.** As a student attains greater and greater oneness with both its higher being above and all life below, it moves toward the next level of Christhood. When it reaches this level, it can graduate from the material realm and no longer have to express itself through a physical body. This is what some spiritual teachings call the ascension, but I will later give more detailed teachings on this. The main point is that a student can reach a point when it can permanently rise above the level at which it started its journey in a given sphere.

Any new student starts with a limited sense of self-awareness that is narrowly focused on its own situation in its particular world (be it the material universe or a sphere that is now part of the spiritual realm). It has no awareness of the Allness or even of the Creator. Yet a new co-creator does have a limited level of Christ awareness in the sense that it knows there is something more than what it experiences in its immediate world. It does not directly perceive anything beyond its level, but it senses intuitively that there is more and it has a longing to discover it. The co-creator also has contact with a spiritual teacher who can teach it how to expand its self-awareness within the framework of the Creator's laws.

Regardless of where a new student came from before it entered a cosmic schoolroom, the essence of its situation is that everything is new, including its sense of identity. It does not fully understand who it is and it does not fully understand its creative powers. How can a new student expand its understanding? Only by experimenting! And since it has no prior experience (at least in this particular sphere), it is natural that it will miss the mark—meaning that it will make choices that are not in harmony with the laws of God. That is why a new student is placed in a protective environment in which its misses have limited effects. And because the student has the loving guidance of a teacher who has attained enlightenment, it can learn from everything it does, whether it misses the mark or hits the mark. When a student is willing to learn from everything, it is on the path of becoming MORE. Becoming MORE does not mean that all of your choices have to be perfect. It means that you have to be willing to learn from all of your choices, which requires you to freely acknowledge when you have missed the mark. In a sense, a choice that is turned into a learning experience is not a mistake but has become a step forward on the path of self-awareness.

If a student chooses the path of becoming less, it is not willing to admit when it misses the mark. It refuses to acknowledge that its choices were out of harmony with the laws of creation. Instead, it seeks to justify why it had a right to do what it was doing or why it wasn't wrong. Instead of learning from its misses – using them to expand its self-awareness – it seeks to justify or explain away its misses, whereby it actually limits its self-awareness.

If you choose the path of becoming MORE, everything you do will help you grow in self-awareness. You will strengthen your sense of who you are without limiting yourself or other beings. You will gradually expand your sense of self, until you become aware that you are part of a larger whole, namely the All, the Body of God.

**

A new student starts in a sphere that is not yet transformed into a sphere of light. Only when there is still room for darkness can a lifestream have the experience of starting out as a separate being. Yet the student starts in a protected environment, much like a child on Earth is ideally born into a harmonious home. The student has a God-given individuality but it is not fully aware of it, much like a child on Earth is not aware of its personality. Thus, the first stage of the student's journey is a period of self-discovery and world discovery.

The new student goes through a phase in which it is meant to experiment. This is much like a child on Earth that needs to experiment in order to gain control of its body, discover its personality and find out how its environment works. As a child grows up in a protected environment, where it has limited opportunities for harming itself and others, so does a student start out with limited creative powers. There is a limit to how much power a new student has, and thus there is a limit to how much it can hurt itself and others. This limits the severity of the consequences of the student's misses.

Earthly parents naturally seek to protect their children by creating a safe environment. However, within the confines of that environment, mature parents are rather tolerant of the child's mistakes. A child might fall down many times in its attempts to learn how to walk, but the parents do not blame the child for not getting it right on the first try. The child might spill the milk many times as it learns to drink from a cup, but no parent cries over spilled milk. Likewise, a new student is placed in a protected environment and it has the loving guidance of one or more spiritual teachers. Within the safe framework of the cosmic schoolroom, the student can do anything it wants. It cannot severely hurt itself or others, and the teacher is highly tolerant of the student's misses. In other words, a student is not expected to get everything right and is not expected to know the laws of God from the beginning. Yet as the student experiments with its creative powers and receives training from its spiritual teachers, it is expected to grow in understanding and maturity. Again, this is similar to what is expected of a child on Earth. No child is expected to stay a child forever.

In the beginning, the student will often go against the laws of God without understanding what it is doing. This is expected and there is no blame or guilt associated with it. However, there is no hiding it either. The teacher will give the student feedback on its actions and their consequences. To understand the significance of the teacher-student relationship, we need to take a closer look at the learning environment in which a new student is placed.

***

I am fully aware that when I talk about a spiritual schoolroom and a spiritual teacher, many people will compare this to the type of learning environments they have experienced on Earth. This is natural and understandable, but the main problem that prevents people from understanding the spiritual side of life is that they project their earthly experiences onto the spiritual world. Thus, if you truly desire to understand the spiritual side of life, you must become aware of this tendency and open your mind to the fact that in the spiritual realm everything is very different from the way things are on Earth. As I have said, in the material universe there is still an absence of light, whereas the spiritual realm is saturated with light. In order to understand the spiritual realm, you must be willing to look beyond the world view you have developed as a result of your experiences on this planet. You must be willing to see the spiritual realm as it is and not as you want it to be—based on your earthly expectations. You must be willing to experience the reality of the spiritual realm instead of projecting a man-made image unto it.

The major difference between a spiritual school and a school on Earth is that neither the teacher nor the new students have developed a human ego. We will later take a more detailed look at the ego and the games it is playing, but for now let us look at how an ego-free environment is different from the learning environments found on Earth. The purpose of a spiritual school is to expand the student's sense of self-awareness without restricting it or even forcing it in a certain direction. In contrast, most learning environments on Earth are designed to limit or at least control the student's sense of self-awareness under the guise of making students fit to enter society. A spiritual school never seeks to force the students but encourages learning from within because only that which is internalized will expand the students' sense of self-awareness. A spiritual teacher has already mastered his or her psychology and is never threatened by anything the students do. Thus, the teacher has no need to control the students through guilt, blame or other fear-based means.

From a student's perspective the spiritual school is completely loving and supportive. There is no blame put upon the student for any mistakes made. Instead, these are pointed out in a loving manner that makes a clear distinction between the student and its actions. In other words, while your actions may not be right, *you* are always right, loved and supported. Ideally, the student responds to this environment by feeling safe, loved and by having a healthy appetite for experimenting. The student is eager to learn from the teacher and has no negative feelings associated with having its misses pointed out. Instead, the student simply turns its misses into stepping stones for progress—it learns the lesson and moves on. When the lesson is learned, both the teacher and the student forgets about the mistake.

My main point here is that when the students go against the laws of God, the teacher does not blame them or criticize them. The teacher is entirely supportive of the students' growth and only seeks to turn every action taken by a student into a positive learning experience. Yet a spiritual teacher is more than just a teacher. As I said earlier, a self-aware being is given free will, but with it comes responsibility for how you use God's energy. You are responsible for maintaining the balance of the universe, so if you use energy in an unbalanced way, you must bring it back into balance. Eastern religions generally call this karma, whereas Western religions call it sin. Human beings often associate guilt or blame with this, but in the spiritual realm, it is seen simply as a debt to life. However, this debt to life can and will limit your creative powers. It can be compared to wearing a backpack on Earth and putting a rock into it for every mistake you make. At some point the backpack might become so heavy that you can hardly move, and this will obviously limit your freedom.

When an imbalance has been created, someone must take on the misqualified energy and assume responsibility for repolarizing it to restore balance. In a spiritual schoolroom the teacher takes on the full responsibility for the students' use of energy, meaning that he actually takes on the karma made by the students under his care. This allows the students to experiment with their creative faculties without being burdened by the weight of any karma they create. This is in some ways similar to parents on Earth who assume the responsibility for the safety and care of their children until they have grown up and become self-sufficient.

This very mechanism is one of the cornerstones of the teacher-student relationship. It is what allows students to express their creativity without destroying themselves and others. The sponsorship of the teacher creates a protected environment, where the teacher serves as a buffer between the students and the destructive consequences of their actions. The teacher will literally neutralize the consequences of a mistake made by a student so that those consequences cannot destroy the student itself or other students in the schoolroom. When you understand the law of karma, you see that this is a major dispensation for the students and can lead to much faster progress than if the students were left to learn the hard way—by carrying the consequences of their choices.

Yet any relationship is a two-way street. What the students vow to do in return for this grace from the teacher is to allow the teacher to teach them. In other words, in return for being protected from the karma of their choices, the students vow to let the teacher describe the consequences of their choices, so that each student can learn from both good and not so good choices. If the teacher simply took on the karma made by the students without making them aware of how the karma was created, the students would learn nothing from the situation. And since the entire purpose is learning, the students are given loving and completely neutral – no blame or guilt – guidance on how to self-transcend. Some might be aware that the Greek word that is often translated as "sin" actually means "missing the mark." The only question in a spiritual school is whether the student's use of energy hits the mark of raising all life or misses the mark and thus produces misqualified energy that limits all life. Concepts such as good or bad, sin or guilt are irrelevant.

Because the teacher's sponsorship prevents misqualified energy from harming the students or other parts of life – the teacher uses his own spiritual attainment to neutralize the karma before it can have physical effects – the students can experiment without any fear of negative consequences. The psychological effect is to create a learning environment that is completely loving and does not have any of the fear, guilt or blame that is so typical for learning environments on Earth. It is somewhat comparable to the innocence of children playing in a sandbox, where they cannot harm the sand, themselves or others and can thus experiment freely. The only condition for this sponsorship is that the students must maintain the connection to the teacher. If that connection is broken, the teacher can no longer carry the students' karma, meaning that the students must carry it and can potentially create so much karma that it limits their creative expression.

***

As I described earlier, every aspect of life has two sides, meaning that there are two aspects to the learning experience faced by the students. To avoid confusion, take note that I am here talking about the period before the student graduates from the spiritual schoolroom—which is what I earlier called the Alpha phase. Yet even within this phase, there are two aspects—life truly has rings within rings and worlds within worlds.

A new student starts in a particular environment and has an individuality and a body that is equivalent to the human body although made of energies that vibrate within the spectrum of its particular sphere. The Omega aspect of the student's learning experience is to discover its environment and how to interact with the environment. The Alpha aspect is to discover its origin as an individualization of a Being from a higher realm than its immediate environment. The Omega aspect is learning about what is seen and the Alpha is learning about what is unseen—but which can become seen when a higher awareness is developed.

It is natural that a student first focuses on the Omega aspect of the learning process. It can directly perceive its immediate environment, and thus its attention is naturally drawn there. This is like an infant on Earth who first has to figure out how to control the physical body before it can begin to develop its personality. The first part of the teacher's job is to help the student learn about its environment and about who it is in relation to that environment. The student needs to learn how it fits into and can interact with its environment. However, let us remember that a student is not created to adapt to a particular environment. A student is in a sphere that has limited intensity of light (the spiritual schoolroom is a protected sphere within the greater sphere but it still does not have the intensity of light found in higher realms). The role of the student is to master its own Being, which opens up for mastery over its environment. Thus, the student can fulfill the command described in Genesis to multiply and have dominion. In other words, a student is not born on Earth in order to adapt to the limited conditions found here. The student is meant to multiply its creative talents and take dominion over the Earth, thereby raising the vibration and light intensity until the kingdom of God becomes manifest on Earth.

***

How does a new student learn to multiply and have dominion? It is taught by its teacher as it experiments! As I said earlier, everything in the world of form is created from the Ma-ter Light which can be molded into any form. The Ma-ter Light cannot take on form by itself but must be acted upon by a self-aware being who is in the role of a co-creator. We now see that the process of co-creation has two aspects:

- The Alpha aspect is that the co-creator must form a mental image of what it wants to create.
- The Omega aspect is that the co-creator must have a portion of the Mother Light upon which it can superimpose the mental image.

In the beginning, students are given both the mental images and a portion of the Mother Light from their teachers, much like an infant on Earth receives everything from its parents. However, the long-term goal of the spiritual teacher is to bring the student to the point of graduation, which means that the student has now become spiritually self-sufficient and thus no longer needs an external teacher in order to co-create (obviously, the student can still benefit from maintaining contact with the teacher). What exactly does this mean? It means that the student graduates by mastering its co-creative abilities:

- I earlier said that God created a safety mechanism to guide the creative efforts of co-creators. This is the universal Christ mind which stores the blueprint of creation and all of the Creator's laws. Only by using the Christ mind can a co-creator make sure its creative efforts stay within the framework of God's laws and raise all life. The spiritual teacher serves as an intermediary between a new student and the Christ mind. The teacher is a representative of the Christ mind, the Cosmic Christ.

As the student comes closer to graduation, it discovers that it is an expression of a spiritual Being who is one with the Christ mind (the master out of which it was created). Thus, any student can – by seeking oneness with its own higher being – gain direct access to the Christ mind from within itself. When you have gained a critical degree of connection to the Christ mind, you can graduate from the schoolroom because you are now able to know on your own when your actions hit or miss the mark of selflessness.

• In order to create anything, you must have power over a portion of the Mother Light. The Mother Light has a pure form that is of very high vibration, and every sphere in the world of form is created by lowering the Mother Light to a certain vibrational spectrum. So before a student can create anything in the material realm, it must have a portion of the Mother Light that is brought into the vibrational spectrum of its sphere. This is ideally done by the student receiving light from the spiritual realm (from its own higher being) and lowering it in vibration. However, only a being who has attained some degree of Christhood/enlightenment can receive light from within. In the beginning a student must receive its light from its spiritual teacher. The teacher brings the light into the relevant spectrum and then gives it to the student.

As the student grows in Christhood, it becomes aware that it is an extension of a Being in the spiritual realm. Thus, through its own inner Being, it can bring forth light directly from the spiritual realm. When a student can bring forth sufficient light to sustain itself and express its creativity, it can graduate from the schoolroom and express itself in its native sphere.

When it reaches graduation, a student has become spiritually self-sufficient in that it can bring light into the material vibrational spectrum through its own efforts and it can create mental images that are in alignment with the Christ mind. Thus, the student no longer needs an external teacher, for it has now become connected to its own higher being, its internal teacher. To bring the student to self-sufficiency is the ultimate goal of all true spiritual teachers and teachings, be they found on Earth or in a higher realm.

Take note that reaching self-sufficiency is not the same as reaching permanent Christhood. As you leave the schoolroom, you can still make mistakes and can potentially leave off the Path of MORE and join the path of less. However, the student can still remain connected to the teacher if it so chooses. And if a student keeps growing, it will eventually attain permanent Christhood and become an immortal being, an ascended master.

***

When we realize that the goal of a spiritual school is to make the student self-sufficient, we see that such a school must have graded lessons. It is much like the school system on Earth that starts out by teaching very simple concepts in kindergarten and progresses to the most advanced lessons at the university level. This also means that as the lessons progress, the teacher must take a less active role, giving the students more room to learn on their own. Only by doing so will the students fully integrate the lessons and become self-sufficient.

This process was illustrated by Jesus in his parable about the master who gave his servants various amounts of talents. Let us look at the actual text:

> 14 For the kingdom of heaven is as a man travelling into a far country, who called his own servants, and delivered unto them his goods.
> 15 And unto one he gave five talents, to another two, and to another one; to every man according to his several ability; and straightway took his journey. (Matthew, Chapter 25)

The different numbers of talents symbolize that each student is an individual and that each student might be working on a specific lesson. It does not symbolize that one student is better than another, but it does show that students can progress at a different pace.

The master then travels away and leaves the servants on their own to decide how to make use of the talents. This symbolizes the fact that, as the students come closer to graduation, a spiritual teacher will give the students specific instructions – adapted to the particular lesson each student needs to learn – and also give each student a certain amount of the Mother Light—again adapted to the student's level on the path to enlightenment. The teacher then withdraws in order to give the students complete freedom to decide what to do with the teacher's instructions and with the light they have.

16 Then he that had received the five talents went and traded with the same, and made them other five talents.
17 And likewise he that had received two, he also gained other two.
18 But he that had received one went and digged in the Earth, and hid his lord's money.
19 After a long time the lord of those servants cometh, and reckoneth with them.

This symbolizes that the goal of the process is for the students to learn, which means that the teacher must eventually come back and perform an evaluation. This is the entire purpose of the spiritual school and the students have originally agreed to this. Let us now see what happens to the students who multiply their talents:

20 And so he that had received five talents came and brought other five talents, saying, Lord, thou deliveredst unto me five talents: behold, I have gained beside them five talents more.
21 His lord said unto him, Well done, thou good and faithful servant: thou hast been faithful over a few things, I will make thee ruler over many things: enter thou into the joy of thy lord.
22 He also that had received two talents came and said, Lord, thou deliveredst unto me two talents: behold, I have gained two other talents beside them.
23 His lord said unto him, Well done, good and faithful servant; thou hast been faithful over a few things, I will make thee ruler over many things: enter thou into the joy of thy lord.

Let us remember that the purpose of the world of form is a growth in self-awareness, and this can be achieved only when a student multiplies the "talents" it has been given as a starting point. However, what Jesus' parable does not convey is that there is more than one way for a student to multiply the talents:

- A student can follow the teacher's instructions to the letter. This will make sure that it uses the Mother Light in a way that is in harmony with God's law and thus raises all life. This will create positive karma for the student and thus it has multiplied the talents. However, the multiplication factor is limited, as in $5 + 5 = 10$.

- A student can realize that the teacher's instructions come from the Christ mind and that it has access to the Christ mind within itself. It can then use this access to gain a deeper understanding of the teacher's instructions, which will allow it to multiply the talents beyond what can be achieved through the literal approach. This creates an exponential multiplication factor that is much more powerful, as in $5 \times 5 = 25$.

- A student can realize that the light it was given by the teacher comes from the cosmic supply and that it has access to that supply through its own higher being. It can then use this access to bring forth more light than what the teacher gave it, which also opens up for an exponential multiplication.

- A student can use both of the above approaches to multiply the instructions and the light. This obviously increases the multiplication factor to the maximum degree, as in $25 \times 25 = 625$.

Let us now look at what happened to the servant who did not multiply the talents:

> 24 Then he which had received the one talent came and said, Lord, I knew thee that thou art an hard man, reaping where thou hast not sown, and gathering where thou hast not strawed:
> 25 And I was afraid, and went and hid thy talent in the Earth: lo, there thou hast that is thine.
> 26 His lord answered and said unto him, Thou wicked and slothful servant, thou knewest that I reap where I sowed not, and gather where I have not strawed:
> 27 Thou oughtest therefore to have put my money to the exchangers, and then at my coming I should have received mine own with usury.
> 28 Take therefore the talent from him, and give it unto him which hath ten talents.
> 29 For unto every one that hath shall be given, and he shall have abundance: but from him that hath not shall be taken away even that which he hath.
> 30 And cast ye the unprofitable servant into outer darkness: there shall be weeping and gnashing of teeth.

To fully understand this passage, we must realize that Jesus' parable was adapted to the level of consciousness that humankind had 2,000 years ago. Therefore, it is adapted to the fact that people on this planet have lost the direct contact with their spiritual teachers and thus cannot fully understand the relationship between a spiritual teacher and its students. Instead, people project human qualities unto the spiritual teacher. In reality, no spiritual teacher ever belittles, condemns or punishes the students.

It is true that the students who refuse to multiply their talents will suffer consequences, but to fully understand this, we need to look at how students lost contact with their spiritual teachers. Before we do so, let us briefly look at the ways to *not* multiply the talents:

- A student can disregard the teacher's instructions out of fear. The student is so afraid of making a mistake that it would rather do nothing. It takes the safe bet to preserve the exact amount of light it was given so it can give the light back to the teacher. However, the teacher is not concerned about conserving the light; he is concerned about helping the student grow. If the student refuses to run the risk of making a mistake, it cannot grow, and thus it goes against the very purpose of creation and its own contract with the teacher. The student will justify this by projecting a limited image upon the teacher, as did the servant in Jesus' parable.

- A student can go beyond the teacher's instructions out of pride. It will now use a lower part of the mind to reinterpret the instructions so they seem to say what it wants them to say. The student can then use the light for self-centered purposes, meaning to raise itself up in comparison to other parts of life. It will justify this by convincing itself that it has a right to do what it did and that it was not a mistake. It might even come to the point of being convinced that it is right and that the teacher was wrong.

- A student can use the light purely for gaining physical pleasure, as you would spend money on consumption instead of investing it in a way that gave a return. Again, the student can convince itself that it has a right to do this and that its actions don't have any limiting consequences for itself and others.

With this in mind, let us look at how students on Earth lost contact with their spiritual teachers.

Key 8
How human beings lost contact with their spiritual teachers

In order to understand how and why human beings separated themselves from their teachers, we need to take a closer look at your total being. I will describe this in generic terms that apply to most of the beings who evolve on Earth. I have said that everything has an Alpha and an Omega aspect, and so does your own being. We might compare your total being to a figure-eight:

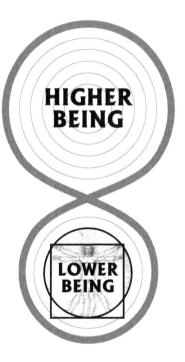

- The upper figure represents the spiritual side of your being, the part that permanently resides in the spiritual realm. This part contains the divine blueprint for your individuality, and it can never be destroyed by anything you do in the material world. It is an extension of an immortal spiritual being and the very basis for your sense of identity. It has been called the I AM Presence in several teachings given by the Ascended Host.

- The lower figure represents that part of your being which is designed to empower you to express yourself in the material world. This lower self has several parts which we will explore later. For now, the important point is that your lower being is centered around your sense of identity, meaning both the sense of who you are as a spiritual Being but also who you are as a being in the material universe.

Your spiritual self is a gift to you from the spiritual being who created you out of its own consciousness. This is your divine blueprint that you can never lose. In other words, no matter what you do in the material universe, you cannot destroy this divine blueprint because it exists in a spectrum of vibrations that is above – and thus cannot be affected by – the frequencies of the material universe. The important point here is that your original divine identity can never be lost. What *can* be lost is your connection to it and even your memory of it. As I have said, the learning process of a student has two aspects, but this truly applies to all beings in embodiment on Earth:

- The Alpha aspect is that you discover and fully embody your divine identity, so that you reach the point of enlightenment where you know and accept who you are as a spiritual being. You can then express your divine individuality in everything you do in the material world. You have become here below all that you are above. A new student does not have this enlightened self-awareness but starts out with a limited self-awareness as a separate being. It is the role of the teacher to guide the student to discover, accept and internalize its spiritual identity.

- The Omega aspect of the learning process is to build a sense of identity that serves as the platform for your co-creative efforts in the material world. In other words, you are meant to *discover* your Alpha identity, but you are meant to *define* your Omega identity. A new student starts out with a limited sense of who it is—both spiritually and materially. As it discovers more of its divine individuality and gains experiences with the material world, it gradually builds the sense of who it is as a spiritual being with the task of taking dominion over the material world and bringing God's kingdom to Earth. At least, this is what will ideally happen.

***

The logical question now becomes who it is that builds this composite sense of identity? Where is your sense of identity centered? What is the *You* which decides who – and what – you are and who/what you are not? Understanding this is the central mystery of existence, the missing link between the material and the spiritual aspects of your Being. Unfortunately, an understanding of this has been missing from most spiritual and religious teachings on this planet. It has been determined by the Ascended Host that it is time to correct this lack, and Mother Mary's book was the first step. I will build upon her revelations in this book.

As I explained earlier, everything in the world of form is created out of an interplay between the two basic polarities, namely the expanding force of the Father and the contracting force of the Mother. Yet a sustainable creation is only possible when these two polarities are held in a dynamic balance. And the element that is designed to create and maintain this balance is the element of the Son, the universal Christ mind.

In terms of the figure-eight of your being, the upper figure represents the Father polarity and the lower figure represents the Mother polarity. For you to reach enlightenment, take dominion over your own being and fulfill your role on Earth, you must balance – or unite – the two aspects. In the nexus of the figure-eight is that part of your being which represents the Son, the Christ that is meant to balance the upper and the lower aspects of your being. This part is what Mother Mary calls the Conscious You, but in this book I will call it the conscious self. You have free will, so you are not a robot or an animal. The meaning is that you have the ability to be aware that you exist, to know you are a spiritual being and to consciously

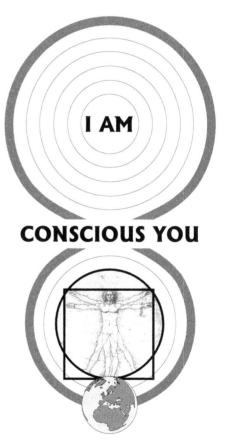

choose to co-create on Earth. The very basis for this is that you have self-awareness, that you have the ability to know that you exist. You exist because there is a part of your being that was created by an immortal spiritual Being, and thus it is permanent. You can know you exist because you were created out of the Being and consciousness of the Creator, for without him was not anything made that was made. Thus, the Creator's omnipresent self-awareness is embedded within your being. We might say that the basis for your self-awareness is your I AM Presence, which gives you the foundation for knowing, "I AM, I exist, I am alive, I have being." Yet the part that actually comes to this recognition is your conscious self. It is the conscious self that says, "I am..." and then defines the characteristics for what comes after the words "I am."

Your conscious self is the center of your total being. It is here you decide who you are, and it is here you decide how to express who you are in the material world. What is the basis for these decisions? It is your sense of identity, who you see yourself as being, what you put after those all-important words, "I AM ..." What you define as your sense of identity determines how you co-create in the material world. Obviously, this has two aspects, namely to what degree you have discovered, accepted and internalized your divine individuality and what kind of material identity you have built for yourself. My point is that it is the conscious self who has the dual task of discovering your Alpha identity and building your Omega identity. The conscious self is the only begotten son of your higher being and it alone can know the Father, meaning your spiritual identity. It is the conscious self that decides who you are, and, as we will see later, every aspect of your life in the material universe is directly determined by your sense of identity. Thus, we might say that the conscious self is the core of your lower being, the very center of your sense of self. It is therefore essential that your conscious self becomes conscious of itself.

***

When a new co-creator is born – or when any student starts out in a cosmic schoolroom – it has a limited sense of self-awareness. It is essential to realize that this is not some kind of punishment or design flaw. On the contrary, the entire purpose of the world of form is to give self-conscious beings the experience of starting out with a limited self-awareness and then growing toward the full God consciousness. We might say that the Creator has chosen to focus part of its own self-awareness as the conscious self in order to experience the journey from that limited self-awareness back to the full God consciousness. However, this is not simply a journey from Allness to specialness and back to dissolution into the Allness. As the conscious self comes back to God consciousness, it will disappear back into the Creator's Being but a new self is born based on the identity that the conscious self has built during its return. This identity does not disappear but becomes immortalized as a new God with full internalization of everything learned on the journey. The identity, the sense of self, of a co-creator is a God in the making.

It is also essential to realize that everything functions within the framework of the Law of Free Will. Thus, you were not simply created without any choice on your part. Your identity is actually not a separate entity but an extension of a spiritual being, namely the master who created you. When a master creates extensions of itself, it decides that it wants to send individual extensions of itself into the material universe, partly to experience the growth in self-awareness and partly to help bring light into this world. To facilitate this process, the master creates individual presences within its own Being, one of which is the I AM Presence of an individual co-creator. Yet even then, each I AM Presence had to make a conscious choice to send an extension of itself into the material universe. Only when this decision was made was the lower part of a co-creator created, and only then did the conscious self take up its place in the nexus of the figure-eight.

Your conscious self is an individualization of God's Being, an individual spark of the greater flame of the Creator, that was given to you as a foundation for self-awareness. We might say that your conscious self is an extension of the Creator's Being that is focused in a particular location in the world of form. Part of the purpose is to give you a spark of the Creator's Being which you can build upon and multiply until you build a sense of identity that can become immortalized. Another part of the purpose is to give the Creator an opportunity to experience creation from the inside, from a particular point of view rather than from the all-encompassing viewpoint of the Creator. The Creator's sense of self-awareness is omnipresent, meaning that the Creator is everywhere in creation and also aware of the Allness. Your conscious self is a part of the Creator's Being that is focused in a particular point in creation, in your case the material universe and planet Earth. Yet because you are out of the Creator's Being, you have the potential to expand your sense of self-awareness until you attain the omnipresent awareness of the Creator while still retaining the individuality you have created throughout your journey from one-pointedness to all-pointedness. I know it is very difficult for human beings – given their sense of self-awareness as separate beings – to fathom that the Creator can divide itself into separate spirit sparks and still remain the One, omnipresent Creator. Yet as you grow toward enlightenment, you will gradually experience how the One can divide itself infinitely and still remain the One.

The essential point is to realize that your conscious self is focused in a particular point but that it has the potential to expand its self-awareness infinitely. In other words, your conscious self has no fixed identity. It is given a starting point and is then charged with the task of building its own sense of identity from there. Thus, the conscious self is what it sees itself as being, it is what it identifies itself as being. You are who you think you are in the sense that you will co-create according to who you think you are.

I am quite aware that many of the people reading this will greet these ideas with mixed feelings. Many people have a limited sense of identity and feel they are stuck in situations that are not of their own making. Some even have mixed feelings about the fact that they exist at all. Yet the very essence of the spiritual path – the path to enlightenment – is to realize that if you don't like who you are right now, you have the potential to change who you are by changing your *sense* of who you are. And as I will explain in coming chapters, once you change your sense of identity, your outer situation will change as well.

In other words, if you don't like your current situation, you have the potential to change it by expanding your self-awareness. Your conscious self is who it thinks it is, but you can change that by changing who you think you are. If you don't like being a human being with certain limitations, then expand your self-awareness and realize you are truly a spiritual being who is beyond all human limitations. You have simply chosen to focus your sense of self-awareness at this particular point as a human being on Earth. Yet you can expand that self-awareness and focus it somewhere else by following a systematic path toward enlightenment.

***

Let us take a closer look at choice. Your conscious self is an extension of your I AM Presence, which made the choice to extend itself into the material universe. And your I AM Presence is an individualization of a greater being which also made the choice to extend itself into the material universe. This being is an extension of a greater being, and if you follow the Chain of Being, you end up at the Creator. The Creator made the choice to create self-conscious extensions of its own Being. Thus, your very existence is based on choice and as an extension of the Creator, your conscious self did choose to come into the material universe in order to serve as the foundation for your growth. My point being that although your conscious self may currently see itself as a separate being, the reality is that you are part of the Body of God. You truly *are* that Body of God and your own greater Being *did* choose to focus part of itself as the conscious self that is currently identifying itself as you.

So a greater part of your own being did make the choice to enter the material universe. Yet even though we might say that *you* – as your current sense of identity – might not have consciously chosen to come into existence, you still have the potential to expand your sense of identity infinitely. In other words, there might be certain aspects of your current life experience that are unpleasant and cause you to feel like you would rather not be alive. Yet if you could remove those aspects, would you still regret being in existence? We might say that your self-awareness is a container and your life-experience is determined by what you put into it. So if you don't like your life-experience, you have the option of changing the contents of the container of self. And once the contents give you a pleasant life experience, you will not regret having self-awareness.

My experience as a spiritual teacher shows that there is no self-conscious being who ever regrets being alive, being self-aware, once it overcomes its limited sense of identity. There may be certain aspects of a person's life-experience that cause negative feelings, yet once these are gone, the person connects to its own higher being and now realizes that it did make the choice to focus itself as an individual being in the material world. Thus, by reconnecting to your own higher being and the choices it made out of love, you can overcome all sense of regret or anger over being in your current situation. And by reconnecting to who you truly are, your outer circumstances will change as if by magic. Yet as we will see later, there is no magic, for it is a fact that your outer circumstances are a mere reflection of your sense of identity, and thus when you change the cause, the effect will automatically follow. It is, of course, the function of every true spiritual teacher to help the students transcend their limited sense of identity and reconnect to their own greater beings.

Let me also make it clear that you were created with a predefined divine identity as the foundation for your growth in self-awareness. When you are in embodiment, it is your task to express that identity in the material universe, and in order to do so, you must first connect to it. You must, so to speak, bring your Omega identity – what you have created since you entered this world – into alignment with your Alpha identity so you can *be* here below all that you are above. For some people this might sound like they are being forced to be something they don't want to be. Yet the reality is that before you came into this world, your own higher being did indeed want to express its individuality in this world. As you lost the connection to your higher being, you forgot this purpose and the choice made by your higher being. Yet you have a subconscious memory of this, and you will never feel truly fulfilled until you are living your reason for being. Thus, coming into alignment with your own higher being is not something that is forced upon you. It is what you truly want and it is the key to your wholeness and fulfillment in life.

***

Let us revisit the fact that you start out your journey in this world with a limited sense of identity. Psychologists have discovered that a newborn baby on Earth sees itself as the center of its immediate environment. The infant basically thinks its environment is a kind of machine in which every part is designed to serve it. It sees itself as the center of its world, a world that is designed to fill its needs. As the child grows, this world view must be replaced by a broader world view. The child realizes that it is an individual being living in an external world, a world that is not designed exclusively to fill its needs. On the contrary, the world contains many inanimate forms and separate beings that often will not fulfill the child's needs.

We might say that the first stage in the child's development is to separate itself from the sense of being the center of its environment. While this separation can be painful, even traumatic, it is actually the basis for the child's growth. Only by doing this can the child develop a realistic sense of identity and build its own personality. This is similar to what happens to a new student in a spiritual school. The student must separate itself from its sense of being the center of its environment and then discover and develop its sense of self from there. This involves several elements:

- **Self.** The student must discover its spiritual individuality and integrate it into its sense of self. It must build a material sense of identity that reflects its spiritual identity.

- **World.** The student must realize that it is not a product of its environment, that it is more than a material being. Only by doing this can the student fulfill its role of taking dominion over the material universe and helping to bring God's kingdom to Earth.

- **Others.** The student must accept that it is not the only being living in its environment. It must learn to balance its co-creative efforts so that they raise the whole rather than seeking to raise itself. In the end, it must realize that the ultimate way to raise itself is to raise the whole because all life is one.

We return to the fact that everything has an Alpha and an Omega aspect and that sustainable growth can happen only when the two are balanced. Each of the above elements has an Alpha and an Omega aspect, and if the two are not balanced, then the student will go too far into one of two extremes. If the student has a dominant Alpha polarity – the expanding force – then things will be taken too far. If the Omega – the contracting force – is dominant, things will not be taken far enough. Let us look at how this affects each element:

- **Self.** The goal is to develop a realistic sense of self, which gives rise to true self-esteem. This comes from developing oneness with your own higher being. If the Alpha is dominant, the student will develop an inflated sense of self-esteem and begin to think it is better than others. If the Omega is dominant, the student will have a very low sense of self-esteem, thinking it is unworthy to fulfill its role of having dominion over the Earth. On planet Earth you see many examples of both. Some people think they belong to a power elite and have the right to dominate the general population. Others think they are miserable sinners who can do nothing right because God designed them to be sinners.

- **World.** The goal is to fulfill the role of having dominion over the material universe while remaining within the framework of God's law. If the Alpha is dominant, a student will think it has the right to force other people or that it can define its own laws. If the Omega is dominant, the student will see itself as a product of its environment, meaning that it has no power or right to change that environment. On Earth you see people who think the ends can justify the means, and they are trying to take heaven – and Earth – by force. They think they can do whatever they want to the Earth and other people. You also see people who think human beings are alien creatures who are not part of nature and who have no right to change their environment. They completely refuse to use their co-creative abilities to take dominion over the Earth.

- **Others.** The goal is to develop a sense of oneness with all other beings, which comes from developing the oneness with your own higher being and realizing that all other beings came from the same source. If the Alpha is dominant, the student will fall into the trap of comparing itself to others, seeking to make itself appear better than others. This can lead into an endless cycle of competition, even an attempt to raise oneself by putting others down or destroying those who threaten one's sense of superiority. If the Omega is dominant, the student will submit itself to the control of others, seeking for those who will make decisions for it. It will basically erase all sense of identity and make itself a biological robot, controlled by external forces. On Earth you see many people who are fighting with others in an endless cycle of seeking control or superiority. You see many people who express no individuality but are like animals that are driven by the heard instinct. They are like jellyfish that mindlessly flow with the currents in the polluted ocean of the mass consciousness.

We now see that the primary goal for a student is to develop a balanced sense of identity. If your current situation is not to your liking, the cause is that in the past you developed an unbalanced sense of identity. Regardless of what sense of identity you currently have, the goal for any sincere spiritual seeker must be to develop a true sense of identity as the extension of God you were created to be. However, to get from where you are now to where you want to be, you need to understand how you lost the connection to your higher being and your spiritual teachers.

***

As I said, a student starts out with a very narrowly focused sense of self-awareness, much like a newborn baby. It has only an intuitive sense of its divine individuality, and it lives in an environment that demands its attention. Thus, it is natural that a new student focuses most of its attention on developing a sense of who it is in relation to its environment. In other words, it begins to define its identity based on the demands of its environment. In the protected environment of a spiritual schoolroom, this is not really a problem—as opposed to the current conditions on Earth. Yet a new student is likely to build a sense of identity that is shaped by its environment and thus to some degree out of harmony with its divine individuality. Thus, as the student matures and begins to discover and integrate its divine individuality, it will have to transcend its former sense of identity. It must replace its worldly sense of identity with its true, divine identity.

We might say that in the beginning it is natural that a student lets its environment have dominion over it, but as it matures it should ideally come to know its divine individuality and take back dominion over its sense of self. It is not a matter of how your environment wants you to be; it is a matter of being who you are. You need to unite with your divine individuality and then express that individuality through everything you do in the material world. This, of course, is completely different from the conditions you have experienced on Earth, where parents and society want you to grow up in conformity with their norms.

As a student matures, it reaches the critical stage of its development, which can be compared to the teen-age stage on Earth. Here, the student must begin to develop self-sufficiency, which means that the spiritual teacher must now withdraw somewhat. At the earlier stages, the student is under constant supervision, as is a small child on Earth. Yet the teacher must now give the student space for self-discovery. The difference between a spiritual school and Earth is that the

teacher is not seeking to control the student, so the student has no reason to rebel. Yet the student *does* need to withdraw from the teacher
in order to stand on its own.

The teacher's withdrawal is an opportunity and a necessity without which the student could not become self-sufficient. Yet it does
carry an inherent risk. As the teacher gives the student space, it
becomes possible that the student can begin to hide things from the
teacher. Because the teacher has absolute respect for the student's free
will, this makes it possible that the student can develop an unbalanced
sense of identity while seeking to hide this from the teacher. In reality, nothing can be hidden from the teacher, but the teacher allows the
student privacy and does not confront the student with anything that
the student chooses to withhold from the teacher. If the teacher did
not take this approach, the student could not become self-sufficient,
for you cannot develop self-sufficiency in a controlled environment—you cannot be forced to stand on your own, you cannot be
forced into becoming free.

At the higher stages of the spiritual education process, the teacher
does take a calculated risk, and this makes it possible that the student
can gradually build a sense of identity that makes it unwilling to work
with the teacher. This can eventually lead the student to consciously
and deliberately make the choice to withdraw from – to hide from –
the teacher, which then breaks the connection between the teacher
and the student. Yet to fully understand why this can happen, we need
to examine one of the mistaken ideas about God that many people
have been brought up to believe without question.

***

As we will see later, the human ego has an insatiable desire for control. The only way to control a situation is to predict what will happen
next, and predictability must be based on order. Thus, human beings
have a great desire to turn the universe into an orderly place that follows rules they define. This has obviously been expressed in many
religions that claim everything is subject to God's will. Ironically, it is
science that has dealt a death-blow to this view, but let us first look at
the history of science.

During and after the Renaissance, many scientists believed the
material universe was nothing more than a huge machine in which all

the individual parts were connected with cogs and wheels. If you knew all aspects of the machine and knew its starting position, you could predict everything that would happen in the future. In other words, there was no room for uncertainty in this deterministic view of the world. Albert Einstein started undermining deterministic science with his theory of relativity, but it was quantum physicists who took science beyond determinism. They discovered that at the deepest level of the material universe – where energy becomes matter in the form of subatomic particles – the universe is not deterministic. It is impossible to predict exactly what will happen in any situation, for one can only predict probabilities. This discovery was too much for Einstein, who responded that, "God does not play dice with the universe!"

In reality, God *does* play dice with the material universe in the sense that the Creator has given dominion over the Earth to its co-creators and has also given those co-creators free will. Free will is free, meaning that it can never be predicted what a self-aware being will choose to do. One can look at the prior choices of a particular being and define probabilities for how it will respond to a given situation, but one can never predict with certainty. The reason is that the conscious self can – at any moment – choose to change how it sees itself, which will inevitably change how it responds to situations.

This is a point that might require some contemplation, for the rational mind will reason that since the conscious self is created out of the Creator's Being, it should respond as the Creator. Yet the Creator has an all-encompassing awareness, and thus it is predictable that the Creator will make choices that are best for the All. In contrast, the conscious self of an individual being is focused at one point in the All, and it sees the universe from a particular – potentially very limited – perspective. Thus, it can make choices that are out of alignment with what is best for the All but based on an evaluation of what serves itself best in the immediate situation. Such self-centered choices cannot be predicted. For that matter, the Creator does not want individual choices to be predictable, for it is only in freedom that self-sufficiency can grow. And the growth in self-awareness, leading to the self-sufficiency of God-awareness, is the entire purpose of the world of form.

My point being that even when a new student is placed in a protected environment and under the supervision of an enlightened teacher, it is impossible to predict exactly how that student will choose to define its identity. Thus, it becomes possible that the student can build an unbalanced and self-centered sense of identity and seek to hide itself from the teacher, gradually building an identity as a separate being until it can no longer maintain a conscious connection to its teacher or its own higher being.

A student can fall into a lower sense of self-awareness as a being that is separated from its teacher, its Higher Self and its God. This can create a downward spiral that eventually can cause the student to identify itself as a human being, a being that is a product of hereditary and environmental factors on planet Earth. What was created as a spiritual Being – designed to take dominion over the Earth – has now descended into a state of letting the Earth take dominion over itself. This is the process that the Bible describes as the Fall of Man, and we will later take a closer look at the Biblical story and the true meaning behind its symbols.

***

We are now at the point where we can see the central problem on planet Earth, the very cause of all human suffering. The problem is that most human beings have separated themselves from their spiritual teachers and have built a sense of identity as separate beings. This has caused them to build an unbalanced sense of identity, and through that identity they have co-created their individual situations. Human beings have collectively co-created the current imbalances on the planet. This was not the original design for Earth but is a result of the fact that human beings separated themselves from their spiritual teachers. They began to use their creative abilities in an unbalanced way, causing them to experience the consequences of their choices.

We can say that the Earth is a giant schoolroom in which all people are the students, no matter where they came from originally. The students learn from experiencing the consequences of their choices, and if their choices are based on a separate sense of identity, they will inevitably lead to suffering. The only way out of suffering for any student is to re-establish its connection to its own higher being. Yet because of the density of physical matter, there is a huge gap between the vibrations of your higher being and the vibrations of the material universe. Thus, it is impossible to reconnect to your higher being without having the help of a mediator, a spiritual teacher who has direct perception of the spiritual realm and can represent the Christ consciousness to the student. The first priority for any spiritual seeker is to re-establish the connection to your spiritual teacher. Therefore, you must come to a deeper understanding of why you lost contact with the teacher and consciously reverse the decisions that caused this. One might say this is the very essence of the spiritual path, at least at the beginning stages.

Each student is an individual and had its personal reasons for separating from the teacher. Yet there are certain general tendencies, and the main ones deserve further description. As I have said, in every situation there is an Alpha and an Omega aspect. Yet the principle of the Son is meant to balance the two, so there are three basic tendencies that caused students to lose contact with their teachers:

- An imbalance in the Alpha aspect, the expanding force. Ironically, the students who became imbalanced in the Alpha aspect were those who were most eager to learn their lessons and do everything right. Yet in their eagerness, they started wanting to control everything to make sure they always did the right thing. This led them to try to take heaven by force by using the expanding force to control and impose their – self-centered – sense of what was right upon themselves, other students, their environment and even the teacher. As I said, any imbalanced use of either force will not work, yet the students became unwilling to admit this. They now became victims of their unbalanced desire to do everything right and attempted to hide their mistakes from the teacher. They reasoned that if only they could have some time without the teacher seeing their mistakes, they would figure out how to undo them. They could then come back to the teacher without him ever seeing their mistakes.

- An imbalance in the Omega aspect, the contracting force. The students who became unbalanced in the contracting force were those who were the least concerned about doing things right. They were not eager to learn from their mistakes and preferred not to have those mistakes exposed. They then started to use the contracting force to conform to the conditions on Earth and avoid having to take dominion over the Earth. When this led to the inevitable suffering, they blamed it upon others or the teacher and eventually felt that the teacher had let them down. They now built an excuse for why they did not have to follow the teacher's advice and withdrew into a state of denial—denying that the suffering they experienced was the result of their own choices. They simply wanted to be left alone, and the teacher had no other option than to let them learn from the consequences of their choices.

- An imbalance in the Son aspect, the Christ mind. The role of the Christ mind is to maintain balance between the expanding and contracting forces. Thus, the previous categories were both caused by a failure to apply the Christ mind to the use of both forces. However, there is a third potential, namely that students can deliberately misuse the Christ mind—or rather that they can use the opposite polarity of the Christ mind, the mind of anti-christ. The role of the Christ mind is to make sure your actions are in harmony with the laws of God, which means that the Christ mind has an absolute standard for defining constructive and non-constructive actions. Any action that raises yourself and all life is a life-enhancing use of your creative powers. Any action that limits other parts of life will also limit yourself, and thus it is a life-degrading action.

  Only the Christ mind can give you a truly free choice, for only when you know God's law and the consequences for going against it, can you make a free choice between following or disobeying the law. Yet the creation of the Christ mind, in combination with free will, gave rise to an opposite, namely the mind of anti-christ. This mind is based on a separation from God's law, and thus it leads students to lose an absolute standard for evaluating their actions. Instead of using the Christ standard, they now define their own standard based on their limited world view and self-centered desires.

  This allows students to sink deeper into separation from the teacher. As long as you realize that your suffering is caused by your unbalanced use of either the expanding or the contracting force, you at least know where the problem is. Yet when you sink into the consciousness of anti-christ, you now define your own standard for right and wrong, good and evil. Thus, it becomes possible that a student can be violating the laws of God while being firmly convinced that it is doing the right thing. The student has lost the connection to the reality of God's law and has now defined a set of self-made laws that it has elevated to the status of God's law. The student thinks it is already doing the right thing, and thus it believes it has no need for the spiritual teacher who represents Christ. In fact, it will use the reasoning of the mind of anti-christ to reject any true teacher or teaching, meaning that the student has now become unreachable to the true spiritual teacher who will never violate the Law of Free Will. The student is unteachable.

We can now see that there are stages in the fall. All students started separating themselves from the teacher because of an unbalanced use of the expanding or the contracting force. Yet the fall became complete only when they used the mind of anti-christ to justify the separation. They could do this only because they refused to reach for the Christ mind within themselves, meaning that their conscious selves refused to hold the position of the Christ in their beings. They refused to take responsibility for balancing the lower and higher aspects of their beings, for bringing matter into oneness with Spirit. Thus, instead of taking dominion over self and then over the Earth, they allowed the Earth – and the consciousness of anti-christ – to define self. To fully understand this process, we need to take a closer look at the consciousness of anti-christ. Understanding this anti-mind is absolutely essential for any spiritual seeker on Earth.

Key 9
Understanding Christ and anti-christ

Have you ever taken a walk in a dense forest or in a foreign city and actually lost your way, not knowing where you were or how to get to your destination? Why were you lost? Was it not because you had a limited perspective, a limited view of the situation? If you could have jumped into a helicopter and seen the situation from above, it would have been easier to find your way. Or if you could have phoned someone in a helicopter, that person could have guided you from a higher perspective.

There are many people on Earth who claim to be religious or spiritual people, seeking for a higher state of life, whether they call it salvation, eternal life, nirvana, higher consciousness, enlightenment or something else. Some of these people have truly found a viable path that leads to a higher state while others are simply deluding themselves. What is the difference between those who have discovered what Jesus called the strait and narrow way and those who follow what he called the broad way that leads to destruction (Matthew 7:13-14)? The difference is that those who have found a true path have realized that the key to making viable progress is to expand your perspective, to change the way you look at everything, to transcend your limited state of consciousness. In contrast, those who are following a false path think they have found the only true belief system and that this external truth will guarantee their salvation.

The most important fact about planet Earth is that human beings have lost their way and have become trapped in a lower state of consciousness in which they have a limited and distorted view of *everything*. It is true that, in the beginning, God created self-aware beings in his image and after his likeness. But since people lost the connection to their higher beings, they have created a God in the image and after the likeness of themselves—as they are now in their limited, self-centered state of consciousness. Therefore, they project human qualities upon God and think he is angry, frightening, remote, unloving, unjust or any other human quality that springs from anti-love.

You probably know that there was a time when many human beings believed the Earth was flat. You probably also know that the Earth was as round then as it is today. In other words, there are certain aspects of life that human beliefs cannot change, because those facts were defined by a mind that is in a higher state than the current state of consciousness of human beings. Thus, I wish all sincere spiritual seekers would contemplate the fact that God is not mocked (Galatians 6:7) and that he is no respecter of persons (Acts 10:34) or their limited opinions. In other words, people's beliefs about God do not change the reality of the Creator.

However, beliefs do change people's perception of and their relationship with the Creator, and thus beliefs change how people see themselves. There is a reason why the first two commandments given to Moses were to not have any other God's before the one true God and to not take unto yourself any graven image (Exodus 20:3-4). When people fell into a lower state of consciousness, they started creating mental images – as well as idols made of wood, stone or gold – and believed they were the true God. Yet the true God is the Creator who is always beyond – while at the same time being everywhere within – its creation. Thus, no image in the world of form can describe the Creator who created the world of form.

When you create a graven image of God – meaning a mental image that you think is infallible and refuse to change – you will inevitably lose contact with the true God and the reality of his law. As we have already discussed, you will then begin to create a world that is not based on the Creator's laws. Thus, your creation will inevitably be unbalanced which can only lead to suffering. The cause of all suffering is that people have lost contact with the reality of God's laws so they are using their co-creative abilities to create an unbalanced world. In other words, all suffering is the result of ignorance, of an illusion. This is proven by the fact that so many people blame their God for their suffering, thinking they were created as sinners, that God wants to punish them or that he is an unjust God.

What I am leading up to here is the realization that most human beings today have a limited perspective on life, a limited world view. Yet they tend to project that limited view upon God and think they can actually know – even define – what God is like based on their present state of consciousness. It would be extremely constructive for your spiritual growth if you would recognize this tendency and make a sincere effort to rise above it.

You can start by contemplating the thought that even though many human beings are confused and cannot understand how the world works, God suffers from no such confusion. The Creator is not unintelligent and has a complete understanding of the laws that guide the unfoldment of its creation. Thus, if you want to escape the confusion that causes your suffering, you need to expand your understanding of God's laws. This might require you to go beyond your current beliefs about life, God and the world. As mentioned before, one of the major problems on Earth is that many people are so attached to their current beliefs that they reject a higher understanding when it is offered to them. Nevertheless, I shall endeavor to offer you a higher perspective on the most basic principles of the universe.

**

As we have discussed, the very purpose of the world of form is to give self-conscious beings the ability to grow in self-awareness, from a sense of identity focused in one point to the full God-awareness that is in every point in the All and is one with the Allness. This requires several elements:

- Beings must start in an environment in which they can have a sense of identity as separate, individual beings. As I have explained, that is why the Creator makes a sphere that is set apart from the void and contains basic structures but is not so filled with light that the illusion of separateness is impossible.

- Beings must have the ability to build their own sense of identity, which is why they have the Creator's own abilities of self-awareness, unlimited imagination and unrestricted free will. Only by choosing to build its own identity will a being truly grow in self-awareness.

- Beings must have a path that leads them toward full God-awareness. Otherwise they might build a limited sense of identity and get stuck in it indefinitely. Obviously, this would be against the most basic principle of creation, namely growth, and thus there must be a safety mechanism that ensures growth.

We now need to revisit our earlier discussion of the kind of safety mechanism the Creator designed. The Creator decided to manifest itself as two forces, namely the expanding and the contracting force. These two forces are designed to be complimentary forces and magnify each other, thereby creating the MORE and raising sphere after sphere until the void is filled with light. Yet if used in an unbalanced way, the two forces become opposites and cancel out each other. The Creator then decided to create a state of consciousness that contains its vision and purpose for the world of form and a record of the principles that the Creator designed in order to ensure the balanced growth of this world. Take note that this all happened before anything was actually created in the void. The Creator then decided that it would only create by using the Christ consciousness. In other words, the Creator itself *only* created through the Christ consciousness, meaning that everything was in harmony with the Creator's vision and laws. The Creator never created anything that was against its own laws, but since it did create self-aware beings with free will, such beings can depart from their original design and go against the Creator's laws.

Once a co-creator has attained enlightenment or mastery, that co-creator likewise co-creates everything through the Christ consciousness. Therefore, the masters who created the original Earth did so through the Christ consciousness, meaning that they created a perfectly balanced planet.

We now need to revisit the fact that the Christ consciousness is the only begotten Son of the Father and that you can know God only through the Christ mind. Yet the purpose of the world of form is to give beings the experience of starting with a limited and separate sense of self-awareness. In other words, this would not be possible if new beings were created with the full Christ consciousness. A new being has only a seed of the Christ consciousness, meaning that it starts out by co-creating without having any awareness of God's overall vision or God's laws. Thus, it is inevitable that a new co-creator will violate the laws of God and use the expanding and contracting forces in an unbalanced manner. And since any unbalanced use of the two basic forces leads to an unbalanced creation that produces suffering, it would seem that co-creators are born into a life of suffering.

If this was true, it would obviously seem unfair. Co-creators are born with a limited awareness of God's laws and thus it is inevitable that they will be unbalanced in their use of their creative powers. They simply don't know better, and thus they cannot do better. If they were "punished" for the ignorance with which God created them, that would seem unfair to most people. One could argue that this would not be truly unfair, since the purpose of life is to grow in self-aware-ness—and by growing, co-creators can rise above suffering. How-ever, the reality is that when a being enters any sphere, it is placed in a protected schoolroom under the guidance of a spiritual teacher. The teacher represents the Christ to the student and gives it loving guid-ance while at the same time protecting the student from the conse-quences of its unbalanced actions. Thus, a new co-creator is *not* born into a life of suffering but is born into an environment that seems like paradise – and *is* a paradise – compared to the current conditions you face on Earth.

It is only when a student chooses to leave this protected environ-ment that it must bear its own burden and experience the conse-quences of its unbalanced actions. It would thus seem highly unlikely that anyone would choose to leave their paradise. Which makes it necessary for us to investigate the mechanism that has led most human beings on Earth to leave the protected environment of a cos-mic schoolroom.

***

What I hope will happen as you read this book is that you will gradu-ally overcome the sense – held by so many people – that you live in a world that is incomprehensible, unpredictable and therefore scary and unfair. I hope you will begin to see that – regardless of outer appear-ances and what you were brought up to believe – you live in a world that is based on certain principles. Once you understand these princi-ples, you can use them to co-create the kind of life-experience you want. My point being that the key to improving your life experience is to increase your understanding of the very principles that shape your life-experience. And the most important of these principles is the Law of Free Will. So let us take another look at free will.

Choice is an interesting concept that most people take for granted without ever thinking about what it means and how it works. As you are reading this book, you are facing a choice: Do you keep reading or do you stop reading? You have two options, yet no one is forcing you to choose either one. Nevertheless, "someone" is forcing you to make a choice. You either keep reading or you stop reading—there is nothing in between. Who or what is forcing you to make a choice? Could it be the very fact that you have self-awareness and that you live in a world that has different forms—each representing an option? In other words, as you are reading this, you are aware that you exist and that you are reading this book. The awareness of yourself and of your environment forces you to make a choice as to how you respond to the environment, in this case the fact that you are holding this book in your hand. Do you continue reading or do you stop reading? You must choose one or the other.

I know some will say that you have an alternative, namely to numb your self-awareness by going to sleep or using a chemical substance to numb your mind or alter your state of consciousness. Yet as near-death experiences have shown, even after the body dies, you still have self-awareness. Thus, even if you numb the body and brain, you cannot escape self-awareness—it is simply no longer focused around the body and the material world. Yet at some level you still have self-awareness and you are faced with choices.

My point is that there are certain things in life that are inescapable. As I mentioned earlier, you live on a planet that has gravity. You could rebel against this and seek to escape the force of gravity. Or you could accept that the force of gravity actually is very helpful and thus get on with making the best of your life on a planet with gravity. Likewise, you can rebel against the fact that you have self-awareness and free will by seeking to numb yourself or refuse to make choices. Or you could accept this fact and get on with using your free will to expand your self-awareness, so your existence is no longer seen as a punishment but as an opportunity. The mechanics behind free will are as follows:

- You must have self-awareness. You must be aware that you exist, you must be aware that you exist as a being with certain capabilities and you must be aware of your environment and its characteristics (such as gravity).

- You must have imagination, meaning that – based on your sense of identity and your knowledge of your environment –

you can imagine the different options you have. You must also be able to imagine the potential consequences of your options.

- You must have will, the ability to evaluate your options and their consequences and then make a decision to choose one option over another.

- You must have the ability to think rationally and evaluate the consequences of your actions, so you can learn from your past actions and avoid continuing to miss the mark.

Once you have made a choice, that choice will become an action that will trigger a reaction from the universe. Because you have self-awareness, you will inevitably experience that reaction, and it will obviously influence your life experience. There are many people who have been programmed to believe that they have little influence on their life experience because it is shaped by factors – be it fate, luck, chance or an angry God – over which they have no control. I am hoping to gradually help you see that you live in a universe that is like a giant bio-feedback machine or a cosmic mirror. The universe responds to your unbalanced actions with an opposite reaction designed to restore balance. Thus, what comes back to you from the universe is dependent upon what you send out. And since what you send out is a product of the choices you make, you have the option of changing not only your choices but also the entire process of making choices, including how you see yourself, how you see the world and how you imagine the options you have.

My point is to show you that the choices you make in life are very much determined by your knowledge or awareness of yourself and the world. Many people think they are human beings and that their options for improving their life experience are limited by their physical bodies. Yet a growing number of people are beginning to realize that they are spiritual beings inhabiting human bodies and that their life experience can be improved immensely by using the creative powers of their minds. There is a fundamental and immense difference between how these two approaches to life shape the options people can imagine—and thus the choices they make. If you look at the progress witnessed in Western civilization over the past couple of millennia, you will see that it is largely a product of the fact that human beings have expanded their awareness of their environment. If you look at some of the problems produced by this external knowledge – such as nuclear weapons and pollution – you will see that it is caused by the fact that human beings have not had a corresponding increase in their awareness of themselves. Yet this has begun to change with more people taking up the old challenge to know themselves. That is precisely why I am releasing this book at this time.

***

We can now see that when people make a choice that leads to undesirable consequences, the mechanics of the situation are that they make a choice that is out of harmony with the principles that the Creator used to define this universe. Yet if people had known that a given choice would have undesirable consequences, would they still make that choice?

We now see the possibility that when people make choices that lead to suffering, the real cause is ignorance. There is something they don't know about themselves or about the world, and this ignorance limits the options they are able to imagine or the consequences they can see. However, even a casual observation of human behavior reveals that people often seem to *know* better, yet they fail to *do* better. In other words, people still do what they know will have undesirable consequences and they often seem powerless to change the equation that leads to such choices. For example, all people know that smoking is dangerous to their health, yet many people continue to smoke anyway. It is as if they do not truly realize or acknowledge that smoking is dangerous. Their knowledge remains a theory and is not translated into action, or they find a way to justify smoking despite its dangers. What is the missing link that prevents people from truly knowing better?

Consider the statement that if people knew better, they would do better. This statement is ultimately true, but only when you understand the dynamics involved in "knowing better." In other words, if people truly knew and understood every aspect of their situation and the options they have, they would not make choices that would harm themselves. The trouble is that there is a certain mechanism in human psychology that prevents people from truly knowing better. They either think they know better or they refuse to expand their awareness. In other words, there is a gray area, an area where it is impossible for people to see reality because they are blinded by a limited or distorted view of reality. They are ignorant, but they fail to recognize their ignorance. For example, people can have an intellectual knowledge of the dangers of smoking, but they fail to connect it to themselves, thinking they somehow will not be harmed by smoking.

Based on our previous discussion, we can see that ultimately, the only way to know better is to have the full Christ consciousness, meaning that you have the full awareness of the Creator's vision and laws. Only then will you fully know who you are, what creative powers you have and how the world works. And only then can you imagine a set of realistic options and actual consequences. Of course, only when you have the full knowledge of your options and their consequences can you make a truly free choice.

One might say that Christ consciousness is true spiritual freedom, whereas anything less than Christ consciousness is a form of spiritual thralldom. Ignorance will inevitably put you in a mental prison that limits the options you can see and thus the choices you make. Only Christ truth will set you free to make truly free choices. We now need to consider what is less than the Christ consciousness.

As I have said, a new student in a spiritual schoolroom does not start with the Christ consciousness. When you have the Christ consciousness, you know you are one with God and one with all life, which would prevent you from having a separate sense of identity. So a new student starts with a self-centered sense of identity and it does not know the laws of God. In other words, a new student starts its journey in a state of ignorance, as does a child on Earth.

This ignorance would condemn the student to a life of suffering, but because it is in a spiritual schoolroom and under the protection of an enlightened teacher, this suffering is mitigated. A student can theoretically grow to Christ consciousness without experiencing the suffering that is so common on Earth. I say theoretically because in actuality most students grow through a combination of theory and experience. As I explained earlier, when a student begins to mature, the teacher steps back and gives the student more freedom to learn from its own decisions. This includes allowing the student to experience some of the consequences of its actions.

If you think about a child on Earth, you will notice that you can tell children not to touch a hot stove. Some will obey, whereas others will test your directions by touching the stove anyway. A good parent would allow the child to have this experience but would make sure the stove was not so hot that it would result in a harmful burn. Like-wise, a spiritual teacher will allow the student to test the teacher's directions – and disobey them to some degree – but will make sure the returning karma only teaches and does not destroy.

My point is that a spiritual teacher does not demand total or blind obedience. In fact, the teacher is seeking to make the students spiritu-ally self-sufficient, which means the students must sometimes learn to follow their own inner directions rather than the teacher's guide-lines. A new student is ignorant because it does not have any internal knowledge of God's laws. It has access to a spiritual teacher, but if the student does not develop internal knowledge, it will become dependent upon the teacher. Thus, the external teacher wants the stu-dent to gradually begin to rely on its internal teacher, meaning that the student must face the test of disobeying the external teacher in order to follow the internal teacher.

As the student matures, disobeying the external teacher is normal and expected. However, there is a subtle but all-important distinction to be made. As I explained earlier, when the teacher starts giving the student more room to make decisions on its own, it becomes possible that the student can build a sense of distance to the teacher. The stu-dent can then begin to deliberately seek to hide things from the teacher. Even this will be allowed, as long as the student still main-tains a connection to the teacher. The big question now becomes whether the student – in exerting its independence – is following its own internal teacher or is following another external teacher?

As I said earlier, the maturing student must face the initiation exemplified by Adam and Eve in the Garden of Eden. That initiation is represented by a certain state of consciousness, namely the knowl-edge of good and evil, and it is personified in the Serpent. We will later take a much closer look at these concepts and what they truly mean. However, for now let us focus on the fact that there are two forms of ignorance.

When a student is new, it has an innocent form of ignorance. It simply doesn't know better, so it makes mistakes. As the teacher and its own experiences demonstrate that the student doesn't know some-thing, the student openly and eagerly learns the lesson, internalizes its new understanding and thus stops making a particular mistake. Yet as the student matures, it faces the test of whether it will continue to learn willingly or whether it will seek to hide or justify its mistakes.

The student now has to wrestle with the temptation to engage in willful ignorance. This is when you truly have the opportunity to know better, but you are not willing to change your behavior and thus you find ways to neutralize your "knowing better." You can see a similar process on Earth where children, and especially teenagers, will begin to refuse to follow directions or refuse to acknowledge that they do know that certain actions are wrong. They will then engage in various schemes to justify that they continue acting in ways that are below their present age and maturity.

We now see that normal ignorance is simply the absence of knowledge, whereas willful ignorance is an entirely different frame of mind. Let us take a closer look.

***

Think back to your childhood and how you faced the initiation of dealing with your fear of the dark. If you analyze the situation, you will see that you were not actually afraid of the dark. You were afraid that in the darkness might hide monsters that could come out and hurt you—monsters that could not exist in the bright light of day. It was the potential for the existence of monsters that caused your fear, which then became transferred to a fear of the dark. This fear became paralyzing because you became afraid to do the only thing that could help you overcome the fear—go into a dark room and experience that there were no monsters. It was only when you confronted your fear, and realized it was not rational to believe in monsters, that you overcame your fear of the dark.

The Christ consciousness is comparable to the light in which nothing is hidden. The Christ mind has an absolute standard for evaluating behavior. Your actions are either in harmony with God's laws or they are not in harmony with God's laws. There is no gray zone, no fuzzy area, and thus you cannot hide, justify or explain away the actions that miss the mark. Your actions are either life-supporting or life-degrading and there is no discussion about what is what.

As I explained earlier, a new being starts in a sphere that still has some darkness left, meaning that it is not as filled with light as the spiritual realm. This is what gives the being the opportunity to start out with a separate, self-centered sense of identity. We might say that the remaining darkness allows the being to be born in a state of ignorance, but it also allows the being to hide its incorrect actions. As the being matures, it can use the darkness to remain in willful ignorance and can even create an outer facade that hides its inner thoughts and intentions. It can create the appearance of being selfless while holding on to selfish beliefs, desires and intentions. You clearly see this on Earth, where people can pretend to be good, even religious, yet their hearts are selfish. As Jesus said, "Beware of false prophets, which come to you in sheep's clothing, but inwardly they are ravening wolves" (Matthew 7:15). This deception is possible only because there is still so much darkness in the energy field of Earth that it is possible to hide your thoughts and feelings. In the spiritual realm no being can hide its thoughts and intentions from others. Thus, lies and deception simply cannot exist in the spiritual realm—total honesty is a way of life.

My point is that planet Earth is (still) a place where there is a veil of ignorance which makes it possible to hide. Yet ignorance is simply darkness. It is an absence of light and has no substance and intentions in itself. However, because of the absence of Christ light, it is possible that the darkness can hide "monsters" that do have substance (although temporary) and intentions that are not in alignment with God's purpose for creating the universe. This is an idea that needs further scrutiny.

As I have explained, everything is created out of the interplay of two complimentary forces, both of which are necessary for creating and sustaining the world of form. There are spiritual and religious teachings on this planet that have taken this to an extreme by saying that God forms one polarity and the other polarity is the opposite of God, namely evil, often personified as a being that is God's opposite, such as the devil. In other words, both good and evil are necessary to complete the cosmic picture and one could not exist without the other. Thus, a being can choose either one and it can return home by following both the path of good and the path of evil. Based on our previous discussion, it should be possible for the alert student to see why these teachings are out of touch with reality.

The Creator first defined a boundary within the Allness and then contracted its being into a single point in a void. The void was not the opposite of the Creator, it was simply the absence of anything. Thus, there is nothing in the void; it has no form or substance and it cannot give existence to evil. Everything that was created in the void was created out of God's substance and being, without him was not any-thing made that was made. Because everything is made out of God's own substance, it follows that when God is all there is, nothing can be in opposition to God. In other words, God has no opposite and there is no need for an opposite polarity to God in order to complete the cosmic whole. The Creator is complete in and of itself and needs no polarity. Take note of what I am saying. Evil has no substance of its own, it has no substance apart from the Ma-ter Light. That which appears to be evil is simply the Ma-ter Light that has taken on a form that is out of alignment with the Creator's laws. Thus, it has only a temporary existence, and eventually the Ma-ter Light will be returned to its original purity and the evil form will be no more.

It was only when creation began that the One Creator manifested itself as the two polarities of the expanding and contracting forces. Yet these two polarities are not opposite but complementary forces. Thus, it makes no sense to say that one is good and the other is evil. Evil did not become possible as a concept until the creation of the Christ consciousness. As I have explained, the Christ consciousness was created because the purpose of creation is to give individual beings the opportunity to grow in self-awareness, which means that they must have free will. Yet the very existence of free will makes it possible that beings can choose to go against the laws of God. There is no need for a being to do this, yet free will would not be complete unless a being had the option to do so. This made it possible for a being to become lost in separation, so the Christ consciousness repre-sents the way back to oneness.

We now see that there are two ways for a being to go against the laws of God. One is out of ignorance, where the being simply doesn't know better. Parents will often let a child get away with things that are selfish behavior because the child simply doesn't understand that what it is doing is wrong. The child can therefore build certain habits of behavior that it thinks are not wrong and that it is reluctant to give up because they seem to give the child a temporary advantage. Yet as the child matures, it is expected to know better and reform its actions accordingly.

As a student in the spiritual schoolroom matures, it is faced with the choice of whether it will reform its actions based on its higher understanding or whether it will refuse to give up its habits. The stu-dent can no longer justify its actions based on honest ignorance, so it must find some other form of justification. It can do this only by making use of a frame of mind that – in contrast to the Christ mind – has no absolute standard for right and wrong. In other words, willful ignorance is based on the existence of darkness that can hide the truth and even make a lie have the appearance of truth.

The Christ consciousness is designed to give students an absolute standard for exercising their free will. By using the Christ mind, students can express unlimited creativity yet still stay within the framework of God's law, meaning that their efforts raise themselves and all life. Yet since the Christ consciousness is meant to guide free will, it follows logically that the Christ consciousness must have an opposite that allows beings to go against the laws of God. In other words, the concept of opposites that are mutually exclusive and cancel out each other does not exist at the level of God and is not built into the expanding and contracting forces. Opposites come into existence only at the level of the Son, the level of self-aware beings who are exercising free will. Thus, evil is not the opposite of God but the opposite of Christ. Good is the result of beings using their free will through the mind of Christ. Evil is the result of beings using their free will – not through the darkness of ignorance that is simply the absence of Christ truth – but through the opposite of the Christ mind, namely the mind of anti-christ.

***

Let me make it clear that the mind of anti-christ does not form a polarity with the Christ mind. The two are not complementary forces. The Christ mind is the only begotten Son of the Father, and it needs no opposite. The mind of anti-christ was not created by God and is not necessary in order to complete the cosmic whole. The mind of anti-christ became an option when the Creator gave its offspring free will. Thus, the mind of anti-christ has no inherent reality. It receives a temporary "reality" only when self-aware beings choose to use the mind of anti-christ. Thus, the mind of anti-christ receives power only through the choices made by such beings.

There is a subtle point here that can be difficult to grasp at first. Nothing in the world of form can be created without using the Mother Light, which is created out of the Creator's own Being. Thus, a being can create nothing without using God's light. However, the Ma-ter

Light will take on absolutely any form imposed upon it by a being with co-creative abilities. Because of free will, it is possible for a being to use the Mother Light to create a manifestation that is out of alignment with the Creator's purpose and laws. The being can do this only by using the mind of anti-christ, which enables it to imagine options and make choices that are out of harmony with God's laws—something that cannot be done through the Christ mind. Do you see what I am saying? A being creates by using the mind to form a mental image and then superimposes it upon the Ma-ter Light. When you create this mental image based on the vision of the Christ mind, you cannot even generate an image that will harm yourself or other forms of life. This can be done only by forming a mental image through the mind of anti-christ—the mind that springs from separation from the All.

Generating a limiting manifestation can be done only by an unbalanced use of the expanding and contracting forces. When the two forces are used in an unbalanced way, they become opposites. In other words, through the mind of anti-christ the two basic forces are turned into opposites that cancel out each other. Yet even when the forces become opposites, it is still possible to create something in the material universe because this world still has darkness left and thus allows for an unbalanced manifestation. Yet any unbalanced manifestation will have a built-in tension that will eventually break it down. Anything created through the mind of anti-christ will be temporary and thus ultimately unreal. It is not a sustainable manifestation, which makes it a constant struggle to sustain it. One might say that you constantly have to recreate an unbalanced manifestation and this requires your ongoing attention and effort, which makes you a slave of your own creation. For example, some people hoard money through unbalanced means and have to spend all their time protecting it from those who seek to take it away by using the same means through which it was gathered.

My point here is that anything created through the mind of anti-christ is simply an appearance, an illusion, a mirage. It is created out of God's own substance – the Mother Light – but it has an appearance that is outside of God's perfect vision. Yet because the light truly is God's own substance, it has the potential to be brought back to the original purity of the Mother Light and then take on a form that is in harmony with creation. No matter how imperfect, ugly or evil an appearance might be, this potential can never be lost. Thus, one of the greatest lies about evil is that it is permanent and that things can get so bad that no power can change them. No matter how bad a situation might appear, it can always be transcended.

A being can use the mind of anti-christ to create a sense of identity that is separated from God, even in opposition to God. Yet because the conscious self is an extension of the Creator's Being, you can always rise above such a limited sense of identity. No matter how evil a being might seem to be, there is always a core of the Creator's Being, a spark of light in the darkness, and thus the potential for coming into oneness with one's source can never be lost.

***

I now ask you to consider the situation I face as a spiritual teacher who is attempting to help you understand the consciousness of anti-christ. The difficulty is that planet Earth – and the collective world view of humankind – is very heavily influenced by the mind of anti-christ. Most people have never experienced an alternative to the mind of anti-christ, or they are not aware that they have had this experience. Consequently, it is difficult for many people to grasp the consciousness of Christ, which makes it difficult for them to see the contradictions built into the mind of anti-christ. They are so used to seeing the world through the filter of the mind of anti-christ that they think this is normal or the way things ought to be. They think the mind of anti-christ represents truth and they often reject the real truth coming from the mind of Christ and the spiritual teachers who seek to bring it to Earth. Yet I shall attempt the seemingly impossible, for I know that if you were attracted to this book, you have already learned to use your intuitive faculties. And if you continue to use them, you will be able to grasp my explanation and the subtle truth that is beyond my words.

I have so far described the two basic forces as two separate forces. I have described them as being complementary and forming a whole, but few people are able to grasp what that truly means. The reason is that you are so used to seeing everything through a world view based on separation rather than oneness. In the spiritual realm all immortal beings have attained enlightenment, meaning that they see the world through the clarity of the Christ mind. Thus, they do not

see the basic forces as separate forces but as complimentary manifestations of the same reality, namely the Creator. In the Christ mind,
there is not even a possibility that the two forces could be seen as
opposites, for how could God be in opposition to itself?

As the Bible clearly states, the Father – meaning the Creator – can
be known exclusively through the only begotten Son (John 1:18),
which truly means the Christ consciousness. The Creator – as the One
Source of everything in the world of form – simply cannot be known
to the mind of anti-christ. The mind of anti-christ cannot see beyond
the expanding and contracting forces because it sees them as opposites and can see no unifying principle behind them. To the mind of
anti-christ everything is defined by two opposites that are defined in
relation to each other—not in relation to, or as an expression of, a
higher reality. The mind of anti-christ thinks in terms of opposites and
it thinks one cannot exist without the other, meaning that everything
must have an opposite. For example, the mind of anti-christ can deal
with the concept of God, but it can see God only as one aspect of a
relative duality in which it must have an opposite, and it sees itself as
that opposite. Thus, the opposite of God and good must be the devil
and evil, meaning that both are necessary to complete the whole. To
the mind of anti-christ, evil is as real as God.

The direct consequence of this is that in the mind of anti-christ
there is no such thing as an absolute truth or an indivisible truth. Truth
is a concept that must have an opposite, meaning that truth is defined
in relation to untruth and vice versa. This is a subtle point that might
require some intuitive contemplation. In the Christ mind, truth is one;
it is undivided. The Christ mind sees God's law and knows it is real,
consistent and absolute. Thus, if an idea is in alignment with the reality of God, it is true. If it is out of alignment with God's reality, it is
untrue. There is no doubt, no room for interpretation, no gray zone,
no veil of ignorance.

The mind of anti-christ cannot see the reality of God. Thus, it
thinks there is no one, absolute, undivided truth. Truth is relative to
how it is defined instead of being one with God's undivided reality.
Truth must have an opposite, meaning that it is not absolute truth –
which can have no opposite – but relative truth. In the Christ mind
truth is defined based on God's reality, whereas in the mind of anti-
christ "truth" is defined based on a view of the world that is outside of
and disconnected from God's reality. The mind of Christ does not

define truth because it is defined by the reality of God. The mind of Christ simply experiences – is one with – this reality. The mind of Christ has no need for a mental image, but the mind of anti-christ cannot experience God's reality, and thus it must create a mental image of everything.

The mind of anti-christ cannot see God's reality and thus it defines both truth and anti-truth. What the mind of anti-christ sees as "truth" is *not* the absolute truth of God but a relative truth of its own creation. The mind of Christ perceives absolute truth, whereas the mind of anti-christ defines its own relative "truth" and then elevates it to the status of being absolute and infallible.

I know this can be difficult to grasp, but do you begin to see the implications of this? We talked about the fact that some students came to a point when they did not want to change their behavior but they could no longer justify their behavior based on honest ignorance. Thus, they had to seek to do so based on willful ignorance, which allowed them to think it was justifiable to continue the behavior. In the Christ mind such a justification is impossible, for there is no doubt about what is life-supporting and what is not. Thus, willful ignorance can exist only in the mind of anti-christ, and it is based on a doubt about what is truth and what is untruth. However, this doubt can exist only because truth has become a relative concept that can be defined within the parameters set up by the mind of anti-christ. There is a gray zone where the experience of God's reality is not possible, and thus there is room for uncertainty, ignorance, deceit and lies. When you cannot experience reality, "reality" becomes a mental image, and the mind can twist such an image to seemingly make it justify what it wants to believe.

The mind of Christ has no mental image because it has a direct experience of reality. The mind of anti-christ has no direct experience and thus has nothing but mental images. When you are in honest ignorance, you see some Christ truth and have a lot of "no knowledge." You might have some mental images, but you don't see them as absolute and you are open to having them replaced by true knowledge. Yet when you are in willful ignorance, you do not admit that there are things you know nothing about. Instead, you form mental images of the reality you have not experienced and you elevate them to the status of being more real than reality itself, so you need not even strive for a direct experience of God's reality. When people are honestly ignorant, they know there is something they don't know and they are striving to expand their knowledge—they are teachable. When people are stuck in willful ignorance, they think they know all they need to know and they are not willing to expand their understanding—they are not teachable. When people are in honest ignorance, they live in a small box, but it is an open box. When people are in willful ignorance, they might think they live in a very big box, but it is a closed box. And no closed box can hold the infinite reality of God.

Key 10
What really happened in the Garden of Eden?

Let us now use these insights to take a fresh look at the Garden of Eden story. This story is one of the pivotal myths in world culture and it is a fruitful source of understanding, especially when it comes to the relationship between people and their spiritual teachers. Obviously, one can unlock this understanding only by looking beyond a literal interpretation. If one does not, one can never resolve the obvious contradictions or answer the questions raised by the story.

First of all, one needs to realize that what the Bible calls God is not God in the ultimate sense, but a spiritual teacher that represented God to the students in the schoolroom that was called Eden. The Creator is beyond all form and thus would not interact with human beings in a form they could see. The Creator leaves this to the beings who hold the appropriate position in the cosmic hierarchy. The word "God" was used differently in Old Testament times, often used to refer to any spiritual being. As I have mentioned before, I, Maitreya, was the teacher of Adam and Eve, which I think makes me more qualified than any human being or institution to explain what truly happened in the Garden. Secondly, one needs to realize that there were many students in Eden. The story focuses on Adam and Eve for the sake of simplicity, and thus Adam and Eve are symbols, archetypes if you will, for what happened to many of the students in Eden. Let us now look at one of the pivotal passages in the story:

> 16 And the LORD God commanded the man, saying, Of every tree of the garden thou mayest freely eat:
> 17 But of the tree of the knowledge of good and evil, thou shalt not eat of it: for in the day that thou eatest thereof thou shalt surely die. (Genesis, Chapter 2)

The first question we will consider is why the spiritual teacher even had to tell the students not to eat of the fruit? Why was there a forbidden fruit in the Garden, why didn't God create the Garden without this temptation? We can now resolve this question by reaching back to our discussion of free will. If students did not have the option to go against the laws of God, they would not have the fullness of free will. Thus, the temptation to deliberately go against God's laws is a companion of free will.

We can now see that the "fruit of the knowledge of good and evil" is a symbol for a state of consciousness, namely the frame of mind that makes it possible for a student to go against the laws of God out of willful ignorance. As we have seen, violating the laws of God is not possible from the Christ mind, for when you perceive the reality of God, you know that violating God's laws will hurt yourself and your greater self (all life). And you would never consciously choose to hurt yourself or your Self.

It now becomes clear that violating God's laws is only possible when you are in a frame of mind in which you do not truly know what you are doing and how it will affect you. You might have come to believe that it will not truly hurt yourself, that it will not have negative consequences or that you can somehow escape those consequences. You might be violating God's laws without truly seeing that you are doing so, or you might be violating them deliberately but still without the full realization of how it hurts yourself.

Violating God's laws is only possible when you suffer from an illusion so that you do not see the reality of the Christ mind. You have neutralized your connection to the reality of God and the clear vision of that reality, which is a product of the Christ mind. How can perception of reality be neutralized and replaced by an illusion? It can be done *only* by entering a state of consciousness that has a more limited perspective on the world than the Christ consciousness. Therefore, you do not see reality but a mental image of reality, an image that is either limited or distorted. In other words, in the Christ mind there is no room for illusions, lies, doubt or interpretation, for there is no gray zone. So you can hurt yourself only by entering into a frame of mind in which there *is* room for illusion and doubt, meaning that there is a gray zone in which things are not clear. There is room to create a mental image of reality instead of the direct perception of God's reality found in the Christ mind. There seems to be a distance between you and reality because you are separated from reality—in your mind.

The frame of mind that separates you from reality is, of course, the mind of anti-christ. This frame of mind cannot see reality but sees only a mental image of "reality." Good and evil have become relative terms and are defined in relation to each other rather than in relation to God's absolute reality. When "truth" is relative, it becomes possible to define it in such a way that although you know you are violating God's laws, your perspective makes it seem like this is acceptable, justified, beneficial or perhaps even your only option.

When you realize that the Garden of Eden was a spiritual school, it becomes obvious that this school had certain lessons or initiations that students had to face and successfully pass before they could move on to the next level. Facing the temptation to go against the laws of God was one such initiation. As mentioned before, a new student does not have enough awareness to know the laws of God. Although it is violating those laws, this is done out of honest ignorance, for when you do not know the laws, you simply do not have the option to willfully violate them. The protection for new students is the teacher's instructions. If they stay connected to the teacher, he will help them develop Christ discernment until they know from within how to avoid violating God's laws.

As a student grows in maturity, it begins to know the laws of God, and thus it now acquires the knowledge that makes it possible to deliberately go against the laws. Thus, the student must now face the temptation to violate God's laws and to justify doing so by using the mind of anti-christ and its relative logic. Do you see the all-important point here? A new student is in a state of innocent ignorance in which it simply does not know better. Ignorance is *not* the same as the mind of anti-christ. Ignorance is a passive state of consciousness caused by an absence of knowledge. If you turn on the light in a dark room, the darkness immediately disappears. In other words, a person who is in ignorance does not resist receiving knowledge that will set him free from ignorance. In contrast, the mind of anti-christ is not innocently ignorant, it is willfully ignorant. It does not recognize that it is ignorant for it has created a mental image of reality and it worships this graven image as the only true God. Thus, it will resist receiving knowledge, as if there was a force hiding in the dark room, trying to prevent you from turning on the light. Or it will get people to keep their eyes closed so they cannot see what is revealed after the light is turned on. When students become blinded by this mindset, they refuse to listen to the teacher, and they justify this by using the logic of the mind of anti-christ. Because this mind defines its own world view, it can justify anything, and thus the teacher cannot help the students escape their circular logic. The students are no longer teachable.

As I have explained, the goal of the true spiritual teacher is to raise the student to become spiritually self-sufficient, which means that the student attains the Christ consciousness and becomes enlightened. Yet this is not a mechanical process that can be forced upon the student from without. It is a creative process that must come from within through the student's own choosing. Before you can attain the mind of Christ – in which you are one with absolute truth – you must overcome the temptation to use the mind of anti-christ to define your own "truth," using it to justify that you do not grow and self-transcend. You must overcome the temptation to separate yourself from your outer and inner teacher by using the mind of anti-christ to justify not transcending your current level of consciousness or even projecting a negative image upon the teacher which seems to justify your withdrawal from him.

***

We can now consider one of the pivotal questions presented by the passage quoted above, namely, "Did God lie to Adam?" I am aware that many people who honor the Bible have never considered this inescapable question and that some have seen it and pushed it aside. Yet the question is essential for understanding the student-teacher relationship.

The parameters are clear and undeniable. God – or rather the spiritual teacher – tells Adam that if he eats of the fruit of the knowledge of good and evil, he will "surely" die (Genesis 2:17). The Bible then describes that Adam and Eve do eat the fruit, but instead of dying, they are cast out of paradise (Genesis 3:24). Since the teacher must obviously have known this, it would seem he lied to Adam. Some people even interpret this to mean that God is trying to hold people in bondage by preventing them from having the fruit of knowledge, while the Serpent is the liberator of humankind. In other words, man did not attain true freedom until he violated God's laws—or so they say.

In our previous discussions we have set the foundation for sorting this out, but we will need to go a bit deeper into what we have discussed earlier. As we have seen, the center of a student's being is the conscious self. This self is an extension of the Spiritual Self that has been sent into the material universe. The purpose was to start out with a limited sense of self-awareness and then grow toward the full realization that you are an extension of God and that you are here to take dominion over the Earth and raise it to become the fullness of the kingdom of God.

In order to co-create anything in the material universe, you must do so through your sense of identity, and it is the role of the conscious self to define your material identity. As you start out in the spiritual schoolroom, you have a rudimentary sense of identity, much like an infant on Earth. However, you quickly build a sense of identity, and it is based on two main factors. One is your experience with and understanding of your environment. The other is the instructions from your spiritual teacher. The first factor is naturally limited in the beginning, and thus you build your sense of identity largely based on ignorance. Even your understanding of the teacher's instructions is limited, for your lack of understanding limits what the teacher can tell you. This is much like small children who cannot be taught advanced knowledge. You do not teach nuclear physics to students in kindergarten.

Child psychologists have discovered that children normally go through several distinct phases as they mature. In reality, each of these phases represents a distinct sense of identity that the conscious self has built. Likewise, a new student goes through such phases, and for each of them it builds a distinct sense of identity based on a specific view of the world. What psychologists have not yet understood is that when a child goes from one phase to the next, the sense of identity built during the previous phase ideally dies.

As I have explained, the conscious self is – at least in the material realm – what it thinks it is. The conscious self is expressing itself through its sense of identity. It can expand its sense of identity gradually, but this evolutionary change can only go so far. At certain intervals, it becomes necessary to take a major leap forward by going through a revolutionary change. This is comparable to the life-cycle of a butterfly. The larvae grows gradually, but then it goes through a revolutionary change and becomes a cocoon. Inside the cocoon, the butterfly grows gradually, but then another revolutionary change breaks the cocoon and the butterfly takes flight.

On a psychological level, a student first builds a sense of identity based on a limited outlook on the world. This identity evolves, but the limitations of the original world view set parameters for how far this growth can go. In order to rise to a higher level, a revolutionary change must occur. The old sense of identity must die and its world view must be left behind as a cocoon. Yet the death of the old sense of identity happens so gradually that most people are not aware of it. They transition into the new sense of identity so smoothly that – even though they may notice a change – they do not realize that they have been psychologically or spiritually reborn.

As a student grew in the Garden of Eden, it gradually built a sense of identity through both evolutionary and revolutionary stages. As it started to reach the stage of becoming more self-sufficient, it had built a sophisticated sense of identity. This identity was based on its understanding of the world and its own individuality. The student had not attained the full Christ consciousness, but it did have an under-standing – backed by intuitive experiences and the teacher's instruc-tions – that it was a spiritual being who originated beyond the material universe and the Garden. In other words, the student's con-scious self was beginning to realize that it was not a product of the world but an extension of a greater spiritual being. This realization was – of course – the master key to the fulfillment of the student's reason for being. You cannot fulfill your role in this world unless you recognize the Creator with whom you are co-creating. Thus, the stu-dent had the seed of Christhood and was on its way to attaining enlightenment, in which you directly perceive – and thus accept with every part of your being – that you are a spiritual Being who is one with your source.

When I told Adam that he would die if he ate the forbidden fruit, I was not lying to him. I knew that Adam – as a symbol for a student who has started to develop the Christ consciousness but is not yet anchored in it – was at a critical stage. This stage is when a student knows enough to realize that it is possible to go against the laws of God, yet the student does not have enough Christ consciousness to perceive that it will hurt itself by doing so. In other words, the student can use its imagination to ask, "What will happen if I go against God's laws?" But because the student does not directly perceive the oneness of all life, it has no direct perception of the consequences. It can only imagine the consequences, which makes it vulnerable to the subtle logic of the mind of anti-christ. The student does not yet have enough Christ discernment to see through the lies of anti-christ.

Take note of a crucial point. Dealing with the mind of anti-christ was an initiation that all students in the mystery school had to face. Yet as a teacher, I tried to make sure that students did not face this initiation before they were ready. You do not send a driving student into rush hour traffic until he or she has sufficient experience to avoid an accident. Only when you have a certain level of Christ consciousness can you successfully refute the temptations of the mind of anti-christ, as Jesus demonstrated when he was tempted by the devil after fasting in the wilderness (Matthew 4:1). My point is that Adam and Eve represent students who took the initiation of the knowledge of relative good and evil before they were ready for it. And that is precisely why they became lost in the mind of anti-christ, as we will see later.

For now, let us return to the question of whether the teacher lied to Adam. As a spiritual teacher, I knew that Adam was not ready for the initiation, yet – forever loyal to the Creator's Law of Free Will – I also had no way of forcing him to stay away from the forbidden fruit. Thus, I had to give him a strong incentive for not eating the fruit. I did this by telling him that he would die if he ate the fruit, and we can now see that this was not a lie. Before Adam ate the fruit, his conscious self had a sense of identity that contained some connection to his Higher Self. Yet once he partook of the mind of anti-christ, that connection was lost. Thus, Adam's sense of identity as a spiritual being in the material universe literally died. Instead, Adam was – without realizing what had happened – reborn into a lower sense of identity in which he saw himself as a material being who was separated from God by an impenetrable barrier. The first Adam had died and a second Adam was born, but the conscious self of the second Adam had no memory of the first Adam and thus did not understand what it had lost. It simply looked at its situation – and its relationship with the spiritual teacher – through the filter of its new identity. This is similar to a teenager who one day realizes he or she is not a child anymore and is now seeing the world through different eyes. This often causes a teenager to rebel against its parents, yet as it matures it learns to understand its parents and comes back into harmony with them (ideally speaking). My point is that Adam's new identity was based on the mind of anti-christ in which truth had become a relative concept. This is crucial to understanding what happened next.

***

The story of the Garden of Eden originated very far back in time. Yet let us look at the official version, according to which the story was given to nomadic tribes roaming the Middle East thousands of years ago. Their knowledge of the world and their understanding of themselves was as far below that of modern humans as the world view of a kindergarten student is below that of a college freshman. Thus, to assume that Genesis gives a complete or completely accurate picture of creation and the fall is simply ignorance. However, to insist that the story must be seen as the infallible word of God and must be interpreted literally in the face of modern knowledge is willful ignorance. My point being that the story has certain shortcomings that can be overcome only by reaching beyond ignorance.

One such shortcoming is that the story describes the fall as a very abrupt process that happened in one momentous event. In reality, the students in the Garden followed a gradual process. The students went through a phase that was as crucial and as turbulent as the teen-age years on Earth. This process of self-discovery was a potentially healthy stage that could lead them to define a new sense of identity, and to do so consciously for the first time. Please make sure you contemplate this point. Up until the student reaches a certain maturity, it defines a sense of identity without realizing what is happening. Yet as it matures, it reaches a turning point, where it can now begin to define a new sense of identity by consciously knowing what it is doing. This is the true meaning of self-awareness.

This is the stage that can lead to the student graduating from the schoolroom, so that it can then go out into the world with a firm connection to its higher being. This will make it far less likely that the student will be overpowered by the world and forget its true identity. Yet before you can graduate, you must define your new identity based on the Christ mind. In order to do this, you must face and overcome the temptation to continue to define your sense of identity based on ignorance. We might say that you have reached a point of no return, where you simply cannot continue in your old sense of identity. A new identity must be formed, and if you define your identity based on the willful ignorance of the mind of anti-christ, you will define a false sense of identity that denies your oneness with your source.

We now see that there is a risk factor because the students had to do this on their own. The teacher could not guide every aspect of the process. No one can define your sense of identity for you, so the teacher was limited to setting up certain parameters in order to define safe boundaries. If the students stayed within those parameters, they would be safe. One such boundary was that students at a certain level should not partake of the fruit of the knowledge of relative good and evil, the consciousness of anti-christ.

A young student will normally follow the teacher's directions without questioning them. Yet as the student matures, it begins to ask itself why the teacher is telling it not to do something. What would happen if it did not follow the teacher's directions? Again, this is a healthy part of becoming self-sufficient – as long as it is not taken too far – because it can lead you to understand the teacher's directions rather than following them blindly. So it is not difficult to foresee that if you tell a group of students not to do something, some of them – the more creative and self-sufficient ones – will do it anyway.

The problem is that the consciousness of anti-christ is very subtle and persuasive. It can be compared to walking into a dense forest. As long as you stay so close to the edge that you can see the light outside the forest, you can always find your way out. Yet once you lose sight of the edge, it is very easy to become disoriented, and now you no longer know which way leads you out. You can quickly become lost in the forest, and now you can no longer see the forest for the trees, as the old saying goes. As a teacher I was well aware when students disobeyed the instructions and started walking into the forest. Yet – again – I was and am completely committed to the Creator's Law of Free Will. Thus, I could not forcefully stop a student and had no desire to do so. Yet I had some consolation in the fact that as long as the student maintained a connection with me, I would always be able to guide the student back out of the forest. Thus, the student's experiments could potentially become valuable learning experiences.

We now see that the decision to experiment with the consciousness of anti-christ was not in itself what led to the fall. As I said, at some point all students had to face the temptation of anti-christ, and if a student was well-prepared, it would normally experiment with the consciousness of anti-christ until it had a sufficient understanding of how it works. It would then dismiss it – as Jesus rebuked the temptations of the devil – and focus all of its attention on the mind of Christ. What really caused the fall was that some students did not maintain their connection to the teacher. They experimented with the mind of anti-christ and then used its relative, dualistic logic to justify cutting the umbilical cord that connected them to the teacher. By doing this, they lost their connection to the reality of God, to the mind of Christ. They now had no lifeline to lead them out of the forest, out of the dualistic illusions of the mind of anti-christ. This was the real cause of the fall, as you can see by reading between the lines in the Genesis story:

> 7 And the eyes of them both were opened, and they knew that they were naked; and they sewed fig leaves together, and made themselves aprons.
> 8 And they heard the voice of the LORD God walking in the garden in the cool of the day: and Adam and his wife hid themselves from the presence of the LORD God amongst the trees of the garden. (Genesis, Chapter 2)

This is one example of how a literal interpretation comes short. There are numerous paintings in the world showing a naked Eve, eating a physical apple. In reality, the students in the Garden were not physically naked, and we are talking about a process that took place in the mind. It was only the primitive frame of mind of the recipients of Genesis that made it necessary to clothe the story in physical symbolism.

Imagine that you are taking a walk in a forest. In the beginning you are keeping a constant eye on the edge of the forest, or at least on a trail or certain landmarks. Yet gradually your attention becomes so focused on the trees and the animals that you forget to look back. Before you know it, you have gone too far and have lost sight of the way out. Yet in the beginning you are so caught up in the scenery that you do not realize what has happened and you unknowingly walk even deeper into the forest. Then, you suddenly remember that you need to go back home and you take a look around. In a moment of truth you realize that you cannot see the way out, and then comes the shocking realization, "I'm lost!" The crucial question is how you react to that realization? Do you keep your calm or do you panic and start running aimlessly through the forest?

As some of the students in the Garden started experimenting with the duality consciousness, they gradually became more enveloped in and blinded by it. This happened so gradually that they did not realize what was happening. Yet at some point every student had a moment of truth and suddenly realized, "I'm lost." The student realized it had violated the teacher's command, that it was now caught in a lower state of consciousness and that it could not hide this from the teacher—it realized it was naked. The crucial question now became how the student responded to that realization?

***

In previous chapters I have gone into great detail in order to convey the truth that the learning environment in the Garden of Eden was completely loving and supportive. Everything the student did was simply an experiment. Every experiment had an outcome, a consequence. That consequence would either expand the student's creative powers or limit those powers. Yet even a limiting consequence could still be turned into a learning experience, and an experiment that caused the student to expand its awareness was not a failed experiment. Thus, as long as the student was willing to learn, it truly could make no mistake. In the Garden, there was no concept of unerasable mistakes or everlasting consequences. There was no mistake that could not be undone.

It is very important that you understand why this is so, so let us take a closer look. In the Christ mind, it is clear that everything in the world of form is created out of the Mother Light which has temporarily taken on a certain form. If a form is in harmony with God's laws, it is sustainable. If a form is out of harmony with the laws, then it will eventually be broken down and erased. The Mother Light will be returned to its pure state as if the imperfect form had never existed. Thus, to the Christ mind, it is perfectly clear that no imperfect form could ever be permanent or unerasable. The meaning is that a student who is in the process of growing toward enlightenment could not possibly make a mistake that could permanently stop the growth process or prevent the student from coming back to a state of innocence. That is why the mind of Christ is the key to what many Christians see as the redemption of sin, the true meaning of which I will explain later.

Let us look at another level of understanding. I have explained how everything is made from the Mother Light that has been lowered in vibration. The spiritual realm is made of higher vibrations than the material universe. Your truc identity is anchored in your I AM Presence which resides in the spiritual realm. Your conscious self is an extension of your I AM Presence that descends into the material universe, where it engages in a process of experimentation aimed at increasing its awareness and self-awareness. This experimentation is carried out by using the energy in the material realm, which has a lower vibration than anything in the spiritual realm.

My point is that no experiment that your conscious self has carried out in the material universe can damage or erase your divine identity, for it is anchored in a realm of higher vibrations. Nothing you do on Earth could possibly damage the sun. The consequence is that no mistake you could possibly make in the material universe could be permanent. The entire material universe is of lower vibrations than the spiritual realm. Thus, the light from the spiritual realm can erase, purify and transform any imperfection created in the material realm.

Any mistake you make results in the generation of energy that has a lower vibration, we might call it misqualified energy. Yet this energy can be requalified, can be raised to its original vibration, by a stream of spiritual energy. The catch is that spiritual light can enter the material realm only through the Christ mind, which forms the open door (John 10:9) between the spiritual and the material realms. In the Garden of Eden, only the advanced students had enough Christ consciousness to erase their mistakes through their internal powers—and those were the students who had overcome the temptation of the mind of anti-christ. Those who had not yet overcome that temptation did not have the power to erase their mistakes. Yet as their teacher, I did have that power. If a non-christed being had the power to erase mistakes, you could keep making mistakes and erasing them without ever leaving behind the state of consciousness that causes you to make mistakes—thus never growing.

The point being that no matter what kind of mistake a student had made, that mistake could be erased by me. Even if the student's identity as a spiritual being had died, I could help the student become reborn into a spiritual identity. However, I was also operating under the rules for the spiritual schoolroom, the most important of which is free will. Thus, I could not erase a student's mistake unless the student asked for it. Here, of course, is the catch. In order for a student to ask for a mistake to be erased, the student had to do two things:

• It had to realize and admit that it had made a mistake.

- It had to be willing to bring that mistake to the teacher's attention (the teacher, of course, already knew, but the student had to be willing to come to the teacher).

If the student did not admit its mistake or if it was not willing to come to the teacher, the mistake obviously could not be erased by me. And since the student could not erase it on its own, the student might believe the illusion that it was permanent and that it could never be free of it. Obviously, as I have sought to explain, that illusion could come only from the mind of anti-christ. Yet it is also the mind of anti-christ that makes the student unwilling to go to the teacher, and it was this mind that made the student make certain mistakes in the first place. My point is that we are now beginning to see that the mind of anti-christ is dangerous because it puts students in what we might call a spiritual catch-22, a situation from which there seems to be no way out. As the popular saying goes, "You can't get there from here," which we can rephrase as, "You can't get to heaven by using the mind of anti-christ." My point is that the real cause of the fall was that Adam and Eve refused to go back to the teacher and openly admit their mistake. Instead, they sought to hide themselves – their nakedness – and their mistake from the teacher, as clearly described in Genesis:

> ...and Adam and his wife hid themselves from the presence of the LORD God.... (Genesis, 3:8)

We now need to understand the psychological mechanism that caused the students to make the fateful decision to hide from their teacher, a decision that has haunted humankind ever since and is still the only real block to people's spiritual freedom.

***

I may seem to be repeating myself, but I am doing it because I know how difficult it is for people on Earth to envision the learning environment found in the Garden of Eden. They are so used to seeing everything through the filter of relative good and evil that they cannot quite envision or accept that the Garden was an environment based on unconditional love. Thus, they find it hard to accept that the teacher had no anger or condemnation toward the students who had disobeyed his instructions. Yet the reality is that I had no negative feelings whatsoever toward the students. And the students had never had an experience of seeing me express any feelings less than unconditional love. My point being that there was nothing in the students' actual experience which gave them reason to believe that I would not receive them lovingly and help them overcome their mistakes.

When you begin to see this, you realize that the central question posed by the Garden of Eden story is why the students decided to hide from the teacher instead of asking for the help that they had every reason to believe would be readily forthcoming? What had happened in the student's minds that made it seem like their best or their only option was to hide from the teacher?

Before we go into that question, let me first set the record straight. Another shortcoming of the Genesis account is that it only tells the story of those students who did *not* go back to the teacher. In reality, there were many students in the Garden who decided to eat the forbidden fruit before they were ready for it, and thus they also fell into a lower state of consciousness. Yet a substantial portion of them *did* cry out for help, and they received every assistance necessary to get them back on the path to enlightenment—obviously within the framework of their willingness to make the necessary choices. Most of these students have long since risen over the need to reembody, although some of them have voluntarily returned to Earth in order to serve as spiritual teachers for humankind.

Let us now return to the question of what happened in the minds of the students who partook of the consciousness of anti-christ. As I said earlier, the beginning students often violated the laws of God because of their ignorance, yet their ignorance was innocent. They had no resistance to being taught, and when they were made aware of a mistake, they instantly corrected it. It was only when the students began to understand how the laws of God work that they gained the knowledge of how to deliberately violate God's laws. As I explained, no student would violate the law if it truly understood the consequences, and it was the consciousness of anti-christ that made it possible for a student to transition from innocent ignorance to willful ignorance. How did this happen? Let us take another look at Genesis:

1 Now the serpent was more subtil than any beast of the field which the LORD God had made. And he said unto the woman, Yea, hath God said, Ye shall not eat of every tree of the garden?
2 And the woman said unto the serpent, We may eat of the fruit

of the trees of the garden:
3 But of the fruit of the tree which is in the midst of the garden,
God hath said, Ye shall not eat of it, neither shall ye touch it, lest
ye die.
4 And the serpent said unto the woman, Ye shall not surely die:
(Genesis, Chapter 2)

We now see that the first element which the mind of anti-christ induces into the mind of the student is doubt, specifically doubt in the teacher's instructions. Up until that point, the student had no reason to doubt the teacher. The teacher's instructions had always been true and in harmony with the student's experience. Yet when it encounters the mind of anti-christ, the student suddenly begins to doubt that the teacher's instructions are true, and this is the opening for the mind of anti-christ to assume control over the student's mind.

Yet why was there room for doubt in the student's mind? Because the student had not yet attained true knowledge, the knowledge of reality that is possible only through the Christ mind. What *is* true knowledge?

***

How would you teach a young child not to touch a hot stove? The child has no concept of what it means that something is hot nor does it – yet – have any experience of what it feels like to touch a hot object. You could try to instill so much fear in the child that it dares not come near the stove, but that is not really teaching the child because it gives the child no understanding of why it should not touch the stove. In order to truly learn why it should not touch the stove, the child needs two things:

- It needs a base of experiences with the material world. It needs to experience that certain things are hot—hopefully without getting severely burned. And it needs to experience that certain things hurt.

- It needs to develop its reasoning mind so that it can transfer one experience to other situations. In other words, by experiencing that one object is hot and causes pain, it can transfer this to other objects. Thus, by being told that an object is hot, it knows why it should not touch it.

When the child has both elements, it can make a decision not to touch the object based on both experience and understanding. Thereby, the child has internalized knowledge, the knowledge has become part of the child's being. My point is that there is a fundamental difference between theoretical, intellectual knowledge and internalized knowledge that is partially based on experience. For example, you see in many work situations that some people have only theoretical knowledge and always "go by the book," whereas some people have developed a deeper sense of the best way to perform a task, a sense that is based on a fusion of theory and experience so the two form a whole. If you have only theoretical knowledge, how can you really know that the theory is accurate? That is why the scientific method is based on testing your theories through practical experiments, and it was because of this willingness to test theory against reality that Western civilization rose above the superstition of the Middle Ages.

The internalization of knowledge allows people to learn without making every possible mistake that could be made. In other words, you do not need to touch every hot object on the planet in order to experience that they all cause pain. You simply need a few experiences and then you know not to touch certain objects. My point is that after you gain some experience, you can use the reasoning mind to learn without having a direct experience. Yet until you have some experience, the reasoning mind is not enough in itself.

We now see that when you mature, you begin to build a foundation for evaluating knowledge. For example, you might be told about a new concept and you immediately compare it to your internalized knowledge. If what you are told seems to contradict your previous experiences, you would naturally be suspicious and possibly reject it without taking a closer look. This is both a strength and a weakness, because your previous experiences can either form a platform for evaluating new ideas or they can become a prison for your mind, causing you to reject new ideas.

Your internalized knowledge becomes part of your worldly sense of identity, the sense of identity you build based on your experiences in this world. You can potentially build a sense of identity that does not allow for the fact that you are a spiritual being in a human body. Most children in the modern world are indeed brought up – even if they are brought up in a religion – without a true understanding of their spiritual identity. Thus, if they are presented with a teaching that says they are spiritual beings, they will tend to reject it and they will use their internalized knowledge to justify this. My point being that your sense of identity can become a closed circle, leading to what is often called circular logic. If the experiences and knowledge you were given during childhood say you are only a human being, you will tend to reject the idea that you are far more than a human being. The difference is whether you are reasoning based on the mind of Christ – which gives you true knowledge of God's reality – or the mind of anti-christ, which gives you a mental image of an illusion that is completely separated from God's reality.

The central problem is that the knowledge and experience you gain in the material world gives you a very limited view of the spiritual world. You cannot see the spiritual world with your physical senses and it cannot – yet – be detected with scientific instruments. Thus, most religious people have an intellectual, theoretical knowledge of the spiritual world, but they have very little experience to back it up. This is why so many religious people find it difficult to actually live the spiritual teachings in which they profess to believe. They cannot internalize the theoretical knowledge, they cannot walk their talk, which is the cause of so much hypocrisy in the field of religion.

What can be done to change the equation? How can you gain a direct experience of the spiritual realm, God's Being and God's Law? You can do so only by using the Christ mind. The challenge here is that many religions claim that you cannot personally contact the Christ mind because you need an outer religion to get to God or God's kingdom. You need some kind of external mediator, be it a church or even an outer savior. Yet the reality is – as Jesus, the Buddha and all other true spiritual teachers have said – that the kingdom of God is within you. God has written his laws in your inward parts (Jeremiah 31:33) and you do have access to the Christ mind right within yourself. Thus, you need no outer person or institution in order to gain true knowledge of the spiritual realm. Which is why the goal of all true spiritual teachers is to bring you to the point of enlightenment, where you realize your connection to your source and thus you become spiritually self-sufficient.

The Christ mind has a reasoning faculty that is higher than the intellect and human rationality and logic. Thus, the Christ mind can give you general, theoretical knowledge about the spiritual realm.

Many spiritual people on Earth have indeed learned to access this higher reasoning. Yet even this reasoning is not enough in itself. The Christ mind also has the ability to give you a direct experience of God's Being, God's reality and God's law. And only when you have both the direct experience and the higher reasoning will you fully internalize spiritual knowledge.

We now come to a subtle point that will require you to go beyond how most people learn on Earth. The Christ mind will not give you external knowledge. Having a theoretical and intellectual knowledge of spiritual concepts is not the same as having Christ consciousness. The Christ mind gives you a special form of knowledge that the ancient Greeks called "Gnosis." The true meaning of Gnosis is oneness between the knower and the known.

On Earth most people learn by acquiring knowledge about an object which they clearly see as being separate from themselves. You will recall our previous discussion about the difference between having a direct experience and having only a mental concept. A geologist might be an expert in mineral formations and he might even have a great intuitive sense of how geological processes work, but he has never experienced what it is like to be a rock. Yet the reality is that nothing was made without the Christ consciousness, so there is Christ consciousness within a rock. The rock does not have self-awareness, but it is still made from the Christ consciousness. Likewise, your conscious self is made from the Christ consciousness. This gives your conscious self the ability to identify itself as anything it chooses, meaning that it can project itself into a rock and experience the consciousness in a rock.

Obviously, this is a silly example, but it illustrates the central point. Some spiritual teachers have actually had their students meditate on inanimate objects until they experienced oneness with the object. This can be a valid preparation for expanding the conscious self's ability to identify itself with its own higher being and with its source, the Creator itself. In order to attain true knowledge about anything in the spiritual realm, you need to get to the point where your conscious self has identified itself with whatever it is you want to know. If you want to get the full knowledge from a spiritual teacher, you need to become one with the teacher and experience the teacher's consciousness. If you want to know God's law, you need to become one with the law, to become one with the mind that defines the law,

namely the universal Christ mind. Thereby, you
action. If you want to know God, you need to be
This oneness is possible through the Christ min·
– after he attained the full Christ consciousnes
my father are one" (John 10:30). We now reac..
many people have been programmed to consider blaspı...,
human opinions have not changed reality: The only way to *know* God
is to *be* God!

My overall point here is that as long as there is a separation
between you – as the knower – and the object of knowledge, there is
room for doubt. Only when you attain oneness between the knower
and the known will doubt become an impossibility. And that oneness
can be attained only through the Christ mind which is the unifying
element in everything that exists.

***

I would now like to give you the master key to understanding what
happened in the Garden of Eden. The essential difference between the
mind of Christ and the mind of anti-christ is that the Christ mind is
based on Oneness whereas the mind of anti-christ is based on separation. The purpose of the Christ mind is to ensure Oneness between all
elements of creation. One aspect of attaining this unity is that the
forms created from the Mother Light must express the Creator's
intent and laws. However, this can happen only when all beings have
a sense of oneness with their Creator and its laws, so they – out of
pure love and the sense of Oneness with God and oneness with each
other – express their creativity within the framework defined by the
Creator. The mind of anti-christ makes you doubt that you can or
want to become one with the teacher and the Christ mind. It makes
you believe you can or should cling to a mental image, instead of
going beyond it to experience oneness—gnosis.

The Christ mind is truly designed to give self-aware beings a way
to always know the truth, whereby their creative efforts will always
support all life. That is why Jesus said, "I am the way, the truth and
the life, no man cometh to the father but by me" (John 14:6). Jesus
came to demonstrate the path that leads to Christ consciousness, and
he did so by walking the path himself until he attained the ultimate
goal of the path. What is that goal? It is to come into oneness with the

.sal Christ mind, whereby you become the Living Christ. You *know* that you are one with the Father, the Creator, and you real-.e that Christ consciousness is the *only* way to come to the Father. The Christ consciousness is the *way* to the one *truth* that gives you eternal *life*.

This is your highest potential on Earth, and when Jesus had attained that state of Oneness, he made his famous remark. Clearly, that remark has been misinterpreted by many Christians to mean that the outer religion of Christianity is the only road to salvation. Yet this interpretation can come only from the mind of anti-christ, for the Christ mind clearly sees that you will not be saved by belonging to an outer religion. You will be saved only by coming into Oneness with the Christ mind itself, which has been the message given by all true teachers on Earth. Jesus came to demonstrate this Path of Oneness, and the *only* way to be a true follower of Jesus is to strive for oneness with Jesus, whereby you become the Living Christ on Earth. Gautama Buddha also demonstrated the Path of Oneness, and the only way to be a true follower of the Buddha is to strive for oneness with the Buddha, whereby you become the Living Buddha on Earth.

The true spiritual path is the Path of Oneness. Ultimately, this means that you attain oneness with your own Higher Self and then oneness with the spiritual hierarchy that leads to your Creator. Yet until you can experience your Higher Self and the Creator directly, you strive to attain oneness with an outer teacher that you *do* see. In other words, the Garden of Eden was a spiritual schoolroom with the sole purpose of helping the students find and successfully complete the Path of Oneness. I, Maitreya, was the head teacher in that schoolroom and I taught the Path of Oneness by offering the students to come into oneness with me as an intermediate step to coming into oneness with their higher beings. Why is the Path of Oneness so all-important? From our previous discussion we can see that you can attain true knowledge about an object only by becoming one with the object. Thus, the only way for a spiritual teacher to pass on his or her knowledge to a student is for the student to come into oneness with the teacher. Only through that oneness will the student know everything the teacher knows. Likewise, the only way to know God is to come into oneness with God. When you realize this, you see why the only way to *know* God is to *be* God.

As I said, this statement will be very provocative to many people, who will instantly label it as blasphemous. Yet where does this judgment come from? It cannot come from the mind of Christ, which is always one with the Creator. Thus, the only place from where it can come is the mind of anti-christ, which is the opposite of the mind of Christ and thus always sees itself as separated from God—or rather from its graven image of God.

My underlying point is that you truly *are* created as a spiritual being. You truly *do* have the potential to grow from your present state of consciousness to the full God consciousness. Yet you can do this *only* by walking the path that leads you to oneness with your own Higher Self and then oneness with your Source. This walk is an inner process, and it should be a matter *only* between you and your God. No force in the world of form should ever come between your conscious self and its direct, inner connection with its Higher Self and its Creator. That is precisely why the first commandment is to never have any other gods before the One true God. And that is why the second commandment is to never let a graven image come between your conscious self and its direct inner experience of its Source. That is also why the Bible states, "Behold, I come quickly: hold that fast which thou hast, that no man take thy crown" (Revelation 3:11). Your crown, your most valuable possession, is your direct inner contact with your higher being.

Do you now see the true meaning of a "graven image?" It is an image that separates your conscious self from having the direct, inner experience of its Source. It is an image that separates the knower from the known. It is an image that comes between you and God and thus separates you from God and from the Path of Oneness. Obviously, an image that separates you from God can come *only* from the mind of anti-christ, which is the only mind that can see itself as separated from God. Thus, a graven image is truly an image of God, the world and yourself that springs from the mind of anti-christ. The most direct effect of this image is that it makes you doubt that you can come into Oneness with your Creator. This doubt causes you to deny your divine potential, causing you to deny God where you are—and this is the true meaning of blasphemy. Any mental image implies distance. True knowledge is when all distance falls away because you are now one with the object of knowledge. You *know* because you *are*. You are worshiping God in Spirit and in truth.

Truly, the mind of anti-christ is the source of all blasphemy. Yet the mind of anti-christ has also created its own dualistic images of blasphemy and many people believe in them. That is why they believe it is blasphemy to accept your divine origin and potential. Which explains why such people accused Jesus of blasphemy when he declared his Divinity (John 10:33). The true meaning of blasphemy is that you have created a mental image of God and you are worshiping this idol. Yet those who are trapped in the mind of anti-Christ think their idol really *is* God, and thus they want you to believe that questioning their mental image is blasphemy and will send you to hell. It is foreseeable that such people will also label this book as blasphemous, whereby they truly demonstrate that they are followers of the false teachers of anti-christ.

We can now see that Genesis does not give the full story of what happened in the Garden of Eden. It only tells the story of those students who decided to leave the Path of Oneness and instead follow the path of separation. Thereby, these students lost the connection to the true spiritual teachers – represented in the Garden of Eden by myself – and they began to follow the false teachers, the teachers who had already become blinded by and identified with the mind of anti-christ. The Path of Oneness is the path of eternal life. The path of separation is the path of spiritual death. That is why I told Adam that if he ate the forbidden fruit, he would surely die. Once he stepped unto the path of separation, the gravitational force would make him descend further and further into the consciousness of death. His true identity would be snuffed out and there would be nothing left. He would be dead in the true sense, namely that his self-awareness as an individualization of God would be erased. That is why Jesus said that in order to enter the kingdom of God, you have to be spiritually reborn (John 3:3).

This raises the questions of why the Serpent was allowed to be in the Garden, who the Serpent was and where it came from. These questions will be answered in a coming chapter, but I first want to give you a deeper understanding of the consciousness of anti-christ and why it can be so difficult to see through this veil of willful ignorance once you have stepped through it and lost your lifeline to God's reality. What happens when a self-aware being becomes a blind follower of the blind leaders who think they see all?

Key 11
What it means to be spiritually reborn

We now need to pull together some of the ideas we have considered in the previous chapters, so we can get a clearer picture of what happened to those students who separated themselves from the teacher. We have seen that a new student starts out with a limited self-awareness and sense of identity, much like an infant on Earth. As the student grows, it builds a sense of identity, but the identity is heavily influenced by the environment—again much like a child on Earth. As a child on Earth is influenced by two factors, so is a student in the cosmic schoolroom. The two factors are its parents and its peers. I represented the parent to the students in the Garden of Eden and, of course, the other students were the peers. A student can develop an identity that goes in one of two directions. It can grow closer to the teacher or it can grow further away from its teacher, much like a child on Earth grows closer to its parents or closer to its peers.

We now come to a subtle but crucial point. I have said that the path I offered my students was the Path of Oneness, whereby students would come into oneness with me. I realize that for people on Earth this will sound like my students had to become slaves or clones of me or that they had to submit their own will to my will. Yet it is essential for you to understand that oneness does not mean sameness.

As I have explained, a new co-creator is an individualization of God's Being and is created for the purpose of starting out with a separate sense of identity and then growing to the full God consciousness. In doing so, the co-creator becomes one with its Creator without blending back into the Creator's Being. If a co-creator – as a unique individual – became the same as the Creator, the individual being would cease to exist. It would simply blend back into the Creator's Being from which it came, much like a wave that blends back into the ocean when a storm subsides.

Yet the true purpose of creation is *not* that you struggle for a long time to build your identity and reach a higher state of consciousness only to disappear as an individual lifestream. On the contrary, the purpose of creation is that your individuality grows until it becomes immortalized—which means it can continue to grow indefinitely. However, because everything was created out of the Creator's Being, your path toward God consciousness is to follow the trail that leads you back to your source. When a self-aware being attains a sense of oneness with its source while still preserving its individuality, it has attained God consciousness; it has become a God in its own right. In order to follow the trail that leads back to its Creator, a lifestream must become one with its higher being and the spiritual hierarchy that leads from itself to the Creator. Yet for new co-creators this can be difficult, which is why they are offered the intermediate step of oneness with a teacher.

The mechanics of the path are simple. The goal is to help you grow out of a very narrow, self-centered sense of identity by helping you become one with something that you see as larger than yourself. As you do this, you will eventually expand the boundaries of your sense of self until you realize that God is not greater than or outside your self because God *is* your Self.

I presented this Path of Oneness to the students in the Garden of Eden. Because it is a huge challenge for a new student to attain oneness with the Creator, I offered the students the Path of Oneness with a representative of the Creator with whom they could interact. By first becoming one with me, a student could go on to become one with its higher being. And then it could work its way up through the levels of the spiritual realm until it attained oneness with the Creator. Because the student started as a separate being, that first step into oneness with the teacher is clearly the most difficult. Once you have experienced coming into oneness with a larger being, it will be far easier to do so again with an even larger being, continuing on to the Creator.

Do you see what this truly means? I realize that many students – and most people in their current state of consciousness – think they suddenly appeared out of nowhere as separate beings. This is precisely what gives a student the opportunity to start out by seeing itself as a separate being and then gradually reconnecting to its source. Yet the reality of the situation is that you did not appear out of nowhere. As I described, the Creator projected itself into the very first sphere in the form of self-conscious beings. These beings then projected extensions of themselves into the second sphere and this process has continued all the way to the material universe. You are not a separate being that appeared out of nowhere. You are an extension of a spiritual being in a realm above the material universe. Yet that being is an extension of a being in a higher realm and so on until you reach the Creator itself.

In other words, all life is truly part of this Chain of Being and the Path of Oneness is a process of gradually expanding your sense of self by coming into oneness with the being out of which you came— continuing to do so until you reach the Creator and attain God consciousness. We might say you have come into being as the last link in a process of spiritual beings, a spiritual hierarchy, projecting extensions of themselves into a lower sphere. Your highest potential in life is to follow that Chain of Being back to your ultimate source. Doing so is the only way to attain a sense of meaning and purpose and overcome the sense of being alone or abandoned. It is only when you realize you are part of a larger whole that you will feel truly fulfilled and at peace. Obviously, every spiritual being that is above you in the Chain of Being, including the Creator, wants you to have that feeling and does not want to see you remain in a state of separation that can only cause constant suffering. Your spiritual "parent" loves you as itself because it sees that you *are* itself. You will feel fully enveloped in love only when you come to the realization that you love God as yourself because God *is* yourself, your Higher Self.

For the students in the Garden of Eden, I, Maitreya, was the lowest representative of the Chain of Being. They could not yet see the Chain of Being itself, so their opportunity was to come into oneness with me as the first step and then go on to become one with a Being on the next level up.

I know very well that many of the more mature spiritual seekers on Earth will look at the imperfect spiritual teachers or religious leaders they see on this planet and reason that they have no desire to come into oneness with such teachers. This is understandable, but the point of this book is to show you that there is an alternative, namely to come into oneness with your own Christ self and ascended teachers who have risen above the consciousness of anti-christ. You can go beyond any outer teachers and messengers and establish a direct, inner, personal contact with the spiritual teachers who are above the duality of the ego. And if you feel a reluctance to come into oneness with the beings who are above you in your own Chain of Being, then I must tell you that it is the ego that feels this reluctance. For the ego knows it will die when the conscious self overcomes separation and comes into oneness.

Yet consider that a physical teacher or messenger can still help you establish your direct inner connection, and thus it is valuable to learn from such teachers and honor those who demonstrate an example of the Path of Oneness. Therefore, heed the teacher, even when he appears in the humble disguise of an ant. The challenge of the ego is that it forms a closed box around your mind, and in order to break free, you must attain a connection to something beyond your own mental box—for while you are inside it, you cannot see beyond it. Thus, other people who are outside your box can become your teachers, and that is one of the main values of a true spiritual community, as we will discuss later.

***

As I said earlier, when a child on Earth grows, it smoothly transitions from one sense of identity to the next. And when this happens, the previous sense of identity dies and a new one is born. Although this is a distinct event – one identity dies and another is born – the child obviously has a continued sense of awareness and thus rarely even notices the transition. This was much the same for the young students in the Garden, who gradually transitioned from a very limited to a far more sophisticated sense of identity.

Yet even a child on Earth eventually reaches a sense of identity where it becomes more self-aware, more conscious of the fact that it has the power to deliberately change its sense of identity instead of having it shaped by outer factors. This is the point where the child takes responsibility for itself and becomes an adult. Obviously, I am describing an ideal scenario, and I am fully aware that many people on Earth can live an entire lifetime without actually taking responsibility for their lives and consciously changing themselves. Nevertheless, my point is that as the students in the Garden matured, they approached the point where they needed to consciously let the old identity die and build a new one. This was a change that was fully as dramatic as the change from a teenager to an adult on Earth, and students responded with a wide range of reactions.

Some sought to postpone the change, seeking to hold on to their childhood sense of identity. Others rebelled against the change and refused to let go of their old identity, while still others pretended like nothing needed to happen. As I described earlier, the Garden was a very loving environment, and I fully respected the free will of the students. Thus, I gave them a great deal of latitude, not only in terms of what kind of identity they would build but also how long they would take to approach the final exam of the cosmic school.

Nevertheless, the Law of Free Will demands that a student cannot take forever to reach the point of taking responsibility for its life and thus becoming self-sufficient. This is a point that has been much misunderstood by people on Earth, so we will look at it in the next section. However, my point here is that there did come a point when I, as the responsible teacher, had to confront students and tell them they could no longer postpone the essential choice, the choice expressed by Hamlet in Shakespeare's famous play, the choice to *be* or not to be.

A student will eventually come to a turning point where it will have to make a choice between the path of life and the path of death, between the path of becoming MORE or the path of becoming less, between the Path of Oneness and the path of separation, between the true path and the path that seemeth right unto a man, but the ends thereof are the ways of death. As the teacher in charge, I had to confront students with the necessity to make that choice, and it was in doing so that I had to run the risk that some students would rebel against having to choose. They could instead choose not to choose, whereby they would separate themselves from me and remove themselves from the Garden of Eden. More on this later, but let us first overcome some common misunderstandings about free will.

***

We have earlier talked about the fact that having free will comes with a price, namely that you cannot stop making choices. Every situation, every moment, presents you with at least two options, and you must choose one. I know that from your viewpoint on Earth, having to make choices might seem like a burden. Yet I hope you can sense that the Garden of Eden was a totally loving and supportive environment in which students had every opportunity to avoid any stigma related to making choices. In reality, making choices is the key to developing your self-awareness and your sense of identity.

By making a choice and experiencing that it has certain consequences, you can evaluate whether the consequences reflect the kind of individual you want to be. If not, then you simply change your choices – change yourself – so they produce the consequences you want. This then brings us to another aspect of free will that many people fail to understand. If a choice does not have consequences, you do not actually have a choice.

I know that when you experience choices that have unpleasant consequences, consequences that haunt you for a long time, you can develop a negative view of consequences. Nevertheless, when you think about it, you see that if your choices did not have consequences, how could you actually have a choice? If nothing happened no matter what you did, how could you have different options? Or if the same happened no matter what you did, how could you have options? In other words, making choices means having more than one option, and it is the difference in consequences that defines the options you have. Without consequences, there is no choice. If you come to a fork in the road, you must choose one way, but if they both take you to the same place, your choice was of no consequence and thus it was not actually a choice.

The final insight you need is that in the material universe, free will is inescapably linked to time. This is so because the entire purpose of the world of form is your growth toward God consciousness. The driving force in this growth is your free will and you have two basic options. You can choose to move closer to God consciousness or further away from it. Yet remember that the Creator has embedded a part of its own Being in you. You literally have a part of the Creator on loan until you attain God consciousness and now attain your own, self-contained self-awareness by uniting with the Allness.

The Creator has given you a part of its own Being and it has given you the free will to do with it whatever you want. Thus, you can literally imprison a part of the Creator's Being in a limited sense of identity and you can even choose to go against the Creator's vision and laws so that you refuse to take the Creator's Being back toward union with the whole. The Creator will allow you to do this, but the Creator does not want to have a part of itself spend forever being separated from the whole. Thus, the very fact that the world of form is evolving toward a goal sets a time limit on how long you can refuse to grow.

This means that a young student in the Garden of Eden had a certain time in which it could refuse to make the choice to commit to the Path of Oneness. Yet the student did not have forever to do this, and thus there would come a point when I had to confront a particular student. If the student then refused to let go of the separate identity it had created, that student simply could not remain in the Garden. It would then be "cast out," but not by an angry God employing angels with flaming swords. That is simply a dramatization born from the consciousness of the people who received Genesis. In reality, the student's consciousness would become so self-centered that it would sink into a lower vibration. Thus, it would not be able to even perceive the Garden and would now see only a realm of lower vibrations.

When you realize that everything is energy, you see that there are different levels of vibrations, such as the spiritual realm and the material universe. Yet even the material universe has several levels; four to be exact. The Garden of Eden vibrated within the spectrum of vibrations that define the highest level, called the identity realm or the etheric realm. Below it is the mental realm, below that the emotional realm and finally you have the material or physical realm, which is the realm you can perceive with your physical senses. This level has a lower level of vibration, meaning that it appears more dense than the other realms. The effect is that once your conscious self descends to the material realm, it will be far more difficult for you to maintain a connection to your Higher Self and spiritual teachers. Your vision will be fully or partly obscured so you cannot see anything beyond solid matter, and that is why you can forget your spiritual origin. You simply have no experience of the spiritual realm to give you direct proof that there is something beyond the material universe.

The Garden of Eden was not a physical garden that existed in a specific location as you see the Earth with your physical senses. The Garden of Eden was on Earth but it was – and is – in the identity realm. This realm coexists in the same "space" as the physical realm, but because of its higher vibrations you cannot see it with the senses. This is much like TV and radio waves of different frequencies that interpenetrate your living room without interfering with each other or being visible to the senses. When you turn your TV set to the right frequency, you see a certain channel. Likewise, by learning to turn the dial of your mind, you can learn to perceive higher realms than the material universe.

When a student had reached the end of its allotted time and still refused to commit to the Path of Oneness, that student would become so blinded by the lower vibrations of the mind of anti-christ that it could no longer perceive the Garden of Eden. It would then literally descend into the physical realm and take on a human body.

This is not all that strange, when you realize that you are more than your body. Most people on Earth were created as beings in the spiritual realm, and they then descended into the material realm. They first descended into the identity realm, where they received training in a cosmic schoolroom. When they were ready, they would graduate and descend into the material realm with a level of consciousness that made it highly unlikely that they would identify themselves with and as the physical body. They could enter the denser vibrations of the material realm without losing awareness of their spiritual source and identity. Thus, life in the material realm would not be a struggle and would not lead to suffering.

However, if a student did not pass the exam of the spiritual schoolroom, it would – when its allotted time ran out – descend into a physical body without having attained sufficient self-awareness. It would then instantly come to identify itself with and as the physical body. It might still have some memory of a higher realm, but it could easily lose this and come to identify itself as a purely material being that is the product of a random process of evolution. And, of course, since the conscious self is what it thinks it is, the student would then start acting like a human being rather than as a spiritual being in a human body. And since the universe is a mirror, what you send out is reflected back to you, so when you project the image that you are a human being, you become a self-fulfilling prophecy.

***

We have seen that a new student starts out with a limited sense of identity. As it matures in the Garden, it will – through both experimentation and by interacting with the teacher and its fellow students – build a more sophisticated sense of identity. Yet this will happen so gradually that the student does not fully realize that there are certain distinct steps on the path, and when you rise to a higher step, your old sense of identity dies and a new one is born. This death and rebirth simply takes place below the level of conscious awareness (for most students), much as it does for a child and teenager – even many adults – on Earth.

Yet there comes a point when the student has to take one of the major steps on the path, namely the step from unconscious growth to conscious growth. This is the point where a student can begin to become self-sufficient. How can you be self-sufficient unless you become aware of the process of growth and take responsibility for directing it yourself? This is ideally what should happen on Earth, and the spiritual definition of an adult is a person who is fully aware of its ability to consciously and willfully change itself. Unfortunately, this definition is not widely known, which is why many people reach adult age without taking responsibility for their lives, often preferring to let outer circumstances define who they are.

Do you see what is at stake here? A young student is not consciously aware of the growth process and its steps. It is simply going along with a process that is in large part determined by outer circumstances. Obviously, the Garden was a schoolroom where every aspect was designed to help the student grow, which is clearly not the case on Earth. Nevertheless, the young students were largely being pushed to grow by factors outside themselves. Some were more eager to work with the tools they were given and grew more rapidly, developing an awareness of the process that helped them take command over their own growth. Others resisted the process and did not develop a clear awareness of what was happening and how they could take command of the process.

The purpose of the process was to make students self-sufficient, and this could happen only when they became consciously aware of the mechanics of growth and decided to take command of their own growth instead of being pushed along by external factors. If you consider teenagers on Earth, you will see that they often go through a period of pulling back from their parents and perhaps even rebelling against their parents and society. Yet this pulling back is simply a necessary phase in the process of the student forging its own distinct identity. The ideal outcome is that the student comes to the realization of who it is and what it wants to do in life. It then sets its sights on this goal and in so doing it rejoins its parent's society on its own terms. Instead of being pushed along by its parents, its peers or its society, the student now chooses to consciously rejoin society because it realizes this is the best way to reach its goals. In other words, instead of allowing itself to be pushed along, the student now attains full awareness of how life works and consciously decides to take command of its own life within the framework of its family and society. We might say that the student had to pull back and look at the big picture in order to rejoin society out of its own, conscious choosing.

This is exactly what I hoped would happen to all students in the Garden of Eden. And in order to give students the opportunity to choose on their own, I gave them a great deal of freedom to pull back and work on developing their identity in private. Yet doing so did come with a built-in risk, and we need to understand why this was so.

***

The risk was that as students pulled back from the teacher, they could fall prey to the temptation to build their sense of identity based on the mind of anti-christ. Or they might use the dualistic reasoning of the mind of anti-christ to seemingly justify that they should not let their old sense of identity – the one built on innocent ignorance – die.

As we have seen, a new student has a limited awareness of its spiritual self and the laws of God. In other words, the student's world view is dominated by ignorance. As the student grows, the student attains more knowledge, but there will still be a fair amount of ignorance in the student's world view, meaning that its sense of identity will be partly based on ignorance. During the unconscious part of the student's growth, the student would regularly acquire a higher understanding of life, whereby the old sense of identity would naturally die and a new one be born. The student was unaware of this, but this lack of awareness could not continue when the student reached the point of having to become self-sufficient. The student now had to consciously transition from a lower to a higher sense of identity, which means that the student had to be willing to consciously let the old identity die. Instead of letting outer circumstances drive the transition, the student would now consciously see that it needed to rise to a higher level, and thus it would let go of attitudes and beliefs that blocked the change.

Most spiritual people will be familiar with this process, for in pursuing your spiritual growth, you have no doubt made some life-changing decisions, decisions where you deliberately decided to make a dramatic change in your life and let go of some of your old behavior, beliefs and self-image. For that matter, even transitioning through life requires such changes, such as going from elementary to high school, graduating and entering the work life, finding a spouse and having children. Perhaps you never thought about it, but in such life-changing situations, your old sense of identity dies and a new one is born, an identity that is adapted to helping you cope with your new situation. For that matter, the death of the physical body is just another transition, as reported by many people who have had near-death experiences.

Many students willingly and lovingly made this transition because they understood that letting go of a limited sense of identity would simply mean that they were instantly reborn into a higher sense of identity, meaning there was no loss but only a gain. Yet those students who had become partially blinded by the duality of the mind of anti-christ simply could not see this. They came to believe that letting the old identity die would mean a loss, and they feared they would end up with no identity. Some felt that I was trying to force them to give up the old identity and that this was unfair. I was fully aware of this, but actually had no intention of forcing a student. Thus, I could only hope that by allowing these students to pull back for as long as possible, they would eventually come to see what was in their own best interest and would then choose to rejoin the process of growth. This is much like parents on Earth who must sometimes be content to hope that their children survive the teenage years and move on to living productive lives as adults.

The critical point was whether the students who were affected by the mind of anti-christ would begin to see through the contradictions and inconsistencies of this mind. Would they realize that this mindset was actually imprisoning them behind a veil of illusions and stopping their growth? Some did indeed realize this and saw that their old sense of identity had become a prison that limited their minds and kept them apart from the process of life itself. Others, however, were so focused on seeing me as trying to force them that they came to resent everything I represented. They especially resented the fact that I had to present them with the absolute necessity of having to make a choice between the Path of Oneness and the path of separation. They had become as spoiled children who resented having any limits set for their behavior, thinking they should be allowed to do whatever they wanted for as long as they wanted.

This leads to another misunderstanding about free will, namely that if there are any restrictions whatsoever, you do not have free will. Certain students in the Garden came to feel that way, led along by the serpents—whose identity I will later expose. My point here is to show you that you do indeed have free will, but there are certain mechanical aspects of free will that you cannot escape. As we have seen, free will without consequences is meaningless. The purpose of life is growth and you grow by making choices and experiencing the consequences of those choices. Thus, you can literally do anything you want but you cannot escape experiencing the consequences of your choices. When you truly understand what I have told you so far, you will see that this is not a restriction of your free will. It is actually a safety mechanism designed to prevent you from becoming stuck at a certain level of consciousness and remaining in that state of suffering indefinitely.

My overall point here is that the Garden of Eden was designed specifically as a spiritual schoolroom in which students followed a process of growth. Thus, growth was the entire purpose of the Garden. A student had free will and could choose to set itself apart from the process of growth. Yet it did not have the right to do this forever, meaning that if the student refused to join the process of growth after a certain point, that student had no purpose for remaining in the Garden. If you do not want to learn from going to college, why remain in college? If you are not learning, you are better off going somewhere else where you might learn from a different environment.

The students in the Garden had a certain time limit, and when it ran out, they had to choose to join the process of growth or remain separated from the teacher. If they chose the latter, they could not remain in the Garden but would descend into a lower realm, usually into physical bodies in the material realm. They would then no longer be able to receive the teacher's instructions, and the teacher would no longer balance the students' karma. Thus, the students would now be in the school of hard knocks, where they would learn by experiencing the full weight of the consequences of their choices.

***

What exactly was it that the students had to give up in order to consciously join the Path of Oneness? Well, it was the sense of identity as a separate being, which the students had naturally built as a result of starting out with a limited and narrowly focused sense of self-awareness. This identity was built on ignorance, meaning that the students did not know and experience that they were extensions of the Chain of Being. Ignorance does not mean that the students knew nothing – they might know a lot about their environment – however they did not know the reality of their true identity and origin. They had built a sense of identity based on the material world instead of their spiritual selves. Consequently, they did not see the oneness with their own higher selves or the oneness with the teacher and they did not see the oneness with each other. They were like waves who did not realize they were connected to and a part of the ocean of Self.

As a side note, let me mention that many spiritual people on Earth have misunderstood the concept of becoming enlightened. They think an enlightened person knows something they don't know, that such people have some kind of secret formula that gives them special powers. Thus, some spiritual seekers study spiritual teachings for the purpose of finding this secret formula, much like some alchemists were searching for the philosopher's stone. Others think that if only they have a very sophisticated intellectual understanding of the spiritual side of life, they will find the secret formula, so they study outer teachings and can discuss any topic under the sun. Yet as Jesus said, unless you become as a little child, you cannot enter the kingdom (Mark 10:15). I am fully aware that some readers of this book are anxiously looking for the page where I will reveal the secret formula. Yet in reality there is no secret formula, and no amount of intellectual knowledge of spiritual topics will guarantee your entry into the enlightened stage. True enlightenment means that you overcome the illusion that you are a separate being, that you are separated from the Chain of Being, your Creator and other beings. So becoming enlightened does not mean you acquire more knowledge but that you change your perspective and now see the reality that was hidden behind the veil of separation. It is not a change in outer knowledge but a change in inner perspective. In fact, having sophisticated intellectual knowledge can often prevent you from attaining enlightenment, as proven by the scribes and Pharisees who used their scriptural knowledge to reject the Living Christ when he stood before them in the flesh (Matthew 5:20).

Let us now return to the Garden. The new students saw the teacher as being outside themselves, which was a natural phase. Yet as a student matured, it was also natural that the student would begin to realize that the teacher only wanted the best for the student. Thus, the student's trust in the teacher would naturally grow until the student realized that the teacher was not an outside force seeking to impose its will upon the student. On the contrary, the teacher represented the higher will of the student's own spiritual self. It was the choice of your higher being to send the conscious self into the material universe to start out with a limited self-awareness. Thus, it is the desire and wish of your own Higher Self that the conscious self grows in self-awareness until it realizes where it came from and why it came here in the first place. The teacher is charged with helping the student come to this realization, whereby you see that God's will is not the will of some external being, some angry God in the sky. On the contrary, God's will is actually the will of your own higher being, which is part of the Chain of Being reaching all the way to the Creator. Thus, following God's will is following your own higher will.

It must also be noted that following God's will or the teacher's will does not mean that you surrender your free will and have no choices. You still have infinite possibilities for expressing your creativity, but you are now doing it within the framework of God's laws, which means that you will not hurt yourself or other parts of life.

Key 12
Following a true teacher or a false teacher

As we have seen, the entire purpose of life is that you grow in self-awareness, which means that you overcome the limited and narrowly focused self-awareness with which you started the journey. You broaden your self-awareness, and in doing so you rise up the Chain of Being that leads toward full God consciousness. Yet in order to rise to another level, you must come into oneness with your own higher being. And the first step in that process is that you come into oneness with the spiritual teacher.

The challenge here is that if a student has been blinded by the consciousness of separation, the duality of anti-christ, it cannot see the Chain of Being and thus it can only see the teacher as being outside itself. Therefore, it will feel that if it gives up its separate sense of identity, it will have no identity left and will suffer a loss. Or it will feel it gives up its freedom to make its own choices by submitting to the teacher. Some students even felt that having to consider how their choices affected other students was a restriction of their free will. Since no self-aware being can bear the thought of having no identity, students who are blinded by the illusion of separation cannot give up their old sense of identity, and thus their new sense of identity cannot be born.

If a student has overcome the mind of anti-christ and seen through its illusions, the student will know that by giving up its old sense of identity, it will instantly be reborn into a new and higher sense of identity. Thus, such a student has no fear of loss and will gladly give up something that is less in order to gain something that is MORE. Yet when a student has become blind, it thinks giving up something can only lead to loss, and thus it will hold on to the old as if it was a matter of life or death. This literally puts the student in a catch-22 from which there is seemingly no way out.

Is there a way out? Of course, but the only way is that the student's conscious self comes to realize that it has been blinded by an illusion. What has really happened is that the conscious self has come to identify itself *as* the student's current sense of identity. Thus, the conscious self thinks it will die if that identity dies.

Let me expound on that thought. I have so far said that the conscious self of the student is charged with building the student's Omega identity, the identity that allows the student to interact with its environment and express its spiritual identity and creative powers. It is perfectly natural that the conscious self identifies with the identity it has built, but the conscious self is always more than any identity. The identity is like the costume in a theater that the actor of the conscious self wears during the play. Thus, if the sense of identity dies, the conscious self will not die, nor will it have no identity. It will instantly create a new sense of identity.

The only way out of the dilemma is that the conscious self realizes it is MORE than its current sense of identity and that its self-awareness is *not* the sense of identity but is simply expressing itself through that sense of identity. However, before the conscious self can attain a higher sense of identity, it must let go of its identification with the old identity. It must let the old identity die, which is exactly the process that Jesus demonstrated when he was hanging on the cross.

The cross symbolizes – among other things – your old identity that has put you in a position where you cannot move. You are paralyzed by your own self-created limitations. Even Jesus felt this way on the cross, crying out that God had forsaken him (Matthew 27:46). This signifies that even Jesus had certain expectations that made it hard for him to give up his old sense of identity. What was the essential key that set Jesus free from the catch-22? It was that he finally resigned himself to his own higher will and gave up the ghost (Matthew 27:50). He gave up the ghost of his old sense of identity, and by being willing to let the old self die, he opened the door for his resurrection into a higher sense of self. The cocoon must be left behind before the butterfly of self can take flight.

***

We now come to a subtle idea that will take some pondering. I have said that it was my goal to raise up the students to become self-sufficient. And I have said that the students needed to come into oneness with me. Does this sound like I am contradicting myself? If so, that is exactly how some of the students felt, but why did they feel that way?

They did so because they had become so blinded by the duality consciousness that they could not see what the path is all about. The reality of life is that you are part of the Chain of Being. You are a separate being in the sense that you have individuality, but you are not separated in the sense that you are disconnected from your source or from other beings. Because you started out with a limited awareness, you built a sense of identity based on the illusion of separation, meaning that you saw yourself as separated from other students, from your teacher and from your source. This sense of identity was based on ignorance and thus it was imprisoning you in a limited state.

What is the natural next step on the path? It is to escape this limited sense of identity, and how can you do this? You can do so only by realizing that although you have individuality, you are not a disconnected being but a part of a larger spiritual being. You are a wave on the ocean of self rather than a drop of water floating around in empty space. What I presented students in the Garden was a way to escape the limited, disconnected sense of identity by becoming part of something beyond that limited sense of self, something bigger than the limited self. The true path to spiritual freedom is to become one with your own higher being, rather than remaining trapped in the limited sense of identity that says you are a disconnected being.

What needed to happen to the mature students was that they would consciously recognize this dynamic and then voluntarily give up the sense of being disconnected from their teacher, their fellow students and their own higher selves. What I truly offered to the advanced students in the Garden was a true sense of community in which all are united – all have **come** into **unity** – around the true purpose of creation, namely to grow in self-awareness and to take command over the material realm. The story of Adam and Eve is the story of those students who failed to see this opportunity or who deliberately refused to let go of the limited sense of identity and come into unity with a greater sense of identity. They would not come into unity and thus could not remain in the community of the Garden.

Do you see the point here? Coming into oneness with me as your teacher did not mean that you would lose your individuality or free will. It meant coming into oneness with the will of your own higher being and the purpose for which your higher being sent you into the material realm. I was not forcing you to become something that you did not want to become. I was trying to help you reconnect to the will and vision of your own higher being, which is the only way you can ever feel fulfilled and at peace. As long as your lower being is out or harmony with your higher being, you are what Jesus called a house divided against itself (Mark 3:25).

The Path of Oneness must start somewhere, and for the students in the Garden of Eden it started by becoming one with me as their teacher. You come into oneness with the teacher in order to escape your old sense of identity as a disconnected being. You do this by consciously accepting a new sense of identity as one with a higher being rather than remaining separated from it. However, oneness means oneness in vision, purpose and the knowledge that following God's laws leads to growth whereas going against them leads to suffering. It does not mean loss of individuality or freedom. In fact, a separate identity is what takes away your freedom, and only through oneness with your own higher being can you experience true spiritual freedom.

***

Let me explain this in another way. A new student started out with a limited sense of identity. Yet you cannot function without a sense of identity, and thus a new student had to build a sense of identity based on its knowledge and experience. In other words, a new student inevitably built a sense of identity that was largely based on ignorance. This, of course, was perfectly in alignment with the purpose of creation, which is that a student starts out with an identity as a separate being and then grows in awareness. This is similar to a child on Earth who builds a sense of identity based on its immediate environment, which is very narrow in the first years of life. It is often defined by its parents and perhaps siblings and its home or a kindergarten. Yet as the child grows, it realizes the world is much larger than its childhood environment and the person gradually builds a broader sense of identity. Some people even go beyond identifying themselves based on their family, ethnic origin and nationality. They build a more universal identity as world citizens or even as spiritual beings who are only in this world on a temporary basis.

How can this growth happen? It can happen only when the student realizes that its previous sense of identity was based on ignorance, was based on an incomplete view of the world. And then the student must be willing to consciously let this former sense of self die so that it can create a new sense of identity based on a higher understanding.

My point is that there was nothing wrong or unnatural about a student having built a limited sense of identity. This was simply part of the natural process of growth. However, it was also part of growth that the student would let this limited sense of identity die and then be reborn into a higher sense of identity. Students had done this a number of times, but what the students in the Garden faced was the initiation of doing this consciously. And in doing this consciously, they had to deal with the temptation that is represented by the "fruit of the knowledge of good and evil."

In order for a student to willfully let its old sense of identity die, it must consciously acknowledge that the old identity is not ultimately real because it is based on ignorance. It will do so by using the Christ consciousness, which is the ultimate measure for what is real and unreal. As the teacher, I presented students with the Christ vision of what was real and unreal about their sense of identity. Yet the fruit of the knowledge of good and evil is a state of consciousness in which there is no absolute reality. In other words, by partaking of this state of consciousness, a student can refuse to acknowledge that its old sense of identity is unreal. The student can use the relative, dualistic logic of the mind of anti-christ to reason that it does not have to give up its old sense of identity or that it is not limiting itself. Thus, a sense of identity that was based on innocent ignorance now becomes turned into a sense of identity that is based on willful ignorance. The student refuses to accept the vision of reality presented by the teacher.

This causes the student to lose its connection to the real teacher, and thus the student ends up in a catch-22. The mind of anti-christ makes the student think that it does not have to examine its sense of identity. The reason is that the student either thinks its dualistic beliefs are absolute or that there is no absolute reality because any statement can be debated or questioned. The student quickly gets lost in a state of consciousness in which it is not consciously examining its life and sense of identity. The conscious self of the student retreats into a little cave in which it seeks to avoid being forced to make conscious choices. Instead of taking command over its life, the student has now turned itself into a victim of forces beyond its conscious control. Instead of driving the car with a clear vision of the destination, the student is just flowing with the traffic and has no idea where it will end up.

This is the unexamined life that Socrates said is not worth living. Yet as long as the student refuses to examine its life, it will not even realize that its life is not worth living. The net result is that the student now becomes unreachable for a true spiritual teacher—the student is no longer teachable. Of course, when a student is no longer teachable for the spiritual teacher, there is no point in the student remaining in the cosmic schoolroom. Thus, the student inevitably sinks into the school of hard knocks, where physical consequences become its teacher, consequences that are more difficult – although not impossible – to ignore or explain away through dualistic logic.

***

My point here is that certain students in the Garden had reached the initiation that could bring them to become awakened and self-sufficient beings by consciously building a new sense of identity based on true knowledge, namely the oneness of all life rather than the illusion of separation. However, this process did require these students to give up certain things that they had so far enjoyed. By having a sense of identity as being separated from your own higher being and other students, it becomes possible for you to act in certain ways that are virtually unthinkable when you see the oneness of all life. For example, you can maintain the illusion that you can hurt others without hurting yourself. Or you can pretend that you are better or more important than other students and that you can raise yourself up in comparison to them. Or you can pretend that you do not really have a higher purpose for your life but can continue to play with your childhood toys. In short, you can pretend that you don't really have to grow up just yet or that you are already fully grown. In any event, you think you don't have to listen to the teacher.

Another thing you could do by maintaining a separate sense of identity was to believe that you could actually hide things from the teacher. As I have said many times, the whole purpose of life is to start out as a separate being. Yet all life is truly one – because it comes from the same source and is created from the Creator's own being – and thus the sense of being separate must be based on ignorance, it must be based on an illusion. There was room for this illusion in the Garden, and I did indeed give students instructions and then withdraw from them in order to give them space to make their own decisions. Yet because I had overcome the sense of separation, I did indeed have a sense of oneness with all life, including the students in the Garden. So in truth, they could hide nothing from me. Yet as long as they held on to the separate sense of identity, they thought they could hide things from me, and that allowed them to do certain things that they would not have done had they realized our underlying oneness. Again, this was allowed so that students could eventually have enough of playing with these childhood toys and decide it was time to grow up. A student had a long time to play around in this twilight zone, but as I have explained, no student could do this forever.

There would inevitably come a point, where the students realized that they could not hide anything from me. Let us look at the quote again:

> 6 And when the woman saw that the tree was good for food, and that it was pleasant to the eyes, and a tree to be desired to make one wise, she took of the fruit thereof, and did eat, and gave also unto her husband with her; and he did eat.
> 7 And the eyes of them both were opened, and they knew that they were naked; and they sewed fig leaves together, and made themselves aprons. (Genesis, Chapter 2)

The reality was that while the students were innocent, there was nothing they needed to hide from the teacher. It was only when they had started partaking of the consciousness of anti-christ that they even began to entertain the conscious thought that they needed or wanted to hide something from me. Thus, it was only the mind of anti-christ that introduced feelings such as shame or guilt into the minds of the students. I did nothing to introduce such feelings; on the contrary I did everything possible to assure the students that they never needed to hide anything or feel badly about anything. Only the relative logic of the mind of anti-christ makes it possible to enter a value judgment that says certain actions are bad and committing those actions makes you a bad person who needs to hide from your teacher or your God.

So what was the psychological mechanism that made the students feel they needed to hide from me, even though I had done everything possible to help them never get to that point? It was that they used the mind of anti-christ to project qualities upon me that had nothing to do with the reality of who I AM. They literally started violating the first two commandments given to Moses. They created a graven image of me as their teacher, and they projected that image upon me, thinking it was the real me. The image made them believe they would be better off hiding from me, and thus how could I – without violating their free will – show them that their image was not real? They started thinking I would be harsh and judgmental toward them, and thus they felt it was better to avoid me altogether. They then withdrew from me, thus making it impossible for their graven image to be compared to reality and proven wrong.

This shows you an essential characteristic of the mind of anti-christ, which we will talk more about later. This mind creates a graven image of everything, it projects that graven image upon reality and then it uses the dualistic logic – which can prove anything – to argue that it never needs to compare the image to reality, that it never needs to question or look beyond its image. And this unwillingness to question your image of the world is precisely what puts you in a catch-22 where you can remain stuck for a very long time. Another problem is that before you can project a mental image unto others, you must first have projected it upon yourself. In other words, the image that the students projected unto me was simply a reflection of the dualistic image they had created for themselves. If the students thought I was an angry teacher, it was because they had come to see themselves as angry. Their anger against me was simply a reflection of their anger against themselves. My only desire was to set them free from such crippling self-images and negative feelings. Yet free will reigns supreme, and thus no one can save you from yourself—except your conscious self. But it can do so only by becoming conscious of itself as being MORE than its outer sense of self.

***

We now come to another subtle point that will require some contemplation. I have explained that as the students grew, they built a sense of identity that was to a large degree based on ignorance. Yet students eventually reached the point, where the next logical step was that they became consciously aware of the "mechanics" of how you build your identity. They could then begin to consciously build a new sense of identity based on a gradually expanding sense of oneness with the teacher, their own higher beings and all life.

Yet if a student refused to step up to that level of awareness, the student would hold on to its old identity as a separate being. However, the student could no longer do this based on innocent ignorance. Thus, what actually happened was that the student's old sense of identity – the identity that the student refused to give up and sought to preserve – would die anyway. That is truly why I said that if students partook of the fruit of the knowledge of good and evil they – meaning their old sense of identity – would surely die. Yet when the old sense of identity died, the student was immediately reborn into a new sense of identity. The problem was that instead of being reborn into a higher sense of identity based on the reality of Christ (the oneness of all life) the student was reborn into a lower sense of identity based on the unreality of anti-christ (that all life is separate).

Now comes the subtle point. Your conscious self is named this way precisely because it is conscious. The meaning is that once you have been presented with the reality of Christ, your conscious self cannot deny that reality and at the same time remain conscious of its denial. It simply cannot consciously deny reality once it sees that reality. Thus, when a student refuses to step up to the point of conscious growth, the conscious self of the student will inevitably retreat into a little cave in which it refuses to be in charge of the student's life. Essentially, the conscious self – which is meant to have dominion over your life – refuses to take command, refuses to make the important decisions in life. It refuses to make the essential decision to consciously take command, and in order to uphold that denial, it must stop making conscious decisions. Yet because the conscious self can never retreat back into innocent ignorance, it must now retreat into a cave of willful ignorance in which it confines itself to making unconscious decisions, meaning that the conscious self refuses to be aware of the real consequences of its choices. We might say that the conscious self refuses to remain conscious, and thus it puts itself to sleep. The process of recovering from this decision is the process of reawakening the sleeping beauty of the conscious self, so that you become conscious again and can take charge of your life. That is why, when asked who and what he was, the Buddha simply answered, "I am awake!"

The problem with the conscious self's decision not to make decisions is that you – meaning the identity that the conscious self creates as it retreats – simply cannot exist without making decisions. So if the conscious self refuses to make decisions – both the big life-changing decisions and the small day-to-day decisions – someone else must make those decisions. And that someone else is a new entity that is created the moment the conscious self makes the fatal decision to refuse to take conscious dominion over your life. This new entity is what I call the ego.

We will later talk more about the ego, but the essential idea you need to ponder at this point is that the ego is an entity created by you. It was not created by God and thus it has no ultimate reality nor does it have the potential to become an immortal spiritual being. The ego was born out of illusion and it simply cannot rise above the basic illusion of the separation of life. The ego is born out of a denial of the oneness of all life, and the ego is much like a computer program. A computer is programmed to do certain things, and it cannot change its own programming. It will continue to do the same thing indefinitely, unless you remove the program from your computer. The ego was born out of the conscious self's decision not to have dominion, not to be the Christ. The ego is programmed to defend and justify the decision not to be the Christ, and it will continue to do so until your conscious self decides to take back command of your life and remove the ego from the computer of the subconscious mind.

In fact, the ego is not a simple computer program, but is more like an operating system that decides how the unconscious computer functions. Within the framework of its basic identity, there are numerous specific computer programs – like the individual trees that make it hard to see the forest – that hide the ego and its true nature. These programs can change, and when you start the spiritual path, the ego can adapt to your new world view. Yet the ego will never change its basic programming of denying the oneness of life and your responsibility to be the Christ. Thus, the ego will simply use your new beliefs and vocabulary to keep you away from the Path of Oneness while believing you are actually making spiritual progress.

***

The most important consequence of the ego's denial of oneness is that the ego will deny the validity of a true spiritual teacher who represents the Path of Oneness. The ego is born out of your unwillingness to let the teacher confront you with the need to take the next step on the Path of Oneness, to step up to conscious growth. Thus, the ego will always deny the Path of Oneness and will deny the need for your conscious self to take command of your life. This is not because the ego is evil. The ego is as neutral as a computer program and has no evil intent. Yet the ego is born from willful separation, which is the consciousness of anti-christ. Thus, the ego simply cannot fathom the reality of the Christ mind, it cannot fathom the oneness of all life. Consequently, the ego firmly believes that you are a separate being and that you will always remain so. It thinks that if your separate identity dies, *you* will die. The reality is that the *ego* will die and *you* will be reborn as the spiritual being you were created to be.

The ego sees you as being separated from your source, from God. The ego can deal with God as a concept but can only see God as an external being who is seeking to impose his will upon you. The ego can never conceive of God as a part of your own higher being. Likewise, the ego can only conceive of you as a being who is separated from other beings. Thus, it sees other people as competition or threats, and this gives rise to all types of selfish behavior. The ego can never fathom the underlying oneness of all life, and thus it can never overcome the illusion that you can hurt others without hurting yourself. The ego will forever deny that your actions have consequences (for yourself) or will seek to explain away those consequences. The ego will never admit that its basic approach to life is wrong and will always look for ways to justify its approach, even using a spiritual or religious teaching to do so. That is why some people can feel justified in killing other people in the name of God.

The ego is born of your unwillingness to make decisions. In one sense the ego wants to make decisions for you because it was created so that the conscious self would not have to make decisions. Yet at the same time, the ego does not feel responsible for your life any more than a computer feels responsible for its actions. The ego is no more capable of admitting a mistake than a computer is capable of thinking that it is wrong for executing its programming. So the ego will never accept any responsibility or admit that its decisions were wrong. And in order to avoid having to take responsibility, the ego wants to follow an authority outside itself so that it can say, "It wasn't me, I just did what I was told."

In a sense, this was an excuse that students in the Garden could use as long as they were in a state of innocent ignorance and were following my directions. Yet as students matured, they needed to step up to the point of not blindly following my directions but doing so based on understanding. If they refused to do this, they would refuse to take responsibility for their lives. As a true teacher, I was absolutely committed to the student's growth, and thus I would eventually confront the student with the need to rise above this level. If a student refused to do this, the student would want to keep following an external teacher rather than taking responsibility for its growth. And since I, as a true teacher, would no longer allow the student to blindly follow me, the student would create the ego which would seek to blindly follow another external teacher. Obviously, such a teacher could not be a true teacher and thus had to be a teacher who was trapped in the illusions of the mind of anti-christ. Thus, the ego is predisposed to follow a false teacher, a teacher who claims the student can "be saved" without making conscious decisions.

This obviously raises the question of where such a false teacher came from and why it was allowed to be in the Garden of Eden, which I will answer in the next chapter. However, let us first look at a question that might have surfaced in the minds of some readers.

***

I have said that a new student is never tossed into the world without a life-line to its higher being in the form of a teacher with whom it can interact. I have said that in order to grow toward enlightenment or oneness, the student must follow a true teacher and come into oneness with that teacher. Yet why do you need a teacher in order to come closer to oneness?

The mechanics of life are quite simple. A new student is born with no awareness or remembrance of the spiritual lineage out of which it came. Thus, it has a very limited self-awareness that is narrowly focused on itself and its immediate environment. It is much like an infant on Earth who simply could not survive on its own but needs someone to take care of it. As I have explained, a new student needs the teacher for these immediate reasons:

- The teacher gives it the vital life energy that allows it to survive and express its creative abilities.

- The teacher gives it instructions on how to use its energy without harming itself.

- The teacher gives it feedback that allows the student to grow in awareness of its environment and of itself.

- The teacher protects the student from the destructive consequences of its unbalanced actions—preventing the student from destroying itself or others.

Consider what would happen if a new student had no teacher. In the material universe, matter is quite dense and the result is that most people on Earth cannot see anything beyond matter. Thus, the material universe could easily become a closed circle in which the inhabitants believe there is nothing beyond it. This is why many people on Earth believe they are nothing more than evolved animals and that their identity will disappear when the brain dies. We might say that a student starts out in a very small box, namely its sense of self. If the student had no direct, visible connection to anything outside its own identity box, it might think it was all alone or that it could not rise beyond a certain level. The identity of the student would become a closed circle in which the student's perceptions would confirm its aloneness and thus its separate sense of identity.

There is an inherent danger in the process of a spiritual being descending into a denser realm. Such a realm still has darkness left and thus contains illusions that hide the reality that the realm is not self-contained but is an extension of a higher realm. So when a spiritual being descends, it will inevitably forget anything outside the new realm, it will forget that it is an extension of a spiritual being in a higher realm. There is a very real potential that a new student can build a sense of identity based on its current environment and forget that it has the potential to rise above that identity and take dominion over its environment. Obviously, this is not what the Creator wants, since the purpose of life is that self-aware beings grow in self-awareness.

I have said that a new student builds a sense of identity that is largely based on innocent ignorance. Without a connection to a source of true knowledge, how would the student ever rise out of this ignorance? Ignorance is like darkness in that it has no substance of its own. You cannot simply remove darkness from a room and you cannot remove ignorance from the mind. Darkness can be removed only by replacing it with something that is different, namely light. But in order to do this, you must have a source of light, for light cannot come out of darkness.

Likewise, ignorance can be removed only by replacing it with knowledge, and knowledge cannot come from ignorance. There is nothing you can do to or with ignorance that will turn it into true knowledge. With that I mean that although you may know everything about how the material universe works – as materialistic science is currently striving to attain – the knowledge of this world will not tell you that there is something beyond this world. My point being that ignorance – in a spiritual sense – is not the same as knowing nothing. Spiritual ignorance means that you are ignorant of the fact that there is something beyond your environment, that everything came from the Creator's Being and that you can become one with the Chain of Being. Thus, a student can overcome ignorance only by being connected to a source of true knowledge, namely a teacher who has attained oneness with its source.

One might say that the overall function of a spiritual teacher is to give the student a connection to something outside its identity box. By interacting with the teacher, the student realizes that it is not alone. It also realizes that the teacher has reached a higher level of consciousness, a broader sense of identity, than itself, and this gives the student something to strive for. The student can then learn from the example of the teacher.

I am not hereby saying that a student could never grow on its own. As we will discuss later, there is an evolutionary force built into the Ma-ter Light that will give a student some growth. Yet that force cannot take the student to the point of enlightenment. Such a change of identity can come about only by interacting with beings who have already attained enlightenment. As I have explained, life begets life. Beings in a higher realm created you and those beings were created out of even higher beings and so on all the way to the Creator. We might say that a person on Earth is the latest link in the Chain of Being, and becoming enlightened means that the person expands its sense of identity until it sees itself as one with the Chain of Being above it. How can a student reach this sense of identity? Only by expanding the narrow identity with which it started its journey. And how can it do that? Only by connecting to something outside its box of identity.

***

The ultimate goal is that the student comes into oneness with the Chain of Being. Yet a new student has such a small identity box that it cannot make that transition in one giant leap. It must gradually expand its sense of identity so that it does not become scattered. Thus, the new student starts out by becoming one with a being that is more highly evolved than itself but not so much more evolved that the student cannot relate to this being. That being is the spiritual teacher, so the spiritual teacher is the open door for the student's entry into the Chain of Being. That is why Jesus said that he was the open door (John 10:9), as he represented the Christ consciousness to people on Earth.

My point is that the process of growth means that you expand your sense of identity by coming into oneness with a being that is MORE than yourself, that is outside the box of your identity—which would otherwise become a closed box. Yet as you come into greater oneness with the teacher, you come to a point when you can begin to see that even though the teacher is beyond your own identity, the teacher is part of something even greater, namely the Chain of Being. At that point, you can begin to attain self-sufficiency, meaning that you no longer need an outer teacher in order to connect to the Chain of Being. You realize the truth in Jesus' words that the kingdom of God is within you, meaning that because your conscious self is an extension of the Creator's Being – created through the Chain of Being – you can connect directly to the Chain of Being within yourself without going through an external teacher.

We might say that the role of a true teacher is to make himself obsolete by taking you to the point where you no longer need an external teacher to serve as an intermediary between you and your source. However, what really happens to enlightened students is that they go beyond seeing the teacher as a being outside themselves. Instead, they come to see the teacher as part of their own spiritual lineage, as part of the Chain of Being. So instead of discarding or bypassing the teacher, they now see that by going through the teacher, they gain access to everything that is above the teacher.

This presents a special problem for those students who have become blinded by the duality of the mind of anti-christ and have separated themselves from their teacher. There really is only one way for such students to come back to the Path of Oneness, namely that they must reverse the process that took them away from the path. They must attain a sense of oneness with their teacher, but this can be very difficult to achieve because of the creation of the ego which can never understand why you need a teacher. Thus, once the ego has been created, it puts people in a catch-22, and the only way out is that the conscious self begins to see the inconsistencies of the ego's illusions, thereby realizing it is more than the ego.

We will talk more about this in coming chapters. Yet my point here is that regardless of the many illusions created by the mind of anti-christ – the illusions that portray you as a separate being and thus say you do not need a teacher – you cannot attain enlightenment except by reconciling yourself with your own higher being. Enlightenment means oneness with your source, so unless you overcome separation, enlightenment is not possible. And overcoming separation also means overcoming the sense of separation from your teacher. There simply is no other way, even though the false teachers – as we will see – have attempted to create what seems like alternative roads to salvation. Yet the only valid road to salvation always has been and always will be the Path of Oneness.

***

Before we move on, let me summarize what we have discovered thus far. The process of life, the process of growth, can be compared to a spiral staircase. A new self-aware being was created at a certain level of (self-)awareness. We might compare this to the ground floor of a building or the zero on a scale, such as a thermometer. The Garden of Eden presented students with a spiral staircase that led them up from the level on which they started. In the beginning, they had no other way to go than up, for they were still so innocently ignorant that they could not even conceive of consciously going against the teacher's directions. Yet as they ascended the staircase, they would eventually reach the essential turning point, the point where they had to consciously commit to the Path of Oneness or consciously reject that path (at least for the time being).

If a student rejected the Path of Oneness, it would start descending the staircase toward progressively lower levels of awareness. This compares to a spiral staircase that leads down to the lower levels of a building and eventually leads below the ground floor to the basement. By following this path, a student would quickly descend below the level of awareness at which it started. At the starting level, the student was as an innocent child and had no selfish thoughts. Yet by following the path of denial, the student would inevitably become more and more self-centered and selfish, giving rise to all kinds of thoughts and actions that would be increasingly inconsiderate of other forms of life.

Obviously, a new student did not actually create the downward staircase, as it did not create the upward staircase. The downward staircase was created by other beings who had already chosen the path of separation and had thus carved out the steps of the downward staircase. These are the false teachers that we will talk about in the next chapter.

My point is that the student had two basic choices, as you have two basic choices right now. You can choose to follow a true teacher and go up the spiral staircase of life, or you can choose to let your ego follow a false teacher and go down the staircase of death. You really have no other choices, for if you are not consciously going up, you will be unconsciously pulled down. Thus, you must choose life or you must choose death, for there is nothing in between, even though the illusions of the mind of anti-christ make it seem that way.

The staircase of life, the Path of Oneness, has a number of floors, just like a spiral staircase in an old castle. Each floor represents a distinct sense of identity. Once you have reached a certain floor, you can spend quite a bit of time roaming the floor and exploring its various rooms. Yet eventually it will be time to go back to the staircase and climb to the next floor. However, in order to do this, you have to be willing to leave the present floor behind, and in doing so you must let the sense of identity built on that floor die.

When you do make the decision that you are willing to rise to the next floor and leave behind the old sense of identity – to put off the old human and put on the new human (Ephesians 4:22) – you have made a LIFE decision. As long as you are on a certain floor, you are making numerous decisions that help you explore that floor and internalize the knowledge it represents. These are not LIFE decisions in the sense that they do not take you to a higher level, but neither do they hinder your growth. In fact, they help you internalize the consciousness on the level to which you have ascended. It is only after a certain time that you need to find your way back to the spiral staircase and make a LIFE decision to rise to the next floor.

Each floor in the building represents a certain level of awareness, a certain sense of identity. Each floor gives you a progressively higher vision of life, much like the higher floors in a building give you a better view of the building's surroundings. If you keep making LIFE decisions, you will eventually reach the top of the building, and from the roof itself you will have a free and unobstructed view of the world. This is comparable to the Christ consciousness in which you see yourself as one with your source and one with the Body of God on Earth and in the spiritual realm.

The downward staircase also has a number of levels, and for each time you go to a lower level, you must make a decision. We might call this a Death decision because it takes you further down into the consciousness of separation and death. While you are on a specific floor, the ego makes the decisions for you, but the ego cannot make the decision that takes you to the next floor down. Only the conscious self can make LIFE and Death decisions. The trick is that as long as the conscious self refuses to take command, you will not be making conscious decisions. You will seek to avoid making decisions and you will allow the ego to present you with the need to make a decision and the information on which you base the decision. The ego cannot make Death decisions for you but it can influence how you make those decisions. The same goes for the false teachers who are using the ego as an inroad into your consciousness. A true teacher will give you accurate and complete information and leave you to make your own choice. The false teachers and the ego will give you incomplete and distorted information that makes it impossible for you to make a truly free choice. With that in mind, it is now time to consider where these false teachers came from and why they were allowed in the Garden of Eden.

Key 13
Why was the Serpent in the Garden of Eden?

At this point, it is foreseeable that some readers will feel that I have spent far to much time and gone into far too much detail in describing what happened to students in the Garden of Eden. Some might feel that my description somehow does not apply specifically to them. One reason might be that they did not originate in the Garden of Eden but in a different spiritual schoolroom, perhaps in a higher realm. As I mentioned earlier, there are other evolutions in the world of form, evolutions that were not designed to be co-creators but to perform other functions. As we will see later, the human beings who currently embody on Earth have come from many different points of origin, so it is difficult to say anything that applies to all people on Earth.

Yet my description of the Garden of Eden has certain universal elements that do apply to all of the people who currently embody on Earth, and that is why I have gone into such detail. For example, every aspect of life on Earth has been influenced by the duality consciousness. The only way to attain spiritual growth on Earth is to rise above the duality consciousness. And in order to do this, it is important to understand how self-conscious beings can become blinded by the duality consciousness without realizing what is happening. It is important for everyone to understand how the duality consciousness blinds you and traps you in a catch-22 from which there is no way out—unless your conscious self takes charge of your life by letting the old identity die, thereby being reborn into a higher sense of identity.

Regardless of where you have come from and how you ended up in a physical body on planet Earth, your only way to enlightenment is to follow the Path of Oneness, whereby you overcome the separate identity and come into oneness with the Chain of Being that leads from you to the Creator. And – as I have explained in the preceding chapters – the only way to overcome the catch-22 of your separate identity is to connect to a teacher who is not inside your identity box and can thus lead you out of it. Only by interacting with a being who is not blinded by your dualistic illusions can you overcome those illusions.

For some this will seem obvious, whereas others will sense a negative reaction in some parts of their being. Some of the beings who currently embody on Earth have a predisposition to reject the Path of Oneness, especially the idea that they need to follow a teacher and come into oneness with him or her. They are, so to speak, programmed against this process, but in reality it is their egos that are programmed. Thus, the only way to overcome this programming is to understand how the egos of these beings were created and why the very illusion that caused these beings to fall also prevents them from overcoming the fall and joining the Path of Oneness. In fact, the consciousness of these fallen beings has affected every aspect of life on Earth, so it is important for everyone to understand how and why spiritual beings can fall from their original state and end up on planet Earth. This is the topic we will explore next, and we will start by looking at the Serpent in the Garden of Eden.

***

In order to fully understand who the Serpent is and where it came from, we need to look beyond some common beliefs about the Bible, especially about Genesis. Obviously, if you believed in a fundamentalist interpretation of the Old Testament, you would long ago have rejected this book, so I assume you have already accepted that the Bible is not the infallible word of God. Thus, you should be aware that it makes no sense to take all of the generations mentioned in the Bible and use them to construct a timeline, according to which the universe was created 6,000 years ago.

In reality, the material universe is very old, as is the Earth. Certainly, modern science is closer to the real age – with their estimate of 4.5 billion years for the age of the Earth – than those who interpret the Bible literally. Yet even science has not fully understood its own theories, namely Einstein's proof of the link between space, gravity and time. It is simply not correct to see time as a linear phenomenon, thinking that one second is a constant that has had the same length from the beginning of time until now. In reality, time is not linear, and the length of a second varies depending on gravitational conditions. There are areas of the universe right now where a second is shorter or longer than it is on Earth. And during the long history of this planet, the length of a second on Earth has also varied, depending on the gravitational fields through which the planet moved and its own gravitational conditions, including the density of matter itself.

As a side note, even Einstein himself did not fully understand his own theories and made certain assumptions that will one day be proven incorrect, the most important of which is the assumption that the speed of light is a constant. Obviously, this cannot be the case if light rays can be bent by gravity—as Einstein proved. If light rays can be affected by gravity, they can also be slowed down or sped up by a gravitational pull. It is possible to measure the speed of light compared to something constant, namely an immovable backdrop of "absolute" space, which is what I have called the void. To an observer who can measure light compared to the immovable void, the speed of light will vary depending on the gravitational conditions through which the light is passing. The immovable void is the true constant – the ground state of absolute rest – that Einstein and other scientists have been seeking. In fact, what the theory of relativity really proves is that there is nothing in the material universe that is constant— everything really is relative, even the speed of light. In order to make their mathematical calculations work, scientists need a constant. Yet the true constant can be found only by looking beyond the relativity of the material universe. Thus, Einstein actually proved that without spirituality, science can never reach its ultimate goal of explaining the origin of the universe and life.

By comparing time to the void, it will be possible to set up an absolute time that does not vary with gravity or the expansion and contraction of space. This will one day become possible, yet even the best supercomputers of today are not up to performing the calculations needed. Furthermore, science has not yet recognized just how complicated a path the Earth is following as it is hurtling through what they call empty space, being pulled in various directions by different gravitational centers. Only by comparing the Earth's path to the absolute constant of the void itself, will science be able to trace the true path of the Earth and calculate her absolute age. This will also open up to the possibility of traveling back through time by following the Earth's exact course through absolute space.

My point for bringing this up is to show you that it is at present meaningless to set up a linear timeline for the age of the Earth or give you a precise date for when the fall took place or when the Garden of Eden was established. What is important is the recognition that the Garden of Eden story goes very far back, yet it does not record the beginning of intelligent life on this planet. There were self-conscious beings living in the energy field you today call Earth long before the Garden of Eden. The records of these beings and their civilizations are currently unsubstantiated by archeological findings and even most ancient myths. Yet Genesis itself has certain hints of the existence of such beings. Let us begin by looking at one of the obvious questions raised by the Genesis account:

> And Cain knew his wife; and she conceived, and bare Enoch: and he builded a city... (Genesis 4:17)

The preceding chapters in Genesis record that Adam and Eve had three sons, of which one was killed by his brother. So if the Bible is to be taken literally, Adam and Eve had only boys, which raises the question of where Cain's wife came from? This, of course, is a mystery that most fundamentalists, be they Jewish, Christian or Muslim, would rather ignore. Yet it is an undeniable fact that there is either a flaw in Genesis or there is something missing, which means you can either reject the Bible or look for the missing insight.

Can we resolve this mystery? We *can*, when we go back to my previous teachings that everything is made from energy and that the material universe is made from vibrations that vibrate within a certain spectrum. We have already seen that beyond the level of vibrations that is visible to the physical senses is the spiritual realm, which has several layers, or levels. We now need to consider that even the material realm has levels, set apart by their vibrational properties, much like the octaves on the tonal scale. There are four basic levels of the material world. Each level has certain subdivisions, but to make this less confusing, we will begin by looking at the four main levels. It is easier to visualize the four levels when you know that they correspond to four levels of your personal energy field, your mind.

***

Most people who are open to this book are probably already aware of this field, or aura, but let me give a very quick explanation. Because everything is energy, your physical body is also an energy field—this is simply a consequence of the theory of relativity. Your body appears dense only because your physical senses are tuned to the body's vibrational spectrum, and thus cannot see beyond matter or cannot see that matter is actually vibrating energy. Another consequence of relativity is that physical matter is made from more fundamental energies, meaning energies of a higher vibration. In other words, the gross vibrations of physical matter are produced from finer energies that were lowered in vibration. Science is already able to measure the vibrational level of the physical body and the vibrational level of feelings and thoughts. The vibrations of certain thoughts are so much higher than the vibrations of the body that it goes against physical findings and common sense to say that the brain produces these thoughts. Higher vibrations are not produced by lower vibrations—it is the other way around, meaning that certain thoughts originate at a higher level of vibration than the physical brain.

The brain simply acts as a receiver and transformer for such thoughts, much like a radio receives a program produced and broadcast by a radio station. The brain can distort thought waves, much as a radio receiver can distort sound waves, and the brain can produce certain lower thoughts (especially related to physical survival, which includes propagation). It should now be relatively easy for you to see that there is an energy field of higher vibrations surrounding and interpenetrating your physical body. This energy field is what makes it possible for you to think and feel, and it also houses your subconscious mind. Thoughts and feelings originate in this field – in your higher minds – and are then sent to the brain which conveys them to the conscious mind—sometimes in a distorted form. Let us now look at the four levels of the material universe and the mind:

- The identity or etheric level. This level is the highest level, meaning that it is closest in vibration to the lowest spiritual realm. This level stores the original blueprint for the creation of the Earth. On the personal level it houses your sense of identity, which is what your conscious self is responsible for creating. Your identity is the foundation for your expression in the material realm.

- The mental level is the level of thought, and this is where your thoughts take a more concrete form.

- The emotional level is obviously the level of feelings and it is here your thoughts are imbued with direction and momentum that translates them into action.

- The physical level is the level that is visible to the physical senses. Some people can perceive the higher levels because they have had their senses sharpened, but most people cannot see beyond the level of their physical bodies. This is the level where you take physical actions and reap their physical consequences. Yet your actions begin at the level of your sense of identity; they are ultimately expressions of how you see yourself.

The main image you need to get out of this sketchy explanation is that there is a flow or a stepping-down of energy from higher to lower vibrations. As I have said, everything is made from the Ma-ter Light that has been lowered in vibration. Thus, the energy in the lowest spiritual realm is lowered in vibration in order to create the identity realm. The energy in the identity realm is lowered in order to create the mental realm, and so on to the physical realm itself. On a personal level, you receive spiritual energy from your I AM Presence, and it enters your identity body. Here, it is colored by your sense of identity and stepped down so it can enter your mental body. Your thoughts will further color the light and step it down to the emotional body, where your feelings will do the same before the energy enters the level of the physical body and is translated into conscious thoughts and physical actions.

As you move from higher to lower vibrations, everything becomes more dense, meaning that it is less fluid and thus harder to change. It should be easy to see that your thoughts are quite airy and can easily be changed. Once a thought has been imbued with emotion, such as anger, it is much harder to change. And, obviously, once a thought/emotion has been translated into action, it will release a physical reaction that can be very difficult to change or neutralize. It is common sense that you can think about a lot of things without actually doing them. Yet once a particular thought has been infused with a strong emotion and reinforced over time, the temptation to carry out the thought becomes much harder to resist. Still, thinking about harming another person and feeling strongly about it is not in itself illegal. Yet once you take action, it is impossible to turn back the clock and make your action – and its consequences – undone.

The vision I am giving you here is that there are four levels of the material universe that co-exist within the same "space," only at different vibrational levels. This is not hard to imagine when you consider that radio waves, television waves and many types of cosmic rays penetrate your living space. Because they have different frequencies, they do not interfere with each other, which is why you can turn the dial on your radio and tune in to different stations. You can even listen to the radio and watch TV in the same room, should you so desire. Likewise, the spiritual realm is not actually above you in a physical sense—heaven is not a canopy covering the Earth as people used to believe. It interpenetrates the same space as the material universe, only at a higher vibration.

We can now see a relatively simple explanation of the mystery of where Cain's wife came from. The fact of the matter is that the Garden of Eden did not exist as an actual location on the physical Earth. It existed in the higher vibrational spectrum of the identity realm, or octave. What really happened when Adam and Eve fell was that they experienced such a drop in the vibration of their consciousness that they were no longer able to perceive the higher vibrations of the Garden. We might say that your conscious mind is much like a radio receiver. As I said, your conscious self has the ability to identify itself as anything it chooses, meaning that it can project itself anywhere it chooses. Before the fall, the conscious minds of Adam and Eve were "tuned" to the radio station called the Garden of Eden. After the fall, their conscious minds were tuned to the material vibrational spectrum.

Because the conscious self is the core of your identity, your total being is a slave of your attention. Where your conscious attention is focused, the rest of your energies will follow. Thus, the lifestreams, the energy fields, the Omega identities, of Adam and Eve literally descended into the physical vibrational spectrum, where they took on – merged with – physical bodies. In that spectrum, there were already many beings living in human-like bodies, so Cain and Seth simply found wives among these and produced offspring.

Obviously, this explanation leads to the additional question of where these human beings had come from. However, I would like to put that aside for now and return to it later, when we have a better foundation for understanding it and when it will not complicate the central issue of this chapter, namely where the Serpent came from.

***

As we have discussed, there are four levels of the material universe, corresponding to four levels of vibrations, four levels of density. But why are there four levels, why not simply one? Well, when the first sphere in the world of form was created, it did have only one spectrum of vibrations. It was created at a certain level, and it was then raised in vibration from there. This also holds true for several of the other higher levels.

I have explained that the purpose of creating a sphere that is set apart from the void is to give self-transcending beings the opportunity to start out as separate beings. This is attained by creating a sphere where the intensity of light is so low that it allows for the illusion of separation to exist. The beings in the sphere are meant to grow in awareness until they see themselves as one with their Creator and one with all life. In the process of raising their own consciousness, they also bring more light into their sphere and raise its vibration, until it ascends and becomes part of the spiritual realm.

Yet as the process of creating new spheres progressed, there came a point when not all of the beings in a sphere were ready to ascend when the sphere itself ascended. Thus, the question arose of what to do with the beings who were not willing to raise their consciousness? The obvious answer was to allow them to descend to the newly created sphere, the next sphere set apart from the void. In such a new sphere, there would still be enough darkness left, there would still be such a low intensity of light, that the beings with a lower level of consciousness could continue an existence there. They could maintain the illusion that they were separate beings, which was no longer possible in their old sphere. Thereby, such beings could receive additional opportunities to get back to the path of becoming MORE and rejoin the River of Life.

When a new sphere is created, it is the original model to create it at a certain level of vibration, a certain level of density. My point being, that according to this model there would have been only one level of vibration in the sphere in which you live. Yet there were several groups of beings in the sphere above yours – some of whom had come from even higher spheres – who were not willing to rise above their old state of consciousness and ascend with their sphere. Thus, it became necessary to design the new sphere so that it could provide a place for these beings, a place that was adapted to their level of consciousness. In other words, the density of the new sphere was adapted to the density of the consciousness of these groups of beings. That is why this sphere was designed with four different levels, ranging from not very dense (the identity realm) to very dense (the physical realm).

This now adds a complexity to the purpose of this sphere. In the higher spiritual realms, there was a very clear and simple purpose. Self-conscious beings could basically focus on their own growth and walk the Path of MORE until they were ready to ascend to a higher level. It was not their concern how other beings grew, as those who did not grow would simply be left behind when the sphere ascended. Yet by the time your sphere was created, there were so many of these "left behind" beings that a shift in purpose occurred. Instead of simply designing a sphere in which beings were meant to focus on their own growth, this sphere was – from the very beginning – designed to serve a dual purpose. One was to give new co-creators an opportunity to start out as separate beings and grow in awareness. The other was to attempt to awaken those who had been left behind when previous spheres ascended.

We now see that there are (at least) three distinct reasons why a specific being might be in the material universe:

- A being might have fallen into this realm because it was not willing to self-transcend when the sphere that is now the lowest spiritual realm ascended. Such a being might actually have originated in a higher sphere and have fallen through several levels.

- A being might be a new co-creator who was created to descend to the material realm and grow from there.

- A being might have voluntarily descended from a higher realm in order to either help the fallen beings or the new co-creators grow in awareness. These are beings who had already become spiritually self-sufficient in a higher realm. Yet instead of continuing their personal growth, they volunteered to help those below them grow. This is a concept that in Eastern religion is known as the Boddhisatva ideal.

We now see that the most general explanation for the origin of the Serpent is that "Serpent" refers to a group of beings who fell in a higher realm and thus descended to this latest sphere. It now becomes clear that the Garden of Eden was not as neat and tidy of a place, not as much of a paradise, as most people have been brought up to believe. In reality, it was a mixed environment, and this obviously raises some questions that we will look at next.

***

Given that so many people have been brought up to think of the Garden of Eden as a paradise, as an ideal place where there was nothing bad, nothing evil, it is understandable that people will have mixed feelings about being told that they were brought up with an incorrect impression. Some people might feel betrayed by God, thinking that God really should have created them in an ideal environment, where there were no temptations and thus no risk of falling. And although it is very understandable that people feel this way, we can now see that this simply is not a realistic expectation. In fact, it is an unrealistic expectation that has deliberately been forced upon humankind by beings who are seeking to hide a certain truth. More on this later.

Let us admit that the expectation that the Garden of Eden was a pure paradise is non-constructive for a spiritual seeker and can only hinder your personal growth. It is simply one of those myths that must be left behind as you grow, much like the myth about Santa Claus or the tooth fairy. However, in order to make this easier, let us look at the reasons why this myth is so persuasive and why it really is a myth:

- Any being on Earth has a built-in longing for a place that is better than what they see around them on this planet. This is a safety mechanism built into the Ma-ter Light itself, making everything long for something more. A being who has descended from the spiritual realm might have no conscious memory of that realm, but it will have a largely unconscious sense that something is missing on Earth, that things are not right and should be better. This is partly a deeper memory of how things are in the spiritual realm, where there is no longer anything evil, where there is no longer room for deception and lies, such as what the Serpent presented to Eve. Yet for co-creators in embodiment, it is also a sense that they are here to make things better, to bring paradise to Earth.

I am in no way saying that you should give up the hope of bringing paradise to Earth, for that is likely the reason you came to this planet and it remains a realistic goal. In fact, the myth about the Garden of Eden, at least in its present form, is deliberately engineered to take advantage of your deepest memories about the spiritual realm and your deepest hopes about the future. It is designed to stir those dreams and hopes and then squash them by giving a subconscious message that this can never happen again on Earth, that Paradise on Earth is lost forever. We will later take a closer look at who engineered this myth and why.

What I am saying here is that you have an inner knowing that there is truth in the dream of a Paradise on Earth. I do not want you to leave behind that inner knowing or the hope of seeing it come to fruition. What I do want you to leave behind is the lie that Genesis describes a real paradise, for such an edenic place has not yet existed on Earth. It is, as I have described before, the plan that this sphere, including the material universe, will eventually be raised in vibration until there is no longer room for anything dark or evil, and thus it ascends and becomes part of the spiritual realm. Yet there never was a true Eden on Earth, although there have, in past ages, been communities, even entire civilizations, that were at a much higher level of sophistication than anything you see today.

- The myth that Eden was a true paradise was never realistic to begin with, and this is proven by the story itself. There could be no Serpent in a real paradise. The problem is that the mainstream religions that honor Genesis have glossed over the existence of the Serpent. This was done because they did not have the knowledge of the true identity of the Serpent, but this ignorance was partly engineered by changing the original story, as we will see later.

- In previous chapters I went to great length to explain the nature of free will. Thus, it should be possible to see that an inevitable companion of free will is the temptation to use it to go against the Creator's purpose, vision and laws. When you understand this, it is no longer realistic to expect that you could ever be in a Paradise where there was no temptation. As long as you have free will, there will be at least a theoretical temptation to misuse it. Yet the higher your level of Christhood – the higher your level of oneness with your own higher being, with all life and with your Creator – the less the temptation. By attaining Christhood you create your own inner Paradise. But it simply is not realistic to expect that God should have created you in such a state from the beginning. This is a dream that springs from what I have called innocent ignorance, so there is no reason to blame yourself for it. Yet it is now time to dismiss it as so many other childhood beliefs.

**

We can now tackle the quintessential question about the Garden of Eden story, namely why God allowed the Serpent to be in the Garden. We can see that the Garden was created for more than one purpose, and one of these purposes was to give another opportunity to a group of beings that had fallen from a higher realm. The Bible only describes one such being, but in reality there were many of them. In other words, there were a number of beings in the Garden who fell as a result of the serpentine consciousness. The Garden of Eden was partly established to give them an opportunity to rise above that state of consciousness. How could this be accomplished?

The Garden did have new co-creators who started out their journey of self-discovery in that environment. By interacting with these innocent lifestreams, those in the serpentine consciousness had an opportunity to reform their approach to life, much like some adults on Earth who are transformed by working with children. Obviously, this arrangement came with the inherent risk that the new co-creators could be led astray by those who had already fallen. Yet this does not mean that the innocent lifestreams were thrown at the mercy of a flock of ravening wolves.

The Garden did, as already mentioned, have a head teacher who had successfully passed the temptation to engage in the serpentine consciousness. Likewise, there were a number of lifestreams who had passed this initiation in a higher realm and who had volunteered to descend to the Garden in order to serve as a counterbalance to the serpentine lifestreams. Thus, there was a balance between those who had risen above the serpentine consciousness and those who had not. By interacting with those who were above this temptation, those who fell had another opportunity to reconsider their choices. Naturally, those who were above the temptation could also serve to help the new co-creators avoid being tempted by the serpents. So the Garden was a balanced yet very dynamic environment, which of course goes against the popular myth of a static place of eternal rest. Yet as I have attempted to explain, there is no place of static rest, as even the spiritual realm is constantly transcending itself. Life is an ongoing process, the River of Life, and it is only the ego and fallen beings – who have separated from this process – who want to create a static place in which their power and control cannot be challenged by the force of life itself. I hope you can begin to see that this is an impossible dream that will never come to pass.

I have already mentioned that the Garden was not located in the physical vibrational spectrum. It was located in the identity realm, which is the highest of the four levels of the material universe. This realm is meant to serve as the meeting point between "heaven and Earth," between the material universe and the spiritual realm. The idea is that a lifestream from any of the other three levels can raise its consciousness to the identity realm and then begin the process of ascending to the spiritual realm. Thus, the identity realm must remain pure, and to ensure this purity, it was divided. The Garden was located in the lowest level of the identity realm, which allowed it to house the serpents and also allowed it to serve as a schoolroom for lifestreams who had risen from the lower realms.

In order to understand how this was possible, we need to reach back to my earlier explanation that the Earth is very old and that the Garden was not established at the beginning of the Earth's history. This is proven by the fact that there were people in the physical realm with whom Cain and Seth could intermarry. Some of the beings who started out in the physical realm had indeed risen in consciousness and were now being tutored in the Garden. I will later talk more about this, but for now it is necessary to give you a greater understanding of why there are four levels of the material universe.

***

Genesis clearly does not explain the origin of the Serpent and thus contains no teaching about beings who fell in the spiritual realm and descended to Earth. Yet we can find hints about such beings elsewhere in the Bible. Let us look at a few quotes:

> 1 And it came to pass, when men began to multiply on the face of the Earth, and daughters were born unto them,
> 2 That the sons of God saw the daughters of men that they were fair; and they took them wives of all which they chose. (Genesis, Chapter 5)

> How art thou fallen from heaven, O Lucifer, son of the morning! how art thou cut down to the ground, which didst weaken the nations! (Isaiah 14:12)

> Therefore rejoice, ye heavens, and ye that dwell in them. Woe to the inhabiters of the Earth and of the sea! for the devil is come down unto you, having great wrath, because he knoweth that he hath but a short time. (Revelation, 12:12)

These quotes clearly indicate that beings in a higher realm descended to Earth for various reasons. The Book of Enoch is not a part of today's official Bible, and it gives even more detail about fallen angels who took on physical bodies on Earth. My point is that in reality a great number of beings – from different spiritual evolutions – fell in one of the spiritual realms, and they now reside in one of the four levels of the material universe, including wearing physical bodies on Earth. These beings can be grouped into four categories depending on why they fell.

I earlier talked about the fact that the universe is created through an interaction of two basic forces, namely the expanding and the contracting forces. The expanding force is what Christianity calls the Father, whereas the contracting force is what some religions call the Mother, an aspect of creation that has been sadly neglected by Christianity, Islam and Judaism (mainly because of a literal interpretation of Genesis and the temptation to blame women for the fall—which is truly the male ego's refusal to take responsibility). We also have the element of the Christ mind, which Christianity calls the Son. Finally, we have the element that is meant to ensure growth in the matter universe by driving all living things to overcome limitations and by giving them a lifeline to the spiritual realm whereby they *can* transcend. This is what Christianity calls the Holy Spirit.

Each of these elements represents a certain state of consciousness, even a set of initiations. Thus, each represents an initiation on the path to Godhood. Consequently, beings can either pass or miss this initiation. You pass the initiation by embodying, by becoming one with, the corresponding state of consciousness. You fail the initiation by refusing to do so. Let us now list the four elements and how they correspond to the levels of the material universe (take note that I am talking about both co-creators and other forms of evolutions, as all must pass these initiations although in slightly different ways):

- The identity realm corresponds to the element of the Father, which is the expanding force. The main principle is self-transcendence, leading not only to filling the void but first of all to having self-transcending beings become all that their Creator is—and MORE. This initiation requires beings to expand their sense of identity, and when they pass the initiation of the Father element, they build a sense of identity that is based on their spiritual identity—the hierarchy of beings out of which they are individualizations, a hierarchy leading back to the Creator. The initiation of the Father requires beings to create or maintain the sense of oneness with their source, oneness with their own higher beings and oneness with all life—which is the only source of peace of mind and ultimate fulfillment. At a higher level, the Father element takes responsibility for all life and works to raise up all life. The Father does what is best for all members of his spiritual family.

  When a being fails the initiation of the Father element, it builds a sense of identity based on seeing itself as separated from God. This is what the Serpent hinted at when he told Eve that she would not surely die, meaning that she could actually build an identity outside the oneness of the spiritual hierarchy. What the Serpent "forgot" to mention was that this would be a life of constant tension and suffering that can never lead to peace of mind. Also, it will be a life that has an absolute time limit, as the Creator will not allow part of its Being to remain indefinitely separated from the whole. The fallen Father consciousness represents an absolute rebellion against God's purpose for the world of form, a rejection of the very purpose of life itself and a refusal to enter into the River of Life. It also represents a refusal to fill the role of Father by helping all members of one's spiritual family grow.

- The mental realm, the level of thought, corresponds to the element of the Son, the Christ mind. This is what gives a being the ability to know what is real – meaning within the framework of God's vision, purpose and law – and what is unreal, meaning outside God's oneness. By passing the initiation of the Son, a being gains the ability to discern between what is real – the one truth of the Christ mind – and what is unreal – the many dualistic "truths" from the mind of anti-christ. Such a being can "rightly divide the word of truth" (2Timothy 2:15).

  By failing the initiation of the Son, a being goes outside the reality of the Christ mind and becomes enveloped in the mind of duality, where truth and error, good and evil, are relative terms. Yet the being cannot see this and thus comes to believe it has the right to define good and evil. It might even begin to believe it is better at doing so than the representatives of Christ or God, which gives rises to intellectual and spiritual pride. This can easily form a catch-22 from which beings find it extremely difficult to extricate themselves.

- The emotional realm, the level of feeling, corresponds to the element of the Mother. When beings pass this initiation, they feel completely nurtured, but this can happen only when they learn to use the Mother Light in unison with the laws of the Father. There will then be harmony – oneness – between the Mother and Father elements of their beings. The initiation of the Mother also requires beings to work toward nurturing all life and raising this sphere toward manifesting the kingdom of God. In other words, such beings are willing to take dominion over their environment instead of being controlled by it. They realize that the material realm, for example, is not an end in itself. Life has a higher purpose, beyond enjoying what the physical Earth has to offer, namely to bring the Mother element into oneness with the Father element.

  When beings fail the initiation of the Mother, they will not feel nurtured but will experience that life does not live up to their expectations. Their hopes are not fulfilled, everything seems to break down and their lives become a constant struggle. Yet instead of seeking the only solution – to bring the Mother back into oneness with the Father – they start blaming the Father for everything that goes wrong, even for the fact that they exist. Others develop a hatred of the Mother principle and the Mother Light, causing them to either seek to control everything in this realm or even become intent on destroying things in the matter realm. Some beings are not aggressive but they become so focused on the material realm that they see it as an end in itself. They focus all of their attention on seeking physical pleasure or possessions—until they eventually realize it can never lead them to fulfillment.

- The physical realm corresponds to the element of the Holy Spirit, and the essence of it is to transform a limited state into a higher state—multiplying your talents and becoming MORE. When beings pass this initiation, they know that their rightful role is to have dominion over the Earth. Thus, instead of conforming and adapting to imperfect conditions, they seek to transform them according to the vision of Christ. They seek to raise themselves above all limitations, but they also seek to raise others, even society or the planet itself.

    When beings fail this initiation, they refuse to take command, they refuse to make decisions based on Christ vision. Instead, they adapt to imperfect conditions, seeking to justify these conditions, portray them as inevitable or even portray them as the best possible conditions. This, of course, is easy to do by using the dualistic logic of the mind of anti-christ. If a critical number of people in a civilization enter this state of consciousness, the society will not be able to transcend itself, and thus it will inevitably become subject to the contracting force that will break a society down until an entire civilization can collapse, even vanish. As we will discuss later, this has already happened to numerous civilizations on the physical Earth. The physical realm is especially prone to this process because matter is so dense that the contracting force has more to pull on and can more easily break down any structure that is not in alignment with God's law.

Let us now look at the state of consciousness of the beings who have failed the initiations and have descended to the four levels of the material universe:

- **Father, identity realm.** The identity realm is designed to help people who have failed the initiation of the Father. The beings here are rebelling against God, especially the oneness of all life. They want to maintain an identity as separate beings, which means they must be outside the Body of God. It also means they refuse to self-transcend (the only way to "maintain" anything), setting themselves outside the River of Life. And they refuse to take responsibility for raising up all life.

  One of the primary motivations for this is that these beings have come to believe they are better than others, and they want to reinforce their sense of superiority. This gives rise to spiritual pride, which, as all pride, blinds you to reality and becomes a catch-22. Many of these beings literally believe they have established an identity outside of God that is better than what they could have inside of God. Obviously, this is an illusion since nothing can really be outside of God, yet these beings not only believe they are outside of God, they also believe they are establishing or have established a world that is better than God's world. They vigorously defend this illusion, and they have to be vigorous because the contracting force of the Mother is constantly breaking it down. In reality, these beings have a desire to *be* God and they are seeking to create a world where they are elevated to the status of gods. They often seek power through any means available, including raw force. Take note that you can be a God by becoming one with your Creator. However, these unbalanced beings don't want to become one with the Creator because they want to elevate the separate self as a god.

- **Son, mental realm.** The mental realm is designed to help people who have failed the initiation of the Son. These beings have a lot of the same desires for a separate existence because they seek superiority. However, they primarily use the mind, the analytical mind or the intellect, to establish superiority—as opposed to power and raw force. As I have explained, the dualistic logic of the mind of anti-christ allows you to "prove" or "justify" anything. So in the mental realm those who are best at using dualistic logic will be able to establish an illusion of superiority. Many of these beings believe they are more intelligent than anyone else. They have a completely dualistic mindset, always comparing themselves to others based on intelligence. Many of them even believe they are better at using reason and logic than God—which, ironically, is true since God does not use dualistic logic at all. Thus, these beings believe they know better than God how the universe should be run. Which they do in the sense that they know their own self-defined dualistic world view better than anyone else—however, the universe does not function according to their illusions. These beings also believe they should be in charge of the universe, although they are not trying to set themselves up as gods but as the true representatives of God. They are trying to present themselves as the true representatives of Christ, as the true spiritual teachers for those below them.

- **Mother, emotional realm.** The emotional realm is designed to help people who have failed the initiation of the Mother. Beings here are consumed by negative emotions against God, against anyone representing God, against anyone who will not conform to their expectations or against anyone who represents the need to self-transcend. These beings often believe some of the illusions created by beings in the two previous categories, but they have taken these beliefs one step further and have used them to create very intense feelings against what they see as their adversaries. They often hate God and everything he stands for, giving them intense anger and a desire for revenge against God. Obviously, they cannot hurt God – even though they often believe they can have some effect – but they can hurt other beings who believe in God. This gives them a murderous intent against any representative of God, especially a true spiritual teacher who challenges their illusions. These beings don't want to be disturbed. They want to keep doing the same thing without being confronted with the need to self-transcend. They have become attached to a limited state and refuse to rise higher.

- **Holy Spirit, physical realm.** The physical realm is designed to help people who have failed the initiation of the Holy Spirit as well as beings who have fallen from the upper three realms. So you do have beings in physical embodiment who are from the three upper realms. You will notice that beings in the three higher realms are still very much centered around God, or at least the concept of God as they see it. So they are not actually denying God's existence, for that would take away their modus operandi of building a better world than God's world, of being smarter than God or of hating God and taking revenge. So the physical realm was originally designed for beings who want to be completely outside of God. The physical realm is the lowest in vibration, making it the most dense, and thus making it possible that beings in this realm can build the illusion that God does not exist, that a creator is not needed. My point being that only in the physical realm is it even possible for beings to create the illusion that there is no God and that the world in which they live was not created by a supreme being. This has some profound implications that will explain many of the conditions you have encountered as you grew up on planet Earth. We will take a closer look at this in a later chapter.

Take note of the importance of this teaching. I have said that when a being refuses to ascend with its native sphere, it falls into the newly created sphere. Yet the mercy of God is unending, so a fallen being is not simply thrown into the ocean to sink or swim. It first descends into a protected environment, in which it has an opportunity to interact with others, including new co-creators and experienced teachers. For example, the Garden of Eden was set up partially to help fallen beings who had failed the initiation of the Father. If such a being refused to take advantage of what was offered in the Garden, it could fall further, going into the mental, emotional or even directly to the physical realm. Yet no matter where a being is, there will always be some link to the cosmic hierarchy that can offer a fallen being a way to come back to the Path of Oneness.

***

To summarize what we have talked about so far, we can now see that you will never understand what is happening and has been happening on the Earth unless you realize that this planet is the temporary home to different lifestreams. I know most spiritual people have felt a sense of disgust over some of the things that have been happening and are still happening on this planet. I know many people are wondering why some people can do things that are so obviously evil or abusive toward others. How is it possible that some people seemingly have no sensitivity or concern for the suffering they inflict upon others or have no awareness of the consequences of their actions? How come some people have an obvious desire to control or suppress others, literally treating other people like property or slaves?

We can now begin to see part of the explanation for human evil. The stark reality is that some of the beings who inhabit human bodies on this little planet were not created to start out their existences on this planet. They were not created to descend to the identity level as new co-creators and eventually take on physical bodies. Some of these beings were indeed created as co-creators, but they were created in a higher realm. When their native realm ascended, they refused to let go of their separate sense of identity and join the River of Life. Thus, they fell into the newly created sphere.

Yet before they fell, some of these beings had attained a sophisticated understanding of their native sphere and how the world of form works. These beings did not fall from innocent ignorance, they fell from willful ignorance. This means that they often had a very high understanding of how the universe works, yet they did not have the Christ consciousness that allowed them to use this understanding in unselfish ways. Thus, instead of using their understanding – and their outer positions in a society in their native sphere – to raise up all life, they had become blinded by the dualistic desire to raise up themselves in comparison to others. This caused them to use their knowledge and power to actually limit and control other beings. They were seeking to elevate themselves by keeping other beings down, and this is an obvious violation of the Law of MORE. This law states that the only true way to raise yourself is to raise all life, so when you seek to raise yourself by limiting all other forms of life, you are truly out of touch with life itself.

Some of these self-centered beings have maintained their separate sense of identity in several spheres, meaning that they have fallen through several levels of the world of form. They have had a very long time to build their current sense of identity, meaning that they are very sure of themselves and their right to suppress other beings. So when they embody on Earth, they feel superior to most other peo-

ple and they immediately seek to set themselves up in powerful positions. Some of these beings are simply self-centered and mainly want
to control others in order to get power and privileges for themselves—all for the cause of expanding their sense of superiority. Yet
some fallen beings have become trapped by the belief that they know
better than God how the universe should be run, giving them a desire
to prove God wrong. Thus, their desire for gaining control over other
people is part of a larger agenda which few people have understood.
This is a topic we will talk more about in coming chapters, when we
have set the proper foundation.

My goal at this point is to make you aware that there are indeed
beings on Earth who do not look at life the same way most people do.
These beings – who wear normal human bodies – have become so
self-centered that they have lost all sensitivity to the suffering of other
people. The equation is simple, for the more you get lost in the duality consciousness – the further you descend down the spiral staircase
– the more self-centered you will become. The inevitable companion
of self-centeredness is an increased insensitivity to other forms of
life. Only *you* matter, and other people simply don't matter. The most
self-centered people believe they have a superior right to pursue their
self-defined goals. They believe the ends can justify the means—
some of them even believe that their superior cause can justify *any*
means, any amount of suffering inflicted upon other people. These
beings are constantly and ruthlessly seeking to control others, which
means they are seeking to take away their spiritual freedom. I know
this is a topic that makes many spiritual seekers uncomfortable, and
they would rather not think about it. Yet if you are a sincere spiritual
seeker, your goal must be to attain spiritual freedom. And how can
you possibly hope to attain spiritual freedom unless you understand
the forces that seek to take away that freedom? So as a mature seeker,
you need to become aware that there is a force on planet Earth that is
deliberately and aggressively seeking to take away the spiritual freedom of all people. Once you understand how this force works, it is
quite easy to avoid its control over you personally. And if a critical
mass of spiritual people come to a full understanding of this force, it
will even be possible to permanently remove it from the Earth. We
will talk much more about this later, but for now let us move on to
look at another type of spiritual beings that have come to embody on
Earth as a result of falling into the illusion of separation.

Key 14
The difference between co-creators and angels

I know some spiritual seekers will be wondering how angels fit into the picture I am describing, so we will look at that next. Some spiritual teachings describe angels as the thoughts of God that are shaped by the purpose for which they were created. Some people see angels as messengers between God and his creation, while others see them as servants of both God and man. Neither view is incorrect, but it must be understood that the evolution of angels is very diverse and angels have vastly different functions. Therefore, it is difficult to make too many generalizations about angels, and a spiritual seeker should be careful not to adopt a simplistic understanding of angels.

It is not my intention with this book to describe the many different types of angels. My purpose is to give teachings that can help people resolve what for some spiritual seekers seems like a contradiction or paradox. There are several spiritual teachers on Earth who firmly claim that angels were not created to take physical embodiment in this or any other world. Yet there are many spiritual seekers who have an inner knowing that they are angels in embodiment. Is it possible that both are correct and that a deeper understanding will resolve the paradox?

***

Let us set a foundation by taking a closer look at the process whereby succeeding spheres are created. As I have explained, each new sphere is more diverse, more expressed, more complex than the previous one. The pattern for creation is that the One Creator diversifies itself, and each new sphere takes this diversification to a new level. So the distance to the Creator's oneness is greater for your sphere than for the first sphere—far greater.

Another aspect is that the first spheres are not standing still. When a sphere ascends, there is no longer room for duality in that sphere, but that does not mean the sphere has reached the level of the Allness.

Consequently, there is still room for growth in an ascended sphere, and all spheres in the spiritual realm are constantly transcending themselves. As a result, the higher spheres are becoming more sophisticated, more evolved, while the new spheres start out as less sophisticated, more dense.

On the one hand we have a growing diversification, which fits well with the goal of giving individual beings the opportunity to experience a separate sense of identity. Yet on the other hand the goal of the world of form is to bring all separate beings back to oneness, meaning that they lose the separateness without losing their distinct identities. As the diversification increases, it becomes easier for new beings to experience a separate identity. Each new generation starts at a denser level, being one step further separated from oneness. Thus, they have a greater "distance" to climb in order to get back to oneness, which naturally increases the risk that they can become lost in separation. We might even say that for each succeeding sphere, the density of that sphere makes the consciousness of duality more persuasive and harder to overcome. The mind of anti-christ forms a veil of illusions, and the veil becomes denser for each new sphere.

The concern now becomes how to prevent the beings in the latest sphere from becoming lost in separation, lost in duality. A related concern is how to make sure the latest sphere stays in harmony with the laws of God and the vision held by the masters in the higher spheres, who are also involved with designing the new sphere. The combination of "distance" and the need to maintain oneness obviously points to the need for communication. Yet the masters in the higher spheres are not meant to descend to a lower sphere and the masters in the lowest level of the spiritual realm are so busy co-creating the new sphere and teaching its new co-creators that they cannot constantly be traveling to the higher spheres. The logical solution is to create a new evolution of beings who are neither masters nor co-creators but are designed specifically to facilitate communication and oneness between all levels of the world of form. Thus comes about the creation of angels. We now see that there are two distinct types of evolutions:

- Co-creators are created in order to descend to the lowest level and work their way up from there. They are created without the Christ consciousness, but only have the seed of Christ consciousness which they can nourish until they become one with

Christ and become the Living Christ. During this process, they experience what it is like to move from separation to oneness.

- Angels are not created to descend to the lowest level but are created to help facilitate the creation of new spheres and the growth of co-creators. Angels are created with some level of Christ consciousness, and although they can expand it, they are not meant to move from separation to oneness as they are not created as separate beings. They all have some awareness that they are extensions of a higher being.

***

As mentioned before, the Creator must create out of its own Being, meaning that the Creator has embedded its own consciousness in the world of form. Regardless of the outer form, everything in this world is created out of the Creator's consciousness, meaning that it has a form of consciousness. As I said, even a rock has a form of consciousness, but there is a difference between the consciousness of an object and the consciousness of a living being. However, that difference is not quite the same as the difference between animate and inanimate objects on Earth. For example, most people would say that a rock is dead and has no consciousness, whereas an animal is alive and does have consciousness. In reality, both have a form of life and both have a form of consciousness, and the difference is largely a difference in the complexity of the entity. A rock is obviously far less complex than an animal, and thus it has a less specialized form of consciousness. We clearly see that the more highly evolved animals, such as monkeys, have a more sophisticated form of consciousness than more primitive animals. In reality, the real distinction in terms of consciousness is the following:

- Inanimate objects, such as rocks or planets. These are objects that do not perform actual actions but are acted upon by living beings.
- Living beings without self-awareness. Such beings have consciousness, but they do not have enough consciousness to have an awareness that they exist or a sense of identity.
- Self-aware beings. These beings do have self-awareness, and this gives them the basis for having free will. For example, a

fish does not know it is a fish, it simply does what a fish does. It cannot say to itself, "I'm a fish, but I'm sick of breathing water and I want to be a dog."

How does this relate to angels? All angels are more than objects, but there are some angels who are – although different in design – functioning at the level of living beings without self-awareness. These lower angels are created to perform a specific function, and they simply do so—much like an animal on Earth which does what it was created to do without having the possibility of changing itself. These angels have very specific functions that relate to stepping down light for your sphere and communicating between your sphere and the lowest level of the spiritual realm. They cannot penetrate into the higher levels of the spiritual realm.

The higher angels have a much more sophisticated level of consciousness, but it does cover a very broad range, depending on the function for which the angel was created and the angel's age or experience. Some angels have a more primitive self-awareness and understanding of the universe than many human beings, whereas others are far more advanced than most humans. Yet with the increase in the level of consciousness comes self-awareness, which involves the ability to change oneself based on one's own decisions.

Angels are created as living beings, and all living beings have the potential to grow, to progress and to eventually transcend the level at which they were created. So angels were not created as a kind of cosmic robots that mindlessly perform a specific function. They can actually progress, and the more sophisticated angels can consciously change their behavior (within certain boundaries). In fact, the higher angels are following the Path of Oneness that leads them toward a higher state of consciousness. While this may sound similar to the path of co-creators, there are some fundamental differences:

• Co-creators are created to descend into what is – at the time they are created – the lowest level of the world of form. Here, they will take on a "body" made of the energies of that level. In your sphere this means taking on a body made from the energies of the material spectrum. Angels are not created in the lowest level and they are not created to descend into it and take on a body. Angels can descend on a temporary basis to deliver a message, but to do this they do not take on an actual body even though they may appear in a human-like form.

- Co-creators are created as extensions of beings in a higher realm and they are created to descend below the level of the beings who created them, working their way up from there. Angels are not created to descend and embody below the level on which they are created. They can work their way up from the level where they were created, but they are not meant to descend below it.

- Co-creators are designed to start out with a rudimentary sense of identity and grow from there. Although I have said that a co-creator has a spiritual identity anchored in the I AM Presence, the co-creator has great freedom to design its Omega identity, the identity through which it expresses itself in the material world. Its Christ-like decisions will even expand and refine the co-creator's Alpha identity. Angels are created with a very clearly defined identity, and since they are not in a physical body, they do not need an Omega identity that is as defined as that of co-creators. Angels can develop their Omega identity, but it must be in perfect alignment with their Alpha identity. We might say that an angel can develop its predefined identity and become more *of* that identity, whereas a co-creator can transcend its predefined identity and become more *than* that identity.

- A co-creator has – in principle – complete free will. It can discover its divine identity and still decide to go beyond it—as long as it creates a new identity that is in harmony with the laws of God. That is why some people on Earth can raise themselves above their upbringing and society. An angel has free will, but since it is created to perform a specific function, it does not have the free will nor the self-awareness to change its basic make-up. For example, some angels are designed to protect human beings and others are designed as healing angels. A healing angel can choose to become a better healing angel, but it cannot choose to become a protecting angel.

- The basic design of a co-creator is to start with a limited sense of awareness and then grow. In other words, its basic make-up is designed to grow, to self-transcend, to become MORE. A co-creator has a built-in longing for a higher state that can be reached only through self-transcendence. We might say the co-creator's attention is directed upward with little attention for anything below its own level. An angel is created to perform a specific function and is not designed to transcend that role. Many angels are created to help co-creators grow, and their attention is focused on those below their own level, although they naturally also have attention on the levels above them that they can see. Angels are primarily created to facilitate the growth of those below them or to serve those above them. Angels grow by being who they are, whereas co-creators grow by becoming MORE than who they were created to be.

• A co-creator is designed specifically to develop its own identity and then take dominion over its native realm. We might say that a co-creator is more self-centered than an angel, but in reality the co-creator is simply doing what it was designed to do, namely defining its sense of self and continually going beyond it to become MORE. An angel is designed to serve others, so transcending its sense of self is not part of the angel's design. While co-creators can grow (up to a certain level) by focusing entirely on their own development, an angel can only grow by focusing on serving others. Self-centered angels can't grow.

• A co-creator is born into a protected environment in which it has a spiritual teacher. We might say that the concept of following a teacher comes naturally to a co-creator because its basic make-up is to learn and grow. An angel is not primarily designed to grow and it is not born into a schoolroom. We might say that a co-creator is born as a child, and an angel is born as an adult with all the training it needs to perform its job. This doesn't mean that angels don't have leaders, for angels are part of groups or bands that have archangels as their leaders. Yet the leaders of angels are not teachers, they are doers. Thus, being in a learning environment and following a teacher does not come naturally to angels, which has an important consequence that we will consider later.

In summary, the most important difference is that a co-creator is meant to start out with a limited and non-specific sense of identity and grow from there toward full God consciousness, whereas an angel starts out with a predefined and very specific identity. This gives rise to a subtle but very important difference in the way the two types of beings exercise free will. We might say that an angel has an all-or-nothing free will in the sense that the angel is created to serve in manifesting God's plan and design for the world of form. Thus, the angel is created to work exclusively within the framework of God's law. A higher angel has free will in terms of how it carries out its tasks, and it does have the option to go against God's law. However, if an angel goes against God's law, it goes against everything and instantly separates itself from the law. An angel is either fully within the law or fully outside the law, there is nothing in between, no gray zone.

In contrast, as I have explained in previous chapters, a new co-creator is created without an awareness of God's law. So the co-creator is meant to learn from experimenting, which means that it is allowed to go against God's law. A co-creator can go against a specific point of God's law without going against the whole. A co-creator is created to learn, and it can go against the law and still learn, whereby it actually comes closer to oneness. An angel is created with some degree of oneness, which means that it can only separate itself by going against the law. It is created to manifest the law and can learn nothing from going outside it.

***

We now need to look at a fact that will surprise many spiritual seekers who are accustomed to thinking that angels were created by God and that they were created as permanent, or immortal, beings. This is a statement that needs to be refined based on a greater understanding of the progression of the spheres. Angels were created to serve the very first sphere and all subsequent spheres, but as the spheres have diversified, the roles of angels have naturally changed. In the first three spheres beings did have free will, but because these spheres were created with a higher intensity of light (they were less dense) it was highly unlikely that they would become trapped in the illusion of separation or rebel against God's law. Thus, beings in these spheres exercised their free will within the parameters set by the vision and laws of God and never truly considered going against God's purpose and design. One might even say that in the first spheres, there was less of a difference between the free will of angels and co-creators. The reason being that the lower density made it easy for all beings to see their connection to something greater than themselves, meaning it was very difficult for them to believe in the illusion of separation.

With the creation of the fourth sphere, a shift occurred. This sphere was created with a level of density that made the illusion of separation more of a temptation. One might say that while co-creators always had free will, it was only with the creation of the fourth sphere that there was a realistic risk of co-creators becoming lost in the illusion of separation. One might also say that in the higher spheres it was easy to tell the difference between what was real – what was in alignment with God's law – and what was unreal. The fourth sphere was created with such density that there was a gray zone, where it was difficult to tell the difference between what was real and unreal. You might say that in the higher spheres, the light was so intense and "matter" so transparent that there were no shadows. In the fourth sphere, "matter" was so dense and the light so dim that shadows appeared for the first time.

The fourth sphere was like a room at twilight, and it was difficult to see things for what they were. Consequently, it now became much more likely that co-creators could become trapped in the duality of the mind of anti-christ. They could become blinded by the shadows and start defining a world view that was out of alignment with the reality of God. Thus, they could create a catch-22 in which their self-defined view of good and evil would become a closed box from which they could no longer see any reality beyond the box.

Do you see my point? In the first spheres, the substance out of which the spheres were created vibrated at such a high level that co-creators inside the sphere could easily see that there was something beyond their sphere and that their sphere was created from energies that came from beyond the sphere. Thus, it was virtually impossible for them to create closed mental boxes. Yet as the spheres became more dense, there would naturally come a point when it was no longer obvious that there is something beyond the latest sphere. It now became possible for co-creators to believe that their sphere was all there was, meaning that they saw their sphere as self-contained, as a closed box. In the upper spheres new co-creators saw themselves as extensions of beings in a higher realm and they knew they had the potential to rise above their native realm. Beginning with the fourth sphere, new co-creators started out with a truly separate sense of identity. They still had contact with a spiritual teacher – there was a schoolroom like the Garden of Eden in the fourth sphere – but it now became possible that new co-creators could come to believe that they were the products of their sphere and had no potential to rise above it. This was possible because the greater density hid the fact that every-thing is made from the Creator's Light. Therefore, co-creators could use the duality consciousness to create a self-contained world view that denied the existence of anything beyond their sphere, whereas in higher spheres this illusion simply was not believable. Since the fourth sphere there has been an increasing risk that co-creators could become lost, that they could leave the Path of MORE and become trapped on the path of less that could eventually obliterate their sense of identity. We might also say that it has become possible for co-cre-ators to choose death over life.

What has this got to do with angels? Well, for each new sphere, a band of angels was created specifically to serve that sphere. Obvi-ously, the very nature and design of the angels was adapted to the specific conditions of the sphere they were created to serve. The angels created to serve the fourth sphere were designed with that sphere's density in mind, meaning that these angels were not actually created as immortal beings. They had to earn their immortality by serving the sphere and the co-creators in it, and they would not become immortal until that sphere ascended.

These angels were still created with a specific identity, so they did not have to define their identity – as did new co-creators – but they had to build on to what they were given. Also, the angels did not have a separate sense of identity but clearly saw themselves as extensions of higher beings. In other words, because the angels were not inside the fourth sphere as were co-creators, they knew there was something beyond that sphere. Because of the density of the fourth sphere, new angels were not simply thrown into the fray with no external connec-tion to the higher realms. New angels were given leaders from higher realms, namely the angels who had served in one or all of the upper spheres. This is what most people call archangels.

***

Here is where things become subtle. To illustrate this, imagine an angel created in the first sphere. It serves this sphere until the sphere ascends and the second sphere is created. The angel can then remain in the first sphere or volunteer to serve the second sphere. Yet because the second sphere is not that much denser than the first sphere, the angel does not lose its memory of its past service. My point is that when the fourth sphere was created, there were some angels who had grown in experience and knowledge, so they had become quite sophisticated in their understanding of God's law.

We now see that there are two parallel evolutions. The evolution of angels produces angels that are increasingly experienced and sophisticated. The evolution of co-creators creates denser and denser spheres, meaning that each sphere and the new co-creators in it are more primitive than the ones before it. So as the angels become more sophisticated, they have to serve more primitive beings and spheres, which gives rise to the possibility that some angels can now begin to think that they are so sophisticated that they should be in charge. This can give rise to a very subtle but persuasive sense of pride, where the angels begin to feel superior to the co-creators they were created to serve. If this spiritual pride grows, angels can begin to feel that the Creator is taking too great of a risk by creating still denser spheres. They can even begin to feel anger against God, whereby they separate themselves from the oneness with God's purpose and law.

Yet angels were created to serve. They were created to help manifest God's overall vision by upholding the laws of God. Obviously, the very purpose for the world of form is the growth of co-creators, so in order to serve a new sphere, the angels are – so to speak – subservient to the co-creators and their use of free will. The angels are also subservient to the masters who oversee each new sphere. Thus, if angels stop seeing themselves as servants, they inevitably become prideful tyrants who want to override the free will of co-creators, which they see as the major problem. Thereby, they obviously go against the very purpose of creation, which means that such angels will inevitably fall. Beginning with the fourth sphere, such angels could stay in one sphere until it started ascending, and they would then fall into the next sphere that was set apart from the void.

As a side note, one might wonder whether masters can become prideful, but this is less of a risk because they create extensions of themselves that go into the new sphere and grow from there. This keeps the masters humble and gives them a greater understanding for the situation faced by new co-creators.

***

Angels are created to serve a specific sphere, the sphere that has not yet ascended. Thus, the new angels are created to help facilitate the creation, growth and ascension of that sphere. As that sphere ascends, the new angels can win their immortality. However in order to do this, they have to face and pass some of the same initiations that I described in the account of co-creators in the Garden of Eden. After the creation of the fourth sphere, angels had to face the initiation of being tempted by and overcoming the duality consciousness.

The world of form is divided into two distinct partitions, namely the spiritual realm and the lowest sphere in which there is still room for duality. No being with free will – angel or co-creator – can become immortalized until it has overcome selfishness, has over-come the temptation of the duality consciousness. I am not saying beings have to partake of the fruit of the knowledge of good and evil, but they have to deal with the temptation to partake of it.

Co-creators are created to descend into the lowest sphere and ascend from there. Angels are, by their nature, created in a higher sphere, but because they have self-awareness and free will, they also have to overcome duality before they win immortality. This, of course, opens up for the possibility that angels can fail their test, that they can fall, and this will be our next topic.

A co-creator is created with a limited sense of identity and is meant to expand it by following the path of becoming MORE. We might say that a co-creator is meant to break boundaries and never become trapped in a mental box. The ultimate challenge for a co-cre-ator is to create a sense of identity within the framework of God's law and to do so by seeing that God's law is created to facilitate the growth of all. Thus, the co-creator understands that God's laws repre-sent enlightened self-interest and it follows them out of love.

An angel is not created to define its identity but to expand it by remaining true to what it was given. We might say that an angel is created to manifest God's law, which is why the angel is created with the fundamental choice to be or not to be—to be in complete align-ment with God's law or to be completely outside God's law. In contrast, a co-creator is created with the choice to be MORE or not to be MORE. In the beginning, a co-creator can actually become MORE by going outside of God's law and learning from it, but eventually it realizes that it can be MORE within the law than outside it—because the ultimate way to become MORE is to be one with the Creator.

For an angel, the basic choice is to remain true to God's law and God's design. As a co-creator grows toward Christ consciousness, it can actually build on to God's basic design. For example, co-creators on Earth can build on to the basic design for this planet. Angels do not go beyond the basic design defined by the Creator and the masters, they work within the framework defined by others. A new angel does not have the full awareness of God's laws and design but only has enough understanding to carry out the task for which it was created. By serving, an angel can grow in understanding, but it still faces the basic challenge of remaining true to the design defined by God. Yet as it attains a more sophisticated understanding, an angel can begin to disagree with God's design or with its own role as a servant for others. This can lead the more sophisticated angels to rebel against God's design, whereby they instantly fall into separation. An angel is either fully within God's law or fully outside it. There is no gray zone in which it can experiment with violating the law without falling.

It is important to understand that while co-creators fall or ascend based on their own choices and actions, angels generally fall because of the way they react to the choices made by others. Ultimately, angels fall by rebelling against the choices made by the Creator and the masters, but what triggers this rebellion is often that the angels become overly concerned about the fate of co-creators. Angels know that a sphere has to ascend, and they tend to look at this as a task that requires specific actions. Thus, they find it hard to understand why co-creators are reluctant or slow in performing these actions and raising their sphere. Angels generally cannot understand that the real purpose of the world of form is not the ascension of a sphere but the growth in consciousness of individual beings. Thus, they cannot understand that it isn't the primary goal of the Creator to get a sphere to ascend as quickly as possible. It is more important to facilitate the growth of co-creators, even if everything takes longer.

This is especially a problem for the more sophisticated angels, who can begin to feel that the Creator was wrong in giving co-creators free will. Instead, co-creators should be controlled – by the sophisticated angels – so they cannot become lost and are – so to speak – forced to be saved. Yet as I have explained in great detail, being saved truly means that you become spiritually self-sufficient, and you cannot possibly be forced to attain this state. It can only come from within by the conscious self attaining oneness with its own higher Being. Thus, angels can rebel out of a complete misunderstanding of the Creator's true purpose.

**

Why does the increasing density of the spheres present such a problem for the more sophisticated angels? Angels are generally very good at performing the task they were created to do. They are specialists and the angels who have decided to expand their capability are extremely competent at their task. Yet even such angels have little understanding for and appreciation of tasks that are vastly different from their specialty. In other words, angels are not very flexible, not very good at adapting to changing environments. In contrast, co-creators have to be very flexible and they have to be the "jack of all trades." Even if that makes them "masters of none," this is acceptable for a co-creator who must be able to adapt to the changing conditions it can encounter on a planet like Earth.

The tendency to become rigid and refuse to self-transcend has increased in both co-creators and angels as the succeeding spheres have become more complex and diversified. We might say that the greater complexity makes it increasingly difficult to predict how a sphere will evolve. Thus, the destiny of a sphere becomes more and more dependent upon the beings who embody within it. Yet in order to grow and take command over their sphere, co-creators face an increasingly demanding challenge. As I have explained, each new generation of co-creators is designed with this in mind and they are also taught by teachers who know what they are facing. Yet the challenge is that in each new sphere the task of both personal and overall growth can seem more demanding, even overwhelming. It thus requires a greater determination, a bigger decision, for co-creators to engage the challenge, and it requires more flexibility and persistence for them to make it through the challenge. This, of course, is part of the Creator's design, but if co-creators are not willing to step up to the challenge, they can more easily feel overwhelmed and become discouraged.

For angels, the problem is that they are created to serve, which means that they generally do not have to make too many decisions on their own. We might say that – much like a new co-creator – an angel starts out in a well-defined environment, but in contrast to the co-creator the angel also has a well-defined identity. Yet in order to serve co-creators in a very complex environment, angels need to be more flexible, and this means they must make some decisions on their own. We might say that the original function of angels was simply to serve as messengers between higher and lower realms. Thus, an angel would be like a mail carrier on Earth, who receives an envelope and delivers it to the recipient without even looking at it. Yet as the spheres have become more complex, this simple form of messenger-ship is no longer sufficient. The angels must now step down the message and adapt it to the situation faced by the recipient. It is not simply their task to deliver a message and leave it to the recipient how it will be received. The angels need to adapt the message, to translate it according to the situation faced by the recipient. The task of the angels is no longer simply to deliver the message but to help the recipient make the best possible use of it—while staying true to God's overall vision and laws.

In reality, this is an opportunity for the angels because it offers them the potential to grow more rapidly. Yet it does require the angels to become better at discerning, and thus they must remain on the Middle Way of Christ discernment rather than going into one of the dualistic extremes. For example, angels must become better at seeing that in a very complex environment, co-creators cannot always perform a task in the most straightforward way. What seems obvious to an angel from its higher perspective may seem impossible to a co-creator who is looking at a situation from the inside. Thus, the angel can be tempted to seek to force the co-creator to do what the angel knows is best. Yet the purpose of creation is that co-creators grow to the point where they do everything not because they are forced but because they understand what is in their own best interest.

***

The failure to understand or respect the nature and purpose of free will is especially a temptation for the more sophisticated angels who have become blinded by pride and the ambition to be in control, to be God. These angels can develop an ambition to prove that the Creator was wrong in giving co-creators free will, and thus they seek to control or override the free will of the co-creators they were assigned to serve. This causes some angels to distort the message they were sent to deliver, whereby they become more and more blinded by the mind of anti-christ. So we now see that while angels do have to be flexible in delivering their message, the question is whether they will use the mind of Christ or the mind of anti-christ. Will they seek to help co-creators make the best choices from within or will they seek to force co-creators to make the choices that the angels think are the right choices? If they choose the latter, the angels seek to usurp the true teachers who never violate the free will of co-creators. Thus, the angels fall, and even after their fall they continue to act as false teachers while presenting themselves as the true teachers or even as the saviors of co-creators.

Contrary to what many people will think based on the rigidity of the Christian religion, the mind of Christ is infinitely flexible. The mind of Christ is designed to maintain oneness between all levels of creation, and it is never moved from that goal. That is why the Bible talks about the Christ being the same yesterday, today and forever (Hebrews 13:8). However this does not mean that the mind of Christ never changes. The mind of Christ has the ultimate adaptability in that it is able to go into any condition and still maintain its oneness with its source—which is truly what Jesus demonstrated by embodying on Earth. The Christ is the savior precisely because no matter how far self-aware beings have descended into duality, the Christ can meet them there and help them come up higher in consciousness. That is why you saw Jesus healing some people physically without giving them a sermon about how to attain salvation. In other words, the mind of Christ seeks to raise up life by meeting it wherever it is and helping it take the next step on the Path of Oneness.

In contrast, the mind of anti-christ has no vision of God's reality. It creates its own vision of "reality," and it then seeks to force its vision upon the world. Angels who are blinded by the mind of anti-christ will use it to define a standard for how co-creators should behave, and they will then seek to force that standard upon them.

Therefore, the angels will adapt their message to fit in the mental box of their dualistic vision. The angels might actually think that they can save co-creators, whereas God's design will lead to their destruction, but this is merely an illusion they have created based on their self-defined world view.

The vision of anti-christ is always a compromise with God's truth, so it might seem to be more flexible in that it has no absolute standard—there is only one Christ truth but an almost infinite number of "truths" in the mind of anti-christ. The vision of anti-christ seems to offer beings a way out of the responsibility to be one with God's reality. Yet the seeming flexibility of anti-christ is more than offset by its judgmental attitude. The mind of anti-christ is seeking to force reality to conform to a rigid mental image, whereas the mind of Christ is always seeking to help all life become MORE. Thus, the mind of anti-christ is actually more rigid than the mind of Christ, and once you are trapped in it, it is very difficult to escape. This is especially true for the angels who feel they are very sophisticated. Once you think you know better than God, you obviously respect no authority beyond your own dualistic beliefs, which means that those beliefs have become the ultimate closed box. Such beings feel they have God under control, meaning that God is now inside their mental box— they worship a graven image but believe it is the true God.

It is extremely difficult for angels who have fallen because of rebellion against God to come back to the Path of Oneness. Beginning with the fourth sphere, a small number of very high-ranking angels – archangels – have fallen and they have caused a great number of lower-ranking angels to follow them. These lower ranking angels find it much easier to accept the Path of Oneness, but they do have to stop blindly following an outer leader. Thus, they have to undo the original decision that caused them to follow the more sophisticated angels.

**

Another aspect of the function of angels is that they serve as transformers to step down the light of God. I know many people have been brought up to believe that people in Old Testament times interacted directly with the highest God, as for example when God talked to Moses out of a burning bush (Exodus 3:2). Yet we can now see that this simply is not realistic. The "distance" in vibration between the pure, undifferentiated Light of the Creator and the light that is used to create the material universe is enormous. If the Creator was to manifest the fullness of its Presence on Earth, the entire planet would instantly be burned up by the intensity of the Creator's Light. That is why the Bible states, "Our God is a consuming fire" (Hebrews 12:29). To a human being, the Creator will appear as a fire that consumes everything—including your mortal identity.

In reality, the Creator's Light only consumes that which is out of harmony with God's laws, that which has not yet become immortalized. And that is precisely why the Creator cannot appear anywhere in the material universe but must use spiritual beings – including angels – to step down its light until the light can perform a function in the material world while still allowing this world to remain in its unascended state. If the Creator's Light entered this world, all shadows would instantly be consumed, and this would be contrary to the purpose of giving co-creators time to grow.

An important function of angels is to step down the light from higher realms. Yet why is that light sent from higher realms? These are the main reasons:

- The material universe is sustained by a "stream" of spiritual light that is stepped down in vibration until it vibrates within the material vibrational spectrum. If that stream was cut off, it would not take long before the universe would begin to collapse due to the contracting force.

- As co-creators multiply their talents, they are given more light, and that light is delivered by angels, who step it down to the vibration of a particular co-creator's consciousness.

- Light can be sent – often combined with a message – in order to help a person on Earth rise above its limitations. We might say that a message from above can contain both instructions for how to overcome a limitation and a packet of light that gives a person the driving force to actually break free of the past—if the light is accepted and multiplied.

When angels deliver light, they must step it down so that it can perform its function in the best possible way. This means that the light must be stepped down to precisely the vibration that will help a person rise without being damaged by the intensity of the light. When Moses was on the mountain, it was an angel who delivered the message by speaking out of the burning bush. Yet the angel also gave Moses a package of light designed to give him the strength to do what he was asked to do. This light was carefully balanced to Moses' ability to receive it, which can be seen by the fact that the bush burned with fire but was not consumed. The function of spiritual light is to accelerate your consciousness without burning up your sense of identity.

The problem comes in when angels become unbalanced. They can then decide to deliver light of a greater intensity in order to – supposedly – produce better or faster results. Yet the inevitable result is that the people who receive the light – while sometimes being able to perform a certain task – end up having their identity damaged or scattered. Their energy fields are torn or rent, leaving them vulnerable to lower energies and a loss of identity and continuity. There are many examples of people who have attempted to "take heaven by force" (Matthew 11:12) by using drugs, unbalanced spiritual techniques or simply by demanding to receive light. Such unbalanced people will often attract unbalanced angels – even the false gods and their beasts – who give them more light than they can handle. And while the people may for a time appear to have great spiritual light or even seemingly supernatural powers, their unbalanced approach will eventually catch up with them as their identity is burned away by the intensity of the light. This gives rise to a pattern that can be described by the popular expression to "crash and burn."

***

I would like to summarize what we have discussed in the previous chapters. We have seen that the spheres are created with an increasing density. Starting with the fourth sphere, a new sphere is created in a mortal or incomplete state. This allows shadows to exist, which gives co-creators the opportunity to start out with a separate sense of identity and grow toward oneness. Yet the shadows also make it possible for the consciousness of anti-christ to ensnare both co-creators and angels, who cannot clearly see the fallacy of its dualistic, relative logic. This makes it possible that such beings will refuse to self-transcend, and this can prevent them from rising when their sphere ascends. Such beings will then "fall" into the sphere that is created as their own sphere ascends.

We now need to add that it takes a very long time – as time is measured on Earth – for a sphere to ascend. This means that the beings in a given sphere have a very long time to grow and develop their sense of identity. This is true for both angels and co-creators. Both can follow a path of expanding their identity and both can work their way up through layers of service in the sphere they were created to serve. Thus, by the time a sphere begins to ascend, both co-creators and angels might have attained high positions in their area of service. For example, an angel might have become the leader of a band of angels, whereas a co-creator might have become the leader of a great civilization on a planet like Earth. Yet neither of them will become fully immortalized until their sphere ascends. This means that when a sphere ascends, the co-creators and angels who were created to serve that sphere will face one final initiation, namely the ultimate test of selflessness.

I will later describe this initiation but I first want to set a better foundation. I will mention, however, that the concept I just described may seem to contradict the teachings on the ascension that the Ascended Host have released previously. In teachings released through several messengers and organizations, it has been stated that a person on Earth can win his or her ascension and become an immortal being – an ascended master – as Jesus demonstrated. It seems I am now saying that co-creators and some angels do not become fully immortalized until the sphere in which they were created ascends. There is, however, a deeper understanding that will resolve this seeming contradiction, and I shall return to it later, when we have a better foundation for understanding it.

What I will say at this point is that if a being – angel or co-creator – does not pass the final initiation of selflessness, it cannot ascend when its sphere ascends. Thus, such a being will "fall" into the next sphere, where it then has to, so to speak, "start from the bottom and work its way up in its Father's company." Such a fallen being will forget where it came from, but it will not lose its past attainment. In other words, although it starts out with a limited sense of identity, it can reconnect to the attainment it has built previously. This means that a fallen angel will be more advanced than a new co-creator, yet in order for it to rise above the state of consciousness that caused it to fall, the fallen angel must follow the same path as new co-creators, starting out in a cosmic schoolroom and seeking to come into oneness with the teacher. Since angels were not created to start out in a schoolroom, this can present a severe test of humility to the more sophisticated fallen angels.

We now see why the Serpent was in the Garden of Eden. The Serpent is a symbol for fallen angels (as well as a group of specific angels). We can now see why Eve was fooled by the Serpent who had an overpowering sense of identity and great skill in using the mind of anti-christ. Obviously, the teacher and some of the other students in the Garden had equal or greater skill than the Serpent, so Eve had a balanced opportunity to follow either a true teacher or a false teacher.

I earlier said that many spiritual people on Earth have an inner knowing that they are angels in embodiment. We can now see that although angels were not created to take embodiment, they will do so after they fall. However, this does not mean that all those who know they are angels in embodiment are necessarily fallen angels. After the first angels fell, other angels volunteered to descend into embodiment on a rescue mission for the fallen angels. More on this later.

***

Take note that even if an angel had great knowledge and skill before it fell, that expertise was acquired in a different environment than the one into which it falls. The reason being that each new sphere is more complex, more dense and has slightly different laws than the one before it. This means that even the highest-ranking fallen angels are not nearly as accomplished in their new sphere as they might think. They have to start by learning how their new sphere works. The difference is that they can eventually begin to tap into their previous experience and can thus master their environment faster than new co-creators.

When a fallen being enters a new sphere, it forgets its previous identity and attainment. Thus, it starts out with a limited sense of identity, much like a new co-creator. It goes through the same kind of rebirth as I described that students experience as they separate themselves from their teachers. The old sense of identity dies and the being is reborn into a new sense of identity in which it now sees itself as separated from its source. This gives the fallen being a chance to start with a clean slate. We might say that as the being grows in the cosmic schoolroom, it can build an entirely new sense of identity that is not polluted by memories of the sense of identity that fell.

The challenge is that as the fallen being matures, it must face a different initiation than that of new co-creators. New co-creators truly do start out with a clean slate, so they have no skeletons in the closet that must be dealt with later. A fallen being must inevitably face the initiation of rediscovering its previous identity. It then faces the difficult test of choosing between the new more innocent identity it has created or reverting back into its old, more sophisticated identity. We might say it faces the challenge of letting its fallen identity die or choosing to embody it once more. We might also say that whereas new co-creators only have to discover their divine identity, fallen beings have to first discover and dismiss their fallen identity before they can discover and embody their divine identity.

Obviously, this is a complex challenge, but rest assured that the teacher in the spiritual school is well aware of it and is prepared to offer fallen beings all possible help to pass it. Some fallen beings accept this help and turn themselves around, but others will not accept the teacher's help. Thus, they usually cannot graduate from the schoolroom but end up going out into their new sphere without having become spiritually self-sufficient. This has a number of ramifications that we will look at in coming chapters.

As a practical matter, I will from now on generally refer to both fallen co-creators and fallen angels simply as fallen beings. The reason is that both types of beings have to follow the same path in order to rise above the fallen consciousness and become immortalized. I will generally avoid using the term co-creator in the following chapters, except where referring specifically to beings who started out as co-creators. The obvious reason is that the beings who embody on Earth are not necessarily co-creators but can also be angels.

If one wants to be technical, one can say that there are no angels in embodiment. The reason being that an angel is a being who is created with a specific identity in which it is an extension of God's will. The angel falls by rebelling against this purpose, thus separating itself from its true identity. The true identity dies and the angel is reborn into a new identity. The new identity is technically not the identity of an angel but a being who sees itself as separated from God's will and law. However, this still does not override the fact that many beings in embodiment were created as angels and fell from that identity.

Let me make it clear that in the coming chapters I will talk about beings or students who were in a spiritual schoolroom with a teacher, possibly refusing to listen to the teacher's advice. This can refer to both co-creators and angels, and the reason is – as already mentioned – that when beings fall, they are first placed in a spiritual schoolroom where they receive another opportunity to abandon duality. If they refuse it, they can descend further, including taking on a physical body on Earth. You can now see why much of what I said about the Garden of Eden also applies to angels who have taken embodiment. Whether angels fell or descended to help those who had fallen, they still have to follow the Path of Oneness in order to ascend. And this requires them to make peace with the teacher and allow him to present them with the initiation that caused the fall. They must then accept the teacher's help in passing the initiation, which means they must come into oneness with the teacher. Angels often think they need no teacher, but the fact is that – once it has become blinded by duality – no being can overcome its own mental box without connecting to a being who is outside that box.

Key 15
A brief history of planet Earth

The purpose of this chapter is to give you a fuller understanding of the environment in which you are currently focusing your attention. Having this understanding will open up many perspectives that will help you accelerate your spiritual growth and overcome some of the blocks to that growth. We will look at these perspectives in coming chapters, but we first need to set a foundation. The information I will give you in this chapter will go far beyond what you learned in kindergarten and it can at first seem overwhelming. Yet as you will see in coming chapters, knowledge is power.

Let us simply summarize what science says about the timeline for the age of the Earth and the appearance of human beings. The universe is estimated to be 15 billion years old, with the Earth being formed 4.5 billion years ago. The origin of life is estimated to have taken place 3.8 billion years ago—that is 3,800 *million* years. Modern humans are said to have appeared 45,000 years ago with modern civilization, and the epoch of historical time, starting 5,500 years ago.

What is being said by science is that it took evolution 3,800 million years to produce modern humans. Yet in only 5,500 years these humans have evolved from being barely more than tool-wielding monkeys to being able to destroy most life on Earth in a nuclear holocaust. It is undeniable that the evolutionary jump from prehistoric humans to modern civilization is enormous. Yet science claims that while it took the evolutionary process 3,800 million years to go from single-cell organisms to humans, it only took that same process 5,500 years to go from prehistoric humans to modern humans.

Obviously, this can be explained by saying that biological evolution is different from social, cultural and technological evolution. Once the slow process of biological evolution had produced a species capable of consciously altering its environment, this species could quickly make a huge evolutionary jump. Nevertheless, does it seem logical that it took 3,800 million years to go from single-cell organisms to modern humans? Or is it possible that modern humans were not the first species capable of consciously altering its environment?

Could there have been other civilizations with this capacity, civilizations not currently known or recognized by science?

Obviously, such civilizations have now disappeared, so what I am proposing here is that evolution – contrary to the claims made by science – is not a smooth, unidirectional process that grinds from very primitive to more sophisticated life forms—and once a certain level has been reached, evolution cannot go backward. Instead, I am proposing that evolution is a cyclical process, more like a sine wave with crests and troughs. A civilization can evolve to a high level of sophistication, then enter a self-destructive process that leads it to disappear. I am even proposing that this could have been happening for such a long time that the slow geological processes could have played a role in erasing much of the evidence of previous civilizations. In other words, the first sophisticated civilization might have appeared millions of years ago, possibly many millions of years ago.

Obviously, there is no scientifically accepted evidence of such a process. However, science has shown that within the very short period of historical time, a mere second on the timeline of biological evolution, several civilizations have arisen only to disappear for various reasons. So it would seem possible that this could have happened many times in the much longer time-span from the origin of life to historical time. Furthermore, modern humans have, within a mere century, developed the capacity to alter the planetary climate, alter their own genetic makeup and produce nuclear, chemical and biological weapons, all of which could lead to the demise – even the disappearance – of modern civilization.

My point here is simply to make you consider that you might have been brought up with a somewhat incomplete view of the potential age of human civilization. While Biblical fundamentalists claim the entire Earth is only 6,000 years old, even the claims made by science – when it comes to the age of intelligent life on Earth – are far too short-sighted. There is simply more between past and present than is dreamt of in your philosophy.

***

Let me now give you a brief description of how the material universe and the physical Earth were created. Let me make it clear that this description is adapted to the linear form of thinking so common on

Earth. In reality, the creation process is not as linear because outside the physical realm time and space do not have the same properties as they have on Earth. Thus, creation is an ongoing process that does not have a clearly defined beginning or end or even a linear timeline. I know this explanation will be somewhat abstract, but we have to set a foundation that we can build on later.

Your planet exists in a universe that exists inside a larger sphere. The creation of your sphere started when a group of masters in one of the higher spiritual realms defined a boundary within the void, setting a sphere aside from the void. They then projected a certain amount of Ma-ter Light into that sphere. Yet the sphere was not filled evenly, being divided into four distinct levels that were set apart by the vibration of the Ma-ter Light. I earlier described these four levels as the identity realm, the mental realm, the emotional realm and the physical realm. Each realm has a range of vibrations, and since the identity realm is the least dense, it has the greatest range, the widest spectrum, the greatest number of levels. The mental realm has a smaller range, whereas the physical realm obviously has the smallest range. Each realm was created with one or two levels of vibrations but was then divided into more by the beings in that realm—the exception being the physical realm which still has only one level.

The consequence of this is that the three upper realms have what we, for want of a better word, might call a vertical extension. They can be divided into distinct layers, ranging from the lowest vibration to the highest. Each layer corresponds to a specific level of consciousness, meaning that a being must be at the corresponding level of consciousness in order to stay at a given level. If the being falls below that level, it will descend, or fall, to a lower layer. In other words, if a being in the identity realm falls below a certain level of consciousness, it enters the mental realm.

The identity realm serves as a bridge between the spiritual realm and the material world. In other words, a being who is working its way up can enter the spiritual realm only through the identity realm. It is a spiritual law that the opportunity to ascend must never be lost, and consequently the higher levels of the identity realm can never go below a certain level of vibration, they can never be polluted by the fallen consciousness. Thus, a being that falls in the spiritual realm will not fall into the highest identity levels but can fall only to the lowest identity level. If a being in one of the higher levels falls below a certain level of consciousness, it will instantly descend to a lower level and will eventually fall into the mental realm.

In the mental realm, all of the levels can contain the fallen consciousness, so a being from the spiritual realm can fall to any level. Thus, any level can be polluted by the fallen consciousness, but obviously the higher levels will be less polluted than the lower ones. The consequence is that at the higher levels of the mental realm it is relatively easy to see through the illusions of duality, whereas this is presently very difficult at the lower levels. Obviously, the mental realm has a lower limit, and if a being falls below a certain level of consciousness, it enters the emotional realm.

The emotional realm is similar to the mental in that all levels can contain the fallen consciousness. However, the emotional realm does not have a lower boundary in the same way as the mental level does. If you reach the lowest level of the emotional realm, you will not simply descend to the physical. Instead, lower levels of the emotional realm will be created in order to accommodate beings with such a low state of consciousness that they are not allowed to embody in the physical realm. The emotional level can actually be lowered in vibration until it becomes so dense that the contracting force of the Mother breaks down any structure, including the identity built by self-conscious beings. That is why some levels of the emotional realm – called the "astral plane" in some esoteric literature – are so dense that they appear as the fiery hell that some people have seen in visions. Hell exists in the lowest levels of the emotional realm, and these levels have become so dense that the contracting force breaks down any imperfect structure, setting the Ma-ter Light free in a process that appears as an all-consuming fire. One might say that you have the all-consuming fire of the Father above and the all-consuming fire of the Mother below. However, rather than the gloomy picture painted by traditional religion, the reality is that spiritual fire only consumes that which is unreal – that which is out of alignment with the vision of the Son – whereas it accelerates and multiplies that which is real.

***

My next idea will be difficult to grasp for the linear mind, but I need to plant a seed in your mind that will eventually sprout as we move on. In the three higher levels of the material realm, time and space do not exist as they exist in the physical realm. This does not mean that there is no way to measure the progress of a self-transcending being. It is still possible for beings in any of these realms to rise higher or fall lower on the spiritual path—to move up and down the scale of self-awareness. However, because the upper levels are less dense, a being that rises in consciousness will simply rise to a higher level than the beings at its former level. When a being rises, it will not say, "I am in a higher consciousness compared to yesterday." Nor will it say that it has moved to a different location in a horizontal space. Do you see the difference? On Earth you are used to measuring change by comparing yourself to a horizontal space and a linear timeline. In the higher realms, change is measured by your position on a vertical scale. It can be compared to ascending to a higher floor in a high-rise building. There is a limit to how far you can move horizontally inside the building, but you can move up or down instead.

The difference may seem subtle, but it is actually quite significant. Think back to what I said earlier, namely that beings in the higher realms do not deny God's existence. They clearly know that there is a scale of consciousness and that they can ascend or descend it. Yet the physical realm is designed to allow beings to create the illusion that God does not exist, and they cannot maintain this illusion if they have a clear vision of an ascending and descending scale as in the higher realms. Instead, the physical realm is designed with a horizontal space and a linear time. You can rise in consciousness while remaining in the same space as beings who have not risen. This is why you see that people on Earth have an extremely wide range in their levels of consciousness, from very spiritual to very materialistic and self-centered. Such a range simply cannot exist in any one level of the higher realms, partly because in none of these realms is it possible to believe that God does not exist and that your world simply appeared out of nothing as the result of an unconscious process guided only by chance. That illusion can only exist because of the density of the energies in the physical realm.

The consequence is that in the physical realm you have the concept that space is very large, possibly infinite in a horizontal extension. In the higher realms, this concept has no meaning and space is not seen as infinite because there is a vertical scale. You simply cannot move in the same horizontal direction indefinitely, as you will soon come back to your starting point and realize you have gotten nowhere. In the physical realm, time is seen as being able to extend into the future indefinitely, and although it has a beginning, it is seen as having occurred so long ago that it almost seems infinite to a human being. Thus, human beings have the illusion that time will change forever – meaning each moment is new and distinctly different from the one before – whereas in the higher realms, beings can easily see (if they are willing) when they are repeating the same cycle over and over again. In other words, only in the physical realm is it possible to make no progress in a vertical direction (by not transcending yourself) while thinking you are progressing in time and space.

The net effect is that in the physical realm it is more difficult for beings to see when they are standing still or going backward rather than rising in consciousness. This, of course, is a necessity in order to make it possible to believe that there is no God. To maintain this illusion, beings must be able to ignore the potential for a vertical ascent to higher levels of consciousness, leading to God consciousness. If you know there is a God and that you are an extension of God's Being, you can no longer ignore the possibility for you to become one with your source and attain God consciousness. Time and space serve to camouflage the vertical scale by creating the illusion that you can move indefinitely in horizontal space or move indefinitely in time without actually rising to a higher level or descending to a lower one. This makes it possible for beings who have become blinded by the circular logic of the duality consciousness to turn the physical universe into a closed circle—in their minds.

In higher realms, this illusion is very difficult to maintain, as beings experience that if they do not rise from their current level of consciousness, they will eventually fall to a lower level that is less pleasant than their current one. Beings in the lower mental and the emotional realms can still create illusions to hide this fact, but they cannot maintain them indefinitely because their environment is not self-contained. It is clearly part of a larger whole—as is the Earth, the difference being that in the physical realm this fact is hidden behind the veil of time and space.

***

I know the previous idea may seem abstract, so let me relate it to your situation on Earth. Imagine that you have a group of women who have dedicated themselves to a spiritual lifestyle. They have built a monastery and grow all their own food, only interacting with the surrounding world – what some might call the "real world" – to help others. Inside the monastery you find only people with a certain level of consciousness, and thus the lies deceit, manipulation and violence so common in the "real world" are not found in the monastery. The nuns would never dream of harming anyone, and thus one would say that these women do not deserve to be harmed by anyone. Nevertheless, one day their country is invaded by the armies of an empire based on an ideology that denies God and anything spiritual. The soldiers enter the monastery, rape all the women and burn down everything.

Obviously, human history has many examples of such events, where people in a very low state of consciousness have physically violated people in a distinctly higher state of consciousness. Such incidents invariably lead spiritual people to ask "Why?" Many even ask why a just and loving God would allow this to happen. I hope you can now begin to see that God is not wanting this to happen and God is not even allowing it to happen. Such questions are quite understandable, but only because you have been brought up with a highly incomplete, even a distorted, view of the real purpose for the material universe and the planet you call home.

What I explained above is that in the higher realms of the material universe, a scenario as the one just described simply is not possible. Even in the emotional realm, those who rise to a higher level of consciousness also rise to a higher level of their world, which brings them out of reach for the beings in the lower levels of the emotional realm. In other words, if the material universe had been functioning the same way, the nuns would have risen to a higher level in which they were completely out of the reach of the ungodly conquerors.

For reasons explained above, the material universe allows beings in both high and low states of consciousness to coexist in the same physical space and the same time. What you need to acknowledge as a spiritual person is that this is not some cosmic injustice or a mistake made by God—it is a deliberate and necessary design, for reasons just explained. In fact, the design of the material universe is a unique opportunity for beings to grow in consciousness. You simply need to raise your understanding of why this world is designed the way it is, whereby you will see that everyone is here because they made certain choices, and many of them had at least some awareness of what they were getting into.

The stark reality is that the physical realm is the densest level of this sphere, and thus it is the melting pot for all types of beings who have fallen from higher realms. Even this simple fact should empower you to leave behind the childhood expectation that God should have created the Earth as a paradise and that he should prevent bad things from happening to good people. As we examine the real history of the Earth, you will see just how unrealistic this expectation is. You will also see why certain beings have deliberately attempted to make you believe in this myth, so that they could set you up to be discouraged and feel powerless to change the status quo.

∗∗

Let me now give more details concerning how the Earth was created, which did happen after the material universe at large was formed. This planet was created by seven spiritual beings, often called the Seven Elohim. The word Elohim is commonly used in the Old Testament. It is normally translated as "God" and assumed to refer to the highest God. This is incorrect, which can be seen by the fact that the original Hebrew word is a plural word. In other words, there must be more than one Elohim, and since there is only one Creator, Elohim must refer to a lower level of spiritual beings than the Creator. In reality, the Elohim are beings in the spiritual realm who have attained mastery in the art of creating very large structures, such as planets and solar systems, even galaxies.

As the first phase of the creative process, the seven Elohim assembled in the spiritual realm and together developed the design, or blueprint, for the solar system and the Earth. At that point a group of even higher-ranking spiritual beings had already provided the basic building blocks for the material realm. For the physical realm, this included space, time, the chemical elements and the laws of nature. So the Elohim took these building blocks and combined them into their own design.

The design had four elements, designed according to the conditions in each of the four levels of this sphere. When the design was set, the Elohim used the power of their minds to impose the blueprint upon the Ma-ter Light that makes up the identity realm, thus creating the etheric version of the solar system. My point being that there is an identity, or etheric, version of the Earth.

As the next step, the mental blueprint was imposed upon the mater Light in the mental spectrum. The same was then done in the emotional realm. The physical realm, because of its unique properties, required a slightly different approach. In the higher realms, the manifestation of the solar system was virtually instantaneous, meaning that the design appeared in a given realm as one finished creation. Because of the density of the physical realm, including horizontal space and linear time, the physical design was brought into manifestation in several distinct phases. This was also done to give the illusion that the Earth could have evolved from nothing—which, of course, was one of the central goals behind the creation of the physical realm.

Genesis is therefore correct in saying that the creation of the Earth took place in seven distinct phases, but these were not 24 hour periods. The seven phases can be interpreted in two distinctly different but equally valid ways. One is that each phase represents the special gifts or God qualities of one of the Elohim, in esoteric literature often described as seven distinct light rays or levels of vibration. Thus, the Elohim started the process of manifestation by imposing the qualities of the first ray upon the Ma-ter Light, and they then built upon the foundation set by the previous step. However, the seven stages can also represent the fact that the Earth went through physical stages that first created the matter itself, then cooled it to form the planet with atmosphere, continents and oceans, then created life and then created successively more complex life forms, leading to man. This is the process crudely and incompletely described in Genesis as seven days.

Since my primary topic is the history of man and religion, I will not describe each of these phases in great detail. What I *will* say is that modern spiritual people need to develop a world view that is a synthesis between some of the ideas from Genesis and some of the ideas from science. In other words, the Earth and life were clearly created by intelligent beings from a higher realm, yet this did happen in a gradual process. And as we will see later, there is indeed an evolutionary process that is not micromanaged according to an intelligent design but can be influenced by forces that are beyond God's (direct) control. In fact, the evolutionary process can indeed happen without any intervention from above.

My point being that when you understand the true purpose of the material universe – as I have just described it – you can let go of the myth that since God is perfect, he must have created the universe all at once and in a perfect form. When you understand what I have explained, you should be able to see that God – or rather the Elohim – did not create a perfect planet but intended the beings embodying on that planet to build on the basic design according to their state of consciousness. And since a substantial portion of the beings who were allowed to embody on Earth were in the fallen consciousness, perfection is a highly unrealistic expectation. Yet even this is completely within the real purpose for the Earth.

***

At this point, I would like you to mentally look at human beings on Earth – including their physical appearance, their behavior and their beliefs – and then select one word that characterizes what you see. I am sure several words could be applied, but one of them would have to be "diversity." Human beings are incredibly diverse. Even their physical appearance shows greater variation than seen in any animal species. Human behavior is infinitely more adaptable than the behavior of animals, which explains why humans can live in a wider range of natural environments. Obviously, human beliefs and thinking show an even greater variety. In fact, you might have experienced meeting a person and, after hearing his or her thinking on a given topic, wondering, "Are we really from the same planet?" Well, in reality, you might not be, as we will see in the following sections.

I have so far given a relatively uncomplicated explanation of where the beings who currently embody in human bodies have come from. Let us look at a more detailed explanation:

• After the Earth was created and human bodies had evolved to a critical level – meaning they had the physical dexterity, nervous system and brain capable of supporting intelligent life – a number of beings in the lowest spiritual realm projected individualized extensions of themselves into bodies on the physical Earth. These extensions were new co-creators, and they started out with a limited sense of self-awareness, thus having the opportunity to grow from that level. This is much like the new co-creators in the Garden of Eden that I described earlier, only their environment was different. Yet they were still given the opportunity to grow under the tutelage of spiritual teachers. It is important to realize that before the spiritual beings sent extensions of themselves to Earth, they knew exactly what type of environment the Earth was, including the presence of the beings I will describe below. Thus, these spiritual beings made a choice to send individualizations to Earth. Strictly speaking, the individual beings did not make that choice, but their own higher beings, their spiritual selves, did. It was a choice made because these beings saw that the Earth provided a unique opportunity for growth.

- The teachers of the new co-creators were spiritual beings from a higher realm who had already ascended the path to Christhood. Instead of continuing their own growth in higher realms, they had volunteered to embody in the much denser realm of the physical Earth in order to help the new co-creators. Thus, these beings were clearly more accomplished and knowledgeable than the new co-creators. However, due to the density of the physical realm, any being who embodies loses most or all of its memory of the spiritual realm. This must be reclaimed, which requires effort. However, a new co-creator obviously cannot reclaim what it has not yet attained.

- There was also a group of beings who had fallen in the spiritual realm, and they were allowed to embody on Earth along with the other beings. These beings had a very low level of consciousness compared to other fallen beings, which is why they fell to the most dense level of the material universe. This means they were very self-centered and very intent on denying God's existence. Obviously, they also lost the memory of their prior existence, but they did have the opportunity to reclaim it. And since some of these beings were quite sophisticated before they fell, they were far more advanced than the new co-creators and even some of their teachers. That is why some of these beings quickly began to set themselves up as leaders who aggressively sought to get everyone, including new co-creators, to follow them. This is a topic we will later explore in more detail.

- Finally, there was a group of beings who had attained an even greater mastery than the spiritual teachers mentioned above.

They also volunteered to embody on Earth, however their concern was not the new co-creators but the fallen beings. They partly came on a rescue mission. The reason was that since the fallen beings were more sophisticated in certain ways than the new co-creators, they could easily build a sense of superiority. If no one on Earth had the attainment to challenge that superiority, there was little opportunity that the fallen beings would ever overcome it—which, of course, is the purpose of giving them another opportunity. Furthermore, if the fallen beings were unopposed, they could quickly drag the Earth down in consciousness, so someone had to embody on Earth to provide a counterbalance. Thus, these beings had the same level of spiritual attainment as the fallen beings had before they fell. They could, so to speak, hold a spiritual balance for the Earth. Thereby, the fallen beings could not themselves drag the Earth down, but the fate of the planet would be determined by whether the new co-creators followed the fallen beings or their true teachers.

We now see that when the Earth first became capable of supporting intelligent life, four distinct waves of spiritual beings descended to this planet and took embodiment in human bodies. It is important to realize that this happened a very long time ago. In fact, if we were to use the linear timeline of science, the first wave of beings came into embodiment over 2.6 billion years ago. Obviously, this is contrary to evolutionary biology, so let me give you a brief explanation of how evolution actually occurred.

Key 16
How spiritual evolution occurs

If you take an honest look at current scientific theories, including the Big Bang theory and evolution, you will see that there are a number of questions that the theories cannot answer. The biggest one is obviously why the process started, which some say is outside the scope of science—claiming science is better at explaining "how" than "why." Yet there are also many "how" questions that science cannot explain. How did the chemical elements evolve in the first seconds after the Big Bang? How did ordered structures begin forming out of a totally chaotic explosion, instead of the energy simply expanding outward in eternal chaos? How did solid matter appear from vibrating energy? How did organic life appear from inorganic matter? How did primitive life make the move from the oceans to dry land? How did primitive life make the leap to vertebrates? How did monkeys make the leap to humans? How did a random process produce sustainable and increasingly complex life forms, instead of reinventing single-celled organisms over and over again? And how did an unconscious process produce a species that is conscious of its own existence and has the ability to consciously alter its environment, its behavior and even its genetic make-up? With that many unanswered questions, one must wonder why these theories ever gained acceptance as scientific facts and why some people have elevated them to the same status of infallibility as some religious doctrines.

We can now answer these questions. I have earlier explained that everything in the world of form is made from the Ma-ter Light. I have said that the Ma-ter Light has a built-in consciousness, even intelligence. It is aware that it is not complete in itself and it has a longing for wholeness, meaning oneness with its source. The Mother Light has a built-in longing for oneness with the divine Father. However, while the Ma-ter Light is conscious, it is not self-conscious, it is not self-aware. Even though it has the potential to take on any form, it cannot take on form by itself.

Imagine that you are watching a far-away planet through a telescope. You assume the planet has a gravitational field, but you cannot tell by looking at it. You can tell only if you observe an object being pulled in by the gravitational field. We might say that gravity is an inconsequential force until it has an object upon which it can exert a pull. Likewise, the life-force built into the Mother Light needs something to pull on before it produces an effect. Compare this to a blanket of snow on a hillside. The snow simply sits there and does nothing. Now imagine you compress a bit of snow and start rolling it into a snowball. There will come a critical point when the ball is big enough that gravity can pull it down the hill. From that point, your intervention is no longer needed, and the laws of nature can "keep the ball rolling," as they say.

This is similar to the process that led to the existence of the physical universe. The Ma-ter Light could not have started this process on its own. But once the process was started and had reached critical mass, the life-force in the Ma-ter Light could take the process forward to a higher level of complexity. The exact form of this complexity was determined by the design principles defined for the physical universe, what scientists call the "laws of nature." It was spiritual masters who defined these principles, and it was the seven Elohim who started the creation of the Earth, thus setting the evolutionary process on its track.

Spiritual masters also started the initial expansion that scientists call the Big Bang. In reality, the expansion did not start in a single point but started in a huge number of points that appeared in a spherical shape. When scientists give up the idea of creation starting in a singularity and look for a spherical beginning, they will get their mathematical equations to work. Yet that will also require them to acknowledge that the original points did not appear as the result of a materialistic process. They appeared because an image had been imposed upon the Ma-ter Light from a higher realm. This image was also infused with a surge of high-frequency spiritual energy that started the expansion. This infusion is continuing to this day, and it is what drives the physical universe to keep expanding (the continued expansion of the universe is another fact that science cannot adequately explain). In other words, the universe is not driven by the initial burst of energy but by a continuous infusion of energy from the spiritual realm.

After the Elohim had started the process of concentrating physical matter and having it form into planets and solar systems, they withdrew and let "nature take its course." In reality, this was not an entirely unguided process because it involved conscious (but not yet self-conscious) beings, often called the "elemental builders of form." However, for the sake of simplicity, we will simply say that the process continued without direct intervention from the masters in the spiritual realm. You might compare this to Jesus' parable about the talents, where the master withdrew after giving the servants their talents. Jesus' parable illustrates a universal principle, namely that more evolved beings start a process and allow less evolved beings to build upon it.

When the process of revolutionary jumps and evolutionary changes had produced the Earth and taken it to a point of being able to sustain life, the masters from the spiritual realm again stepped in and provided the surge to jump from inorganic matter to organic life forms. When this process had reached critical mass, the masters again withdrew until their intervention was needed to take life to the next level. Thus, what biologists call the missing link between monkeys and humans is missing because it was not a physical link. The missing link in evolutionary theory is the intervention of masters in the spiritual realm, beings who have the vision and the power to accelerate the evolutionary process into a revolutionary jump.

It has long been known from the fossil record that evolution is not a smooth or constant climb toward more complex life forms. It starts with a revolutionary jump, followed by an extended period of gradual expansion, adaptation and complexification. Then another revolutionary jump occurs, followed by another evolutionary phase. This process is undeniable from the fossil record, but it has largely been ignored, mainly because materialistic scientists can find no material cause for the evolutionary leaps. Let it be known to those who have ears to hear that there is no material cause, only a spiritual one.

What are some of the implications of this? Well, for starters, we now see that materialistic science is correct in describing an evolutionary process but incorrect in postulating that is has a material cause. In fact, the evolutionary process is a consequence of the spiritual purpose for the physical universe, namely plausible deniability. The universe is designed to give fallen beings from the spiritual realm an environment in which they can find plausible reasons for denying the existence of God. These reasons are only plausible and not absolute, so as to give these beings an opportunity to grow out of the need to deny God and get back into the River of Life. Great care has been taken to design the universe in such a way that there are plenty of opportunities for beings to rediscover the reality of God. That is why a growing number of scientists are beginning to realize that scientific theories, especially the Big Bang and evolution, raise questions that cannot be satisfactorily answered by looking only at materialistic causes. Internally consistent answers can be found only by incorporating the existence of intelligent beings who give the impetus for the revolutionary jumps. Now for the real reason why I brought up the process of evolution.

***

Let us return to the timeline developed by science. For the sake of simplicity, I will ignore the reality that time is non-linear and refer to the official timeline. The Earth was created 4.5 billion years ago and life emerged 3.8 billion years ago. So after the revolutionary leap that created the planet, it took 700 million years for the evolutionary process to bring the Earth to the point of being able to support life. I earlier said that the first intelligent life appeared 2.6 billion years ago. In other words, it took 1.2 billion years to take life from its initial stages to the level where a species with a human-like intelligence appeared. It follows that it took 1.9 billion years from the creation of the Earth until intelligent life could inhabit the planet.

Science will disagree with this timeline because it will be argued that the process of evolution simply could not have produced intelligent life in a mere 1.9 billion years. In reality, this is correct, given that the mechanical process of evolution could not have produced life at all. As I have said, there is a built-in process in the Ma-ter Light that can drive the evolutionary process, once the revolutionary leaps have taken place. Several such leaps were necessary to produce intelligent life, and that is why it took "only" 1.9 billion years to produce such life.

The entire purpose of creating the Earth is to create a platform for intelligent life, and the evolutionary process was given a lot of help in order to produce intelligent life much faster than if it had been left alone. In other words, it would have been possible to produce intelligent life with much less assistance from above. It only took a minimum of seven evolutionary leaps to produce humans, but in reality more were given in order to compress the timeline. My point being that the Earth has been a platform for two parallel evolutionary tracks:

- The fast track is the one that was given maximum assistance from above. It did produce intelligent life 2.6 billion years ago, so for that long of a time span, spiritual beings from above have been descending into human-like bodies, as I described earlier. Obviously, this has been an important part of the Earth's purpose, and it has given growth opportunities to countless beings.

- The "natural" track is a track that was given only the minimum assistance from above. In other words, this track has produced intelligent life with seven revolutionary leaps, and then the rest has been due to the evolutionary force that is built into the Mater Light and directed by the laws of nature (of which not all are currently known or correctly understood by science). Obviously, as science is correctly pointing out, this track will take much longer to produce human life. In fact, the timeline that science currently gives for the emergence of modern humans is not too far off the actual timeline for the natural track.

Why is this important? Because it describes the origin of another group of beings that are currently embodying on Earth. You will notice that so far I have only talked about beings who originated in a higher realm and who descended to Earth by merging their energy fields with the energy field of a human body. Such beings are individualized extensions of spiritual beings that were originally created by the Creator. In other words, they are part of a spiritual hierarchy that has descended from higher realms to lower realms. Obviously, many of these beings started out their journey on the Earth and can then ascend from there. Nevertheless, they did come out of beings from the higher realm and thus can tie in to their spiritual "family tree." They can draw on this for guidance and even for spiritual energy (when they attain some measure of Christ consciousness).

Yet because of the built-in intelligence of the Ma-ter Light, there is a parallel track of beings who have evolved from below. As I said earlier, the Ma-ter Light cannot create by itself, but once a certain critical mass, a critical complexity, has been created, the evolutionary process can and will bring it toward greater complexity. Thus, this process has taken over after the initial revolutionary leaps and has produced intelligent beings from "nothing," so to speak.

It is only within the timeline that science gives for the emergence of modern humans that such beings have attained the complexity that gives them not only human intelligence, but even the ability to grow beyond the material realm. In other words, such beings have now attained the opportunity to rise above the material universe and work their way up through the emotional, mental and identity realms, until they can actually ascend to the spiritual realm and become immortal spiritual beings.

This is a complex process that I will not here describe in detail. What I *will* say is that everything is created out of the Creator's Being, so when an individual being, evolving from below, reaches a level of sufficient complexity, it can receive a conscious self, whereby it awakens to the reality that it is out of the Creator's Being. In other words, such a being must *earn* a conscious self, whereas a co-creator starts out with one. You currently find a large number of people on Earth who can trace their origins to this process. Many of them have a deep sense of how the Earth works and they have a great mastery of their physical bodies. Many of them also have a great love for this planet and are more sensitive to it than some of the beings coming from higher realms. Some of them still embody as so-called native peoples around the world, but many are found in all areas of modern society.

In a spiritual sense, these beings are generally less evolved than those who have descended from above. Thus, they tend to join religions in which they can follow leaders who have descended from above. They need to imitate those who have spiritual attainment, often for many lifetimes, before they themselves can receive a spiritual spark that makes it possible for them to transcend from within themselves. My point is that a being who has descended from above has a built-in ability to consciously self-transcend. Beings who evolve from below must earn this ability. Beings from above can lose it, and in that case they must also earn it back. There are actually some beings from above who have descended far below the level to which many of the beings from below have evolved.

***

I realize the picture is beginning to look complex, but we have to add another layer of complexity. I have described how new co-creators were sent to the physical realm. In reality, new co-creators were sent to each of the four levels of the material universe. In other words, there were four initial waves of co-creators. So there was a wave for the identity realm, one for the mental, one for the emotional and one for the physical.

It was the original intention that the members of each of these waves would enter the Path of Oneness and gradually ascend from their level toward the spiritual realm, whereby they would not only raise their own consciousness but also raise the vibration of their native realm. In other words, a co-creator would never descend below the level of its initial descent. Yet as I have explained, each of the four levels also gave an opportunity to certain beings who had fallen from above. Thus, on each level there was a risk that some of the fallen beings would refuse to grow and that some of the new co-creators would start following these false teachers instead of their true teachers.

Some beings from the identity realm did indeed follow the false teachers and fell into lower realms, including the physical realm. In reality, it was only a small fraction of the beings in the identity realm who fell, whereas the rest stayed true to the Path of Oneness, which is why the identity realm is relatively pure. On the mental level, a slightly higher fraction fell, but it was still the majority that ascended. In the emotional realm, the majority ascended but a substantial portion did not. In the physical realm, most beings have become blinded by the dualistic illusions and only a few have so far completed the Path of Oneness and have risen to higher realms.

My point is that besides the beings described in previous sections, the Earth also houses some members of the three higher waves, those who have not – so far – chosen the Path of Oneness. Not all who fell from the identity realm (for example) have descended to Earth, because some are in the mental or emotional realm. So what determines whether a lifestream keeps descending until it can go no further? It is one of two things:

- A being can make itself a blind follower of another lifestream, usually a being who has fallen from a higher realm and thus has greater attainment. If that fallen being falls further, the blind followers will simply fall with it.

- A being can cross a dividing line of selfishness, whereby it will inevitably fall to a lower level. That dividing line is where you cause other beings to fall into the duality consciousness that you have embodied. The Law of Free Will basically says that you have a right to enter into any state of consciousness you choose. Even a being in the lower identity realm will be allowed to enter into a very low state of consciousness—as long as that being does not directly cause others to fall with it. Yet when a fallen being causes another being to fall, the "tempter" will inevitably fall also. This can be seen in the account of what happened to the Serpent who tempted Eve:

> 14 And the LORD God said unto the serpent, Because thou hast done this, thou art cursed above all cattle, and above every beast of the field; upon thy belly shalt thou go, and dust shalt thou eat all the days of thy life:
> 15 And I will put enmity between thee and the woman, and between thy seed and her seed; it shall bruise thy head, and thou shalt bruise his heel. (Genesis, Chapter 3)

My point here is that the physical Earth has become a collection place for the beings who have fallen from or through the three upper realms. Some of these beings fell because they blindly followed their leaders, so they are relatively benign. However, they often want to keep following a leader and thus are not likely to take any kind of initiative to self-transcend or improve life on this planet.

However, the Earth has also become the home to many beings who fell because they were very aggressive in violating the free will of others. This, of course, is something you were not told in kindergarten or even in Sunday school. So I am sure you can see that if you are to successfully walk your own spiritual path, it is extremely helpful to be aware of precisely what kind of an environment you live in. You can then be alert to the presence of fallen beings who will aggressively seek to pull you down to their level of consciousness. Some of these beings have fallen all the way from the spiritual realm, while others have fallen from one of the three higher levels of your sphere. For that matter, there are some who have fallen in the physical realm and have not yet gone to the astral plane. They can also be very aggressive, for the old saying is true, "Misery wants company."

Even what I have explained so far is not the full picture. There is still more complexity.

***

As I said before, the three higher realms of this sphere are made from energies that are less dense than those of the physical realm. Because of the more fluid energies, the higher realms are easily divided into distinct levels, where each level represents a level of consciousness and houses only beings whose spiritual attainment, or lack thereof, is within a certain spectrum. In general, the higher realms were created with only one level (the identity realm was created with two), and the division into more levels happened only as the beings in a given realm lowered or raised their consciousness. In other words, the beings in a given realm have created the levels in that realm. For example, the beings in the emotional realm have created the lower levels of that realm, what I have called the astral plane and which many people have seen as hell. Many people have also seen parts of the astral plane during dreams or while being affected by drugs or alcohol.

As mentioned, the purpose of allowing this division into levels is to protect the more highly evolved beings from direct contact with the beings who are selfish and abusive. Obviously, the beings in the physical realm were meant to have that same protection, but because the physical realm cannot be divided into levels, this was accomplished by spacing galaxies and solar systems so far apart that no physical travel between them is practical.

What I am saying here is that there are millions of planets in the physical universe upon which there is life, similar in principle – although in some cases very different in actual design – to what you see on Earth. Yet these life-supporting solar systems are spaced so far apart in horizontal space that direct physical contact between them is in all practicality ruled out. It is actually possible to travel between solar systems, but this can be accomplished only by very sophisticated technology. And such technology can be developed only by beings with high spiritual attainment, meaning that they would have no aggressive purpose for traveling to other planets. They would also understand the purpose of the universe, namely to give beings on a certain planet an opportunity to evolve on their own, and thus they would have the wisdom not to interfere with the process.

My point here is to help you see beyond some of the popular myths that have been created by science fiction literature and movies. Life on Earth was *not* created or planted by space aliens coming to this planet in flying saucers. Nor will this planet be ravaged by space scavengers on a never-ending quest for the resources they depleted on their own planet. And neither will the Earth be saved by space aliens with such sophisticated technology and wisdom that they can solve all of humankind's problems. Interplanetary travel is possible for lower civilizations over short distances, such as within your solar system. However, none of the planets in your solar system do – any longer – support life in the physical realm. The many theories and even sightings of UFOs are due to the fact that such forms do appear in the astral plane. Some people have tuned their minds to the astral plane and have had experiences that were so real that they appeared physical. There are even places on Earth where the vibrations of the physical realm have been lowered so that there – at least at times – is a certain crossover between the physical and the astral plane. This effect can even be reinforced by people becoming obsessed with UFOs and thus actually creating some of the phenomena they observe.

Take note of the subtle but all-important ramifications of what I am saying between the lines. Everything in the physical realm is created through a process that started in the etheric realm, where you find the pure thoughtforms that have been created by masters in the spiritual realm. Etheric thoughtforms were superimposed upon the Ma-ter light, thereby lowering its vibration to the mental level. Based on the etheric thoughtforms, more concrete mental images were created and the light was lowered to the spectrum of the emotional. Here, the images were imbued with emotion that lowered the Ma-ter light to the physical spectrum, where it became manifest as physical forms. This process involves self-aware beings on all levels, and because some of these beings have been blinded by the duality consciousness, the lower levels of the etheric, mental and emotional realms contain many impure thoughtforms that distort the light as it passes through. My point is that if the light follows the purest possible path, it can reach the physical without being greatly distorted. Yet if the light has to pass through the lowest levels of the mental and emotional realms, it can become distorted to the point that the original etheric thoughtform is completely obscured or even replaced by an impure thoughtform.

You now see that the conditions on the physical Earth depend on whether people in embodiment are able to bring into manifestation the pure etheric thoughtforms or whether they bring into manifestation the distorted thoughtforms on lower levels. If people have a relatively pure consciousness, they can bring etheric thoughtforms into physical manifestation without having them distorted. They will then create what seems like heaven on Earth. Yet if people lower their consciousness, they will bring into physical manifestation the thoughtforms that exist in the lower mental and emotional realms. This happens on a planetary scale with certain groups of people tuning their collective consciousness to certain levels of the higher realms. Yet this collective attunement can also become concentrated in certain physical areas. That is why you can see some areas that have a very high and spiritual vibration, whereas other areas seem like hell on Earth. This is outpictured in the myth of a Shangri-la that is an ideal society, but in the past many golden age civilizations have physically manifested such a society.

We now see that if people tune their consciousness to the lower levels of the emotional realm, you will see the absolute lowest thoughtforms ever created by human beings and the false gods. Now add to this that the beings who exist in the lower emotional realms must steal people's energies in order to survive, and you see that these beings are always trying to find an inroad into people's consciousness. Their primary inroad is fear, and they are always seeking to induce a fear of something against which people think there is no defense. For example, during the Middle Ages many people believed in demons and evil spirits that could attack them physically. They even believed in beings that they thought were physical, such as dragons, trolls and many other so-called mythological creatures. Did such beings exist? Yes, they did and they still exist in the lower emotional realm. Could such beings ever be seen by people and could they affect people physically? The answer is a yes, but only in the sense that people had collectively attuned their consciousness to the lower levels of the emotional realm. This had created a "bridge" of consciousness that blurred the border between the physical and the emotional realm. We might say that since everything is consciousness, people's collective consciousness had tuned the vibrations of the physical realm to the emotional realm so that a crossover effect occurred. At certain times and in certain areas, people actually encountered dragons and other mythological creatures. Were these creatures actually physical? Well, that depends on how you use the word. For example, people could have an encounter with a mythological creature that they experienced as a fully physical encounter, yet that creature could not move around freely or propagate in the physical realm. It could only exist in a localized area and only as long as people's consciousness made the crossover possible.

This explains why there were many people in the Middle Ages who claimed to have seen various mythological creatures, whereas hardly anyone in a modern, rational society encounters such creatures. Because of the advent of science, people either do not believe in such creatures or do not believe they are physical. Consequently, the bridge between the physical realm and the emotional levels where such creatures exist has been reduced to the point where there is no longer a significant crossover effect.

The false gods and fallen beings in the emotional realm obviously were not happy with the fact that their power to terrorize people into misqualifying their light was reduced by the advent of science. So they were looking for another way to induce a primal fear by making people believe in a phenomenon from which it seemed there was no defense. This did not become possible until science had advanced to a point when most people realized the universe was extremely vast and believed that life was produced through an evolutionary process. It now became possible to introduce the concept that in this vast universe, sophisticated civilizations had evolved on other planets. As humankind had started to use up resources on this planet, other civilizations had already ravaged their planets and were now roaming the universe in spaceships, seeking for a planet that still had resources left. Because such space aliens had technology far beyond that of humankind, no defense was possible. And since people who believe in science tend to *not* believe in God, they thought no power – in heaven or on Earth – could protect them from an alien invasion.

My point is that much of the science fiction phenomenon has been a tool for the false gods to create a new scientifically based primal fear to replace the religiously based primal fear of the Middle Ages. Thus, they have now created a new fear from which there seems to be no defense. You might find it ironic that the science that helped humankind overcome the fear of the Middle Ages has become the instrument for creating a new version of the same fear.

Do UFOs exist? Yes, they exist in some of the lower levels of the astral plane. Are they physical? Not in the sense that they were built on other planets in the physical spectrum and have physically traveled to Earth. So why does it seem like UFO sightings are becoming more and more common? Because as people have collectively tuned their consciousness to the levels of the astral plane where UFOs have been created by the false gods, a crossover effect has been produced. This effect can potentially be increased, and the best thing the most spiritual people can do is to refuse to focus their attention on the UFO phenomenon and instead focus it on the spiritual realm. My point is that most spiritual seekers can – and should – pursue spiritual growth without being concerned with the UFO phenomenon. The fact is that the more you focus on the UFO phenomenon, the more you tie yourself to the astral plane and open yourself up to its energies and thoughtforms. Thus, by invoking spiritual protection and keeping your focus on the spiritual realm, you can rise above any connection to the astral plane and the UFO phenomenon. The prince of the astral plane will come in his flying saucer and have nothing in you (John 14:30).

**

Since the physical universe cannot be divided into distinct levels, what happens when a large number of the beings who embody on Earth fall into the duality consciousness and become increasingly self-centered? If the physical realm had been as fluid as for example the emotional realm, there would have been many physical versions of the Earth, each version housing only beings at a certain level of consciousness. Obviously, this is not the case since the Earth is home to people with an incredible variety from very high to very low states of consciousness.

In reality, the law will allow beings to continue to embody on Earth even when they fall to a very low state of consciousness. There is actually a lower limit (beings who go beyond it go to the astral plane), but it is presently rather low, as can be seen from the headlines of any given day. However, the planet itself is still affected when humankind's consciousness goes up or down. As I have explained before, everything is made from the Ma-ter Light and this light is made from the consciousness and Being of the Creator. Thus, the Ma-ter Light has consciousness, meaning that the Ma-ter Light that makes up planet Earth will be affected by the state of consciousness of the people who embody on the planet. Obviously, this truth will be denied by most people, but this is due to the fact that their conscious-ness has become so low that they cannot directly perceive anything beyond what can be detected by the physical senses. They can see no direct link between their state of consciousness and the physical con-ditions on the entire planet or in their own bodies. This is due to a refusal to accept full responsibility for one's life and salvation, which is the main characteristic of the duality consciousness. The more self-centered people become, the less willing they are to accept responsi-bility for their actions, feelings, thoughts and sense of identity.

My point here is that because most of the beings who embody on the physical Earth have become blinded by the duality consciousness – a process that began over a billion years ago – the physical condi-tions on this planet have been altered drastically compared to their original design. When the Earth was first created/evolved, it had a much more pristine and balanced physical environment than what you see today. In fact, the matter that made up the planet vibrated at a higher level than today. There were literally no natural disasters, such as hurricanes, earthquakes or volcanoes. Neither were there any poi-sonous or predatory animals, no parasites and no physical diseases. Thus, the life-span of the physical bodies was much longer than today. In fact, it was possible to sustain a physical body indefinitely.

As a side note, the most significant effect of this shortened life-span is that it made reincarnation a necessity. Beings who fell into the duality consciousness misused the Ma-ter Light and thus created a debt to life. The Law of Cause and Effect says that you have to purify, or raise the vibration of, any misqualified energy you have generated in the physical realm before you can permanently ascend above that realm. And since many beings could not purify the misqualified energy, could not balance the karma, in the short life-span, it became necessary to give them additional opportunities by having them come back into other physical bodies. The process demonstrated by Jesus is that when you have balanced all of your karma, you can permanently ascend to a higher realm and no longer have to reincarnate on Earth.

Some beings ascend directly to the spiritual realm and are thus free of any ties to the material world. Yet others rise above the need for physical re-embodiment, but rise to one of the three higher realms in this sphere, having to work their way up from there.

The real cause of the pristine conditions found in previous ages was that matter itself was less dense, which means that there was less "mass" for the contracting force of the Mother to pull upon. This force is not quite the same as gravity, although gravity is one of the effects of this force. To illustrate what has happened, imagine that the Earth used to be bigger and less dense than it is today. Now imagine that the gravitational force was increased, causing the planet to start shrinking, thereby compressing the same amount of matter into a smaller space. It should be obvious that this would give rise to various pressures and forces within the Earth. This would cause the Earth's core to heat up and give rise to all of the forces that geologists have discovered in the Earth's mantle and crust, setting the stage for volcanoes, earthquakes, continental movements, polar shifts and so on.

Obviously, this is a crude illustration, and the reality is that the physical universe was created at a certain level of vibration that was far above what is now the vibration of the lower emotional realm. The vibration of the Earth has been lowered below the original level, causing physical matter itself to actually become more dense. This is what has brought the vibration of the Earth closer to that of the lower emotional realm, causing the crossover effect described earlier. This densification of matter has created the forces that cause upheaval on the physical planet, and they are a signal to humankind that their state of consciousness affects every aspect of their physical environment. Obviously, most people have not gotten the message, but an awakening is always possible. As a side note, the fact that matter in earlier times vibrated at a higher level is part of the explanation why science – so far – has found no fossil evidence of advanced civilizations or ancient humans. Another part of the explanation is that scientists have not been looking with open minds.

As humankind's consciousness became lower, the physical matter that makes up this planet became denser, and this drastically altered the environment. I have also explained that self-conscious beings co-create by envisioning images and then superimposing them upon the Ma-ter Light. It should be obvious that when humankind's consciousness was lowered, they focused on lower and less pure images. Many of these images were subconscious, but they were still projected unto the Ma-ter Light. Obviously, this did not happen overnight, but over a long time-span the collective consciousness of humankind gave rise to virtually all of the imperfect and unbalanced conditions you see today, including the many physical diseases that plague your bodies.

My main point here is that co-creators were sent to Earth with the command to "multiply and have dominion." Thus, God's law will allow humankind to collectively lower their consciousness and "densify" an entire planet to the point where it begins to break down, as is evident in anything from climate extremes to physical disease. It is, in fact, possible that the inhabitants of a physical planet can lower their consciousness to such a point that they literally cause their planet to disintegrate because the contracting force of the Mother pulls matter apart. This has happened to a number of planets throughout the universe.

Obviously, neither God nor the spiritual overseers of Earth want to see this planet disintegrate. So even though humankind has free will, the Law of Free Will gives us some safety measures to try to prevent the inhabitants of a planet from destroying themselves and their physical home. We will take a look at one such safety measure.

***

As a mature spiritual seeker, it is extremely important for you to begin to understand that in the material world nothing is – presently – ideal. You have an inner longing for the spiritual realm, perhaps even a subconscious memory of it, so you feel that things should be better than what you see on Earth. Yet the material universe is still a world in which there is much darkness left, which means that the duality consciousness – and beings who are trapped in it – can continue to exist here. And what you need to understand is that the duality consciousness can distort and pervert anything—which is why there is nothing ideal in the material universe.

My point here is that the Earth was originally intended to be home to only a few groups of lifestreams, meaning that these lifestreams had some common characteristics, especially in their way of thinking. This was done as a protection mechanism in order to minimize the risk of irreconcilable conflicts. The more homogenous the population of a planet, the less likely that it will split into factions that cannot communicate – because their way of thinking is too different – and thus cannot resolve conflicts. Yet even this scenario can be perverted by the duality consciousness.

The simple fact is that while homogeneity of thinking can prevent certain conflicts, it can also prevent the inhabitants of a planet from pulling themselves out of a downward spiral once they have passed a critical point. When most of the inhabitants think alike, it is likely that they will all move in the same direction. After a critical mass of people on Earth had become blinded by the duality consciousness, they pulled the majority with them and then most people were moving together down the staircase of consciousness. Only a few people resisted this downward movement, and they could not pull the rest up. And precisely because most people thought alike, they could not see what they were doing. They could not see that they had entered a self-destructive spiral, and their similar thinking caused them to reinforce each other. There were simply not enough people with a different way of thinking to cry out with sufficient force, "But the emperor has nothing on!"

You can now see why nothing is ideal in the material world. The duality consciousness operates with two extremes, and it will always seek to pull any situation into one of those extremes. So when you have a planet on which most inhabitants think alike, the duality consciousness will tend to pull everyone into following the crowd, so they all go down together without realizing what is happening. Their similar way of thinking blinds everyone to the warning signs that would have been more obvious to people with a different way of thinking. Yet on a planet with a greater variety of thinking, the duality consciousness will polarize people into groups and create conflicts between them. And precisely because people think so differently, they will think there is no way to reconcile such conflicts. One might refer to the old saying, "You are damned if you do and damned if you don't," which is perfectly true for beings trapped in the illusions of duality.

Obviously, the spiritual overseers of humankind don't feel damned, but we do have a very realistic assessment that once a planet has fallen into a state of duality, there is no guaranteed way of pulling it out. Everything is up to the free will of the inhabitants, and if a critical mass of them are bent on destroying their planet, we can do nothing to prevent them from doing so. What we *can* do, however, is to try to counteract the conditions that caused a planet to go into a self-destructive spiral, so let us look at how we have attempted to do this for Earth.

***

As mentioned, I am a member of a group of spiritual beings called the Ascended Host. I am part of a group that is specifically assigned to planet Earth. Yet the Ascended Host is a vast body with billions of members in this sphere and the spiritual realm. Because the spiritual realm, even the identity realm, is beyond time and space, we can communicate with each other and can, so to speak, compare notes. We do indeed hold council meetings and we can invite members from other groups to such meetings so we can learn from each other. I might mention that we obviously are beyond the duality consciousness and thus have no rivalry or sense of competition. We are fully focused on doing our job of helping unascended beings reach the ascended state, and we learn from each other whenever possible.

There are two common scenarios that cause planets to self-destruct:

- The conflict scenario in which warring groups emerge. When they develop destructive technology, they can literally blow their planet apart. If all of the nuclear weapons on Earth were detonated at once, this planet would disintegrate and fracture into millions of pieces, none of which could sustain life.

- The stagnation scenario in which the inhabitants of a planet refuse to grow and transcend themselves. This causes a gradual slide, until life simply becomes extinct as a result of the contracting force.

Over time, we have seen many planets self-destruct for both reasons. Referring to my previous explanation of the two basic forces, we can see that the two scenarios are both the result of a perversion of these forces:

- The conflict scenario is the result of a perversion of the expanding force of the Father. When people become unbalanced in the expanding aspect, they tend to enter into black-and-white thinking, which causes them to think that their way is the only right way. They also feel it is their duty to force all other people to follow their way and that they should do so with any means available. Because of the nature of the dualistic mind, there will always be at least two groups who think this way, and this will set up a conflict between them that they are unable to resolve on their own. The result is often an escalation of warfare until it reaches a scale that blows their planet apart.

- The stagnation scenario is the result of a perversion of the contracting force of the Mother. This causes the inhabitants of a planet to stop transcending themselves, thereby going against the very basic principle of life itself, namely to raise the vibration of a planet until it can ascend to a higher level. They become so content with the way things are, that they want to continue – indefinitely – to live the way they do now. When people become unbalanced in the contracting aspect, they think they don't have to transcend but that they should seek to preserve everything the way it is instead of causing it to grow. They think the imperfect conditions in the material universe are either meant to *be* that way or are beyond change. This leads to a mental and spiritual inbreeding, which is a similar mechanism to what you see in a population where the gene pool becomes too shallow. Birth defects will start to appear and the population will collapse, eventually becoming extinct unless new genes – meaning new information – can be introduced.

On a number of planets you have seen one of these scenarios cause a planet to either be blown apart or become barren. The question is what has happened to the beings that caused a planet to disintegrate or be unable to support life? Well, according to the Law of Free Will, those who violate the free will of others will eventually lose their opportunity to influence others. Thus, some of the most aggressive beings from a dead planet can be dissolved. This will happen only to those who have fallen in a higher realm and have had numerous opportunities to give up the fallen consciousness yet have rejected all of them. The less aggressive beings would be taken out of the physical realm and allowed to stay in the lower levels of the emotional realm. These levels serve as a holding place for beings that have nowhere else to go (until they either change their ways or their sphere ascends and they go to the next sphere).

At some point it became apparent that many planets had followed this pattern of self-destruction. As a side note, the vast majority of the planets in the physical universe are in an ascending spiral. Even the other planets in your system have ascended to the point of having no life in the physical spectrum but only in one or more of the higher levels. At a high-level council meeting a decision was made to conduct a cosmic experiment. It became clear that in every case where a planet self-destructed, a major factor was that the inhabitants had become blinded by the duality consciousness. Thus, they simply did not recognize – through willful ignorance – that their actions could cause their own destruction and even the destruction of their planet. They simply would not believe that their minds had that kind of destructive power. Yet when beings had actually witnessed the destruction of a planet through one of the two scenarios, most of them had a rude awakening and were filled with remorse. Thus, it was decided to allow some of the beings who had taken part in destroying a planet to embody on planets that had entered a downward spiral (and passed the "point of no return") but had not yet been destroyed.

After the Earth had entered the stagnation scenario and had descended to a point where life was beginning to break down, it was decided to allow a large number of beings from other physical planets to embody here. These were beings who had witnessed the destruction of planets for both reasons. They had at least a subconscious memory of what can happen to a planet and could provide a perspective that the inhabitants of Earth did not have. It should also be noted that the beings who came to Earth were selected to represent a very broad range of backgrounds and mindsets. The purpose was to truly "stir the pot" by bringing in beings who could provide a different and often challenging perspective to the stagnant inhabitants of the Earth. It was hoped that because of the diversity, the different groups of beings would counterbalance each other with no one group attaining dominance.

It was fully clear to the Ascended Host that this was by no means a foolproof plan. In fact, the greatest risk was clear from the beginning, namely that the many different lifestreams would congregate in distinct physical groupings and create conflicts with each other until they eventually developed technology that could cause them to blow up the Earth. Yet because the Earth was already in a downward spiral that would have ensured its destruction (had nothing drastic been done), the experiment was allowed to go forward.

Yet we did not simply stir the pot and sit back waiting to see what would happen. On the contrary, millions of lifestreams from the spiritual realm, from the higher realms of this sphere and from more evolved planets than Earth, have – over time – volunteered to take physical embodiment in an effort to counterbalance the most destructive lifestreams and help raise the consciousness of humankind.

Despite the fact that the inhabitants of the Earth have developed weapons that could blow up the planet, I can tell you that the Earth has been in an upward spiral (although with a lot of ups and downs) for quite some time. In fact, we have now reached a point where it has become possible for the Earth to take a quantum leap forward. However, this will require that those who are willing to be a part of this process awaken to their cosmic purpose and make an extraordinary effort to raise their own and the collective consciousness. And it is precisely this realization that is the purpose for this long explanation of the Earth's complexity. Yet rest assured that we will build on the teachings in this chapter as we begin to look at how you can use this knowledge to fulfill the purpose for your being on this Earth. That purpose might be to contribute to an experiment that – if it works – is of cosmic importance. If the Earth can be raised, the experiences from this planet will be used as a model for many other planets, which can have a major impact on the universe as a whole.

Before we move on, let me mention that although the previous explanation does talk about many different lifestreams or evolutions, it does not give the full picture of every being currently embodying on Earth. Yet it does give enough knowledge to help you understand the basic dynamic of this planet, and I will fill in more of the details as we move along.

Key 17
Where did you come from and why are you here on Earth?

One of the master keys to spiritual freedom is the realization that there is more to life than meets the eye, coupled with the desire to find a deeper understanding of that more. You will be free only when you develop a desire for greater understanding – with all thy getting, get understanding (Proverbs 4:7) – and when you become willing to look for that understanding beyond traditional sources, meaning your personal mental box and the one created for you by society, even by humankind at large.

The beginning of wisdom is when you realize that there is much more to understand about life than what is seen by the senses or known by current human belief systems, be they scientific or religious in nature. For example, you are beginning to see that the Earth had an original purpose and that it now has a modified purpose. Yet the underlying purpose is always to give the maximum opportunity for growth to the maximum number of lifestreams.

Everything you see on Earth is simply a facade, an appearance, that hides a deeper reality behind it. The material world hides the underlying spiritual reality. That is why Jesus told people not to judge after appearances (John 7:24), for when you do so, you inevitably condemn yourself to living a life based on superficial knowledge and incomplete assumptions. You will be basing your life on visible effects rather than the hidden, underlying causes.

The reason why it is possible for people to deny the existence of God is that physical matter is so dense, yet matter has become even more dense than the original design because of the fall in humankind's consciousness. This is what creates a self-reinforcing downward spiral. The density of matter made it possible for people to deny the existence of God, deny that they are spiritual beings and justify not transcending their current level of consciousness. This caused them to violate the most fundamental spiritual law, namely that of self-transcendence. The contracting force of the Mother magnified people's choices, making their consciousness more dense, and they actually projected that density upon the Ma-ter Light that makes up planet Earth. Over a long period of time this caused matter itself to become even more dense, which made it even easier for people to deny their spiritual purpose, again lowering their consciousness and projecting an even denser image upon the Ma-ter Light. Obviously, once such a downward spiral reaches a critical mass, the beings who created it can no longer see what they are doing and thus cannot pull themselves out of it.

That is why there is a need to introduce "new blood" into the system in the form of beings who have not created that particular spiral and thus have a fresh perspective on conditions on Earth. These beings can then be like the little child in the fairy tale about the emperor's new clothes. They can see what none of the native inhabitants of the Earth can see, giving them an opportunity to cry out, "But the emperor has nothing on!" The problem is that these beings have to embody in physical bodies and enter into the density of the energy field of Earth, which can cause them to forget why they came. The question is whether these beings will recognize who they are and whether they will awaken to their roles of crying out to awaken humankind – the sleeping beauty – from its long sleep.

You now begin to see that the main purpose of this book is to awaken you to the realization of who you really are and why you are here on this small planet that you somehow find it difficult to call home—the reason being that this planet may not be your spiritual home. Will you consciously acknowledge who you are and why you came here? And will you fulfill that purpose by following Jesus' example of bearing witness to the truth (John 18:37)? However, in order to bear witness to the truth, you first have to *know* the truth, namely the one truth of the Christ mind, as opposed to the many dualistic "truths" of the mind of anti-christ.

***

In the previous chapter, I described the origins of most beings on Earth and divided them into a number of groups. There is always an inherent danger associated with doing this, which is why – in the past – much esoteric knowledge was only available to more advanced students or was veiled behind convoluted or imprecise language. By making this knowledge publicly available in a form that is easy to understand, it is foreseeable that some of the people who read this information will still be trapped in the duality consciousness. These people will be spiritually blind, and they will project their dualistic images upon my teaching. Let me outline how some people are likely to interpret and use the material.

The very first thing that spiritually blind people will do is to impose a value judgment upon the material. They will say that some lifestreams are clearly in a lower, more selfish, state of consciousness, and they will then define this as "bad" compared to a higher state of consciousness – their own – that is seen as "good." They will seek to set up outer criteria – such as people's behavior, race, nationality, sex or beliefs – in order to identify the bad people and set them apart from the good—meaning themselves. They will divide the world into good people and bad people based on outer criteria, based on appearances.

This will lead to the next step, namely an attempt to define certain groups of people as being inherently bad while others are inherently good. In other words, all members of certain groups are bad and all members of other groups are good. This can then lead down the slippery slide of discrimination that – during the course of history – has given rise to many atrocities, including discrimination based on religion, race, sex, nationality, ethnicity and any number of outer characteristics. The actual form of such discrimination ranges from mild dislike to genocide.

Once you start identifying certain groups of people as bad, it is but a short step to reasoning that all of your problems, all of your society's problems or even all of humankind's problems are caused by the bad people. So if we could only remove these bad people from the planet, all problems would be solved and there would be paradise on Earth. If you take an honest look at history, you will see that even religious people have reasoned this way and have been persuaded by the subtle logic that the end can justify the means. They have fallen into the trap of thinking that even though their religion – as virtually every religion on Earth does – defines killing as being against the laws of God, it is acceptable to kill the people who violate God's law. In other words, it is acceptable to violate God's law in order to bring God's kingdom—which is based on the even more subtle logic that you *can* actually bring God's kingdom through a violation of God's law. This, of course, is not so and we will later look at where exactly this kind of reasoning comes from.

In order to make sure that as few people as possible fall into this dualistic trap, let me make certain things very clear. It is absolutely impossible to set up any system based on outer characteristics and say that all members of certain groups are bad people or are fallen beings, whereas all members of other groups are good people or highly evolved souls. There never has been nor ever will be such criteria. The reason for this is very simple, namely the principle I have described of allowing many different beings to embody on Earth for the purpose of stirring the pot. In order to stir the pot to the maximum extent, beings with high and low states of consciousness can be found distributed in *any* conceivable group of people.

It is meaningless to set up outer criteria and attempt to identify certain types of beings, because this cannot be done based on outer characteristics but only based on the inner characteristic of people's state of consciousness. People who look for outer characteristics demonstrate that they are still trapped in duality – they judge after appearances – and thus they simply cannot read people's state of consciousness. Only people who are almost free of duality can read the state of consciousness of an individual, and such people would never seek to discriminate or judge. Those who *want* to identify good and bad people can't do so and those who *can* have no desire to do so.

Yet I obviously have a reason for describing the fact that there are many different types of lifestreams embodying on Earth. So let us look at a model that – while not being beyond manipulation by the duality consciousness – can give us a reasonable foundation for understanding the planetary dynamics.

***

I earlier explained that there are two basic options in life. The purpose of life is to grow in self-awareness, meaning that you transcend your current sense of self and become more until you unite with your source and your individuality becomes immortalized. This is the Path of Oneness, the Path of MORE. Obviously, the other option is to reject the Path of MORE and become less by refusing to self-transcend, seeking to hold on to or even reinforce the sense of identity as a separate being. By choosing this option, you will gradually become less – when you seek to preserve your separate life, you will lose it (Matthew 16:25) – until the Ma-ter Light out of which your being is

made will eventually return to its pure form. We might say that the
light that was you has returned to its source, but your self-awareness
has been obliterated in the process because the conscious self will
eventually blend into the Creator's Being. *You* have not returned to
your source as a distinct individual, and thus the Creator has not
become MORE through you.

Yet a third options exists – at least temporarily – in the sense that
some lifestreams refuse to make a clear decision. Thus, they put
themselves in a gray zone, a twilight zone, in which they have neither
committed to the true path or the false path. In reality, all beings who
are not going up are going down, but I am talking about those who
deliberately rebel against life and those who simply refuse to make a
decision. Those who will not decide often follow either a true teacher
or a false teacher, so that they do not have to make their own decisions. We now see that humankind can be divided into three groups:

- The top ten percent are the people who have stepped on to the
  Path of Oneness. Doing this is first of all an inner condition,
  and when you embody in a physical body in the dense energies
  of Earth, you tend to forget your past attainment, having to
  reclaim it. So there are many of these people who are not consciously aware that they are spiritual people on a mission. This
  is especially true in Western societies, where such people tend
  to reject both traditional religion and materialistic science, feeling like they have no place to go to express their spirituality.

  All people in this group have the potential to experience a
  dramatic awakening that will make them consciously aware of
  who they are and why they are here. Obviously, there is a range
  of consciousness, from spiritually evolved people – who are
  usually fully aware of who they are – to less evolved people
  who might have to go through a period of spiritual study and
  practice in order to fully awaken.

- The lowest ten percent are the people who have deliberately
  rejected the Path of Oneness and who are seeking to reinforce
  their separate sense of identity by building up their egos. Again,
  there is a range from people who might seem to be driven by a
  quest for money, success or power to people who are overtly
  selfish, even those who are often labeled as evil. Some are not
  aware that they are following the false path (and would deny it

if they were told), while others are fully aware that they are working against God's plan and everything it stands for (while of course often hiding this from their followers).

All of these people do have an opportunity to experience a spiritual awakening, but for most of them it will take a very dramatic change in consciousness that can only be achieved over time. This is due to the fact that such people have layers upon layers of dualistic lies that must be consciously discarded before they will be free to fully understand and embrace the path that leads beyond duality. People simply cannot discard every lie at once, as that would shatter their sense of identity.

- The general population, the middle 80 percent. These are the people who are still in the gray zone and who have not committed to the upward or the downward path. These people do not want to make their own decisions, they do not want to take responsibility for their lives or their salvation, so they always look for a leader to follow. Again, there is a range of consciousness, and the least awakened people will follow the bottom ten percent. The more mature people can often be awakened to the spiritual path and begin to follow the top ten percent. The problem is that the top ten percent are often reluctant to take up leadership positions, a fact we will later discuss in greater detail.

My point here is simple. For a long time there has been somewhat of a balance between the top ten percent and the bottom ten percent. They have been evenly matched and their respective effects on the planet tend to neutralize each other. Thus, the future of planet Earth – as has been the past – will be determined by the middle 80 percent, the general population. If they follow the bottom ten percent, the planet will enter a downward spiral, and if it goes beyond a critical point, it is very difficult to turn back. If they follow the top ten percent, the planet will be in an upward spiral. If it reaches a critical point, there will be a large-scale awakening that will free the majority of the human population from the dualistic illusions that keep them trapped in a life of suffering and limitations. This can then lead to the planet ascending and throwing off those beings who will not commit to the Path of Oneness.

In the past, this planet has been in a downward spiral that would surely have caused it to disintegrate. Yet for a very long time, the Earth has been in an upward spiral, thanks to the fact that some spiritually evolved lifestreams volunteered to embody here and pull the population up. The population has responded to this pull, although reluctantly and without understanding what has happened. Thus, the upward climb has not been a steady progress but has gone in ups and downs, as can be witnessed in recorded history.

Yet as I mentioned before, the planet has now come very close to a positive turning point, and if an extraordinary effort can be made by the top ten percent, it can literally bring about the large-scale awakening of the population that will bring the upward spiral past the point of no return. It is, of course, the purpose of this book to give the members of the top ten percent the understanding they need in order to bring about this awakening.

***

You might wonder how the top ten percent of the population can possibly influence the other 90 percent. One of the most common concerns among spiritual people is how one person can make a difference. The belief that you are an insignificant being who can do nothing to improve planetary conditions is a lie that is deliberately manufactured to prevent the top ten percent from fulfilling their mission. So let us take a look at the reality behind materialistic appearances.

As I have explained, everything is made from the Ma-ter Light and this light has consciousness. Thus, everything is made from consciousness – everything *is* consciousness – which even some modern scientists are beginning to realize, a realization that will become clearer within a couple of decades. I have explained that the Ma-ter Light cannot create something by itself, but when a complex structure has been formed, the Ma-ter Light has a built-in drive that will cause such a structure to evolve. The Earth is a very large and complex structure that has plenty of mass and complexity for the evolutionary force to work upon. This force will pull on everything within its reach, and that includes you and every other human being.

As I said, there is an energy field that surrounds your physical body – actually your physical body is the most dense part of this field

– and it is made up of the four levels of your mind. Likewise, the physical Earth is the most dense part of the energy field of the emotional, mental and identity versions of the planet. No energy field is an island, so your personal energy field exists within the larger energy field of the entire planet. There are some spiritual teachers who have likened the physical Earth to a living organism, and while this is not incorrect, my concern here is to show you that within the energy field of the physical planet is another energy field made up of the collective consciousness of humankind. Your personal energy field is tied to that collective field, your mind is tied to the collective mind.

Creation happens through the formation of complex structures, and when a structure becomes sufficiently complex, it forms a unit. The Earth is such a unit, and every human being who lives upon it is part of the unit. Inside this unit you have the energy fields of all human beings, and they combine to form the collective consciousness. Your energy field – your mind – is part of this collective mind, it is an individual unit that exists within a larger unit. Your mind will inevitably be affected by the collective mind so that you are pulled either up or down by the mass consciousness. Yet the influence goes both ways, meaning that you can also pull on the collective consciousness—which, after all, is made up of individual minds that are combined into a superstructure. The influence that an individual mind has on the collective mind and the degree to which the individual mind is influenced by the collective mind depends entirely on the individual's level of consciousness.

Beings in the top ten percent and the bottom ten percent usually have individual energy fields that are relatively shielded from the collective energy field. That is why they have the potential to become leaders who are not overwhelmed by the collective mind but can pull the collective mind up or down. Yet, as I have said, the influences of these two groups have often neutralized each other. The general population, the middle 80 percent, are usually quite overwhelmed by the mass mind and follow along with it in anything from religion to fashion. So the real key to improving the planet is to shift the collective mind in a positive direction—something must exert a decisive pull.

Again, this can seem overwhelming, but it will seem less overwhelming when we consider the fact that the very force of life itself is in our favor. As I have said, the built-in evolutionary force will pull any structure, any unit, in an upward direction. Thus, if the collective consciousness was left alone, was left in the neutral state exemplified by the general population, the Earth would inevitably be pulled into an upward spiral by the evolutionary force. My point being that the Earth can enter a downward spiral only because the general population is being manipulated by the bottom ten percent. These selfish lifestreams must constantly work to neutralize the evolutionary force by aggressively manipulating the general population. And while they sometimes do this through physical force, the very basis for their power is ignorance. Only by deceiving the population can the bottom ten percent keep them ignorant of what is going on. Yet the general population is not made up of stupid or evil people, so if they were aware that they were being manipulated, they would change their ways accordingly. The consequence is that the master key to bringing spiritual freedom to the entire planet is to raise the awareness of the general population.

As mentioned before, if people knew better, they would do better. This statement is the logical consequence of the fact that the evolutionary force pulls on all life to become MORE. Thus, all people have a built-in tendency to go from a limited state to a more affluent state, to go from suffering to fulfillment. If you take normal people and offer them something that is clearly better than their present conditions, people will always choose what is more over what is less. My point being that people will only hurt themselves – and each other – because of ignorance. This ignorance is always a result of the duality consciousness that makes it possible for people to do something without seeing the consequences. Thus, people can harm themselves and each other without realizing that they are doing so. As Jesus said on the cross, "Father forgive them, for they know not what they do" (Luke 23:34).

My main point is that the very life force itself is working to awaken humankind. The bottom ten percent are creating a pull that is seeking to prevent this awakening, but they are constantly having to fight against the basic life force. Thus, it is actually much easier for the top ten percent to pull the population up than it is for the bottom ten percent to pull the population down. The problem in the past has been that the bottom ten percent have been more aware, more aggressive and more determined in their efforts than have the top ten percent. Thus, they have so far managed to prevent a large-scale awakening, whereas the top ten percent have not been able to generate the decisive pull that could bring about the awakening. The bottom ten percent have been absolutely determined that they have a right to pull the population down, whereas the top ten percent have not been equally sure about their right to pull the population up. We might say that, so far, the bottom ten percent have been more willing than the top ten percent to have dominion over the Earth.

What can the top ten percent do to change the equation? They can become more aware and more determined, which involves two aspects:

- The Alpha aspect is that the top ten percent must make an extraordinary effort to raise their own consciousness. When one person raises his or her consciousness, it pulls the entire collective consciousness up. A person who wins permanent freedom from the duality consciousness, call it the ascension or enlightenment, will have a planetary influence. The Buddha, Jesus and others literally had an influence that raised the entire collective consciousness to a higher level. That is why Jesus said, "And I, if I be lifted up from the Earth, will draw all men unto me" (John 12:32). *You* have the same potential as both the Buddha and Jesus, for what one has done all can do—a fact that is vehemently denied by the bottom ten percent. Yet winning your ascension is not the only way to raise the collective consciousness. Thousands or millions of people who raise their consciousness to some degree will also have an effect—there is strength in numbers. Yet what is really required in order to generate a decisive pull is that the top ten percent come to realize the true goal of the spiritual path, namely what I have described as attaining personal Christhood.

- The Omega aspect is to do what Jesus said, namely to let your light shine (Matthew 5:16) and to bear witness to the truth (John 18:37). The general population are followers, so they need examples to follow. They need someone who can demonstrate the Path of Oneness—which is above and beyond any single religion. In other words, the traditional dualistic, black-and-white thinking is that we must convert everyone to the only true religion. Yet that is not what I am implying. Instead, we must help people see the universal spiritual path, the Path of

Oneness, that transcends all outer religions and cannot be confined to any one religion.

An essential part of this process is for spiritual way-showers to teach people about the spiritual side of life and the path to Christhood. This includes making people aware of the duality consciousness and the illusions of the ego that make them vulnerable to following false teachers instead of true spiritual teachers. An important aspect of this is to challenge the many subtle, dualistic beliefs spread by the false teachers – the blind leaders – as both the Buddha and Jesus demonstrated. We will later talk more about the specifics of what you can do, but for now I want to stay with the overall perspective, the big picture.

***

I have said that the influence of the top ten percent and the bottom ten percent have often neutralized each other. For quite some time, the Earth has been in an upward spiral, but it has been a very slow climb. This is comparable to what happens when you put a car in first gear and start driving. As you step on the gas pedal, the engine starts turning faster, yet the power is not transferred to the wheels, so the car simply makes a lot of noise without going faster. The car will not go faster until you change to a higher gear. So what is needed on Earth right now is that the top ten percent, the most spiritually aware people, shift their consciousness into a higher gear. With that I mean that they come to the basic, the most fundamental, the most essential, realization about the spiritual path. That realization is to understand the essence of the duality consciousness.

Let me make this more concrete and relate it to what we are talking about here by explaining why the influence of the top ten percent has so often been neutralized by the influence of the bottom ten percent. The essence of the consciousness of anti-christ is that it is dualistic. Duality means that in any situation, the dualistic mind defines two polarities, two opposites. The dualistic mind can look at opposites in only one way, namely that one is good and one is bad, one is true and one is false. Thus, there will inevitably be a battle between the opposing forces, and the dualistic mind will look for only one outcome, namely that one polarity obliterates the other one. To the dualistic mind, there is only one way to establish God's kingdom on

Earth, namely by obliterating the force that opposes God's kingdom, including killing all of the people who are identified as being aligned with the evil force.

In reality, one opposite polarity can *never* obliterate the other one. Surely, this can sound like a startling statement, but take a realistic look at the history of humankind. Look at all of the warfare and bloodshed that has been happening throughout recorded history. Then consider that recorded history is only a split second of the real time-span for the existence of intelligent life on this planet. Now consider that for millions of years there has been a warring in the members of the inhabitants of Earth. Then consider that in virtually all of the battles and wars this planet has seen, both sides believed that they represented good and that they had to fight the other side because it represented evil. Virtually every war has been fought based on the justification that it was necessary to wage war in order to destroy evil. Yet after all of this fighting and warfare, evil has not been obliterated but is still a force on this planet.

My point here is that it is indeed possible to eradicate evil from planet Earth. But it will *never* be possible to eradicate evil by fighting it in a dualistic battle, a battle that is based on the dualistic consciousness. *Only* by rising above that state of consciousness can you make a *real* contribution to removing evil from this planet. As I explained earlier, evil is not the opposite of God, it is the opposite of relative good. Both good and evil are defined based on the dualistic mind, and thus you can never eradicate evil as long as you are trapped in that mindset. You must be willing to rise above *both* evil and relative good in order to take yourself and your planet to a higher level. This requires you to be willing to question *everything* and see that even what you think is good or true might indeed be based on the duality consciousness, the consciousness of anti-christ. Traditionally, most people in the general population and even many spiritual people have not been willing to do this. However, cycles are changing and people are becoming more open to asking questions that just a decade or two ago would have been considered unthinkable. We might say that one of the master keys to spiritual freedom is to ask the kind of questions that external forces say you are not allowed to ask and that your own ego says you do not need to ask. Wisdom is hiding behind the questions that are not asked, so the key of knowledge is to ask better questions, questions that go beyond duality.

***

The real key to understanding why the top ten percent have not won the battle for the minds of humankind is to see that so far the top ten percent have not understood what I have just explained. They have acted based on a true desire to free this planet from evil, to do good and to bring God's kingdom to Earth. Yet their true desire has been perverted by the duality consciousness, which has fooled them into believing that the *only* way to eradicate evil is to fight it in a dualistic struggle for supremacy. This is nowhere more clearly illustrated that in the history of the Christian religion, which – for anyone willing to see reality – has often engaged in a dualistic struggle to eradicate what it defined as evil. The crusades, the inquisition, the persecution of scientists, the witch hunts and many other atrocities were misguided attempts to eradicate what the church defined as evil. Yet how could this happen in a religion that supposedly is based on the teachings and example of Jesus, who said:

> But I say unto you, That ye resist not evil: but whosoever shall smite thee on thy right cheek, turn to him the other also. (Matthew 5:39)

Can you begin to see that what Jesus was truly saying here is that when you resist evil, you are engaging in a dualistic struggle against evil, and thus you are already caught in the consciousness of duality? What Jesus was teaching is an eternal principle, namely that you cannot solve a problem as long as you are trapped in the same state of consciousness that created the problem. The existence of evil is a product of the consciousness of duality, which is based on the illusion of separation. When people think they are separated from their own source, they also think they are separated from each other, and this illusion is what makes it possible to set themselves up in opposition to each other. If all people realized that they are part of the Body of God and that by harming others they hurt themselves, would there be any warfare left on this planet? So how could you ever remove evil by fighting it based on the consciousness that created evil? As Jesus tried to explain – as best it could be done 2,000 years ago, given the state of consciousness of humankind – you can remove evil *only* by rising above the consciousness that created it. So you must start by refusing to resist evil and therefore turn the other cheek *no matter what* other people do to you.

Can you now see that the bottom ten percent have a very simple way to neutralize the influence of the top ten percent and prevent them from pulling humankind to a higher level? All they have to do is to engage the people in the top ten percent in one of the numerous dualistic battles they have created in every area of human life and in every geographical area on this planet. Once a person from the top ten percent has been drawn into such a battle – thinking he or she is doing God's work and helping to eradicate evil from the planet – all the person is doing is to reinforce the dualistic struggle and thus keep humankind stuck in this state of consciousness. The fallen beings and false gods are deliberately trying to prevent the top ten percent from awakening the population, and their most efficient strategy is to divide and conquer. They divide people into two camps and get them to fight each other, thereby preventing them from being united in Christ vision and overcoming the forces of duality. As we will later explore in more detail, the beings of the bottom ten percent survive from the energy released in such dualistic battles, so any time you fight them, you only reinforce them and the entire force of evil that is hanging like a black cloud over this planet.

What is truly needed in this age is that the top ten percent of the people begin to understand the dynamics of how the consciousness of duality works and how it has influenced *every* aspect of human society, including religion. They must then make an extraordinary effort to free themselves from that state of consciousness and then go out and demonstrate this to the world, including exposing the dualistic lies wherever they are found. This is exactly what Jesus did, but because humankind has risen higher in consciousness, you can do even more today than Jesus could do 2,000 years ago—and you can do it without being nailed to a wooden cross or killed in other ways. That is why Jesus said, "He that believeth on me, the works that I do shall he do also; and greater works than these shall he do; because I go unto my Father" (John 14:12). The fact is that because of the growth in humankind's consciousness that was initiated by Jesus' victory, many more people are now ready to come to a conscious understanding of the duality consciousness and the influence of the human ego. They need to have these topics presented in a way their outer minds can understand and accept, and they need examples to follow.

Take note that turning the other cheek is not a passive or pacifist measure. Jesus was not simply sitting in a cave and experiencing a higher state of consciousness. He went out into the world to challenge and expose the bottom ten percent, the false leaders, who were misleading the population. And then, when they attacked him based on their dualistic consciousness, he refused to fight back and instead turned the other cheek. This had several purposes, as we will discuss later, but one of them was to make the evil of these people more visible. By allowing them to attack him and by not responding in kind, Jesus made the evil of his attackers visible for people to see. In some cases, they even saw the evil in themselves and were transformed by the realization of what they had done. Yet even if they refused to see their own evil, other people had the opportunity to see the evil of those who would attack someone who was not attacking them.

When I talk about making the evil of some people more visible what exactly do I mean? Always keep in mind that the real issue is to raise the awareness of the general population so they will no longer blindly follow the blind leaders, meaning the leaders who are blinded by the duality consciousness. The real key is to expose the fact that these leaders are acting based on the duality consciousness. In other words, it is not the object to expose certain people as being bad or evil. The real object is to expose the fact that people commit evil acts because they have been blinded by a certain state of consciousness. Therefore, overcoming evil is not a matter of getting rid of evil people but a matter of getting rid of the consciousness that blinds people to God's reality. What people really need to understand is that the battle is *never* against other people but *always* against the duality consciousness. And, of course, you can win that battle only by rising above the duality consciousness. A dualistic battle can *never* lead to the ultimate victory but will only prolong the dualistic struggle indefinitely.

Before we move on, let me clarify what we have discussed in the last few chapters. We have seen that the Earth is a mixed environment with beings from many different backgrounds. However, let me make it clear that the Earth was created as a platform for a specific group of new co-creators. After the Elohim had created the physical Earth, these co-creators were sent into embodiment with the command to "multiply and have dominion." My point is that it was given to these specific co-creators to have dominion over this planet, and this divine decree still stands. The destiny of the Earth is still in the hands – or rather minds – of this specific group of co-creators. As I have explained, many other beings have been allowed to embody on Earth, including fallen beings from above, beings from other parts of the material universe and beings with mastery descending from above. Yet even though these beings now outnumber the original co-creators, the destiny of the Earth is still decided by the co-creators for whom the planet was created. All other beings have no direct influence on the destiny of the Earth, but they can obviously influence that destiny indirectly by affecting the original co-creators.

If the original co-creators accept their God-given responsibility to take dominion over this planet, if they join the Path of MORE and transcend themselves, then this planet will continue in the current upward spiral and can – within the foreseeable future – manifest a Golden Age. Yet if these co-creators refuse to take responsibility, the planet will – once again – enter a downward spiral. One characteristic of the original co-creators is that they have a deep love for this planet and they really care about the Earth. In contrast, many of the beings from other parts of the material universe see the Earth as a somewhat primitive or annoying planet. The fallen beings see it as a planet that is beneath them, and they only want to use it as a tool for gaining power. Even the spiritual beings who have descended on a rescue mission do not feel at home on this planet and often can't wait to get back to higher realms.

The important point about this fact is that the top ten percent are not all members of the original co-creators. In fact, the majority of the top ten percent are not from the original co-creators. Their task is to awaken and enlighten the original co-creators without knowing who they are. However, what they *can* know is that it is God's will that the original co-creators take dominion over the Earth without being forced by anyone from the outside. Thus, the top ten percent must be absolutely committed to not falling into the subtle trap of the fallen beings, whereby they seek to force the original co-creators into being saved. I trust this will underscore the need to avoid engaging in any dualistic battles, as I have explained in this chapter. I trust it will also help the top ten percent have a realistic assessment of their role on this planet, thereby avoiding the even more subtle trap of feeling superior. You are not here because you are better than the original co-creators. You are here to serve them with utmost humility as an extension of the spiritual teachers of the Ascended Host. It is in being the humble servant of all that you can attain the greatest possible growth from your sojourn on this planet.

Key 18
Why good people commit evil acts

In this chapter we will take an in-depth look at why people commit selfish – or evil – acts and why they can actually believe such acts are justified, necessary, beneficial, for a higher good or their only option. This is truly the central mystery of human existence, as it has been known on planet Earth. And thus, understanding this mystery is one of the master keys to attaining spiritual freedom. We might say that feeling forced or compelled to commit evil acts or doing so without realizing it is an obvious violation of your spiritual freedom. I have already given you the keys that are needed in order to put together the big picture:

- Everything is made from the Ma-ter Light.

- The Ma-ter Light has consciousness, or rather, it *is* consciousness.

- A self-aware being has the ability to imagine an image or belief and then use the power of the mind to superimpose that image upon the Ma-ter Light. Because the Ma-ter Light has consciousness, it can take on any form imposed upon it.

- A self-aware being can construct mental images by using either the consciousness of Christ or the consciousness of anti-christ.

- An image based on the consciousness of Christ will uplift all life by helping it become MORE, and this is the purpose of life itself. Such an image is sustainable because it is in oneness with the forward movement of life, the River of Life. An image based on the consciousness of anti-christ will cause all life to become less, which goes against the basic life force. Thus, such an image will eventually be broken down by the contracting force of the Mother that is built into the Ma-ter Light.

We now see that when an image is superimposed upon the Ma-ter Light through the consciousness of duality, that image will not instantly be erased. It will continue to exist for some time, which has the purpose of giving beings an opportunity to learn by experiencing

the consequences of their creative efforts. Thus, whatever you co-create, you will inevitably experience. However, we now need to take
this one step further and understand that because the Ma-ter Light has
consciousness, what beings create can take on a life of its own.

To explain this, let us look at the creative process that I described
earlier. We have seen that there is the spiritual realm, in which there is
no room for darkness or evil, and there is a sphere that is set aside
from the void but still has a mixture of light and darkness. The lower
sphere has entered the process of ascending, leading toward that
sphere becoming part of the spiritual realm. In other words, in the
past some of the spheres that are now in the spiritual realm were in
much the same state as your sphere is in today. As the intensity of
light increased in those spheres, the beings in them began to face the
initiation I described earlier, namely that they had to overcome their
innocent ignorance and begin to consciously create a higher sense of
identity based on the Christ mind. Some of these beings refused to do
so, and instead they entered into a state of willful ignorance that they
justified by using the duality of the mind of anti-christ. These beings
refused to come into oneness with the purpose of life, and instead
they insisted on maintaining a separate sense of identity as being outside the process of life itself—what I have called the River of Life.

From the beginning of creation, self-conscious beings have
always had free will, and thus they had the opportunity to go against
God's vision by using the mind of anti-christ. Several spheres had
ascended without anyone using this option, yet there did come a point
when some beings for the first time chose the mind of anti-christ.
When that happened, the mind of anti-christ was simply an option
that had never been expressed. In other words, nothing had been co-
created through the mind of anti-christ. Yet as the first beings made
their choice, they started creating something through the mind of anti-
christ. And because a number of beings used the mind of anti-christ,
they created something that was bigger than themselves. In other
words, the whole became more than the sum of the individual contri-
butions. How can this be?

The explanation is, as I have already described, that the Ma-ter
Light has a built-in evolutionary force that pulls on any organized
structure, urging it to become more. So what actually happened was
that the initial group of beings created a structure out of the consciousness of anti-christ. When this structure reached a critical mass

of complexity, the evolutionary force built into the Ma-ter Light gave it a separate state of consciousness, a sense of awareness as a distinct being with certain qualities (as defined by the beings who created it). In other words, the beings actually created a new state of consciousness, a new mind, a new entity. And this new "mind unit" inevitably became subject to the evolutionary force, causing it to develop a basic level of consciousness. This does not mean that this new entity was self-aware, but it does mean that it had a basic sense of identity that gave it a survival instinct. Part of this survival instinct was the drive to propagate, the drive to grow, to evolve.

At this point, I am aware that the more perceptive students might think I am contradicting myself. I earlier said that the contracting force of the Mother will break down any structure that is not based on the Christ mind. Yet I am now saying that the evolutionary force – also built into the Mother Light – will cause any complex structure to evolve—even structures based on the mind of anti-christ. So let us now take a closer look at the basic forces of life, as this will open your understanding to your true role as a spiritual being on Earth.

***

As I explained earlier, the world of form in which you live started when the Creator defined a boundary and then withdrew itself into a singularity in the midst of a void. In that singularity, there was no differentiation whatsoever—there was nothing expressed. Yet the purpose of life is to give self-conscious beings an opportunity to grow, and for this to happen, they must start out as separate beings and then grow into oneness with their source. Obviously, for anything to be separate, there must be differentiation. The Creator started this differentiation by projecting itself as two different but complementary forces, namely the expanding and the contracting force, the Alpha and the Omega, the beginning and the end. Everything else – everything between the beginning and the end – is created by the interplay of these two forces.

The two forces are manifest as the polarity of Spirit and Ma-ter, which I have also called Father and Mother in order to tie it into a traditional religious terminology. Spirit is represented by self-conscious beings who impose images upon the Ma-ter Light, which then takes on expressed forms. A linear – and thus incomplete – illustration of this would be the figure eight, with the upper half representing Spirit and the lower half representing Ma-ter. Spirit also represents the spiritual realm and Ma-ter represents the sphere that has not yet ascended to Spirit.

We now need to understand that although there are two distinct polarities, each one representing one of the basic forces, we still find both forces within each polarity. In other words, Spirit represents the expanding force because this force is the primary or strongest force in the realm of Spirit. Yet Spirit also has a contracting force, and the interplay between the two forces is as follows:

- The expanding force of Spirit is the force of self-transcendence that drives all life to become MORE. The drive to become MORE is what gives rise to differentiation, because it drives co-creators to express their individuality and in so doing build on to, complexify, that individuality. If this was the only drive, all life could become scattered and the differentiation could soon become self-destructive. Co-creators could define their respective individualities in ways that conflict and thus break down each other.

- The contracting force of Spirit is what ensures that while life is differentiating, all life is pulled into a oneness with the Creator's purpose. This oneness is not sameness, and this ensures that all life grows in the same direction so that differences enhance each other instead of canceling out each other. We might say that the expanding force gives life the drive to become MORE and the contracting force concentrates or aligns that drive so the movement of life becomes a coherent stream, what I have called the River of Life. The stream moves all life toward becoming MORE rather then becoming less.

The basic interplay of these two forces gives rise to a cyclical movement, namely what some spiritual teachings have called the in-breath and the out-breath of God. It is essential for you to understand that this does not mean that God creates a world in an out-breath and then – after a certain time – obliterates that world in an in-breath, repeating the cycle indefinitely without getting anywhere. In other words, God does not go back and forth between creation and destruction. Instead, God has created an ever-expanding movement, namely 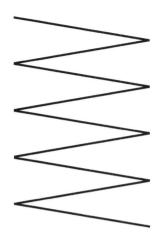 the River of Life. A world is not destroyed in the in-breath—it is accelerated to a higher level so that it transcends its former state. To give you a crude illustration of this, consider the drawing above.

It depicts a zig-zag line that can represent the out-breath and the in-breath, creation and destruction. Seen from this perspective, it seems to go back and forth, creating a world and then destroying it. Yet life is not a two-dimensional line. The zig-zag line is simply a spiral seen directly from the side.

When seen from a different angle, you see that what seems to be a back-and-forth movement actually forms the coils in an upward spiral. The back-and-forth movement now forms an ascending movement, where one out-breath and in-breath form the foundation for a continued growth to a higher level. In other words, nothing is wasted, for every cycle sets the stage for a higher cycle. With this in mind, let us look at how the expanding and contracting forces work in the realm of Ma-ter: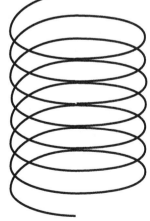

- The expanding force is what I have called the evolutionary force. It will bring life toward greater complexity, but it can do so only within a certain level or range. For example, once vertebrate animals had been created by a revolutionary leap, the evolutionary force caused such animals to evolve toward greater and greater complexity, eventually producing primates that have many human-like features. Yet it took another revolutionary leap to bring life to the human level, and such a revolutionary leap can only come from Spirit. The expanding force in the Ma-ter realm is evolutionary and cannot produce a revolutionary leap on its own. It needs the influence from the Spirit realm to make a revolutionary leap.

- The contracting force in Ma-ter has the effect of making sure that any structure which does not – after a cycle moves to the next level – make a revolutionary leap is broken down, so that the Ma-ter Light is not permanently trapped in an imperfect form but is returned to its original purity. In other words, when a revolutionary leap has occurred, the

evolutionary force is allowed to work for a certain cycle—the outbreath. Yet when a new cycle – the inbreath – begins, any structure that is not raised up by the next revolutionary leap will become subject to the contracting force and will begin to break down.

On Earth (and in any unascended sphere), you have to add to this that God has given dominion over the Earth to the beings who embody here. So these beings can create structures based on the mind of anti-christ, and for a cycle they will be allowed to not only exist but even to evolve in complexity. Yet when the cycle ends, the beings who cre-ated such structures should ideally transcend their limited state of consciousness and thus become able to create better structures—meaning structures that are more in alignment with the Christ mind. The beings themselves will erase the imperfect structures they have created and create better ones instead.

If the beings refuse to do so, their structures become subject to the contracting force and will eventually be broken down. Due to the nature of space and time – the density of matter – this will take some time, and the beings can delay the process, as we will discuss later. Yet the final outcome is inevitable. Everything is created from the one source, which is both the beginning and the end, meaning that the end is guaranteed from the beginning. Thus, everything that is not part of the River of Life will eventually cease to exist, as the river reaches the ocean of the Allness.

I earlier said that a new co-creator had a long time to experiment with its creative abilities but that it eventually had to face the final exam in the cosmic schoolroom. We might say that the experimental phase was the outbreath in which a co-creator had freedom to do anything it wanted. Yet the final exam represented the start of the inbreath in which a co-creator needs to come into oneness with its own higher being. Likewise, when a new sphere is created, the beings in it have a long time to experiment, and this is the outbreath. Yet when the sphere starts ascending, the inbreath starts and this is when all beings associated with a sphere need to face the initiation of self-lessness.

Can you begin to see the ingenious design that causes the evolutionary force in matter to inflate everything? I have talked about the need to multiply the talents, which means that you use your co-creative abilities in alignment with Christ truth. When you do this, your own higher being and spiritual hierarchy will multiply what you have created, but the effect of this is to raise your consciousness. In other words, this multiplication makes you MORE than you were before. If you co-create by using the mind of anti-christ, the reason is that you have been blinded by duality. Thus, you are unreachable for a spiritual teacher and you cannot see that what you are doing is limiting for all life. Because of free will, you cannot be forced to see this, but the expanding force of matter will multiply what you have created so it becomes more of the same thing. Instead of becoming more *than*, you become more *of.* The effect is that the limiting consequences of your creation become more pronounced and easier to see, hopefully awakening you to the fact that you need to change the way you use your mind's abilities. The Bible talks about those who sow the wind but reap the whirlwind (Hosea 8:7).

As a side note, the four categories or forces described above do correspond to the four elements of Father, Son, Mother and Holy Spirit mentioned earlier.

***

Let us now return to the first group of beings who became ensnared by the mind of anti-christ. Because of the Law of Free Will, these beings were allowed to create their separate sense of identity. This was possible because the sphere in which they lived still had some darkness left in it, and this darkness allowed these beings to maintain the illusion that they had set themselves aside from the rest of the beings associated with their sphere. Because of the nature of the dualistic mind, these beings – both co-creators inside the sphere and angels working with the sphere – desired to feel better and more important than others, and they were allowed to set themselves up in what seemed to be powerful positions. This was done partly to give them an opportunity to live out their desire for superiority, so that they might eventually have enough of it and decide to return to the Path of Oneness.

Yet despite the fact that these beings thought they were the most important beings in their sphere, they were few in number and – due to the fact that they were co-creating through the mind of anti-christ – their actual power was rather limited. They could not see this, but it was obvious to anyone in the Christ mind (when you are in the Christ mind, you never feel threatened by anything, for you realize nothing can override the law and the power of God). While the misguided beings were consumed by the drive to raise up themselves, the majority of the beings in their sphere were devoted to raising up their entire sphere. Thus, there inevitably came a point when the sphere had reached critical mass and was ready to start ascending to the vibration of the spiritual realm, meaning that there would no longer be room for the consciousness of duality. The illusions that spring from duality can only thrive in the shadows, and when a sphere ascends, the light becomes so intense that there are no shadows left.

The beings who were still in the duality consciousness were now given a final opportunity to let go of duality and join the River of Life. They were given the opportunity to serve all life instead of serving what they had defined as their self-interest. Here comes a subtle point. The Law of Free Will states that no one can be forced to see the unreality of their illusions. A being can be given an opportunity to choose between its illusion and a higher understanding, but there must always be a choice. In other words, a being cannot forcefully be brought into a vibration where it is no longer possible for it to deny the truth and cling to its illusion. Thus, the beings who were blinded by duality could not be forced to rise higher as their sphere ascended. And since they refused to let go of their dualistic illusions, only two options were possible. One was for these beings to have been erased as if they had never existed. The other option was for them to descend into the sphere that had recently been created and in which there was still sufficient darkness left for them to maintain their illusions. Obviously, since the Creator is a loving and merciful God, the latter option took effect and these beings fell into a lower sphere.

Yet the fallen beings did not fall alone, for in order to maintain their illusions, the consciousness – the entity – they had created fell with them. This was the superstructure, the mind, the separate identity, that they had created through their use of the mind of anti-christ. Thus, the sphere into which they fell now experienced a unique situation. In the previous spheres, the mind of anti-christ had been an option that no one had chosen. Thus, nothing had ever been created through the mind of anti-christ. New co-creators transitioned from innocent ignorance to the understanding of the Christ mind without willfully separating themselves from their teachers while angels kept serving in a balanced way. Thus, each new sphere had, so to speak, started out with a clean slate in the sense that there was no structure based on the mind of anti-christ. This mind remained an unexpressed option with no gravitational force that could pull new beings into choosing it. Take note that it is quite possible to co-create based on innocent ignorance without using willful ignorance. Innocent ignorance means that you have some true knowledge and a lot of areas where you have no knowledge. Willful ignorance means that all of the knowledge in your mind is distorted by duality so you have no true knowledge but you think you know everything. That is why Jesus said the devil had "no truth in him" (John 8:44).

After the first beings fell, the situation in the newly created sphere was dramatically different than the previous spheres. As these first fallen beings descended into the newly created sphere, the mind they had created by using the consciousness of duality fell with them. This mind had become bigger than any of the individuals who created it, and it exerted a certain magnetic or gravitational pull. In other words, a new entity* had been created, and as an expression of its survival instinct, it actively and aggressively sought to pull beings into its own sphere of influence. It is essential for you to understand the mechanics of how this happened.

* * *

As I explained earlier, a being in an unascended sphere can co-create only by using spiritual light that has been brought from the spiritual realm into its sphere. Only the Christ mind can serve as the open door for such a transfer of light, which is why a new co-creator must receive its light from a spiritual teacher who has the Christ consciousness. As a being grows in self-awareness – without becoming arrogant in building up itself in comparison to others – it begins to attain a degree of Christ consciousness, which allows it to bring forth light from within itself. It is a law that as you sow, so will you reap (Galatians 6:7), meaning that if you co-create by using the mind of Christ – even if you do so imperfectly – you will receive more light. If you multiply your talents, you will receive more light, for to him or her who has, more shall be added and he or she shall have abundance (Matthew 13:12). Angels can likewise receive more light as they serve faithfully.

Here comes another subtle point. Having some degree of Christ consciousness does not mean that you have attained full union – oneness – with the Christ mind and become the Living Christ. This full union will happen only when you rise above all ignorance, which normally happens when you ascend from your native sphere. As long as you are still in a sphere that has not ascended, it is possible that you can be tempted by the mind of anti-christ and fall into duality. This is the situation faced by those who graduate from a spiritual schoolroom and go out into their sphere to express their co-creative abilities. Obviously, the higher the degree of Christhood you have attained, the lower the probability that you will be tempted, but it is still possible to achieve some degree of Christhood and then fall. In fact, the scenario described in the Book of Revelation indicates that Lucifer had a high position in his native sphere before he fell (Revelation 12:12),

---

* NOTE: The word entity is used here in its most generic form as a distinct being. In spiritual literature, the word entity can also be used more specifically for beings that are created from people's misqualified energy. For example, there is a specific entity behind every form of addiction.

with some spiritual teachings saying he was an archangel. It should be noted that he was created as an archangel that had not yet become immortalized and thus could fall until his sphere ascended and he passed the final initiation. Lucifer fell because of pride, which makes beings think they are better than others or that they know better than God how things should be done. Such beings will eventually lose what they have created in order to set themselves above others. That is why Jesus said that the meek shall inherit the Earth (Matthew 5:5).

How is it possible that a seemingly highly evolved being who holds a powerful position can still fall? This is due to the scenario I described earlier, namely that a being can begin experimenting with the mind of duality while still being allowed to grow and reinforce its separate sense of identity. The purpose is to give that being the maximum opportunity to experiment with duality until it hopefully has had enough and chooses oneness over separation. My point being that some of the first beings who fell did have some spiritual attainment before they fell. Thus, they had gathered to themselves a certain amount of light, and that light was not taken from them, even when they fell to a lower sphere. If it had been taken, they would have ceased to exist.

We now have a scenario where a group of beings had fallen into a lower sphere. And while they still retained their light, the very fact that they had rejected the Path of Oneness and had fallen meant that they could not get any more light from within themselves. Yet they were using light to live, so it was not difficult for them to see the handwriting on the wall, namely that one day they would run out of light and be no more.

At the same time, they also faced another problem. The entity they had created was generated from the light they had received and then misqualified. Obviously, this entity was not created by God, and thus it did not even have the option of receiving light from inside itself. In other words, such an entity can only receive light from outside itself, from a being who has light. The entity also needed light to survive, and thus it also faced extinction unless it received more light. And precisely because the fallen beings had created this entity, they had a tie to it, meaning that the entity could draw light out of them. Thus, the monster that had been created by the fallen beings now turned on them – as in the story of Frankenstein's monster – and attempted to consume their light for its own survival, thereby hastening their demise.

You now have a group of beings who are in the unique situation that they cannot receive light from a spiritual teacher and they cannot generate it from within themselves (unless of course they had gone back to the teacher and the path). So where do they get the light that is needed for their survival or even their growth in power? Well, the logical solution is, of course, that when you cannot get light from a higher realm, from a vertical direction, you must get it from the realm in which you live, from a horizontal direction. Thus, the fallen beings had to steal the light from those who could still get it from a teacher or from within themselves. So the fallen beings now started seeking to deceive un-fallen co-creators and newly created angels into giving them their light. And the entity they had created started pulling new co-creators and angels into believing in its lies in order to steal their light. These fallen beings used their previous attainment to deceive less accomplished beings, as for example the Serpent deceived Eve. Thus, after being blinded by duality, these beings turned their previous accomplishment into a negative force. This is what Jesus talked about in the following quote: "But if thine eye be evil, thy whole body shall be full of darkness. If therefore the light that is in thee be darkness, how great is that darkness!" (Matthew 6:23).

This is essentially the process that has given rise to the myth of vampires that suck people's blood. This myth is a crude illustration of an underlying fact, namely that there are beings who must suck the light from others in order to survive. The difference between myth and reality is that this is not done in an obvious way but through manipulation that is often unrecognized by the victims.

Take note that the entities I am talking about are not physical and thus have no physical power to harm you. They exist mainly in the emotional and mental realms, so they can only influence you by pulling on your emotional and mental bodies. A primary example of such an influence is what happens to an entire nation before it goes to war. The inhabitants of that nation are being pulled into hating their enemies, and when the hatred becomes strong enough, they are ready to kill the enemy at all cost. This can only happen because people's emotional bodies have become overpowered by a mass entity of hatred that has blinded them so they no longer look at their enemies as human beings. They can see no other way to resolve the tension than by going to war.

***

Now comes another subtle point. A fallen being – as opposed to the entity – can take light through force from other beings at the same level. In other words, a fallen being in embodiment can take light from other people through force, such as rape, murder, torture or other forms of physical, mental or emotional violence. If a fallen being uses force to take light from another being, then that fallen being clearly violates the Law of Free Will. A fallen being has a right to be in a dualistic state of consciousness, but if it forcefully steals light from others, it violates the law. Stealing energy can still be done through force, and it can give a fallen being an injection of light. However, when a being falls, it will have a certain time span to turn around and start the upward path. When a fallen being violates the free will of others, this time span is reduced. It is like an addict who gets a high from a fix but who reduces his natural life-span and will eventually end up completely empty.

The Law of Free Will gives any being the right to do whatever it wants with its energy, meaning that an unfallen co-creator or angel has a right to give its energy to a fallen being. Thus, if a fallen being can deceive another being into voluntarily – although it is a decision based on ignorance – giving it light, then the fallen being is not subject to as severe of a penalty as if the light was obtained through direct force. In other words, fallen beings can experience a greater gain through deception than through force. The more intelligent fallen beings know this, which is why Genesis states that the Serpent was more "subtil" than any of the other beasts of the field (Genesis 3:1). My point is that the Law of Free Will does not allow force, but it does allow deception, for the free will of the un-fallen beings demands that they must have a right to make mistakes and experience the consequences of them. This means they have a right to let themselves be fooled and learn from that experience.

Also, all beings with free will must face the temptation of antichrist and be given the opportunity to overcome it. Before any beings had fallen, that temptation was more personal and theoretical. After the first beings fell, the fallen beings now embodied the mind of anti-christ and thus they served as the tempters for un-fallen beings. Yet take note that this does not mean fallen beings are necessary. The fact that they are allowed to tempt others serves a dual purpose. One purpose is to present un-fallen beings with the temptation of anti-christ and the other is to give the fallen beings more opportunities for abandoning the mind of anti-christ.

How can a fallen being deceive inexperienced beings into giving it light? One way is obviously by presenting the being with a deception that is based on the dualistic logic of the mind of anti-christ. It was such a deception that the Serpent presented to Eve in the Garden of Eden. Yet why would students believe in such a lie? Well, the real reason is that these students have stopped listening to their spiritual teacher. Thus, they must fend for themselves and because they are inexperienced, they are easily overpowered by the logic of the fallen beings and the gravitational force of the entity that pulls on their minds and emotions. As I have explained, everything is consciousness and all consciousness within a given unit is interconnected, meaning that the consciousness of an entity that exists within the energy field of Earth can pull on the consciousness of a person in embodiment. Obviously, this cannot happen against the person's free will, but once a person has opened its mind to the deception of a fallen being, the entity to which the fallen being is connected (is a part) can now pull on the person's mind. This can often provide the extra force needed to draw the person into making the decision to partake of what it is being offered.

We now see another reason why I was not lying when I told Adam that if he ate the forbidden fruit, he would surely die. Once you open your mind to the lies of anti-christ, you will become subject to the gravitational pull of the entire mind that is behind a given lie. And until you have attained a high degree of Christhood, you simply cannot withstand that pull. Thus, the only sure way to avoid being pulled down is to never open your mind to the subtle logic of the fallen beings who parade their fruits before you. Obviously, this is rather difficult to do when you have been brought up in a culture that does not recognize the existence of the duality consciousness and fallen beings or belittles it as superstition. It is hard to protect yourself from a danger that you do not know exists. Just consider how vulnerable people were before they knew that bacteria exist and can cause disease.

***

I know full well that this teaching can seem frightening or depressing and that many spiritual seekers would rather avoid thinking about anything dark or evil. Yet how can you possibly attain spiritual freedom unless you understand the forces that are trying to take away your freedom? Furthermore, these forces can only influence you against your knowledge, for when you see what they are doing, you can overcome their illusions and stop feeding them your light. As always, understanding is freedom and ignorance is bondage. It is the truth that makes you free and the lie that imprisons you. As I have explained, fallen beings can only influence you with your consent, and you will give your consent only because you are ignorant of the nature and consequences of the temptation. Thus, when you become aware of the deception, you can withdraw your consent, you can undo your ignorant choices by making informed choices. By doing this, you will take back your power and stop the bleeding of your light, so that you can make faster progress on the Path of Oneness. So allow me to explain the fullness of what you are up against as a being in embodiment on Earth.

After the first beings had fallen, they had to start trying to deceive other co-creators and angels, and they were successful to some degree. The mind of anti-christ was used to create a number of illusions, and for each illusion a group of inexperienced beings fell. Thus, for each illusion, an entity or identity was created, and there is a symbiotic relationship between such an entity and the fallen beings who created or reinforced it. The fallen beings serve as the tempters for other beings in the new sphere, and the entity pulls on these beings' minds and emotions so they more easily fall for temptation. Yet if the fallen beings are unsuccessful in attracting new victims, the entity will begin to devour their light and thus shorten their life-span. My point being that once such a dualistic entity has been created, it can give fallen beings more power, but it is also a strict taskmaster who demands constant sacrifices. This is actually the origin of the many myths or religions in which a god requires constant and ever more severe sacrifices of its worshippers—such as has been seen in cultures that performed human sacrifices to appease their deities. This is the real cause behind all mass killings, from ancient sacrifices to the modern Holocaust. Likewise, all war is a sacrifice on the bloodstained altar of the gods of war.

The creation of these entities began several levels above the material universe, and for each time a sphere ascended, the fallen beings and their entities fell into the newly created realm. In some cases such entities have eventually been starved to death, but in other cases they have continued to grow, becoming stronger all the time. And since your sphere is – presently – the lowest level of the world of form, all of the dualistic entities and their fallen beings have ended up here, where they truly exert a formidable force that can easily overpower those who are unaware.

As I said, there are many individual entities, but together they form a conglomerate. The Book of Revelation calls such a conglomerate a beast, but all the beasts together form what is called "the beast that was, and is not, and yet is" (Revelation 17:8) or the dragon. This is an apt description in the sense that this conglomerate entity has a survival instinct but does not have any self-awareness and thus cannot be reasoned with. It will mechanically seek to devour the light of any being that it can influence, and it can influence any being who is open to being tempted by the lie that created it. Thus, both the dragon and the individual beasts fit the description in this quote, "Be sober, be vigilant; because your adversary the devil, as a roaring lion, walketh about, seeking whom he may devour" (1Peter 6:8). The Earth is presently the hunting ground of a number of such beasts that roam about, seeking whom they may devour, and together they form a superstructure, a dragon.

Yet – again – while this may seem frightening, remember that a beast can influence you only if you believe in its lies. Thus, by being vigilant, by seeking the one truth of the Christ mind, you will rise above the temptation of any dualistic lies. How can a beast ultimately be eradicated? One way is by starving it to death. The beast can continue to survive only as long as some beings – those who have not yet been cut off from receiving light from above – continue to feed it. We might say that when beings give their light to a beast – even if they do so without fully understanding what they are doing – they are actually using their free will to allow the beast to continue to exist in their sphere. Thus, the contracting force of the Mother cannot consume the beast, for the beings in embodiment have dominion over the Earth. This not only allows the beast to continue to exist, but it also allows it to aggressively seek to do what the Bible describes as follows, "And the dragon was wroth with the woman, and went to make war with the remnant of her seed, which keep the commandments of God, and have the testimony of Jesus Christ" (Revelation 12:17). The planetary beast, the dragon, will seek to pull all beings on Earth into the duality consciousness, so that this world becomes the domain of the dragon and not the kingdom of God. The dragon is essentially trying to set itself up as the superior god of the Earth.

My overall point here is that it is only as long as a majority of the people on Earth remain ignorant of a particular beast – and keep believing in the lie that created it – that such a beast can exist on this planet. Once a critical mass of people see through the lie and decide that they will have nothing to do with it, the contracting force of the Mother will break down the beast, thereby freeing the Ma-ter Light that has been trapped in an impure matrix.

There are also spiritual forces who can bind a beast once a critical mass of people have refused to support it. The leader of these forces is a spiritual being known as Archangel Michael, who is appointed to defend the faith of those who are committed to the Path of Oneness. If a critical mass of people withdraw themselves from a beast and abandon its lies, they gain the authority to call – on behalf of humanity – for this beast to be bound so it can no longer influence people. This can remove such a beast much faster than by simply starving it to death, especially because it is difficult to get every human being to stop feeding energy to a given beast.

Once you personally start freeing yourself from the lies of a particular beast, Archangel Michael can and will cut you free from its influence—if you ask him to do so. Once a critical mass of people do the same, Archangel Michael can bind such a beast, thereby preventing it from influencing people until the contracting force can break it down completely. In fact, you can protect yourself from the gravitational pull of all beasts by invoking the spiritual protection of Archangel Michael, which is most efficiently done through affirmations or a spiritual ritual called Archangel Michael's rosary. Yet take note that the ultimate defense is to become transparent by rising above all dualistic elements in your being. A beast can only pull on misqualified energies and beliefs that spring from the mind of anti-christ. Thus, by transforming or purifying the energies (techniques for doing this can also be found on the website below), you will become transparent to all dualistic entities. This is what Jesus described when he said, "for the prince of this world cometh, and hath nothing in me" (John 14:30).*

Before we move on, let me make one thing clear. Once a beast has been created, the evolutionary force will actually drive that beast to grow. Yet the beast was not created by the Christ consciousness, so it can never transcend its level of consciousness, it can never rise above the lie that created it. The beast cannot grow in a vertical direction and instead must grow in a horizontal direction. What I desire you to understand here is that such a beast can *never* be resurrected, can never be purified and become part of the spiritual realm. It has no chance whatsoever of ascending to a higher state, and thus it will inevitably be broken down by the contracting force. The beast itself is simply an illusion created from the consciousness of anti-christ. The illusion has no substance, but the beast has absorbed misqualified energy, which does have substance. Yet this energy – which is the Ma-ter Light that has been given an imperfect vibration – can indeed be purified and returned to its pristine state. When sufficient energy is purified, there will be nothing to uphold the illusion and the beast will dissolve.

Why is the evolutionary force allowed to make a beast evolve in a horizontal direction? Because the beast was created by beings who exercised their free will. The beast is allowed to grow in order to give these beings the maximum opportunity to overcome the illusion that caused them to create or support the beast. As the beast becomes more powerful, its mechanical nature becomes more obvious. We might say that its evil becomes more obvious, but in a sense a beast is not evil. It is simply like a computer that acts based on its programming, and that programming is defined by its creators through the mind of anti-christ. Since the beast was never created by God and has no self-awareness (has no conscious self) it cannot evaluate what is good and evil, what is in alignment with God's law and what is not. The beast no more questions its actions than a computer questions its programming.

* For more information about Archangel Michael's rosary and other techniques for spiritual protection and for the transformation of impure energies, see www.askrealjesus.com and www.marysdivinedirection.com.

As a beast becomes more powerful and even begins to control or devour those who created it, these beings receive additional opportunities to see what they have created and thus realize their mistake. In other words, a beast can never be resurrected, but the fallen beings who created or are upholding the beast can indeed be resurrected. And that is precisely why the beast is allowed to exist, for the laws of God are set up to give many opportunities for fallen beings to come back to the Path of Oneness. In fact, as I have explained, the entire material universe is presently functioning as one big opportunity for such beings to finally see the light.

Key 19
Separating yourself from dualistic identities

We have now come full circle and can answer the question of why people do evil things and are unable to see what they are doing, often even justifying them as being good. Yet, once again, we are dealing with a subtle point that will require some contemplation and explanation.

Let us begin by reconsidering and clarifying our previous discussion about your origin as an individual being. Your origin goes back to an immortal being that exists in the spiritual realm. This being started its existence as an individualization of a being in a higher level of the spiritual realm, and this Chain of Being goes all the way back to the Creator. Your spiritual source was created in a particular sphere that was, at the time, the lowest level of the world of form, a sphere that was not yet filled with light. Your parent won its immortality by partaking in the process of raising its native sphere until it ascended and became part of the spiritual realm. When that victory was attained, a new sphere was created, and your spiritual parent desired to be part of the process of raising that sphere. Yet because it had already won mastery, it could not project the fullness of itself into the new sphere. If a number of beings with a high level of mastery entered a newly created sphere, they would instantly raise it, and that would defeat the purpose of allowing new co-creators to grow gradually. So your spiritual parent participated in the process by creating extensions of itself that were designed as one of the following types of beings:

- New co-creators with a minimal sense of predefined identity and designed to embody within the new sphere.
- New angels serving the new sphere from the spiritual realm or (in the case of your sphere) possibly from the identity realm.
- Spiritual teachers working inside the new sphere (the parents themselves serve as teachers from the spiritual realm).
- Beings with a more developed identity and mastery than a new co-creator. These are the beings who hold the counterbalance

for fallen beings and are sent in an attempt to rescue them. Such a being does not have full mastery, but it has a much more defined identity than a new co-creator. It takes embodiment like a new co-creator, meaning that it must awaken to its true identity and can potentially fall.

No matter where you came from, you are an individualization of your spiritual parent, who incorporated its own experience and mastery in designing your individuality. You were designed as a unique individual, and although there are billions upon billions of individual beings in the world of form, there is no one who is exactly like you. You have a unique spiritual individuality and thus you have the opportunity to bring a gift to the world of form that no other being can bring.

For co-creators, their unique individuality was defined by their spiritual parents and incorporated into creating a spiritual being that I have called the I AM Presence. This I AM Presence is permanently residing in the spiritual realm, and it is an individual being within the greater whole of the spiritual parent. It was the I AM Presence that projected itself into the lower realm in which a co-creator first took form as an individual being (which might not have been the material universe). Since angels are not created to take embodiment in a lower realm, they have no I AM Presence. But if they fall, their spiritual parents do create the equivalent of an I AM Presence to hold an unerasable blueprint of their individuality. The spiritual being who represents the Divine Mother, which is currently the ascended master Mother Mary, then breaks her body to create a Christ self for the fallen angels that can serve as a mediator between their lower and higher beings. All beings who lose contact with the spiritual teacher have such a Christ self created, but for beings other than angels, this Christ self can be created by various masters who sponsor different groups of beings.

The core of your individual being, or lifestream, is the conscious self, which gives you a sense that you exist. For co-creators the task of the conscious self is to build an identity as a co-creator with God in its native realm. For angels the task of the conscious self is to expand the predefined identity and become an even better angel. In other words, the task of the conscious self is to build the identity through which a being expresses itself and serves in the world of form. The conscious self can then refine this identity as a result of your experiences.

In the beginning, all newly embodied beings were tutored by a spiritual teacher whose task was to help them build a sense of identity that was a combination of two elements. One was the individuality anchored in the I AM Presence. By reconnecting to this spiritual identity, a being would gain a framework in which it could build its own sense of identity based on choices made by the conscious self. We might say that as everything else, the identity has two aspects:

- The Alpha aspect is the identity anchored in the I AM Presence, which has been predefined by the spiritual parent.

- The Omega aspect is the identity a being builds as it expresses itself in the sphere in which it resides.

If you have harmony between the two aspects, you will feel ultimately fulfilled and at peace. You will be one being, a whole being – as opposed to being a house divided against itself (Mark 3:25) – and thus you can complete the Path of Oneness, whereby your total identity – a combination of the Alpha and Omega aspects – becomes immortalized and can ascend to the spiritual realm. It is the task of your spiritual teacher to help you build this identity on your own. In other words, the teacher is not trying to force you or manipulate you into building a particular type of identity. However, the teacher is trying to guide you toward having harmony between the Alpha and Omega aspects, which is the only way you can become immortalized.

The teacher is also trying to help you see that becoming immortalized means that your lower sense of identity, your Omega identity, comes into complete harmony with the laws of God and your spiritual identity. Take note that this does not mean you have no freedom to define your Omega identity. You have great freedom, but in order to attain wholeness, you must exercise that freedom within the parameters set by your Alpha identity. The Father and Mother aspects of your Being must come together in harmony before new life – the immortal you, representing the Son aspect of God (regardless of your physical sex) – can be born.

We might compare this to driving a car. You have certain traffic laws that guide how you can drive, but if you follow the laws, you can go anywhere the road will take you. As you started out building your identity, you did not have a clear understanding of the laws of

God or your Alpha identity, so you created an Omega identity that was not in harmony with your higher being. For you to become immortalized, this identity must be spiritually reborn and brought into harmony with the upper part of the figure-eight flow of your total Being. The reason is that only beings who have passed the test of selflessness can become immortal beings, as God obviously would not want a selfish being to become immortal.

There did come a point when your teacher had to give you the opportunity to make the choice as to whether you would consciously choose to align yourself with your spiritual identity. You had to give up the sense of identity you had created during your neophyte phase and be reborn into oneness with your true identity. As I have tried to explain, this was *not* something that was forced upon you from without. It was truly your own higher will to come into this wholeness rather than remaining in the divided state that can only cause suffering. Obviously, your ego is born from a separation between your higher and lower being and can only see the will of your higher being as coming from outside itself. So it is up to the conscious self to overcome the illusion of the ego. This is the choice between defining your identity based on the mind of Christ – who alone knows your spiritual identity – or the mind of anti-christ, that can never know your true identity.

***

In the first three spheres that were created in the world of form, all beings successfully passed this initiation and became immortalized beings. Yet in the fourth sphere a group of beings rebelled against the very process itself. They refused to bring their Omega identities into alignment with their Alpha identities. They refused to bring the will of their conscious selves into alignment with the will of their own spiritual selves (or for angels, with the beings who created them). Thus, instead of creating a sense of identity based on the Christ mind – becoming one with all life – they created an Omega identity based on the mind of anti-christ. Thereby, they set their Omega identities apart from their Alpha identities and from all other parts of life. In other words, what these beings created was a separate sense of identity, and because they all rebelled for the same reason, they created a superstructure that became what I have described as a separate mind, entity or beast.

As the process of the fall continued, other separate or dualistic identities were created, and there are now a number of them that have been reinforced by many beings. My point here is that when the first beings rebelled, there was no separate identity, no identity based on the mind of anti-christ. Yet after the first such identity had been created, it now became easier for beings to fall. For co-creators the problem was, as I explained earlier, that many of them refused to take command over their lives because they did not want to make their own decisions. Co-creators were allowed to do this for a season, but there came a point when they had to make a decision. And once a fallen identity had been created, it now became possible for co-creators to choose to enter into that state of identity instead of building their own separate identity. For angels the problem was that they became judgmental and rigid, which also caused them to refuse to self-transcend. So they were likewise tempted to enter a predefined, separate identity.

When a being refused to step up and consciously create an identity based on the reality of Christ, it often did so because it seemed like too much hard work or too great a responsibility. It was easier for such a being to keep following someone else. Many students *did* want their teachers to continue to tell them what to do. Obviously, a true spiritual teacher must eventually refuse to play this role, and at that point, the student is faced with the inevitability of making its own choice.

Creating a separate sense of identity based on anti-christ was originally much more of an effort than building an identity based on the mind of Christ with the help of a spiritual teacher. Yet once the first separate, dualistic identities had been created, students had an alternative to doing the work themselves. They could simply choose to step into the mold of a predefined identity based on the mind of anti-christ. They could choose to partake of the "fruit" of such a predefined identity, which had knowledge of relative good and evil because it was created from the duality consciousness. Once beings had taken a bite of the forbidden fruit, they would no longer have to make their own decisions. They could simply flow with the stream of this new identity, just as a flock of sheep follow the lead sheep. So if a being did not want to follow a true teacher – who demanded that it step up to becoming self-sufficient – it could choose to follow a false teacher who would make no such demand. Thus, for beings who did not want to make their own decisions, following a false teacher seemed like much less of an effort. False teachers will gladly tell you what to do and never demand that you think for yourself, as they want you to follow them blindly. Furthermore, the dualistic identities are tied to the beasts behind them, and this creates an aggressive pull on the emotional and mental bodies of beings who have stepped into the gray zone of doubt. This pull is often the factor that overwhelms the minds of the beings who have become houses divided against themselves (Mark 3:25). Thus, it is the gravitational pull that makes it seem like following a false teacher is easier than following the true teacher, who – by the law of free will – can exert no pull on the student's mind.

Once beings stepped into a predefined identity, an ego would be created for them, and this ego would then make most daily decisions so the conscious self could withdraw into a little "cave." Also, there would be other beings who had long ago chosen the false identity and who could act as leaders. Finally, the gravitational force of the beast itself would pull them along. In other words, once beings had chosen to join the club, they could get away with not making their own decisions. What does it take to join such a club? Every separate sense of identity is based on a specific dualistic lie, so in order to enter that identity, you have to accept the lie—which, of course, is presented as an absolute truth. Here comes the essential point. Once you have accepted the lie, you must pledge to never question it again!

If you do decide to question the lie, then the combined force of your own ego, other fallen beings who accept the lie and the beast itself will do anything in their power to prevent you from seeing through and abandoning the lie. My point being that while entering the club requires no effort – can be done by making the decision not to make a decision – it requires an entirely different effort to get out of the club. An identity based on the mind of anti-christ is a club that has no provisions for allowing you to resign your membership. Once you are in, you are supposed to stay forever, continuing to feed your light to the beast, which has now become your new god.

Of course, you were not told all this before you joined, but the reason was that you had made the decision not to listen to your spiritual teacher, and thus you could not be warned. Instead of taking the

Path of Oneness, you took what seemed to be the path of least resistance. Yet in reality it turned out to be the path of maximum resistance, the path of separation, the path of death. As they say when signing a contract, "Always read the fine print." The only problem is that the mind of anti-christ provides no fine print, for the fine print is in the mind of Christ. Even fallen beings and beings blinded by duality have access to the Christ mind through their Christ selves, which is what Jesus described as the Comforter, "But the Comforter, which is the Holy Ghost, whom the Father will send in my name, he shall teach you all things, and bring all things to your remembrance, whatsoever I have said unto you" (John 14:26). The question is whether they will listen to this inner teacher or to an external teacher—even the "external" teacher of the ego.

***

We can now see why people can commit evil acts without seeing what they are doing, without realizing that what they are doing is against what they profess to believe, thus becoming hypocrites. The reason is that they are not actually thinking about what they are doing, and thus they do not see that what they are doing is evil. Since they are not thinking, they cannot see the inconsistency between what they profess to believe and what they are actually doing. That is why people can believe that God will reward them for killing those who are not members of their religion, even though their religion contains the command not to kill. Killing another human being in the name of God is truly the ultimate form of hypocrisy known on Earth.

Yet why can't people see that this is hypocrisy; why are they not thinking? It is because their conscious selves refused to step up to the next level of the path, the level where you take full responsibility for creating your identity, thus taking full responsibility for your own growth, even for your own salvation. Instead of accepting this responsibility, the conscious self refused to think and decide for itself. It then joined a mass identity, and now it is blindly following along with what the leaders in that state of consciousness are saying. It has become a blind follower of the blind leaders, and thus the blindness prevents it from seeing the obvious. The false identity is based on a lie, and this lie uses the duality consciousness – which can justify anything – to justify the actions and portray them as not being evil.

That is why people are able to commit the most evil acts while feeling fully justified in doing so, even feeling that they have the ultimate justification of being told by God to do what they did.

As an obvious example of this, consider the Crusades. We have two groups of people who both claim to be devoutly religious and completely devoted to following the will of their God. As the ultimate irony, both Muslims and Christians say their religious tradition is based on the Old Testament. They both claim to be worshiping the God of the Old Testament, which they see as the only true God and define as the God of Abraham. They also believe that this God used Moses to bring forth the ten commandments, one of which states in no uncertain terms, "Thou shalt not kill" (Exodus 20:13). So how can it be that these two groups of people are now killing each other, while both of them feel their actions are justified by their God? How can the true God of Abraham give his followers the command not to kill and then tell two groups – who both claim to be worshipping this God – to kill each other in his name?

I know full well why this can happen, namely that the Old Testament contains many passages where – supposedly – the "one true God" told his chosen people to kill those who were not so chosen. And throughout history, Christians, Muslims and Jews have used these passages as a justification for a wide range of atrocities that all violate the unconditional command not to kill. Yet what is the truth here? Is it really possible that the true Creator of the world of form – who gave self-conscious beings a part of its own Being – would command a group of people on a very small planet called Earth to kill another group of people that were also out of the Creator's Being? Or is there possibly some other explanation?

What might such an explanation be? Well, it seems we have arrived at a point where our next logical step must be to examine the role of religion on this planet. After all, the topic of this book is how you can attain spiritual freedom. Ideally, religion should be a tool for giving you that freedom. Yet it now seems necessary for us to consider whether the duality consciousness could possible subvert the original purpose and turn religion into a tool for taking away your spiritual freedom. We will do so in the next chapter, but first I want to make a crucial point.

***

One does not have to be a prophet – merely a student of human psychology and history – to predict that some people will take the teachings in this book and reason that the main cause of all of humankind's problems is that a number of fallen beings are embodying on this planet. Thus, the way to solve all problems is to identify these people and either get them off the planet by killing them or by making sure they have no power in society.

I trust the more aware students can see that such people are reasoning this way because they are trapped in the fallen consciousness. They are seeing everything through the filter of duality, and thus they think in terms of "us" versus "them," which is precisely how fallen beings think. The people who would use my teachings to initiate hostility toward other people are themselves trapped in the same state of consciousness that created all of the problems on this planet. Thus, they obviously cannot contribute to the solution—until they free themselves from that consciousness.

Therefore, I will – in the strongest possible terms – encourage everyone who reads this book to consider that the fallen consciousness has been influencing this planet for a very long time. It is virtually impossible to embody on this planet without being influenced by this consciousness. In fact, the vast majority of the people who are in embodiment right now have fallen or have become blinded by the fallen consciousness, which happened many lifetimes ago. Thus, they have had a very long time to incorporate elements of the fallen consciousness into their lower beings, into their identity, thoughts and feelings—what most spiritual and religious people call the soul.

In reality, the "entity" that people normally call the soul is not something that is created by God. Technically, it is a vehicle that is created by the spiritual parents, as they have to allow an extension of themselves to go into duality. Thus, out of their love for you, they give you a vehicle that you can then use as a foundation for your expression in the material universe. However, the contents of that vehicle are created by you as you make decisions based on duality. This will require further explanation, but before we go into it, let me remind you that even fallen beings had the opportunity to be in a spiritual schoolroom with an enlightened teacher.

***

One can say that the soul – or at least the contents of the soul vehicle – is an outgrowth of what I have so far called the Omega aspect of your identity, namely what your conscious self is charged with creating. However, there is a crucial distinction to be made. In an ideal scenario, you would be completely committed to following the Path of Oneness according to your teacher's instructions. Thus, there would be nothing hidden between you and your teacher. When you made a decision based on the mind of Christ, the decision and the memory of it would rise to your causal body so that your attainment would not be lost. This is what Jesus called your treasure in heaven (Matthew 19:21), and it is basically a conglomerate of all decisions that are based on the Christ consciousness. Your conscious self could then draw on this attainment when making future decisions.

When you made an imperfect decision – whether based on ignorance or the mind of anti-christ – the decision obviously could not rise. Yet as long as you did not seek to hide it from your teacher, the teacher would help you learn from the decision, he would take on and resolve the karma and then he would help you overcome the memory of it. In other words, your mistake was turned into a positive learning experience – which could rise to your causal body – and the imperfect aspects of the incident were consumed as if they never existed. Thus, a decision would leave no elements of innocent or willful ignorance in your Omega sense of identity—it would be aligned with your Alpha identity, although you might not yet be consciously aware of the latter. Yet there would be no division or "space" between your higher or lower identity.

When you first decided to start hiding things from your teacher, the learning process was – at least partially – interrupted, and your imperfect decisions could not be erased. Thus, a "space" had to be created that could store them until you decided to go back to the path and turn your imperfect choices into perfect learning experiences. As long as you were in the schoolroom, that space was in the teacher's Being, for everything in the schoolroom is inside the teacher's Being. Yet after you decided to break the tie to your teacher and became subject to the process of reincarnation, you needed a vehicle that could carry your memories from lifetime to lifetime, so that you did not have to reinvent the wheel – or rather, reinvent yourself – and make the same mistakes in every new embodiment. That vehicle, that separate space, is what most spiritual teachings call the soul. Of course, when you withdrew from the teacher, the conscious self refused to make decisions, and thus the ego took over. The ego can *only* make decisions based on the duality consciousness, so since then the ego has had a greater control over your soul than your conscious self.

The soul is made up of decisions based on the duality consciousness. Some of these decisions might be what people normally call bad or evil while others will be what people normally call good. Yet my point is that all of those decisions were influenced by the duality consciousness, or they would have become part of your treasure in heaven. Nevertheless, even though these decisions are imperfect, they still have the potential to be turned into learning experiences that can become part of your causal body and can help you grow spiritually. That is why virtually all spiritual teachings say that the soul can be resurrected or saved. In reality, it is not the soul but the decisions and energies that make up the soul that are resurrected.

The resurrection of the soul is not a process that will happen because some external savior will do the work for you. It is a process that requires your conscious self to be willing to look at its past decisions and – by working with a spiritual teacher – turn them into positive learning experiences, meaning experiences that help you transcend the consciousness that caused you to make the decisions in the first place. Rather than being a source of pain, your past decisions should be seen as a resource that can help you ascend the spiral staircase of life. They can be turned into learning experiences, but you have to look at them, understand why they are dualistic and consciously replace them with better decisions. Yet until the conscious self begins to take responsibility for itself, people cannot look at the past. They seek to avoid looking at it or they seek to justify and defend their actions instead of neutrally looking for the lesson. This causes them to repeat the same patterns over and over, which in a sense is another opportunity for them to see the need for change. Always keep in mind that the purpose of life is to learn and grow, so even your mistakes can become stepping stones for growth—as long as the conscious self is willing to transcend itself and be spiritually reborn.

This leads to a very important realization. There are some people on Earth who are completely identified with their physical bodies. Yet most spiritual people are aware that they are more than their bodies, and many see this "more" as the soul. Thus, the vast majority of spiritual and religious people identify themselves as the soul and think the soul needs to be resurrected or become immortal. In reality, the soul – as I have just defined it – cannot become immortal. Which means that the soul – and the individual decisions that form it – must be allowed to die. It must be given up so it can return to its source. This is the process that Jesus illustrated through the crucifixion. The cross symbolizes how you are immobilized by the dualistic decisions in the four levels of your mind. These decisions are what make up the soul, and since they are dualistic and unreal, they must be replaced by decisions based on the Christ mind. Yet in order to replace a dualistic decision, you have to accept that it is unreal and then you have to let the decision – let part of the soul – die. By dying on the cross, Jesus illustrated that in order to be resurrected, the conscious self must let the soul die, it must give up the ghost (Matthew 27:50) of its dualistic sense of identity, namely the soul. The soul – the separate, mortal you – dying on the cross is the prerequisite to the real you, the conscious self, being resurrected into a new identity based on the oneness of the Christ mind.

If you identify yourself as the soul, you will think that if your soul is gone, *you* will die and be no more. Thus, you cannot let go of the soul, cannot let go of the past, and this becomes a spiritual catch-22. Your identification with the soul blocks the very process of life, the act of self-transcendence, whereby you let the soul – the imperfect identity – die so that the real you – the conscious self – can be reborn into a higher sense of identity. Thus, the master key to spiritual growth is to realize that the core of your being is the conscious self, which is more than any aspect of your lower being, more than the soul. Only when the conscious self pulls itself out of your lower identity will you truly start moving forward on the spiritual path.

***

My reason for giving this teaching at this point is that it leads to a very important conclusion. Virtually every person on Earth has a soul that is influenced by the fallen consciousness. As the Bible puts it, "For all have sinned, and come short of the glory of God" (Romans 3:23). This should give reason for great humility that can prevent people from developing a negative attitude toward anyone else. It is true that some people are beings who fell in a higher realm. They have completely identified themselves with the fallen consciousness and they have built such an intricate sense of identity that it is very difficult for them to see beyond it. Yet these beings still have a conscious self that has the potential to project itself outside the separate identity and stop identifying itself with and as that identity. Thus, every human being has the potential to rise above its current sense of identity, and it is essential for the most spiritually aware people to focus on this potential. You must, as Mother Mary explains it in her book, hold the immaculate concept for all.

A basic drive of the fallen consciousness is to define some people as being better than others. So if spiritual people start identifying others as fallen beings or fallen angels and begin to feel superior to them, then these people have not risen above the fallen consciousness. They have simply fallen prey to one of its more subtle aspects. That is why you need to commit yourself to doing what Jesus described in the following statement:

> 3 And why beholdest thou the mote that is in thy brother's eye, but considerest not the beam that is in thine own eye?
> 4 Or how wilt thou say to thy brother, Let me pull out the mote out of thine eye; and, behold, a beam is in thine own eye?
> 5 Thou hypocrite, first cast out the beam out of thine own eye; and then shalt thou see clearly to cast out the mote out of thy brother's eye. (Matthew, Chapter 7)

My point here is that you must first of all focus on overcoming the elements of the fallen consciousness in your own being, rather than seeking to identify them in other people. I am not thereby saying that the top ten percent of the most spiritual people on Earth should refrain from speaking out against the duality consciousness and those who embody it. For if they did so, how could the general population ever be enlightened to the existence and influence of the fallen consciousness?

What I am saying here is that it is counterproductive (at least until you reach a certain stage of Christhood) to identify people as fallen beings. Instead, it is far more productive to focus on identifying the fallen consciousness in all of its variations and showing how it influences individuals and society. By depersonalizing the topic, you will minimize the risk of setting up dualistic battles between individuals and groups of people. And once society begins to recognize a certain state of consciousness as dualistic, it will be easier for people to withdraw from it. If some people refuse to do so, they will eventually isolate and expose themselves, but that is a different matter than when someone begins to label others. My point being that much can be accomplished by identifying a certain state of consciousness and thus giving people an opportunity to withdraw from it in the privacy of their own minds.

As a spiritual person, it is extremely important to strive to attain a perspective that is beyond duality. One characteristic of duality is that it always seeks to judge others, so you must be aware of judgment. With this I mean a judgment that labels some people as "bad," giving rise to the belief that they are beyond help and thus cannot be saved. There is even the belief that God does not want to save certain people but wants to punish them forever in hell. There is a fundamental difference between seeing that a person's beliefs and actions spring from duality and labeling the person as a bad person or a fallen angel. You should never accept any imperfect images – of yourself or others – as permanent but always focus on people's spiritual potential to be resurrected in Christ.

We of the Ascended Host never judge, for we are absolutely committed to the growth and resurrection of every lifestream. Thus, we do everything possible to help any lifestream disentangle itself from the fallen consciousness and come back to its true sense of identity as an individualization of God. I expect all who are sincere about the spiritual path to make that same commitment—and then to exercise it with discernment, as we will discuss later.

Key 20
The ungodly truth about religion

The quintessential problem with religion on planet Earth can be summarized very simply. Most people have an inner knowing – a knowing that transcends all outer teachings or scriptures – that God is ultimately and wholly good. Because of this knowing, people expect that a religion and its leaders – who claim to represent God on Earth – are sincerely striving to be ultimately and wholly good. So when they see behavior from religious leaders that is not good, people often lose their faith in religion. And if they do not differentiate between religion and God, they can also lose all faith in God. This has happened to billions of people over the course of history, and it is happening at an ever-increasing pace in modern society.

Destroying a person's relationship with God is the greatest crime that can be committed in this and any other world. Yet I think we have now set the foundation, whereby we can shatter your illusion that religion is ultimately and wholly good without shattering your personal relationship with God—who is ultimately and wholly beyond any religion on Earth.

If you take a look at history and consider how human beings have been treating each other, you will see that one of the central questions raised by the human experience is man's inhumanity to man. Why do people treat each other the way they do? Why do people do harmful things, why do they keep doing them over and over again, and why can't they see what they are doing? Such questions often lead to another question, namely why God allows all this to happen. Why doesn't God simply remove evil from this planet?

We can now see that these questions actually have reasonable and logical answers. The central realization that can open your mind to these answers is the very fact that the Earth was not designed to be a paradise. It was designed to be a mixed environment that gives home to a variety of lifestreams in different states of consciousness. The most important consequence of this fact is that there are lifestreams on Earth who are completely identified with the fallen consciousness, the consciousness of duality. Yet the vast majority of the people on

Earth have been influenced by this state of consciousness, and it has affected every aspect of human existence.

When I say that the fallen consciousness has affected every aspect of human existence, I am not exaggerating. And the consequence is that religion has also been affected by the fallen consciousness and the beings who are choosing to embody it. This one realization – when you understand all of its ramifications – has the power to set you free from all religious thralldom. You can then claim your spiritual freedom, a freedom that religion often limits rather than expands. So let us take a look at precisely how religion has become a tool for reinforcing the fallen consciousness and its influence over humanity.

* * *

Based on my long experience as a spiritual teacher, I find it necessary to say that the truth I am about to reveal will often be met with fierce resistance from people on Earth. And ironically, it is usually met with the fiercest resistance from the kind of people one would think would be most open to the reality of God, namely the most spiritual and religious people. Those who are most concerned about religion and spirituality are often very reluctant to acknowledge a fundamental problem with religion in general and with their religion in particular. It is, consequently, important for us to discus why this is so.

The underlying cause is, as I stated above, that all spiritually aware people have an inner knowing that God is ultimately and wholly good. Thus, they feel that even though there is evil in this world, God will ultimately win and the movie about Earth will have a happy ending. These people are truly optimistic and they hold a positive vision for Earth and the future of humankind. Thus, they feel that even though there is much evil in human affairs, there must be some aspect of life where evil cannot get a foothold. There must be something on Earth that is sacred, that is above being corrupted by evil—and they would like that sanctuary to be religion, especially their own religion.

Spiritual people often feel that if there is nothing sacred on Earth, then how can they maintain the hope that good will ultimately win? And if they cannot maintain that hope, then how can they continue living on a planet with so much imperfection? It is as if they know life could and should be so much more than what they see around them, and this puts a constant burden on their hearts. They can endure that burden only because they have the hope that ultimately things will turn out for the best, and thus their sacrifice of being in this environment will not have been for naught. They simply cannot bear the thought that there is nothing sacred, that there is no aspect of human affairs where evil cannot triumph. And therefore, they often will not look at how evil influences religion.

I must tell you that even though I have maintained a neutral tone throughout this book, I very much feel the pain and anguish of the many spiritual and religious people who feel the way I have just described. I understand the dilemma that tortures their souls. Yet I must also tell you that it is precisely people's unwillingness to take a critical look at religion that continues to give evil a foothold in religious movements.

Thus, it is my duty to tell you that unless the top ten percent of the most spiritually aware people on Earth will open their minds to reality, religion will not fulfill its potential on this planet. Allow me to show you that your basic expectation is true – namely that good will win out in the end – but that you have an incomplete understanding of how this will come about. And once you attain the complete understanding, you will be able to acknowledge the truth about religion without losing your hope that the Earth will rise above all evil. In fact, only if religion is set free from the influence of duality is there a realistic hope that this planet will rise above evil.

***

One of the big problems that blocks a renewal of religion is that people tend to identify themselves with their religion. In fact, the more religious they are, the more they see the outer religion as an essential and inseparable part of their identity. They feel that if the outer religion was proven wrong, part of their identity would be lost. And as I have explained earlier, no one can bear losing their identity. This is why I spent so much time in previous chapters explaining that the core of your identity is the conscious self. Your conscious self is an individualization of God's own being, and thus it is above and beyond anything on Earth, including a religion. Likewise, I trust it should be clear by now that the Creator of this world of form is more than anything *in* the world of form, including any religion on this small planet called Earth.

When you realize that you are more than religion and that God is more than religion, you clearly see that your identity is not threatened by looking at religion – and your particular religion – with critical eyes. In fact, it may well be that part of your purpose for descending to Earth was to help raise religion above the consciousness of duality so it can fulfill its original purpose. By refusing to look at how the fallen consciousness has influenced religion, you will keep yourself from fulfilling your divine plan.

Once you overcome the illusion that your identity depends on an outer religion, you can look at the fact – as stated in Genesis – that God sent co-creators to Earth with the command to "multiply" and "have dominion" (Genesis 1:28). In other words, it is clearly God's will that the Earth should ascend and become part of the spiritual realm, but God has suspended his own will by giving dominion over the Earth to the beings who are in physical embodiment. This includes those beings who are fully or partially influenced by the fallen consciousness, even those who have fallen from a higher realm and for whom the Earth has become the latest, possibly the final, opportunity to turn around. The consequence of this fact is that everything that happens on Earth is subject to the free will of people in embodiment. There is literally no area of life on this planet where God or God's representatives are allowed to step in and override the free will of human beings. This includes the field of religion.

Free will means that you have a right to choose anything you want. Consequently, every aspect of human affairs is subject to the choices made by the people who are involved with that activity. Even the area of religion, including any and all specific religions, is subject to the choices made by both the leaders and members.

The next fact you need to consider is that there is no guarantee that the Earth will rise above evil. How can there be, when everything is subject to the choices made by people in embodiment? Free will means that you have the right to do anything you want and you also have the right to experience the consequences of your choices. For as I have carefully explained, if you do not experience the consequences, how will you know that you actually made a choice?

The Earth will rise only if a critical mass of people choose to free themselves – to free their own minds – from evil, meaning from the fallen consciousness. As I explained earlier, if the Earth was left alone, the evolutionary force built into the Ma-ter Light would gradually raise humankind's consciousness. Yet the reality – as I have attempted to explain to you – is that the Earth is not being left alone. The Earth is designed to be a mixed environment in which a number of beings are receiving another opportunity to disentangle themselves from the fallen consciousness that imprisons them and sucks the very lifeblood out of them. These beings, and the beasts behind them, are currently exerting such a strong gravitational force that unless something is done, they will inevitably pull the Earth into a downward spiral that will lead to the disintegration of the entire planet. This is simply the stark reality, but it is by no means a given. However, what I am trying to make clear is that unless some force can counteract the downward pull of the fallen consciousness, the Earth will indeed self-destruct because God will allow humans to experience the consequences of their choices.

What is the positive force I am talking about? Well, ultimately it is the force of God, which can conquer any force of darkness found anywhere. That is why Jesus said that with man this is impossible, but with God all things are possible (Matthew 19:26). Yet the reality is that the Light of God can work on planet Earth only when it is allowed to enter the energy field of this planet. And the light must enter through those who have dominion over the Earth, namely people in embodiment. That is why Jesus clearly stated that as long as he was in the world – meaning in a physical body – he was the light of the world and he was the open door for the Light of God (John 9:5). The Light of God can easily consume all darkness on this planet, but it can do so only when a critical mass of people decide to become the open doors through which the light can enter. And people will make this decision only when they come to a full realization of how evil is pulling the planet down. They must then make the firm decision that they will not allow this to happen. There is enormous power in people making a decision that a certain type of action or a certain type of consciousness is no longer acceptable to them. That is why Jesus said about those who are striving for the Christ consciousness:

> Ye are the light of the world. A city that is set on an hill cannot be hid. (Matthew 5:14)

Why do you think human society has progressed beyond the stage of the cave dwellers? Because some people were willing to look at present conditions and decide that they were no longer acceptable to them. As Jesus said, the call compels the answer:

> Again I say unto you, That if two of you shall agree on Earth as touching any thing that they shall ask, it shall be done for them of my Father which is in heaven. (Matthew 18:19)

When a critical mass of people cry out for a certain problem to be removed from the Earth, then God's answer will inevitably follow. Yet if people do not cry out, there is nothing for God to answer, so he must remain passive. And before people can cry out, they must know what to cry out about. You must understand a problem, and understand it fully, before you can call forth a solution to that problem from above. You must also be willing to take action, for in many cases God's answer to a problem requires the participation of people. Surely, there were people who cried out against oppressive governments, but if no one had been willing to do what it took to bring forth democracy, then all nations would still be under some form of totalitarian rule. When you consider my teachings that beings need to reach self-sufficiency, you will see that God will not simply manifest what you ask for but will release the ideas and the light that can help you manifest it through your own efforts. You must be willing to follow the example of Jesus when he said, "My Father worketh hitherto, and I work" (John 5:17). In other words, God will do his part, but you must also do your part as an extension of God in the material realm.

My point here is that the main purpose of the Earth is to give self-aware beings an opportunity to grow in self-awareness. This means that God will not do the work for you, for that would take away your victory. So if you are a spiritual or religious person, your concern for religion and your desire to see religion be raised above evil is not enough in itself. You must be willing to look at the problem and understand it, so that you can make precise calls to God and God's emissaries. Yet you must also be willing to take action, to let your light shine, to bear witness to your truth, so that you can *be* the solution to the problem. It has been said before, that for evil to triumph, it only takes that good people do nothing, and it is a statement that sums up the very basic dynamic that determines the future of planet Earth, including the future of religion. So let us move on to take an open look at how the original purpose of religion has been subverted by the fallen consciousness.

***

What was the original purpose for religion on the physical Earth? Well, if you look at the story of the Garden of Eden, you will see that it does not say that Adam and Eve went to church every Sunday. It does not even say that there was a church in the Garden, so one might conclude that Adam and Eve did not have any religion. Why didn't they have a religion? Because they walked and talked with God, or rather with a spiritual teacher. If you have direct contact with a spiritual teacher, why would you need an outer religion to serve as an intermediary between you and the spiritual realm? If there is nothing between you and direct contact with the spiritual realm, you obviously need no intermediary outside yourself. Thus, we might say that the Garden of Eden needed no church because it *was* a church, it was an environment where most beings lived their religion every moment.

My point is that the physical Earth is designed as a place for beings who have lost the direct contact with their spiritual teachers. This is illustrated by the fact that most people on Earth have no direct awareness of or contact with spiritual teachers who are beyond the physical realm, including their own higher selves. When people do not have such direct contact, there is a real danger that their state of consciousness becomes a closed circle that leads them into a downward, self-reinforcing spiral. In order to prevent this, people on Earth were given religion as a replacement for the direct contact with a spiritual teacher.

This is an essential realization that will give you an entirely new understanding of the purpose of religion. You have probably been brought up to believe that the role of religion is to save you and that only members of the right religion will be saved. However, the true role of religion is to serve as an intermediary between you and the real saviors of humankind, namely the spiritual teachers of the Ascended Host who can help people save themselves.

The essential realization about religion is that religion was *never* meant to be an end in itself. There is no one who can be saved as a result of following a religion on Earth. What a religion *can* do for you is to help you establish a direct, inner contact with your spiritual teacher, who will then help you attain the state of spiritual self-sufficiency that is the real key to your salvation. In other words, the outer religion itself is insignificant, for the real purpose of religion is to help you attain the inner contact. That is precisely why Jesus said that the kingdom of God is within you (Luke 17:21).

If a religion helps you attain a direct, inner contact with your spiritual teacher, then it has fulfilled its purpose. If a religion fails to do this, possibly even blocks that contact, then its purpose has been perverted and it has become a dualistic religion. Yet why would anyone want to pervert the purpose of religion? Well, how about doing what all good detectives do, namely look for those who have a motive, those who stand to gain from the crime.

***

If you look at many of the things people do, you will see that the individual acts have no rational or logical purpose. Why do some men rape women or molest children? Why does a serial killer decide to kill dozens of people? Why does a mother decide to drown her children in the bathtub? Why do two groups of people allow hatred to build until is seems like violence is the only solution? Why do people engage in organized crime? Why do people destroy their bodies and minds with drugs, alcohol, tobacco or impure foods? Why do nations engage in the mass hysteria called war? Why do huge companies seek to concentrate money in the hands of a few shareholders by exploiting the workers, when spreading the wealth among the workers would give those companies a greater market? Why does an entire civilization allow a few large companies to pollute its environment and deplete natural resources in order to make a short-term profit, when doing so threatens the long-term survival of both the companies and the civilization?

Taken at face value, none of these individual actions are logical or rational, so why do people allow them to go on and on in an endless cycle of repeating the same mistakes? My point is that if you look at surface appearances, you will never find a rational or logical answer, for there *is* no such answer. The fact is that people do not know why they perform self-destructive actions, they have no logical or rational reasons. If people knew better, they would do better, meaning that people can engage in self-destructive actions only when they are trapped in ignorance. So if you want to understand what is really happening on this planet, you have to look for the reason why people are ignorant. Is there perhaps a force on this planet that wants to keep people ignorant? Is there a force that benefits from people's ignorance, whether it be innocent ignorance – people simply don't know – or willful ignorance—people don't want to know? What could such a force possibly be?

Obviously, I have answered that question in previous chapters, so let us briefly summarize. There is indeed a force on Earth whose very existence is dependent on keeping people ignorant. That force is made up of the following elements:

- Beings who fell in what is now the spiritual realm and have kept falling until they ended up on Earth. Some of these beings are in physical embodiment while others reside in the lower levels of the emotional realm, what people call hell.

- Beings who fell in one of the three higher levels of the energy field of Earth.

- Beings who fell in the physical realm, most of whom are still in embodiment.

- The identities and beasts created by fallen beings who wanted to maintain and expand a separate sense of identity. The creation of these identities started in several higher realms, and the identities have now fallen to the material world. They reside primarily in the emotional and mental realms.

- Certain identities or entities that have been created by people in the physical realm, specifically as a reaction to conditions in this realm. An example are entities created out of people's addictions to physical substances, such as alcohol, tobacco or sex. These reside primarily in the emotional realm, from where they pull on people's emotional bodies in an attempt to make them engage in the activities that feed the entities.

- An overall identity that ties all of these parts together in a superstructure, what I called the dragon.

The essential fact about this entire conglomerate is that both the individual beings – the fallen beings – and the mass entities can no longer receive light from spiritual teachers or from within themselves. They are literally cut off from the spiritual world, which is the source of life for the entire material world. Therefore, in order to survive or even grow in power, these beings must obtain energy from those beings who are still either receiving it from a spiritual teacher (although most are not aware of this) or are bringing it into the material world from within themselves.

As I said, the material world is so dense that even a being with high spiritual attainment will forget its true identity and origin when taking embodiment on Earth. Thus, there are many people on Earth who have some spiritual light, yet if they are ignorant of this and ignorant of the many ways this light can be stolen from them, they can unwittingly give it to the fallen beings. Obviously, a person with spiritual attainment would never do this if it understood what is happening. Which is why it is so essential for the fallen beings to keep the people on Earth ignorant about the existence of the fallen beings and the methods they use to get people's light. Ignorance truly *is* bliss—for the forces of duality! *Your* ignorance is *their* bliss.

***

Let me briefly describe the main principle that allows fallen beings to steal people's light. The reality is that a fallen being has become fully identified with a sense of identity based on the mind of anti-christ, which can only exist in the shadows, meaning in a lower vibration. Thus, if a fallen being was to receive a portion of pure spiritual light, the fallen being could do nothing with it. On the contrary, the pure light would be extremely uncomfortable for such a being, making it feel like it was burning up. And if the light was concentrated enough, it literally could burn up and consume a fallen being.

The basic equation is that a fallen being can only absorb light of a lower vibration, which is why such a being cannot steal spiritual light directly from others. It must get those who have spiritual light to misqualify that light, to lower it to a vibration that the fallen being can absorb. It does this by getting people to engage in any type of activity that lowers the vibration of their mental and emotional energies. An obvious example is any activity that causes you to feel anger or fear. Yet many activities will feed your spiritual light to the conglomerate of fallen beings and beasts, which is why Jesus told you to be aware so you do not cast your pearls before swine (Matthew 7:6).

You now see that although human beings commit many acts for which they have no rational or logical explanation, there is a rational and logical explanation for why people commit such acts. The stark reality is that these people have become tied to the conglomerate of fallen beings and beasts, and thus their minds are – at least part of the time – controlled by, even taken over by, this force. The dualistic force can manipulate people – by pulling on their mental and emotional bodies – into committing actions that misqualify light. When you look at the action itself, you can clearly see that it accomplished nothing positive and had no constructive purpose for anyone on Earth. As just one example consider how many battles have caused people to be killed without actually accomplishing anything decisive or constructive for any society. Yet the action was not motivated by a desire to accomplish a constructive purpose on Earth. It was triggered by the desire to produce misqualified energy that feeds the fallen beings and the beasts behind them.

Most people are completely unaware of this mechanism, and part of the reason is that they have never been told about the dualistic forces. The obvious reason is that their religion does not give them the full truth about the forces which oppose God's purpose. Yet another part of the reason is that because people would do better if they knew better, most people who are not completely spiritually blind assume there must be some kind of rational reasoning behind people's actions. They assume others are doing what they do because they think they are getting something out of it. And when people cannot find any possible rationale, they don't know how to make sense of a situation and they often ignore it. Some even deny the existence of a dualistic force that wants to steal people's energy. It is an unfortunate mechanism that when a problem seems too overwhelming and incomprehensible, people will ignore it. Which is precisely why Jesus said that with man – with the human perspective – many things are impossible, whereas with God – meaning with the vision of Christ – all things become possible.

If you only step back and look at the bigger picture, you will see that the people who commit evil acts often have no personal rationale for doing so. In other cases they do have a rationale, but it is so flawed that most other people clearly see that it makes no sense. For example, consider how those who were blinded by the illusions of Nazism could push children into the gas chambers. How could they get themselves to do something that most people today see as one of the most horrendous acts imaginable? How can people commit evil acts for no reason or based on a flawed reason? The answer is that their minds are so overpowered by the illusions of duality and the emotional pull of the beasts that they mindlessly carry out their acts without thinking about what they are doing, why they are doing it and what consequences their actions have for themselves and others.

There is no rational reason in the minds of the people performing many evil acts, but there is an explanation for why the acts are committed, namely that they misqualify light and feed it to the fallen beings and the beasts. I am not saying this is a justifiable reason, I am only saying it is a reason you can understand with the rational mind. And when you do understand it, you can withdraw yourself from the influence of the fallen consciousness and also seek to set other people free from the blindness that pulls them into these downward spirals over which they seem to have no control. For is it not true that if people have no awareness of dualistic forces, they are not making a free choice to act on behalf of such forces? And thus, if you care for such people, would you not naturally want to at least give them a free choice by telling them what is happening?

The stark reality is that the vast majority of the people on Earth have ties to the dualistic force, and people will – from time to time, for some even all of the time – do things for which the only purpose is to produce misqualified energy that feeds the beast. Ideally, your actions should be based on Christ discernment, so they only generate energies of a higher vibration. Anything done in true love and kindness will generate energies of such a high vibration that they will rise to the level of your I AM Presence. Once here, the energies will be multiplied and sent back to you so that you now have more creative energy. Thereby, you establish a figure-eight flow between your lower being and your higher being. When you do things based on a lower motivation, such as in anger or out of a desire to punish others or put them down, you generate energy of such a low vibration that it cannot rise up. Thus, such energy stays in the material, emotional or mental realm, and it will often be consumed by the dualistic forces.

Any action that springs from a motivation below unconditional love will feed the beast. I know this is a startling truth, but it is an absolute truth. An even more startling truth is that you are still partly responsible for the energy that you have misqualified. Thus, you become partly responsible for what fallen beings or beasts do with that energy, especially when it is used to overpower other people.

A substantial number of the people on Earth have their minds so controlled by dualistic forces that they are literally like cows that live only to have their energies milked by the dualistic force. One obvious example is how addicts live and breathe only to get their next fix. Yet even many so-called normal people feed one or more of the planetary beasts through seemingly innocent activities, such as smoking, drinking, watching excess TV, sex addiction, gossiping, pornography, buying the latest consumer gadget or fashion, or watching a violent sports activity. Basically, any activity that can be addictive will feed one of the planetary beasts, as will any activity that causes you to feel negative emotions or think negative or selfish thoughts.

Most people are not completely taken over by dualistic forces, but they do have ties that allow these forces to steal their energies on a more or less frequent basis. These are the people who have the potential to take action and free themselves and the Earth from the influence of dualistic forces. The first step is to become aware of how they are personally influenced by dualistic forces and then extricate themselves from that influence. The second step is to cry out to God for the Light of God to banish these forces – and the state of consciousness out of which they spring – from the Earth. And the third step is to go out and challenge the influence of such forces on individuals and on the institutions of society. If people knew better, they would do better, but who will help them know better? Certainly not the forces of duality and the institutions they control, including most religious institutions.

Once you begin to understand how every aspect of life has been influenced by the duality consciousness, you realize that all of the institutions of society have been manipulated by dualistic forces—at least to some degree. As a result, these institutions have become tools for keeping people in bondage, in democratic nations mainly through ignorance. So there is an obvious need for people to speak out against duality in every area of society, according to their expertise and experience.

However, since this book is about spiritual freedom, I will focus on how the institution of religion has been influenced by the duality consciousness. The fact is that if religion could be set free from duality, it would become much easier to free all other areas of society.

Religion was meant to be the primary institution for giving people spiritual freedom by maintaining an activity on Earth that cannot be manipulated by the duality consciousness. If such a bastion of truth is maintained, it will then filter into all other areas of society. Consequently, the dualistic forces have done everything possible to pervert the institutions of religion. What I am actually saying here is that instead of being the primary force for setting people free, religion has become the primary force for keeping people ignorant, and thus keeping them in the bondage imposed by dualistic forces. If you will be honest, you will see that most religions actually close people's minds to a higher understanding of life. They close people's minds to Christ truth by imprisoning them in a mental box defined by the duality consciousness—often through a perversion of a true religious teaching.

***

Before we move on, I would like to make one thing clear. I know that I have so far described the dualistic forces in terms that might invoke images of an evil empire that is perpetrating actions that are obviously evil. Thus, it is possible that some people will feel that I am being unreasonable by saying that religion is being used by a dualistic force. Some people will say that religion is by and large a force for good in this world. Obviously, one might respond that the millions of victims of religiously motivated violence, such as the Crusades, the Inquisition or modern terrorism, would disagree with that assessment. The stark reality is that some of the worst atrocities in history have been committed by people who thought they were doing God's work and thus felt fully justified in violating the commands of their own religion. However, my larger point here is that it is not only actions that most people see as evil that are feeding the dualistic force. I have used such examples in order to make it more obvious how the dualistic force can steal people's energies. Yet the reality is that the dualistic force is very subtle.

As I explained earlier, the Serpent is the most subtil – meaning the most deceptive – beast of the field, and thus it knows that the best way to steal people's energy is to deceive them into giving it up voluntarily. And the best way to accomplish this ploy it to make people think they are contributing to a good cause. Therefore, what you truly need to understand is that many of the activities that most people would label as good are still feeding the dualistic force. This includes many activities that religious people consider necessary for their salvation.

The real point I want to make is that, for a very long time, the primary role of religion has been to keep people in a state of ignorance in which they cannot free themselves from the unseen manipulation of dualistic forces. This has been done by using religion to create graven images, mental images that people are afraid or at least reluctant to question. As a thought experiment, consider what would be the best way to get energy from people on Earth. Obviously, you want to get energy from the people who have the most of it, namely those with the most spiritual attainment. Yet these people are also the least likely to give their energy to anything they see as dark or evil. So the only way to get these people's energy is to make them believe that they are contributing to a good cause. And what is the ultimate good cause on Earth? Well, it is God's cause—as defined by a religion that claims to be the only true religion.

Once people believe in this claim, they will gladly give their energy – even their lives – to what they see as the highest possible cause. Many of them will even do so without ever questioning what they are doing, why they are doing it and what the hidden consequences of their actions are. They will make themselves blind followers of those they believe to be true leaders. Yet if these leaders are tied to or blinded by the dualistic force, they will be the blind leaders who can only lead their followers into the ditch (Matthew 15:14), meaning one of the dualistic extremes. This is what the Bible calls the way that seems right unto a human, but the ends thereof are the ways of death (Proverbs 14:12). It is what Jesus called the broad way that leads to destruction (Matthew 7:13), as opposed to the straight and narrow way – the way that has no room for duality – that leads to eternal life.

We will later talk about this in greater detail, but let me remind you of one characteristic of the duality consciousness. The reason this consciousness is so difficult to see through is that it defines a complete world view, meaning that it defines both good and evil. Obviously, religion has been the primary force in defining for believers what is good and what is evil. Yet once religion became influenced by the duality consciousness, both the definition of evil *and* the definition of good became based on duality, based on the mind of antichrist. Thus, it became possible that people can do what their religion defines as being good, yet the activity generates lower energy that is feeding the dualistic force. I trust that anyone who is concerned about religion will want to understand this fully, so that we can free religion from duality and make sure it returns to its original purpose—which is to set people free from duality.

***

We can now see that we need to make a distinction between non-dualistic religion and dualistic religion. As I have attempted to explain in previous chapters, the key to attaining what many religious people call "salvation" is that you must rise above the consciousness of duality and put on the mind of Christ. I hope you have fully understood that this is the *only* way to be saved. As I have explained, you are meant to become a completely self-sufficient spiritual being – a true SUN of God – who radiates spiritual light from within yourself. And you can become such a being *only* when you realize that because the conscious self is an extension of God's Being, you have access to the fullness of God's Being – through your own higher being – right within yourself. That is why Jesus said that the kingdom of God is within you and that you will never find God's kingdom as long as you look for it outside yourself.

Let me say this even more directly. There is *no* way to be saved besides going through a transformation of consciousness from the ignorance of duality to the enlightenment of Christ. There are no outer or physical means on Earth that can guarantee your salvation. You can be a member of a church for a lifetime and attend services every Sunday, believe in the doctrines and follow the outer rules, yet if you do not transform your consciousness – by making choices only the conscious self can make – you *will not* be saved. As Jesus clearly stated in his parable about the wedding feast, you can enter God's kingdom only by putting on the wedding garment, which is a symbol for the Christ consciousness that makes your lower being – symbolizing the feminine polarity – a bride of Christ (Matthew 22:11).

The point here is that you need *nothing* from outside yourself in order to be saved. You do not even need an outer religion, for it is indeed possible that people can transform their consciousness without following a formal religion. A religion should ideally help you go through this inner transformation—it should encourage that transformation without in any way hindering it. In other words, a true religion is seeking to bring out what you already have inside rather than claiming it can give you something you don't have. When a religion has helped you establish an inner contact to your spiritual teacher and higher being, then it has fulfilled its role and has now made itself obsolete in terms of telling you what to believe or what to do. Obviously, you can still be involved with such a religion in order to fulfill the Omega aspect of your salvation, which is to help others, as we will later explore in detail.

We can now see that the definition of a dualistic religion is a religion which does not fulfill this requirement. This is a religion which states that you do *not* have everything you need inside yourself and that God, in effect, created you as an incomplete and perhaps even a flawed being. As such, you need *something* or *someone* from outside yourself in order to be saved. Some religions say you need the outer organization or its leaders. Some say you need an external savior, but they still set themselves up as the only mediator between you and that savior. The consequence of these beliefs – which come in a number of subtle disguises – is that you cannot be saved without the outer religion, and thus you will always need the religion. In other words, instead of seeking to make itself obsolete, a dualistic religion has become an end in itself. It is seeking to keep you in a codependent relationship with the outer organization and its leaders. Of course, you will also be in a codependent relationship with the dualistic forces behind such a religion.

***

Let me illustrate this with a couple of historical examples. Most Westerners know little about Buddhism and often think that the Buddha appeared in a spiritual vacuum and started a new religion. In reality, neither assumption is true. The Buddha was born in a culture that was dominated by Hinduism, but it was not the original form of Hinduism. Instead, it had come to emphasize the outer religion and its leaders as the key to salvation. It was a very elitist religion with a group of Brahmins (priests) who thought they were above the people and that they could administer salvation to the people. They also felt the need to withhold certain teachings from the people, thinking they were not advanced enough to understand them. The Buddha gave forth a teaching which emphasized an inner transformation of consciousness as the key to enlightenment, or salvation. He also said that what you needed in order to obtain this salvation was to master your own mind. This could only be done from within yourself, not by following outer rules or rituals and not by having anyone do it for you.

Yet what the Buddha gave was not a new religion. It was a universal teaching, describing the Path of Oneness. This teaching could – and still can – be practiced by anyone, no matter what outer religion they might follow. In other words, the Buddha was truly trying to give Hindus a teaching that could bring them back to the essence of Hinduism—the essence of all true religion. Because the leaders of the Hindu religion saw this as a threat, and because so many people followed them, Hinduism was not reformed by the Buddha's teachings, and thus a new religion eventually emerged. Yet that was not the Buddha's intent, nor was it his intent that this new religion would split into factions, some of which have become just as stuck in outer doctrines and rituals as the Hinduism the Buddha sought to transform.

Let us now look at Jesus, who appeared in a society dominated by the religion of Judaism. This religion is based on the Book of Genesis and thus it traces its origin back to the Garden of Eden, namely Maitreya's Mystery School. Nevertheless, this religion had become as stuck in rituals, doctrines and rules as Hinduism was at the time of the Buddha. The Jews believed that the key to their salvation was the remission of sins and that only the priesthood of their religion had the power to remit sins. Thus, if you did not obey the priests, they could refuse to remit your sins and send you to hell. We might therefore say that the priests of the Jewish religion had absolute power over their followers.

Jesus did not seek to draw the Jews out of Judaism to a new religion. Instead, he sought to free Judaism from its reliance on outer rituals, such as animal sacrifices and an elitist priesthood. He directly challenged the leaders of the Jewish religion, and the two main aspects of this challenge were:

- Jesus stated that the kingdom of God is within you, meaning that the key to salvation is inside yourself (Luke 17:21). Thus, you do not need an outer religion or its priests in order to be saved.

- Jesus claimed to have the power to remit sins and he gave that power to his disciples (John 20:23). Yet in reality, that power comes from the universal Christ mind – manifest on Earth as the Holy Spirit – which is the *only* force that can transform your sins. For only when you put on the mind of Christ and rise above the consciousness of sin will you be fully free of sin. Jesus did not mean to imply that he would remove all of humankind's sins. He meant to show people how to put on the mind of Christ, and then the universal mind of Christ will remit their sins.

It should be easy to see that by these two measures alone, Jesus had challenged the very essence of the Jewish priesthood's power over the people. If the people had believed Jesus, the priests would have lost their power and their privileged positions. Since they were not willing to give this up, their only option was to kill Jesus. They even managed to make it seem like this was done in the best interest of the people. After all, it was expedient that one man should die (John 11:50) rather than a whole nation perish (as if those were the only options). Because most Jews did not accept Jesus and his teaching and did not stand up to their leaders, Christianity emerged as a separate religion. Yet Christianity quickly became as rigid and ritualized as Judaism, and this trend has continued to this day. In reality, Jesus did not come to start a new rigid religion. He came to bring forth a universal teaching about the inner path to salvation, the Path of Oneness. It was his hope that all people would discover this universal path and thus follow it regardless of their outer religious affiliation (or lack of it).

If you take a look at the history of religion on this planet, you will quickly see that the pattern described in these two examples has been repeated numerous times. A religion starts out by promoting a universal teaching about inner transformation, but after a while, it is transformed into a rigid system that claims you cannot be saved from within yourself. A religion starts out with a non-dualistic teaching and is then transformed into a dualistic religion. If you are to claim your spiritual freedom, you need to understand why this happens.

Key 21
How a non-dualistic teaching becomes a dualistic religion

There is a very pragmatic reason behind the fact that a non-dualistic teaching is so often transformed into a dualistic religion, namely that the dualistic forces want to get energy from religious people. A non-dualistic teaching will make it very difficult for this force to steal energy from its followers. Thus, the dualistic forces must seek to pervert a non-dualistic teaching by inserting very subtle dualistic ideas. Thereby, they can eventually turn a non-dualistic teaching into a dualistic religion without the followers being aware of what has happened. The effect is that the followers believe they are following a true religion – perhaps the only true religion – yet almost everything they do within that framework gives spiritual energy to the dualistic force that has managed to pervert the religion. Let us look at the most obvious differences between non-dualistic teachings and dualistic religions:

- A non-dualistic teaching describes the reality that God is your source. You have a spark of God's Being within you, and therefore you have the potential to attain oneness with your source. You can say with Jesus, "I and my Father are one."

  A dualistic religion portrays God as a remote being in the sky who is above and beyond his creation and thus inaccessible to you. There is a distance between you and God and thus you and God are in a dualistic relationship. Only very special people, such as Jesus, can attain oneness with God.

- A non-dualistic teaching describes the reality that because God is your source, you can attain a direct inner contact with your own higher being, with your spiritual teacher and with God. In fact, it teaches you to let nothing come between you and God, to let no man take your crown (Revelation 3:11).

  A dualistic religion says that you need someone or something from outside yourself to mediate between you and God.

You need the outer religion and its leaders or at least an external savior.

- A non-dualistic teaching describes the reality that God is a loving God who loves you unconditionally. Thus, it encourages you to build a personal relationship with God and God's representatives (the spiritual hierarchy out of which you are an individualization), a relationship based on love. It also gives you intermediaries for helping you build this relationship, the Ascended Host, but we will neither do the work for you nor block your own growth.

  A dualistic religion portrays God as an angry being in the sky, who is ready to condemn you for your mistakes and send you to hell if you do not obey his commands—as defined by the outer religion and its leaders. Thus, it teaches you to fear God and blindly obey the leaders of the outer religion, causing many people to build a relationship with God that is based on fear. This fear makes you a house divided against itself, for you are fearing what is truly your own higher being.

- A non-dualistic teaching helps you attain inner communion with the spiritual realm, whereby you can know God's law from within yourself. You can then begin to spontaneously follow that law because you experience that it is enlightened self-interest.

  A dualistic religion teaches that you cannot know God's law on your own. You can know it only through the outer religion, which has a monopoly on revelation from God. Thus, the law is inevitably portrayed as an external influence that is being forced upon you under the threat of going to hell. You do not follow God's law out of love but out of fear.

- A non-dualistic teaching helps you attain Christ discernment so you can know what is right and wrong from within your own higher being.

  A dualistic religion claims that you cannot know right from wrong on your own. Therefore, you need an external authority to tell you what is right and wrong, namely the outer religion and its doctrines, rules and leaders. You should follow the outer religion rather than trust your own inner guidance.

- A non-dualistic teaching describes the reality that by putting on the mind of Christ – by walking the Path of Oneness until you become one with the Christ mind and your own higher being – you can know the truth about God from within yourself.

  A dualistic religion claims that because you are an incomplete being, you cannot know truth on your own. Human beings can know truth only through divine revelation. And only the leadership of the only true church can determine what is true revelation and what is false revelation.

- A non-dualistic teaching describes the reality that you were originally created as an individualization of God. Thus, you have the potential to become all that God is by following the Path of Oneness. In other words, you will be saved not by following an outer religion but by following the inner Path of Oneness.

  A dualistic religion teaches that you were created imperfect and incomplete – for example, that you are a sinner – and thus you can be saved only through the intercession of an external savior. That savior might be a spiritual being, such as Jesus, but you still need the outer religion in order to receive the salvation from this spiritual being. You simply cannot be saved without the outer religion.

- A non-dualistic teaching describes the reality that as you walk the path of Christhood and become sufficiently mature, you need to follow your inner guidance, even if it conflicts with the outer guidance from an earthly institution or a spiritual teacher.

  A dualistic religion claims that if you do not obey the doctrines, rules and leaders of the outer religion, you will not be saved.

- A non-dualistic teaching describes the reality that in order to receive reliable inner guidance, you must strive to rise above the human ego. Thus, a non-dualistic teaching promotes Christ discernment.

  A dualistic religion does not talk about the ego or Christ discernment. It encourages you to blindly follow the outer religion. It essentially says that you do not need to pull the beam – the ego – from your own eye. You can ignore that beam, for the outer religion will guarantee your salvation.

- A non-dualistic teaching describes a path of love. You follow God's law because you know it is in your own best interest to do so. It will make you more, and you love becoming more.

  A dualistic religion seeks to motivate you through the fear of something bad happening to you, such as burning forever in a fiery hell. Thus, you should not seek to go beyond the level of a normal human being, you should not seek to become more, which effectively puts you on the path of becoming less (for if you do not multiply your talents, you slide downwards).

- A non-dualistic teaching describes the reality that salvation is not a matter of the arbitrary and unknowable decisions of a remote God or some kind of miracle. It is solely a matter of applying God's law so that you raise yourself above duality and put on the mind of Christ. This is a rational, scientific procedure, and although it involves creative decisions, anyone can follow it.

  A dualistic religion traps you in the dualistic state of fearing the punishment of an angry God and hoping for a reward that is administered in mysterious ways, thus given to some while withheld from others based on unknowing and seemingly arbitrary decisions.

- A non-dualistic teaching encourages you to ask questions beyond its outer teachings, for it knows that it is only by asking questions that you internalize the truth.

  A dualistic religion strongly discourages any questions that cannot be answered by official doctrines. Such questions are portrayed as dangerous, often combined with the threat of damnation for those who continue to ask them and an eternal reward for those who blindly follow the outer religion. Thus, a dualistic religion gives you both a carrot and a stick, appealing to both pride and fear.

- A non-dualistic teaching will do everything possible to take you to a point where you no longer need the teaching for your own growth—you have become spiritually self-sufficient. It will then give you opportunities to use your attainment to help other people.

A dualistic religion will want you to stay codependent on the outer organization and its leaders. It will seek to keep you at a certain level where you are not spiritually self-sufficient.

- A non-dualistic teaching will promote leaders exclusively based on their spiritual attainment, meaning whether they have risen above their personal egos and the duality consciousness.

  A dualistic religion will promote leaders based on their willingness to conform to the doctrines and rules set by the outer organization. Only those who are willing to put the outer organization above anything else – such as the truth – will attain positions of power.

- A non-dualistic teaching is always open to the truth, and it will receive the truth no matter where it comes from.

  A dualistic religion is not open to anything beyond its doctrines, for they are seen as absolute and infallible. Only those who have attained power can bring forth any new idea, and only if it preserves the status quo of the organization.

- A non-dualistic teaching is open to change coming from below or from the outside, such as changes in society. Such a religion will adapt to changes in society so that it can continue to meet the spiritual needs of its members. It functions to *serve* its members, not to *pre*serve the status quo.

  A dualistic religion is not open to anything coming from beyond its leadership and tradition. The only people who can bring change are the ones in the established leadership, and you can only become part of leadership by demonstrating that you are committed to preserving the organization at all costs. Only those who have power can change the status quo, but you can attain power only by demonstrating that you don't want to change the status quo. A dualistic religion becomes a closed circle.

- A non-dualistic teaching is open to new revelation from the spiritual realm. Thus, the Ascended Host can take a non-dualistic teaching to a higher level, as the consciousness of humankind is raised.

  A dualistic religion is not open to such input, claiming revelation stopped with the founder of the organization or can only be brought forth by the leaders and only within the mental box of past teachings and tradition. Nothing can overthrow the status quo.

- A non-dualistic teaching is focused on bringing forth the highest possible expression of truth, and it is focused on serving people in the best possible way. It sees itself as a means to an end, namely the spiritual growth and ascension of its members.

  A dualistic religion is focused on preserving or expanding itself, meaning the outer organization and the power of its leaders. It is focused on preserving and defending existing doctrine and it acts as if the members are there to serve the organization. It has become an end in itself and neither God, truth or people are more important than the organization.

- A non-dualistic teaching has no superior leadership in the three lower levels of this sphere. It recognizes that the true spiritual leaders of humankind are the Ascended Host who are completely beyond the duality consciousness and thus only serve to set people free.

  A dualistic religion is led by people in embodiment and by fallen beings and beasts in the mental and emotional realm.

- A non-dualistic teaching has ultimate respect for free will. It needs nothing from its members, and thus they are free to leave at any time and with no penalty or threats.

  A dualistic religion creates its own beast that needs to be fed by people's energy. Thus, the beast seeks to suck people into the religion and makes it very difficult – physically, emotionally and mentally – for people to leave.

- A non-dualistic teaching places great importance upon humility and the fact that all people are equal in the eyes of God.

  A dualistic religion often raises its leaders far above the members but it also raises its own members above all other people. Thus, it appeals to and encourages pride and a sense of superiority (combined with the fear of hell, of course).

***

Obviously, this list could go on, but I hope you can now see the pattern, namely that a non-dualistic teaching is based on the consciousness of oneness, the mind of Christ, whereas a dualistic religion has become changed in subtle and not-too-subtle ways by the consciousness of separation, the consciousness of anti-christ. A dualistic religion portrays God as a remote being in the sky, as a being that is unreachable for you but is still seeking to force you into his kingdom. This creates a gulf between you and God, which is exactly what the fallen beings have created between themselves and God. They are literally seeking to force their own beliefs about God and salvation – namely that God is wrong and that if they prove him wrong they will be saved – upon humankind through an outer religion. In reality, a non-dualistic teaching describes the inner path, where the key to salvation is the transformation of consciousness, leading to spiritual self-sufficiency. A dualistic religion teaches an outer path to salvation, claiming that the only way to be saved is to follow the doctrines, rituals, rules and leaders of the outer religion. In many cases, a dualistic religion will make absolutist claims about its ability to save people, making it seem like those who *do* follow the outer religion are guaranteed to be saved. It portrays salvation as a mechanical process of living up to certain outer claims, such as sacrificing animals, lighting candles or saying prayers. Obviously, because of the nature of free will, no such guarantee is possible. Salvation is not a mechanical but a creative process.

I hope you can now begin to see that when you participate in a religion that is based on the consciousness of separation, anything you do that conforms to the framework – even if it seems perfectly benign – will serve to uphold the status quo, meaning that it supports the consciousness behind the outer religion. Obviously, there is a question of degree. A religious person who is very sincere will not feed the dualistic force to the same degree as a person who goes out and kills other people in the name of religion. However, as the old saying goes, if you are not part of the solution, you are part of the problem. If the good people in religion do nothing to overthrow the influence of duality, then they are – in reality – helping to uphold the status quo in which most religions on this planet are dominated by the consciousness of separation and duality.

What I am trying to help you see here is that there is no middle way when it comes to the consciousness of duality. It is so subtle that if you are not vigilant, you will be pulled down by it without noticing what is happening. I know I have talked about duality as creating black-and-white thinking, where you are polarized toward one of two extremes. I know it might seem as if I am now talking in black-and-white terms, but there is a higher understanding that I am trying to show you. The key is to realize that the duality consciousness defines two extremes. Thus, dualistic religions have defined a standard for what is considered good behavior, and many people think that by living up to that standard, they can do nothing wrong. In other words, if you live up to your religion's standard for what it means to be a good person, you will not do anything wrong and you are sure to be saved. In reality, it is quite possible to be a "good" person and still give energy to the dualistic force, and you will inevitably do so if you have made yourself a blind follower of blind religious leaders.

The *only* way to avoid giving energy to the dualistic force is to attain Christ discernment, whereby you will become aware of what activities lower your light to a vibration that is below unconditional love. You will know there is such a thing as dualistic love or dualistic goodness that is below the critical vibration, even though most people will insist it is truly good. If you participate in any dualistic activity – while conforming to the outer standards defined by the consciousness of duality – you will be giving your light to the forces of duality behind that activity.

However, it is also necessary to recognize that given the current state of affairs on planet Earth, just about every human activity is influenced by the consciousness of duality. Thus, to avoid having anything to do with duality, one would have to sit in a cave and meditate on God 24 hours a day. And while some spiritual people have done that, this is not the approach that is needed in this age. In other words, I am not saying that you should withdraw from all religious activities.

What is truly needed is to find the real Middle Way, namely the way demonstrated by Jesus and the Buddha, where you can be *in* the world but not *of* the world. You are participating in human activities, but you are doing it in such a way that you challenge the status quo and raise the activity to a higher level. In other words, you can free your mind from any influence of duality, and then you can participate in an outer activity without feeding the forces of duality. At the same time you are helping other people rise above duality by giving them an example of a person who is beyond duality. This is a concept we will talk more about in coming chapters, but for now I want to take a closer look at how the forces of duality pervert a non-dualistic teaching.

***

I assume that if you have read the book up until this point, you will – while not necessarily being able to accept every point I make – have an inner knowing that my testimony is true (John 8:13). The reason is that you have started the process of separating yourself from the duality consciousness. You have elements of truth in your own consciousness, and that is why you feel a resonance between my teachings and something inside yourself. Thus, when you read the above description of the differences between dualistic and non-dualistic religions, you probably see how most religions – including the religion or religions you might have been exposed to in your life – have been affected by duality. You probably feel a strong sense that this is wrong and needs to be corrected.

I now ask you to consider that the vast majority of the religious people on this planet – if they were to read my description – would not agree with you. Many would say that they see nothing wrong with what I describe as the characteristics of a dualistic religion. On the contrary, they would say that my description of a non-dualistic teaching is completely false and the works of the devil. Only a religion which really *is* the only true religion can save you, and when a religion really is the only true one, it is perfectly natural that it expresses its superiority (by doing most of what I say is done by dualistic religions). In fact, some people will say that what might seem like a religion forcing its members through fear is simply necessary for their salvation and thus fully justified. Other people will say that while some of my points apply to all other religions, their religion really *is* the only true one. While other religions make a false claim when they say they can save people, the only true religion is not making a false claim, because it really *can* save people. For these people it is not a matter of bringing all religions back to their original purpose by raising them above duality. The only option they can see is that everyone must be converted to their religion, and then all problems related to religion will be solved.

Many people are so blinded by the duality consciousness that they cannot see the duality consciousness – they cannot see the forest for the trees – and they will not be able to even fathom my teachings on it. They truly believe there is only one way to think and that the dualistic way of thinking is the only right way. Thus, everyone who thinks differently is by definition wrong. So when it comes to religion, there can be only one true religion, and all others are per definition false. To such people the very fact that there are other religions in this world proves that there is a struggle between God and the enemies of God, call them the devil or anything else. Thus, it is perfectly justified that they defend their religion against all attacks from the enemies of God, for doing this is truly doing God's work, even if it involves fighting against other people. The idea that to truly do God's work one must rise above duality will be utterly alien to them.

My point here is to show those who have eyes to see that there are millions of sincere and devout religious people who truly believe they are on God's side, but in reality they have been tricked into taking one of the sides in a dualistic struggle, the origin of which is the consciousness of anti-christ. Thus, neither their religion nor their efforts support the true cause of God, which is to raise all people above the duality consciousness so they can attain the Christ consciousness— the *only* thing that gives them access to the true kingdom. These people have become victims of a deliberate ploy by the more sophisticated fallen beings associated with this planet. This ploy is to draw all religious people into the ongoing dualistic struggle.

The main serpentine lie that sets the stage for this ploy is that because there is only one God, there can be only one expression of God's truth, and thus there can be only one true religion on Earth. Consequently, all other religions are false, and it is the duty of the followers of the only true religion to eradicate all false religions by doing whatever is defined acceptable by their religion and culture. Once people have been drawn into this dualistic struggle, they will serve to maintain the status quo, because nothing they do will help raise humankind out of the duality consciousness. On the contrary, their every effort gives energy to the fallen beings, thus feeding the planetary beast of duality while also reinforcing the lie of the dualistic world view.

I trust those who are open to this book can see that the idea that there is one true doctrine and that all others are false is dualistic in nature, and thus it inevitably sets up a struggle between people who belong to different religions. This idea is based on an entirely false premise that has no bearing in God's reality. Let us look at why it is false.

***

For starters, let us consider the concept that there can be enemies of God. On the face of it, it might seem as if the fallen beings that I have been talking about are enemies of God and are successfully opposing God's plan for the material universe by turning people away from the Path of Oneness. In other words, one could interpret my teachings to mean that instead of fighting against other people or other religions, the more enlightened people need to fight against the fallen beings. Yet this is far from being the case, which is what Jesus demonstrated when he told people to not resist evil but instead turn the other cheek (Matthew 5:39). Let me make it very clear that it is in no way my intention to set up a higher-level dualistic struggle between the top ten percent and the bottom ten percent. My real intent is to inspire the truly spiritual people to rise above the consciousness of duality and thereby inspire others to do the same. I have no intention of enticing you to seek to defeat the fallen beings. Instead, I desire to see you make them obsolete, insignificant and irrelevant because you have risen above duality and are now out of their reach.

In reality, God has no enemies. How could the Creator have enemies, when everything in the world of form is created out of the Creator's substance and when every self-conscious being has an individual spark of the Creator's Being? Without him was not any thing made that was made (John 1:3). How could an all-knowing and omnipresent God be in opposition to itself? Thus, seen with God's eyes, there are no enemies of God.

It is true that there are some beings who believe they are enemies of God and act accordingly. These are the beings who fell in a higher realm and who have used the duality consciousness to create a world view according to which it seems like the Creator is wrong. Based on their own dualistic view of the world, these beings truly believe they are right and that the Creator is wrong. They think they know better than the Creator and that they could run the universe better than the Creator. This explains why they are attempting to control the material universe and prevent parts of it – such as planet Earth – from ascending. They think that if they can thwart God's plan for the Earth, they can prove that the Creator was wrong all along, and then they will be left to be the true rulers of the world. I am not saying this belief is rational or logical, I am simply describing what is going on in the minds of these beings. As I said, the duality consciousness defines its own "reality," and thus it can justify anything. When you define "reality" a certain way, you can make it seem like even the Creator is wrong. When you set up a certain viewpoint as being absolute, complete and infallible, the conclusion is a given—as long as you don't question the basic assumption upon which the conclusion is based. This is how the duality consciousness creates closed mental boxes from which no being can escape—until it becomes willing to question its most fundamental beliefs and assumptions.

My point is that while these beings see themselves as the enemies of God, the Creator does not see them as its enemies. It sees their conscious selves as extensions of its own Being. It also sees that these conscious selves have simply stepped into an identity that is entirely built from the consciousness of anti-christ and therefore has no reality to it whatsoever. It also knows that when the void is filled entirely with light, all unreal identities will be dissolved in the final judgment. Thus, the Creator allows individual beings to take on an unreal identity, while hoping they will eventually outplay this identity to the point where they see its unreality and decide that they want to be more—thus rejoining the River of Life.

In fact, the Creator has allowed the material universe to be designed specifically to give these beings the ultimate opportunity to live out their fantasies. The Creator does not feel threatened by anything these beings could possibly do. For even if they manage to destroy an individual planet, the overall plan of the Creator will proceed on schedule. The material universe in its entirety is in an ascending spiral (it was designed to be too large for the fallen beings to pull it all down), and the force that pulls on everything to transcend its former state is becoming stronger every second. Even though some fallen beings have managed to slow down the growth of individual planets, they have to constantly fight harder to maintain their illusions. The fallen beings associated with Earth are literally resisting the upward pull of the entire universe, and I trust you can see that the Earth does not have the mass to resist the gravitational pull of the rest of the universe. The fallen beings on Earth have no chance of resisting the force of life, but the Creator allows them to maintain the illusion that they can do so. So far, a majority of the people on this planet have cooperated in this endeavor, which is why the illusion has been maintained. The illusion will be maintained until a critical mass of people are willing to cry out, "But the emperor has nothing on!"

When you see the reality that the Creator has no enemies, I trust you can also see that it is a complete illusion that humankind can be divided into two groups, namely those who are fighting *for* God and those who are fighting *against* God. The reality is that all people who think they are fighting an enemy – however it is defined – are trapped in the consciousness of duality. Thus, even if they claim to be doing God's work, they are only serving to maintain the forces of duality, which is definitely not doing the work of the real God.

I trust you can see that if a religion defines itself as the only true religion and defines certain other people or religions as its enemies or as enemies of God, this is a clear proof that the religion is influenced by the duality consciousness. Thus, the religion is simply one player in the ongoing dualistic struggle created by the fallen beings in order to help them survive and even expand their power over the Earth. A non-dualistic teaching does not define itself in opposition to anyone. It simply offers its teachings to all and it ministers to those who partake of them without thinking it has to save every person on Earth. This does not mean a teaching cannot state the truth it sees and even state why it sees the doctrines of other religions as being less than truth. However, this can be done without fueling the dualistic struggle.

***

What about the argument that since there is only one God, there can be only one reality, and thus there can be only one true representation of that reality, meaning one true religion? How can we explain that there are so many religions on Earth and that they often have outer teachings that are in direct opposition to each other? If several viewpoints are in conflict, they cannot all be true, so one must be true and all opposing ones false.

I hope it should now be obvious that there is an alternative to this black-and-white line of reasoning. The alternative is that all of the viewpoints could be false, or at least incomplete. Another alternative is that it is people's dualistic interpretations of religious teachings –

not the teachings themselves – that set the stage for religious conflicts. How can you know if an interpretation is dualistic? All interpretations that operate with a duality of truth and falsity spring from
the consciousness of duality. It is the duality consciousness that is
responsible for creating the contradictions between religious teachings. When you rise above duality, you see that there are no contradictions between the inner teachings of all non-dualistic religions.

In the beginning of this book, I attempted to make it clear that
there is a fundamental difference between truth – God's reality – and
people's mental images of truth. A mental image is needed only when
you do not have a direct experience of truth. And precisely because
the mental image is separated from God's reality, it is fertile ground
for the forces of duality. These forces cannot exist in God's reality, so
they can exist only in a realm that is removed from reality—so that
shadows can still exist. That is why they exist in the world of mental
images, in which everything is an idol, a graven image. Jesus said that
God is a Spirit and that those who worship him must do so in Spirit
and in truth (John 4:24) because he understood the need to go beyond
all mental images in order to know God. If you really want to know
God, you cannot settle for *any* description. You must reach for the
direct experience of God's Spirit. And because your conscious self is
an extension of the Creator's own being, that experience is open to
you.

Do you see the essential difference? When you have even a brief
glimpse of God's Spirit, you know that no doctrine or scripture could
ever give a complete and accurate description of God. You realize
that a religious teaching is only a road sign but is not the final destination. So what is the point of acting as if one description is the only
true one, when in reality no description can do justice to the transcendent reality of God? This realization sets the basis for a non-dualistic
approach to religion—both your own and the religions of other people. Imagine that you are on the way to a city and come across a road
sign which says the city is 100 miles away. Yet around the road sign
you see a group of people who are celebrating, and when you ask
them, you realize they think they have arrived at the city. You would
probably think this was silly, so it should be obvious that fighting
over which road sign – which religion – is the only true one is equally
silly—especially since they might all be pointing to the same destination when understood in a non-dualistic way. Just follow the sign you

like in a non-dualistic manner and keep going until you reach the destination, namely a direct experience of the Spirit of Truth.

My point is that there is no religious scripture that can give a full representation of God. It can only give an image, and if people think it is complete and infallible, they will inevitably turn it into a graven image. They will worship the image as if it *was* God and refuse to reach for the direct experience of the Spirit that is beyond all images. The purpose of a religious scripture – even one inspired by the Ascended Host – is *not* to bring forth a complete and infallible representation of God's truth, for this is impossible. The real purpose is to inspire people to go beyond the outer scripture and reach for a direct, inner experience of the Spirit behind the outer description.

The dilemma for a spiritual teacher is that matter is so dense that it is not obvious to people that there is something beyond the material world. Thus, we must give them a religious scripture in order to show people that there is something beyond, we must give them a road sign that points to the unseen destination. Yet the main purpose of such a scripture is *not* to describe the destination in every detail but only to give people enough information to awaken their desire for a direct experience. A religion is like a brochure that promotes a vacation destination. Yet if people only look at the brochure and never actually travel to the destination, then the brochure has failed.

Because the human ego cannot have a direct experience of the Spirit of Truth – only the conscious self can – people have allowed the fallen beings to lead them into believing that they cannot or are not allowed to go beyond the outer description and the outer religion. And they don't need to because the outer religion itself will take them to the destination. I hope you can begin to see that this mindset is the real cause of all religious rivalry and warfare.

***

Why are there so many religions on Earth, why not simply give forth one superior religion so as to avoid all the fighting? I trust that given your understanding of free will, the duality consciousness and the influence of fallen beings, you can see that it would not be possible to bring forth only one religion. Various groups of people have created their own religions, and fallen beings have created others, so there is no religion that would be acceptable to all people. Even if we did bring forth a non-dualistic teaching – as we have done several times – people in a dualistic state of mind will turn it into the "only true religion." When they do that, the teaching has entered the dualistic struggle for supremacy.

However, the Ascended Host have no desire to bring forth only one religion on this planet, and the reason is simple—one size doesn't fit all. In a previous chapter, I went to great length to describe the fact that the Earth is currently home to groups of lifestreams from vastly different backgrounds. It should be obvious that these many groups are so different in their way of thinking that they need different religions. One teaching has no chance of appealing to all lifestreams on Earth. Our goal is to bring every lifestream home, and thus we are constantly seeking to bring forth teachings that are designed specifically for lifestreams in a certain state of consciousness. When you see the overall goal, you see no contradiction in the fact that different groups of lifestreams are given different directions for how they can reach the same destination. After all, they *do* start out from different locations, or rather states of consciousness. People who start out from vastly different locations will need different road maps, even if they are all going to the same destination.

The Ascended Host are also aware of the fact that as humankind's consciousness is raised, we can bring forth more sophisticated teachings than could be released in the past—which is why I am bringing out this book. Yet let me make it clear that I make no claim as to the infallibility or superiority of this book. This book is the result of genuine revelation, but as all other forms of revelation – including all of the scriptures of the main religions – it is brought forth through the consciousness of a person in physical embodiment. Thus, it will to some degree be affected by the consciousness of the messenger and the consciousness of humankind at the time it is revealed. In reality, this is not a limitation—once you understand the need to always reach beyond the outer teaching for a direct experience of the Spirit of Truth. No teaching will hold you back as long as you see it as a road sign and keep going toward the final destination. It is when people start dancing around the road sign – as the Israelites danced around the golden calf (Exodus 32:19) – that you set the stage for religious conflicts. The tendency to turn an outer religion into a graven image is due to the ego's inability to fathom the Spirit of Truth. Thus, people who are blinded by their egos want something visible to worship instead of worshiping the transcendent Creator who is beyond all form.

In conclusion, the reality that all truly spiritual people need to see is that it is utterly pointless to go on fighting these dualistic battles between various religions. The devil never has more enjoyment than when he watches two groups of religious people fight each other in the name of the same God. If spiritual people still need an enemy to fight, let them fight the consciousness of duality and its influence on every aspect of human society, especially religion. And let them fight it by realizing the truth in Jesus' statement that you should start by pulling the beam – the consciousness of duality – from your own eye before you attempt to remove the mote in the eye of another. By doing this, people will eventually rise above all duality and thus no longer have a need to fight anyone or anything. Instead, they focus all their attention on letting the light of their spiritual selves shine, so that the Light of God can consume all darkness on Earth. When enough spiritual people let their light shine, there will be no shadows left in which the forces of duality can hide. And that is the real work of God on planet Earth.

Key 22
Understanding how beings fall

In previous chapters, I described how all beings in a given sphere – whether they are new co-creators or have fallen from a higher sphere – start out in a protected environment, such as the Garden of Eden. The beings who fell in what is now a higher sphere in the spiritual realm did not fall as new or inexperienced co-creators or angels. In fact, some of them had very powerful positions. It is important to understand how such beings can fall, so let us take a closer look.

As explained in the chapter on angels, the original fall happened in the fourth sphere. This fall happened because certain angels, who had started out in the three higher spheres, decided to deliberately rebel against God's purpose and design. However, since then many beings – both angels and co-creators – have fallen and this chapter is primarily concerned with how such beings fall. In other words, we will be primarily talking about how the angels and co-creators created to serve a specific sphere can fall as their sphere ascends. However, the teachings in this chapter will to some degree apply to beings who have fallen in a higher sphere and started out in a cosmic schoolroom in their present sphere.

Beginning with the fourth sphere, the density of the Ma-ter Light was sufficient to make the fall a realistic possibility. Therefore, up until the moment when a given sphere attains critical mass and actually ascends, it is still possible for the beings in that sphere to fall. This is true even for beings who hold high positions in that sphere. As long as there is any shadow left in a sphere, there is room for the duality consciousness to hide, and this means it is possible for a being to be ensnared by the subtle illusions of the mind of anti-christ. Thus, even beings who seemingly have a very sophisticated knowledge of the spiritual side of life can fall without seeing what they are doing. If they had known better, they would not have fallen, but because they still have elements of duality in their consciousness, they do not truly know better—they know not what they do (Luke 23:34).

It is also important to understand that a cosmic schoolroom is not meant to take the students to the fullness of Christhood. You simply cannot create a curriculum and guarantee that all students who go through it will come out as Christed beings. Christhood is not a mechanical skill but a creative process that you attain only by making decisions and having certain insights within yourself. You become the Christ as a result of "Aha experiences" or breakthrough experiences that cannot be produced mechanically. You either "get it" or you don't get it. A teacher can help you make the right decisions and set the foundation for breakthrough experiences but cannot force such an experience. What the schoolroom is aimed at doing is taking a student to the point of being spiritually self-sufficient, meaning that the student has some contact with its own higher being and can thus receive light and directions from within. Even this does not mean you have the fullness of Christhood for in a sense there is no fullness. Christhood is an ongoing growth process that leads to full God consciousness.

How do you attain the critical degree of Christhood that makes you an immortal being? Only by coming to the state of oneness with all life, which – as Jesus said – makes you the servant of all (Mark 10:44). This means that Christhood cannot be attained only by sitting in a classroom and learning theoretically. As everything else, Christhood has an Alpha and an Omega aspect. The Alpha aspect is to go within and find the kingdom of God that is within you and cannot be found by looking outside yourself. Yet once you have attained some contact with that inner kingdom – your own higher being and Chain of Being – you need to engage in the Omega aspect of sharing it with others, meaning that you serve to raise up the All. This is comparable to a college education on Earth. For several years you learn theoretically and after you graduate, you go out into the world to learn by practicing your skills. Many people know that they learn more from working than they did in college. Likewise, you make the fastest progress on the path of Christhood by serving others, for it is in teaching that you truly learn. Thus, after students had reached a sufficient level of learning in the spiritual schoolroom, they were sent out to practice what they had learned. For example, some of the students that graduated from the Garden of Eden were sent into physical embodiment while others went to the emotional, mental or identity realm.

Another consideration is that not all students reached the same level of Christhood when they graduated, much like college students are not equally skilled. On top of that, some students did not graduate but had to be sent out without being self-sufficient because they separated themselves from the teacher. A teacher still has the hope that these students will learn from life outside the school and will eventually grow in Christhood.

My overall point is that after students leave the spiritual schoolroom, they go out in their native sphere and grow from there. It now becomes possible that students can become very good at performing an outer skill without growing further in the inner skill of Christhood. Obviously, students can even grow in outer skills and become more self-centered in the process. This is seen on Earth in the fact that some leaders of nations are very skilled at exercising power but have no true compassion or love for other people, thus misusing their power. Other people are very focused on developing their skills in a certain area, but they are driven by a desire to compete with others. While this can give some growth, it doesn't necessarily mean growth in Christhood, for as long as you are competing with others, you are obviously in a dualistic frame of mind.

***

We now see what happens when co-creators and new angels (angels created specifically for a given sphere) fall. Some co-creators and some angels develop their outer skills to such a degree that they attain what they see as high positions compared to others. Even though such beings do provide a valuable service that helps their sphere ascend, they can still do so out of self-centered motives. Yet even self-centered beings are allowed to attain leadership positions, and the reason is simple. As a sphere is growing, co-creators – and to some degree angels – grow by experimenting. Thus, they are given some latitude in being allowed to experiment, co-creators having more latitude than angels. In other words, a co-creator can become almost anything it wants to become, even if it is driven by a self-centered desire. The reason for this is that even increasing your own skill in comparison to others is part of the process of becoming more. It is clearly at a lower level, but it has the potential to be transformed into selfless service.

That is why the Book of Revelation talks about those who are hot and cold as being in a better place than those who are lukewarm (Revelation 3:15-16). Those who are lukewarm are those who are not taking responsibility for improving themselves but who would rather follow a leader. Those who are cold are those who are working hard to improve themselves but for selfish reasons. Yet even so, there is a potential that they can experience an awakening that turns their striving into selfless service. Having acquired the advanced skills to glorify themselves will then empower them to give better service to others.

We now see – once again – that the true spiritual teachers and masters do not judge anyone. They attempt to give every self-aware being the maximum opportunity to grow, and the world of form is designed to be very flexible in allowing beings to create an environment that facilitates their growth. If a being develops a strong desire to raise itself compared to others, this being will be allowed to do so (in a sphere where there is still room for shadows). The reason is that any attempt to become more leads to some growth and has the potential to be turned into true growth.

Many beings have striven for a long time to increase their skills for their own glory, but have then experienced a change of heart, a turn of the dial of consciousness, that made them see the vanity of living this way. They have then become more altruistic and have been able to use their skills and experience to serve others. You see many examples of this on Earth, for example a business owner who spends decades accumulating wealth only to turn into a philanthropist who gives it all away in order to raise the All. So the difference between being hot and cold is only a slight turn of the dial of consciousness, which is why those who are cold are given many opportunities to take their self-centered desires to the extreme. The hope is that they will eventually have enough and will be awakened from their dualistic mindset. Take note that as spiritual teachers we must remain true to the nature of the Holy Spirit, and thus we can never allow ourselves to create an image that a being is beyond hope. We must always hold the immaculate concept that a being can be awakened and start the Path of Oneness.

***

We now see that when a sphere comes close to ascending, all beings in that sphere will face the ultimate test of Christhood, namely the test of selflessness. A spiritual school teaches the Path of Oneness, meaning that you are meant to fully internalize the fact that all life is one. So after students leave the school, they go out into the world to integrate what they have learned, and they do so by experimenting. Some continue to follow the Path of Oneness and come ever closer to oneness, thus becoming hot. Others leave the Path of Oneness and follow the path of, to use a popular expression, "looking out for number one," which makes them cold. Still others bury their talents in the ground and are neither looking out for themselves nor the All, so they become lukewarm. All of this is allowed as a sphere grows, which is the phase we can call the cosmic out-breath. Yet when a sphere reaches critical mass, the process of the in-breath begins, which is when beings must face the test of selflessness.

Some beings become so focused on attaining a high position and doing all the duties associated with such a position that they set aside the need to fully integrate the teachings on oneness. They become focused on the desire to do everything right – which is a constructive desire – but they color it with the desire to be better than others, to raise themselves in comparison to others. Such beings often attain very high positions in their societies, for example in religion and government, and they can have many followers who look to them as their leaders. Some of these followers are very loyal to their leaders and would basically do whatever their leaders told them to do, meaning that they follow them blindly.

When a sphere reaches critical mass, the leaders who have attained high positions based on self-centeredness face a set of very difficult initiations. The nature of these initiations is unknown to the leaders, for if the initiations were known, they would be too easy to pass. The initiations are carefully designed to help beings overcome all separation and all remnants of a separate sense of self. Thus, as a sphere rises in vibration, the initiatic process will inevitably expose any selfish tendencies in all beings, even those of the highest rank— who might actually think they are above being tested. One might say that all initiations are tests of humility, and no one is exempt from these tests—even (or especially) those who think they should be because of their rank in the outer society. God truly is no respecter of persons (Acts 10:34).

What is the ultimate test of oneness and humility? As a new sphere is being formed, the beings in the ascending sphere are asked to help create the next sphere. Yet how is a new sphere created? It is part of the creative process that started with the Creator. As I explained earlier, the Creator created the first sphere out of its own Being and consciousness. The Creator then created self-conscious co-creators out of its own Being and gave them free will. One could say that the Creator allowed part of its own Being to be imprisoned in form and then allowed the self-aware co-creators to do whatever they wanted with that part of the Creator's Being over which they had control. This is the process that has continued, as the beings – both angels and co-creators – in an ascending sphere embed their own beings and consciousness in the creation of the next sphere.

When one sphere is close to ascending, the beings in that sphere will be asked to allow part of themselves to be embedded in the new sphere. And, of course, the new sphere will be inhabited by inexperienced co-creators with free will – even some fallen beings – who can then do whatever they want with what is embedded by the beings in the higher sphere. I trust you can see that this is the ultimate test of oneness and of humility. I trust you can also see the wisdom of this, as the beings who embed part of themselves in the new sphere will have a deep sense of oneness with the new sphere and thus a vested interest in helping the beings in that sphere ascend, thereby freeing up their own Beings to ascend as well.

***

We can now see why this initiation could be quite difficult, even traumatic, for some beings in an ascending sphere. If these beings had not fully overcome their separate sense of identity – still seeking to raise themselves up in comparison to others – the initiation I have described would come as a great shock to them. They would likely feel that they had spent so much time and effort in working to attain their high positions – hoping for some ultimate recognition and reward – and now it was as if everything was going to be taken away from them. Instead of getting the promotion and recognition they had been working for, they would think they were being demoted and degraded. Instead of achieving some ultimate recognition in comparison to others, they thought they were being humiliated in front of the whole world.

Most beings happily took the opportunity to be part of the creative process, but a few thought they were being treated unfairly.

Instead of seeing the initiation as a great opportunity to grow in one-ness, they thought they were being unfairly stripped of their rank and position and being made the underlings of completely inexperienced beings who were likely to make all kinds of mistakes. They literally felt like a general in a huge army who, after a lifetime of flawless ser-vice, is asked to go down and clean the barracks and take orders from a group of new recruits. Yet I trust you can see that this viewpoint was only possible for those who were still affected by the consciousness of separation. For if you see the new co-creators as extensions of your own being, how could it possibly be humiliating for you to serve them and help them grow in self-awareness? How could it be unfair for you to be asked to extend the same opportunity to others as those before you — starting with the Creator – had extended to you? You were actually being asked to participate in the greatest adventure of all, namely the process whereby life begets life.

We can now see that the fall is not something that happens by accident, necessity or design. It happens as the result of a decision, a decision based on the duality consciousness. Beings deliberately refuse to serve those below them in rank and they rebel against the basic design of the world of form. They refuse to give up their sepa-rate sense of identity because they are not willing to give up the need to feel superior to others—which is only possible when you feel sepa-rated from them. So these beings rebel against the very process of life itself, particularly rebelling against the concept that they should allow part of their own beings to be controlled by co-creators of a lower rank and attainment than themselves (on their own dualistic scale). Some beings in lower spheres fall because they come to believe in the original lie of the first fallen angels, namely that it was a mistake by the Creator to give new co-creators free will and that the Creator should have designed the universe in such a way that new co-creators did not have the opportunity to rebel against his laws but were guar-anteed to be saved.

I trust you can see the great irony of this belief. It is precisely the fact that the Creator gave all beings free will that makes it possible for beings to rebel against the creative process. So in reality, self-cen-tered beings are not against free will in general, they are only against free will for others. They have actually built a separate sense of iden-tity that is so strong that they believe they should have free will but that they – because they are so superior – should be allowed to control the free will of those they consider to be below them in rank.

The consequence of this rebellion is that these beings cannot remain in their native sphere as it ascends. Thus, they end up in the newly created sphere. One might say that instead of allowing a part of their total Beings to be embedded in the new sphere (while the main part of their Beings ascends to the spiritual realm), they now have the totality of their beings embedded in the new sphere. The difference is that they have full control over their beings in the new sphere, and for self-centered beings this is their overall concern. Yet they still feel that they have been treated unfairly by God, and they are very angry over the fact that they have now been "cast down" (for they feel they were forced rather than suffering the consequences of their own choices). Thus, it is entirely accurate when the Bible describes the mindset of these fallen beings as follows:

> Therefore rejoice, ye heavens, and ye that dwell in them. Woe to the inhabiters of the Earth and of the sea! for the devil is come down unto you, having great wrath, because he knoweth that he hath but a short time. (John 12:12)

Note that "Earth" is a symbol for the physical realm and "sea" is a symbol for the emotional realm, as the fallen beings described in Revelation descended to both. In reality, this quote refers to the original fallen angels, but it also is true of all beings who have fallen to this current sphere. They all descended with anger against God, against co-creators and against the Divine Mother, the Ma-ter Light, that makes them experience the consequences of their self-centered choices.

***

Before we move on, I will use the teachings in this chapter to explain what I hinted at earlier. Many spiritual teachings contain the concept that you can escape the wheel of rebirth and rise to a state of consciousness where you no longer have to re-embody on Earth. The general idea is that once you have balanced all karma made on Earth, you no longer have to come back.

Within the last century, the Ascended Host have released several spiritual teachings as a part of our ongoing and progressive revelation. These teachings have given much more detail about the ascension process, as it is generally called. This has caused many people throughout the New Age movement to believe that once you ascend from Earth, you become an ascended master, an immortal being. Some students are aware of a new dispensation that makes it possible for a person to ascend with only 51 percent of its karma balanced, which makes it seem like ascending is relatively easy. And while it has been our goal to make the ascension seem like an attainable goal, the more perceptive students should have asked certain questions.

For example, does balancing 51 percent of your karma really set you completely free from the duality consciousness? And if you have not fully overcome the duality consciousness, how can you become an ascended master and permanently enter the spiritual realm? How can a being who is still affected by duality become immortal—and if you were not affected by duality, how could you have unbalanced karma? I will now give you a deeper understanding of these concepts.

Let us begin by making a distinction between ascending from the Earth – meaning that you do not have to come back into physical embodiment – and ascending to the spiritual realm, whereby you become an immortal being, an ascended master. As I have explained, there are certain beings whose origin is tied to this particular sphere. They include beings who evolved from below, co-creators who were created to descend into this sphere (in all four levels) and angels who were created to serve this sphere. These beings cannot permanently ascend to the spiritual realm until this sphere reaches critical mass and begins the ascension process. They were created to help this sphere ascend, and thus their individual ascensions are tied to the ascension of the entire sphere.

Let me make it clear that I am not hereby saying that the ascension is a collective process. You will not "automatically" ascend by following the crowd. The ascension is an individual process that requires you to permanently overcome duality and come into a sense of identity that is based on oneness. You must attain spiritual self-sufficiency, whereby you become a spiritual Sun that radiates light from within itself. No one from outside yourself can do this for you, so you must walk through the pearly gate entirely on your own inner oneness with your own higher being and Chain of Being. Take note of the subtle distinction here. You cannot ascend based on outer skills or the help from external beings, for this cannot be accomplished. You can ascend only through your inner oneness with your own higher being and your Chain of Being. You can ascend only by resolving the enigma of a separate self and a greater self.

We can now see that while the ascension is an individual process, it is not a self-centered process. So if you were created to serve this particular sphere, you can ascend only by overcoming all self-centeredness. And when you do so, you will not want to ascend until your sphere has been brought past the critical point and is guaranteed to ascend. At that point you can then pursue your individual ascension and can indeed ascend before other beings from your sphere ascend.

What I am saying here is that beings who were created to serve this sphere can indeed ascend from Earth so they do not have to come back into a physical body. Yet this does not mean that they become immortal beings or ascended masters. They will still have to serve this sphere in the emotional, mental or identity realms. In performing this service, they will be exposed to the temptations of duality until this sphere reaches the point of having no more room for duality. Thus, they can theoretically fall right up until they face the final initiation I just described.

I know this will seem to contradict previous teachings that gave people the impression that once you ascend – even if you have only balanced part of your karma – you will become an ascended master. Some will refer to Jesus who became an ascended master after his ascension from the Earth. Yet as I explained earlier, not all people on Earth were created specifically to serve this sphere. Some have descended here from what is now the spiritual realm. One such group are beings who descended with greater mastery and who were sent into physical embodiment in order to help humankind grow. This is what some spiritual teachings call an avatar.

When a being with such mastery comes into embodiment, that being forgets who it is and can thus be tempted by duality and fall. An immortal being is immortal and thus cannot fall, which means that it cannot send the totality of itself into embodiment in a lower sphere. So it sends an individual extension of itself, but this being has a higher degree of awareness and mastery than a new co-creator. It forgets this attainment, but it can recover it and thus use it on Earth instead of having to start from the bottom and work its way up.

The descending avatar is an independent being, which means that it can become lost and that it must walk the Path of Oneness in order to qualify for its ascension. The difference is that once such a being does overcome duality and qualifies for the ascension, it will immediately become immortalized as an ascended master. In other words, since it was not created to start as a new co-creator within this sphere, it can ascend independently of the sphere into which it descended. The being whom you know as Jesus started out as an avatar who descended here to demonstrate the process of the ascension. Yet this being had several embodiments before the one in which it became known as Jesus, which means that the being made karma and could have fallen. After such a being ascends, it becomes a new ascended master rather than blending back into the master that sent it down.

Take note that all beings who descend – including new co-creators – are extensions of beings in the spiritual realm. Yet the question is how much of its own consciousness a spiritual being embeds in the descending being. This is similar to investing money in a business venture—how much of your fortune will you risk? When an immortal being embeds part of itself in a descending being, that part can become lost, which is one reason an immortal being cannot descend in the fullness of its being. A new co-creator has only a small portion of a spiritual being embedded, whereas an avatar has a greater portion—the size depending on the purpose for which it is created.

What about beings who fell from a higher realm? Since they were not created specifically for this sphere, they too can ascend and become immortalized without waiting for this sphere to ascend. This might seem unfair, but remember that fallen beings have some serious hurdles to overcome. They have to overcome all of their past momentum of the duality consciousness, and if they have fallen through several spheres, this is a very demanding task. So if they make it, they truly deserve to quickly rise back up to the place in the River of Life where they would have been had they ascended as planned.

So the deeper understanding of the ascension is that there is a partial ascension and a final ascension. You can ascend from the physical realm, from the emotional realm and from the mental realm without making your final ascension. And only when you overcome all duality and ascend to the spiritual realm do you become an ascended master, an immortal being.

Key 23
Understanding how the blind leaders approach religion

We can now see exactly how those who are partially or completely blinded by the duality consciousness approach religion. These beings have either fallen from above or they have fallen here below by becoming blinded by the duality consciousness. Obviously, they do not see this and many of them truly believe they are doing God's work or even that they are God's true representatives on Earth. Thus, we will call them the blind leaders. These people have the following beliefs about the role of religion in human life and about their own role in religion:

- The blind leaders believe they are superior to God in knowledge and intellect, meaning that they have no respect whatsoever for divine revelation, spiritual teachers or for the representatives of God in embodiment. That is why they killed Jesus and many other people who attempted to change the status quo. That is why they are completely convinced that they have the right to take God's revelation – such as a religious scripture or the teachings of Jesus – and change it as they see fit. They also feel they have the right to impose an outer doctrine upon a scripture that goes beyond or distorts the original revelation. In short, they feel they have the right to create their own religion on Earth and that they should be the supreme judges of what is a true religion. They literally feel they own the Earth and that God has no right to interfere by giving humankind new revelation and sending prophets to awaken the people.

- The blind leaders fundamentally disagree with free will and believe people on Earth should be saved through control by themselves as superior beings. They disagree with the goal of a non-dualistic teaching, namely to make people spiritually self-sufficient by connecting them with their higher beings and spiritual teachers. They believe they are the true leaders of humankind and that people should be forced to follow them. This is, of course, only for people's own good, since the blind leaders know better than God how the universe should work and how people should be saved. These beings believe religion should be a force for controlling people, herding them as sheep into the orthodox fold and then keeping them there indefinitely.

- The blind leaders believe they know best, so it is in people's best interest to be kept ignorant of any viewpoint that contradicts or goes beyond the doctrines defined by the leaders. That is why they seek to use religion as a way to control people's minds by keeping them ignorant of anything beyond the mental box created by themselves. They feel completely justified in suppressing all alternative knowledge through any means available, whether it be burning books, killing people or torturing their own followers.

- The blind leaders are always trying to create the perfect religion, which they see as a religion that forms a completely closed box. Once people are in, they have no way of escaping the control of the blind leaders, they have become unreachable for God and the true spiritual teachers. The blind leaders do this by all means, but primarily through deception and intimidation. That is why so many religions have an obvious culture of fear. Any religion that does not make an all-out effort to raise people beyond fear is influenced by the blind leaders.

- The blind leaders have an insatiable desire to prove that they are right and God is wrong. In their blindness, they believe this can be achieved when all people on Earth follow the religion they have defined. They are actually trying to set themselves up as being infallible on Earth, or at least set themselves up in positions where their word is law and cannot be questioned or gainsaid.

- The blind leaders are essentially trying to set themselves up as gods on Earth and they have no compunctions about having people worship them as if they were gods. That is why you have seen certain civilizations where the leader was worshipped as a god or as the only representative of God on Earth. That is why so many religions have a hierarchy in which the leaders are seen as infallible or at least as above being questioned. They claim this hierarchy represents God, but it is a creation that springs entirely from the duality consciousness and thus comes between the people and the true God.

- For the blind leaders religion is simply a means to an end, namely the attainment of all of the goals described above, including power and privileges for themselves. For them religion is completely disconnected from the reality and the truth of God. God's truth has no place in their religion, only the "truth" they have defined based on their dualistic world view—that places them at the center of the universe.

- The blind leaders believe they have a right to be doing what they are doing, and when they are challenged, their default reaction is anger, often even a rage that goes beyond all rationality or proportion to the challenge. That is why the Jewish leaders were so angry with Jesus and so quick to kill him. That is why Jesus said about them:

> 15 Beware of false prophets, which come to you in sheep's clothing, but inwardly they are ravening wolves.
> 16 Ye shall know them by their fruits. Do men gather grapes of thorns, or figs of thistles? (Matthew, Chapter 7)

- The essence of the fallen consciousness is a refusal to self-transcend by serving all life instead of serving the separate sense of identity. Thus, the blind leaders are always seeking to create a state of control that will be permanent and can never be overthrown. In doing this, they are going against the very essence of life itself, which is self-transcendence, the process of becoming more until the void is filled with light and all self-conscious beings have attained full God consciousness. The consequence is that the blind leaders can never succeed and that their creations will eventually be broken down by the force of life itself. The blind leaders are on an impossible quest, and if only humankind would realize this, people could free themselves from spending lifetime after lifetime on this treadmill—while never getting closer to fulfilling their reason for being.

- The true teachers of humankind are always seeking to give people teachings and examples to show that all human beings have the potential to attain the Christ consciousness. The blind leaders are always seeking to counteract this effort, and they do so by elevating the example to an exception, thus turning the person who was sent to set people free into an idol. This is what the blind leaders have done to the example of Jesus. Thus, the stark reality is that mainstream Christian churches are not following the true Jesus – who is a member of the Ascended Host – but a false Jesus. The blind leaders have used the example of Jesus to create a religion that is largely based on the mind of anti-christ, meaning that most mainstream Christians are actually following anti-christ rather than the true Christ.

***

The blind leaders have no compunction about starting a new religion that is based on their own world view and which often sets themselves up as gods on Earth or worships gods that are fashioned after themselves. Even in modern history there are examples of such religions, and there are many more from earlier ages. Such religions have generally been of localized reach and have been relatively short-lived. The reason is simple. In order to maintain a religion, it must be infused by spiritual light, or it will quickly be broken down by the contracting force of the Mother. The blind leaders and those who follow them do not have this light, so it must come from those who still have some connection to the spiritual realm. Yet such people also have at least some Christ discernment, and thus they are not likely to be converted to a religion that is entirely based on the duality consciousness.

Obviously, the blind leaders cannot see beyond the dualistic state of mind and thus cannot – on their own – come up with teachings that are beyond duality. For this reason, the more sophisticated blind leaders have used the tactic of seeking to distort or pervert a teaching that was inspired or revealed by the Ascended Host. In other words, they have taken a teaching that was sponsored by the Ascended Host and have distorted some of its beliefs, thereby gradually pulling it into the dualistic struggle.

This can be done in various ways, but in this context, I will focus on the falsification of scripture. There are no religious scriptures on Earth that fell from the sky, even though many modern Christians seem to think this happened with the Bible. The reason is that the law of God states – as I have explained earlier – that there must be plausible deniability on Earth. Thus, a religious scripture is brought forth through one or more persons in embodiment—meaning that people can always deny the scripture by discrediting the messenger, as many Jews did with Jesus.

Scriptures can be revealed through various processes, but they all go through the mind of the person who serves as a prophet or messenger or whatever people choose to call it. The law states that the Ascended Host are not allowed to give forth a truth that is higher than what someone in embodiment has internalized. We can multiply the contents of a person's consciousness, but we cannot give forth ideas that are beyond the messenger's state of consciousness and spiritual attainment. Thus, to receive a non-dualistic teaching, the messenger must have risen above duality, at least to some degree. This obviously puts certain limitations on what can be revealed, and it is possible that a messenger can have certain personal or cultural beliefs that put an overlay on a teaching from the very beginning.

Yet this demand also has the advantage that a teaching will be expressed in such a way that it is adapted to the cultural background of the messenger, making it more easily accessible for other members of that culture. Always remember that the purpose of a spiritual teaching is to reach a certain group of people and take them to a higher state of consciousness. So even if a teaching is affected by the consciousness of the messenger, it can still take people higher—if they are willing to use the outer teaching as a stepping stone for a direct inner experience.

The danger is, of course, that once a new spiritual teaching begins to gain widespread acceptance, it can become influenced by the culture in which it is given. Thus, instead of allowing the teaching to raise their consciousness, people can – both unwittingly and deliberately – pull the teaching down and use it to justify the state of consciousness they refuse to transcend. People interpret the teaching in such a way that it seems they do not have to change their ways or their consciousness (obviously, a change in consciousness is the purpose of any true spiritual teaching). The blind leaders are very skilled at exploiting this tendency by making – often subtle but sometimes very blunt – changes to religious scriptures that were brought forth as a result of genuine revelation.

***

Let us look at one example of just how far blind leaders are willing to go in terms of changing a religious scripture. Many Bible scholars are aware that Genesis seems to give two accounts of how human beings were created. We first read:

> So God created man in his own image, in the image of God cre-
> ated he him; male and female created he them. (Genesis 1:27)

Then, in the very next chapter, we find this account:

> And the LORD God formed man of the dust of the ground, and
> breathed into his nostrils the breath of life; and man became a
> living soul. (Genesis 2:7)

So were human beings created in the image of God, or were they created out of the dust of the Earth? It might seem as if there is little contradiction between the two accounts, but when you understand the reality of different vibrational frequencies, you see the incompatibility. Here are the relevant questions to ask:

- Were what you call human beings created in a higher realm, a higher vibrational spectrum, or were they created in the physical spectrum?

- Were what you call human beings created to descend to Earth and take command over it, or were they created on the Earth for the purpose of tilling the garden of their master?

- Where was "God" when man was created—in a higher realm or on the Earth?

It would seem logical that God – or a spiritual being – would not have to descend to Earth in a physical form in order to create man. Being all-powerful, God could certainly create man from the spiritual realm. This supports the idea that human beings were created in a higher realm. This is the only way they could be created in God's image and after his likeness, for how could the Creator of the world of form himself have a form that would allow him to be in the physical spectrum while creating man? In other words, God does not have a physical body like human beings. Being created in God's image means that human beings have the capacity of consciousness to co-create by imposing mental images upon the Ma-ter Light. The consequence is that human beings are co-creators and are meant to do the work of subduing the Earth according to God's design. This is supported by Genesis:

> 28 And God blessed them, and God said unto them, Be fruitful, and multiply, and replenish the Earth, and subdue it: and have dominion over the fish of the sea, and over the fowl of the air, and over every living thing that moveth upon the Earth. (Genesis 1:28)

Yet in Chapter 2 we are told that man was not created in a higher realm, but was formed out of the dust of the Earth, which is a symbol for the energies in the material spectrum. We are also told that the being who created this "living soul" – as opposed to a co-creator designed to have dominion – planted a garden and made man the farmer:

> And the LORD God took the man, and put him into the garden of Eden to dress it and to keep it. (Genesis 2:15)

There is nothing here about subduing the Earth and having dominion, and it seems like the second account has a much more passive role for man than the first. Thus, one might question whether the two accounts are talking about the same "god?" Why would the "god" in the second account need a garden on Earth—it would seem that this god was actually *on* Earth.

We can also approach this by using common sense. If Genesis really is the revealed word of God, why would God repeat himself and give two accounts of the creation of man? Why not simply stick to the one, which opens the question of whether the second account was added later and perhaps mixed in with the first one, so that it can be difficult to sort out which verses were original and which were inserted. This, of course, raises the question of who would have inserted a second account and why? Based on what we know now, I can give you the answer.

As I have explained, there have been many civilizations on Earth that are not known by today's science. Some of these civilizations had reached a very high level of technological ability, including in some cases the ability to perform genetic engineering far beyond today's science. One such civilization was ruled by a particular emperor who was a fallen being. He had set himself up to be not only the secular ruler of the civilization but also as being their god. He was supported by a large group of other fallen beings in leadership positions and some of these had advanced knowledge of genetic manipulation. As always happens with such a civilization, it was constantly under threat of being broken down by the contracting force. The expanding force was also working and it manifested as a growing rebellion against the idea that the ruler – who was obviously in a physical body – was really the highest God. A growing number of people started having direct experiences of the spiritual realm and thus attained proof that there was much more to God than what the state-controlled religion taught.

As an attempt to counteract this growing threat, the ruler and his priests and scientists came up with a plan to genetically alter human bodies. They were aware that although people's spiritual longing is not coded into the genes, there are certain centers in the brain that facilitate the experience of something beyond the material universe. Thus, they attempted to create a sub-race of humans in which these spiritual centers had been degraded to the point where it became very difficult for people to have a direct spiritual experience. These people would thus be prone to blindly follow their spiritual leaders and did not have the opportunity of attaining a direct experience that could go beyond outer doctrines. As a beneficial side-effect, these people did not have any longing for anything beyond the material universe and were thus far easier to satisfy within a modest material lifestyle. They were, so to speak, the perfect worker bees.

The ruling elite was successful in creating such a slave race (by mixing human and animal DNA), and they were very proud of their creation. Thus, they decided to leave a veiled testimony to their work by altering their religious scripture. They altered what was the forerunner for what is now known as the Book of Genesis. This scripture was originally released as genuine revelation by the Ascended Host, although it was released in a culture with a limited understanding of spiritual concepts. Thus, Genesis was never meant to give a full account of creation, nor was it meant to be taken literally. The ruling elite of the civilization altered Genesis by inserting the second creation story which describes how they created man out of the "dust of the Earth," as a symbol for the genetic material and then "breathed life into" their creation in a test tube. This second "creation" brought forth a human that was designed to till the garden of his master without asking any "dangerous" questions. At the same time, the elite also removed certain material from Genesis that exposed the true origin of the Serpent and themselves.

As a side note, let me make it clear that while it is acceptable that a civilization has some knowledge of genes and some ability to manipulate them, it is not acceptable that a civilization takes away the spiritual potential that is the very purpose of life on Earth. When a civilization breaks this law, the contracting force will begin to break down that civilization. Thus, soon after the ruling elite thought they had created a paradise for themselves on Earth – having plenty of worker bees to do all the hard work for them – the civilization began to break down. The outer vehicle was rivalry within the ruling elite that weakened the civilization from within and opened the door for an outside enemy to attack the civilization. The ensuing warfare was fought with nuclear weapons, and it released such intense natural disasters – even the event that triggered the myth of a world-wide flood – that the civilization collapsed and was erased from the historical record.

Obviously, not all of the members of the civilization died, but they were scattered far and wide and within a few generations lost all memory of the old civilization, except for a few myths (such as the myths of the sunken continents of Atlantis and Lemuria). There are even people in embodiment today whose genes are still affected, although the expanding force of life has compensated somewhat for the manipulation. Yet there is a genetic component behind the fact that so many people on Earth either have no spiritual interest or blindly follow an outer religion without ever reaching for a direct inner experience.

One group of survivors managed to preserve part of their spiritual tradition, including what is now known as Genesis, but it was the altered version that was preserved. I know this might seem like a far-flung story that can make some people feel like nothing is beyond manipulation. Yet it illustrates the extent to which fallen beings are willing to go in order to distort a religious scripture. Once they have accomplished what they want, they will then create a culture that venerates the scripture as the infallible word of God, using it as the foundation for a religion that becomes a closed box. These beings have no respect for genuine revelation and have no hesitation about altering it for their own ends, even for their own glorification. That is why true spiritual seekers must be willing to look beyond all outer scriptures and seek for the Christ discernment that is the only way to know God's truth.

*****

If you will take an honest look at the history of religion, you will see that many religions have followed a very distinct pattern. They were started by one person who had attained a direct connection to the spiritual realm. This person could serve as a messenger for bringing forth a non-dualistic teaching from the Ascended Host. You will also see that most such leaders were very spiritual or mystical people, meaning that their attention was focused on the spiritual realm and they had little interest in worldly matters, especially in power. So what they started was a mystical movement that was focused on the following:

- Bringing forth and disseminating mystical knowledge, meaning knowledge from the spiritual realm as opposed to doctrines created through the consciousness of duality. Such a movement always puts God and spiritual revelation before human opinions. And the movement often allows more than one person to receive such revelation.

- Serving the people they reach. A mystical movement is service-oriented, meaning that serving the people is more important than the organization itself. The organization is a means to an end. Serving the people meant, among other things, to help them attain a direct inner experience of the Spirit of Truth. As a result of this service-oriented focus, the leaders of the movement were usually mystics who had little interest in worldly power and privileges.

There have been many such organizations even in known history, but most of them did not survive for long and did not spread beyond a localized area. This was mainly due to the fact that humankind's consciousness was not yet at a level that allowed the general population to recognize such mystical teachings, a condition that has finally started changing. A few mystical movements did start growing, and at some point they reached a critical mass and a shift started to occur. After a gradual period of transition – sometimes lasting several generations, sometimes just a few years – the organization had been transformed and now had the following characteristics:

- It was no longer focused on revelation from above. In fact, it was often stated that such revelation was no longer needed since the official scriptures gave people everything they needed in order to be saved. The members were discouraged from developing their inner connection to their own higher beings and the spiritual realm. They were told to follow the outer organization and its doctrines and leaders.

- The organization was no longer open to changes in its doctrines or structure—neither from above nor from below. It had become solidified and rigid, while at the same time claiming this was mandated by God. It had become a closed box.

- It was no longer focused on serving the people but on serving the organization itself or its leaders. The organization was no longer a means to the end of serving the people, but the people had become a means to serving the end of strengthening the organization. The survival and expansion of the organization – and the power of its leaders – had become an end in itself.

- The organization now attracted leaders who wanted power. Some thought they knew better while others clearly used the organization as a way to get power over people or influence in society. Power quickly became paramount and it was centered around a very small hierarchy. The organization no more attracted mystics to its leadership and often deliberately kept them away from leadership positions.

In short, what started out as a true spiritual movement had now become an outer religion that exhibited most or all of the characteristics of dualistic religions that I described earlier. While the young organization was inclusive, the solidified organization had become exclusive. It had built a culture that can be described with the popular saying, "You have to go along to get along." Unless you were willing to blindly follow the organization's doctrines and leaders, you would be excluded from the organization, perhaps even branded as heading straight for hell. If you want a prime example of such a transformation, study what little is available about the early Christian movement and compare it to the organization that formed after Christianity became the official state religion of the Roman empire.

***

What can explain such a transformation? Many religious people have seen this happen to their own or other churches and they have been wondering why. You might find part of the explanation by looking at human psychology, the mechanics of organizations or by saying that sometimes bad things happen despite people's best intentions. However, the problem with this approach is that it does not explain why religious organizations are so unwilling to correct themselves when the errors become apparent. Why is the Catholic Church, for example, still so reluctant to adapt itself to the fact that modern society is vastly different from the society of the Middle Ages? Why have some religions refused to change even to the point of bringing about their own demise? What is it that prevents an organization from changing?

The key to understanding the real cause is to acknowledge the existence and modus operandi of fallen beings. The simple fact is that when a spiritual movement is new and small, it has little to offer the fallen beings in embodiment—for it gives them no opportunity to attain significant power. That is not to say that such people cannot be attracted to a new organization, for a few of them are often there from the very beginning and they attempt to influence the movement at the earliest possible stage. Nevertheless, when an organization reaches a critical size and begins to have a real influence on the population, it will inevitably act as a magnet for fallen beings who want power and who want to set themselves up in positions of superiority and privilege.

As soon as fallen beings enter an organization, they begin to transform it into a vehicle for their own power and glorification, as I described earlier. Once they have attained power, the overall goal of the organization is to expand or at least preserve the power of the leaders. This explains why an organization cannot transform itself—the leaders will resist anything that threatens their power and they will keep doing so beyond all rationality. As times change, the organization can no longer meet the spiritual needs of its members. Yet the leaders refuse to see this, and thus the organization holds on to the old ways because every new thing is seen as a threat by the leaders who are blinded by their dualistic thirst for power.

The inevitable effect is to create a climate that effectively weeds out the very people who have the potential to transform an organization, namely those who are mystical, intuitive and service-oriented. They simply have no chance of attaining powerful positions, for they will not be willing to compromise their principles and inner beliefs in order to rise in the hierarchy of the outer organization. Once an organization has become polluted by the quest for power, those who will not compromise principles and truth in order to maintain power simply cannot exist in the leadership of the organization. Such people will either withdraw voluntarily or they will be forced out, often through great humiliation and condemnation from the dominant leadership. We might say that as a spiritual movement starts, it attracts people primarily from the top ten percent, but as it grows, it begins to attract those from the bottom ten percent. Those from the top ten percent are then frozen out and the power-hungry people take over the organization. I am not saying this can explain everything that happens to spiritual movements, but it is a very clear tendency that needs to be more widely understood.

***

Why does a religious organization attract people who want power, why don't they become emperors or generals who can exercise power through brute force? Well, a substantial portion of the fallen beings on Earth have indeed become emperors or generals and they have taken power through force. Yet there are different bands of fallen beings and some of them are more sophisticated – or subtil – than others. The more subtle ones know that brute force is a primitive way to exercise power. When people are being suppressed through obvious force, they will always long for freedom, and sooner or later they will revolt. So it is far better to suppress them in such a way that they do not realize they are suppressed. When people do not think there is an alternative to their current situation, they will submit to it much more readily. That is precisely why religion is so attractive to fallen beings—it gives them an opportunity to create doctrines that have the highest possible authority, namely that of God himself.

The fallen beings are very skilled at using religion to create a culture in which they set themselves up as leaders who have absolute authority over their followers. Their word cannot be gainsaid, for if you speak out against the church, its doctrines and leaders, you are rebelling against God, and that carries the ultimate penalty, namely that you will burn in hell—for all eternity. If you really believe that a church and its leaders have the power to condemn you to eternal torment, you are likely to submit to anything they demand of you. Which explains why the people of the Middle Ages submitted to the overt abuses of the Catholic Church and its leaders. They did not want to make their own decisions, did not want to step up to Christhood, and thus kept following the external leaders.

Another part of the puzzle is, of course, that a dualistic religion also promises you that if you *do* obey the outer doctrines and rules, you are guaranteed to go to heaven. Between the threat of eternal punishment and the promise of eternal reward, most people will feel that submitting to a certain amount of oppression on Earth is the lesser of two evils. Which explains why the Catholic Church could continue to get away with suppressing people for over a thousand years.

Do you see the subtle psychological mechanism that is being used here? Many spiritual and religious people surely know in their hearts that there is something wrong with their church. But they are more interested in reaping an eternal reward in heaven, and thus they do not take a stand against the church here on Earth. On the other hand, the fallen beings who have taken over a church know they have forsaken all chance of reaping a reward in heaven. So they only want to have the greatest possible power here on Earth, and they have no compunctions about using a religion to get that power—while justifying it by claiming they are doing God's work.

Of course, fallen beings are always part of an invisible beast, and when a religion begins to become powerful, it actually creates its own beast as an outcropping of a larger beast. As I have explained, a beast is basically like a computer, and a computer cannot change its own programming. From the perspective of the beast, the outer religion only exists to serve it by getting the members to give their spiritual light to the beast. A beast will resist any changes that can bring a religion closer to becoming a true religion which gives its members self-sufficiency. The beast will seek to keep the members in bondage to it by pulling on their mental and emotional bodies through the reward-punishment scenario and other means.

This explains why it can be almost impossible for a large religious organization to change and why it can be so difficult for people to leave a religion. Change can be brought about only by individuals, but in order to create change, they must go against the entire gravitational force of the beast and the collective consciousness of the members who don't want to change. Most individuals, even groups of people, do not have the spiritual attainment to withstand the force of the beast but are overpowered by it. Or they are frozen out or forcefully suppressed.

Thus, an organization often becomes so rigid that it cannot change with the times, and that will eventually lead to its collapse. The beast behind it does not have sufficient awareness to realize that if it does not change, it will die. This explains why people who are overpowered by such a beast will refuse to change their behavior, even to the point that an entire civilization collapses. People cannot go beyond the beast and the beast cannot go beyond its programming. So if no one cries out that the emperor has nothing on, self-destruction will be the inevitable result. This is simply the ultimate consequence of free will. Those who will not self-transcend will inevitably self-destruct.

***

I hope I have made it clear in previous chapters that the Creator of the world of form is utterly beyond the consciousness of any human being. The Creator is not a being that resembles an old man with a long white beard, nor is it a god-man who has human characteristics, such as anger or hatred. In fact, the Creator itself has absolutely no need to be worshipped by human beings. What could the Creator possibly need from human beings on Earth? Certainly, when people put their attention on something, they direct energy at that something over the bridge of their attention. So when people go to church and worship their God, they direct energy at that God. Yet how could the Creator of the world of form need energy from human beings, when the Creator is the source of all of the energy that makes up the world of form?

Can you see that the idea that God needs to be worshipped by human beings must have originated in a time when people's world view was very narrow? There was indeed a time when people believed the Earth was much smaller, that it was flat and that the sky was a dome that covered the Earth, with God living right above the dome. People thought the universe was very small, that the Earth was the center of it and that God was very close to the Earth. Based on this world view, it is understandable that they would create the traditional theistic view of a personal God who is very involved with human affairs and who needs worship or even sacrifices from human beings. This is not surprising, but it certainly *is* surprising that this theistic view of God survives in an age when just about every person realizes that the material universe is infinitely larger than what people believed in Old Testament times.

The reality is that the Creator needs nothing from human beings but only desires to give its light and truth to human beings so they can use it to co-create God's kingdom on Earth. As Jesus said, it is the Father's good pleasure to give you the kingdom (Luke 12:32). Obviously, the Creator is not living right above the clouds, and the Creator is not a remote being in some distant heaven. In fact, there is no place where the Creator itself can be found in any form—for the Creator is beyond all form. There are levels of the spiritual realm in which are found representatives of God in the form of beings who have attained the Christ consciousness in its varying degrees. And right above the material universe is the lowest level of the spiritual realm, in which are found the spiritual teachers of humankind.

My point being that while the Creator is not the personal God envisioned in the Old Testament, human beings are not alone. We, the members of the Ascended Host, are very much involved with human affairs and are always ready to guide people toward fulfilling their roles of co-creating the kingdom of God on Earth. Yet both the Creator and all members of the Ascended Host are completely beyond the duality consciousness. We have no need to be worshipped, nor do we need energy or sacrifices from human beings. We only desire to give, but we cannot fully give our light until people rise above duality. Thus, in all of our dealings with human beings, we are seeking to raise them above duality, *not* to make them more firmly anchored in duality.

***

If the Creator and all true representatives of God desire only to give to human beings, how come so many religions portray a God that needs something from human beings, such as prayers, worship, obedience or sacrifices? To help you understand this, I would like to ask you to read some quotes from the Old Testament.

> 2 And when the LORD thy God shall deliver them before thee; thou shalt smite them, and utterly destroy them; thou shalt make no covenant with them, nor shew mercy unto them:
> 3 Neither shalt thou make marriages with them; thy daughter thou shalt not give unto his son, nor his daughter shalt thou take unto thy son.
> 4 For they will turn away thy son from following me, that they may serve other gods: so will the anger of the LORD be kindled against you, and destroy thee suddenly. (Deuteronomy, Chapter 7)

> 13 And when the LORD thy God hath delivered it into thine hands, thou shalt smite every male thereof with the edge of the sword:

> 16 But of the cities of these people, which the LORD thy God doth give thee for an inheritance, thou shalt save alive nothing that breatheth:
> 17 But thou shalt utterly destroy them; namely, the Hittites, and the Amorites, the Canaanites, and the Perizzites, the Hivites, and the Jebusites; as the LORD thy God hath commanded thee:
> 18 That they teach you not to do after all their abominations, which they have done unto their gods; so should ye sin against the LORD your God. (Deuteronomy, Chapter 20)

> 19 And when the LORD saw it, he abhorred them, because of the provoking of his sons, and of his daughters.

> 21 They have moved me to jealousy with that which is not God; they have provoked me to anger with their vanities: and I will move them to jealousy with those which are not a people; I will provoke them to anger with a foolish nation.
> 22 For a fire is kindled in mine anger, and shall burn unto the lowest hell, and shall consume the Earth with her increase, and set on fire the foundations of the mountains.
> 23 I will heap mischiefs upon them; I will spend mine arrows

upon them.
24 They shall be burnt with hunger, and devoured with burning
heat, and with bitter destruction: I will also send the teeth of
beasts upon them, with the poison of serpents of the dust.
25 The sword without, and terror within, shall destroy both the
young man and the virgin, the suckling also with the man of
gray hairs. (Deuteronomy, Chapter 32)

Many spiritual people have wondered about these and many similar quotes from the Old Testament. I hope you can now see that these words simply could not be the words of the true Creator, nor of any true representative of the Creator. For no being who is beyond duality could possibly utter words that so obviously originate in the duality consciousness. As I have just explained, God has no enemies, so it makes no sense that God would tell one group of people to commit genocide against another group of people. How could the Creator of the universe feel threatened by a group of people worshipping false gods, when the Creator itself has no need to be worshipped and when it has given people free will?

My point here is that the Creator and all true spiritual teachers have nothing to gain from directing people to engage in dualistic struggles with other groups of people. On the contrary, doing so would only work against our goal of raising *all* human beings above duality. Which also means that we would never seek to set one group of people up as being superior to others, as being the chosen people who have a divine mandate to kill their enemies.

When you see the logic of this, you realize that the words that are recorded in Deuteronomy and other parts of the Old Testament could not possibly have come from the true God. So where *did* they come from? Well, let us once again use the time-honored method of detectives and look at who has a motive for creating dualistic struggles on Earth. Obviously, this is the fallen beings, but beyond them is the superstructure of the identities or beasts they created in a higher realm and which have now grown more powerful than their creators.

Consider that the Old Testament often describes a God who has very human feelings, such as anger, wrath or jealousy. In reality, such feelings describe a being that is obviously threatened by something, and the sense of being threatened can only come from fear. If this being was the almighty Creator, what could it possibly have to fear? We can see that this must be a being that exists in a lower realm. And since this being has very strong feelings, it is reasonable to assume that it exists in the emotional realm, what has been called the astral plane.

Consider also that the ego can only see God as being outside itself, but the ego also wants an absolute justification for its actions. And what higher justification can there be than having God's approval for your conquest of other tribes who have the land you want? You now see a symbiotic, codependent relationship between the false gods and the people who follow them. People trapped in duality do get certain advantages from following a false god, but the price they pay is that they sacrifice their spiritual freedom—the freedom that can be won only when you have no other gods before the one Creator who is your source.

***

From the beginning of this book, I have talked about the ability to know truth based on direct experience. All people are meant to have an ability to tune their minds to a level of reality beyond the material universe. Yet their ability to do this will be affected by their own state of consciousness. If a group of people are heavily influenced by fear, anger, jealousy or other negative feelings, they cannot raise their inner attunement beyond the emotional realm. Thus, they will be unable to contact the true spiritual teachers of humankind in the identity realm and above. Instead, they will come in contact with beings in the emotional or mental realm. Like attracts like, so people will attune to beings who correspond to their own level of consciousness.

The stark reality is that there are beings in the mental and emotional realms who have set themselves up as gods for the Earth, namely the beasts created by fallen beings. You can even find hidden evidence of this in Genesis:

> For God doth know that in the day ye eat thereof, then your eyes shall be opened, and ye shall be as gods, knowing good and evil. (Genesis 3:5)

This is the Serpent talking to Eve, and you should know by now that when the Serpent talks about God, he is not talking about the highest God, the Creator. For how can a being trapped in duality ever see the highest God? In reality, the "gods" that Eve shall be like are the dualistic gods that *do* know good and evil because they have *defined* good and evil based on the mind of anti-christ. The true God, the Creator, does not know relative good and evil because God is completely beyond the duality consciousness.

Once again, the Serpent does not tell Eve the full story, making her believe the fruit will give her god-like powers, while in reality it will make her a slave to the consciousness of duality and the false gods who have grown out of it. Once you allow yourself to be pulled into the world of duality, you will indeed know good and evil, meaning that you will inevitably experience the dualistic conditions in this shadowy world. You will actually know something that the true teachers don't know, namely a world in which everything is an illusion, created by an interplay of dualistic opposites that are perversions of God qualities.

These false gods were created before the material universe was formed, so they have had a long time to grow in strength. To a human being on Earth, they can seem very powerful. If a group of people do not have Christ discernment, they can truly believe that such a dualistic "god" is the almighty creator of heaven and Earth. And once they believe this, they will be trapped in a spiral of fear that makes it very difficult for them to break free.

You might wonder why such beings would tell their followers to make war with other nations since it could potentially destroy their own followers. However, these false gods do not use common sense, for they are blinded by the duality consciousness. In fact, they believe they will win either way, for whether their followers win or lose, they will still be able to absorb all of the energy that is misqualified in the dualistic struggle, and this will make them stronger—at least temporarily. They simply don't care about their followers—they only care about themselves. This is a degree of selfishness that can be difficult to fathom for most human beings, yet it is a temporary reality.

Obviously, if all people killed each other, these false gods would eventually lose their source of energy, but they are not able to think that far because of their spiritual blindness. Another factor is that these false gods are in a constant rivalry with each other, which is the only reason they have not completely taken over – and then destroyed – the Earth. This is partly by design, as I described earlier when I said that many different lifestreams – including their "gods" – were allowed to come to the Earth so they could counterbalance each other.

My main point is that when you actually realize that certain religions have been created or distorted by these false gods, you can truly begin to free yourself from the many dualistic beliefs that have found their way into the religions of this planet. And although this will likely require you to let go of some deeply held beliefs, it will also put you in a unique position to claim your spiritual freedom. For the real problem with a false god is that once it has been accepted, it will create a religion that is a closed box, meaning that the members are mortally afraid of questioning their "god." And unless you are willing to think the unthinkable thought that perhaps there is such a thing as a false god, how could you ever free yourself from worshipping such an idol? It is only the truth that can set you free, and before you can find the Spirit of Truth, you must be willing to question the illusions that keep you trapped in your current mental box.

You must also be willing to go beyond the pride of the ego, which will make people refuse to consider that they or their religion could possibly be wrong. Yet think about this logically. If you have grown up in a religion that has been distorted by fallen beings and thus can no longer take you to heaven, *wouldn't you want to know?* Or would you rather remain ignorant and thus condemn yourself to remaining in the shadows of duality? Which God do you want to follow, the true Creator or one of the many dualistic gods out there? I fully respect your free will, but if I might make a suggestion...

Key 24
Discovering your mission on Earth

Let us now consider why I am giving you all this information. What can you do with it all? Well, for starters you can attain a new perspective on what it will take to attain true spiritual freedom while you are in embodiment on planet Earth. You can now see that spiritual freedom means that you rise above the duality consciousness and attain the true vision – the non-dualistic vision – of the Christ mind. And in order to attain this freedom, you must separate yourself from the sense of identity that is based on dualistic beliefs, including the many dualistic religious or spiritual doctrines found on this planet.

There simply is no other way to attain spiritual freedom, for any state of consciousness that is influenced by the duality consciousness will imprison you in a mental box. And as long as you are in such a box, you will be fully or partially enslaved by whatever taskmaster created the box, be that your own ego, fallen beings in embodiment, fallen beings in the mental or emotional realm, other people, the mass consciousness or the false gods created out of the mind of anti-christ.

You can also see that every aspect of life on this planet has been influenced by the duality consciousness. Thus, no matter where you have grown up, you will have been affected by this state of consciousness. The effects are:

- You have been exposed to physical abuse, which can be anything from violent acts by individuals to being treated by society as a sheep who should follow the crowd.

- You have been exposed to emotional abuse, which can range from being told you are stupid or unworthy to being told you are a sinner who was born as an incomplete being.

- You have been exposed to mental abuse, which means being brought up to accept certain beliefs about yourself, God and the world, ideas that sprang from the consciousness of duality but were presented as the infallible truth, perhaps even as God's absolute truth.

- You have been exposed to identity abuse in the sense that you have never been told who you really are and where you came from. Instead, you have been given a vastly distorted image of your origin and identity, making you believe you are a human being rather than a spiritual being. You have been programmed to become a "good" human being but *only* a human being.

The basic message is to never rock the boat, to never go beyond what your society has defined as the norm for a human being. In essence the message is to remain a "normal" human being and never seek to become a Christed Being. This abuse has caused you to deny your spiritual potential, which has given you various types of wounds and scars in the four levels of your mind.

Your mind is made of energy and can be wounded as easily as your physical body. And although the mind has some ability to heal itself, it will need help to overcome the effects of growing up in the treacherous environment found on Earth. Thus, as a sincere spiritual seeker, you can now begin to see that attaining spiritual freedom means that you must heal the wounds in the four levels of your mind. And when you add the perspective of reincarnation, you can see that you must heal the wounds from past lives as well. Given the violent history of humankind, it is likely that you have been exposed to even more severe abuse in past lives than what you have experienced in this lifetime. Thus, there could indeed be many wounds to heal.

I am not in any way trying to make you feel overwhelmed. On the contrary, the very fact that you are open to this book demonstrates that you have already healed many of your wounds. Yet it is prudent to recognize that there could still be certain wounds left that keep you in the shadows and block you from walking the last steps into the sunlight of spiritual freedom. Thus, by recognizing the need for healing, you can make much more rapid progress than by continuing to believe what you were brought up to believe—which probably did not involve the need for you to actively take charge and seek spiritual healing.

There are, of course, many valid teachings and techniques available for psychological and spiritual healing, and it is not my aim to say that only one will work and that all others are false. You should feel free to follow your intuition, but I would like to make you aware of the tools given by Mother Mary, for they are designed by us to supplement what I am giving you in this book. In her book, *Master Keys to the Abundant Life*, Mother Mary presents a gradual and gentle path to seeing through many of the false beliefs that cause emotional wounds. She has also released a large number of rosaries, which are spiritual techniques designed specifically to help you resolve both dualistic beliefs and the energies that have been misqualified as a result of such beliefs.*

It is a simple fact, demonstrated by the experiences of numerous people throughout the ages, that you will attain the fastest progress by employing a two-fold approach of study and the practice of spiritual techniques. Thus, Mother Mary's book and her rosaries are designed to offer you such an approach, and I recommend them highly. What I will do in this book is to give you the bigger picture of how to free yourself from spiritual thralldom, especially the slavery caused by dualistic religion.

***

When you step back from your own personal life and society, you might say that planet Earth is a giant rescue operation. The original purpose of any planet is to give a group of co-creators the opportunity to start out with a separate sense of identity and then grow toward Christ consciousness. Obviously, many of the beings that embody on Earth started out on this track. However, because of the descent of fallen beings, the purpose of the Earth was modified. Most of the new co-creators on Earth have now fallen into the duality consciousness and most of the beings who fell to Earth or came here from other parts of the material universe are likewise trapped in duality. Thus, the current purpose for the cosmic schoolroom that you call planet Earth is to raise as many beings as possible above the duality consciousness. How can this be done?

As I have attempted to explain in previous chapters, the main problem with the duality consciousness is that it becomes a self-fulfilling prophecy, a closed circle, a self-reinforcing downward spiral. Once a critical mass of people in a society have entered the duality

---

* These techniques and others are available for free at *www.askreal-jesus.com* and *www.marysdivinedirection.com*. For a more direct description of the spiritual path, see the book *Save Yourself*, which is a revelation from Jesus.

consciousness, they will be so blinded by it that they literally believe there is no other way to look at life. They are like a person with a blindfold on who is walking toward an abyss while thinking he is on the road to heaven. Even recorded history has many examples of how an entire civilization could believe in a completely false idea while being absolutely convinced that it was an infallible truth. Consider how the population of medieval Europe believed the Earth was flat. The effect was that no one dared to sail beyond the horizon, so even though the population was living as literal slaves of a small noble class, no one could discover the New World and escape the tyranny of the ruling elite. The population was enslaved by actual physical conditions, but there was a way out. Yet because of the belief in a wrong idea, no one could discover that way—that is, until someone finally broke the spell and cried out, "But the emperor has nothing on."

If you have not read the fairy tale about the emperor's new clothes, I encourage you to do so. It illustrates beautifully how people can become trapped in the duality consciousness, and everyone is going along with the illusion because no one dares to speak out and shatter it. How can the spell be broken on Earth, so that humankind can begin to consciously see the duality consciousness and its effects? Well, expanded awareness is always the first step toward the escape from any limitation, but humankind's awareness will be expanded only if some people are willing to demonstrate for the rest of the population that they are not trapped in the duality consciousness. Someone must cry out that the emperor of duality has nothing on, and someone must dare to demonstrate the true path that leads beyond duality, namely the Path of Oneness. And this leads us to consider why you are on Earth at this particular time.

***

I know that the history of the Earth might seem very chaotic, even completely random. And I freely admit that the Earth is a chaotic planet, where no one is truly in control—for even the false gods are warring amongst each other so none of them have ultimate control. My point being that there are many religious people and even many New Age people who believe that God or the Ascended Host are ultimately in control of what happens on Earth. They think that one day, a savior – or a UFO – will appear in the sky and solve all of humankind's problems. This is simply another illusion created by the human ego, and we will later consider why this illusion is so widely believed. Yet for now let me simply point out – as I have said many times – that everything on Earth is subject to the free will of those in embodiment. God will literally allow humans to destroy this entire planet if they decide to do so. And we of the Ascended Host are committed to the law of God, which means that we cannot step in and solve people's problems for them. What we *can* do is to enlighten and empower people in embodiment so they can solve their own problems. We are constantly trying to teach people that with men this is impossible but with God all things are possible. Only, it is God *in you* – the God who rules the kingdom of God that is *within* you – who will solve all problems. Thus, you will never solve your problems as long as you look for the solution – or for God – outside yourself. We have been teaching this universal truth for a very long time, and we do this by orchestrating certain spiritual cycles that gradually take humankind higher in consciousness.

As many spiritually minded people will know, there are certain cosmic cycles, or ages, each lasting a little over 2,000 years. Jesus came to inaugurate one such cycle, namely what is often called the Age of Pisces. His purpose was to bring forth a teaching and set an example of the path to personal Christhood. The entire purpose of his mission was to give people the tools to manifest their own Christhood, and if thousands of people had followed in Jesus footsteps, it would have produced a massive transformation of humankind's consciousness. Obviously, this has not happened, and the main reason is that certain fallen beings infiltrated the Christian movement and turned Jesus into an exception – the *only* Son of God – rather than an example showing that all can become SUNs of God.

As a result, humans are currently behind where they were meant to be in consciousness, yet we are still moving into the next cosmic cycle, namely the Age of Aquarius. This is designed to be an age of spiritual freedom, meaning that there is a huge potential that humankind can finally break the spell of duality and manifest a Golden Age of such spiritual and material freedom and abundance that it is beyond the imagination of most people. The potential is there, and the Earth is actually moving closer to a turning point that can produce a large-scale awakening, whereby millions of people will suddenly be able to see that the emperors of duality – in their many disguises –

have nothing on and have no power over them. However, for this to happen, someone must dare to demonstrate that there is an alternative to the duality consciousness. Someone must do what Jesus declared as his reason for coming to Earth:

> To this end was I born, and for this cause came I into the world, that I should bear witness unto the truth. Every one that is of the truth heareth my voice. (John 18:37)

Someone must flow with the inbreath of Pisces and put on the Christ consciousness, whereby they can become instruments for the out-breath of Aquarius that demonstrates truth for all to see.

***

What is needed in this age – the X-factor that can fundamentally change the equation on Earth – is that millions of people come to the conscious realization that they too came into this world in order to bear witness to the truth. And the truth that must first of all be made clear is that there is an alternative to the duality consciousness, there is something beyond duality.

Yet this cannot simply be explained intellectually. It must be demonstrated by people who are willing to walk the Path of Oneness and thereby – in both words and actions – demonstrate that anyone can indeed rise above the duality consciousness and put on the mind of Christ. Why is the mind of Christ the key to spiritual freedom? Because the mind of Christ empowers you to discern what is of God and what is of the duality consciousness. As I have attempted to explain, people are enslaved by the mental boxes created from the duality consciousness, so you can never be free until you can discern what is a dualistic illusion and what is real. That is why Jesus came to inaugurate what should have been an age of Christ discernment that could lead to the age of spiritual freedom. Discernment is truly the foundation for your freedom, for without it, you might think you are free while being enslaved by a clever dualistic illusion.

There are millions of beings who chose to come into embodiment at this particular time precisely because they saw how critical this time is for the Earth. They wanted to be here in order to help bring about the large-scale awakening that is planned. Yet in order to do this, these lifestreams naturally had to take on a physical body, which means they forgot their purpose for coming here. Thus, the first priority for these lifestreams is to awaken themselves and reclaim the conscious awareness of their origin and their purpose for coming to Earth. Then, they can begin to truly fulfill their purpose by witnessing to others. As Jesus said, you must first remove the beam in your own eye before you can see clearly how to remove the mote from the eye of another.

If you have read this book up until this point, you should seriously consider that you are – or have the potential to be – among these lifestreams. I know you might have done things in your life or have descended into a state of consciousness that is not very spiritual. Yet you need to understand that you came here to demonstrate how to rise above the duality consciousness. Thus, many beings volunteered to take on certain aspects of the duality consciousness and to live them out for a time. This was done so they could demonstrate that even though you have been trapped in certain forms of dualistic behavior or beliefs, you can still rise above it all and follow the Path of Oneness. My point being that you need to seriously consider that whatever you have been into is not a true expression of who you are.

As I have explained, you are truly an extension of a spiritual being, and the core of your lower identity is the conscious self, which has the ability to step into any sense of identity it chooses, including one of the many identities created from the duality consciousness. Thus, whatever non-spiritual behavior you have manifested is a result of your conscious self stepping into a dualistic identity. What you need to do now is to realize that you are more than that identity. You can then step out of the dualistic identity to reclaim your true spiritual identity. By doing this, you will demonstrate for other people who are trapped in your particular dualistic identity that it is possible to rise above it and be spiritually reborn. And this is precisely why you decided to come to this troubled planet. You wanted to do what Jesus told his disciples to do:

> Let your light so shine before men, that they may see your good works, and glorify your Father which is in heaven. (Matthew 5:16)

The light that must shine is the light of your higher being and God Flame. By letting it shine through your lower being, you demonstrate that there is something beyond duality, that there is a divine solution to every problem that is created from the duality consciousness. Thereby, people can learn to glorify "your Father which is in heaven," meaning that people realize they can receive help from spiritual beings who are completely beyond duality, even beyond the false gods and the blind spiritual leaders who are trapped in duality. Therefore, these true spiritual teachers can help people overcome duality, and then people will see that they too are extensions of spiritual Beings. When people see the divine in you, they can be helped to see the divine in themselves.

What are the good works human beings will see from you? It is the kind of works that Jesus talked about when he said:

> But Jesus answered them, My Father worketh hitherto, and I work. (John 5:17)

Jesus came to demonstrate that it is possible for a person in embodiment to act in a way that is not based on the duality consciousness. And when you do so, you will have dominion over the Earth, meaning you can perform acts that seem impossible to the duality consciousness. As Jesus said:

> With men it is impossible, but not with God: for with God all things are possible. (Mark 10:27)

With the duality consciousness it is impossible to solve the problems and conflicts created by the duality consciousness. But when you bring the Light of God and the vision of the mind of Christ, the solution suddenly becomes obvious. When people realize that the emperor – the duality consciousness – has nothing on, they are set free from illusion and can now see the obvious solution.

Key 25
Overcoming the dualistic mindset

There is indeed a forward movement that is raising the consciousness of humankind. That movement is overseen by *us*, meaning the Ascended Host, but it is carried out by *you*, namely beings in embodiment. Millions of people have the potential to be part of this movement, but in order for you to take up your personal position, you will have to first overcome the condition that caused you to become blinded by the duality consciousness, whereby you started withholding or misqualifying your light. In other words, before you can let your light shine, you must rise above the condition that caused your light to stop shining. Before you can bear witness to your truth, you must overcome the dualistic "truth" of your ego. Your conscious self must see through and then separate itself from the dualistic identity with which you have identified.

To help you do this, I will reach back to my previous description of the four main reasons why lifestreams become blinded by the duality consciousness. This ties in with the four elements and their corresponding states of consciousness, as we discussed earlier:

- The identity or etheric level represents the Father element and can thus give rise to a perversion of the Father principle, the active principle. This is the temptation to maintain an identity as a separate being, based on the belief that you are better than others. When beings are blinded by this illusion, they refuse to serve those who are below them. This results in spiritual pride, making beings feel they know better than God and anyone else how to run the universe. Such beings have a desire to be god and they are seeking to create a world where they are elevated to the status of gods.

   How can you escape this illusion? Well, only by coming to a point of total realism, making you see and truly understand that all life comes from the same source and thus all life is one. Separation is a complete illusion, and because of the contracting force of the Mother, it can only lead to suffering. The force of life itself will inevitably tear down all the towers of Babel built through pride. The question is whether people trapped in this state of consciousness really are as smart as they think they are. Will they recognize the reality of oneness and voluntarily come back to the River of Life? Or will they continue to act upon the illusion of separation until they finally tire of having their creations broken down? How much suffering must they experience before their pride gives way to realism? Can they overcome pride through insight or only through the experience of utter humiliation?

How can you help demonstrate the path of overcoming the perversion of the Father? The most common effect of this perversion on Earth is the misuse of power in the form of tyrants of every kind, leaders who have misused their power to take advantage of their people. You can demonstrate the path of overcoming by becoming a leader and exercising power in a just manner. You can also do it by refusing to submit to tyrannical leaders and standing up to their abuse—however, you must do so with peaceful means only. There is no point whatsoever in standing up to a tyrannical leader in a way that perpetuates the dualistic struggle. Another way to demonstrate the path of overcoming is to selflessly serve others in any number of ways.

In order to do this, you must overcome all desire to use power to force others, even the desire to force others to be saved. You must attain absolute respect for the free will of others and allow them to strike you on one cheek, even both cheeks. You must keep turning the other cheek – there is *always* another cheek to turn – and seek to enlighten others – so they can make the best possible choices – and never seek to force them to make the choices you think are best.

- The mental realm represents the misuse of the element of the Son, the mind. Beings in this trap use the mind, the analytical mind or the intellect, to establish superiority. They become extremely adept in justifying and proving that they are right, and their modus operandi is that they can never be wrong. By their adept use of the duality consciousness, they can always prove their point—at least to their own satisfaction. If others disagree, it is simply because they are not intelligent enough to see the point. These beings are trying to set themselves up as the true representatives of God, the true spiritual leaders of humankind, and they seek to use their superior intellect to get others to follow them blindly.

How can you demonstrate the path out of this trap? By refusing to engage in dualistic arguments, but this does not mean withdrawing from the debate. You must engage the debate in a non-dualistic way. Obviously, this requires you to first overcome all desire to be right among men, so you only strive to be right with God. You can also stand up to the false leaders in church and state, but again this must be done peacefully. You want to expose their dualistic way of thinking instead of allowing them to drag you into another dualistic struggle.

• The emotional realm represents a misuse of the Mother element. These beings are consumed by negative emotions against God or anyone who will not conform to their expectations. The Mother element is the passive polarity to the Father's active polarity. People trapped in a misuse of the Mother often see themselves as victims. They refuse to take responsibility for themselves, want to follow leaders and doubt that they can do anything to change their lives. They often make themselves blind followers of those who misuse the Father and the Son.

How can you demonstrate the path out of this misuse? By taking full responsibility for your own life and spiritual path, seeking to strive for your own Christ discernment instead of wanting a leader to tell you what to do. However, this also involves discerning between true and false leaders. You must not be afraid to expose the false leaders and embrace the true leaders. To do this, you must overcome all tendency to see yourself as a victim of forces beyond your control. You must overcome the temptation to blindly follow those who claim they can lead you to heaven. You must be willing to make your own decisions and be willing to learn from whatever consequences you experience.

• The physical realm represents the perversion of the element of the Holy Spirit. Beings in this trap have often built the illusion that God does not exist, which is really a desire to do whatever they want without ever being held accountable by a higher authority. Yet there is an opposite polarity to this, which is to elevate an outer system, such as a religious, scientific or political philosophy to the status of infallibility and then refusing to change it. Such people often believe that by strictly following the beliefs, rules and practices of an outer religion, they can buy their way into heaven, they can force God to accept them even though they have not changed their state of consciousness and put on the mind of Christ. This is the illusion of salvation without self-transcendence.

The Holy Spirit is truly the force that allows people in physical embodiment to transcend the limitations of the material world. Thus, those who pervert it refuse to transcend, thinking they are either mere human beings or that they cannot go beyond a particular religious tradition. These are beings who refuse to self-transcend, those who bury their talents in the ground—as a symbol for the material universe and the lower mind. Some of them simply want to live a good material life and enjoy what this world has to offer—they don't want to be disturbed by any spiritual teaching.

How can you demonstrate the path to overcoming? By being willing to rise above the temptations and pleasures of the material world. By being willing to question belief systems of any kind and show that you can find a more fulfilling life by going beyond such man-made limitations. You can demonstrate that by being willing to make the best out of whatever situation you were given in life, the universe will respond by multiplying the talents that you have multiplied. You can demonstrate that the law of God really works and that self-transcendence is possible. To do this, you must overcome the temptation to see the material universe as an end in itself. You must come to see it only as a means to an end, namely the growth in self-awareness, leading to full God consciousness.

***

If you look closely at the descriptions of the four categories, you will see that there is a common denominator behind all of them. Each category represents a certain way of thinking, a certain way of looking at life. In each group you find people who are completely convinced that their way of thinking is the only right one. Thus, when they are confronted with people who do not think as they do, they feel threatened. This sense of being threatened is the hallmark of beings trapped in duality, because it is built into duality. The consciousness of duality is based on separation, and when you think you are separated from God – from your source, from the whole – you inevitably fear that you can be lost. The concept that you can be lost can exist only in the realm of separate identities, for when you fully realize that you are one with the All, how could you possibly be lost? So the sense of separation gives rise to the fear of loss, which people simply cannot live with.

In order to compensate for the fear of loss, fallen beings must establish a world view that makes it seem like living up to certain conditions will prevent them from being lost. Thus, they create a world view that portrays their way of thinking as superior and they seek to create a world or a society in which everyone submits to their way of thinking. This gives them a sense of equilibrium that allows them to live with their fears. They have used outer conditions to make themselves believe that they can ignore their innermost fear of being lost, the fear that inevitably springs from their refusal to rejoin the River of Life. Only the Path of Oneness will empower you to overcome the primal fear of being lost as an individual—only the perfect love that comes from feeling one with all life will cast out all fear. Yet in order to rejoin the River of Life, you must give up the illusion of separation. Beings who are not willing to do that inevitably become trapped in an endless game of seeking to neutralize their inescapable fear. They are seeking to build towers of Babel that they think will reach into the heavens, but the contracting force of the Mother is constantly breaking them down, so these people always feel threatened by life.

The inevitable result is that when such people encounter those who refuse to accept their way of thinking, they will feel threatened by them. If you follow the party line, you are welcome, but if you refuse to go along, you will be seen as a threat. And as a pure survival mechanism, the beings trapped in duality must seek to destroy the threat. How far they are willing to go in eliminating the threat will depend exclusively on how trapped they are in duality—which gives rise to the belief that the ends can justify the means. Their attempts to destroy the threat might range from seeking to ignore you to actually killing you in order to silence you. You will see a wide range of scenarios being outplayed throughout history, but the underlying mechanism is always that people feel threatened and seek to eliminate the threat to their sense of equilibrium.

Why am I telling you this? Because in order for you to fulfill your role in the spiritual awakening, you must recognize that awakening people inevitably means threatening their sense of equilibrium. As long as people can maintain the sense that they are guaranteed to be saved, they will refuse to change. So the first step toward awakening people and showing them that there is a better way to live is to disturb their sense of equilibrium. And this will always be a task that will be met with hostility. Once you learn to understand and expect this, you can learn to avoid reacting to it in ways that either pull you into the dualistic struggle (thereby misqualifying your light) or cause you to shut off your light. Of course, you must begin by overcoming the sense of being threatened that is the hallmark of your own ego. As always, in order to be part of the movement to set humankind free, you must be willing to start by pulling the beam from your own eye. You cannot help free others from duality as long as you are blinded by your own dualistic identity. Obviously, by reading this book you have demonstrated that you are willing to start this process. What remains to be seen is how far you are willing to go.

**

My larger point here is that there were only a few beings who deliberately rebelled against God, and even they did not fully understand what they were doing. Yet they created the separate identities, the false gods, that I have described. And once these gods had been created, they became more powerful than any individual being. Thus, they seek to survive and grow by manipulating individual beings into surrendering to them. They seek to get beings to submit to their world view—the illusions out of which they were created.

When a society is trapped in a certain dualistic illusion, the illusion itself forms a superstructure in which individuals are overpowered by the larger mind, reaching from the mass consciousness to the false god. All of the people who accept that they are part of this society will serve to uphold the status quo, to uphold the equilibrium that allows the false god to stay in a position of being unchallenged.

People do this by setting up certain ideas as being beyond questioning. Behind every society that has ever crumbled, you will find a set of ideas that the members refused to question. And it was precisely the blind adherence to these ideas that put the society in a downward spiral that led to its destruction. The same, of course, holds true for individuals, for the force of life itself will always break down the illusions that keep you imprisoned. Unfortunately, people can be so imprisoned that they cling to their illusions and feel that life is a hostile force that is trying to take away what gives them a sense of security and identity. This explains why they resist the very force that is trying to set them free, making them unreachable for a spiritual teacher. You will see throughout history how societies resist what is later seen as obvious progress. And you will see in the lives of individuals how they resist making the life changes that can prevent their destruction and lead to their freedom. And when you see this in others, perhaps you will one day come to the point of seeing it in yourself—which is the breakthrough point where your spiritual progress will truly begin.

There are four main false gods seeking to control the Earth, namely a god for each of the perversions described above. And the practical consequence of this is that most of the people on Earth have fallen because they submitted to one of these gods and the societies that are based on their illusions. By embodying on Earth, it is almost impossible for you to avoid being affected by one of these false gods. In order to grow up in any normal fashion, you will have to go along to get along. You will have to submit to the basic mindset of your society, and that mindset is affected by at least one, possibly more than one, of the perversions of the Father, Mother, Son and Holy Spirit.

You might have come here with the best of intentions, namely to bear witness to your truth and let your light shine. But you have likely been overpowered by the collective mind, and the effect is that you have been forced to shut off your light and to keep silent about your truth in order to get along with other people. You were likely met with blank rejection from the people who did not want to have their sense of equilibrium disturbed by your truth and your light. If you want a universal illustration of this, simply look at how Jesus was rejected by the leaders who felt threatened by his presence and by the people who did not want to change. I know you have been brought up to believe that Jesus was unique, but his life demonstrates what has happened to millions of lifestreams who came to Earth to be part of the cosmic rescue operation. And it demonstrates how anyone who desires to be part of it today must be willing to stand up to the temptation and intimidation to follow the party line, to go along with the majority, to not challenge people's illusions, to not disturb their sense of superiority, their sense of being powerless victims or their belief that their salvation is guaranteed by an outer religion.

If you want to fulfill your mission of helping awaken humankind, you must be willing to disturb people. Let me say this again. The only way to awaken people is to help them see what they cannot see right now. Yet why can't they see it? Because their egos and the dualistic forces have managed to get them in a state of mind in which they do not want to see it, in which they do not want to change their lives. That is why anyone who represents Christ truth must be willing to do what Jesus did, namely disturb people's sense of equilibrium by challenging the dualistic illusions that uphold the status quo in people's minds and in their societies. Obviously, this will be a thankless job on Earth but with an incalculable reward in the spiritual realm. We might say that while it is a tough job, the retirement benefits are out of this world.

In order to fulfill your reason for coming to Earth, you must come to a state of non-attachment, so that you do not let other people's reactions make you feel that they are rejecting you personally. For when you feel personally rejected, you can so easily fall for the temptation to either engage them in a dualistic struggle or to withdraw and withhold your light and truth. Millions of well-meaning lifestreams have come to Earth with the best of intentions only to be lured into one of these reactions, thereby aborting their missions. It is my goal with this book to give you the teachings that will allow you to extricate yourself from this reactionary pattern. If you will truly internalize my teachings, you will be empowered to adopt the essential attitude – the Middle Way of the Christ and the Buddha – that will enable you to fulfill your mission of demonstrating the way above duality. In the next chapter, we will take a closer look at what it will take for you to establish an approach that will allow you to do right action while being non-attached to the fruits of action.

***

Before we move on, I would like to summarize the ways beings fall and how that relates to how they approach religion. We have talked about four elements, namely the Father, Son, Mother and Holy Spirit. Obviously, other names could be used, but I have used the ones most familiar to people in the West. In Hindu cosmology, we find the trinity of Brahma, Vishnu and Shiva, who represent the Creator, the Sustainer and the Destroyer and correspond to the Western trinity of Father, Son and Holy Spirit. Obviously, Hindu cosmology has a far greater awareness of the Mother than Western religions and sees it as the fourth element of creation, as I have described it in this book. Let us look at the four elements and the beings who were meant to serve them:

- **Father, creators.** Beings who serve the Father element are meant to step down or make more concrete the Creator's overall vision for their sphere and the vision held by the Beings in the sphere right above them. In reality, these beings often do not take on the lowest form in their sphere. For example, in your sphere they would not normally descend below the identity realm. These beings are what various cultures have seen as gods, such as in Greek mythology. Since there are many of them, it is not necessarily wrong to have a religion that talks about many gods, as long as it is recognized that there is a supreme God, and that some "gods" have not yet become immortalized. Some cultures have had as their gods beings in the identity realm who had not fallen but who had not yet ascended either, which explains why such gods seem to be not fully beyond human-like idiosyncrasies. Yet it should also be noted that some cultures have worshiped beings in the mental or emotional realm as gods.

- **Son, sustainers.** Beings who serve the Son element are meant to keep oneness between the growth of their sphere and the vision and laws of the Creator. They help keep their sphere on the right track until it ascends to the spiritual realm. Some of these beings have descended as co-creators who are in physical embodiment in order to take dominion over the Earth and manifest God's kingdom here. There are also angels who represent the son, and they serve as messengers between the spiritual teachers, the co-creators and other beings.

- **Mother, creators of form.** These beings are charged with doing the actual work of building form, meaning that they cause the Ma-ter Light to take on the form of the mental images projected upon it. These beings have a lower sense of self-awareness than humans and are created to serve. They are what people have traditionally seen as gnomes, elves, and fairies. There are four distinct groups of these elemental builders of form, one for each of the four levels of this sphere. We might say they serve as a form of translators or messengers that bring a vision from the identity into the mental, then into the emotional and finally into the physical where it takes on a form that is visible to humans. Yet these beings can take on physical bodies by evolving through service.

- **Holy Spirit, transcendence.** In Hindu mythology, the Holy Spirit, represented by the God Shiva, is seen as the destroyer. In reality the Holy Spirit is what brings about self-transcendence and thus causes individual beings and an entire sphere to increase its light intensity until it can ascend to the spiritual realm. The Holy Spirit destroys that which imprisons beings, meaning that it is not really destruction but liberation from limitation. The beings who represent the Holy Spirit will descend to the lowest level of a sphere and will, so to speak, do the most dirty work in order to demonstrate the path out of duality. In the material universe, these beings are the ones who descended on a rescue mission in order to help the beings in embodiment overcome duality. Yet new co-creators can also grow into fulfilling the role of the Holy Spirit. Certainly, the top ten percent of the most spiritual people are all called to fill this role to some degree.

Obviously, one could go into much more detail to describe the various evolutions and their roles, but that is not my intent with this book as I want to stay with the big picture. The important fact is that there are representatives of all four evolutions in embodiment, meaning that there are people who have fallen because of a perversion of each element. There are also people who have not yet fallen because of such a perversion but who have been so blinded by it that they cannot attain spiritual freedom until they see through the perversion. Finally, there are beings who descended in order to take on a perversion and demonstrate the way to rise above it. Obviously, they also need to see through the perversion in order to fulfill their missions.

The lifestreams who are now part of the top ten percent have come from all four evolutions, so it is helpful for them to understand that even though all evolutions fall because of the same mechanism, there are variations for each group. Beings from each group fall because they fail the essential initiation of having to give up their lives – everything they have attained since they came into being – in order to serve those below them in the next sphere that is created. They seek to hold on to their lives instead of giving them up in order to follow Christ and join the River of Life. They fail this initiation because they are afraid that a part of their own Beings can be lost when self-conscious co-creators in the new sphere exercise their free will. Each group has its own version of this fear, and let us look at them:

- **Father, creators.** These beings are focused on the Father's overall vision and purpose, and they can become very concerned about seeing God's purpose fulfilled in a timely manner. They are concerned that their own beings can be imprisoned by the lower co-creators for an indefinite period of time. They want to control how long co-creators can take to attain Christhood, and it is this desire for control that causes them to fall. People who originally fell from this group are often very good at seeing the overall picture and are often very concerned about time. In a religious setting, they will often seek leadership positions and they will use them to control their organization and its members according to their vision. They will often be motivated by some kind of time element, such as the imminent destruction of the world or the return of a spiritual figure, such as Jesus.

- **Son, sustainers.** These beings are charged with making sure their sphere evolves within the framework set by the Creator's vision and laws. After they fall, they are not original or creative thinkers and they often refer everything to the letter of the law. Yet keep in mind that the Creator did not create a world that mechanically follows a predefined track. There is plenty of room for creativity and individual expression, so the role of the sustainers is to allow for creativity but to make sure it stays within the law so that it is sustainable. When the sustainers become trapped in fear, they cannot allow creativity but want to restrain it so that it cannot go beyond a strict interpretation of the law. People who originally fell from this group are very concerned about the law and the letter of the law. They can often be very judgmental, feeling justified in comparing the actions of others to what they see as an absolute standard. In a religious context, these people are often very focused on a literal interpretation of scripture and on keeping tradition. They will not allow their religion to change, yet when you seek to sustain something through control, you stop the creativity of self-transcendence and you will inevitably lose what you seek to preserve. These people are often very good at using the mind to argue their case by always referring to the law or an infallible scripture. They are often so concerned about avoiding mistakes that they would rather do nothing and prevent others from being creative—which is burying your talents in the ground.

- **Mother, creators of form.** These beings were created to translate the vision and mental images of other beings into physical form by causing the Ma-ter Light to vibrate and take on form. To do this they must imbue the light with energy, namely emotions that represent energy in motion. We might say that they imitate or take on the design created by others and then expresses it through emotion. The challenge for these beings is that as their sphere comes close to ascending, they have to stop imitating and step up to actually creating from within themselves. If they refuse to do that but want someone else to make the decisions for them, they will fall. Since they are emotional beings, they can be very powerful. People who originally fell from this group can become powerful leaders who carry out an ideology but cannot renew it or allow others to do so. They can also be singers or actors who are good at portraying emotions but could not write the script. In a religious context, they want to be told what to believe and how to live, and they don't want anything to change. These beings are prone to repeating the same patterns over and over again without ever changing them.

- **Holy Spirit, transcendence.** These beings are designed to descend to the lowest level of their sphere and then work their way back up. They are meant to never accept anything for what it is but to always make it more by transcending themselves and transforming everything around them. Their challenge is to always go beyond, and they fall by becoming attached to anything they have created – refusing to give it up to become MORE – or by refusing to challenge the limitations of others. People who originally fell from this group are often very content to do exactly what they are doing and don't think it is necessary to go beyond their current level. Such people may in fact seem to be transcending themselves by becoming better at a particular activity, yet they refuse to go beyond that activity. For example, some people seek to become the best possible in business or sports while refusing to look for a higher activity that will actually take them and the world to an entirely new level. We might say such people are striving to become better at anything but the task for which they came into embodiment— namely to challenge the status quo. They focus on a particular tree and refuse to see the forest, the big picture. In a religious setting, these people are often very willing to work within their own religion, even to the point of adapting it to the times. Yet they refuse to go beyond the framework of their religion by developing a universal and non-dualistic approach to religion. They refuse to take their religion beyond certain boundaries, so once these beings are trapped, it is very difficult for them to free themselves.

***

As you grow in spiritual awareness, you will eventually come to realize that you have been affected by one of the perversions I describe, perhaps even more than one. You might even realize that you fell because of such a perversion, either in a higher realm, after coming to Earth on a rescue mission or while evolving in this sphere. Yet the important point is that you never use such a realization to create a permanent image of yourself as a fallen being or fallen angel. The core of your Being is the conscious self, and no matter how you have fallen, you can step out of that sense of identity and thereby demonstrate the Path of Oneness for others. Regardless of how you came to be on Earth, this is your highest potential and your true reason for being.

My point is that at the lower levels of the spiritual path, people are blissfully ignorant of the potential that they could be fallen beings. Yet as you grow, you must eventually come to recognize why you are in your current state of consciousness. And, as I said, most people on Earth have become trapped in the fallen consciousness. Only by seeing how you got to where you are can you reverse the process and rise above your current state of consciousness. Only by knowing the dualistic choices that brought you here can you undo them and replace them with choices based on the vision of Christ. In pondering this, keep in mind that the duality consciousness will always seek to polarize you toward one of two extremes:

- Some people readily admit that they have fallen, but they become so burdened by guilt or shame that they feel like they could never again face God or a spiritual teacher. This, of course, will keep them under the control of the false teachers, and it might be because of letting such teachers control them that they fell in the first place. You need to put this entire scenario behind you, and you do so by – once again – realizing that the conscious self is *not* a fallen being. The conscious self is created out of God's own Being and it simply cannot be permanently trapped in any lesser identity. Yet the conscious self is what it thinks it is, so it can step into or build an identity as a fallen being. And once it looks at itself from inside that identity, the conscious self will think that it really *is* a fallen being— which it *is* in the here and now of time and space but not in the eternal now of God's reality. You need to realize that you simply cannot make up for the mistakes you have made while in the fallen consciousness, you cannot fix anything from the past. All you can do is let go of the consciousness that caused you to make mistakes and then let go of the past. The moment you let the fallen identity go, at that moment you are forgiven by God. And you need to accept that you are reborn as the spiritual being you were created to be.

- The opposite reaction is that some people will not admit that they have fallen and will not even contemplate the possibility that they might have been blinded by the duality consciousness.

This is a form of spiritual pride, and it truly is pride that goes before the fall. So when pride prevents you from admitting the mistakes you have made, it becomes a catch-22 that can be very difficult to break. As I just explained above, you cannot undo duality, you simply have to leave it behind, you have to give it up. The problem is that you literally cannot give away what you do not own. As long as you have not admitted that you have been trapped in the fallen consciousness – as long as you have not taken ownership of your condition – you cannot let it go. Once again, the only way out is to realize that your conscious self is more than the pride of the ego or the sophistication of a fallen identity. You have to realize that you are more and that you want MORE—which you can only receive by giving up that which is less. So take ownership of your fallen identity and then allow it to die, as you give up the ghost of the past and allow your conscious self to be reborn into a new identity in Christ.

It is a spiritual law that you are never presented with an initiation before you are ready to pass it. So no one will be able to see that they are fallen beings until they are ready to rise above it. However, being ready to pass an initiation does not mean that it will happen without effort. In order to pass any initiation, you have to transcend yourself and go beyond a certain level of consciousness. In fact, the very purpose for any initiation is to help you go beyond a certain state of consciousness (and not to achieve certain outer skills or results as immature seekers often think). When you come to the realization of why you have fallen – or at least been blinded by the fallen consciousness – you can pass the initiation only by going beyond the consciousness of self-judgment and self-condemnation. Take note of the subtle point. If you have fallen, it is necessary to recognize why you fell. Yet if you pass judgment upon yourself by saying, "I am a fallen being," you affirm the condition as permanent. This is especially true if you allow yourself to fall prey to the belief that once you have made a mistake, you can never escape it. My point is that realizing you are a fallen being has only one purpose, namely that you transcend the condition.

You are fully capable of doing so, but you must make a conscious effort to avoid the trap of condemning yourself for your past choices and simply determine – based on love for something MORE – to rise above the past. Instead of fearing that the past is permanent or will prevent you from rising above it, you must let go of the former sense of identity and be reborn. You must realize that God gave you free will, and no matter what choices you have made in the past, God wants you to rise above them and come home to oneness. Self-condemnation or the self-elevation of pride are feelings that spring from the fallen consciousness, and you need to leave them behind also. When you leave behind a particular dualistic illusion, you are instantly forgiven for the actions committed while you were blinded by that illusion. You must accept God's forgiveness and forgive yourself. You cannot fix, undo or compensate for the choices of the past by using the duality consciousness. You can *only* overcome the past by letting go of the dualistic choices—and continuing to do so until the prince of this world has nothing in you. In Mother Mary's book, she gives much more detailed teachings on this process, and I strongly recommend that you study them for the purpose of learning how to let go of the past.

***

As I have said, the conscious self is who it thinks it is. If you think you are a fallen being, then you *are* – at least temporarily – a fallen being. The moment you separate yourself from the fallen consciousness and accept your true identity as the offspring of God, you are no longer a fallen being. The trick is to get to the point where who *you* think you are is the same being that *God* thinks you are.

We now see that the core of the human psyche is your relationship with God, and the essence of spiritual growth is to make peace with God. As beings fell, they created graven images of God and projected them upon reality. It is your graven images that prevent you from making peace with God and coming into oneness with your Creator That is why you must question your images of God and keep doing so until there is nothing between you and God. You must keep going beyond all images until you finally have a direct experience of oneness with your Source.

If you can overcome the fallen consciousness, you can obviously become an inspiration that can help others do the same. It really doesn't matter who you have been; what matters is who you are willing to become—who you are willing to *be*. You are who you think you are, but only until you think you are MORE.

As a final remark, let me say that there were representatives of all four evolutions who fell in higher realms and are still embodying on Earth. Yet one might say that those who fell because of a perversion of the Son face an especially difficult challenge. Because the Son is the Christ mind that separates the real from the unreal, those who pervert the Christ mind find it very difficult to overcome their self-created illusions. They are simply so convinced that their illusions are true that it is extremely difficult for them to see and admit otherwise.

Furthermore, these beings often tend to be so judgmental of others that they do not look for the beam in their own eyes. Because they have such developed minds, they can so easily see when those around them stray from the laws of the Creator, and thus they are more easily tempted into seeking to judge and control them. By seeing the many mistakes made by others, they are more easily tempted into thinking the Creator was wrong by giving humans free will and that they could do a better job of administering the law by forcing people to comply.

The majority of the beings who fell in higher realms did indeed fall because of a perversion of the Son. There is still a large number of these beings in embodiment on Earth, and it can be very difficult for them to rise above the dualistic illusions that caused their fall. Such people are often very spiritual and are easily attracted to a spiritual or religious movement. They often come across as being very advanced and as having great knowledge of the spiritual side of life. As a result, they often seek leadership positions, thinking they know how things should be done. Yet it is very difficult for a spiritual teacher to help such people see the true nature of the Path of Oneness and the need to transcend all dualistic illusions. In other words, while being outwardly spiritual, they are often not teachable. The reason is that these people are, to use another popular expression, too smart for their own good.

It is my hope that the teachings in this book might make it easier for such people to see beyond their present conception of the spiritual path and realize the need for true self-transcendence. After all, I volunteered to lead the Garden of Eden as a mixed environment for both new co-creators and fallen beings. I would like to see both groups transcend their way back home.

Key 26
How to fulfill your mission on Earth

I hope you can begin to see that what I am seeking to create in this age is a new movement, an initiative unlike anything seen on Earth in recorded history. I am seeking to establish a movement of people who see the fallacy of duality and who are absolutely committed to rising above it, thus demonstrating the path to others. Yet for this to happen, it is essential that those who want to become part of this movement truly understand how subtle and pervasive duality can be. Let me give you an example.

Beings who are trapped in duality have created an illusion which allows them to hold their primal fear at bay. Thus, they want to maintain this state of equilibrium, and when you challenge their illusions, they will feel threatened. They will seek to destroy the threat, and in so doing, they are seeking to pull you into one of two reactions. Most people are not doing this consciously, but the effect is the same. The reactions are:

- They want you to accept their illusion, to become one of them through submission.
- They want you to oppose them, to become their enemy through opposition.

It might seem as if these two reactions are opposites and that one affirms their illusion while the other opposes their illusion. Yet when you go beyond the surface, you see that there is a more subtle understanding. The basic illusion of all fallen beings is that they are separated from God and other forms of life—they are separate beings. If you submit to their way of life, you affirm that their way of thinking is superior to your old way of thinking, meaning that you affirm its separate status. If you oppose their way of thinking, you affirm that it is in opposition to your way of thinking, which also affirms its separate status.

Can you see that either reaction will affirm the basic illusion of the fallen beings, namely that they are separate from other parts of life? Whether you submit to them or oppose them, you affirm that they are different from you. The basic illusion they do not want to give up is the illusion of separation. So either way you respond, you are actually empowering them to continue in that illusion. If you submit, you voluntarily give them your light, and if you oppose, you engage in the dualistic struggle that misqualifies God's energy, whereby you also give your light to the false gods who thrive off the dualistic struggle. The real issue is that whether you submit or oppose, you place yourself in one of the dualistic extremes that are the inevitable result of separation. When you separate from the oneness of Christ, you inevitably step into the duality of anti-christ, in which there must be two opposing polarities. Regardless of where you place yourself on the scale that has two opposite polarities – right or left or anywhere in between – you are inside the dualistic struggle.

Either way, the cause of non-duality is lost, so it is imperative that you stay out of this pattern by *always* seeking to respond in a non-dualistic manner. You must begin by recognizing that other people are trapped in the illusion of separation, and you must then refuse to become part of it. You do this by neither submitting to their illusion nor engaging in a dualistic struggle with them. As the next step, you must avoid reinforcing the illusion in their minds. Again, this requires that you neither submit nor oppose, but then what is left—how can you possibly react when those trapped in duality reject your light and your truth?

It was part of the mission of both the Buddha and Jesus to demonstrate how to respond to dualistic people in a non-dualistic manner. That is why Jesus told you to not resist evil but to turn the other cheek. Let me give you a practical example. One of the places on this planet where the dualistic struggle has been outplayed the longest is in the Middle East. You have various factions that oppose each other and have been doing it for so long that no one can remember how it all started (the reason being that it did not start on this planet). What we see is a downward spiral where one group is seeking revenge for offenses committed by another group. Yet those offenses were acts of revenge against offenses committed by the first group. So each side is seeking revenge for revenge in a frenzy that no one seems able to stop.

Can you see that what is really happening here is that the two sides are reinforcing each others illusion of separation? Nothing can break the spiral until one side refuses to respond in a manner that reinforces the other side's illusion. Say Group A has built up a great hatred against Group B, feeling its members are bad people and are responsible for their own problems. At some point the self-reinforcing spiral of hatred reaches a flash-point, and some of the weakest members of Group A (they see themselves as the strongest members) commit an act of violence against Group B. Group B reasons that the members of Group A are bad people and deserve to be punished, so they commit an act of violence in retaliation. What have the members of Group B just done in the minds of the members of Group A? They have reinforced Group A's illusion that Group B are made up of bad people who are responsible for their problems. They have also reinforced the underlying illusion of separation between the two groups. Thus, Group A feels justified in having committed the first act of violence and in seeking revenge for the revenge of Group B. And before they know it, a couple of millennia have gone by with countless acts of revenge and countless people killed while neither side has made any real progress. What can break the spiral?

Suppose Group B decides not to respond to violence with violence. They decide to follow Jesus' advice and turn the other cheek. The immediate response from Group A is surprise, because Group B didn't respond the way they usually do. What is going on, what are they up to now? It is likely that Group A will test the waters by committing other acts of violence. For a time, Group A might even interpret the non-violent response as weakness and become emboldened to commit more violence. Yet what happens if Group B consistently refuses to respond to violence with violence? At some point, the more mature members of Group A will begin to question their own beliefs about Group B, and they will even begin to question their own self-image. If Group B refuses to affirm the separate sense of identity of Group A, the members of this group will eventually begin to question that identity. If the members of Group B are really so bad, how come they are not shooting back? And if we keep shooting at someone who is not shooting back, does that mean *we* are the bad people and they are not?

I realize that so far human history does not have a lot of examples of people who responded to violence with non-violence. But there are certainly some, and one magnificent example is how the Indian nation, under the generally non-dualistic leadership of Mohandas Gandhi, responded to the suppression of the British empire. The Indians eventually succeeded in making the evil of the British so obvious that the British began to question whether their actions in India were in alignment with their self-image of being a highly civilized nation. When the discrepancy finally became obvious to the British, they changed their behavior in India. A similar approach could literally resolve all of the conflicts seen on this planet.

Yet for such an initiative to start and be carried through to completion, there must be people in embodiment who have risen above duality so they can avoid being pulled into a dualistic reaction. How can you become one of these people?

***

The essential step is to recognize the very mechanism whereby you became trapped in the consciousness of duality. This most likely happened because you were misled by the fallen beings who are the false teachers of humankind—even though they cleverly present themselves as the true teachers of humankind. These beings exploited your most vulnerable period, namely – as described in previous chapters – when you came to the point when you had to consciously take charge of building your identity. This is the point where you have the potential to become spiritually self-sufficient, to become the Living Christ.

For this to happen, you must be willing to accept full responsibility for your own path and your own salvation. You must be willing to make the essential decisions – the LIFE decisions – that propel you beyond all sense of separation and empower you to be reborn into a new sense of identity based on oneness with your own higher being, oneness with your Creator and oneness with all life.

As I have explained, you were most likely created in order to descend into a sphere – be it the material universe or what is now the spiritual realm – in which there were already fallen beings. Thus, your higher being knew you would encounter fallen beings and run the risk of being trapped by their state of consciousness. Yet it also knew this was part of God's larger plan, and therefore your higher being – your real self – decided to run the risk. I am saying this because I am hoping to help you accept the decision of your Higher Self, the decision to send you into a sphere where there is a mixture of light and darkness. By coming to this acceptance, you can quickly adjust your approach to life, whereby you can connect to the determination of your Higher Self, the determination *not* to be or remain ensnared by the fallen consciousness. You can thereby come to the realization that you need to make a very one-pointed effort to free yourself from all of the dualistic illusions that have been admitted into the four levels of your mind. And once you have made that decision, you have taken the most important step toward freedom. In fact, making this LIFE decision wholeheartedly is half the victory—the rest is largely a matter of cleaning up the mess.

I realize that the duality consciousness can seem very subtle, and thus you might fear that you cannot escape its illusions. Yet once you decide that you are willing to become free, you can quickly begin to attain the discernment that will allow you to see through the illusions of duality. In this endeavor, you are not alone, since you can make use of your own Higher Self, often called your Christ self,* and the Ascended Host who will gladly serve as your teachers. Yet in order for you to take advantage of this divine direction from within, you must first overcome the major block that the false teachers have managed to insert into your mind. You can see this illustrated in the story of how the Serpent tempted Eve in the Garden of Eden.

The situation was that Eve had been told that she would die if she ate of the forbidden fruit. The Serpent undermined this belief and thus made Eve doubt the true teacher and her ability to understand and follow the divine direction from a true teacher. Because of this doubt, Eve was not able to respond to the Serpent's temptation by making a LIFE decision. Instead, she made a Death decision and the rest, as they say, is history.

The story of Eve illustrates that you also fell because you doubted your ability to receive accurate direction and your ability to make LIFE decisions—your ability to be the Christ in embodiment. Ever since then, the false teachers have attempted to uphold your doubt in your ability to get accurate directions and make LIFE decisions. They have done this by using your fear to scare you into following them blindly.

Most people on Earth tend to blindly follow their leaders, but the most spiritually mature people have attained enough self-sufficiency to avoid being blind followers. Yet the false teachers have attempted

* For more information on your Christ self and higher being, see *www.askrealjesus.com.*

to prevent you from becoming self-sufficient by reinforcing your doubt in the true teacher and your ability to follow the teacher. If they cannot get you to blindly follow them, they seek to destroy your ability to follow any teacher or make your own decisions, seeking to plunge you into spiritual paralysis. They do this by setting up outer standards and making you believe that if you don't live up to them, you have failed. Thus, it is safer not to try than to run the risk of failure.

How do you overcome doubt? Doubt can exist only in the shadows, a fact that is captured in the popular saying, "Without the shadow of a doubt." Doubt exists in the gray areas of your mind, areas where you have not taken dominion because there is something you have not taken a conscious look at. To overcome doubt, you need to make a conscious effort to seek out the gray areas and expose them to the light of truth, whereby the shadows of doubt will disappear. This is the *only* way to overcome doubt, and take note that it is not nearly as hard or intimidating as it might seem. Again, the ego and the forces of duality seek to put you in a catch-22 in which you fear to take a look at the gray areas, you fear what might be hiding there. Yet all fear is a fear of the unknown and things are never as bad when you actually get them out into the light. As the popular saying goes, you have nothing to fear but fear itself, and once you experience how taking a look at your doubts can set you free, you will build a positive momentum on overcoming doubt.

For example, when I talk about people attaining personal Christhood, I am well aware that for many this will seem like an unrealistic goal. Yet the primary reason for this is the intense cult of idolatry that the fallen beings have built up around Jesus over the past 2,000 years. He has been portrayed as being so perfect that no one else could possibly become like him. If you listen to the false teachers, you will feel so overwhelmed by Jesus' supposed perfection that you will not even try. You will think that being the Christ on Earth means that you have to be perfect. Yet this entire book has presented life as a gradual path. Thus, Christhood must be attained in stages and you have a right to express your current level of Christhood even though it is not the full Christhood. In fact, until you begin to express your Christhood in selfless service to others, you cannot go beyond a certain level of Christhood. You have essentially buried your Christhood in the ground, where it cannot be multiplied. The false teachers know this and that is why they seek to abort any attempt at expressing your Christhood in this world. They want to stop you before you can take dominion and set forth the example that all people can follow in Jesus' footsteps. So the question is whether you will listen to the false teachers or to Jesus, who clearly said:

> Verily, verily, I say unto you, He that believeth on me, the works that I do shall he do also; and greater works than these shall he do; because I go unto my Father. (John 14:12)

Another way the false teachers work is by getting people to doubt that anything is real, using the illusory nature of the duality consciousness to make some people so confused that they can't accept anything as ultimately real. This is easy to accomplish for people who do not have a direct inner experience of the Spirit of Truth and have only encountered dualistic appearances. Because these are all unreal and because spiritually mature people begin to see this, they can be made to doubt everything. How can you overcome such a Catch-22?

The key realization is – as already mentioned – that all fear of loss springs from a separate sense of identity. When you identify yourself as a separate being, you will inevitably believe that your identity can be opposed by other people's identity. And this opposition implies loss and victory, meaning that someone else could potentially destroy or control your identity.

The price you pay for establishing a separate sense of identity is that you inevitably come to believe that your identity, your individuality, could be lost. And the separate identity you create really *can* be lost. In contrast, when you see the truth that all life is one, you realize that everything came from God and thus nothing could be separated from God in reality. And since separation is an illusion, it follows that loss is also an illusion. Only that which is unreal can be lost, whereas that which is real – your spiritual identity – cannot be threatened by anything.

Another way to describe this is to say that your true identity and individuality is defined in your I AM Presence, which, as explained earlier, is above and beyond the material universe. Nothing that happens in this world could negatively affect your I AM Presence, and therefore your true identity can never be lost. The sense of loss can come only because your conscious self has lost contact with your I AM Presence and has entered into a temporary, separate identity created from the duality consciousness. Yet your conscious self is an extension of the Creator's own Being, and thus it can never be lost either. What *can* be lost is only the temporary sense of identity with which you have identified up until this point. By letting go of this identity, you can overcome the sense of separation and thus the fear of ultimate loss of identity. When you give up separation, you will feel the unconditional love of your own higher being and the entire Chain of Being above you. This is the perfect love that will cast out all fear. The problem is that you will not be able to accept this love as long as you hold on to the separate sense of identity.

***

It can be difficult to let go of the separate identity until you realize that the real problem here is that because you have become enveloped in the consciousness of duality, you look at everything through the filter of duality. This makes you vulnerable to the illusion that because you have separated your sense of self from the All, you have made such a terrible mistake that you can never come back. The false teachers truly believe this illusion, and they want you to believe it as well. The difference is that they think they don't want to come back, whereas you know you *do* want to come back. However, your ego – the separate sense of identity – can never come back since it did not come from God in the first place. That is why Jesus said, "And no man hath ascended up to heaven, but he that came down from heaven" (John 3:13). Only what was created from the Christ consciousness descended, and only what your conscious self has created from the Christ consciousness can return.

The reality of the situation is that your conscious self is who it thinks it is. If you identify yourself as a separate being, you are lost— as long as you uphold that belief. Yet the moment you let go of this dualistic sense of identity, you will be saved. And you can do this at any moment.

The consciousness of duality gives rise to the concept of loss, which implies that you can make mistakes, even mistakes from which there is no escape. As I have hopefully helped you realize, the material universe is only a temporary world, and the concept of separation and loss can exist only until a critical intensity of light is reached, whereby these illusions will disappear as darkness disappears when you turn on the light. Nothing in this world is permanent, meaning that nothing can permanently prevent you from coming back to oneness. What prevents you from coming back to oneness is the dualistic beliefs in your four lower bodies and the energy – the karma – you have misqualified since you fell. Yet both can be transformed, and then you will eventually begin to see beyond the trees in the forest of your mind. You will begin to glimpse that you are more than your mind, more than your past and more than your beliefs. You are more than your mortal sense of identity.

As you begin to see beyond the filter of duality, you will realize that there is a higher perspective in which there is no fear of loss and no sense of failure. You then see life as a learning process, as a process of building your self-awareness. Doing this is naturally a process of experimentation. And the real key is to realize that every experiment can become a stepping stone for your progress. In fact, it is meaningless to even talk about an experiment as failing or succeeding. Anything you do will have a consequence. The real question to ask is whether the consequence was in alignment with who you want to be or out of alignment with your highest vision of yourself. If the answer is the latter, then you change your actions to bring them into alignment with your being. Either way, the experiment can help you raise your definition of who you are—which means that every experiment becomes a step forward. The concept of failure or success becomes irrelevant. Or perhaps one might say that you rise above the consciousness in which everything must be judged on a relative scale defined by two opposites, such as success and failure, victory or defeat.

***

Let me give you a couple of practical examples. When Thomas Edison was attempting to create an electric light bulb, the central question was finding a material to create the filament, the thin thread that radiates the light. He tried hundreds of materials without finding one that works, but he simply looked at them as learning experiences. As he said, "I discovered 2,000 ways not to make a light bulb," Had he instead come down upon himself as being a failure for not finding the material on the first try, he would have destroyed himself emotionally before he found the material that worked.

As another example, imagine you are lost in an underground mine. You come to a chamber from which radiates five tunnels. You pick one and follow it until it dead ends. Have you failed in choosing that tunnel? Or have you taken an important step forward by eliminating one possibility? If you collapse and judge yourself to be a failure and vow never to try again, you will inevitably die in the mine. Yet if you go back to the chamber and pick another tunnel, you will eventually find the one that leads you out of the darkness and into the light of a new day.

Can you see that the false teachers and your own ego are seeking to control you through your fear of loss, the fear that springs from separation? Can you see that you can escape this control by adopting a new approach to life, an approach that takes you beyond success and failure as defined by a dualistic standard? Beyond duality is a higher standard, namely the standard of God, and it will empower you to use any experience as a step forward on your path to defining your true identity. What will it take to rise to this higher approach? You must be willing to question *everything*, to examine yourself, to look for the beam in your own eye!

The fear of loss makes many people unwilling to look at themselves. They are afraid that if they discover a beam in their own eye, they will condemn themselves—or be condemned by other people or God. As a survival mechanism, they refuse to acknowledge anything that needs to change in the way they look at life. Yet by going beyond success and loss, you also go beyond guilt, shame, condemnation and self-condemnation. The fear of loss makes you think that if you make a mistake, it proves that you are a bad person and bad persons will go to hell. So people would rather not see a fault, apparently based on the assumption that if they do not recognize a fault, it does not exist and thus cannot hurt them.

Yet where does this assumption come from? It can come only from the duality consciousness, which believes that the material world is the only world and that light and darkness are both real. Therefore, it believes it is possible to hide one's faults in the shadows. This gives rise to the popular illusion that if people can hide something from each other, it is also hidden from God. The reality is, of course, that nothing is hidden from God and from the spiritual teachers of humankind. I earlier explained that what separated you from your spiritual teacher is that you began to think you needed to hide something from the teacher, and your desire to hide made it impossible for the teacher to help you.

The reality is that you can hide nothing from me. Yet it is also a reality that I do not judge you for anything you have done. Please consider carefully that the popular concept of value judgments is another consequence of the duality consciousness and the fear of loss. The false teachers want you to believe that once you have turned your back to the true teacher, you can never come back. If you accept this, you will remain in the sense of separation, where they have the potential to control you, which is exactly what they want. I see the real you and I also see that any imperfection is simply something that the conscious self has taken on temporarily. As soon as you see it as unreal, you can let it go and return to being who you really are. I am not interested in judging you for anything you have done in the past. I am only interested in seeing you be here below all that you are above.

***

It is not my role to condemn you. It is my role to help you become spiritually self-sufficient by building an identity based on oneness with your own higher being. I have no desire to see you remain trapped in a limited sense of identity for one second. I only desire you to rise above any limitations, and I am always willing to help you do so. The problem is that I cannot do this *for* you. You chose to accept a dualistic illusion and you must choose to let it go and replace it with the truth of Christ. You can choose a dualistic illusion without truly knowing what you are doing, but you cannot overcome it without doing this consciously. Thus, in order to be free from an illusion, you must be willing to look at the illusion. And in order to do that, you must acknowledge that you were fooled by the illusion and acted based on the illusion.

Many people have been manipulated by the false teachers into believing that God or their true teachers will judge them harshly for their mistakes. One example is the story of Adam and Eve being cast out of Paradise by angels with flaming swords. In reality, God and God's representatives make no value judgments of anyone. It is the false teachers who use the duality consciousness to judge and condemn people based on a dualistic standard. The false teachers have projected their own state of consciousness onto God and the true teachers, making people fear the true teachers while trusting the false teachers. So when people fear to turn to the true teacher because they think the true teacher will judge them, it is actually the dualistic judgment of their own egos that they fear. Consider a couple of the more mystical statements made by Jesus:

> 15 Ye judge after the flesh; I judge no man.
> 16 And yet if I judge, my judgment is true: for I am not alone, but I and the Father that sent me. (John, Chapter 8)

Yet Jesus also said:

> For judgment I am come into this world, that they which see not might see; and that they which see might be made blind. (John 9:39)

What Jesus was saying between the lines was that it is the consciousness of the Son that is designed to judge, but it is *not* a dualistic value judgment. The true judgment is to separate what is real from what is unreal so that people can make a real choice between the dualistic illusion and the truth of Christ. The role of the Christ mind is to make it possible for people to make a real choice, and those who reach for the Christ mind will see the difference between reality and unreality. Those who refuse to do so will be made blind by their own dualistic beliefs that make it impossible to distinguish between what is real and unreal, for everything is a dualistic illusion.

The Christ mind does not judge based on a dualistic standard that says you are a bad person or a good person based on your outer actions. The Christ mind has no value judgments and does not in any way condemn you as being below others or elevate you above others. The Christ mind only judges whether your actions are life-enhancing, meaning that they raise up yourself and all life, or life-degrading, meaning that they limit yourself and all life. And if an action is life-degrading, the Christ mind simply wants you to let it go and rise above the consciousness behind it. Always keep in mind that the Christ only wants to set you free, never to keep you imprisoned. So if the true teachers really did condemn you and made you feel guilty, we would serve to keep you trapped in the duality consciousness. That would be entirely against our mission and our – non-dualistic – nature.

Do you see what I am saying? A dualistic judgment says that if you have done this or that, you are a bad person forever after. The Christ judgment makes you see that some of your actions sprang from beliefs that are not real. Yet the purpose is *not* to condemn you forever but to set you free forever. How do you become free? By accepting the reality of Christ vision and letting go of the dualistic beliefs. As soon as you do that, you are completely forgiven in Christ. The "you" that made the mistakes dies and the real you, the conscious you, is reborn into a new identity. This new you did *not* make the mistakes in the past – even though it has learned the lesson from them – and therefore should not feel burdened by them.

***

Now take this one step further. Who is the Christ in your Being? Well, your conscious self is meant to fill this position, and when it does, it will quickly expose any dualistic beliefs and actions and let go of them without any negative feelings whatsoever. When you fully realize that you are MORE, you can effortlessly let go of all that is less.

When you decide to take up your rightful role, you can overcome *all* sense of fear, guilt and shame, for you now see that God only wants you to attain spiritual freedom by rising above all dualistic illusions, including the illusion that feeling bad about your mistakes – thereby keeping yourself trapped in a dualistic reaction – somehow compensates for what you did. As the old saying goes, two wrongs don't make a right, so there is no point in feeling bad about what you did. You simply need to let go of the dualistic illusions that gave rise to your actions and allow yourself to be spiritually reborn.

The very moment you ask me to help you see through one of the dualistic illusions, I will be ready to help you. As long as you do not ask, the Law of Free Will prevents me from helping you. But as soon as you ask, you will begin to reestablish your relationship with me, and over time it can grow to the sense of oneness that permanently frees you from the temptations of duality and separation. As the Bible says:

> Fear not, little flock; for it is your Father's good pleasure to give you the kingdom. (Luke 12:32)

> Bring ye all the tithes into the storehouse, that there may be
> meat in mine house, and prove me now herewith, saith the
> LORD of hosts, if I will not open you the windows of heaven,
> and pour you out a blessing, that there shall not be room
> enough to receive it. (Malachi 3:10)

The basic strategy of the false gods is to lure you into partaking of the duality consciousness and then making you believe that you can never escape, that you can never make up for your mistakes. They want you to think that God and the true spiritual teachers will judge you harshly if you try to return. It is better for you to keep hiding from the teacher so you can avoid his judgment. Yet all judgment springs from the duality consciousness, and it is really your own ego and the forces of duality that judge you. By hiding from your teacher, you only condemn yourself to staying in the state of consciousness in which you constantly experience this judgment. You must then continue to engage in the game of seeking to neutralize the fear of loss in an attempt to avoid the judgment that you believe will condemn you to burning forever in whatever hell you imagine. All this is nothing but an illusion, and there truly is nothing that can prevent you from coming back to the Path of Oneness, where you will be received with unconditional love by the true teachers of humankind.

My point being that if you are willing to learn even from what seems to be your mistakes, then any action you have ever taken can help you take a step toward a higher self-awareness. God only wants you to grow in self-awareness, so if you use an action to grow, God does not judge that action as being a mistake. God does not judge your actions based on a dualistic standard with success at one end and failure on the other. So why would you continue to judge yourself – or accept the judgment of others – based on such a standard?

***

Once you have taken the step of disassociating action from the duality of failure and success, you can take the ultimate step. Yet let me make it clear that you cannot take this step until you have accepted full responsibility for your actions, your state of consciousness and your salvation. For only by accepting full responsibility can you take the step of disassociating actions from results, of disassociating action from reaction.

You can then overcome the essential duality of the material world, the duality that causes you to commit actions that generate a reaction from the universe in the form of karma that must be balanced before you can be free of this world. Instead, you can learn to act without generating karma that binds you to the material world, you can learn to act without generating the ultimate duality of a reaction. And when you act without generating a reaction, there will be nothing that binds you to the material world in which the coexistence of light and darkness makes it possible for the ultimate duality of action and reaction to occur. Surely, this sounds mystical, so let me explain.

As I have explained earlier, a great number of beings have descended to the material universe from a higher realm for the purpose of sharing their light and truth. Many of them have fallen into the trap of the duality consciousness, and the single most common cause is that they have become attached to seeing specific results of their actions in the material world. They have come to expect, desire and even demand that if they perform certain actions, they should see certain results. And if the results have not manifested, they have then gone into a negative reaction that has brought them further down the staircase that leads to the pit of duality, the pit of despair.

This desire for a certain reaction to your actions has often been fueled by religion, and I am aware that even what I have said in previous chapters can fuel the desire. Many religions talk about the need to save yourself, save the world or save other people. Many religious people expect that if they make the sacrifices prescribed by their religion or seek to convert others to their religion, they are entitled to certain results. My teachings in this book talk about awakening humankind and raising the Earth, even the entire material universe, to become part of the spiritual realm. Thus, many spiritual people have used their particular spiritual teachings to build a certain expectation about the results of their involvement with religion. Many expect that by following the outer rules and making the sacrifices prescribed, their personal salvation will be guaranteed. Others build a strong desire to convert others, possibly even wanting their religion, political system or the religion of scientific materialism to dominate the Earth. For example, many mainstream Christians believe they will be saved by Jesus without having to truly change themselves, and they are often very disappointed when they leave embodiment and find out this it not true and that they will have to reembody. Many of them come back with a distrust or anger against Christianity and often join scientific materialism as a form of revenge. Yet hopefully these people will eventually come back to a balanced approach and discover the true way that Jesus – as opposed to the churches – taught.

I hope you can now begin to see that such expectations and desires will only bind you to the duality consciousness. For is not the essence of duality the sense of separation? So when you separate actions and results – making it possible that your actions might not produce the best possible results – have you not bound yourself to the treadmill of separation? And how can you escape that merry-go-round until you overcome the expectation that a certain action should produce the result your outer mind desires? The key here being to overcome the very expectation that certain results should follow certain actions, especially the expectation that your actions should produce a certain reaction from other people.

I know I have called you to become one of the people who can help the Ascended Host bring about the large-scale awakening that is possible in this cosmic cycle. Yet in order to bring about this awakening, you need to demonstrate the path of overcoming duality, the Path of Oneness. And you obviously cannot demonstrate this path by remaining trapped in any of the illusions of separation. Thus, you must overcome even the most subtle illusions, and the most subtle of all is the desire to have other people or the material universe respond to your actions in a certain way. When they do not, you feel justified in responding with feelings that are less than unconditional love, inevitably leading to actions that spring from less than unconditional love, actions that misqualify God's pure light and thus create karma for yourself and perpetuate the dualistic struggle. In other words, when your actions do not produce the expected results, there is a reaction inside your mind, and it is precisely this reaction that binds you to the dualistic treadmill. How can you escape this dilemma?

***

You must begin by recognizing that your most basic desire, or drive, is the desire to become spiritually self-sufficient. This means that you become whole, meaning that you realize you are a complete being who needs nothing from outside yourself. Only when you are whole, and know you need nothing from other people, will you be able to give to others without expecting a certain reaction in return. You can give without expecting to get anything as a result of your giving— you give selflessly. Only by attaining this wholeness can you break the cycle of action and reaction.

When you are trapped in the illusion of separation, you will inevitably feel incomplete. When you refuse to consider yourself as part of a larger whole, you do have the possibility of doing whatever you want without considering how your actions affect the whole, but the price you pay is that you will never feel complete in yourself. Only when you overcome all separation from your source, from your Creator, can you feel complete. For when you realize that you are an individualization of the Creator's Being – and thus you have access to the fullness of the Creator from within yourself – you will feel truly whole. You will know that you need nothing from outside yourself in order to be complete. You only need to establish a correct sense of identity that allows you to be here below all that you are above.

Take note of what I am saying. When you first came into existence as a separate being, you did have a sense of connection to a larger whole. This was the seed of oneness – the body of Christ which was broken for you (1Corinthians 11:24) – and you were meant to expand it to the full God consciousness without ever experiencing the loss of your inner connection. When you fell into duality, you lost the direct inner connection and the inevitable result is that you were reborn into a new identity as a completely separate being with no direct connection to your source. This identity is what gives you a fear of loss, a sense of being threatened and a sense that life is suffering. Yet as long as you cling to this separate identity, you can never overcome the sense of separation that causes these feelings. In order to overcome separation, you must let the separate identity die and be reborn into a new identity as a being who is – once again – connected to your source. You must accept the body and blood of Christ – meaning the consciousness of Christ – into your being and allow it to become the leaven that will raise the whole loaf of your consciousness (Matthew 13:33). Yet because you have fallen into duality, you can no longer get this from inside yourself but must receive it from a being who has risen beyond duality, namely a member of the Ascended Host. Thus, you must reconnect to your own Chain of Being and place yourself in a student-teacher relationship with the spiritual hierarchy above you. You cannot overcome separation through the separate identity but only through the spiritual lineage out of which you came.

***

As you become whole, you realize that the purpose of having an individual identity is that you can descend into a sphere where there is still darkness. You can then share the Light of God with others, thereby awakening those who have not yet come to the realization of who they are. When you are whole, you can share your light and your truth without expecting anything in return, without even expecting that others should be enlightened as a result of your efforts. As an example of such service, consider the sun which gives light to everything on Earth yet needs or expects nothing from the Earth in return. Your rightful role on Earth is to become a spiritual sun, the SUN of God, who radiates your light selflessly and unconditionally, never expecting or demanding anything in return. You are content to share your light and you feel complete in sharing your light. In other words, your job on Earth is to radiate light and bear witness to the truth, leaving other people free to respond according to their own choices. You give without expecting any return from other people, and by giving selflessly, you will receive a return from above, because your I AM Presence will multiply everything given with unconditional love. You can then give to others without expecting a return from them, but with full expectation of a return from God so you can give even more, eventually becoming the fullness of a SUN of God.

In contrast, when you are trapped in the illusion of separation, you cannot find wholeness within yourself. Thus, you will seek wholeness from outside yourself, which means you will want other people to complete or validate you. So when you share your truth with them and they reject it, you will feel they are rejecting *you*. This will make it impossible for you to remain non-attached, and thus you cannot fulfill the role of demonstrating the path out of duality. For as long as you are attached to a sense of identity that springs from a lack of wholeness, how can you demonstrate how to become whole? As long as you are wanting something from others, how can you demonstrate spiritual self-sufficiency?

When you are whole, you can see that when other people reject what you radiate, they are not actually rejecting you. Their response really has nothing to do with you personally, for they are simply responding based on their state of consciousness. And the more trapped they are in duality, the more self-centered or hostile their reaction will be. You are not causing their hostility, and thus you have no reason to take it personally. You are simply bringing it out so they have an opportunity to see it. They are projecting their dualistic images upon you, and when you remain non-attached, you might help them see beyond the images. If you respond in a dualistic way, you only reinforce their images.

Incidentally, doing this is perfectly within the Law of Free Will. You do not have a right to force others to make choices, but you do have a right to bring out their unresolved psychology so they get an opportunity to rise above it. Even if they do not rise above it but take it out on you, you should remain non-attached. You must understand that they are truly acting out their own limited state of consciousness, and you have no desire to be pulled into it by responding in a dualistic manner. You can then remain in a state of unconditional love, whereby you give both yourself and others maximum freedom.

***

Take note of what I am saying here. By overcoming duality, you can become part of the movement to awaken humankind from the illusions of duality. Yet your job as part of this movement is *not* to awaken others or save them or save the Earth. Your job is to radiate your light and bear witness to your truth. When you have done that, your job is done, and it is of no consequence to you what other people do or don't do with what you have offered them. Your reward is not dependent upon other people's reactions. It is dependent solely on your willingness to give with unconditional love. Your reward does not come from the material universe—it comes from God and is independent of what other people do. It depends only on your willingness to give with unconditional love and to remain in unconditional love.

When you have escaped the most subtle illusion of duality, the illusion of action and reaction, you do not act in order to produce a particular reaction in the material world. Yet neither are you passive and do nothing. You act to share your light and truth and in the act of sharing, you are complete. You act based on the pure joy of the action itself. It is in seeing your light radiate that your joy is full, not in seeing the light produce particular changes in the world. Regardless of any visible results, sharing your light freely will increase the intensity of light in this sphere. Thus, whenever you selflessly share your light, you are helping bring about God's overall purpose. What better reaction could you possibly want? Thus, you see that no matter how other people react to you, there is no reason for you to go into a dualistic reaction. And if your actions do not lead to a dualistic reaction in yourself, you stay out of the action-reaction duality that is the basic challenge of any unascended sphere.

Please take some time to carefully consider these concepts, for they are of supreme importance. I have explained to you that the true teachers of humankind have absolute respect for the Law of Free Will, and we are seeking to inspire people to be saved as a result of their own choices, choices made in total freedom and based only on love for God. In contrast, the false teachers have no respect for free will and they are seeking to force people to be "saved" by manipulating them into making choices based on a lack of knowledge and motivated by fear. I have no desire to see anyone misinterpret my teachings and use them to justify seeking to force others to overcome duality—for this is impossible. I desire to see everyone who reads this book escape duality and find their place in the true movement that seeks to awaken people by giving without expecting a return.

The reality is that people are trapped in mental boxes created from the duality consciousness, meaning that they are simply illusions that have no reality to them. The true teachers are trying to show people that their conscious selves can walk out of those boxes at any moment, that you can simply leave them behind as if they had never existed. The catch-22 is that because people look at life from inside the mental boxes, they think the boxes have reality and they cannot imagine that it is so easy to escape them. Therefore, they tend to believe the false teachers who say they either cannot or do not need to escape the dualistic boxes.

For when you truly give unconditionally, selflessly and without expecting that your action should produce a certain reaction from others, then your efforts cannot fail. No matter how other people respond or don't respond to your actions, your efforts will be a success. You will win either way, and so will the Earth and the efforts of the Ascended Host. Let me explain.

***

The purpose of the material universe is to give beings an opportunity to grow in self-awareness. You can grow only through a voluntary and conscious effort, meaning that you grow only when you make free choices based on understanding. If you are forced to take certain actions or accept certain beliefs, you have not grown, for you have not internalized a higher understanding, you have not reached a higher self-awareness.

You do not help to awaken humankind by forcing others to become members of a certain religion or even by forcing them to accept your beliefs. Spiritual awakening simply cannot be forced or produced through mechanical means. It is a creative effort that requires people to make enlightened choices, meaning that they make choices that are not dualistic. They choose to abandon duality and they do so with the full understanding of what they are doing and why they are doing it. Thereby, they can raise themselves out of the reach of duality, so they are not as easily ensnared again.

The problem on Earth is that the vast majority of human beings are not in a position where they can make free, enlightened choices. The reason is that they have been brought up in a society and culture that is almost entirely dominated by the consciousness of duality. Most of the ideas they have ever encountered have been influenced by or have sprung from duality. Thus, most people have no awareness that there is anything beyond duality, that there is a higher way to look at life. They don't understand what duality is and they don't see its effects on their lives. And if people have no awareness that there is an alternative to duality, how can they choose to separate themselves from duality? If people cannot even conceive that there might be a new world beyond the horizon, how can they ever set sail for that world? If people are not aware of the potential to *know* better, how can they follow their built-in desire to *do* better?

What is needed is *not* that the top ten percent of the most spiritual people on Earth create a new religion and promote it as the superior religion. What is needed is that the most spiritual people raise themselves above duality and then let their light shine and bear witness to their non-dualistic truth, so that other people can see that there is an alternative to the duality consciousness. When you have demonstrated to other people that such an alternative exists, your job is done. You can and should leave it completely up to people's free will how they respond or don't respond. Your job is to show them the alternative, your job is *not* to make choices for them. When you have let your light shine, you have done your job. What other people do as a result has no consequence for you whatsoever.

This does not mean that if they reject your light and your truth, your effort will have had no effect on the progression of this planet. The law of God gives beings the right to free will, but it does not give them the right to a free ride. The law mandates that lifestreams who have fallen into duality must be given a certain number of opportunities to forsake duality and make a choice based on non-duality. So when people encounter a person who can demonstrate non-duality, they have received an opportunity to rise above duality. If a person rejects the opportunity, then that rejection is subtracted from the number of opportunities the lifestream has left. This number varies from lifestream to lifestream, depending on their past history, including their spiritual attainment before they fell. Yet each person on Earth only has a certain amount of opportunities before it will lose its right to re-embody on Earth.

For example, a person like Adolph Hitler spent all of his opportunities and will not be allowed to ever re-embody on this planet. Thus, the planet and all humans have been permanently set free from the gravitational pull of the personal consciousness of Adolph Hitler. When Jesus was rejected by the leaders of the Jewish religion, these lifestreams brought about their own judgment and some of them were not allowed to re-embody on Earth. That is why Jesus said, "For judgment I am come" (John 9:39). By rejecting the Living Christ in embodiment, and especially by persecuting or killing the Living Christ, a fallen lifestream will use up its opportunities and can quickly lose its right to return to the Earth. A fallen being can eventually lose all opportunities and can be dissolved in a ritual that Revelation calls the second death (Revelation 20:14, 21:8).

***

When you truly let your light shine with unconditional love, your efforts cannot fail to produce an effect that will raise the consciousness of humankind. One option is that the people you encounter will be awakened by your example and use it to raise themselves above duality. The other option is that some people reject you, whereby they eventually are removed from the planet. Either way, the downward pull of the fallen consciousness is reduced, allowing humans to rise to a higher level.

By doing right action – sharing your light and witnessing to your truth – while being non-attached to the fruits of action, you will perform the ultimate service to planet Earth and the cause of the Ascended Host. And whether other people are inspired or judged is of no consequence to you and thus should be of no concern to you. You need to know that people can be judged by rejecting you, but you do not need to judge them for rejecting you. You must have no negative feelings whatsoever, for such feelings show an attachment and any attachment will cause you to make karma. As I have tried to explain before, even actions that many people label as good can cause you to make karma. The stark reality – that many spiritual and religious people are reluctant to acknowledge – is that any action which does not spring from unconditional love will create karma and work against your own salvation and the salvation of humankind.

Let me say this another way. Everything you do is done with God's energy, and you are responsible for all of the energy that flows through the four levels of your mind. If you misqualify the energy, if you send it forth with a vibration that is less than unconditional love, the energy cannot flow back up to your I AM Presence and be multiplied. Thus, you break the figure-eight flow between Spirit and matter, whereby the stream of light from your I AM Presence will be reduced. At the same time you create an imbalance in the matter world by adding misqualified energy to the gravitational force on Earth. You simply will not be free from the Earth until you have purified the misqualified energy so that the Earth is no worse off than before you first descended here.

However, when your I AM Presence decided to send you to Earth, it did not do so with the hope that you would come here, make karma, balance that karma and then leave. It did so with the purpose of having you send forth unconditional love so you could make your contribution to raising up the vibration of this planet. The ideal is that you act with unconditional love – you multiply your talents by approaching every situation with a completely loving and non-attached attitude – whereby all of the energy that passes through your four lower bodies will return to your I AM Presence and be multiplied. The multiplied energy will then add to the positive energy on Earth by becoming part of the causal body of the planet in the identity realm, thus creating a magnetic pull that raises up the entire planet. This is why you came to Earth, and you will not feel fulfilled in leaving until that purpose has been accomplished. The key to fulfilling this divine plan is to attain wholeness, so you can witness to the truth and let your light shine with unconditional love. When people become attached to results, they try to fulfill their divine plans through the duality consciousness, which simply cannot be done. When people do not get the results they want, they think they have to push harder, but this only traps them on the dualistic treadmill of force and counter-force. It is when you are non-attached to seeing visible results of your efforts that you will produce the greatest results in terms of lifting up the entire planet. To produce the greatest results, stop focusing on the results and focus on the action itself. Focus on *being* rather than *doing*.

***

I know full well that this can seem like a very strict and unrealistic demand that no one could possibly live up to. After all, the serpents are very good at making you doubt yourself, including your ability to know when you are acting selflessly and when you are not. How can you actually know when your actions spring from unconditional love and when they do not?

I have no desire to leave you in the grips of doubt, so let me give you a way to evaluate whether you are acting based on unconditional love, a way that simply cannot fail—if you are willing to be honest. As I have explained, the basic goal of your personal path is to attain wholeness. When you are whole, you know you need nothing from other people. Thus, the actions and reactions of other people can never be a threat to your wholeness. Other people can only take away your wholeness if you allow them to, and if you are whole, you simply will not allow them to come between you and your God.

My point is that as a sincere spiritual seeker, your fundamental desire in life should be to attain wholeness. You should be willing to acknowledge and correct *anything* that takes you away from wholeness. And it should be obvious that as long as you feel threatened or rejected, you have not overcome duality, you have not become whole.

Therefore, be willing to acknowledge when the actions and reactions of other people cause you to feel threatened and when something in your own being causes you to resist life, to resist self-transcendence. When you discover an element of resisting, be willing to look for the illusion that binds you to the dualistic state of consciousness. Be willing to look for the lie that separates you from your own higher being, from God.

Let me say this another way. It is the Father's good pleasure to give you his kingdom, meaning that God really wants you to have the spiritual freedom that can only come from wholeness. When you are above dualistic attachments, you freely flow with the River of Life, and everything seems to come to you effortlessly. It is as if the entire universe is supporting your actions, *which it is*. My point is that you were designed to express your creativity by remaining in the River of Life where you are freely flowing with life. When you leave the River of Life and become trapped in the illusion of separation, you enter into an unnatural state. I know that because they have been trapped in the consciousness of duality for lifetimes, most people believe the limitations and suffering on Earth are natural. Yet in reality, the abundant life is the natural state for a human being. And when you are in the River of Life, you have no need to resist anything in life. Thus, it is the very act of resistance that sets you apart from the river, it is the sense of struggle – the dualistic illusion that you need to resist life – that creates the struggle.

When you step into duality, you separate yourself from the flow of life, but since this is an unnatural state, it takes effort to remain separate. In other words, in order to remain in a separate sense of identity, you have to resist the natural flow of life. Thus, your ego is based on resistance, the act of resisting the natural flow of life. If you will pay attention to this, you can relatively quickly develop the ability to sense when you are resisting life.

***

I know this will take some contemplation, for how can you realize that you are resisting until you have had at least a glimpse of what it is like *not* to resist but to flow with the River of Life? Yet most spiritual people have had such experiences of inner peace, inner freedom or an expanded, innocent state of consciousness. The very fact that you are open to this book means that you already have a foundation upon which you can build your ability to know when your ego is resisting life. You can then use this awareness to uncover the dualistic beliefs that cause you to resist, resolve them through a higher understanding from the Christ mind, surrender them and then move into the innocent mind of the child. You might remember that Jesus clearly stated that unless you become as a little child, you shall in no wise enter the kingdom (Mark 10:15). The meaning is that unless you attain the state of innocence in which you no longer resist the flow of the River of Life, you cannot be in the state that is natural and thus requires no resistance. You don't really believe that the resistance and struggle you see on Earth is found in God's kingdom, do you?

If you will ponder my teachings honestly, and ask for the direction from your Higher Self and spiritual teacher, you will make immense progress. And you will soon come to the point of knowing that you can no longer be threatened by any of the games played by those who identify with the consciousness of duality. You will be able to say with Jesus, "The prince of this world comes and has nothing in me" (John 14:30). The forces of duality will have nothing in you whereby they can force you into a reaction that is less than love. Thus, they will have no way of controlling you, and you will have no reason to fear them any longer. You can do what the Buddha did, namely resist the temptations of Mara and claim your right to be the Living Christ, the Living Buddha, on Earth. And when thousands, even millions, of people make this claim, you will see an awakening that will spread around this planet like a tidal wave that sweeps aside the fortifications erected by the forces of duality. When people stop resisting the forces of duality, these forces will not be able to resist the force of non-resistance, the force of unconditional love. With human beings this is impossible, but with God – acting through his extensions on Earth – all things are possible.

Key 27
Who can free the world from dualistic religion?

It is virtually impossible to grow up anywhere on this planet without being affected by one dualistic religion or another. Even scientific materialism is a dualistic religion in that it claims to present an infallible truth about the existence of God, your identity and the purpose of life, but in reality it simply presents the doctrines of those who have made a religion out of the plausible deniability built into the material universe. My point being that as a sincere spiritual seeker, you can now see that unless you make an effort to free yourself from the effects of dualistic religion, you cannot manifest your spiritual freedom. However, take note of what I am saying here. I am saying that you need to free yourself from the *effects* of dualistic religion, I am not saying you need to free yourself from *all* religion or even a particular religion. The difference may seem subtle, but it is extremely important—as will become clear in this chapter.

The first step toward rising above dualistic religion is to overcome the basic manipulation behind all such religion, namely that if you do not follow the right religion – submitting to all of its doctrines and practices – you are sure to burn forever in hell. This fear-based approach to religion has been influencing people on this planet for a very long time, and in this cosmic cycle it is time for the most spiritual people to dispense with it once and for all. The concept that you need a religion on Earth in order to be saved is one of the biggest lies ever perpetrated upon humankind.

As I have explained in previous chapters, you are more than religion, and God is more than religion. Thus, God – who created the entire world of form – cannot be confined to any particular religion on this planet—which is like a speck of plankton in an infinite ocean. You are an extension of the Creator's Being, and thus you cannot be confined to any particular religion, and neither do you need any religion in order to be saved. Because you are an extension of God, the key to your salvation is *not* to do something on Earth but to unite with your own higher being. The key to salvation is not *doing* something but *being* who you were created to be. Thus, the most important task for you is to never let any man – or anything outside yourself – take thy crown (Revelation 3:11). Let nothing come between you and the direct inner contact with God and your own higher being that is your ultimate birthright.

What you *do* need in order to be saved is a transformation of consciousness, a rebirth of your sense of identity, whereby you attain oneness with your own higher being. You absolutely can never be saved by maintaining a separate identity. You must become one with your own greater Being while retaining your individuality—not as a separate being but as an individualization of the greater Being out of which you came. I realize this can sound like an enigma or contradiction, but it is one that can be solved by rising above duality. Only the illusion of separation makes this seem like a contradiction. Once you see beyond the filter of duality, it becomes perfectly obvious how you can be one with your source without losing your individuality.

My point being that the *only* true path to salvation is the Path of Oneness. Yet this path is an inner process. The meaning is that it cannot be guaranteed by following any outer religion. On the other hand, it cannot be stopped by any outer religion. So you can follow the Path of Oneness while being a member of any religion or no religion.

The master key to spiritual freedom is to realize that you can be free only when you are whole, when you are self-sufficient. You are whole when you realize that you get everything from God via your direct inner oneness with God—due to the fact that your conscious self is an extension of the Creator's Being. So you need nothing from any other person or from the material world, including an external religion or savior.

Take note of the subtlety here. I am not saying that you need nothing besides your conscious self or lower being in order to be saved. Your lower being truly cannot save itself, which is why there is some truth to the belief among many religions that you need God's grace or help from spiritual beings in order to be saved. The problem is that these religions tend to portray God as the external being in the sky, and thus his grace is seen as coming from an external source. There is separation between you and God and thus there is a gap between God's grace and your receipt of it. And as long as there is such a gap, how could you possibly receive God's grace?

The all-important distinction that the most spiritually advanced people need to make is that God is not an external Being. Your source is ultimately the Creator, but you reach the Creator by going through the hierarchy of Beings that have descended from the Creator, the lowest link of which is your I AM Presence. You are an individualization of that hierarchy, and the only path to salvation is for you to come into oneness with it. Thus, you are not saving yourself in the sense that your lower being – which includes your ego – can bring about salvation. You save yourself by bringing your lower being into alignment with, into oneness with, your higher being. Thus, it is your higher being that saves your lower being, not your lower being that saves itself through its own efforts or light. The grace of God is the Light of your own I AM Presence. The trick is to realize that you can receive that light only from inside yourself—the kingdom of God is within you and you cannot find it anywhere else.

In order to ascend, your conscious self must receive grace, namely the light of a being in the spiritual realm. You cannot receive this light as long as you see yourself as separated from God. Thus, you must come into oneness with your own higher being and Chain of Being, and then you can receive the ascension flame. Take note that the ascension flame will accelerate the vibration of your entire lower being, and in doing so all dualistic images and sense of identity will be burned away. That is why you cannot receive the ascension flame until you have purified your lower being from a dualistic sense of identity. If such a mortal identity was suddenly burned away, you would end up in a spiritual vacuum, potentially feeling like you had no continuity and identity. Thus, the Path of Oneness is a gradual process of rising above your mortal, separate sense of identity until you are ready to be accelerated into the ascension without losing your sense of identity.

Take note that the true teachers of humankind will not claim that they can save you. They will help you transform your consciousness until you reach the state of wholeness that *is* salvation. In contrast, the false teachers are trapped in separation, and the very idea that there is a distance between you and God inevitably gives rise to the concept that you need an external savior in order to cross that distance. In other words, any religion, person or non-material being who claims to be able to save you is making a false claim, whether knowingly or unknowingly. Many immature religious people actually want to believe in this claim, because it seemingly sets them free from taking full responsibility for their own choices. As a mature spiritual seeker, you need to stop believing in such claims and accept the ultimate responsibility that you are the one who must change your consciousness and thereby open the door for the true salvation, the salvation from within.

***

The ultimate question to ask concerning your involvement with religion is not whether your religion will save you. The real question is whether your religion helps you come closer to wholeness or takes you away from wholeness? The most sure way to evaluate this question is to honestly consider whether there is any trace of fear in your approach to religion.

As we have seen, fear can only come into play when there is separation from your source. So if you detect any fear in your approach to religion, you know you have not yet attained wholeness. You then need to use the right tools, such as Mother Mary's book and rosaries, to overcome your fear. You need to strive for a state of mind in which your involvement with religion is based on love and joy, with no sense of fear or obligation. You should not be involved with religion because you fear hell or feel obligated to do God's work. You should be involved with religion because you love your own Higher Self, you love the Creator, you love other people, you love the Earth, you love truth. And it gives you supreme joy to be involved with an activity that expresses your God Flame while helping other people and bringing God's kingdom to this planet.

Consider what I have told you in this book about the true God – the Creator – and the false gods. How do you think the true God wants you to approach religion? How do you think the false gods want you to approach religion? The true God wants you to approach religion exactly as Jesus described, when he said that God is a Spirit and that you must worship him in spirit and in truth" (John 4:24) and when he said that you must become as little children (Luke 18:17). The Creator has nothing to hide and wants you to discover the truth that will set you free from all illusions, whereby you will experience the incredible joy that the Creator has in being creative—you will experience the Creator's blissful Spirit. In contrast, the false gods can motivate people only through fear, for in their state of separation they have forfeited all true joy. They know only the dualistic joy that is in a polarity with its opposite. The false teachers want you to be fearful of religion. Why? Because if you knew better, you would never follow them, so their survival depends on keeping you in ignorance. And the primary way whereby they use religion to keep people in ignorance is to create a culture based on fear so there are certain questions people don't dare to ask. And when you don't ask, how can you receive an answer? And thus, how can you escape the illusion that keeps you trapped in a limited sense of identity?

The simple fact is that you will never escape your current mental prison unless you adopt a willingness to question any and all of your current beliefs, including those imposed upon you by an outer religion. The false gods want you to think that if you ask the forbidden questions, terrible things will happen, but if you follow them blindly, your salvation is guaranteed. As I have now hopefully helped you see, nothing bad will happen from asking questions, but following the false leaders blindly will not take you to heaven. Thus, be willing to question every aspect of your present approach to religion, from the most general – your attitude to God – to the most specific—the doctrines or rituals to which you have been exposed.

Obviously, by reading this book you have already started this process, but you cannot expect the process of cleansing your mind from dualistic beliefs to be completed in the – relatively – short time it takes to read this book. You should consider this a life-long process, and if you will ask for inner direction, study teachings that give you a broader view of religion and practice spiritual techniques, you will be amazed at the transformation that will begin to take place.

***

I realize that your willingness to read this book shows that you have already started questioning your childhood religion, perhaps even all religion. After all, if you had been a blind follower of any outer belief system, this book would have caused you to close your mind long ago. Consequently, you might already have overcome so much fear that you have abandoned your childhood religion, perhaps even withdrawn from all religion. You might be looking for an alternative to your present or past religion, or you might have resigned yourself to never again becoming involved with any form of organized religion. Yet I hope to help you see that this is not necessarily the highest possible course of action.

As I have explained, millions of beings volunteered to come into embodiment at this particular turning point in the Earth's history. The main reason was that these beings wanted to help bring about the large-scale spiritual awakening I have talked about. Yet how can this awakening come about?

I realize that based on the very subtle programming from the false gods, it is very tempting for even the most mature spiritual people to think that the awakening must come about through the emergence of a new religion that finally is the one and only true religion on Earth. There are millions of people who have left traditional or mainstream religions and started a search for a new religion or guru that will be the right one. Yet I hope you can now begin to see that this mindset is fundamentally dualistic. For millions of years the false gods have created their own religions and have always attempted to make it seem like their particular religion was the only true one. So it is tempting even for spiritual people to continue this subtle way of looking at religion, namely by thinking that there has to be such a thing as the one true religion or the highest possible spiritual teaching. If they come to doubt the religion in which they grew up, they think they have to abandon it and go in search of this mysterious new religion that will meet all of their criteria for the perfect religion.

Yet the stark reality is – as I have explained – that there is no single religion that will work equally well for all of the many different lifestreams on this planet. The dream of a superior religion is simply a dualistic dream that springs from the mindset of separation. The mechanism is simple. If you are a member of the superior religion on Earth, then you must be among the spiritually superior people, and thus your ego can make you believe that your salvation is guaranteed. Your fear of being lost can then be suppressed so you can live with it.

What really needs to happen in this age is the emergence of an entirely new approach to religion, an approach that is non-dualistic in nature. Such an approach must incorporate an understanding of the human ego, the duality consciousness and the false gods. However, this approach must be truly universal, and thus it is not meant to become the basis for the emergence of the "one and only" religion. It is meant to become the basis for a new approach that can be used to rejuvenate almost all of the existing religions. I am not saying the new approach will not give rise to new movements, but if a religion claims to be the only true one or the superior one, then it has not fully embodied the nature of the new approach.

My point here is that before you decided to come into embodiment in this age, you very likely made a vow to work for promoting the new universal approach to religion. And you most likely also vowed to help apply it to one of the existing religions. Which is precisely why you chose to embody in a family and culture affected by a particular religion. By growing up in that environment, you experienced directly how people in that culture think. Thus, you are in a unique position to help these people go through the same transformation of consciousness that you have experienced and will continue to experience. In other words, it might not be in your divine plan that you abandon your childhood religion or withdraw from all organized religion. It might be part of your plan that you remain somewhat associated with religion and make a contribution to renewing it according to a non-dual, universal approach.

I am aware that many sincere spiritual seekers have been profoundly hurt through their involvement with a rigid, dogmatic and fear-based religion. Many feel they have been spiritually raped because the outer religion inserted so much fear and so many dualistic beliefs that it severely distorted their innocent relationship with God. Yet I ask you to consider that by going through the spiritual healing process I am outlining in this book, you can overcome these wounds. You can also demonstrate that a person from your background can rise above fear-based religion and find a new love-based approach to religion and God. This has the potential to become an incredible inspiration for other people, and this might be precisely what you intended when you decided to embody in that environment.

Can you see that what hurt you and many other people is the fear-based approach to religion? Sadly, there has not – in recorded history – been a truly love-based large religion on this planet. So imagine the incredible impact it can have if millions of people begin to adopt a universal, love-based approach to religion and begin to express it in the context of the traditional fear-based religions—demanding that they be transformed into love-based religions. Can you see that this can potentially change the religious landscape forever? It is the perfect love that will cast out all fear, so if unconditional – non-dualistic

– love is introduced into the religious life on this planet, it can have a healing effect that is unprecedented. It can heal billions of people and also transform the outer religions in a way that the false gods and the fallen beings simply cannot imagine—and thus will find it very difficult to counter-act. As the popular saying goes, they won't know what hit them—mainly because nothing – meaning nothing dualistic – will actually hit them.

***

If you will take an honest look at the religions found on this planet, you will see a very clear pattern. Most religions are affected by the consciousness that there can be only one true religion, and the members of each religion believe that their religion is the one. This creates a culture that fosters exclusivism, elitism, extremism and even fanaticism. The result is that many of the people who see themselves as highly religious tend to be very aggressive in promoting their own religion and denouncing all others as the works of the devil. They tend to be very judgmental of any spiritual ideas that go beyond or contradict the doctrines of their religion. And they tend to look down upon the members of any other belief system. The reason being, of course, that they feel threatened by other religions, and the reason for feeling threatened is that they have not fully integrated their own beliefs. For if you know that you are devoted to seeking the Spirit of Truth, why would you feel threatened by other people's beliefs?

I am sure you are perfectly aware of this judgmentalness and that it is probably one of the main reasons why you might have withdrawn from religion. I am quite aware that the vast majority of the top ten percent of the spiritual people have withdrawn from religions that exhibit this kind of unbalanced behavior. I am not saying this isn't understandable. Yet I ask you to consider a very simple question. The reason why so many religions are trapped in an unbalanced approach is that they are trapped in duality. The only people who have a realistic potential for overcoming duality are the top ten percent. So if all of these people withdraw from a particular religion, how can that religion ever be transformed? The obvious answer is that these religions will not be transformed, and what will be the inevitable result? The result will be that these religions will stay in the dualistic game, trapping their members in that game because they will not see that there is an alternative.

You might think that if a new non-dualistic alternative emerges, then the members of other religions can see an alternative to dualistic religion in the new one. The problem is that as long as an old religion remains stuck in duality, the members will see a new religion – even a non-dualistic one – as an adversary. They will look at the new religion as a threat, and thus they will see it only through the filter of duality, completely failing to see its non-dualistic nature. Yet if some people within their own religion begin to talk about a non-dualistic approach – and if they present it by using the teachings and terminology of that religion – it will be more difficult for the leaders and members of the old religion to label them as enemies of that religion.

I am not here talking about taking a religion beyond duality in one giant step. I am talking about a gradual movement of renewing the old religion by calling attention to the non-dualistic elements in that religion's own teachings. Virtually all of the world's religions have teachings that – when understood with the clarity of the Christ mind – are non-dualistic or point beyond duality. So by using these elements, it will be possible to make at least some of the members of an existing religion think—without making them feel so threatened that they instantly close their minds.*

The underlying purpose for any true representative of Christ truth is to give people a real choice between duality and non-duality by allowing them to encounter an idea and a person who is beyond duality. Therefore, working from within existing religions can often be more effective than creating a new religion that will clearly be seen as an adversary. Take note that Jesus sought to reform Judaism and the Buddha sought to reform Hinduism. Eventually, both the teachings of the Christ and the Buddha were turned into separate religions, but as I have explained earlier, that was not the original intention. The intention was to reform the old religion by bringing a breath of non-dualistic air.

In summary, I hope you can see that it is only the top ten percent of the people, namely the ones who have started to move beyond the veil of duality, who have a realistic potential for taking religion

---

* For an example of a non-dualistic approach to Christianity, see the book *I Love Jesus, I Hate Christianity* by Kim Michaels.

beyond duality. So if all of these people withdraw from traditional religions and either join new ones or attempt to create the ultimate religion, this planet will remain stuck in the same old patterns that have been repeated for millions of years.

Key 28
How to help free people from the dualistic mindset

In order for the top ten percent of the spiritual people to have the maximum impact, they need to recognize how they tend to respond when they are confronted with religious people who are openly fanatical, hostile and aggressive. Let us begin by looking at the lowest half of the top ten percent.

These people have recognized that there is a spiritual side to life, so they can see beyond the rigidity of traditional religion, but they have not yet fully understood the nature of duality. The result is that they are often drawn into a dualistic struggle of arguing with those who are fully trapped in duality. They clearly see the error of a traditional religion, and they become very zealous in trying to convince other people, often feeling they are doing this for God or some great cause. Yet because those in the top ten percent have risen above the lower manifestations of the duality consciousness, these people are not willing to go as far as the bottom ten percent in order to defeat their opponents. They do not fully believe that the end can justify the means, at least they realize that there are certain means that are never justified. The result is that the top ten percent almost invariably lose any power struggle with the bottom ten percent, who will often exclude them from leadership positions in traditional churches. This often makes the more spiritual people very frustrated and causes them to go into a passive-aggressive response of feeling like victims or martyrs.

Many of these people feel that they have already attempted to reform their childhood religion and they failed, so now they want to have nothing to do with that or any religion. Yet I hope you can now see that this is a black-and-white form of thinking, where you jump from one extreme to the other. If the leaders of your religion won't listen to you, then you won't have anything to do with them, so you withdraw. Yet such people withdraw with great frustration and often become hostile toward all religion or a particular religion. Obviously, this shows that these people are still attached to the results of their actions, and thus they have not overcome duality.

I am quite aware that many of these people are truly well-meaning and very sincere. I am also aware that they often feel stuck, because they feel that if others won't listen, then they have no other alternative than to withdraw. Yet I hope these people can use the teachings in this book to realize that there is an alternative that goes beyond the two dualistic extremes. That alternative is to truly rise above duality, so you can engage in the religious debate without expecting particular outer results. Thereby, you can avoid feeling rejected and that will actually open up for the desired results to manifest.

Let us now look at the top half of the top ten percent, what we might call the top five percent. These are people who have seen the futility of engaging in any kind of dualistic struggle. Yet because they have not consciously seen the reality of the non-dualistic approach, they have felt there is no way to constructively engage the more fanatical people. Some of these people are members of traditional religions, and they often participate in religious activities without ever saying anything. They engage in the outer rituals while thinking for themselves in the privacy of their own minds. Others have simply withdrawn quietly from a particular religion or from all religion, still being spiritual but without any outer practices.

These people have often adopted a form of gray thinking, where they believe you should simply live and let live, believe and let believe. You should believe what you want to believe and let other people do the same, not interfering with their beliefs or challenging them in any way. So while the group described above are often in a passive-aggressive response, the people in this latter group have overcome aggression – which is good – but they have now gone into the blind alley of being entirely passive. Yet what could possibly be wrong with this approach—aren't these people simply refusing to resist evil and turning the other cheek?

We have now arrived at the central question that will determine whether the top ten percent will rise and fulfill the roles they planned to play or whether they will sit passively by while the religious debate continues to be controlled by those trapped in duality. The question really is whether the top ten percent will take this planet into a Golden Age of spiritual freedom and abundance or whether they will let the bottom ten percent reverse the upward trend built over thousands of years and instead take the planet into another downward spiral. Let us take a closer look.

***

The basic dynamic that shapes everything on planet Earth is very simple. As I have explained, everything is created from the Ma-ter Light, which has consciousness. All structures in the world of form are organized into units, and within a given unit, there is a collective consciousness that affects everything within that unit. In the unit called planet Earth, the dominant factor is the consciousness of humankind. Thus, every aspect of life on this planet, including human society, the balance of nature, natural disasters, the movements of the Earth's crust, even the density of matter, is affected by humankind's consciousness. Because of free will, the greatest impact is caused by the state of consciousness of the middle 80 percent of the population. The lowest ten percent cannot destroy the planet on their own, neither can the top ten percent pull it up on their own. It is the 80 percent of the general population that largely determine which way the planet will go. What the top and bottom ten percent *can* do is to pull the general population up or down.

In the past, this planet has seen golden ages in which the knowledge, technology and abundance far surpassed what the most optimistic science fiction writers can even imagine. That happened in periods when the top ten percent decided to take dominion over the Earth and pull the general population up with them. As Jesus said, "And I, if I be lifted up from the Earth, shall draw all men unto me" (John 12:32). The planet has also seen downward spirals that led to the collapse of huge civilizations, and some of them were literally erased through cataclysmic natural disasters. There were periods when the human population was greatly reduced in numbers and reduced to a state of existence not much higher than monkeys. What today's archaeologists consider the beginning of humankind, namely the cave dwellers, was only one such low point. These downward spirals occurred when the top ten percent decided not to take dominion and thus allowed the bottom ten percent to drag the general population down to their selfish level of consciousness. We might say that if the bottom ten percent are not counterbalanced by an infusion of light, they will drag society down until the contracting force breaks it down.

The Ascended Host have been working with humankind for millions of years, and we are always seeking to prevent a downward spiral and bring about a golden age. Yet we are always loyal to the Law of Free Will, meaning that we can work only through people in embodiment. In practical terms that means we must work through the top ten percent, for they are the only ones who have a sufficient level of spiritual maturity to recognize our existence and see the validity of our non-dualistic teachings and direction.

What you see on planet Earth today is that, after the last low point, the Ascended Host have very carefully and gradually brought humankind close to a breakthrough point. We have done this by working with the top ten percent, but it has – quite frankly – been an uphill battle, for even the most spiritually mature people have been very reluctant to take dominion.

The planet is right now on the threshold of a Golden Age, but it can only come about if the top ten percent awaken to the reality of the situation and decide to take dominion. And for this to happen, these people must overcome one of the most common illusions about love and kindness, namely that love is only soft, gentle and passive. So many spiritual people have gotten themselves into a frame of mind where they think that all they have to do in order to serve God is to be loving and kind. This is not actually wrong, but the problem is that too many people think that being loving and kind means that you have unlimited tolerance toward other people and their behavior. They think love is passive or that it tolerates everything.

Many spiritual people think love means being non-judgmental of others, and while this is true, the problem is that duality perverts everything, even people's concept of love. What you see in many religions is a form of dualistic judgment of anyone who does not live up to the standard set by the outer religion. Many spiritual people see the hypocrisy of this, but they think they have to jump into the opposite dualistic extreme of passively tolerating everything. This is a very dangerous illusion, for the reality is that the top ten percent must use Christ discernment to overcome both dualistic extremes. True love is not passive and it does not tolerate everything. True love is unconditional love, and it is a force that wants all life to be free. Thus, while it does not put people down through judgment, neither does it allow them to suffer needlessly by doing nothing to help them. That is the reason Jesus told the parable about the good samaritan who helped the person that the self-righteous Jews ignored (Luke 10:30). Unconditional love is a very active force that always seeks to set people free from conditions that prevent them from becoming more. Unconditional love is the very force of life itself. I know the Creator has given beings free will, but you don't really think a loving Creator wants them to use it to destroy themselves, do you? Which is precisely why the Creator sends representatives to Earth – in the form of beings with some degree of Christhood – to awaken humans from their self-destructive ways. You might be one of these representatives, the question being whether you are willing to fill this role or whether you will use a dualistic excuse for remaining passive.

I am fully aware that there are many among the top ten percent who will be unwilling to read or accept this book because I so directly talk about fallen beings, the presence of evil and the duality consciousness. Many of the most spiritual people have entered into a state of gray thinking in which they want to believe there is no evil, that there is nothing really wrong on this planet or that evil will go away if they ignore it. Everything will work out in the end—if we are nice to everybody. It is continually amazing to the Ascended Host how the most spiritually inclined people can be open to spiritual teachings that talk about love and peace while at the same time ignoring the reality of what is happening on this planet, such as the potential for war, terrorism, the increasing sexual abuse of children, poverty, starvation and many other conditions that clearly could not exist in a golden age. This is especially amazing because the most spiritual people usually took embodiment because they wanted to help humankind rise above such conditions. My point being that all people forget their divine plans as they take embodiment but that it is high time for the spiritual people to overcome this amnesia.

The simple – yet unpopular – truth is that many among the top ten percent have reached a certain level of spiritual maturity, but instead of going on to full Christhood, they have allowed their egos and the false teachers to take them into a blind alley of a very subtle form of selfishness. These people have become so focused on themselves and their own spiritual growth that they think the goal of life is for them to strive for personal enlightenment. And as long as they do that, they will send out so many positive vibrations that the Earth will be lifted and all darkness will disappear. Yet let me remind you that Jesus told you not to *resist* evil—he did not tell you to *ignore* evil (Matthew 5:39). Instead, he told you to be wise as serpents and harmless as doves (Matthew 10:16).

The simple fact is that the Earth will go up or down based on who decides to take dominion over the general population—the top ten percent or the bottom ten percent. The sad fact is that – so far – the bottom ten percent have been far more determined, aggressive and organized in their efforts to take dominion than have the top ten percent. In fact, the top ten percent largely ignore the existence of the bottom ten percent and the dualistic force that is aggressively seeking to pull humankind down into their self-created hell. And as mentioned before, for the dualistic force to triumph, it only takes that the top ten percent do nothing.

***

As I have already explained in great detail, it is absolutely essential that the top ten percent do not engage in another dualistic battle with the bottom ten percent. Yet it is equally essential that the top ten percent realize that because there is still so much darkness in the energy field of Earth, the evolutionary force built into the Ma-ter Light will not bring about a golden age automatically. The dualistic force on Earth is presently so strong that it will inevitably pull the planet down unless it is counteracted by an upward force. And – as I have now explained many times – that force can come only through the top ten percent.

If the Earth is to cross the threshold and enter a truly golden age, the top ten percent must awaken to the reality I have described. They must acknowledge the dynamics of the tug of war between the top and bottom ten percent, and then they must decide to engage in it—in a way that is neither dualistic nor pacifistic.

The key to finding the Middle Way – that is above and beyond dualistic extremes – is to realize that there is a fundamental difference between what most human beings see as love and what I have consistently called God's unconditional love. Human love is generally self-centered and possessive. Many people profess to love others, but the reality is that they do so because they hope to get something for themselves. Their love is possessive in the sense that they are trying to use it to control others so they can get what they want from them. They control others by setting up certain conditions that others must live up to in order to be worthy of their love. And then they seek to get other people to conform to their conditions in order to receive their love.

In contrast, divine love is unconditional and is like the light of the sun that is freely given to all life on Earth. Yet divine love is *not* pacifistic. It is more intelligent than sunlight in that its effect on the recipient is determined by what the person does with the love. We might also say that divine love magnifies whatever is in the consciousness of the recipient. If the person is willing to grow, the person will multiply his or her talents and divine love will then accelerate that growth. If the person is not willing to grow, the person will bury his or her talents in the ground, and then divine love will magnify the person's selfishness, making it more visible and harder to ignore. Why is this so?

Unconditional love is unconditional. One aspect is that it is given freely to all. This is the passive or Mother aspect that nourishes all life. Yet the other aspect is the active or Father aspect that will not allow any being to remain stuck in a limited identity forever. Divine love is truly the driving force of the universe, and it is the force that propels all life to grow and become more. Thus, unconditional love will not accept any conditions that prevent the growth of all life.

Divine love naturally works within the context of free will. So it accepts that a being has the right to resist the force of life itself, the force of growth and self-transcendence. The being can do this only by setting up conditions that seemingly justify that it should not self-transcend. And even though a being has the right to define such conditions – which can be done only through the duality consciousness – the being does not have a right to uphold them indefinitely. Thus, the force of unconditional love has a right to challenge the conditions that prevent a being from growing. It does this in two ways.

- One is the gentle way represented by the spiritual teachers of humankind. We seek to positively inspire people to question their conditions, and we do so by offering spiritual teachings. If people accept such teachings, they will come to understand that they have defined conditions that limit themselves, and they will naturally grow to the point of voluntarily looking at them and then letting them go.

- If people resist this inspiring force, they become subject to the second force, the school of hard knocks. Unconditional love will then inflate their conditions in order to make them more visible so that people will hopefully see what they are doing and decide to stop doing it. This happens because the universe is a mirror that reflects back to people – multiplied by the force of unconditional love – what they send out. The more hatred people send out, the more hatred comes back, and this downward spiral will go on until people decide they have had enough and become willing to change themselves.

The force of unconditional love will simply keep presenting people with opportunities to grow until they decide to take advantage of them and leave behind some or all of their dualistic illusions. Yet take note that this is always an effort to set life free. The basic dynamic is that if people knew better, they would do better. Some can come to know better through the inspiration of a spiritual teaching, while others are blinded by certain conditions. So how can people overcome those conditions? They can do so only through choices, but they cannot make such LIFE decisions until they see the conditions and see them as a problem that limits themselves. So even though it might temporarily disturb people, challenging or inflating their dualistic conditions is actually the only opportunity for helping people see what is best for themselves.

***

The top ten percent of the people on Earth have the potential to become part of the force of unconditional love. They can do this by becoming the mouthpieces for the Ascended Host and helping awaken people through spiritual teachings and by example. Yet they can also become extensions of the force of unconditional love that reflects back to people what they send out, thus making their dualistic beliefs more visible. This gives people an opportunity to choose between duality and non-duality because they have now seen that there is an alternative to duality. This is what Jesus did when he actively challenged the scribes, the Pharisees, the temple priests and the lawyers.

Jesus had unconditional love for all people, and that is why he did not leave them alone in their misery. He reached out to all those who were considered outcasts, he ministered to all who were afflicted and he challenged the proud who would not let go of their control over the people. Too many spiritual people have the vision that being a spiritual person means sitting in a cave in the Himalayas and meditating on God 24 hours a day. Yet if that was so, why didn't Jesus stay in the wilderness after he had meditated for 40 days? Why didn't he avoid being humiliated and crucified by simply staying in the mountains? Why didn't the Buddha stay in Nirvana after he had attained that state of consciousness? Why did he return to society and start teaching others? It was because neither Jesus nor the Buddha had self-centered love—they had unconditional love. As a result, they could not remain in their higher state of consciousness as long as the people were trapped in the duality consciousness. They simply could not accept the conditions that prevented the people from experiencing the state of consciousness that they had attained. The reason for this was that they had overcome the separate sense of identity and thus saw themselves as one with all life, which naturally generates a desire to help raise all life. When you are lifted up from the Earth, you naturally want to draw all men unto you (John 12:32).

If you see a person with blinders on who is walking toward an abyss, how would you respond? Would you reason that it is the person's choice to put on the blinders and to start walking, and you should let him be so he can learn from his own choices? Or would you reason that as long as he doesn't realize he is wearing blinders – because others put them on and he has never experienced what it is like not to wear them – he cannot make a free choice?

The stark reality is that many among the top ten percent think they are very loving and spiritual people. Yet they have adopted the passive attitude which is simply the opposite dualistic polarity to the aggressive or fanatical attitude. Such people are watching humans walking toward the abyss with blinders on, and they are doing nothing to awaken them. They are so focused on themselves – and their dualistic image that they only have to be loving and kind – that they are not doing the only sensible thing, namely to climb the housetops and cry out that the emperor of duality has nothing on. Do you think this is being truly loving? Do you think this is being truly spiritual? I do not—I think it is being truly selfish!

***

Let me now take this one step further by looking at selfishness and taking it to the ultimate extreme. Most spiritual people think selfishness is wrong, so they are very concerned about not being selfish. Thus, they will be very reluctant to admit it when I call them selfish. Yet what is wrong with selfishness? Let us explore the overlooked virtues of selfishness.

What is truly best for yourself? Well, that depends on how you define "self." Do you define self as the separate self or do you define self as the All, as the Body of God? If you define self based on the illusion of separation and duality, you will inevitably condemn yourself to an endless cycle of struggles and suffering, and is that truly what is best for you? If you define self based on the reality that all life is one, you will enter the River of Life, whereby your life becomes an endless growth process toward more and more of everything that is positive.

What does it take for you to enter the River of Life? Very simple! All you have to do is to let go of the illusion of a separate self and accept the reality of the one Self. Then you start working on what is best for the greater self, whereby the entire universe will support and multiply your every effort. Life simply cannot fail to become an upward spiral for both your individual self and the larger self, of which you now know you are a part.

There truly is a phase on the spiritual path where it is natural and acceptable that you focus on your own spiritual growth. You cannot grow spiritually by following the mass consciousness, for it will pull you away from spiritual endeavors. That is why most people will have to withdraw from a "normal" materialistic life in order to focus on spiritual growth for a time. Yet what I am also saying is that there are millions of people among the top ten percent who have now completed that phase in their lives. They have reached the most crucial turning point in the growth of any being, namely the point I described earlier. This is the point where you must take full responsibility for your growth and become spiritually self-sufficient. Yet you can do so only by letting go of the separate sense of self and no longer work for your own growth, instead starting to work for the growth of the All, the one Self. You must be willing to lose your life – your separate sense of life – in order to follow Christ into the eternal life of oneness with the All.

If you will study the lives of the Christ and the Buddha, you will see that they both had a period where they focused on raising their own state of consciousness. Yet they both reached a turning point, where they were at the threshold to a non-dualistic state of consciousness. At that point they faced a choice, a choice that has not been fully understood by those who idolize the Christ and the Buddha, thinking they could not possibly have failed. The choice they faced was simple. Would they continue to focus on the individual self or would they focus on the All? This is the choice to give up the separate self and let the conscious self become the awakened self, the enlightened self, that realizes it is one with all life. Why is this such a crucial choice?

I earlier described what caused the fallen beings to fall in the spiritual realm. The reason was that they refused to give selfless service to all life but wanted to serve only the separate self. There is a naive belief among spiritual people that once you rise to a certain level of consciousness, you cannot fail or go backward. Yet the stark reality is that as long as you are in a non-ascended sphere, you can indeed fail, no matter how high a level of spiritual understanding you have attained. There are indeed people on Earth who have attained some degree of mastery of mind over matter, whereby they can perform what seems like miracles to most people. Yet they do this to elevate the separate self, and thus they are truly the people Jesus warned you about:

> For there shall arise false Christs, and false prophets, and shall shew great signs and wonders; insomuch that, if it were possible, they shall deceive the very elect. (Matthew 24:24)

Many among the top ten percent are right now facing the crucial choice that will either take them into Christhood or will take them into the selfishness of the fallen beings. The equation is simple. Christhood that is not expressed in selfless service to others is not Christhood. It is simply selfishness masquerading as spiritual attainment, and even though it may show signs and wonders, it is nothing more than the fallen consciousness in disguise. For did not Paul say:

> 13 For such are false apostles, deceitful workers, transforming themselves into the apostles of Christ.
> 14 And no marvel; for Satan himself is transformed into an angel of light. (2Corinthians, Chapter 11)

My point is to show you that if you have read this book up until this point, you are most likely one of the top ten percent of the most spiritual people on this planet. Thus, you have the potential to become part of the movement that will propel this planet into a truly golden age. Yet for you to fulfill this potential, you must overcome the very subtle dualistic illusions I have described in this chapter. You must overcome the last vestiges of the illusion of a separate self and start truly working to raise the one self. This includes exposing and challenging the bottom ten percent—even when they attack you for doing so. And it includes awakening the middle 80 percent, even though they would rather remain asleep in their mortal state and most likely will show little gratitude for your efforts to awaken them to eternal life.

Key 29
How to free yourself from false teachers

I have now explained that the only people who have the potential to free the Earth from dualistic religion are the members of the top ten percent. Yet for you to fill this role, you must – as always – begin at home, begin by removing the beam in your own eye. What I am essentially asking you to do is to help set the rest of humanity free from the influence of the false teachers. And how can you possibly do this unless you have set yourself free from the influence of false teachers?

I must tell you that one of the most delicate problems faced by the Ascended Host is how to get the most spiritually mature people to recognize that they have been influenced by false teachers and then withdraw themselves from these teachers and their false ideas. There are several aspects to this problem, and I will review them in this chapter.

Let us begin with what should be the most obvious problem. All spiritual people recognize that there is something beyond the material universe, whether they call it God, Source, the Ascended Host or something else. Naturally, a spiritual person feels a great sense of loyalty toward that something, feeling it is necessary to remain faithful to God or the spiritual teacher. Obviously, there is nothing wrong with this, as it is indeed appropriate to feel such loyalty toward the beings who are above you in the spiritual hierarchy. As I have explained, you do not progress as a separate individual, you progress by becoming one with your own spiritual lineage, the River of Life. Spiritual people know this subconsciously, and that is why they feel a conscious need to be loyal to their vision of those whom they see as above them in hierarchy.

Yet while we have a constructive and necessary drive for loyalty, there are two potential problems with this. The first one is that even if you are loyal to a spiritual being who is beyond the Earth, you could potentially be loyal to one of the false gods that exist in the emotional or mental realm. Or you could be loyal to a being in one of these realms who portrays itself as a spiritual teacher, perhaps even as a

representative of the Ascended Host. There are beings who imperson-
ate ascended beings and claim to be the real Jesus or the real Maitreya, thus being impostors. If you have become loyal to such a false
god or teacher, it can be very difficult for you to break free. For how
can you break free unless you question the being, and how can you do
that when questioning will be seen as a lack of loyalty? So this can
form a catch-22, and the only one who can break it is *you*.

You must be willing to realize that questioning your God or
teacher is not a lack of loyalty. Why not? Because if your God or
teacher is true, they will have no problem with being questioned. The
real representatives of God have nothing to hide and know that you
will grow only by asking questions. Thus, it is natural that there
comes a point when you do question your teacher or even your God.
As I have attempted to explain, the Creator is beyond the world of
form, so there is no image or spiritual teaching that can accurately
portray the fullness of the Creator's Being. So how can you get to
know that fullness? You can do so only through direct experience,
and you will attain this experience only by being willing to go beyond
any outer teaching. You can go beyond only if you are willing to
question, and thus the Creator knows that questioning is the Alpha
and the Omega, the beginning and the ending, of all progress. Those
who think they know everything are always far from the Creator's
true Spirit, no matter how sophisticated they think they are.

The first problem is that spiritual people can be loyal to a false
god or false teacher who is beyond the physical world. The second
problem is that many spiritual people have come to believe that being
loyal to their God means being loyal to an organization, doctrine, religious leader or guru who claims to represent that God on Earth. Thus,
they dare not question the outer organization, its doctrines or its leaders, feeling that doing so would be disloyal to God. However, as I
have attempted to explain, most spiritual and religious organizations
have been affected by the duality consciousness. And how can they
ever be set free from that consciousness unless the members are willing to ask questions?

The forces of duality, including your own ego and fallen beings,
are not in the least loyal to the true God. Thus, if you do not question
their influence on your religion, you are actually being loyal to *them*
instead of being loyal to God. They have perverted your religion and
taken it away from what God wants it to be, and you are allowing this

to go on by remaining silent. Remaining silent in the name of loyalty to God makes no sense at all. Those who are truly loyal to God or a true spiritual teacher will question anything in an outer organization that is influenced by duality. And they will keep doing so until they either see positive change or until they decide to move on and go elsewhere.

Only the false gods and the false teachers have something to hide, and that is why they will seek to make you believe that you should not question them in the name of loyalty to God. They know they cannot stand up to scrutiny, and the only way they can continue to fool spiritual people is to get them to stop asking questions. For as soon as people do start asking questions, they will clearly see that there either are no answers or that the answers don't make sense. And then people will begin to see through the false doctrines and realize they need to look for a true teacher. So if the top ten percent are to fill their role of freeing the Earth from the influence of false teachers, they need to start questioning everything about their spiritual lives, including their God, their doctrines, their outer organization or an outer guru. If you are not willing to question – if you have mental holy cows that you see as untouchable – you are not on the true path to spiritual freedom.

***

There is misplaced loyalty – you are loyal to the wrong being – and there is false loyalty – you are loyal to an outer representative and not to the transcendental God – and you need to overcome both. How do you begin? In the end it all comes down to discernment, the ability to distinguish between the one truth – the truth with no dualistic opposites – of the Christ mind and the many "truths" of the mind of antichrist. Obviously, this is one of the main characteristics of Christhood, but it is not an intellectual or analytical capability. It is intuitive, meaning that it is based on a direct inner experience. As you attain Christhood, you attain a direct experience of the reality of God, and thus you can experience the difference – the difference in vibration – between what is one with God's reality and what is separated from that reality. For example, you can listen to a spiritual teacher, and even though your outer mind cannot find any flaws in the words being said, you experience that there is something lacking in the person's vibration or intentions. You know there is something not right, even though you cannot express it in a way the analytical mind can grasp or accept.

My point here is that all spiritual people have some degree of Christ discernment—or they would not be interested in the spiritual side of life. So even though you might think discernment sounds abstract or difficult, you already have it. There is no question that if you are reading this book, you have some measure of Christ discernment. However, there are two questions you need to ask.

The first one is whether your discernment is developed to its full potential, and the answer is most certainly a "No!" How can I say that? Because if your discernment was fully developed, you would not be in embodiment on Earth but would have ascended. I am not saying this to discourage you but to help you recognize that as long as you are on Earth, it is prudent to work on sharpening your discernment. And how do you do that? You do it the same way you develop any other skill, namely by practicing it. And that brings us to the second question you need to ask.

I have said that all spiritual people have discernment, but the real question is whether they are using it? Or rather, are they using it selectively, feeling there are some areas of their spiritual lives where they no longer need to ask questions? The ego is on an eternal quest to feel secure, to feel that it is saved. One aspect of this is that it is always looking for a God, a spiritual teacher, a teaching or an outer organization that is the ultimate and can guarantee your salvation. In other words, by merely being a member of this organization or being a follower of this guru, your ego feels that it is saved. And once it accepts this belief, your ego does not want you to question the source of its sense of security. Thus, the ego will try to set up "safe zones" or mental holy cows in your mind, areas where it seems you do not have to question, you do not have to apply your Christ discernment. You might question other spiritual teachers, but you do not question your own. You might question the gods of other religions, but you do not question your own. You might question other religious doctrines, but you do not question your own. You might question the behavior of other spiritual leaders, but you do not question the behavior of your own. You might question many ideas, but there are certain beliefs you never question. In other words, you might question the motes in the eyes of other people, but you do not question the beam in your own eye.

In order to make maximum progress, you need to become aware of these gray areas, these shadowy areas, where you are not applying your Christ discernment. And then you need to start letting your light shine so it can consume all shadows—in which the ego and the false teachers seek to hide. This is a matter of making some clear decisions. Are you truly willing to be part of the movement to set humankind free from the false teachers? If so, start by setting yourself free and you will see more clearly how to set others free. Are you willing to acknowledge that there are false teachers in this world and beyond this world? Are you willing to acknowledge that you have been affected by them, or would you rather remain in ignorance?

Let me give you a useful measure for evaluating whether you have spiritual holy cows, areas of your spiritual life where your ego resists questions. As I have said before, the essence of the ego is resistance to the flow of life, the River of Life. Therefore, the ego is constantly seeking to defend its illusions against the light of truth. In reality, no illusion can stand in the light of truth, as the darkness cannot remain when you turn on the light. So the ego is constantly trying to prevent you from turning on the light in your mind by finding and accepting an understanding that goes beyond the ego's dualistic illusions. Whenever you detect any hesitancy toward having your beliefs questioned or any reluctance to consider new knowledge, you know the ego is at work.

The equation is very simple, and it was described by Jesus in the parable about building your house on sand versus building it on rock (Matthew 7:24). If your spiritual beliefs are built on the shifting sands of the duality consciousness, they will inevitably be threatened by the light of truth, and thus you will resist truth, you will resist questions. Yet if your beliefs are built upon the rock of Christ, you have no need to resist truth and thus you can openly examine any idea that comes to you, dismissing the ones that do not vibrate with truth and accepting the ones that do. As the Buddha put it, "Accept nothing that is unreasonable. Reject nothing as unreasonable without proper examination." It is only the ego that resists properly examining new ideas before you dismiss or accept them.

***

Let me make it clear that there is no shame in having been fooled by the forces of duality. They are very subtle, and it is virtually impossible to grow up anywhere on Earth without being so indoctrinated with dualistic ideas that you do not even think to question them. Yet the eternal question is whether you would rather admit that you have been fooled and thus no longer be fooled, or whether you prefer to remain in the ignorance that some – the false teachers – say is bliss? The hallmark of a true spiritual seeker is that he or she would rather be free than remain enslaved by illusions. And in order to overcome an illusion, you must bring it out of the shadows, out into the light of Christ truth. And in order to do that, you *must* exercise your Christ discernment—which begins by asking questions that no one else is willing to ask or that you have not been willing to ask in the past.

Be willing to honestly examine your spiritual life and beliefs. Are there areas where you are reluctant to ask questions? Are you afraid to ask questions out of a desire to remain loyal or a fear of going to hell? Are you reluctant to admit that a spiritual leader is not walking his talk, so you allow your analytical mind to find excuses or rationalize why the leader does not have to live up to his own teachings?

While you are at it, take this to a higher level by being willing to ask whether you are reluctant to ask questions because a part of you does not want to find out that you have been wrong? The most obvious temptation on the spiritual path is fear and the most subtle temptation is pride. Pride is dangerous precisely because it will make you reluctant to ask the questions that might reveal that you have been wrong. So once you are stuck in a gilded cage of pride, it is very difficult to escape unless you become willing to break the chains of pride.

Yet where does pride come from? I can assure you it is not part of your conscious self or the spiritual identity anchored in your I AM Presence. Pride comes only from the ego, and it is not part of your true Being. Thus, be willing to actively look for signs of pride and use them to force your ego out of the shadows from which it is trying to control you through pride. You need to realize that no matter how persuasive the ego might seem, the ego exists only in the realm of duality, so all of its beliefs are illusions. Thus, the ego is *always* wrong, even though it is desperately trying to create the impression that it is *never* wrong. Once you realize that duality is always wrong, it becomes obvious that it is better for the real you, the conscious self, to see when you have accepted dualistic beliefs. It is better to admit that you have been wrong – and thus stop being wrong – than to continue to be wrong indefinitely. As the popular saying goes, "Fool me once, shame on you. Fool me twice, shame on me." Obviously, I am not encouraging you to feel shameful, I am encouraging you to willingly admit when you have been fooled and then simply move on.

I can assure you that once you begin to consciously see through and separate yourself from the pride of the ego, you will experience a sense of spiritual freedom that most people – even most spiritual people – cannot imagine. The reason being that while you are still trapped on the treadmill of constantly seeking to defend the ego's pride and illusions, you have no idea what spiritual freedom really feels like. That freedom will make you realize that it was completely illogical to hold on to the fear and pride, even though it seemed to offer you certain emotional advantages, such as a sense of security and superiority. Yet why do you need a false security when you are free in the oneness with your own higher being in which you can never be lost? So allow yourself to leave behind the ego's prison and run into the bright sunshine of your own I AM Presence. For when you are willing to let the truth make you free, "there is nothing covered, that shall not be revealed; and hid, that shall not be known" (Matthew 10:26).

***

One of the dilemmas faced by the Ascended Host is how to help spiritual seekers overcome their loyalty and attachment to a false teacher without destroying their belief in any teacher or teaching. There are indeed many people who have come to the conclusion that they have followed a false religion or teacher only to decide that they never want to be fooled again. And they reason the only way to avoid being fooled is to never again trust any teacher or teaching.

The best way for you to overcome this problem is to realize that it is a deliberate plot by the false teachers who are aided by your own ego. As I have said, the forces of duality want to prove God wrong, and one way they think they can do this is to prevent as many people as possible from discovering and following the true path to Christhood. They think that if no one on Earth becomes the Christ, then they have conquered the Earth and taken it away from God. Therefore, the false teachers want you to keep following them, for as long as you do so, you obviously will not become the Christ. They try to set up all kinds of dualistic spiritual movements that can satisfy people's needs to feel that they are spiritual while making sure they never reach Christhood. They create the appearance that their followers are making spiritual progress while keeping them from reaching the true goal, which is the spiritual self-sufficiency that I call Christhood.

Once you have started following a false teacher, the forces of duality do not want you to stop, so what happens when you begin to question the teacher and reach for something more? Well, the overall goal is to prove God wrong by keeping you from the true path, so when you begin to reach for a true teacher, the false teachers and your ego will attempt to prevent you from doing so by destroying your faith in all teachers. They would rather destroy your faith in anything spiritual than to see you find the true path. Once you realize this, I trust you can see the need to go beyond this plot and simply leave the false teachers behind. I also trust you will remember that the Serpent manipulated Eve by sowing the seed of doubt in her mind.

Yet I also know that once you recognize that you have followed a false teacher, it can create a wound that needs to be healed. After all, if you have been fooled once, what is to prevent you from being fooled again, so how can you trust anything? My first comment is that the very fact that you have recognized that you were fooled once has made you wiser and thus lowered the probability that you could be fooled again. My next comment is to remind you that you grow only by experimenting, so even if you have been fooled more than once, you can still turn it into a valuable learning experience—as long as you admit that you were fooled *and* move on. Nevertheless, I also encourage you to recognize that it is the ego who is trying to create the sense of ultimate security by looking for an ultimate teacher or teaching. As I have attempted to explain in this book, there is no ultimate security outside yourself. Even a perfect teacher cannot guarantee your salvation, for it is a matter of your own growth in consciousness. When you fully acknowledge this, you can dismiss the ego's dream of finding an infallible teacher.

The real problem with following a false teacher is that you think the teacher is infallible and thus you can shut off your Christ discernment. As I have tried to explain, you can *never* shut off your discernment, so one might say that there are no infallible teachers. I do not want you to turn this book into an infallible teaching, for surely more will be given as the consciousness of humankind is raised. My point is that the ego tries to get you to follow a false teacher and then it gets you to believe the teacher is infallible so you should never question him or her.

Some people recognize that the teacher they have followed is not infallible, so they immediately start looking for another teacher who *is* infallible. Some people even jump from teacher to teacher for years, decades or lifetimes. Yet a more mature response is to abandon this "Guru-hopping" and give up the entire idea that you need an infallible teacher. What you need is to anchor yourself on the true Path of Oneness, the path that transcends all outer teachers or teachings by leading you to self-sufficiency. When you have a direct inner experience of the Spirit of Truth, you no longer need an outer teacher or teaching. This does not mean that you engage in no outer teaching or religion, but it does mean you never think the outer activity can guarantee or prevent your salvation.

Do you see the fundamental difference? People who are looking for an infallible teacher are looking for a teacher who can do it all *for* them. Once you give up that dream, you can step on to the path of self-transcendence. You can then stop looking for some ultimate expression of truth, for you recognize that there is no such expression in the material world. Instead, you trust your intuition while continuing to refine it. You trust that it has taken you to where you are now and that, as you continue to sharpen it, it will take you the rest of the way to Christhood. With this approach you can never lose your faith in the spiritual path, for you know the path is an ongoing process and not a matter of finding some kind of external savior.

Instead of looking for the ultimate teacher, you are simply looking for the teacher who will take you to the next level. You realize that the real teacher is within, namely your Higher Self. Outer teachers or teachings are only tools used by your inner teacher in order to awaken your outer mind. Thus, when one teacher has served its purpose, your inner teacher might direct you to another one. So instead of thinking in terms of true and false, you simply see each teacher as a stepping stone in the ongoing process of growth. As I have said, even your failed experiments can be turned into progress, and you can actually learn immensely from an involvement with a false or imperfect teacher.

***

All spiritual seekers can benefit from pondering the saying that when the student is ready, the teacher appears. The trick is to realize that the teacher you find is a reflection of your current state of consciousness. Thus, the teacher is the one that is best suited to helping you learn the specific lesson you need to learn at this stage of your personal path. So if you attract a false teacher, the reason is that you need to learn something that helps you go beyond false teachers. Instead of trying to defend your past decisions or explain them away, you simply look for the hidden lesson and then you move on. If you will observe people, you will see that if they do not learn the lesson they need to learn, they will simply attract another teacher who will present them with the same lesson. Yet as soon as you learn the lesson, you will rise to a higher level of the path and now you will attract a higher teacher. Thus, learn what you need to learn so you can rise above false teachers and find the true teachers of humankind.

If you have followed a teacher that you now realize is false, there is a reason why you chose to become involved with that teacher. You might have decided to follow this teacher as part of your divine plan. There can be several reasons why you might choose this:

- You wanted to learn something from following a false teacher.

- You wanted to force yourself to overcome any naiveté and increase your discernment. Following a false teacher and possibly being the subject of various forms of abuse was the fastest way to accomplish this.

- You wanted to help bring about the teacher's judgment.

- You wanted to help expose the teacher – or false teachers in general – to the world, and in order to do that you needed to know what it was like to be inside such an organization.

- You wanted to demonstrate the path. And since most people on Earth are following false teachers, you wanted to demonstrate how to rise above being a blind follower and step onto the true path of Christhood.

When you realize this, you can forgive yourself for following a false teacher, you can forgive the teacher and you can move on. I am in no way trying to justify that false teachers often abuse their followers. I am simply saying that for you it is a non-productive response to go into a consciousness of anger and blame. Doing so only ties you mentally and emotionally to the teacher and stops your growth. It also shows an identification with the ego that wants to blame the teacher. In reality, there is no need to blame others or yourself. You simply learn from the experience and use it to take the next step on the path. Let your basic approach be to never deny, resist, justify or blame but to simply consider whether something helps you grow or hinders your growth. If it hinders your growth, you look for the lesson and once you have learned the lesson, you simply let go of the past and move on. This leads to another important consideration.

***

As I have explained, it is a natural part of the path to Christhood that you begin to share your truth and your light with others. Jesus told his disciples to bear witness to the truth (John 18:37) and to let their light shine (Matthew 5:16), so other people could see that both come from God. Yet does that mean you have to reach some state of perfection before you can attempt to teach others? Should you retreat to a cave in the Himalayas and wait until you have attained full enlightenment, or should you begin to teach based on your current level of consciousness and attainment?

I am not here denouncing that some people do find it right to retreat until they have attained a higher level of consciousness before they start teaching. Yet in this age, there simply isn't time for everyone to take that approach. As I have explained, human beings are behind where they should be in terms of understanding and applying Jesus' teachings on personal Christhood. So there is a great need for people to start teaching the path as they see it with their present level of consciousness. That is why it is indeed in order that many people do step into the role of being spiritual teachers of various kinds.

It is obvious that some of the people who act as spiritual teachers are not in any way perfect. Yet that is not really a problem—if both they and the spiritual seekers who learn from them can let go of the ego-dream of finding an infallible teacher. Thus, it can be recognized that no being on Earth has the ultimate understanding but that some do have a more advanced understanding that allows them to inspire and help others. Yet those who teach also need to acknowledge that they are not done learning, and thus they must be willing to transcend themselves, even by going beyond or correcting something they have taught earlier.

My point here is that there are many people on Earth – and hopefully more will dare to take up this role – who are right in serving in the capacity of spiritual teachers. Yet those people will not always be right in what they teach, for they teach based on their current level of understanding and Christhood, which is not the highest possible. This does not mean that they should not teach, nor does it mean that they are false teachers. In other words, you cannot define this in black-and-white terms by saying that a true teacher can never say anything "wrong" and that anyone who says something wrong is a false teacher. I want you to distinguish between false teachers and imperfect teachers.

It is another plot of the fallen consciousness to define a standard of perfection and say that anyone who does not live up to it is a false teacher. The false teachers do this by using the duality consciousness, so they make it seem like they are the only true teachers and that anyone who differs is a false teacher. So what is the real difference?

What I have attempted to explain in this book is that spirituality is not about finding an infallible outer teaching, organization or teacher. True spirituality is about following the Path of Oneness, which is a path of ongoing self-transcendence. In other words, being a true teacher is not about saying something that is ultimately true, for ultimate truth cannot be expressed in words. Being a true teacher is about always reaching for the Spirit of Truth that is beyond all outer teachings. It is about living and demonstrating the true path of self-transcendence.

How do you do that? By *never* thinking you have found the ultimate truth and by *always* seeking to transcend your current level of consciousness. My point is that there are many teachers who still have a somewhat limited understanding of spiritual concepts and still have some human flaws and idiosyncrasies, yet they are still true teachers in the sense that they demonstrate the path of self-transcendence.

***

Then what makes a person a false teacher? It is that the person is *not* following the path of self-transcendence but is trying to set himself or herself up as some kind of infallible authority who cannot be wrong and thus should not be questioned or gainsaid. If you look at the history of religion, you will see this pattern repeated over and over again, where people and institutions have made the claim to infallibility. You see it very clearly in the Catholic Church whose leaders claimed that if you questioned the pope, you were questioning God. As I have explained, there is nothing wrong with questioning God, for the true God has nothing to hide and wants you to find his truth. Which is precisely why Jesus said, "Seek, and ye shall find; knock, and it shall be opened unto you. For every one that asketh receiveth; and he that seeketh findeth; and to him that knocketh it shall be opened" (Matthew 7:7-8). Jesus knew that questioning is the beginning of wisdom.

You also see some people who have tried to set themselves up as an unquestionable authority by claiming to be an incarnation of some ultimate being, such as God or even Maitreya. Such people are always making a false claim, for the Creator or an ascended being does not descend into incarnation. I realize this is a subtle point, so let me explain. The Creator is ultimately nothing more or less than a specific identity. It is an identity that is very far beyond the identities of most humans, yet it is still an identity. That identity *is* the Creator and will remain so for as long as this world of form exists (until the void is filled). So the identity that is the Creator will not descend into a physical body on planet Earth and claim that God has now taken incarnation. This is true for Jesus – who never claimed to be God – and for any present guru who might make this claim.

The conscious selves of all beings are extensions of the Creator's Being. Yet they are endowed with an individual identity. Thus, although they are out of the Creator's Being, they are not the same as the Creator. As I have explained, attaining oneness with God does not mean attaining sameness with God. You are meant to retain your individuality while expanding your sense of identity to the level of a God, thus becoming an individual God who is at the same level as – but not the same as – your Creator. Yet this expansion of identity simply cannot be attained while you are on Earth, for this planet is in a sphere that is not yet ascended.

My point is that it can be said that a person is the incarnation of God—but this claim is only true when it is understood that if one person is an incarnation of God, then other people are also incarnations of God. Therefore, there never has been and never will be a human being on Earth who can rightfully make the claim to be the exclusive or the full incarnation of God. Meaning that if a person makes that claim, then he or she is trapped in the most subtle form of dualistic illusion possible—the desire to elevate the separate self above all others, to turn the separate self into a god. Making this claim turns a person into a false teacher.

It is valid to say that a person has come to remember and accept that he or she is God incarnate and is an extension of, an individualization of, the Creator. Coming to the full realization that "I and my Father are one" (John 10:30) is indeed part of the path to Christhood, and it obviously sets you apart from most other people. Thus, one can say that Divinity appears in a human form, but that is not the same as saying that the Creator – in its fullness – is incarnated in a human body or is incarnated exclusively in a particular body.

When you really have attained oneness with your source, you realize that all other people are also extensions of the Creator's Being. Thus, you are not here to set yourself up above others by having them revere or worship you as a god on Earth. You are here to help them see that if God is in one person, God must be in all people. Thus, if they see something divine in you, it is because they are seeing a reflection of their own Divinity. And instead of putting you on a pedestal, they need to follow the path you have followed until they too can accept their own inherent Divinity. In other words, if you really are God incarnate, you are here to raise up God in all people, not to have them raise you up to be a god on Earth. The Creator is the ultimate servant, so anyone realizing that he or she is an extension of the Creator's Being will naturally serve as the Creator serves. Only the false teachers have a need for other people to serve or worship them. Thus, as Jesus said, by their fruits ye shall know them (Matthew 7:15-20).

***

We can now see that the Path of Oneness is an ongoing and an inner process. No teacher can produce your progress for you. You have to produce that progress by expanding your understanding and internalizing it, whereby you raise your consciousness. A teacher might help you take one or several steps on your path, and even a false teacher can – when you see through the deception – be instrumental in helping you overcome certain illusions. Many people have had a tendency to avoid taking responsibility for their own growth, thus wanting to blindly follow a leader. Only by experiencing the severe abuse of a false teacher have they decided to accept that they are ultimately responsible for their own salvation.

My point is that the path is an ongoing process, and your true loyalty should be to the path and your continued progress. If a teacher is helping you rise higher, then learn from that teacher. But be aware that there might come a point when that teacher cannot take you higher. Thus, remain alert for the inner prompting to look for another teacher. It is a law of God that when the student is ready, the teacher appears. Yet it happens over and over again that a student is ready for a new teacher, but the student is so attached to its old teacher that it does not even see the new one as it appears. Misguided loyalty to a specific teacher – rather than to the universal teacher – has held back many students on the spiritual path. It is time for you to step up to a new approach, whereby you always follow the highest possible teacher you can see, while constantly striving to expand your vision so you can see an even higher teacher.

That, of course, holds true for this book as well. As said before, I am not claiming this book is the ultimate revelation possible. I am claiming it is the most direct revelation on this topic yet given on this planet. It is *not* the final revelation, for there will never be a final revelation. Much more can be said, much more detail can be given, for what is given here is a reflection of the consciousness of humankind and the messenger who is bringing forth the teaching. Yet be not dismayed by this, for the book can still help you and millions of others raise their consciousness and anchor themselves on the Path of Oneness. And as you climb to higher levels, you will be given a higher revelation, either through an outer teacher or directly within your own Being.

Always be willing to question and look beyond your current teacher. If it is a true teacher, it will only strengthen his or her ability to teach and it will only increase the students' understanding of the teacher. And if it is a false teacher, your questions will serve to set yourself free and potentially bring about the exposure or judgment of the teacher. This can then set others free to move on to a higher teacher rather than remaining stuck at their present level. Sincere questions can only serve to further the cause of the ongoing growth in people's consciousness, the growth that the false teachers are doing everything they can to stop. Make your contribution to having them fail by finding your role in the process of setting the world free from dualistic religion.

Key 30
Creating a new openness in the religious debate

Based on our previous discussion, it should not be difficult to see what needs to happen in order to free the world from dualistic religion. We obviously need to free religion from all elements of the fallen consciousness, the duality consciousness. The way to do this should also be obvious, for as we have seen, the duality consciousness can only survive in the shadows, where it is not seen or seen for what it is. If people knew better, they would do better, so the duality consciousness can influence people only because it hides behind a veil of deception and manipulation.

However, forcing the illusions of duality out in the open will require a special effort, which can be seen from the fact that no mainstream religion openly talks about the duality consciousness and the human ego or gives a deeper understanding of the beings who deliberately oppose God's plan by deceiving humankind. In fact, no human effort can bring this about, but with God – acting through human beings who are willing to rise above duality – it will be possible to completely change the tone and content of the religious debate.

There are already enough people in embodiment to bring this change about, namely the top ten percent. These people have reached a state of consciousness where they can quickly come to see through the smokescreens created by the forces of duality. Yet having the understanding of duality is only half the battle, for the spiritual people also need to overcome the stranglehold of intimidation that prevents a free debate about religious issues. This intimidation works in individual churches – to varying degrees – and it works on a world scale. After centuries, even millennia, of oppression and intimidation, many religious people are simply afraid to publicly ask any kind of critical questions about religion, particularly their own religion. The top ten percent can quickly overcome this intimidation, but the challenge will be to help a critical number of the members of particular religions to overcome their fear of thinking and talking freely about issues relating to religion and God.

The forces of duality are very determined and quite skilled in terms of manipulating humankind. They have also had a very long time in which they have had virtually free reign on this planet—caused by the fact that people simply have not known about fallen beings and their influence. This condition was obviously created by the fallen beings in past ages, when they removed any reference to their existence and identity on this planet. Thus, humans have been as unprotected against the manipulation of fallen beings and the false gods as they were unprotected against disease before they knew about bacteria. Ignorance truly is not bliss.

Because of this, it is foreseeable that many people will have some resistance toward acknowledging many of the facts I have exposed in this book. As I said in the beginning, I have presented truth in a direct manner, and the reason is that I know many among the top ten percent are ready for this truth. Yet I also know that many among the general population are not ready for the full truth. Modern psychologists are aware of the mechanism called the flight-or-fight syndrome. When presented with a threat, people will instinctively seek to avoid it, and if they cannot escape, they will turn and fight it. Yet there is a related mechanism that most people are not aware of. When people are faced with a threat that seems too overwhelming, they will neither flee nor fight, but they will instead refuse to acknowledge the threat, as an ostrich buries its head in the sand. They will use the relative logic of the duality consciousness to belittle the message or the messenger, or they will find other ways to justify ignoring the threat.

For many people the full truth I have given in this book will be so overwhelming that they will be unable to acknowledge it. If people do not yet have the inner knowing that the power of God is far superior to any dualistic forces, they will refuse to see that there is a dualistic force. This is precisely the reason the dualistic force has remained unknown and unrecognized for so long, and this is the very mechanism that will prevent many people from removing the veil of ignorance. Once again, a catch-22.

Another reason why many people will rather remain ignorant is that if they acknowledge the existence of the dualistic force, they know it will be such a serious threat to their freedom that they simply cannot ignore it. And since they do not yet believe God can defeat this force (through them), they would rather continue to know nothing about it. Likewise, they sense subconsciously that if they acknowledge the threat, they cannot continue to live as they do now. And since they are unwilling to change their lifestyle, they will look for ways to justify ignoring the message.

My point here is that it is not my intention to see the top ten percent go out and preach a message based on the direct truth I am giving in this book. My intention with this book is to educate those who are close to rising above duality, so they can take the final step and attain the full truth that will set them free from both the consciousness and the forces of duality. Once you have claimed that freedom for yourself, you can go out and serve to set other people free, but in doing so you must practice the art of the possible. As I have explained, you probably chose to embody in a particular environment in order to learn how people in that environment think. You can then use this experience to sense what those people are ready to hear and how you can best present it to them.

I realize this will be a challenge, and some will want me to give them more detailed instructions. However, please remember that the more mature students must face the test of becoming spiritually self-sufficient. In Mother Mary's book and this book we have given you everything your outer mind needs in order to connect to your own higher being. And when you *do* connect, you will receive directions from within as to how you can express a higher truth to the people with whom you are familiar. In other words, the real purpose of this book is *not* to tell you everything you need but to awaken in you the memory of who you are and why you came here. You must then accept who you are and accept that it is part of your mission to go within and get the exact directions from your own higher being rather than from a source that will be seen as external. You must embody the teachings so you can teach them to others by example. It is when the general population see the top ten percent rise above duality and demonstrate this publicly that *they* will gradually be empowered to rise above duality.

What I will give you in this chapter are some general instructions about what needs to be exposed and what most people are ready for at this time.

***

A majority of the people in the Western world know – within their inner beings – that something is wrong with religion. Many realize that things are not as they should be in their churches, which is demonstrated by such things as the pedophilia scandal in the Catholic Church and other events that demonstrate how religious leaders are not walking their talk, are not living up to the standards set by the spiritual teachings of their religion. Many people also realize that there is an element of deception in many religions and that things were taken out of the Christian religion centuries ago. Many people have been disappointed by the behavior of religious leaders or by the rigidity of the outer institutions. Many people feel that the churches in which they grew up can no longer meet their spiritual needs in this modern age. Many churches are stuck in the past and simply *cannot* or *will not* adapt to the challenges presented by life in a fast-changing world.

My point here is that in the Western world there is a general discontent among a majority of the people, but so far these people have had no clear vision of why they feel something is wrong with or missing from their religion. Yet people are rapidly becoming more open to looking for explanations beyond traditional sources, and this is where the most spiritual people and the Ascended Host have an opportunity to expand people's vision. A majority of the people in the Western world are ready to receive the understanding that what causes things to go awry in religion – as well as in their personal lives and in society – is the human ego and the duality consciousness. These people can quickly be helped to see that everything they sense is wrong with religion is caused by the ego that uses the duality consciousness to pervert the original purpose of religion—a purpose that most people have some awareness of in their hearts.

Many people are ready to look for the beam – the ego – in their own eyes, for they have already received some awareness of the ego from the self-help movement. This movement has for decades opened people's minds to a deeper understanding of psychology, including the existence of the ego. People are ready for a breakthrough that connects the dots and shows them how the human ego has influenced religion for thousands of years and how the characteristics of the ego have distorted virtually every aspect of religious life. This will cause many of the people who are still involved with religion to see that it is possible and necessary to take religion to a higher level. It can also cause many of the people who have abandoned religion to see that it is not actually religion itself, but ego-based religion, that they cannot accept.

My point is that a critical mass of people are ready to see that religion is the one area of society where the duality consciousness should not be allowed to operate. They are also ready to see that in order to counteract the influence of the ego, it is absolutely necessary that the duality consciousness must be openly discussed and exposed. Time has simply run away from the approach of remaining silent or pretending nothing could be wrong with your religion. People are ready to call a hypocrite a hypocrite and they are ready for a new initiative to remove all hypocrisy from religion. In other words, people are ready for a new openness, whereby it becomes possible, even necessary, to discuss many of the things that were previously considered taboos in the religious debate.*

In fact, this is a development that the fallen beings and the false gods are quite aware of. Some of them know this tide can be slowed down but that it cannot be stopped. They are still trying to slow it down as best they can, for example in the attempt to use fear to make people turn to fundamentalist religion that insists on the infallibility of the scriptures of the past. Yet some of the more advanced fallen beings have realized that openness cannot be stopped, so they are trying to direct the debate into areas of their choosing. The motto of the fallen beings has always been that if you can't beat 'em—join 'em, and they are seeking to steer the religious debate into a blind alley that will obscure the real cause of the problem and allow them to stay in control of this planet. Some fallen beings are quite ready to destroy modern people's faith in all religion and elevate scientific materialism as the "one true religion." Therefore, it is necessary that the most spiritual people engage in the debate and put it on the right track, namely the track that will lead people to see what is taking away their spiritual freedom so they can find the truth that will make them free.

This is your challenge, namely to engage in the religious debate and take the initiative away from those who are trapped in the duality consciousness—whether they do so unwittingly or with some knowledge of the forces they serve. The main goal is to establish a new

---

* For an example of how to expose the ego and duality in religion, see *I Love Jesus, I Hate Christianity* by Kim Michaels.

approach to religion, an approach that makes it clear that in the modern world it is time to raise religion above duality and the human ego. It is time to establish non-dualistic religions on this planet. Let me give you some pointers on the specific areas in which the influence of the ego needs to be exposed.

***

Many people are becoming aware of what some see as the danger of all religion, but which is truly the danger of an unbalanced and extremist approach to religion, an approach that fosters fanaticism. Historically, this has been seen in the crusades, the Inquisition, the witch hunts and other obvious atrocities, including a string of religiously motivated wars. In the modern world, it is most clearly seen in radical Islam and the justification of terrorism, suicide bombing and so forth. There is growing talk of a clash of civilizations between the Muslim and the Christian world, and this has made many people open to taking a critical look at the role of religion in society. Potentially, this is a positive development, but it will be so only if the debate is taken beyond just discussing outer religions and their influence.

What needs to happen is that the debate is opened to the fact that religion in itself is not causing atrocities. Thus, creating an entirely secular society will not guarantee a peaceful world. On the contrary, religion has an important effect on setting limits for the worst forms of human behavior, in that it raises the fear of an eternal punishment that no one can escape. I am not saying this is the highest possible motivation, I am only saying that in a secular society this motivation is gone, and it will inevitably lead to more extremist behavior. This can already be seen in some Western nations, where young people organize in gangs and have no respect for any restrictions of their behavior. Likewise, you see a rise in organized crime, based on the philosophy that since there is nothing beyond the material world, you might as well take what you can while you have the chance. This is the inheritance left by the Western world's flirtations with scientific materialism and secularism, going back to the split between science and religion—a split that was obviously caused by the duality consciousness.

What needs to happen is that the debate about the role of religion in society begins to incorporate the human ego and the duality consciousness. In reality, religious fanaticism is caused by the ego and its tendency to take every issue toward one of two dualistic extremes. This causes black-and-white thinking, which naturally leads to the extremist view that there is only one true religion, and if "our" religion is not victorious, the entire planet will be destroyed and humans will burn forever in hell. Thus, it is justified to use violence and other extreme measures in order to prevent the ultimate calamity. It is acceptable to kill people's bodies in order to save their souls from eternal damnation.

Many people are ready to understand that the entire concept that the end can justify the means springs from a dualistic view of life. They are ready to see that this is a typical example of the hypocrisy of the ego that causes selfishness to be disguised as altruism. It is exactly what Jesus addressed when he talked about those who focus on the mote in the eye of another – making them the scapegoats that must be fought with all means – as an excuse for ignoring the beam in their own eyes. Many people are ready to understand the true cause of religious fanaticism, and they are ready to acknowledge that it is high time to dispense with the idea that there is only one true religion.

It is possible to help people see that the concept that one religion is superior to others springs from and fuels the pride of the ego, which is always comparing itself to others. Thus, religion has been hijacked by the ego and in some cases this has caused religions – and no religion has ever been completely exempt from this – to go too far toward an extremist approach, often leading to violence. It is thus high time for the people of the world to become aware of this tendency and decide to take their religions back, wrestling them from the grip of the human ego.

Many people are ready to see that a lack of balance is always made worse when there is no openness and debate. Fanaticism thrives in the shadows because people are intimidated into not asking logical and rational questions. This has led to all kinds of violence, including the madness of the Crusades where two religious groups killed each other in the name of the same God. In today's world, you see it outplayed in Islam, where the moderate elements are too often intimidated into silence by the radical elements. In the West you have seen how the pedophilia scandal in the Catholic Church was kept secret for

decades because too many church members and leaders were intimidated into silence, fearing that the church would condemn them to
hell if they blew the whistle on the priests. You even see some modern fundamentalist churches that are as filled with fear as the Catholic
Church of the Middle Ages. And you see more moderate Christians
who are reluctant to speak out against fundamentalism.

It is absolutely necessary to help people realize that in this age it
is time to create a new openness and honesty in the religious debate.
It is time to dismiss the idea that an outer church has the power to
send you to hell, and thus you should remain silent in the face of
obvious abuses of power. For truly, all religious leaders who use religion to incite violence are guilty of the worst form of abuse of power.
They are making a karma for themselves that it will be very difficult
for them to balance, and thus it is a mercy toward them to expose
their fanaticism and get the public to put an end to it by refusing to be
intimidated. The same holds true for some Western fundamentalist
leaders who likewise encourage an extremist approach to religion.

The world is ready to dispense with the entire idea of religious
fundamentalism, including the belief that any religious scripture
could ever be the infallible word of God and thus should stand
unchallenged for eternity. People are open to the understanding I have
given in this book, namely that any scripture is adapted to the state of
consciousness of the recipients, and thus God can tell modern people
much more than he could tell nomadic tribes living thousands of
years ago. Genesis was never meant to be the final word on how the
world was created, and much more can be given today.

And while many people may not be quite ready for the teachings I
have given in this book, they are certainly ready for a higher teaching
that unites science and religion. In fact, many people are ready for a
world view that reconciles science and religion, for they know within
that the so-called war between science and religion is simply another
dualistic battle. In reality, science and religion are two parallel ways
for expanding the consciousness of humankind, and by removing
fanaticism on both sides, they could learn from each other, leading to
a greatly expanded and refined world view.

***

As I have explained, there are certain spiritual cycles that guide the growth in humankind's consciousness. The planet is entering into the Aquarian Age, which is an age of spiritual freedom. As a result, the Ascended Host are releasing certain spiritual energies that will affect people and turn their awareness toward the importance of freedom in all of its aspects. I am not saying all religious people are ready to hear about the Age of Aquarius, which will be too "New Age" for some, yet all are affected by the energies. You can see this in society, for example how communism was overturned without a third world war. You also see a growing awareness around the world of the value of freedom, causing people to take a stand against oppression. In the West, many people have been lulled asleep, but they are ready to be awakened to the awareness that there are forces who will try to take away their freedom and that in a democracy they always work in the shadows. Thus, eternal vigilance is the price of freedom.

In fact, many people are ready to see that throughout history there were always a small elite of people who would do anything to attain power, including suppressing the general population by all means available to them. People are ready to understand how the hidden hand of such a power elite can be seen behind most of the atrocities of history. Thus, the struggle for freedom is truly a process of the general population becoming aware of the existence of a power elite and deciding to no longer submit to its oppression. People may not be ready to identify the power elite as fallen beings, but they are ready to see that a power elite does exist and that its members are blinded by their egos. When you understand the ego, you see that when the ego is not directly addressed but allowed to thrive in the shadows, the inevitable outcome will be a power elite who seeks to suppress the general population in order to gain the power and privileges that their egos crave. And in a democracy this suppression happens primarily through a suppression of information so the general population is kept unaware of what is happening.

In the religious arena, many people are ready to understand that putting people in a physical prison is a very primitive way to control them. When people know they are oppressed, they will long for freedom and sooner or later they will revolt. Thus, the most efficient way to control the population is to use the mind by programming people to enter and stay in a mental prison. Once there, they will either think there is no other way to live or they will think there is no way out—at

least not while they are on Earth. Many people are ready to acknowledge that religion has historically been the most efficient tool for
brainwashing the population into accepting a status quo that allowed
a small elite to maintain a position of near absolute power. When people believe that the priesthood of an outer religion has the power to
send them to eternal damnation, that priesthood has near absolute
power over the people. And as has been said, absolute power corrupts
absolutely, for the human ego will always take things to the extremes,
and thus no person can handle having absolute power over others.

The simple fact is that religion has been used to suppress the population through a clever combination of fear and the promise of a
reward. On the one hand, people have been brought up to believe that
if they do not obey the outer church, they will burn forever in hell. A
worse form of punishment could hardly be imagined, but as I have
explained, such a punishment was never imagined by the Creator. It is
the exclusive product of the duality consciousness and has no reality
to it whatsoever. God never sends anyone to hell. People can create
their own mental hells, and they have even created a collective hell in
the emotional realm and in certain places on the physical Earth. Yet
the force of life itself will make sure that no one can remain trapped
in such a hell forever. In fact, in an ever-transcending universe, there
is no such thing as forever.

Combined with this fear of the ultimate punishment is the promise of an ultimate reward, in the form of eternal life in a remote
heaven. The psychological effect is that many people have been programmed to accept abuses and suppression here on Earth because
they think that by doing so they will qualify for an eternal reward in
heaven. This has – for long periods of time – allowed a small power
elite to use religion to maintain a status quo that kept them in power,
not only in religious organizations but also in society. An unholy alli-
ance between church and state has often suppressed people to the ultimate degree.

Many people are ready to see that this suppression is not an inevitable by-product of religion itself. It is an inevitable by-product of
allowing religion to be ruled by those who are blinded by the duality
consciousness and controlled by their own egos. Thus, it is high time
to expose the influence of the ego and how it creates a power elite,
even in religious organizations. In fact, religious organizations have a
tendency to attract people who are so blinded by their egos that they

want ultimate power over others. As I have explained, religion is unique in offering leaders an almost godlike power on Earth, a power that those who believe in the outer religion simply cannot question or oppose. Obviously, this is why fallen beings in embodiment are often attracted to leadership positions in the most powerful churches.

I caution that many people are not yet ready for the truth that a number of prominent religious leaders have been and are indeed fallen beings who are absolutely committed to the cause of anti-christ, even to the cause of proving God wrong. Yet many people are ready to understand that religion offers a unique opportunity for those who are so blinded by their egos that they seek power for its own sake. They seek power as the ultimate way to create the illusion that their salvation is guaranteed. If people have a position of absolute power in a church and if they use it to do what they have defined as God's work, they think God simply has to save them. I am not saying this is true, I am only saying that this is what some people believe.

In conclusion, people are ready for a message that makes it clear that it is necessary to eliminate all fear and force from religion. Religion must be set free from the ungodly influence of the ego and its attempts to use fear to control the population. In fact, it is high time to take religion beyond the age-old dualistic struggle between two opposing polarities, the struggle that has created all of the violence and atrocities seen throughout history. There simply is no longer room for fear and force in religion. Instead, we must establish an approach to religion that is based on joy and love. Only it must be unconditional, divine love and not the self-centered, ego-based love that seeks to control.

The more spiritually mature people are ready to recognize that the hallmark of the fallen beings and the false gods is an atmosphere of fear mixed with subtle pride and the sense of superiority. The result is that no one dares to question anything, so there is no openness, no dialogue. Many people will be able to understand that the duality consciousness thrives in the shadows, and when there is no openness, shadows can remain indefinitely, allowing the human ego to remain in control of religion. This must be changed, and it can only happen when the most spiritually aware people decide to speak out rather than withdrawing from organized religion.

***

Many people are ready to see that intrigue, secrecy, elitism and power plays should no longer be allowed to dominate religious life behind the scene. They are ready to see that it is an unacceptable contradiction to have any kind of secrecy and manipulation in religion. Why is this so? Because all power plays on Earth are based on keeping things secret so that only the elite who make decisions are "in the know," whereas the members of a religion are considered unfit for the full knowledge of what is going on behind the facade. Yet consider that this is happening in the field of religion, which is supposedly an endeavor that is an intermediary between human beings and God. What is the insanity that makes some people think that what they can hide from other human beings on Earth is also hidden from God?

Well, that insanity is the spiritual blindness of the human ego, which literally makes people believe that they can hide from God, thinking that if they can fool other people, they can fool God. This goes back to the belief that students in the Garden of Eden could hide something from the teacher. Yet isn't it time to expose this logical fallacy and root it out from the religious life of this planet? Isn't it time to recognize that if a religion and its leaders feel they need to hide something from their own members, then that something most likely would not be acceptable in the eyes of God? And if it isn't acceptable in the eyes of God, it should not be happening. Furthermore, if it isn't acceptable in the eyes of God, it should not be allowed to be hidden from the eyes of human beings – who are extensions of God – and thus it has no place in a modern, non-dualistic religion.

**

As I have explained earlier, the ego can never be saved, it can never become acceptable in the eyes of God. Thus, it is constantly trying to create an outer appearance according to which God simply has to save the ego and the people who are blinded by its dualistic logic. This has led to the belief that an outer religion on Earth can guarantee your entry into heaven, and one offshoot is that there is only one true religion. Another offshoot is that the leaders of the one true religion are in a special class. Not only is their salvation extra guaranteed, but they will also attain a superior position in heaven, just as they now have it on Earth.

Once a religion has become affected by this dualistic logic, it will inevitably attract the kind of people who are completely blinded by the duality consciousness, and they will take the religion and its doctrines even further into the jungle of duality. They will attempt to create a system in which they are on top and no one can challenge or even question their superiority. Once such an elitist system has been established, it will be very difficult to reform it, and it is important to understand why.

If you will take an honest look at how certain religions select leaders, from priests to even higher positions, you will see a clear pattern. Logically, one would think that the leaders of any religion should be those who had embodied the principles of the religion to the highest degree. They should be the most selfless, meaning the ones who have overcome their egos and established a high degree of Christhood. In reality, such people are kept out of leadership positions in many churches. Instead, these organizations select people who are willing to uphold the status quo, those who will not challenge the church's doctrines or organizational structure, including the elitist system of leadership. In other words, those who are selected for leadership positions are those who are willing to compromise truth in order to get along in the organization, those who are willing to go along with duality in order to attain a position in the outer organization. In contrast, those with Christhood are not willing to compromise the truth – as Jesus demonstrated by challenging the religious elite – and thus they either will not apply or are deliberately kept out.

I am not saying this unnatural selection happens consciously, for in most cases religious leaders think it is their duty to preserve the status quo. They think they have a responsibility to keep their religion pure from what they see as a compromise with tradition or scripture. They truly do not think to question whether the status quo is out of alignment with the true teachings of Christ (or the founder of their religion), for had they been prone to such questioning, they would never have attained leadership positions in the first place. My point being that once a church has passed a critical mark, the selection of leaders becomes a circular process. Only the leaders have the power to change the status quo, but you can become a leader only by demonstrating that you do not want to change the status quo.

How can this closed circle be broken? Only by demanding a new openness and accountability in religious leadership. People must

become aware that secrecy creates shadows, and the duality consciousness will always grow in shady areas. The equation really is
quite simple. There should be nothing going on in a religious organization that is not acceptable in the eyes of God. And if everything is
acceptable to God, then there is no reason to keep it hidden from the
eyes of God's people. Thus, people need to stand up to their religious
leaders – in a non-aggressive and non-dualistic way – and demand
openness and accountability, including greater involvement and over-
sight by members. By demanding openness and by demanding leaders with true humility and spirituality, people can fundamentally
change their religious organizations and take them away from the
forces of duality. People get the leaders they deserve—until they
demand better ones.

***

Why did elitism ever become such an ingrained part of the religious
life on this planet? Because from ancient times there has been a subtle
belief that not all people are equally suited to knowing the truth of
God. Some people are more spiritual than others, and thus they have
the ability to serve as intermediaries between God – the spiritual
realm – and the general population. Hence, the concept of a spiritual
elite was born and has persisted to this day.

    In a sense it could be said that this book promotes the idea of a
spiritual elite. I talk about the top ten percent of the most spiritual
people, and I say that the general population will not bring about
change. Even Jesus had a small circle of close disciples, and while he
taught the multitudes in parables, he expounded all things to his disciples (Mark 4:34). So the real question is how we can recognize the
fact that human beings have different levels of spiritual awareness
without falling into the trap of pride and elitism?

    The only way – the absolutely only way – to avoid the pitfalls of
elitism is for the top ten percent to recognize the profound truth in
Jesus' denouncement of the hypocrites, those who look for the mote
in the eye of another while ignoring the beam in their own eyes. The
top ten percent *must* recognize that pride is the most subtle enemy of
spiritual growth. In fact, the very logic of the Serpent itself was based
on a subtle form of pride, namely the thought that I know better than
God and thus I can ignore the teacher's instructions. I am somehow

so special that I am above the laws of God that apply to most other people. The real danger of religious elitism is that it uses a religious teaching to justify that some people feel they are above others and thus above the laws of God that only apply to those others. This trap is so subtle that it is extremely difficult to escape once you have been caught in its spiritual quicksand.

The only way out is to recognize that the entire idea that some people are above the law is a complete fallacy, an illusion that springs from the duality consciousness. As the Bible says, God is no respecter of persons (Acts 10:34), and God's laws apply to all people. You will not enter the kingdom without putting on the wedding garment of the Christ consciousness (Matthew 22:11-12). No scheme thought up by the duality consciousness will ever fool God, and thus there simply is no way to cheat your way into heaven. Only when you recognize that the duality consciousness creates a complete fantasy world, and sets up rules that make it seem like an elite are above the people, will you be able to see through this trap. You must recognize that there is no point in pretending, no point in creating conditions on Earth and thinking that living up to those earthly conditions will guarantee your entry into heaven. Hypocrisy in the field of religion is truly the greatest fallacy of all, for even though you may fool all people on Earth, your ego has no chance of fooling God. As Jesus so clearly stated, "For what shall it profit a man, if he shall gain the whole world, and lose his own soul?" (Mark 8:36). Consequently, those who are truly the most spiritually mature people will always be the ones who are the most humble.

Yet even humility can be perverted by the ego, and many people put on a facade of humility. The true humility I am looking for is not the false humility of belittling yourself. I am talking about a humility that is based on realism, namely that all beings came from the same source. When you see that all life is one, you see that all value judgment is meaningless. All beings have the same infinite value in the eyes of God, for all are extensions of the Creator's own Being. There are no comparisons in infinity, and thus no being is better or worth more than any other. Once you realize this, you can recognize that some people have attained a certain maturity that makes them wiser than others in certain areas. Yet this can be recognized without imposing the value judgment that this makes them better than others or entitled to special positions or privileges in a human society or reli-

gious organization. That is why Jesus chastised his disciples for fighting over who would be the leader after he left. He told them that those
who would be greatest among them should be the servants of all
(Mark 10:44). For when you realize the value of all life, you seek to
raise up the All rather than raising up yourself in a dualistic comparison to other people.

The hallmark of pride is judgment that degrades others, which is
why Jesus told people not to judge after appearances (John 7:24). It
truly is a divine law that as you judge other people, so will you be
judged at the end of your current lifetime when you receive a cosmic
performance review. I can assure you that in such a review – as
reported by some people who have had a near-death experience – all
pretence and all hypocrisy falls away and you see your life with
greater clarity. So why *pretend* to be a spiritual person when we have
given you the knowledge of how to truly *be* a spiritual person? Why
go for the fool's gold when you have access to the real thing by building your house on the rock of Christ truth instead of the shifting sands
of the illusions of the ego?

***

In order to fully understand elitism, it can be helpful to understand the
codependent relationship between those who want to be in an elite
and those who want to follow an elite. I am not saying everyone is
ready for this understanding, but the top ten percent need to have it so
they can free themselves from the superiority-inferiority dynamic.

As I have explained, there were some beings in higher realms
who rebelled against God's vision and laws. These leaders had
attained powerful positions with a great number of beings under
them. Many of these beings followed their leaders when they fell and
many of them have blindly followed their leaders ever since. In the
long time span that has passed since the original fall, two distinct
identities have been created, and they have been reinforced by many
beings, including some on the physical Earth. So you now have these
two distinct identities:

- The identity of the false leaders, the power elite. This is an
  identity that thinks it knows better than God and better than all
  other people. It obviously cannot maintain this sense of superiority by interacting with God, so it needs to do so by comparing

itself to other people. Thus, its survival is dependent upon having a group of followers who act as if they are subservient to the superior leaders. This identity often defines an adversary, a group of people who are the scapegoats and who must be fought with all means. This battle helps the elite justify taking freedom away from their own subjects.

- The identity of the followers. This is an identity that will not take full responsibility for its life and salvation. When people enter into it, they refuse to step up and become spiritually self-sufficient by making their own decisions. These beings refuse to become the Christ, whereas the leaders think they are superior to Christ. In order to maintain this identity, these people need a group of leaders who will tell them what to believe and how to live. And they need their leaders to ensure them that as long as they follow the leaders without question, they are guaranteed to be saved. In order to uphold this belief, people also need an adversary, a group of people who – since they are not following the superior leaders – are guaranteed to receive eternal punishment in hell. This allows the followers to feel inferior to their leaders but superior to their adversaries, thus neutralizing their fear of being lost.

What you see here is a distinctly codependent relationship between leaders and followers. Without followers, the leaders could not maintain their illusion of ultimate superiority. And without leaders, the followers could not maintain the illusion that they can be saved without making their own decisions. To maintain their illusion, the followers need to feel better than other people, so even though they are too inferior to make their own decisions, their association with the superior leaders still gives them a sense of superiority compared to the "damned" who are not following the leaders. The followers refuse to step up and become the Christ, so they turn their leaders into false Christs who will do it for them. They even elevate the false leaders to the status of infallibility, which justifies that they follow them blindly.

My point here is that what psychologists call the inferiority and the superiority complexes are simply two sides of the same coin. We might say that when a being separates itself from its spiritual teacher, it creates the ego, the separate sense of identity. The ego can never be acceptable to God, so it has a chronic, built-in inferiority complex.

Yet the ego cannot live with the sense of being inferior, of being damned, and to compensate it creates the sense of superiority. In other words, the superiority complex is simply an attempt to cover over the underlying inferiority complex. Yet the inferiority complex came after the fall which was caused by the belief that you know better than God. This belief is obviously a form of superiority. However, why would you even think that you knew better than God – why would you even need to compare – unless you already had a sense of inferiority? My point here is that we end up with the same kind of problem illustrated in the old question, "Which came first, the chicken or the egg?" The real point is that inferiority and superiority are simply two sides of the coin of duality—what Jesus called Mammon. And as he said, you cannot serve both God and mammon (Matthew 6:24), meaning that both inferiority and superiority has to go before you can win your spiritual freedom.

***

Inferiority and superiority cannot be separated because they are part of a classic dualistic polarity. One simply cannot exist without the other, and the real cause is a lack of Christ vision, an inability to see God's reality. When you do see Christ truth, you see that you are an extension of God's Being, so you are inherently worthy. By being all that you are, by being here below all that you are above, you have no need to feel inferior to anyone, not even the Creator—for you are out of the Creator's Being. At the same time, all other people are also out of the Creator's Being, so you have no need to feel inferior or superior compared to anyone. You have no need to compare, for comparisons spring from duality. You were created as a unique individual and your task is to express your individuality to its fullest measure. When you are focused on being all you can be, you have no attention for comparing yourself to others. When everyone is unique, how can comparisons have any meaning?

What the top ten percent need to see is that the entire dynamic of inferiority and superiority springs from the duality consciousness. It is likely that you have grown up in an environment in which there is an elite, a group of followers who gain pride from being inferior to the elite and a scapegoat that is inferior to the followers. Thus, you need to demonstrate that it is possible to step out of this codependency and live as a God-free individual who is neither a blind follower nor a power-hungry leader. You need to demonstrate that people are more than these outer identities, that their conscious selves can step outside these roles and be on Earth the spiritual beings they were created to be. This will open the way for people overcoming the need to feel that their religion is the only true one or is better than all others. And only when people overcome the inferiority-superiority dynamic can there be real religious tolerance on this planet.

Key 31
How religion needs to change

Let us look at some of the concrete changes that must be brought about by the top ten percent. It is extremely important to bring forth a widespread understanding of the fact that the role of an outer religion is *not* to save people. The major goal of true religion has always been the transformation of consciousness, and in this age you see it exemplified in the self-help movement. Obviously, most members of the top ten percent have already understood this and are living it. Yet what most have not understood is why there is so much resistance to this idea from traditional or mainstream religions. In fact, most people in the top ten percent see spiritual truth as so obvious that they cannot understand why others cannot see it. I hope you can now understand that other people cannot see truth because they are still blinded by the duality consciousness. Thus, you need to help them become aware of their blindness and its cause before you can help them see the truth that is obvious to you. You think truth is obvious because you are no longer looking through the filter of duality, so you need to help other people go beyond that filter as well.

The idea that religion will not save you but will help you transform your consciousness will meet fierce resistance from both the blind leaders and their blind followers. The reason is that this very concept threatens the fragile illusion upon which the inferiority-superiority dynamic is based. If people can bring themselves closer to salvation through their own efforts, then the blind followers no longer need the leaders to save them, and they no longer have an excuse for not making their own decisions. Likewise, the leaders can no longer maintain the sense of superiority that has become more important to them than anything else. Thus, you can see why both groups fiercely resist the idea of personal transformation and why they will resist seeing religion as a tool for self-transformation. They will cling to the idea that people cannot save themselves and that they need an outer religion and its leaders in order to be saved.

How can you help such people? It will often be necessary to be non-threatening and to allow them to maintain their basic illusion while getting them to accept the concept of self-help for other reasons. For example, Jesus clearly said that the kingdom of God can be found only by going within (Luke 17:21). He also told his followers to remove the beam from their own eyes (Matthew 7:5), and in this age people can be helped to understand that he was referring to the human ego and its dualistic reasoning that prevents them from having the single eye – the non-dualistic vision of Christ – that makes their whole bodies filled with light (Luke 11:34).

Jesus also told Christians not to be blind followers (Matthew 15:14) and he warned them about false leaders who would appear in his name (Matthew 24:24). So there are many elements of Jesus' teachings that can be used to open people's minds to the need for personal transformation.* Yet it is necessary for you to realize that some people are not ready or willing to take responsibility for themselves, and thus you must be content to demonstrate the path while being non-attached to the reactions of others.

***

Another area that needs to be exposed is the fact that women should be given equal status in all churches. The basic fact is that women are *not* responsible for the fall of man. Every individual being made its own choice that led to the fall. Eve is not a symbol for women but a symbol for your lower being, which is the feminine polarity of your total being, as your spiritual self is the masculine polarity. Thus, the feminine-masculine polarity of your lower and higher being is independent of the sex of the physical body you are wearing in this life. In past lives you have been embodied in both male and female bodies, so it is meaningless to blame women for the fall and to relegate them to secondary positions in churches. I realize this discrimination is based on Biblical references, but it is high time to recognize that these references were not the infallible words of God but the distortions of a male-dominated culture. It is thus high time to dispense with them and to allow women to hold any position in any church.

In fact, it is high time to recognize that the entire concept of inequality, even conflict, between the sexes is another expression of the duality consciousness. The strategy of the fallen beings has always

---

* For an example of how this can be done, see *I Love Jesus, I Hate Christianity* by Kim Michaels.

been to divide people—by making them houses divided against them-selves and by setting groups against each other. Setting men and women against each other in a struggle for superiority is simply another ego game that must be brought to a halt before a golden age can be manifest. Only when men and women work together in har-mony can they and their society reach the full potential.

Because women have been suppressed for so long, it is necessary to compensate for this by allowing women to take more prominent positions in society, including in religious life. This does not mean that we need a role-reversal in which women seek to take the superior roles that men have had or seek to punish men for the oppression of women. It means that women need to find their rightful role as full equals in every respect, so that there can be complete harmony between the masculine and feminine polarities in human society. Yet this will also mean that women must not stop being women or seek to adapt themselves to a male-dominated culture. We do not need women pretending to be men, we need a society that respects the unique qualities of both men and women, allowing both to be expressed in full measure.

* * *

The role of sacred scripture in religion needs to be discussed openly, so that many of the dualistic beliefs about scripture can be examined and replaced with a non-dualistic view of scripture. I have already talked about this in previous chapters, but to quickly summarize, it needs to be seen that any religious scripture was given to a specific group of people and that it was a reflection of their state of conscious-ness and their understanding of the world. Thus, it was never meant to be seen as the infallible word of God that could guide all people for all time.

The way fundamentalist people approach scripture is actually an attempt to control God. For example, many Christians are effectively saying, "Okay God, you brought forth the Bible, but we will never allow you to bring forth any additional revelation. As far as we are concerned, you will never again be allowed to speak to humankind." Obviously, this mindset is simply an outgrowth of the fallen con-sciousness and its attempt to prove that God was wrong by shutting him out from this world. This mindset wants to create the appearance that this world is separated from God and that God can work in this world only on special occasions and through special people. It thus denies the fact that God is not bound by any of the limitations created by human beings and institutions and that the Ascended Host can – at any time – bring forth new revelation through people with open minds and hearts. It also denies that every human being has the potential to become a Christed being, thereby becoming an open door for God's light and truth to stream into this world.

What is the logic in recognizing that God did bring forth a sacred scripture through direct revelation but that the almighty God could only do so once? Well, the logical explanation is that the fallen beings have taken over the religious life of this planet, and they want to keep God and the Ascended Host from breaking their stranglehold over the people. When religious leaders fiercely defend their scripture, the hidden goal is to hold back a new revelation that can overthrow the status quo. And it is only the fallen beings and false gods who benefit from upholding the status quo.

There is a great need for the emergence of an openness to new revelation from the Ascended Host. Obviously, this raises many questions, such as how you determine what is valid revelation – what truly comes from the Ascended Host and what comes from the false gods – but this is part of the point. For in wrestling with such questions, human beings sharpen their Christ discernment and put on personal Christhood. By blindly adhering to a so-called literal interpretation of past scriptures, no one has ever moved closer to Christhood.

The entire cult of idolatry built around Jesus has the sole purpose of preventing anyone else from following in his footsteps and declaring their Christhood. The fallen beings had so much trouble with Jesus that they never want to see another one like him on "their" planet. They think they have made it, but it is time for the most spiritual people to prove them wrong!

***

It is necessary to bring attention to the fact that there is nothing wrong with religion following the times. It is obvious that human beings know much more about the world and themselves, including the human psyche, than people knew 5,000 years or even 2,000 years ago. Thus, it should be obvious that people have a better foundation for understanding all aspects of the spiritual side of life, which has two obvious implications. One is that humankind can now receive a higher revelation from the Ascended Host than at any previous time in recorded history. The other one is that it is time for religions to give clear and rational explanations for their doctrines, beliefs and rituals.

It is untenable to maintain the dualistic struggle between science and religion. Thus, religion must recognize that one of the beneficial effects of science is that it has demonstrated that the natural world makes sense and is guided by consistent laws that can be understood rationally. Science has also shown that if something seems mysterious, it is simply because people do not yet know how it works. Yet by systematically seeking to understand, and by performing experiments, people can increase their understanding, and all phenomena will eventually be understood. It is high time for religious people to recognize that the same holds true for the spiritual side of life. Jesus' miracles were not supernatural events. They were produced by a person who had attained a state of consciousness in which he could make use of higher spiritual laws – not known by science or most religions – whereby he could supersede the natural laws that are known by science.*

I sincerely hope this book has demonstrated that there truly is nothing about the spiritual side of life that cannot be explained and understood in a rational, consistent and intelligible way. It is no longer acceptable that religious leaders defend their doctrines by brushing people's questions aside with the remark that, "It's a mystery." There is nothing that you are not allowed to know, for the Creator has no secrets and has nothing to hide from its offspring. In fact, as you strive for the Christ consciousness, everything shall be revealed to you. For it is your own state of consciousness that limits what you are able to know about God. How can you know the one reality of God until you are willing to look beyond the veil of duality?

As I have attempted to show, only the forces of duality have something to hide, so they are the ones that want to maintain a sense of mystery in religion. This is simply a smokescreen to hide the fact that many religious doctrines are dualistic and thus are contradictory or have no rational explanation. To keep people believing in such

---

* For a more detailed discussion of these concepts, see *Beyond Religious Conflict* by Kim Michaels.

doctrines, churches must prevent people from thinking about them in a rational manner. It is time to help religious people see that you will not be sent to hell for asking questions. In fact, by *not* asking questions, you condemn yourself to remaining in the dualistic hell that people call "life." You condemn yourself to staying in the mental prison created for you by the fallen beings, just as people during medieval times stayed in a mental box that made them believe the Earth was flat.

You live in a modern age, and in this age religion should make sense. People have a right to demand that their religion either gives consistent and rational explanations for its doctrines, culture and practices, or that it reforms itself so that it *does* make sense. God and God's laws *do* make sense, so if a religious doctrine doesn't make sense, it is because it is out of alignment with God's reality and influenced by the duality consciousness. It is time to prevent the forces of duality from hiding behind a facade of infallibility or the fear that you will go to hell for asking perfectly logical questions.

It is necessary for spiritual people to learn certain lessons from science and apply them to the field of religion. Using the scientific method to investigate spiritual experiences is an opportunity to increase people's understanding of such experiences, even make it easier for people to have them. Many other aspects of religious life can be investigated by science. Obviously, in the current climate of open warfare, science is so materialistic that most scientists either will not or do not dare to investigate religious phenomena. This must be changed by challenging the false leaders in both science and religion.

Certainly, science has also been influenced by the fallen consciousness. In fact, materialistic science has become one of the most powerful tools for the fallen beings who want to prove God wrong by destroying humankind's belief in God and getting people to deny their spiritual origin and potential. However, I can assure you that as non-duality begins to reform religion, science will be reformed as well. There are already many people in the field of science who have a spiritual outlook on life, and it is only a matter of time before a critical mass is reached and the materialistic stranglehold on science will be broken. Yet my concern in this book is to reform the field of religion, because it truly is the key to reforming every other aspect of society.

The bottom line is that you can indeed find logical and rational answers to all questions about God and spirituality. If a particular religious teaching cannot answer your questions, then be willing to look outside that teaching. Stop allowing the false teachers to put you in a mental box that gives you only the answers they want you to have, the answers that will not overturn the status quo in which they feel they have control over life on this planet. As Jesus said, seek and ye shall find, knock and the door to understanding shall be opened unto you (Matthew 7:7), for there is not any thing kept secret, but that it should come abroad (Mark 4:22).

***

Behind the more specific topics mentioned above – and obviously there are too many such topics to mention here – there is one overall topic that needs to be brought out in the open. It is absolutely necessary to wrestle with the topic of why religion so often divides people rather than serving as a unifying factor. When you think about this, you realize that all religions claim that they seek to reconcile people with God and they recognize that God created everything. So if the members of a religion are becoming increasingly reconciled with their God, and if their God created everything, should they not realize that their God must also have created all other people? And therefore, isn't it logical that religious people should start feeling closer to other people, even if these people call God by a different name or worship him in different ways? If religion is meant to help people go beyond appearances on Earth, why do religious people so often become stuck in focusing on earthly appearances?

Obviously, we have now seen why religion is so divisive, including the influence of the human ego and the existence of false gods who are warring amongst each other and want people to fight each other so they can steal their energy. Nevertheless, it is time for the more mature spiritual people to recognize that if religion is not unifying people, it is not true religion. It is indeed dualistic religion that is ruled by the ego and the duality consciousness. Thus, the more mature people must rise above this divisive approach to religion and adopt a unifying approach.

In doing so, they must stay out of the classical dualistic trap, namely the belief that religious unity must be brought about by one religion exterminating all others and becoming universally recognized as the one true religion. True religious unity will not eradicate all religions except one but will bring unity between the members of different religions. This will happen when a critical mass of spiritual people become aware of the duality consciousness and decide to rise above it, thus seeing that they all came from the same source and are simply following different roads back to their source.

What needs to happen is the emergence of a universal movement of religious people who are openly committed to oneness, including the Path of Oneness that I have described. Such people can create a true interfaith dialogue that can become an essential vehicle for bringing about the new, non-dualistic approach to religion that I am describing in this book. I have said that it is not my goal to start a new religion. Yet it may be advantageous to create a new organization that is dedicated to oneness—as long as it does not position itself as the only true alternative to existing religions.

To avoid this, one might envision an umbrella organization with individual chapters, such as Catholics for Oneness, Lutherans for Oneness, Hindus for Oneness, Muslims for Oneness, Buddhists for Oneness and so on. In other words, the organization is not seeking to replace other religions but to increase the awareness of the concepts of oneness and non-duality in all religions. The central organization serves only for the coordination of dialogue between the specialized groups. It is a contact point, not a controlling entity. While such an organization might find some inspiration in this book, I do not expect it to be based on, to promote or to demand allegiance to my teachings. It must be truly universal and present its teachings independently of this or any other specific source.

***

Let me make it clear that in freeing the world from dualistic religion, the above measures are not enough in themselves. Surely, if the top ten percent and the 80 percent of the general population all decided to become aware of and abandon dualistic religion, humankind could eventually remove all such religion. Yet this is not a scenario that is likely to come about in the foreseeable future. So what is the point of even doing any of these measures, if they cannot remove dualistic religion? Well, the point is that what is done by people in embodiment will be multiplied by the Ascended Host, as Jesus described in the parable about multiplying your talents.

The people in the top ten percent do not have the power to remove evil from the Earth, but they can give the Ascended Host the authority to remove a particular evil. One might say that people in embodiment have the authority to remove evil, but they do not have the power, whereas the Ascended Host have the power but not the authority. The obvious answer is to combine the authority of people in embodiment with the power of the Ascended Host, which is precisely why the false leaders have been trying to insert themselves as intermediaries between the people and their ascended teachers. Because of the influence of dualistic religion, this plot has been quite successful, but it is not that difficult to overturn the false teachers. This will involve the following elements:

- The false teachers derive their power from the beasts who in turn are largely conglomerates of misqualified energy. Since everything is made from energy, the concentration of a certain type of energy into a beast creates a gravitational pull that can overpower or at least influence people's thoughts and emotions. One way to diminish this pull is for a critical mass of people to stop feeding their energies to the beast, and this can be done through expanded awareness. Yet another way is for a smaller number of people to actively call for the transmutation or consuming of the misqualified energy. All lower energies can be consumed by invoking higher spiritual energies. This will reduce the magnetic pull of the beast and thus break the vicious cycle of a beast overpowering people. As the pull is reduced, it becomes easier for people to free themselves from the influence of the beast, which feeds it less energy and so on until a positive spiral or momentum is created.

    How do you transmute misqualified energy? Through appropriate spiritual rituals! In fact, many religious rituals were originally given as a means for people to free themselves from negative energy. Yet the Ascended Host have continued to release such rituals and the latest effort is the release of Mother Mary's Miracle Freedom rosaries and other techniques.*

---

* See *www.askrealjesus.com* and *www.marysdivinedirection.com*.

- Everything is subject to the free will of people in embodiment, so the Ascended Host cannot remove a beast or a group of fallen beings until a critical mass of people separate themselves from the consciousness of the beast and decide that it is no longer acceptable on the Earth. There is enormous power in people deciding that a certain manifestation is no longer acceptable to them. One example is how people in the 1800s decided that slavery was not acceptable. This led to the removal of a large part of the planetary beast of slavery, but unfortunately it has to some degree been recreated by those who are still willing to treat other people as property that can be bought and sold. Yet as the awareness of modern slavery grows and people develop the determination to overcome it, the beast can quickly be further reduced.

- People in embodiment can, when they have removed the beam from their own eyes, call for the judgment of Christ upon the false gods and the people who embody the fallen consciousness. This will then give the Ascended Host the authority to bind or neutralize a beast so that it can no longer exert a pull on people's minds. The beast can remain bound until the contracting force of the Mother breaks it down and the Ma-ter Light is purified. Or a beast can remain bound until humankind is ready to face the final initiation to overcome the consciousness it represents. This is explained in the following quote:

  > 1 And I saw an angel come down from heaven, having the key of the bottomless pit and a great chain in his hand.
  > 2 And he laid hold on the dragon, that old serpent, which is the Devil, and Satan, and bound him a thousand years,
  > 3 And cast him into the bottomless pit, and shut him up, and set a seal upon him, that he should deceive the nations no more, till the thousand years should be fulfilled: and after that he must be loosed a little season. (Revelation, Chapter 20)

Many fallen beings have been taken out of physical embodiment for a time and are now in the astral plane. Some of them are or will be allowed to reembody – either now or in the future – in order to test whether humankind has risen above a certain state of consciousness.

- There are people on Earth who are absolutely committed to the fallen consciousness, but they are allowed to embody here because most people have not separated themselves from that consciousness. In a sense, we might say that this is allowed because these fallen beings can make the evil of a certain state of consciousness more visible so people can see it and receive another opportunity to rise above it.

  The danger is that the gravitational pull of such people can pull humankind further into a downward spiral. Yet when people do begin to see through a dualistic illusion, they can call for the judgment of the people who embody that illusion. When this is done with sufficient Christ authority, such beings will not be allowed to re-embody and the Earth will be free from their downward pull. However, the law requires that for a fallen being to be removed, someone on Earth must have risen to the level of consciousness that the fallen being had before it fell. Jesus caused the removal of certain very dark beings, as explained in the Bible quote above. This is indeed why he said, "For judgment I am come" (John 9:39).*

  It must be understood, however, that some fallen beings will be allowed to embody to test whether the people will follow them again. Will people refuse to follow the Living Christ and instead follow the false leaders in religion, music, government and business? If people do not follow such "wolves in sheep's clothing" (Matthew 7:15), they will be permanently removed and the planet will have risen to a higher level.

- Before a certain beast and the beings who embody it can be fully removed from this planet, the Christ truth that sets people free from the dualistic illusion must be preached to a critical mass of people. People must have the opportunity to choose between Christ truth and the illusions of anti-christ, and they will not have that opportunity until they encounter a person who has embodied Christ truth. This is explained in the following quote:

---

* For specific techniques designed to allow people to call forth both spiritual protection, the transformation of misqualified energy and the judgment of the fallen consciousness and false gods, see *www.askrealjesus.com*.

> And this gospel of the kingdom shall be preached in all the world for a witness unto all nations; and then shall the end come. (Matthew 24:14)

The gospel that shall be preached is the true gospel of Christ, namely the gospel of non-duality. The end that shall come is not the end of the world but the end of duality, the end of the world that is based on the duality consciousness, in fact created from the duality consciousness. You will then see the following prophecy fulfilled:

> And I saw a new heaven and a new earth: for the first heaven and the first earth were passed away; and there was no more sea. (Revelation 21:1)

We now see that there is an Alpha and an Omega aspect to freeing the Earth from dualistic religion. The Alpha aspect is that the top ten percent free themselves from the dualistic illusions and free their own beings from all misqualified energies. As they do this for themselves, they can then do the spiritual work of calling for the transmutation of energy on a planetary scale and calling forth Christ judgment upon the beings and beasts who embody a certain type of evil. In a sense, this is something people can do on an individual basis or in separate groups. It can be done without interacting with the general population.

Yet the Alpha aspect will not be enough in itself, for it must be supplemented by the Omega effort of awakening the general population and all members of the top ten percent. Obviously, the two efforts go hand in hand. As more and more energy is transmuted and as more and more fallen beings are judged, the gravitational pull will be lessened and it becomes easier for people to see through a certain dualistic illusion. Thus, it becomes easier to awaken people to the illusion and get them to separate themselves from it. As they stop feeding the beast, a positive spiral is created that will awaken more and more people, and eventually an entire beast and all beings who embody its consciousness can be removed from the Earth.

This process has been going on for a long time, but as I explained earlier, it has been a slow progression. In this age there is the potential that large numbers of people can be awakened and can join this effort consciously, which can accelerate the process tremendously.

Yet as I said, this will happen only if the top ten percent decide to not only do the Alpha effort but also go out and demonstrate to the people that it is possible for all beings to be the Living Christ in embodiment.

Key 32
Non-dual interactions

We have now arrived at a crucial point that has traditionally been the one thing that has prevented the top ten percent from taking dominion over this planet. That point is how you deal with other people, and it is absolutely essential that the spiritual people of this age make an uncompromising commitment to finding a way to treat each other that is not dualistic in nature. This chapter will offer some suggestions.

One of the most persuasive dualistic lies is the concept that the end can justify the means. Another equally subtle lie is that everything that happens in the material universe is ultimately real or permanent. And the third lie is that what happens in the material universe really matters in this world. When these three lies are combined, you have the perfect storm that causes people to be completely enveloped in, blinded by and emotionally attached to an activity in the material world. They now start acting as if the outcome of their efforts is a matter of some ultimate importance, such as life or death or the end or salvation of the world. And since their efforts have an epic importance, it is justifiable that in order to accomplish their goals, they treat people in a way that is clearly against their own religious teachings. After, all what does it matter that we mistreat people if we do it to save their souls or save the world—or so the ego reasons.

This form of religion-based insanity simply must come to an end, and I am calling on those who have read this book to be the forerunners for a new culture that treats people on Earth the way beings in the spiritual realm treat each other. That means without deception, manipulation, pretension, judgment, controlling love, unkindness or any of the other dualistic games. I am calling on people to find a way to have non-dual interactions.

The reality – as I have explained it in previous chapters – is that nothing in the material universe is ultimately real in the sense that nothing in this world has yet attained the permanence you find in the spiritual realm. This world is not a quarry where people chisel sculptures in stone, it is a sandbox where mistakes can – relatively speaking – easily be erased. Thus, the actual events that happen in this world cannot have ultimate or everlasting importance. Your salvation does not ultimately depend on your outer actions in this world but on your state of consciousness. Of course, what you do in this world *is* a reflection of your state of consciousness, but the point is that it is by reforming your consciousness, not your outer actions, that you qualify for eternal life.

What has ultimate importance is not what happens outside of you – the results of your actions – but what you allow to happen inside of you in response to what happens outside of you—your *re*actions. Consequently, it is not appropriate to act as if any activity on Earth can mean the end or the salvation of the world. The Earth should be viewed as a theater where everything is simply the stage, set pieces and props. "All the world's a stage" as Shakespeare – a messenger for the Ascended Host – put it. Human beings are actors who have temporarily taken on a costume, namely the physical body and outer personality. You know that what happens in a play is just a story, so what is the purpose of the play? Well, a good play has the effect of transforming both the actors who perform it and the people who watch. My point being, that planet Earth is a theater that is designed to give the actors – human beings – an opportunity to engage in a play – in which they can play any part they want – and thereby be transformed and reach a higher state of consciousness. The important thing is not what actually happens in the play but that the actors are transformed. The process is more important than the results, the journey more important than the destination.

The spiritually mature people need to develop a realistic sense of what is important and what is not. For example, it is not of cosmic importance that a particular religion gathers members and becomes the dominant one in your country or the world. The measure of success from a spiritual viewpoint is not the same as it is from the viewpoint of most humans. The Ascended Host have no desire to see one religion become dominant, for we see religion only as a tool for raising people's consciousness. If a religion – however small – truly transforms people and helps them come closer to Christ consciousness, then the religion is a success. Yet if a religion only takes people into a state of spiritual blindness or fanaticism, then it is not a success, even if it managed to convert the whole world. What shall it profit a religion if it gains the whole world yet loses the souls of its members?

My point is that the real goal of the Ascended Host is to raise people's consciousness, *not* to achieve any particular outer goal on Earth. Surely, we would like to see the manifestation of a Golden Age of peace and prosperity, for such an age would give people a better opportunity to focus on spiritual growth. Yet the emergence of such an age is only a side-effect of raising the consciousness of a critical mass of human beings. Thus, our real goal is always the raising of consciousness, and it should be your goal as well.

An extreme example of the unbalanced approach to earthly activities is war, where the individual is unimportant and where any number of individuals can be sacrificed for the goal of defeating the enemy. The mission is more important than people. Yet I hope you can now see that this is in complete opposition to how the Ascended Host work. For us, the mission is never more important than the people, for the mission *is* the people. We are *only* concerned about raising people's consciousness and we *never* compromise that goal in order to accomplish an outer goal on Earth. Thus, I want the spiritual people to adjust their thinking and likewise never compromise the true goal of raising up people.

What would be the point in the spiritual people using this book to start a new religion and start acting as if it is the ultimate religion that must replace all others, thus treating people the way every other religion does? *There would be no point,* and thus it is essential for you to spend some effort on adjusting the way you look at the purpose of religion. You need to study how religions treat people and learn from them for better and for worse. There are plenty of bad examples, but there are also some good ones.

***

In order to develop non-dual interactions, you will – as always – have to start at home by pulling the beam from your own eye. The foundation for dealing with others in a non-dualistic manner is that you first learn to deal with yourself in a non-dualistic manner. When Jesus told you to do unto others what you want them to do unto you (Luke 6:31), he was really saying that what you do unto others, you have already done to yourself. If you treat other people with anger, it shows that at subconscious levels you are angry with yourself.

The most important step in the right direction is for you to *de*personalize your life. You need to seriously consider my teachings on your true identity and fully internalize that the core of your being is the conscious self. This self is more than your body and outer personality, even more than the personality you have built over many embodiments. And when you begin to reconnect to your higher being, you realize that anything that happens on Earth is of lesser importance than your progress on the Path of Oneness. Therefore, you should never let anything on Earth come between you and that oneness, you should never allow anything to prevent you from taking the next step on the Path of Oneness. The only way to attain this goal is to never take anything personally, to overcome the attachment that – as the Buddha said – causes all suffering.

You need to overcome the sense that you are a victim, which is one of the hallmarks of the fallen consciousness. So let me ask you to consider a simple question. Do you have a written contract, signed by God, which says that if you agree to take embodiment on Earth, you are guaranteed certain benefits and you are protected from certain unpleasant circumstances? And if you have no such contract, why would you live your life as if you *did*, thereby thinking you are entitled to certain things and becoming dissatisfied when you don't get them? Many people seem to think that it is a basic human right that life lives up to their expectations. In reality, your basic right is to experiment and to experience the consequences of your choices, whereby you can rise above your dualistic expectations, even rising above the human condition.

The single cause of all human unhappiness is unrealistic expectations, and those expectations are created by the human ego and the false teachers. These beings are very skilled at putting people in a catch-22 in which they expect that life should be a certain way, but the expectation is completely unrealistic. Thus, people spend their entire lives chasing a carrot dangling in front of their noses, while having no chance of ever reaching it. People are condemned to living unfulfilled and unhappy lives in which they rarely grow spiritually because they don't overcome their false expectations and often simply "give up on life."

As I have explained, planet Earth is currently a mixed environment, so it simply is not realistic to expect some kind of heavenly perfection. To avoid expecting too much and taking life too seriously, you need to become conscious of the fact that nothing on Earth is ultimately real or is of epic importance. You are like an actor and your body and outer circumstances are simply the stage for a play. You know very well that an actor in a play is a real person who puts on a costume and makeup. If the actor is good, he might identify himself with the part to the point of temporarily feeling as if he really *is* Hamlet. Yet when the play is over, he takes off the costume and reverts back to his real identity. If an actor refuses to take off the costume and continues to act as Hamlet outside the theater, you would immediately see this as a form of insanity. So as a spiritual person you need to separate yourself from the collective insanity of identifying yourself with and as the role you are playing here on Earth, thereby taking life too seriously and taking everything that happens to you personally.

Ideally, you should never take anything that happens to you personally, for you should realize that you are a spiritual being who cannot be affected by anything that happens on Earth. As Jesus said, fear not him who can kill the body, but fear him who can destroy both the body and the soul in hell (Matthew 10:28). Yet who can destroy your soul? You might have been conditioned to believe that the devil or other dark forces have the power to destroy your soul against your will, but I hope my teachings have shown you that this is not so. No force in this world can destroy the real you—except of course the being who controls your free will, namely yourself. You are the only one who can destroy your soul, for you are the one who defines your identity. Surely, you can reject this responsibility and allow others – including your ego – to make decisions for you, and then they can potentially destroy your lower identity. Yet you have to allow them to do so and you can – at any time – take back your power to define your identity. In reality, there is no such thing as a hell from which you cannot escape—it is a concept created by the false gods to scare people into submission.

You need to take back command over your mind and redefine your sense of identity, so you realize that you are a spiritual being who is temporarily playing a role in the stage production called "Planet Earth." Thus, you should take it no more seriously than you would take a stage play. You have heard the saying that beauty is in the eye of the beholder. Likewise, offense is in the mind of the person taking offense. Surely, some people may deliberately try to offend you, but you are the one who must decide whether you will let them offend you and thereby allow them to have power over your mind. Your mind is your castle, and the conscious self should be in complete command of what happens inside your mind.

The most important realization for any spiritual seeker is the fact that there is no direct cause-and-effect relationship between what happens *outside* your mind and what happens *inside* your mind. For everything that happens outside will affect your mind *only* by going through you—that is, if you accept the call to have dominion over your mind. You are the one who decides how outside events affect your state of mind, and the – often overlooked – key to spiritual mastery and freedom is to have dominion over how outside events affect – or rather, do not affect – your mind. In order to have dominion over your life, you must take dominion over your responses to outer situations. You must get yourself in a frame of mind where you are never forced by outer events to go into negative thoughts and feelings. Instead, you have complete freedom of choice as to how you react to outer events. You never let other people force you into a negative reactionary pattern, and thereby you never give them power over your mind. This can be done only when you depersonalize your life so you do not take anything that happens to you personally. You can control your actions only by first controlling your *re*-actions.

What other people do to you, they are only doing to the outer person they see, and you know you are far more than that person. In fact, you might consider that what other people do *to* you, they are not actually doing *against* you. They are simply acting out their roles in the planetary drama—acting out their own unresolved psychology. Even if they have identified themselves with *their* roles, that does not mean you have to identify yourself with *yours* or identify them as theirs. Let us take a closer look at this concept.

***

I have said that a Christed being goes into the world to give people a real choice between the reality of Christ and the illusions of antichrist. Yet you cannot make people understand the difference through intellectual reasoning, so you must demonstrate the difference. One way to do this is to demonstrate that you do not react and respond to life and other people in a dualistic manner. You do not allow outer circumstances or other people to take away your peace of mind, your inner oneness with your higher being. You can say with Jesus, "The prince of this world – meaning the entire dualistic force – cometh and has nothing in me" (John 14:30). The dualistic force has no element of duality or attachments in your being whereby it can force you into reacting in a dualistic manner. In order for you to be in a state of mind in which you are not tempted to respond dualistically, you must enter into a state of perpetual and unconditional forgiveness.

As always, you must begin at home by unconditionally forgiving yourself. Let us look at the concept of unconditional forgiveness. You have been programmed by the ego and the false teachers to believe that everything should be conditional, including love and forgiveness. This is a direct result of the duality consciousness, which makes every concept dualistic. Forgiveness is truly a non-dualistic concept, but the ego makes it dualistic by saying that it must have an opposite. From this springs the concepts of holding a grudge and of not being saved if you are not forgiven, concepts that have no reality in God but only exist in the shadows of the dualistic mind. We now have a mental construct which says that if you are not forgiven, something terrible will happen to you. It also says that forgiveness can be obtained only by living up to certain conditions in this world, conditions defined by the duality consciousness. If you do *this*, you are forgiven, if you do anything else, you are *not* forgiven.

In reality, the very reason you need forgiveness is that you have partaken of the forbidden fruit, the duality consciousness. If you believe in the dualistic lies about forgiveness, you can never find true forgiveness. You will think you need to live up to certain dualistic conditions before you can receive forgiveness. Yet God gave you free will, so God gave you the opportunity to partake of duality. Obviously, God does not want you – does not want part of itself – to remain stuck in duality. So God will instantly forgive you, the very moment you decide to let go of a dualistic illusion and take a step higher on the Path of Oneness.

Do you see what I am saying here? You do not need to meet any conditions in this world – any conditions defined by duality – in order to receive God's forgiveness. The eternal rain of God's forgiveness descends upon the just and the unjust (Matthew 5:45). The problem is that the unjust cannot accept it for the very reason that they cannot let go of their dualistic illusions. For that matter, the just often cannot accept it either, thinking they have to live up to certain outer conditions in order to be forgiven by God. Yet as I have tried to explain, God's forgiveness is unconditional, so all you have to do to receive it is to abandon the dualistic conditions you have set up in your own mind—the very conditions that make you think there is a distance between you and God's forgiveness. Once you realize that this sense of distance is another dualistic illusion, you will be fully immersed in God's Flame of forgiveness. You then realize that you do not have to earn God's forgiveness by *doing* anything on Earth. You simply have to accept it, which means you have to *stop doing* things on Earth, you have to stop acting and reacting based on the duality consciousness. Every step you take toward forgiveness based on a dualistic illusion will only bring you one step further into the dualistic jungle.

To give you an example of this, consider how the Jews at Jesus' time believed that by sacrificing animals they could compensate for their sins. Yet their sins were committed out of a non-sensitivity to all life. So how could killing innocent animals compensate for that? You could sacrifice thousands of animals – turning the temple of God into something resembling a slaughter house – without coming closer to God's forgiveness. The only way to be free from your sin is to rise above the dualistic illusion that caused you to sin.

There is a very pronounced tendency for people who engage in religious or spiritual movements to use their outer teachings to set up conditions that keep them from accepting that they are already forgiven by God. Every outer religion defines a set of conditions that must be met before you can attain salvation or the forgiveness of sins. I hope you can now begin to see that such conditions are always defined by the duality consciousness and are often set up by the false teachers. The purpose is to make you believe you need them and the outer religion in order to be saved or to get you to pursue an impossible goal. So once again, the *only* condition you must meet in order to be saved and forgiven is that you abandon all of the dualistic conditions that keep you outside the kingdom of God—because they make you focused on the outer world and thus prevent you from discovering the kingdom of God within you (of course, this involves balancing your karma or purifying all misqualified energy). Can you see that because God's forgiveness is unconditional, you do not need to meet any conditions in order to receive it? In fact, focusing on conditions will keep you from receiving what is given unconditionally and can only be received unconditionally.

***

There is a built-in dynamic in the concept of the spiritual path that your ego and the false teachers will try to use against you. The entire idea of the path is that you are now in a lower state and that you can move toward a higher state. In this book I have defined the primary goal of spiritual growth as the Christ consciousness, and it is possible you will take a look at yourself and realize you are not yet in the Christ consciousness. This can be used by the ego to try to get you to feel inadequate or guilty for the fact that you have not yet reached the goal. In other words, your ego will try to take my description of the Path of Oneness and turn it into a set of outer conditions you must meet—thus engaging you in another dualistic treadmill that leads nowhere. To avoid this, let me suggest the following approach.

There is a spiral staircase that leads you out of this sphere, and at the top of it is the immortality of the ascension. Each step represents a specific initiation, and in order to pass it, you have to see through and abandon a particular dualistic illusion. How do you pass the initiation? Well, you must expose the dualistic illusion so you can see it for what it is. How do you do that? You do so by doing what you were designed to do, namely by experimenting with your co-creative abilities. God gave you free will and the right to experiment, and the best way to learn is to conduct an experiment and evaluate the result. The material universe is simply a giant spiritual feed-back machine designed to give you a response to your creative efforts by giving you a physical outpicturing of the mental images you project upon the Ma-ter Light. The challenge is to overcome your fear of experimenting, so you can come back to the natural state – the innocence of the child – in which you love to experiment. You do so with no negative feelings, simply learning from every experiment, no matter how it turns out.

How do you project these mental images? You do so through the four levels of your mind, meaning that the images will be shaped by the contents of your mind. You have now been in the material universe for potentially many lifetimes, and as we have seen, this is a treacherous environment in which it is virtually impossible to avoid being affected by duality. So you have picked up certain dualistic beliefs, received certain psychological wounds and accumulated misqualified energies in the four levels of your mind, all of which will affect the images you project upon the Ma-ter Light. Every aspect of your outer situation is a reflection of the mental images you hold in your mind. The ego and the false teachers want you to think of this in the dualistic terms of success and failure. If you do something that has an unpleasant consequence, *you* made a mistake and if your life does not live up to a certain worldly standard, *you* are a failure.

In reality, everything that happens to you is an opportunity to examine your mental images, to overcome a dualistic illusion and heal a psychological wound. So an action really is not a mistake but is an opportunity to take the next step up the spiral staircase. Any consequence makes it possible for you to expose the dualistic illusion and psychological wound that caused you to project an imperfect image into the cosmic mirror. And by openly examining yourself, you will be able to turn any action – even what the world calls a mistake – into a stepping stone for progress. The moment you *do* leave behind a dualistic illusion, you are instantly forgiven for any actions taken from that state of consciousness (you may still have karma, or misqualified energy, to balance, but the forgiveness is instantaneous).

When you accept this approach, you can enter into a state of perpetual forgiveness of yourself, whereby you will not take your own mistakes personally. What do I mean by taking things personally? As I have explained, your conscious self is in charge of defining your sense of identity. After you fell into the duality consciousness, you started creating a mental image of who you are instead of basing your sense of identity on a direct experience of the reality anchored in your I AM Presence. That mental image is simply a picture you have imposed upon yourself, and although it is unreal, it is upheld by your belief that it is real and permanent. For example, if you make a mistake, you might fall prey to the temptation to think, "I am a bad person," and thus you impose the image of a bad person upon your identity, thinking it is real and permanent.

There is an essential difference between saying, "I acted in a nonconstructive manner" and saying "I am a bad person." An action is something you can easily change, whereas the sense of being a bad person is perceived as permanent. You might have heard the concept of not taking God's name in vain. Well, the name of God is "I AM" (Exodus 3:14), so whenever you say something limiting or negative after the words "I am," you are taking God's name in vain by using it to reinforce a negative image of yourself, an image that denies your oneness with God.

When you realize that you are more than any image you have created in the dualistic world, you can very quickly let go of these limited self-images. You can then develop the attitude that when you "make a mistake" you do not condemn yourself, for that only reinforces the sense that you are permanently bad. Instead, you openly look for the lesson you can learn and then you let go of the dualistic belief behind it. The strategy of the ego and the false teachers is to make you believe that once you have made a mistake, you are condemned forever and can never be free of it. I have now shown you that you are free the very moment you let go of the dualistic illusion that limits you. So please go and sin no more (John 8:11).

When you accept the concept of unconditional forgiveness, you will no longer feel threatened by your mistakes, and thus you can admit them freely, learn from them and move on. Once you have entered into this perpetual forgiveness of yourself, you can then transfer it to perpetual forgiveness of other people. You are behaving the way you do right now because you are at a certain step of the spiral staircase. You have certain psychological wounds and certain dualistic beliefs that cause you to sometimes act in a way that does not live up to your highest ideals. Yet instead of condemning yourself for it, you must forgive and move on. The same holds true for others.

Even the most seemingly evil people simply do what they do as a result of the outer personality that is shaped by their psychological wounds and dualistic beliefs. Let me make it very clear that God never created any evil beings. In reality, there are no bad or evil people. There are bad or evil identities which have been created based on the duality consciousness, and some people have chosen to step into one of them. Yet the identities are simply like the costumes worn in a play, and behind that outer facade is the conscious self of a co-creator or an angel of God. The goal of life on Earth is to rise above the false identities and become who you really are. Thus, you always strive to set yourself free from the false identity. And when interacting with others, you always strive to set *them* free. Unconditional forgiveness of yourself and others sets you free from the sense of being threatened. And when you no longer feel threatened by others, you have the foundation for interacting with them in an entirely new way, a nondual way. This leads to an extremely important concept.

***

You have probably seen a magician who pulls a rabbit out of a hat that you perceived to be empty. Thus, magic is based on perception. With that in mind, one might say that the material world is created as a result of magic, namely the magic of holding a mental image in your mind and then projecting it upon the Ma-ter Light. White magic is when you hold a life-transforming image and black magic is when you hold a life-degrading image.

If you hold a negative or limiting mental image of yourself and your abilities, you are actually practicing black magic against yourself, and you can make karma with yourself for doing so. Likewise, if you project a negative image upon another person, you can, depending on the person's vulnerability, limit the person's growth. In fact, many people practice black magic against the people whom they claim to love the most, such as their immediate family. They do so by holding dualistic images of these people, images based on selfish love that seeks to control others and make them conform to their opinions and meet their needs.

My point is that the most spiritually mature people need to become aware of the importance of the mental images they hold of themselves and other people. In this respect, nothing is more important than to understand what Mother Mary explains in her book, namely holding the immaculate concept. As she was raising Jesus, she constantly looked beyond his outer personality and behavior, holding the vision for the fulfillment of his spiritual mission. She had to do this to the very end, even when standing at the foot of the cross.

As you interact with other spiritual people, you need to overcome all sense of being in competition with others. You are all extensions of the Creator's Being, you are all unique individuals, so there is no need for any sense of competition amongst you. Again, those who would be greatest should focus on having the greatest sense of oneness. And in that oneness, jealousy and competition fades away. You clearly see that only by raising up others can you truly raise up your

Self. When people approach any activity with this attitude, their efforts will multiply each other and that is the true meaning of multiplying your talents. Too often we see spiritual people who engage in a religious activity with an inharmonious attitude toward each other, and thus their efforts actually neutralize or cancel out each other with the result that their activity either fails or does not reach its highest potential. Yet when people are in harmony, their individual efforts will multiply each other so the whole becomes more – potentially far more – than the sum of the parts.

Yet what do you do when an activity has a mixture of people, some of whom are on the true Path of Oneness and others who are still on the path of separation? What I have told you in this book is that every spiritual and religious activity will attract some people who are blinded by the duality consciousness and are using the activity for the fulfillment of ego goals. An activity might even attract those who are so trapped in the fallen consciousness that they use the activity to gain power and control, or even some who simply seek to destroy anything that is constructive and spiritual. These latter beings are called the spoilers and they have come to identify with a fallen identity created by a desire to destroy everything that confirms God's reality and beauty.

I can assure you that many spiritual activities have been destroyed by those seeking to gain power or seeking to destroy, so how can this be avoided? It can be avoided by creating an environment in which it is made abundantly clear that the entire goal of the community is oneness. This includes oneness in a vertical direction, where each person strives for oneness with his or her higher being, and oneness in a horizontal direction, where all members of the community strive for oneness with each other. When the members of such a community follow my advice to depersonalize their lives and stop feeling threatened, those who are trapped in duality will find it very difficult to control the community. Thus, they will often leave, and if they do not leave, they will find it difficult to gain power. Some of them might actually be transformed by interacting with less dualistic people. If they refuse to be transformed, then that refusal will inevitably be their judgment, and they might lose the opportunity to re-embody on Earth. Thus, the overall goal of raising the consciousness of humankind has indeed been helped by allowing such a person to remain in a spiritual community without allowing him or her to destroy the activity.

***

How do you hold the immaculate concept? By always envisioning that behind the outer facade and personality is the conscious self. That conscious self is an extension of the Creator's Being, and you should treat it with utmost respect—in yourself as well. You always see beyond the person's immediate actions and state of mind, and you envision his or her spiritual potential. You envision in your mind how the person awakens and suddenly sees its dualistic beliefs and behavior, then throwing it off as you take off a heavy overcoat that restricts your movement.

Yet holding the immaculate concept does not mean that you become blind, for it is only conditional love that makes you blind. When you love someone conditionally, your "love" is motivated by your own desires and thus you refuse to see that the person might not be able to fulfill those desires. This makes you spiritually blind, but when you depersonalize your life and overcome the need to control others, you become spiritually seeing.

I am not saying you should ignore a person's imperfections. I am only saying you should see them as temporary and never affirm them as permanent. You always see that when a person is acting in a dualistic manner, it is because the conscious self has stepped into, has identified itself with, a dualistic identity. You realize that as long as the conscious self upholds this identification, the person will act in a dualistic manner, and thus you take the necessary precautions. Yet you never allow yourself to see this as permanent or to judge the person as being a "bad person." You do everything possible to help the person see his or her dualistic beliefs, but you do so in a non-attached and loving manner. It is not your job to change other people but to give them a choice by helping them see beyond duality. Thus, you should do your best and be non-attached to the choices made by other people.

In fact, as you become more skilled at identifying and seeing through these dualistic identities, you can begin to treat people as their real selves, talking to them in a way that does not affirm their dualistic identities. In some cases, this can be enough to help a person snap out of its identification with the external identity and reconnect to its spiritual self. Consider how many people have grown up with a certain personality, for example as being a bully. When other people allow themselves to be bullied, when they withdraw or when they fight the bully, they only affirm the person's self-image. Yet when you refuse to respond to the person as most people respond to a bully – when you turn the other cheek – you do not affirm the person's self-image. And this gives that person an opportunity – perhaps for the first time in that lifetime – to step outside the temporary identity, examine it and ask the question, "Is this really who I am, or am I more than this sense of identity?"

When the more mature members of a spiritual activity are constantly seeking to rise above duality and constantly seeking to come into non-dualistic oneness with each other, they can create an environment in which duality cannot thrive and thus people blinded by duality cannot play their ego games. For example, in a spiritual activity that openly talks about the ego and the duality consciousness, it can rightfully be assumed that all members are striving to overcome their blindness. Thus, there is no reason to beat around the bush and avoid openly exposing when someone acts in a dualistic manner. Yet this can be done without any negative feelings, so that you do not give people an excuse for responding with negative feelings.

An all-too-common pattern is that you see someone's imperfections but you say nothing. As the other person continues his or her actions, your own frustration keeps building until you can no longer hold it inside. You then challenge the person, but you do so with a burst of negative feelings. The other person reacts to your negative energy in such a way that he or she feels you are being unreasonable, and thus your message can be ignored, explained away or refuted. In other words, by engaging in negative feelings, you gave the other person's ego a perfect excuse for ignoring the truth behind your actions and words. In this way, two people are often tricked into creating a negative spiral between them that cuts off communication and perpetuates the dualistic struggle. In contrast, if you express your observations without any negativity or judgment, you do not give the other person's ego an excuse for rejecting your message. The ego can always find an excuse, but there is a far greater chance that the other person will actually listen to what you say instead of allowing his or her ego to sweep it under the rug.

Keep in mind that you have a right to express how the actions and words of other people affect you. If you have depersonalized your life, you can avoid responding by wanting to hurt the other person.

Depersonalizing your life does not mean that you have no feelings, but it does mean you are not absorbed in and blinded by those feelings. Thus, you simply describe your feelings without seeking to hurt the other person in return. And when you do not accuse the other person but simply state how his or her actions have affected you, there is a better chance of reaching the real person who might have hidden itself behind a wall of dualistic defenses.

Obviously, an entire book could be written on how to interact with other people, yet my overall point here is that when people depersonalize their lives, they will also depersonalize their relationships. And when they are no longer threatened by other people, many of the ego games fade away. The overall goal of a non-dualistic spiritual activity should be to bring people into oneness. Thus, you can approach people with the basic attitude that you are willing to come into oneness with them in the Christ mind and that you assume they are willing to come into oneness with you. When the message you send out is, "Come into oneness with me in Christ," you are not as likely to attract people who are very attached to their egos and the duality consciousness. For such people have no intention of giving up their separate identities in order to come into oneness with others in Christ.

***

In this book I have clearly explained that there are some beings who fell in a higher realm and who are so identified with their fallen identities that it is extremely difficult for them to separate their sense of self from the duality consciousness. Obviously, there is always a potential that these beings can be awakened, and that is why some of them are still allowed to embody on Earth and why they are allowed to enter spiritual organizations where they can mix with those who are sincerely following the Path of Oneness. Yet to be realistic, it may not be possible for you to transform such a being no matter what you do. Thus, always remember that you are not here to change or save others. You are here to give them an opportunity to change themselves by showing them an alternative to the duality consciousness. And sometimes the only thing you can do is to allow a person to mistreat you in order to make the person's dualistic identity more obvious.

As you attain Christ discernment, you will be able to see that some people are totally identified with the fallen consciousness and are acting it out by seeking to control others and destroy those who will not be controlled. You might then challenge them in a very direct manner, as Jesus did when he called the scribes and Pharisees the sons of the devil (John 8:44). Yet I suggest that until you attain a high degree of Christ consciousness, you take a more subtle approach and never actually call someone a fallen being or a fallen angel. It is so easy for the ego to misuse these concepts and start to call anyone who disagrees with it a fallen angel. This will obviously be a form of black magic that will make karma for yourself.

I suggest that spiritual people create a culture in which one can talk openly about the ego and the duality consciousness. Thus, one can easily say that a person is acting in a dualistic manner without judging that person with a permanent label. I suggest you treat every person as a conscious self that is temporarily stuck in a dualistic sense of identity. You hold the immaculate concept and do everything you can think of to help awaken the person to the reality that he or she is far more than the outer identity. Again, remember that outer results are not important. You are only here to give people an opportunity to choose. If people choose to cling to their dualistic identity, the members of a spiritual organization have the right to keep them away from positions of power. You also have a right to face them with a final opportunity to either abandon a certain type of dualistic behavior – which you expose to them with all possible clarity – or be asked to leave your activity.

***

As mentioned before, you must always be aware of the ego's tendency to misuse any concept. The ego can easily take these concepts and use them to judge other people, even as feeling superior to them. It can use them to get rid of people who disagree by judging them as being fallen angels who are beyond hope. However, the opposite dualistic polarity to judgment (wanting to get rid of people) is the tendency to become emotionally attached to changing or saving another person.

I have explained that there were many beings in the spiritual realm who fell because they followed their leaders. Because these beings did not personally choose to rebel against God, they can often find the spiritual path and they can relatively easily begin to rise above duality. Yet the last thing they overcome is often the attachment to their leader. In order to overcome that attachment, they often have to embody with the leader and consciously make the choice to let go. This will often require such beings to see the leader as a being who is stuck in the fallen consciousness and then consciously let the leader go. However, this can be very difficult to do unless you fully understand what I have explained in this book. Thus, some people have continued to follow a certain leader lifetime after lifetime without being able to free themselves and move on.

There are also some beings who allowed themselves to fall because a being to whom they were attached fell. They did not blindly follow a leader but allowed themselves to fall because they thought they could save the other being. Again, some of these beings have now risen to the upper levels of the spiritual path, but as I have explained, Christhood is a matter of becoming spiritually self-sufficient. And you cannot be self-sufficient if you are attached to any other being. You must give the other being complete free will, for if you do not, you are in a way practicing black magic by seeking to force the other being to awaken. My point being that there is a subtle difference between holding the immaculate concept – which gives the other person total freedom – and holding a vision based on your own desire to save the other person.

Some lifestreams descended from the spiritual realm on a rescue mission, and some of them have – while in embodiment – become attached to saving another person. Even some who started out on Earth and have grown in consciousness have developed such attachments. My point is that there comes a point on the path to Christhood where you must let go of all such attachments. As Jesus said, those who love father or mother or brother or sister more than Christ are not worthy of him—meaning that you simply cannot attain spiritual self-sufficiency while remaining attached to other people (Luke 14:26).

Another aspect of this is that when you are emotionally attached to saving others, you simply cannot depersonalize your relationship with them, and thus you cannot have the non-dualistic relationship I am talking about. The most spiritually mature people must make an effort to overcome such attachments, so they can let people exercise their free will without in any way taking it personally when others do not choose as you think they should have chosen.

***

An essential element of a non-dualistic approach to spirituality is to find a way to communicate that is above the dualistic games people play. And one valid guideline is to let all communication be based on kindness.

In the East, the name Maitreya is associated with kindness, yet the kindness that I embody is divine kindness, unconditional kindness. This form of kindness is above the dualistic extremes. One aspect of this is that it is above human emotions, such as fear, anger, blame or anything else that seeks to put people down instead of raising them up. The top ten percent obviously need to find a way to communicate that is free of such emotions, and this will naturally begin to happen as people depersonalize their lives, as described already. In fact, many of today's spiritual people have indeed made great progress in terms of developing a way to talk to others that avoids the obvious forms of unkindness.

Unfortunately, many spiritual people have gone into the opposite dualistic extreme, as described earlier, of becoming passive. They think being kind means never challenging others, which means you must tolerate anything they do. As already described, this is neither true love nor true kindness. True kindness is when you do not want people to remain trapped in a dualistic illusion. You give them every possible opportunity to experience that there is an alternative, that there is something beyond duality. You do this even if it means being very direct and very firm in challenging the illusions of their egos.

After all, the ego has a very clear agenda of not being exposed, challenged or gainsaid. Thus, it will say that if you do challenge a person, you are being unkind to that person. Yet you are only being "unkind" to the ego, while you are being extremely kind to the real person. For the real person is the conscious self, and it is extreme kindness to empower that self to become free from the prison of the ego.

In reality, it is extreme kindness to help another person see his or her dualistic beliefs. This is especially true for those who are so trapped in duality that they are acting in ways that are evil, whether they fail to see this or no longer care. Such people are likely to resist your challenge, often in very aggressive ways, and this causes many spiritual people to withdraw and give up. Yet those who really have unconditional love and kindness will keep challenging duality, while being non-attached to other people's reactions.

***

You need to become very clear about the fact that you have a right to bear witness to the truth you see, even to the point of exposing and challenging the dualistic beliefs of other people. You have a right to be the Christ on Earth, no matter how many people – who are blinded by their egos – tell you the opposite. This must be done without fueling the dualistic struggle, and therefore you must be impersonal about it. You must strive to avoid being dragged into a dualistic reaction, even when others react in a dualistic manner.

As always, there are two dualistic reactions, one is to respond with negative feelings, the other is to withdraw and remain silent. Both must go so that you – depending on how deeply the other person is trapped in duality – can do what is most likely to lift that person out of illusion. For some it may help to be very gentle and understanding, for others it may be best to be very enthusiastic and inspiring while for others it will be necessary to act in a very direct yet non-emotional manner.

One aspect of awakening another person is that the ego has erected a fortified wall around the person's mind, and you must find a way to penetrate the wall and reach the conscious self inside. This conscious self is often like the princess in the fairy tale about the sleeping beauty. It is put to sleep by the evil stepmother – the ego – and is now unconscious behind walls of thorny bushes—the dualistic illusions and psychological wounds. My point being that the conscious self is often so identified with the dualistic identity that it cannot awaken itself from its sleep. Thus, you must find a way to reach through the defenses and help the conscious self see that there is an alternative to duality.

While this is an individual matter, I must tell you that for many of the people trapped in duality, your only way of reaching them is to be very direct and to be completely unyielding. You must literally stand on the rock of Christ and not allow these people to move you. Many people are so trapped in the ego's game of seeking to control others that they subconsciously seek to control you when you challenge them. If you give in to this control – perhaps thinking you have to be kind – you will only reinforce their belief in the ego's illusions. For example, if people are trapped in superiority, giving in to them will obviously reinforce the illusion that they are superior.

The only way to free people is to challenge them and continue to do so without ever giving in to their attempts to silence you. You must oppose their attempts to silence you without engaging in a dualistic battle with them. You do this by never seeking to prove them wrong, but by simply stating your truth, over and over again if necessary. This is literally the only way to reach the people who are completely trapped by their egos, and that is why Jesus so firmly opposed the scribes and Pharisees. Will it always work? Certainly not, and that is why you must be clear that you are not doing it to change others but to give them the opportunity to choose change. Therefore, when you give people this opportunity, your effort is a success—regardless of how others respond.

For people who are less trapped by their egos, it may be sufficient to seek to outmaneuver their egos by confusing them and responding in a non-dualistic manner. The ego is extremely good at using dualistic logic to explain away any challenge and to justify its beliefs and actions. You literally can never outmaneuver the ego through analytical or intellectual thinking. You can never win a dualistic argument, and as soon as your interaction with another person becomes dominated by duality, the spiritual purpose is lost. Thus, you must go beyond dualistic thinking and use a non-dualistic form of logic. This is why some spiritual teachers teach by giving their students koans, riddles that cannot be comprehended by the analytical mind.

You can often help people by presenting them with real-life koans, which means you must ask questions that help them look at themselves and life in a new way, a way that goes beyond their traditional way of thinking. Once you begin to attain some Christ discernment and a firm understanding of the difference between duality and non-duality, this is not difficult to do. When you remove the beam in your own eye, you will see clearly how to help other people overcome their illusions. Duality always has two opposites, which means that no dualistic viewpoint is entirely self-contained, logical and consistent. By taking a dualistic belief to its logical extreme, its flaws often become apparent.

Finally, there are some people who are starting to go beyond duality, and they can often be helped by inspiration. Yet many of these people have sunk into a state of quiet desperation and depression, often feeling that life in this world is so bad that they really don't want to be here. To awaken such people, it can be necessary to be firmly optimistic and counteract all of their millions of excuses with all-consuming enthusiasm. These people are usually not doing anything bad that needs to be exposed. Their problem is that they are not doing *anything*, and it can be challenging to help them escape this state of spiritual paralysis. Many people will understand and agree with everything you tell them about the spiritual path, yet they will be unwilling to do anything about it. Thus, it can require great firmness and persistence to pull people out of this passivity. That is why Jesus said it is easier to work with those who are hot or cold, whereas it is much harder to help those who are lukewarm (Revelation 3:15-16).

It is indeed possible to create an environment where people can talk openly and freely about the ego and its quirks, so that the ego finds it very difficult to hide and play its games. And when such an environment can be established by a few people, it can become the catalyst for spreading to larger spiritual organizations. Eventually, the entire tone of the worldwide religious debate can be changed and based on true kindness—kindness that is loving yet never tolerates any conditions behind which the ego can hide.

***

When you have a group of people who are committed to the Path of Oneness and who are in the process of depersonalizing their lives, you can have the creation of what many spiritual people long for and what the Ascended Host want to see established on Earth, namely a truly spiritual community. Many people have been drawn to spiritual and religious movements precisely because they long for the kind of community that exists in the spiritual realm, and of which they have an inner memory. Community means "coming into unity" and it can – obviously – be attained only when you have individuals who are following the Path of Oneness. Only when you attain a degree of oneness with your source, with your own higher being, can you attain true oneness with other people.

Yet I must tell you that as with everything else, the duality consciousness can pervert the concept of community and create a false desire for community. In far too many cases, spiritual or religious movements have manifested a false community in which the leaders form an elite with absolute power and the members follow them blindly. This has been an outpicturing of the dynamic I described earlier of those who have a desire to be superior to others and those who have a desire not to make decisions. Unfortunately, a religious community has often become a refuge for these two types of people, which has caused it to deteriorate into power games and other egoic manifestations.

Such a community typically becomes very rigid and focused on outer rules. It creates a mental image of how the ideal member should be, and then it seeks to force everyone to fit that mold. The result is that the more mature spiritual seekers feel as if they have to put on a straightjacket in order to fit in, and they would rather withdraw. As I have said before, oneness does not mean sameness. You do not help people grow spiritually by forcing them to suppress their individuality. You help them by putting them in touch with their higher beings and then allowing them to express their divine individuality.

There is a widespread dream among some spiritual people of a collective salvation that you qualify for by simply being a member of an outer community and following its rules. Yet this is – no matter how cleverly disguised – simply the ego's unrealistic dream of an automatic salvation that makes the ego acceptable to God because it fulfills earthly conditions. As I have described in this book, the Path of Oneness is the path of individualism. However, as you start uncovering your spiritual individuality, you will not feel threatened by being in a community and working with other people.

The Age of Aquarius is the age of community, and it is time to overcome the image of the spiritual person wandering the world alone or sitting in solitude in a cave in the mountains. It truly is the challenge of this age for the spiritual people to embody and express their individualism while working together in a community. I can assure you that in the spiritual realm we are all individuals, but we still work together in a true spirit of community. The reason being that we have overcome *all* manifestations of ego, including the very subtle desire to stand apart from others that causes some spiritual people to seek solitude. There are two main reasons why spiritual seekers need a community:

- The simple fact is – as I have attempted to explain many times – that you will not manifest full Christhood unless you help other people, and this must obviously happen in a community setting.

- You need other people to help you see what you cannot see from inside your own mental box. Obviously, when you interact with people who are actively striving to follow the Path of Oneness, you can help each other overcome duality.

***

One model for such a community is what was established by the Buddha and by Jesus, yet in the Aquarian Age this must be taken one step further. Both Jesus and the Buddha were far ahead of any of their followers, and thus they were in the situation of being the clear leaders. They acted as the teachers and all other members were the students. In this age, many more people are close to manifesting Christhood, and we do not desire all of these people to create their own little following, working independently of each other. In the spiritual realm, we all have Christhood, and we all work together, which is what needs to be duplicated on Earth. For this to happen, a community must be formed in which many people with a high degree of Christhood can share the roles of leaders and teachers.

In fact, an ideal community will realize the truth in Jesus' words that he could, of his own self, do nothing (John 5:30) but that it was the Father within him who was doing the works (John 14:10). Thus, the members of a true spiritual community – even the most spiritually advanced (or rather, especially the most spiritually advanced) – know they can do nothing of their own. It is the Holy Spirit who is doing the works through individuals, and the Holy Spirit bloweth where it listeth (John 3:8).

In one situation the Holy Spirit might bring forth an idea through one person, and in another situation it might use another person. In other words, instead of the age-old model of having a fixed leadership that cannot be replaced or challenged, an Aquarian community sees the true leader as the Holy Spirit, and it allows the Spirit to use whomever it chooses for a particular task. This would ideally involve a community in which a group of people are all mature enough to be instruments of the Spirit and can thus step in and out of leadership positions as directed from above.

Yet such a community must also recognize that the Spirit can use anyone, and as a spiritual master is fond of saying, "If the teacher be an ant, heed him." In other words, a true community must recognize that rank in an outer organization should never overshadow the true leadership of the Spirit. So if the Spirit uses a seemingly insignificant person to bring forth a new idea, the idea should be used. There is no longer time for the ancient ego game that people do not look at the validity of an idea until they know it has been presented or approved by an "important person."

Of course, such a community must be based on Christ discernment so people's egos, fallen beings or false gods cannot gain a foothold. Although anyone can be used by the Spirit, this does not mean that everything that seems spiritual really is from the one Holy Spirit. It can also come from the legions of dualistic spirits.

Why have so many spiritual communities failed or become rigid? It is because, as mentioned earlier, when they reach a certain size, they attract the kind of people who are blinded by the dualistic quest for power and control. Thus, a human leadership emerges, and it replaces the leadership of the Spirit. A true spiritual community recognizes that its primary responsibility is to establish and maintain a direct connection to the spiritual realm and the Ascended Host. Thus, such a community becomes an outpost of the Ascended Host, and we are the true leaders. The community does not allow the emergence of a leadership which is blinded by duality but allows the Ascended Host to be in command through the agency of the Holy Spirit.

***

I could give more teachings on establishing a spiritual community, but I have actually given enough for those who have ears to hear and eyes to see. It is not my intent with this book to bring forth a set of rules for how to establish the true spiritual community. This would only lead to the creation of another rigid framework that forces people to conform to outer rules and suppress their individuality.

The purpose of the material universe is to give God's co-creators and other evolutions the opportunity to use their co-creative abilities and get feedback from their physical circumstances and each other. Yet as beings grow in Christhood, they spontaneously come into alignment with the Creator's overall purpose, which also brings them into oneness with each other. Many beings are still experimenting with expressing their abilities and defining their identity, so they will naturally be less able to work well with others. Yet the more mature beings are beginning to know who they are – as individualizations of a greater Being – so they can begin to express their creativity within the larger framework of the Creator's vision and goals. When understood correctly, this will not be a restriction of your creative efforts, and it will not require a suppression of your individuality.

It is only the duality consciousness that makes it seem like people's real personalities clash. In reality, your spiritual individuality was defined by spiritual beings who were quite capable of defining billions of individualities without creating conflicts between them. Why do we work harmoniously together in the spiritual realm? Because we have become one with our divine individualities, and thus we naturally and effortlessly supplement each other. Our individual characteristics do not cancel out or oppose each other. They magnify each other so that we can create far more together than each of us can do alone. And as a natural expression of the drive to be more, we work together instead of working alone. This is not a chore or sacrifice for us, for we fully enjoy seeing each other's individual expressions, and we are filled with joy over what we create together. The Alpha aspect of co-creation is that you co-create in harmony with your own higher being. The Omega aspect is that you co-create in harmony with your spiritual brothers and sisters, with whom you feel oneness.

The coming together in oneness on Earth is the foundation for establishing the right figure-eight flow between the spiritual realm and the material realm. You here below can form the Omega polarity to the Alpha polarity of the Ascended Host. And only when a critical mass of people join together in a true spiritual union, can the kingdom of God be manifest on the physical Earth. Why do you think Jesus said:

> Again I say unto you, That if two of you shall agree on Earth as touching any thing that they shall ask, it shall be done for them of my Father which is in heaven. (Matthew 19:19)?

The material universe was not created so that one being could set itself up as being superior to all others—although some fallen beings seem to think so. The material universe will become the kingdom of God only when a critical mass of people come together in true spiritual unity. Even the quote above does not give the full story, for the term "two of you" does not refer simply to two people. It refers to people – individually and collectively – overcoming the dualistic illusions so that they attain what Jesus described in another quote:

> The light of the body is the eye: therefore when thine eye is single, thy whole body also is full of light; but when thine eye is evil, thy body also is full of darkness. (Luke 11:34)

As long as humankind's vision is divided by the dualistic illusions, their whole planet will be filled with darkness. Yet when the top ten percent come together in a single vision – the vision of Christ – and a true commitment to oneness, their community – and eventually their entire planet – will be full of light. Thus, the establishing of a true spiritual community that transcends all dualistic boundaries and differences is the most important task that could be accomplished by the top ten percent in this age. Therefore, I say to you, "Come into oneness with me in Christ," and then come into oneness with each other.

***

I know there are many people who will feel that I have presented you with so much information that it can seem overwhelming. I also know that some people will feel I have not given them enough information. Many people will feel a great sense of responsibility for their individual growth and for helping others, even for raising the entire planet into the kingdom of God. Many of the most responsible people will feel a strong desire to succeed, and they will want more specific directions than what I have given.

I understand this desire, but I ask you to see beyond it. It is not my purpose for this book to tell you how to do everything. Why not? Because I have no intention of releasing a book that – as has happened to so many religious scriptures – becomes a replacement for your Christhood. I have no intention of giving you an excuse for following outer rules instead of seeking oneness with your higher being. My goal is to awaken you to the Path of Oneness and give you sufficient pointers that you can anchor yourself firmly on the true path to Christhood.

Take note of what I explained earlier, namely that Christhood means becoming spiritually self-sufficient. This means that you no longer need a book or an outer guru to tell you what to do or how to do it. You get such directions from within, from your own higher being. Thus, everything you do becomes a true expression of who you are, namely the unique individual God created and the unique individual you have co-created based on your divine foundation.

It is not my desire to turn you into a sheep who blindly follows me. It is my desire to see you manifest the fullness of your personal, individual Christhood, whereby you can express – here below – the fullness of who you are above. Therefore, I cannot tell *you* how *you* should be the Christ. For when you become the Christ, you stop acting through a dualistic identity created in this world. You now act exclusively through your whole identity, which is a perfect union between your Alpha identity, that is anchored in your I AM Presence, and the Omega identity that is above all duality. Thus, you can truly say that "I and my Father are one" and that "My Father worketh hitherto and I work."

The challenge of Christhood is that there is no standard for how to be the Christ—which the ego cannot understand and will not accept. Thus, those who are still trapped in duality will want me to define rules so that by following them to the letter, they can feel that they are being the Christ. Christhood is supreme individuality, yet it is individuality that is in harmony with the whole. Thus, true Christhood must be expressed in helping others, in raising up the whole. As I have explained, it was the refusal to pass this initiation that caused the fall and sent the Earth into a downward spiral. Thus, in order to overcome the fall, a critical mass of people must pass this initiation and put on the fullness of their Christhood while still walking the Earth in a physical body.

While you are trapped in duality, you do things because you have a mental image which makes you think you have to or ought to do this or that. You do it to escape punishment or to receive a reward—you act to receive a certain *re*action. Christhood means that you let go of all such dualistic mental images of yourself, who you are and how you should behave. Instead, you do what you do as an expression of who you are—meaning your divine individuality and Christlike identity. You no longer act based on the punishment-reward duality but act based on the pure love of expressing who you are in service to the all. You are now worshiping God in spirit and in truth instead of dancing around a golden calf of a dualistic identity. You no longer have a mental image between your higher and lower beings but allow your Alpha identity to be expressed freely through your Omega identity. Thus, the Alpha and the Omega aspects of your being have come together in perfect harmony, the beginning and the ending have merged in the eternal NOW.

Key 33
Preach a non-dualistic gospel to all creatures

In the previous chapters of this book, I have attempted to give you an understanding of the reality you face as a person in embodiment on this little planet that you call Earth. I have attempted to give you a relatively concise explanation that appeals to the mind, the reasoning mind, so that you might understand what you are up against and what you have been up against for a very long time in many past lifetimes. Yet I will not leave you without giving you a more full experience of my total being, for truly I, Lord Maitreya, am more than mind. I am also heart, I am feeling and I have very strong feelings for the lifestreams on Earth and for this planetary home itself, even for Mother Earth, who is truly a living Being, holding the vision and the balance for the evolutions that grow – or do not grow as the choice might be – on this planetary home.

Thus, my beloved, I truly want to greet you in the love of Maitreya's heart, for I represent the love of the Father to the evolutions on Earth. Truly, I am aware that many of you have been brought up in a religious tradition that portrays the Father as a very remote being, as the external God in the sky, perhaps even as the angry God in the sky. Thus, my beloved, I am aware that many of you have never really seen any kind of love associated with God, with the Father figure of God. Some of you have been fortunate enough to have been exposed to the feminine aspect of God, be it as Mother Mary or as one of the feminine goddesses revered in the East. And thus, you have at least received a more balanced experience of the love of God. Yet I desire for you to have a more full experience of the love of God, so that your love might be full because you realize that God the Father, the Creator itself, has an infinite and unconditional love for your being, for your Alpha identity, for your conscious self and for the Omega identity you have built on the Rock of Christ.

Oh my beloved, could you even for a split second experience a glimpse of the Creator's love for you, you would be totally transformed by that love. Away would fall all of the elements of the dualistic consciousness that reside in your four lower bodies. Away would fall the ego, and you would be plunged into a complete sense of oneness with the Creator's Being.

As I have explained, your conscious self truly is an extension of, an individualization of, the Creator's own Being. For when God decided to create individual lifestreams with free will, he did indeed say, as did Christ, "This is my body which is broken for you" (1Corinthians 11:24). Thus, the "body" of God, the consciousness of God, the Being of God has been broken in the creation of innumerable individual lifestreams that all form the Body of God in the world of form. Thus, you who are embodying on planet Earth are part of the Body of God on Earth, and I would love nothing more than to see each of you individually reconnect to the infinite love that the Creator has for your own individual Being, whereby you could accept yourself as a worthy member of the Body of God on Earth. And when you accept this individually, you can then come together collectively and form the true community of the Holy Spirit of the Aquarian age, the true community of unconditional love, the true community that then becomes Maitreya's Sphere of Oneness, wherein each person feels as one part in the Body of God.

***

Oh my beloved, what I attempted to establish in the original Garden of Eden was just such a community, where all had the maximum opportunity to feel loved and to feel part of the greater whole. It was with great sorrow that I saw some of the lifestreams in the Garden embody the fallen consciousness instead of letting go of it and coming into oneness. It was with great sorrow that I saw these lifestreams draw even some of the innocent ones with them, as they decided to leave the protected sphere of the Garden of Eden, which was maitreya's Sphere of Oneness.

I can assure you that these beings did not leave because they had not experienced my love for them. For as the representative of the divine Father in the Garden of Eden, I did indeed express the love of the Father. Yet the unfortunate fact is that when you are trapped in the consciousness of separation, you cannot receive the love of the Father, for you cannot experience the Being of the Creator. Once you have become trapped in the illusion of separation, your conscious self cannot accept that it is an extension of the Creator's Being. And when you cannot accept this, how can you reconnect to the fullness of the Creator's Being out of which you came?

You see, my beloved, when you are trapped in the consciousness of separation, you are like a puddle that has been left behind after the high water of the river moved on toward the ocean. And thus, you see yourself as a separate puddle and you are not able to conceive that you were created out of the River of Life and that if you follow that river back to its source, you will find your own source as the Creator itself.

So my beloved, it has been my role to see many lifestreams that were entrusted to my care go the way of separation, the way of death. I could do nothing to stop them, nor did I really want to stop them. For you see, my beloved, I represent the consciousness of the Father, the love of the Father. And the love of the Father is unconditional, which means that the Creator will allow extensions of itself to separate themselves from its Being, from the River of Life. The Creator itself feels no sorrow over this. But my beloved, as a Being who does not have the full God consciousness, I did indeed feel a certain sorrow. This was not the human sorrow that comes from possessive love, where you feel a personal loss. But it was the greater sorrow that comes from seeing clearly what awaits the lifestreams that separate themselves from the Sphere of Oneness.

For in representing the Father, I also represent the Father's mission. And thus, I can clearly see that those who follow the path of separation will condemn themselves to a future that can only be filled with conflict and suffering. Thus, these lifestreams can never attain peace of mind. And as the teacher who was charged with raising beings up to attaining the peace of mind that comes from spiritual self-sufficiency, it was with some sense of loss and sorrow that I saw these beings choose to reject the gift I offered them, the gift of the Path of Oneness.

Yet my beloved, you must understand that in my mind nothing is ever lost. For as long as a lifestream continues to be in existence, there is always the potential that it can turn around and decide to start climbing back up the staircase of life. And what I want to assure you is that you can do that at any moment. And when you decide to turn around, I will be there, greeting you with open arms and a love that has not diminished no matter how long you have been traveling in the duality of space and time.

***

You see, my beloved, it is the tactic of the false teachers, the fallen beings and the false gods to make you believe that if you have made a certain mistake, you can never make up for it. So they want you to believe that if you have ever had any kind of negative feelings about God – if you have ever had doubts, if you have ever believed in any atheistic idea or other wrong ideas about God – then you cannot come back to God. They want you to think that because of what you have done, or believed, or said, or thought or felt about God, God will not receive you, for he somehow holds a grudge against you. My greatest desire is that you will come away from reading this book with an inner knowing that this is nothing but lies and illusions, designed to keep you from turning around and stepping on to the Path of Oneness—that will surely take you home to your Father's kingdom.

I desire you to understand and accept that no matter what you have done in the past, no matter what you have thought or felt, it has not in any way diminished God's love for your being. Thus, there literally is nothing – past, present or future – that can prevent you from rejoining the Path of Oneness and from entering the Sphere of Oneness. If you sincerely want to let go of the past, then I and all other ascended beings will offer you any assistance you can accept in order to help you leave the past behind and be spiritually reborn into the true identity that is anchored in your I AM Presence and has not been touched by anything that has happened in the matter world. This, my beloved, is my true desire—that you will realize the fallacy of the fallen consciousness and its claim that you could be permanently lost, that you could burn forever in hell because an angry God will not accept you into his kingdom.

It is not God who sends beings to hell. It is the self-aware beings themselves who condemn themselves to their self-created hell and to the collective hell created by the fallen beings because they will not accept God's forgiveness. Maybe they think they are unworthy of it or maybe they are too prideful to bend the knee and accept that they need to be forgiven for anything. Yet in either case, it is all illusions, springing from the egoic mind. And if you are willing to see through these illusions and let them go, then they can fall away from you, literally in the blink of an eye, as the scales fell from the eyes of Paul, when he encountered the blinding light of Christ on the road to Damascus (Acts 9:18). Take note that Paul had been persecuting, even instigating the killing of, Christians. Yet by being willing to completely turn his life around, he became one of the foremost apostles of Christ.

This my beloved, is the potential that all have. For did not Christ say, "I wish thou wert either hot or cold, but because thou art lukewarm, I will spew thee out of my mouth" (Revelation 3:16). The meaning is that even if you are cold, even if you have denied God or held negative images of God, you can still turn your life around. Yet if you are lukewarm, if you are not willing to make the decision to take responsibility for yourself, to examine yourself and your beliefs, well then Christ has nothing to work with. And thus you will, as so many among the general population, simply continue to live an unexamined life that is neither fully happy nor fully unhappy, for you have numbed yourself, even to the conditions found on this Earth. And these conditions truly are such that if you will examine them, you will see the absolute logic that there must be more to life than what this planet has to offer. For how could an infinite and all-powerful God create such an imperfect planet?

My beloved, this makes no sense at all, and thus those who are willing to take a look at life will see that there must be MORE. And in that recognition and the desire to find that MORE, you have the start of progress, the start of the Path of Oneness, where you will no longer settle for imperfections, for the mediocre. You want the reality of God instead of continuing to live in the shadows of duality.

***

My beloved, in this book I have explained to you a truth that has never before been fully explained in any of the spiritual teachings given on this planet, namely the fact that there are beings on this planet who are completely blinded by the fallen consciousness, the duality consciousness, the mind of anti-christ. Many of these beings do not in any way live up to the stereotypes of evil people that have been promoted in popular culture. You see, my beloved, life is not like the old Western movies, in which the bad guy always wore black and the good guy was the prince on the white horse.

So my beloved, you need to understand that the essence of the duality consciousness is deception. It is putting on a facade that hides something behind it. For as I have explained, the fallen consciousness thrives only in the shadows where nothing is seen clearly. And thus, you know that in the twilight things look different than what they are. And so you need to realize that the people who are the most blinded by the duality consciousness have become very skilled at putting on a facade as being good people. You find many of them in the field of politics, you find many of them in the field of business. But my beloved, you also find some of them in the field of religion. That is indeed why Christ said that he sent his disciples out as the sheep amongst wolves (Matthew 10:16). Unfortunately, most Christians have not understood that some of the wolves have attained prominent positions in Christian churches and have used their power to distort the true teachings of Christ.

I too am sending you out as those who will take a stand for a non-dualistic approach to religion. And I know that there are those in the field of religion and in other areas of society who will oppose you and your efforts to reform religion. What you need to understand is that some of these beings have literally come to believe that they own the material universe or at least planet Earth. Some even believe that God has given this world to the devil or that the devil created this world. My beloved, as I have explained, many conditions on Earth are surely not created by the representatives of God but are expressions of the imperfect consciousness of humankind. So in a sense one might say that there are certain conditions on Earth that are created by the devil and those who represent him, those who are blinded by the duality consciousness. Yet this does not mean that this universe was created *by* the devil or was created *for* the devil or that the devil and his representatives own this world.

My beloved, this world is only a temporary schoolroom for those who are still trapped in the duality consciousness. It is a place where they can receive still more opportunities to live out their dualistic fantasies to the point where they have finally had enough and desire more in life than what they can create with the duality consciousness. And when they become aware of that desire for the MORE, they might begin to see that the duality consciousness has certain built-in limitations, and thus it can never bring them beyond a certain level. And if they truly desire more than the dualistic appearances of highs and lows, of good and evil, of happiness and unhappiness, of success and failure, then they must reach for the mind of Christ that can take them beyond to the very consciousness of the Creator itself.

Thus, my beloved, you need to be aware that when you go out to spread the non-dualistic truth about religion, those who are trapped in duality will surely oppose you. They will oppose you in many ways. One way is that they will attack your arguments, your teachings. But I must tell you that some of them will go beyond this and will attack you personally. They will literally seek to destroy you in order to silence you. They will act as if it is a matter of life and death and that if they do not silence you, they will die. This is actually true when it comes to the false gods and the egos of the beings who are fully identified with the duality consciousness. If they do not silence the representatives of Christ on Earth, they will lose the Earth as their playground. And without people giving them energy, they will eventually burn out and die.

**

Fortunately, you live in a world that has become at least somewhat more civilized than the world into which I sent Jesus 2,000 years ago. I know that there are still people in this world who are willing to kill in the name of God and who are willing to kill those whom they feel are a threat to their religion or their God. Yet at least in the Western world it is not as likely that you will be killed for taking a stand for the non-dualistic truth of Christ. Neither is it likely that you will be nailed to a wooden cross and executed as a common criminal. Thus, I take some consolation in this, but I will still give you a very direct warning that there are those in this world who will seek to destroy you emotionally, even if they cannot destroy you physically.

They will seek to destroy your sense of self-worth, your sense of identity. And they will seek to destroy your sense that you have a right to do what you are doing. They will challenge your right to challenge them, and they will seek to make you believe that you have no right to challenge their dualistic beliefs and the institutions and organizations they have built based on duality. You see, my beloved, some of these beings have been in embodiment for a long time and they have built elaborate castles. These castles are built on the shifting sands of the duality consciousness and not on the rock of Christ. So truly, they cannot withstand the winds of the Holy Spirit.

Yet the winds of the Holy Spirit must flow through someone in embodiment, as I have carefully explained. And thus, you must be that open door for unleashing the winds of the Holy Spirit. But you can do so only when you know that you have an absolute right to be the open door for the truth of Christ and the winds of the Spirit—you have a right to be the open door even if the winds of the Holy Spirit blow apart the institutions created by man.

Thus, my beloved, I need you to understand that as you walk the Path of Oneness and attain your Christhood, you attain the absolute God-given right to challenge the illusions, the lies and the institutions created by the fallen beings on this planet. This, my beloved, is what you saw Jesus do, and you saw that he received no thanks for doing so. Nevertheless, had Jesus not done what he did, this planet would have gone into a downward spiral that could potentially have led to its destruction.

Thus you see, my beloved, even one person walking the Earth in the fullness of his Christhood was enough to accelerate the upward spiral and keep the Earth from going in the opposite direction. And so you will see that if we could have 10,000 people in the fullness of their Christhood and millions more with some degree of Christhood, much more could be achieved. And thus, Jesus' prophecy could indeed be fulfilled, the prophecy where he said that those who believe on him shall do the works that he did, and even greater works than these shall they do because he has gone to the Father—and has thereby carved a path that others can follow to the fullness of their Christhood (John 14:12).

So you see, my beloved, Jesus was not in doubt about his right to challenge the fallen consciousness and those who embody it on Earth. He claimed that right, he exercised that right, and he dared to be the open door for the truth of Christ and the winds of the Holy Spirit. Yet Jesus did not arrive at this point in the blink of an eye. He too followed the Path of Oneness, and it took him some time, some experimentation and some trepidation to come to the point where he was willing to stand up to the fallen beings in embodiment and to call them what they were, namely the sons of the devil.

One major initiation was the temptation by the devil after his fasting in the wilderness, where the devil sought to derail him, even by offering to give Jesus all the kingdoms of this world, so that he could rule them (Matthew 4:8). This might seem like a wonderful opportu-

nity for a spiritual representative to bring about the changes that he
was working for. After all, if Jesus was ultimately in control, he could
change religion on this Earth and create an institution that was
according to his ideal. Yet as I have tried to explain throughout this
book, this is not God's vision. For people must choose on their own
and must not be forced by institutions. It is indeed the fallacy of the
fallen beings that they are seeking to force people unto the path that
supposedly leads to God's kingdom. But as Jesus said, it is only the
broad way that leads to destruction and not the straight and narrow
way that leads to the inner kingdom (Matthew 7:13).

***

My beloved, I desire you to realize that in order for you to fulfill your
mission of bearing witness to the non-dualistic truth and letting your
light shine, you must be firm. You must stand on the rock of Christ,
and you must know that no matter what they throw at you, it cannot
remove you from that rock. And to attain that, you must strive for the
non-attachment that I have taught you about.

I also desire you to learn from the example of the Buddha. Study
the story of how Gautama sat under the Bo tree, and as he was ready
to enter into Nirvana, he had to pass one last initiation. He had to face
the demons of Mara, the forces of this world, the representatives of
the duality consciousness. These beings not only attacked him, but
they tried to tempt him in any way possible. What they truly wanted
was to get him to act or react in a dualistic manner, whereby he would
have been caught in the dualistic game. Yet Gautama refused to be
tempted, and finally he claimed his right to be the Buddha on Earth.
He touched the Earth with one hand and exclaimed the fiat, "Vajra,"
as a way of expressing his absolute knowledge of his God-given right
to manifest a non-dualistic state of consciousness in the midst of
duality. And the Earth itself rose up to bear him witness, that he had
the right to be the Christ, to be the Buddha, on Earth.

Yet even after entering Nirvana, the Buddha had to face another
initiation, another temptation. For again, the consciousness of duality
presented him with the temptation to believe that even though he had
attained this high state of consciousness, there was no way for him to
make other people understand non-duality. And thus, he should simply leave the Earth behind and go on in the spiritual realm, thereby

leaving the Earth in the hands of the dualistic forces. Yet the Buddha also passed this initiation by holding firm to the knowledge that some would understand his teaching, some would accept it, some would realize that they too had the potential to become the Buddha. For indeed, everything is the Buddha nature.

So my beloved, this is what you need to hold firmly in your mind. When those who are blinded by duality attempt to destroy your sense that you have a right to be on Earth, you *know* you have the right to bear witness to the non-dualistic truth and let your light shine. You have the right to walk the Path of Oneness, you have the right to be the Christ or the Buddha on Earth. You need to know and anticipate their attacks, not in the sense that you build walls around your mind, but that you reach the complete non-attachment that makes you transparent to the forces of duality so that there is nothing in you that resists duality or resists self-transcendence.

***

My beloved, the essence of the human ego is that it resists the River of Life. And in creating this resistance, you create a block to the flow of the River of Life, and this block is what the forces of duality can use to control and manipulate you. For what you resist will become a target, and as they strike at the target, you will think you have to resist even more in order to defend yourself against the attacks. And thus, you build an even stronger wall of resistance, but they will simply attack you even more. And thereby you have to build the walls thicker and higher, and this leads you into the endless dualistic game of resisting the dualistic forces. And in resisting duality, you also resist life, so the walls that you think are protecting you from the dualistic attacks are actually keeping you in the prison of the dualistic mind.

So my beloved, what is the way out, the *only* way out? Well, it is that you stop resisting the River of Life, that you stop resisting self-transcendence and that you instead commit yourself to the Path of Oneness that is perpetual and eternal self-transcendence. Do you see that by resisting duality, you are actually resisting self-transcendence? For the forces of duality cannot reach beyond the realm of duality, the vibration of duality. So if they can hurt you, it shows that you have elements of duality in your being. And thus when they *do* hurt you, the low response is to build a wall against their attack. Yet the high response is to look for the beam in your own eye and pull it out, so that you overcome the attachments that make you vulnerable.

When you do this, you flow with the River of Life, and then the blocks you have built over many lifetimes can gradually be resolved by invoking spiritual light and letting go of the dualistic illusions. And thus, you are on the upward path, and as you go higher and higher, you become more and more transparent seen by the forces of duality, for they have nothing in you. The prince of this world – the forces of duality – will come and have nothing in you, whereby they can influence you in any way (John 14:30). And thereby, you will not be vulnerable to their attacks, to their temptations. And you will not fall for their attempts to destroy your sense of self-worth, to destroy your sense that you have a right to be here. Neither will you fall for their attempts to make you pity them or feel that you are destroying something of value by destroying the institutions they have built.

***

My beloved, I must tell you that many of the current world religions are indeed towers of Babel (Genesis 11:4), houses built on sand. And before a golden age can be manifest, they must indeed crumble. For the old must crumble in order to give way to the new. This is an eternal principle that you see outplayed in the change of the seasons in nature.

My beloved, have I not attempted to explain to you that one of the greatest problems on Earth is that people become attached to the outer circumstances they see, and they think they could not be better, they could not become MORE? So people think they have to uphold and preserve the past institutions instead of allowing them to be transformed into something better, something that is MORE. If you will be honest, you will see in the field of religion a very clear tendency that people think they have to hold on to the structures, the doctrines, the scriptures of the past. They think that it is somehow their sacred duty to defend these structures from any change. Yet as I have attempted to explain, the mainstream religions are all affected by the duality consciousness. So what is the point in seeking to preserve something that is created from duality? Are you not thereby preserving a graven image that prevents you from having a direct experience of the Spirit of Truth that is hidden behind the dualistic images?

Do you see, my beloved, these dualistic structures must be broken down, must be abandoned, in order for humankind to be free to receive and accept a non-dualistic form of spirituality. Therefore, you must realize that as you embody the Christ consciousness and begin to express it, you will, in a certain sense, become an instrument for the destruction of the religious structures that many people do not want to see destroyed. For they have an emotional attachment to these towers of Babel that they have helped build, sometimes over many lifetimes.

Take note that I am not hereby saying that all traditional religions must be broken down or will disappear. What I am saying is that a structure can be preserved only by transcending itself. And thus, the structures that are not transformed by a non-dualistic vision will indeed be broken down by the winds of the Holy Spirit.

You need to realize that there is indeed a force of God, a force of nature itself, that is designed specifically to break down the structures that have become prisons for the minds of human beings in embodiment. For only by breaking down these prison walls can people be set free to embrace a higher future and be MORE. That force is known in the East as Shiva, which is the destroyer. Yet Shiva does not destroy that which is built on the rock of Christ and the vision of Christ, but only that which is built on the duality consciousness. In the West this force is known as the force of the Holy Spirit. Yet unfortunately many Christians have not understood the true role of the Holy Spirit. Thus, there are even those who claim that they have the Holy Spirit, but it is a false spirit. For it is a spirit that only works within the dualistic belief systems they have created.

Thus, my beloved, if a force – no matter how spiritual it might seem – does not challenge your beliefs, then it is not the Holy Spirit. The Holy Spirit will challenge *anything*, for as I have attempted to explain, any belief in this world can become a trap for your mind. For it can keep you from flowing with the ever self-transcending River of Life.

***

Thus, I ask you to recognize and fully internalize that I am calling you to a mission of the Holy Spirit. It is the mission of establishing the true community of the Holy Spirit, a community that transcends all boundaries defined by people, all boundaries defined by the duality consciousness. This means that it transcends all outer religions, all outer religious teachings and all outer divisions, such as race, sex, nationality or ethnicity.

My beloved, the Holy Spirit accepts nothing as permanent. And thus, the community of the Holy Spirit must never accept anything as permanent either. It must be a community that is always seeking to transcend itself and come up higher in the true Spirit of Oneness. For my beloved, yesterday's level of attainment is not sufficient for today. And thus, today's level will not be sufficient for tomorrow.

I have no desire to see people take the teachings in this book and elevate them to the status of an infallible scripture that can never be expanded upon or replaced by an even higher teaching. For my beloved, even though it has been my goal to give you the full truth, I must tell you that there is always more that can be revealed in the future. I can assure you that as humankind raises its consciousness – and I sincerely hope this book will contribute decisively to that process – even more profound revelations can and will be given by the Ascended Host.

Thus, I desire to see the emergence of a community of the Holy Spirit, which is open to receiving new revelations and will not stop this process by saying that we have now received the ultimate revelation, or we now have the ultimate messenger, and that nothing further could possibly be given. My beloved, the community of the Holy Spirit must be eternally committed to progressive revelation from the Ascended Host. And if a spiritual community, movement or organization defines some ultimate revelation and claims that now revelation has come to a stop, well then that community is no longer the community of the Holy Spirit. For it has indeed left off from the very essence of the Holy Spirit itself, which is self-transcendence. Do you see, my beloved, the moment you stop self-transcendence – and use any teaching, any structure, as an excuse for saying that now you do not have to transcend yourself anymore – at that very moment you have left off the Path of Oneness. You have separated yourself from the River of Life and you have said to the Holy Spirit that although it bloweth where it listeth, it has to blow elsewhere, for you are no longer willing to be the open door for its flow.

***

My beloved, I know that when I tell you that the people who are blinded by the duality consciousness will seek to destroy you as you challenge their beliefs and their institutions, this might cause some fear and trepidation, given your current state of consciousness. Yet I want to let you know that there is an absolute law of God that you cannot be faced with an initiation until you have reached the state of consciousness in which you are able to pass that initiation.

You see, my beloved, what you saw in the lives of Jesus and the Buddha was the initiations you face at the highest levels of Christhood. Yet you will not face those initiations until you reach that level of Christhood. In other words, while you are at lower levels, you will not face the same severe initiations as Jesus and the Buddha faced. And the meaning of this is that you will never face an initiation that you do not have the ability to overcome.

You can pass every test that you face, yet I must tell you that no matter what level you are at on the Path of Oneness, there is only one way to pass the test you face at that level. You can pass a test *only* by transcending your current level of consciousness. That is precisely why it is so important that you never allow yourself to think that you do not have to self-transcend anymore. For the moment you stop transcending, you will inevitably fail the test that you are presented at your current level of consciousness, and thus you will not be able to go higher. In fact, if you try to stand still, you will inevitably slide into a downward spiral, often without noticing what is happening. We might say that when you refuse to transcend, you fail the test of Self, the challenge to keep expanding your sense of self until you reach full God consciousness. This is the challenge to never settle for any graven image, to never settle for anything less than oneness with your Creator.

I hope to help you understand that no matter what happens in this world, no matter what situation you might be facing, you *do* have the ability to overcome that situation—if you are willing to transcend your current level of consciousness. This does not mean that you have to – in one leap – jump from where you are now to the consciousness of Jesus or the Buddha. It simply means that you have to transcend your current level, so that you come up one step on the spiral staircase of life. You have to go beyond the limitations that you currently see for yourself, you have to go beyond what you have been conditioned to think are the limits for your sense of self. And if you are willing to go beyond self, then God will multiply your efforts, and you know that with God all things are possible. Therefore, *you* – meaning the separate self – cannot pass the test, but the you that is willing to become MORE can indeed pass every test—for every test is a test of whether you will cling to your current sense of identity or whether you are willing to become MORE.

***

My beloved, how do you ultimately overcome the opposition from the fallen beings, those who are trapped in the duality consciousness? Well, you do so by realizing that the more a being is trapped in the duality consciousness – the more a being is blinded by the illusions of duality – the more that being will take itself and everything it believes and does seriously. The most blind people are the ones who take themselves so seriously that they personalize everything and see everything as a personal attack. These are the people who will say that if you do not submit to them one hundred percent, then you are against them. And therefore, they feel justified in using whatever means they have at their disposal to silence or even destroy you.

It is true, as the old saying goes, that if you laugh at the devil, he will run away from you. For the devil takes himself seriously, and he manipulates people by getting them to take him seriously as well. So when the devil meets a person who refuses to take him seriously, the devil does not know what to do, and thus he will eventually run away.

I know that when you look at the life of Jesus, you might say that he was not exactly cheerful and joking when he faced the fallen beings. Yet you must understand that times were very different 2,000 years ago. Jesus faced a very difficult situation, for he was the forerunner for humankind's step up to the path to Christ consciousness. Before Jesus set forth his example, it was extremely difficult for people to attain the Christ consciousness. And therefore, Jesus faced a much heavier opposition than you will face today. In this day and age many more people have attained some degree of Christ consciousness, and thus it is easier for everyone to rise higher.

This is not to diminish your accomplishment but to make you realize that you can fulfill the prophecy of Jesus to do even greater works than he did. Therefore, in expressing your Christhood, you are learning from the example of Jesus but that does not mean you are copying everything Jesus did. Not only are you expressing your individual Christhood, but you are also expressing the Christhood that can be expressed at this particular time, as we move from the Age of Pisces into the Age of Aquarius. This new age is an age of spiritual freedom, and freedom cannot thrive under control. Freedom thrives when there is joy, when there is enthusiasm. And thus, what I desire to see happen is that those who are willing to be instruments for bringing about a non-dualistic approach to religion go out there with joy, with enthusiasm.

My beloved, look at so many religions on Earth and how they have caused people to be so serious that they almost go around with long faces all the time. So many people have been turned off to religion because of this fear, this tendency to take everything so seriously, being so afraid to make a mistake that you dare not experiment with life. In this age, you are meant to embody the command of Jesus, when he said that unless you become as little children, you will not enter the kingdom of heaven (Mark 10:5). Children are joyful, children are enthusiastic, children are free, and those are the qualities that must be embodied as you go out and preach a non-dualistic approach to religion. Be known as the ones who are excited about spirituality, who are enthusiastic about it, who are joyful about spirituality and who are free to talk about it with no taboos. Be known as those who cannot be disturbed no matter what opposition they run into. Let not people take away your joy, your enthusiasm. No matter what they throw at you, remain at peace, remain joyful.

And when you speak, speak with joy, speak with enthusiasm. Do not come across as if you are presenting the most serious topic in the world and that life and death or the end of the world will depend on whether people accept or reject you. Be joyful and enthusiastic so that people will want to accept you because they want the joy and the enthusiasm – the spiritual freedom – that you have.

We are not trying – as the fallen beings have been doing for thousands of years – to force people into accepting what we preach because they are afraid of going to hell. In this age, we need a complete change in the approach to religion, so that people do not attempt to go to heaven because they are trying to get away from hell. We want people to strive for heaven because they *want* to be in heaven, because they know it is a place of love, of joy, of enthusiasm, of spiritual freedom. They know this because they see that *you* are in the kingdom of heaven. And how do they see this? They see this because you are radiating the love and the joy that is found in heaven.

My beloved, the Creator has no worries and concerns and fears whatsoever, for the Creator is almighty. Well, if you were almighty, would you go around with a long face all day? Would you be concerned about the future? So if you were almighty, how would you feel? Well, you would feel what can only be described partially by any of the words in this world. But the word that comes closest to describing how the Creator feels is "bliss." The Creator is in a constant state of ever-expanding bliss.

And when you walk the path of Christhood and reach a certain level on the path, you will begin to experience that bliss. And I want you to strive for it, I want you to accept it and I want you to express it, so that you radiate that quality of bliss. In that way, other people look at you and say, "I may not understand what they are saying, I may not agree with what they are saying, but I see that these people have something I don't have, and I want it." Thus, people listen to you, and beyond the words that you say they will listen to and absorb your vibration, the vibration of joy, enthusiasm and bliss.

I will *almost* say that it does not matter what you say, as long as you say it with enthusiasm and joy. For it is not truly the words that awaken other people. It is the vibration, the light, that streams through your heart into their hearts and suddenly rekindles that memory of who they are, the memory that there is more to life than what they experience on this Earth, and there is more to them than the person they thought they were. And this is when people see that if you can become MORE, maybe *they* can become MORE. And that is when they start the path of becoming MORE, the path of self-transcendence that will lead you from your present state of consciousness to the fullness of the bliss of God. I want all of you to have that bliss, and I know you will find it if you keep walking the Path of Oneness.

***

Look at how many religions have squeezed all joy and enthusiasm from the lives of their own members. And in so doing, they have shut out the Holy Spirit from their activities. For the Holy Spirit is indeed not a dark, angry, fearful or brooding spirit but a spirit of joy that experiences the bliss of constant self-transcendence. Thus, you cannot attract or retain the Holy Spirit when there is no joy, which explains why so many religions have lost the spirit.

This, my beloved, has indeed happened to virtually every spiritual movement on the face of this planet. And I desire to do everything that can be done to make sure it will not happen to any movement that might decide to use the teachings that the Ascended Host are giving forth in this age. For I desire you to know that the Holy Spirit can never be restrained or captured into any framework on Earth. The Holy Spirit cannot be institutionalized. The very moment you think that you have reached some ultimate state of spirituality, at that moment you have lost the Holy Spirit.

My beloved, it is indeed one of the most subtle temptations on the spiritual path that many people – individually and collectively – come to believe that the goal of the path is to reach some ultimate state of enlightenment or salvation or whatever they call it. And once they have reached that state, they no longer have to transcend themselves but can now rest on their laurels and perhaps even begin to feel that they belong to an elite who is above and beyond the rest of the population and therefore should have special authority or special privileges.

Do you see, my beloved, that as long as you are here on Earth, you can fall prey to the temptation to stop self-transcendence? And this will plunge you right back into the fallen consciousness, for it was indeed this very temptation to stop self-transcendence – in one of its myriad disguises – that caused the beings in what is now the spiritual realm to fall. They thought they were so high and mighty that they did not have to transcend themselves by serving those they considered to be below them. This was the very illusion that caused the original fall and has caused the fall of all beings since then.

So you see, my beloved, this is the very temptation that you must be aware of, that you must anticipate, so that when the tempter comes to you – as he will surely come in a very clever disguise adapted to your personal state of consciousness – you will be ready. You will know that this is the tempter in disguise. You will see it, and therefore you will rebuke the tempter as Jesus and the Buddha rebuked him.

***

My beloved, I desire to leave you with an open end, so you realize that this book is not an end in itself but is a means to an end, namely that you enter the true spiritual path, the Path of Oneness that has no end. For it is the path of perpetual self-transcendence leading to full God consciousness, which *is* perpetual self-transcendence. For is not even the Creator constantly transcending itself, as I have explained that the Creator becomes MORE as all life becomes MORE.

My beloved, *hear me!* Hear my words! And hear the hidden meaning beyond the words! Read my words over and over, contemplate them many a time. I know, my beloved, that at your present level of consciousness my words may seem mystical, abstract and difficult to understand. But I tell you that if you will keep contemplating these words over and over again – contemplating the need to self-transcend, to never ever allow anything to stop your transcendence – if you will keep contemplating this, you *will* eventually break through. There will come a point when the clouds in your mind will part and you will see the light of your Higher Self shining through. You will see the truth of Christ shining through. And you will *know* – you will experience, you will be one with – the mind and the reality of Christ. You will be one with your own higher being.

That is why I want to leave you with this thought—that you ALWAYS take the next step. No matter where you are in consciousness, no matter what outer situation you face, keep this one principle in your mind: ALWAYS take the next step! Always transcend your current conditions, both inner and outer conditions. And if you will keep doing this – if you will keep striving to take the next step, to go one step higher on the spiral staircase – I will promise you with absolute certainty that one day you will break through and you will see the shining reality of God.

I have said that the spiritual path is not automatic, and indeed it is not a mechanical path. But what I am talking about here is not taking mechanical steps. I am talking about taking creative steps of transcending yourself, your understanding, your wisdom so that you come to see something that you did not see before. And if you will keep repeating this creative process – of *always* looking beyond your current mental box, no matter how big, sophisticated or complete you think that box might be – then you will indeed reach the goal of Christhood that I have set before you.

This, my beloved, is not a promise, it is the law of God. For there is indeed nothing hidden that shall not be revealed, and what may seem abstract or mystical to you in your present state of consciousness will indeed become clear when you transcend that state of consciousness. And if you will keep asking the questions – keep contemplating that which you do not understand, keep looking at it from different angles and keep asking for an inner revelation and inner understanding – well, my beloved, if you will keep transcending limitations, you *will* reach the goal. You will reach the state of oneness with your higher being. And at that moment you will *know* that you are permanently free from the duality consciousness. You will know you have entered God's kingdom, for you have found the kingdom that Jesus told you is within you.

My beloved, you do not even have to believe in what I am telling you. You simply have to be willing to put it to the test. If you will keep striving to transcend your current state of blindness, you *will* break through. This is the law of God that Jesus taught, that the Buddha taught. It is the law that they demonstrated and that other people have demonstrated throughout the ages. And in this age, *you* have the potential to demonstrate that law so that others can follow the example that you set. My beloved, there is no greater legacy you can leave on this planet than to demonstrate the Path of Oneness so that others can see it and believe that they too can follow it.

My beloved, it has been said that the greatest legacy you can leave is to plant an idea. But indeed, there is an even greater legacy and that is to set an example by *living* an idea. When you embody and become one with an idea, it becomes a living reality because you are not talking about being the Christ in abstract terms. You are *being* the Christ, you are demonstrating what it means to manifest Christhood and to express that Christhood in working selflessly to raise up all life and set all people free from the dualistic illusions that keep them trapped. This, my beloved, is the greatest legacy that you can leave on this planet, it is the greatest gift you can give to humanity, to God, to the future. And my beloved, it is a goal that is realistic for many of you—if you will only keep putting one foot in front of the other, taking small believable, attainable steps of transcending yourself.

If you *will* keep transcending, you *will* reach the goal. This is the reality that the fallen beings do not want you to accept. And thus, it is the reality that I ask you to accept, or at least put it to the test until the acceptance comes from within because you experience that the path really *does* work, that there really *is* a way out of duality.

I have now set before you the challenge of life and death, and I say with the true prophets of all ages: "Know the difference between life and death. And then, Choose LIFE!"

Epilogue
The eternal challenge of Christ

Let me make it clear that what is going on behind everything I have told you is that people must be presented – over and over again for as long as it takes – with the challenge of Christ. The challenge of Christ is that you encounter the Living Christ in the form of a person who embodies the Christ consciousness on Earth. Thus, you have an opportunity to accept or deny Christ. Yet the challenge of Christ has several levels:

- The first level is when you encounter a person who has attained the Christ consciousness on Earth. This is not limited to Jesus, the Buddha or Krishna, for it is sufficient to encounter a person who has attained some degree of Christhood. You do not necessarily have to meet such a person physically, for at this level you merely need to learn that it is possible for the Living Christ to appear on Earth and that the Living Christ represents an alternative to the duality consciousness. You learn that it is – in principle – possible to be the Christ on Earth. At this level, you clearly see the Christ as being outside yourself and if you accept Christ, you will become a follower of Christ (possibly a student of the person who embodies the Christ consciousness). This is the challenge to accept or reject Christ outside yourself.

    The ability to recognize Christ is what Jesus talked about in the following passage:

    > 15 He saith unto them, But whom say ye that I am?
    > 16 And Simon Peter answered and said, Thou art the Christ, the Son of the living God.
    > 17 And Jesus answered and said unto him, Blessed art thou, Simon Barjona: for flesh and blood hath not revealed it unto thee, but my Father which is in heaven.
    > 18 And I say also unto thee, That thou art Peter, and upon this rock I will build my church; and the gates of hell shall not prevail against it. (Matthew, Chapter 16)

    Jesus was not talking about the person of Peter but about an ability that all people have, namely the ability to recognize that there is something beyond duality and the willingness to follow the Christ that you see. This ability is built into the conscious self because it is out of the Creator's own Being, which is why it can see beyond duality – flesh and blood – and receive direction from the "Father which is in heaven," namely the spiritual hierarchy. Obviously, Peter as a person had overcome this first challenge of Christ. The ability to see beyond duality is the rock upon which all true religions are built, but the gates of hell – the forces of duality – will only be held back as long as people continue to look beyond duality and follow the highest expression of Christ that they see, always looking for a higher one. Which brings us to the second challenge of Christ.

- At the next level, you need to accept that the role of the Living Christ is to challenge all of your dualistic beliefs and to take you out of your mental box and into the "promised land" of non-duality. This can be a severe challenge when people are not aware of what I have explained about mental images. Many people recognize a spiritual leader, but they immediately seek to fit him or her into their mental boxes. They seek to impose a dualistic image upon the Living Christ who has come to take them beyond duality—whereby they actually refuse to follow the Living Christ and end up continuing to follow the leaders of anti-christ (while thinking they are sure to be saved). This is the test that Peter failed, as recorded in the following quote (which is often "overlooked" by mainstream Christians):

> 21 From that time forth began Jesus to show unto his disciples, how that he must go unto Jerusalem, and suffer many things of the elders and chief priests and scribes, and be killed, and be raised again the third day.
> 22 Then Peter took him, and began to rebuke him, saying, Be it far from thee, Lord: this shall not be unto thee.
> 23 But he turned, and said unto Peter, Get thee behind me, Satan: thou art an offence unto me: for thou savourest not the things that be of God, but those that be of men. (Matthew, Chapter 16)

Peter was not willing to let the Living Christ take him beyond his mental box and his view of what should happen to the Living Christ on Earth. He preferred his own dualistic images – the things that be of men – over the non-dualistic truth of Christ – the things that be of God – and thus he failed the second challenge of Christ. So far, humankind – including the majority of all Christians and Christian churches – have failed this exact same test. Even many among the top ten percent – especially among those who think they are the most spiritual people – have so far failed this test. The planet simply cannot move into a golden age until a critical mass of people master the second challenge of Christ.

- At the next level, you go beyond being a mere follower of Christ and you begin to accept that you have the potential to embody the teachings of Christ. As you put on the mind of Christ, you realize that you have the potential to *be* the Living Christ. You stop seeing Christ outside yourself and start seeing Christ as the ruler of the kingdom of God that is within you. This is the challenge to accept or reject Christ inside yourself.

- At the next level you begin to realize that being the Christ is not simply a matter of transforming your own consciousness. In fact, being the Christ is really not about you but is about awakening other people. You now begin to see that the true role of the Christ is to go into the world and present people with the challenge of Christ, the challenge to accept or reject the Living Christ. Again, you have the opportunity to either accept or reject this role, and let me assure you that many spiritually advanced people have in fact refused to go out and expose themselves to the condemnation and rejection of the world, the fallen beings and the planetary beasts.

My point is that it is possible to fail the initiation of Christ even when you have reached a high level of spiritual attainment. Which is why the Ascended Host keep presenting the top ten percent with the opportunity to become the Christ, as I have now done in this book.

One of my major goals with this book is to set forth a teaching that more plainly than ever before spells out the challenge that too many among the top ten percent have so far refused to take on, namely the challenge to stand before the world and declare their Christhood by letting their light shine and bearing witness to the non-dual truth. As I have explained, only by taking on this challenge will you rise to the fullness of Christhood and become permanently free from planet Earth. Only by becoming the Living Christ on Earth can you rise and become the Living Christ in the spiritual realm. You have – in past lives, some of you even in the Garden of Eden – rejected this challenge by postponing the choice. Yet how long will you continue to reject me – the representative of the Cosmic Christ for the Earth – before you realize that it is far easier to face the challenge than it is to keep rejecting it, thereby fighting the force of life itself and condemning you and the rest of humanity to a seemingly endless spiral of suffering?

Surely, this message has been released over and over again in many different spiritual teachings. Yet it has often been shrouded in mystery or obscure language that made it hard to understand. This book is the first one to explain the challenge of Christ in such plain language that anyone who is willing can understand it. You can still reject the challenge, but do not come to me after this lifetime and accuse me of not explaining it to you with sufficient clarity. For in this book, everything that is secret has now come abroad (Mark 4:22). Will you accept my challenge or will you take another round of seeking to hide from me, your cosmic teacher?

You see, by rejecting me, you are also rejecting him that sent me, namely the Creator whom I represent for the lifestreams on Earth. One of the illusions created by the false teachers is that everything is a matter between people and their teachers. It was actually by getting Eve to doubt me that the Serpent was successful in causing her to fall. Yet in reality, it is not about me, it is not a matter between you and me. In reality, everything is a matter between you and your Source, which is the Creator itself. Your salvation will happen only when you attain a sense of oneness with your Creator. I am here to help you attain that oneness, but if you do not see beyond me, you will not understand my purpose. As a true teacher, I am here exclusively to help you become one with the Creator, so as long as you focus on me – or a false teacher – you cannot go beyond that level. Thus, even a true teacher can be turned into a block that stops your progress on the Path of Oneness. Obviously, that is not what I desire, which is why I have gone into such great detail to explain the dynamics of your situation. Those who have ears, let them hear.

CPSIA information can be obtained at www.ICGtesting.com
Printed in the USA
LVOW04s1107130215

426934LV00019B/352/P

9 780976 697176